T5-BQA-465

THE AGE OF SOLOMON

STUDIES IN THE HISTORY AND CULTURE OF THE ANCIENT NEAR EAST

EDITED BY

B. HALPERN AND M.H.E. WEIPPERT

VOLUME XI

THE AGE OF SOLOMON

Scholarship at the Turn of the Millennium

EDITED BY

LOWELL K. HANDY

BRILL
LEIDEN · NEW YORK · KÖLN
1997

This book is printed on acid-free paper.

Library of Congress Cataloging-in-Publication Data

The age of Solomon : scholarship at the turn of the millennium / edited by Lowell K. Handy.
p. cm.—(Studies in the history and culture of the ancient Near East, ISSN 0169-9024 ; v. 11)
Includes bibliographical references and indexes.
ISBN 9004104763 (cloth)
1. Solomon, King of Israel. 2. Bible. O.T. Kings, 1st—History of Biblical events. 3. Bible. O.T. Kings, 1st—History of contemporary events. 4. Middle East—History—To 622. 5. Bible. O.T. Kings, 1st—Antiquities. 6. Jews—History—1200-953 B.C.—Historiography. I. Handy, Lowell K., 1949- II. Series.
BS580.S6A34 1997
222'.53092—dc21 97-19311
CIP

Die Deutsche Bibliothek – CIP-Einheitsaufnahme

The age of Solomon : scholarship at the turn of the millennium / ed. by Lowell K. Handy. - Leiden ; New York : Köln : Brill, 1997
(Studies in the history and culture of the ancient Near East ; vol. 11)
ISBN 90-04-10476-3

ISSN 0169-9024
ISBN 90 04 10476 3

PRINTED IN THE NETHERLANDS

CONTENTS

ARCHAEOLOGY AND THE REIGN OF SOLOMON

SOCIOLOGICAL APPROACHES

HISTORIOGRAPHY

SOLOMONIC AGE AS CONSTITUENT PART OF THE HISTORIES

LITERARY-HISTORICAL VISIONS OF THE AGE OF SOLOMON

PREFACE

The origin of this volume was the 1994 idea of Dr. F. Th. Dijkema, then an editor at E. J. Brill. He believed that there should be a single volume on the reign of Solomon that would collect the scholarship current in the fields of biblical studies and archaeology. To this end he contacted Prof. Diana V. Edelman, who was then organizing a section of papers on the Age of Solomon for the joint American Schools of Oriental Research and Society of Biblical Literature annual conference to be held in Chicago, Illinois, on November 20, 1994. Prof. Edelman, in turn, referred Dr. Dijkema to myself. I agreed to the project on the condition that not only the historical reconstruction of the time period of Solomon as historical event, but also the historiographical recreation of the period be included.

Each of the presenters of papers at the conference was invited to publish in this volume. Four agreed such that two of the presented papers are included herein (Na'aman, Hopkins). Knauf had been unable to attend the conference, so his paper appears here for the first time, while Lasine wrote a new contribution for the volume. John S. Holladay's presentation at the conference was a selection from his forthcoming book on the archaeology of the Solomonic period and was already to be published elsewhere.

To expand the scope of the present volume, a "shopping list" of scholars (both established and new to the field) was developed. For the opening chapters on the current approaches to the "Age of Solomon" two of the most distinguished and respected biblical historians who have published extensively on the United Monarchy were asked to submit summaries of their approaches and conclusions; Alan Millard and J. Maxwell Miller have graciously contributed the requested chapters, giving the volume a solid grounding in the current stage of Solomonic research. Both scholars also agreed to critique each other's chapters for the volume; their own chapters having been composed prior to seeing the other chapter. A section on the surrounding territory seemed necessary and so scholars specializing in the regions neighboring Judah and Israel were asked to provide short descriptions of their cultures in the 10th century BCE. A section on sociological approaches to recreating Solomon's history was also included as this methodology was at its peak of popularity when editing began. Finally, a series of essays on the historiography of the reign make up the final section of the volume, less interested in "what happened" than in "what was said to have happened." In all, the present volume should provide a good overview of the state of Solomon scholarship at this particular point in time.

I am very grateful to Diana V. Edelman, Robert D. Biggs, Louis H. Feldman and Steven W. Holloway for their suggestions regarding contributors for the volume. The contributors themselves have done a fine job of providing chapters suitable for the purposes of the book and I thank them for their work (which most completed with little or no prompting from myself, an appreciated variation from the norm for edited works I understand). A very few manuscripts came in too late to be carefully edited; I apologize for some of the inconsistences in their format, but we (Brill and I) did try to keep to the deadlines. And only three of the original chapters did not, in some form, make it into the volume; not too bad for an invited-contribution edited work. A special thank you is extended to Prof. Kitchen for producing and delivering the chapter on Egypt and East Africa at the last minute (quite literally: the last month), when the original contributor was unable to submit the chapter on time. The editor produced the section on the Phoenicians when the deadline arrived but the projected chapter did not (a case of computer crash). Several libraries in the Chicago vicinity have been "raided" for correcting footnotes in manuscripts; I thank United Libraries (Seabury-Western & Garrett-Evangelical Theological Seminary), Elizabeth Cudahy Memorial Library (Loyola University Chicago), Joseph Regenstein Library (University of Chicago), Oriental Institute Archives (University of Chicago), JKM Library (Lutheran School of Theology in Chicago), and the Evanston Public Library for use of their collections. Another special thank you is extended to Carolyn Coates and Steven W. Holloway for salvaging the index to this book when my computer crashed taking these files with it.

While it was F. Dijkema who got the project off the ground at Brill, it has been Patricia Radder who has handled the worrisome editorial task since the volume actually got into production and I thank her for her patience, concern and work on the project. In addition, Baruch Halpern, co-editor of SHCANE, has made several suggstions concerning the manuscript.

Lowell K. Handy
December 30, 1996

ABBREVIATIONS

AASOR	Annual of the American Schools of Oriental Research
ÄAT	Ägypten und Altes Testament
AB	Anchor Bible
ABD	*Anchor Bible Dictionary*
Abod. Zar.	*Aboda Zara*
ABRL	Anchor Bible Reference Library
AbrN	*Abr-Nahrain*
ADPV	Abhandlungen des Deutschen Palästina-Vereins
AfO	*Archiv für Orientforschung*
AIR	P. D. Miller, P. D. Hanson, S. D. McBride (eds.), *Ancient Israelite Religion*
AJBA	*Australian Journal of Biblical Archaeology*
ANET	J. B. Pritchard (ed.), *Ancient Near Eastern Texts*
AnOr	Anelecta orientalia
AnSt	*Anatolian Studies*
Ant.	Josephus, *Antiquities of the Jews*
AOAT	Alter Orient und Altes Testament
AR	D. D. Luckenbill (ed.), *Ancient Records of Assyria and Babylonia*
Ass	Excavation numbers from the German excavations at Assur
Ass Ph	excavation photographs from the German excavations at Assur
ARI	A. R. Grayson (ed.), *Assyrian Royal Inscriptions*
ASTI	*Annual of the Swedish Theological Institute*
ATANT	Abhandlungen zur Theologie des Alten und Neuen Testaments
ATD	Das Alte Testament Deutsch
ATD Erg	Das Alte Testament Deutsch Ergänzungscriehe
B. Bat.	*Baba Batra*
B. Meṣ.	*Baba Meṣi'a*
B. Qam.	*Baba Qamma*
BA	*Biblical Archaeologist*
BAH	Bibliothèque Archéologique et Historique
BAR	*Biblical Archaeology Review*
BASOR	*Bulletin of the American Schools of Oriental Research*
BBB	Bonner biblische Beitrage
BDB	F. Brown, S. R. Driver and C. A. Briggs, *Hebrew and English Lexicon of the Old Testament*
BEATAJ	Beiträge zur Erforschung des Alten Testaments und des Antiken Judentums
Ber.	*Berakot*
BeO	*Bibbia e oriente*
Bib	*Biblica*
BibEnz	Biblische Enzyklopädie
BibRev	*Bible Review*

BJRL	*Bulletin of the John Rylands University Library of Manchester*
BKAT	Biblischer Kommentar: Altes Testament
BM	British Museum, London
BN	*Biblische Notizen*
BO	*Bibliotheca orientalis*
BTAVO	Beihefte zum Tübingen Atlas des Vorderen Orients
BWANT	Beiträge zur Wissenschaft vom Alten und Neuen Testament
BZ	*Biblische Zeitschrift*
BZAW	Beihefte zur Zeitschrift für die Alttestamentliche Wissenschaft
CAH	*Cambridge Ancient History*
CBQ	*Catholic Biblical Quarterly*
CBQMS	Catholic Biblical Quarterly Monograph Series
CBS	Babylonian Section, University Museum, Philadelphia
ConBOT	Coniectanea biblica, Old Testament
CRBS	*Currents in Research: Biblical Studies*
CRINT	Compendia rerum iudaicarum ad novum testamentum
CTM	*Concordia Theological Monthly*
DBAT	*Dielheimer Blätter zum Alten Testament*
DDD	K. van der Toorn, B. Becking, P. W. van der Horst (eds.), *Dictionary of Deities and Demons in the Bible*
DSB	Daily Study Bible
EKL	*Evangelisches Kirchenlexikon*
ErFor	Erträge der Forschung
ErIsr	*Eretz Israel*
EstBib	*Estudios bíblicos*
ETL	*Ephemerides theologicae lovanienses*
E T Bulletin	*Bulletin. Europeäische Gesellschaft für Katholische Theologie*
FAT	Forschungen zum Alten Testament
FCB	Feminist Companion to the Bible
FOTL	Forms of Old Testament Literature
FRLANT	Forschungen zur Religion und Literatur des Alten und Neuen Testaments
FTS	Freiburger Theologische Studien
HAR	Hebrew Annual Review
HAT	Handbuch zum Alten Testament
HOE	Handbuch der Orientalistik Ergänzungsband
HSM	Harvard Semitic Monographs
HSS	Harvard Semitic Studies
HTIBS	Historic Texts and Interpreters in Biblical Scholarship
HTR	*Harvard Theological Review*
HUCA	*Hebrew Union College Annual*
ICC	International Critical Commentary
IEJ	*Israel Exploration Journal*
IM	Iraq Museum, Baghdad
JANES	*Journal of the Ancient Near Eastern Society* (Columbia University)
JAOS	*Journal of the American Oriental Society*
JARCE	*Journal of the American Research Center in Egypt*
JBL	*Journal of Biblical Literature*

JCS	*Journal of Cuneiform Studies*
JESHO	*Journal of the Economic and Social History of the Orient*
JHNES	Johns Hopkins Near Eastern Studies
JNES	*Journal of Near Eastern Studies*
JPOS	*Journal of Palestine Oriental Society*
JQR	*Jewish Quarterly Review*
JSJ	*Journal for the Study of Judaism in the Persian, Hellenistic and Roman Period*
JSOT	*Journal for the Study of the Old Testament*
JSOTSup	Journal for the Study of the Old Testament Supplement Series
JSP	*Journal for the Study of the Pseudepigrapha*
K	Kouyunjik collection, British Museum, London
KAI	H. Donner and W. Rollig, *Kanaanâische und aramäische Inschriften*
LÄ	*Lexikon der Ägyptologie*
LAI	Library of Ancient Israel
LCL	Loeb Classical Library
LSJ	Liddell-Scott-Jones, *Greek-English Lexicon*
LXX	Septuagint
Mesopotamia	Mesopotamia: Copenhagen Studies in Assyriology
MT	Masoretic Text
N	Excavation numbers from the Oriental Institute excavations at Nippur
NBD	*New Bible Dictionary*
NCB	New Century Bible
Nid.	*Niddah*
NRSV	New Revised Standard Version
NSK-AT	Neuer Stuttgarter Kommentar—Alttestament
NTS	*New Testament Studies*
OBO	Orbis biblicus et orientalis
OIP	Oriental Institute Publications
OLA	Orientalia Lovaniensia Analecta
Or	*Orientalia* (Rome)
OrAnt	*Oriens antiquus*
OTG	Old Testament Guides
OTL	Old Testament Library
OTP	J. H. Charlesworth (ed.), *The Old Testament Pseudepigrapha*
OTS	*Oudtestamentische Studiën*
PEQ	*Palestine Exploration Quarterly*
Phil.-hist. Kl.	Philosophische-historische Klasse
QD	Quaestiones disputatae
RA	*Revue d'assyriologie et d'archéologie orientale*
RB	*Revue biblique*
REB	Revised English Bible
REg	*Revue d'égyptologie*
RHA	*Revue hittite et asianique*
RIMA	Royal Inscriptions of Mesopotamia, Assyrian Periods
RIMB	Royal Inscriptions of Mesopotamia, Babylonian Periods
RLA	G. Ebeling, et al. (ed.), *Reallexikon der Assyriologie*

Rm	H. Rassam collection, British Museum, London
Ros.	*Ros Hassana*
RSO	*Revista degli studi orientali*
RSR	*Recherches de science religieuse*
RSV	Revised Standard Version
RUB	Reclams Universal Bibliothek
SAAS	State Archives of Assyria Studies
SAM	Sheffield Archaeological Monographs
Sanh.	*Sanhedrin*
SBAB	Stuttgarter biblische Aufsatzbände
SBAlt	Saarbrücker Beiträge zur Altertumskunde
SBAW	Sitzungsberichte der bayerischen Akademie der Wissenschaften
SBLDS	Society of Biblical Literature Dissertation Series
SBS	Stuttgarter Bibelstudien
SBTS	Sources for Biblical and Theological Study
SESJ	Suomen Eksegeettischen Seuran julkaisuja
Šabb.	*Šabbat/Shabbat*
SHANE	Studies in the History of the Ancient Near East
SHCANE	Studies in the History and Culture of the Ancient Near East
SU	Tablets from the British excavations at Sultantepe in Ankara
SWBA	Social World of Biblical Antiquity
TCS	Texts from Cuneiform Sources
ThStud	*Thelogische Studien*
ThZ	*Theologische Zeitschrift*
TLZ	*Theologische Literaturzeitung*
TOTC	Tyndale Old Testament Commentary
TRu	*Theologische Rundschau*
TSSI	J. C. L. Gibson, *Textbook of Syrian Semitic Inscriptions*
TynBul	*Tyndale Bulletin*
VA	Vorderasiatisches Museum, Berlin
VAT	Tablets in the collection of the Vorderasiatisches Museum, Berlin
VTSup	Vetus Testamentum, Supplements
War	Josephus, *The Jewish War*
WBC	Word Biblical Commentary
WMANT	Wissenschaftliche Monographien zum Alten und Neuen Testament
WTJ	*Westminster Theological Journal*
WVDOG	Wissenschaftliche Veröffentlichungen der deutschen Orientgesellschaft
Yebam.	*Yebamot*
ZA	*Zeitschrift für Assyriologie*
ZAH	*Zeitschrift für Althebraistik*
ZAW	*Zeitschrift für die alttestamenliche Wissenschaft*
ZDPV	*Zeitschrift des deutschen Palästina-Vereins*

CONTRIBUTORS

Mark W. Chavalas	Associate Professor; History Department, University of Wisconsin—La Crosse, La Crosse, Wisconsin
William G. Dever	Professor; Department of Near Eastern Studies, University of Arizona, Tucson, Arizona
Diana V. Edelman	Assistant Professor; Department of Philosophy and Religion, James Madison University, Harrisonburg, Virginia
Carl S. Ehrlich	Assistant Professor; Division of Humanities, York University, Toronto, Ontario
Louis H. Feldman	Professor; Classics, Yeshiva University, New York, New York
Lowell K. Handy	Senior Lecturer; Department of Theology, Loyola University Chicago, Chicago, Illinois; Indexer/Analyst, American Theological Library Association, Evanston, Illinois
Steven W. Holloway	Indexer/Analyst, American Theological Library Association, Evanston, Illinois
David C. Hopkins	Professor; Wesley Theological Seminary, Washington, DC
David Jobling	Professor; St. Andrew's College, Saskatoon, Saskatchewan
Kenneth A. Kitchen	Personal & Brunner Professor Emeritus of Egyptology; Department of Archaeology, School of Archaeology, Classics and Oriental Studies, University of Liverpool, Liverpool, England
Ernst Axel Knauf	Professor; Biblisches Institut, Evangelisch-theologische Fakultät, Universität Bern, Bern, Switzerland
Gary N. Knoppers	Associate Professor; Head of Department of Classics and Ancient Mediterranean Civilizations, Pennsylvania State University, University Park, Pennsylvania

Stuart Lasine	Associate Professor; Department of Religion; Director, Master of Arts in Liberal Studies Program; Wichita State University, Wichita, Kansas
Niels Peter Lemche	Professor of Old Testament; University of Copenhagen, Copenhagen, Denmark
Alan Millard	Rankin Professor of Hebrew and Ancient Semitic Languages; Archaeology and Oriental Studies, University of Liverpool, Liverpool, England
J. Maxwell Miller	Professor, Division of Religion, Graduate School of Arts and Sciences, Emory University, Atlanta, Georgia
Nadav Na'aman	Professor; Department of Jewish History, Tel Aviv University, Tel Aviv, Israel
Hermann Michael Niemann	Professor; Theologische Fakultät—Alttestamentliches Seminar, Universität Rostock, Rostock, Germany
Linda S. Schearing	Associate Professor; Department of Religious Studies, Gonzoga University, Spokane, Washington
Sandra Shimoff	University of Maryland, Baltimore County, Baltimore, Maryland
Mark A. Throntveit	Professor of Hebrew and Old Testament; Luther Seminary, St. Paul, Minnesota
Pauline A. Viviano	Associate Professor, Department of Theology, Loyola University Chicago, Chicago, Illinois

FOREWORD

Diana V. Edelman

The present volume has grown out of a panel presentation on the Age of Solomon that took place at a session of the Hebrew Bible, History and Archaeology Section at the 1994 Annual Meeting of the American Schools of Oriental Research and the Society of Biblical Literature. The focus of the panel was an evaluation of the available textual and archaeological testimony about the purportedly historical figure, Solomon ben David, who would have been part of the political landscape of Syria-Palestine in the 10th century BCE. The panel concluded with two historical recreations of Solomon's reign. Brill publishers expressed interest at that time in publishing a volume devoted to the figure of Solomon in history and tradition and Dr. Lowell Handy graciously agreed to undertake the task of editing the volume. Five papers were originally given at the session and four have been included in revised form in the present collection: the ones by Stuart Lasine, Nadav Na'aman, David Hopkins, and Ernst Axel Knauf. The fifth paper on the archaeology of Palestine in the 10th century by John S. Holladay was an extract of a larger work in progress and has not been included. Instead, William Dever has agreed to contribute an essay on this topic.

The remaining papers have all been commissioned by L. Handy. He has done an admirable job of widening the scope of the original panel that only lasted two and a half hours and assembling a set of essays that covers the many literary and historical issues involving Solomon. A quick perusal of the list of authors will demonstrate that the editor has not favored any particular "camp" in what often remains heated debates; he has allowed a wide range of positions to be voiced and has chosen an inclusive approach that addresses five subject areas: Solomon and the historical endeavor, the cultural-political environment of the ancient Near East in the 10th century, archaeology and the reign of Solomon, sociological approaches, and historiography. The final section includes hermeneutical studies of Solomon in the Roman and early Rabbinic periods, while the conclusion includes a brief overview of depictions of Solomon in Islamic literature, a subject ripe for systematic study.

The editor's failure to endorse particular positions or to take sides may annoy some readers who want a definitive view of Solomon to emerge from the work that can be used to teach or to write future histories of Israel and Judah. The aim of the volume seems not to be to provide definitive answers, however, but to indicate that there is no concensus emerging at this time, and why. This message is not stated explicitly by the editor; it emerges clearly from the voices of individual scholars, who at times overstep bounds of scholarly debate and use personal attack or defense to try to persuade the reader to "their" view as opposed to that of a well-known "opponent." At the same time, the volume moves beyond a focus on the historical Solomon to explore the richness of the literary Solomon, which in turn reinforces the relativity of the historical issue. Whether or not one is already familiar with the "camps" and scholarly personalities involved in various debates, the present volume will prove to be entertaining as well as enlightening.

Can the Real Solomon Please Stand Up?

Solomon ben David, real person or fictional folk hero? If real, ruler of an extensive Israelite empire, king of Israel and Judah, or head of a fledgling chieftaincy located in the central hills of Cisjordan? As more critical histories of ancient Israel and Judah are being written, views about the historicity of Solomon vary widely. Three of the most recent recreations of the reign of Solomon will be summarized below as a prelude to discussing why such diverse pictures can continue to emerge.

In his recent monumental history, the late G. W. Ahlström recreates a Solomon who truly was a unique phenomenon, who moved Israel and Judah out of their status as backwater petty states into the cultural and commercial world of the ancient Near East for the brief period of his reign. For him, the biblical writer had access to fairly extensive records created by the Solomonic court. While the so-called Deuteronomistic writer responsible for the account of Solomon in 1 Kings has exaggerated the boundaries of the Solomonic kingdom, most of the reported incidents from his reign are deemed historically reliable. Solomon cannot be a fictional folk hero because too much is said for him not to have been a real person: "A king would not have been built up to such proportions if there were no basis for it."[1] Remains datable to the 10th century BCE in

[1] G. W. Ahlström, *The History of Ancient Palestine from the Palaeolithic Period to*

urban centers in Palestine are cited to support this interpretation.[2]

Thomas Thompson, on the other hand, rejects the historicity of Solomon all together, arguing that there was no state of Israel until the Omrides in the 9th century BCE[3] and no state of Judah until the end of the 8th century BCE, with the rise of Assyrian economic interests in the area. For him, our inability to confirm the existence of Solomon in sources outside of the Bible means that we cannot accept his historicity; there is no way to prove his existence or the existence of 10th century sources that the Deuteronomistic writer used to depict his alleged reign. Settlement patterns in Judah as well as limited excavations in Jerusalem are cited to support this recreation.[4]

Ernst Axel Knauf represents a middle ground between these two. He accepts Solomon as a real personage, but recreates him as head of a fledgling chieftaincy in the late 10th century BCE, arguing that his depiction in the Bible is the result of the retrojection of political alliances and commercial ventures from the court of the Omrides in the 9th century BCE. He compares David and Solomon with Gideon and Abimelech, suggesting that the absence of Jerusalem from the list of cities conquered by Sheshonq is the most authentic evidence for the existence of Solomon's principality. He agrees with T. Thompson that there is no way to prove the existence of sources that were quoted by the Deuteronomistic writer to recreate the career of this individual, but concedes the possibility that some of the information in the account of Solomon's reign might reflect older, genuine traditions. In his opinion, settlement patterns in Palestine in the 10th century reflect a poor country with incipient, decentralized urbanism.[5]

Each of these three recreations is based on the same set of literary and archaeological sources of information: the Bible, the victory list of Sheshonq for his campaign in Palestine sometime near 925 BCE, and material cultural remains from various sites in Palestine in the 10th century BCE. The differences arise from disagreements over the conversion

---

Alexander's Conquest (ed. D. V. Edelman; JSOTSup 146; Sheffield: Sheffield Academic, 1992) 539.

[2] *Ibid.*, pp. 501-42.

[3] T. L. Thompson, *Early History of the Israelite People: From the Written and Archaeological Sources* (SHANE 4; Leiden: E. J. Brill, 1992) 313.

[4] *Ibid.*, pp. 332-33.

[5] E. A. Knauf, "King Solomon's Copper Supply," *Phoenicia and the Bible: Proceedings of the Conference held at the University of Leuven on the 15th and 16th March 1990* (ed. E. Lipiński; OLA 44; Leuven: Peeters, 1991) 167-86.

of the testimony provided by the texts and archaeology into evidence. Each historian is working with a different data pool that contains what he has deemed to be historically reliable information preserved in texts and material cultural remains. The core of the dispute over the historical Solomon, therefore, centers in the process of evaluating the commonly agreed upon testimony and converting it to evidence.

The determination of what constitutes historically reliable material in the biblical account is primarily influenced by a scholar's assessment of the purpose of the biblical writings: were they intended to be historical, in our modern sense of the word, meaning consciously critical and evaluative of sources, or not? Is the Bible a collection of historical writings or of theological reflections about the past? How did inhabitants of ancient Judah or Yehud understand the literary genre we call historiography and did they think of information in Kings and Chronicles in this way or not? If the Bible can be classified as historiography, what are the differences in principles and practice between their world and ours? What kind of sources dealing with Solomon were available from the second half of the 10th century BCE or subsequent eras at the time 1 Kings was composed? What was the nature of the only source cited for the Solomonic narrative, the Scroll of the Deeds of Solomon (1 Kgs 11:41), which apparently included deeds from the king's reign as well as discussion of his wisdom; was it annalistic or anecdotal and when was it compiled or composed? Conscious or unconscious assumptions about these crucial issues underlie maximalistic, minimalist or middle-of-the-road portraits of the historical Solomon that rely on biblical testimony for raw data.

Sheshonq's list of conquered cities and towns in Palestine is not without its problems, either. The badly preserved state of the inscription prevents us from reconstructing the entire campaign and knowing the full extent of conquered territories. There appear originally to have been some 180 name rings. The lower half of the inscription is largely destroyed, as are major parts of the fourth and fifth columns of the upper half. In the fifth column, out of some fifty name rings, only the first twenty and the last five are legible. Bearing this in mind, the failure of Jerusalem to appear in the preserved portion may or may not mean it was not conquered by Sheshonq. Similarly, the failure of any mention to be made of either the state of Israel or Judah in the preserved sections may or may not be significant. Not only could such mentions have fallen in a portion of the text that is now destroyed, but ideologically, the Egyptian scribe may have deliberately avoided reference to any territorial states in the region that had been the domain of Egypt from *ca.* 1200-1050 BCE. The listing of towns and settlements as though they were independent entities may, therefore, either reflect the political reality of the day or Egyptian ideology that did not want to admit loss of control over this territory.[6]

Finally, the archaeology of Palestine in the 10th century is undergoing intensive reevaluation at the moment, a situation that has developed during the preparation of the current volume. Unfortunately, the essay by William Dever was written before Israel Finkelstein published his two articles that suggest the need to lower the date of the pottery sequence that has traditionally been used to date objects and structures found associated with this pottery from the 10th century to the 9th century instead.[7] Most archaeologists would openly acknowledge in principle the inability at this time to date material cultural remains specifically to the reign of Solomon because diagnostic pottery forms that have served as the basis of the dating scheme for the 10th century BCE cannot be limited to the first or second half of the century, let alone to specific decades within a given century. In fact, the current set of diagnostics cannot be limited to the 10th century alone; it is not distinguishable from 9th century forms in most instances. In practice, however, some archaeologists have identified various remains at the sites of Megiddo, Hazor, and Gezer with the reign of Solomon, using the six-chambered gate and 1 Kgs 9:15-19 as criteria, rather that standard ceramics.[8]

With I. Finkelstein's recent challenge to the ability of archaeologists to use what have traditionally been considered 10th century ceramic diagnostics to date associated remains to some point within the 10th century, there looms the critical issue of defining what will be considered

---

[6] For the various problems and proposed reconstructions, see conveniently, G. W. Ahlström, "Pharaoh Shoshenq's Campaign to Palestine," *History and Traditions of Early Israel* (eds. A. Lemaire and B. Otzen; VTSup 50; Leiden: E. J. Brill, 1993) 1-16.

[7] I. Finkelstein, "The Date of the Settlement of the Philistines in Canaan," *Tel Aviv* 22 (1995) 213-39, and *idem*, "The Archaeology of the United Monarchy: An Alternate View," *Levant* 23 (1996) 177-87.

[8] For the classical formulations, see for example Y. Yadin, "Excavations at Hazor, 1957: Preliminary Communiqué," *IEJ* 8 (1958) 1-14; *idem*, "Solomon's City Wall and Gate at Gezer," *IEJ* 8 (1958) 80-86; Y. Aharoni, "The Building Activities of David and Solomon," *IEJ* 24 (1974) 13-16; and W. Dever, "Excavations at Gezer," *BA* 30 (1967) 34-47. For a good collection of articles that represent the subsequent debate among archaeologists over what archaeological criteria might allow the dating of the six-chambered gates to the reign of Solomon, see *BASOR* 277-278 (1990).

diagnostic forms that have clearly definable chronological implications at the end of the Iron I period and the beginning of the Iron II period and how wide a span of time is covered by each form. The current 10th century repertoire may be shifted down almost totally into the 9th century if Finkelstein's views prevail, could remain indicative of both the 10th and 9th centuries if the current position is maintained, or could remain partially in the 10th century but extending into some or most of the 9th century, if a compromise is struck. Bearing in mind this new and heated controversy, all uses of material cultural remains allegedly relating to the 10th century in discussions of the historical Solomon might wisely be set aside or bracketed until some sort of resolution is reached among the archaeologists.

The historian must be careful to evaluate each type of testimony, literary and archaeological, using methods appropriate to each before placing the results into a common data pool to be linked together into cause and effect relationships using creative imagination. There is no way for us to know what transpired exactly during the career of Solomon; at most, we can try to piece together bits of those events from critically evaluated literary and archaeological remains. There can be no single "history of Solomon;" the testimony is too complex and limited to allow total agreement about his life. At most, we can strive for a "consensus" view that agrees on most of the raw data and the way to interrelate it. Yet, ultimately, while this can be helpful for teaching introductory-level courses where all issues cannot be explored, it is not necessary or even desirable: history, as the recreation of the past, is an act of individual interpretation. The pretense that there is ever "a" history of a given event is a potentially dangerous message to instill in minds of any age in any time period. In addition, recognizing the legitimacy of a number of historical Solomons might have the positive effect of leading to a better appreciation of the range of literary Solomons that appear in biblical and post-biblical tradition, regardless of the amount of underlying historicity in a given account.

SEPARATING THE SOLOMON OF HISTORY FROM THE SOLOMON OF LEGEND

J. MAXWELL MILLER

1. THE SOURCES OF INFORMATION

Everything we know, or think we know, about the historical Solomon rests ultimately on the Hebrew Bible. Solomon is not mentioned in any ancient inscriptions or other available documents from pre-Roman times and there is archaeological evidence for him only in so far as one is prepared to interpret the silent[1] monuments and artifacts in light of biblical materials. Josephus, whose own account of Solomon's reign essentially paraphrases the Hebrew Bible, found references to him in the writings of Dius and a Menander of Ephesus, both of whom according to Josephus had access to ancient Phoenician records.[2] Neither the Phoenician records to which they supposedly had access nor the works of Dius and Menander have survived however. Nor, even if they had access to such records, does it necessarily follow that Dius and Menander's references to Solomon were derived from these records. Josephus is vague on the matter, perhaps intentionally so, and both authors reported the same story which sounds rather like a folk legend which might have circulated in Jewish and Phoenician circles during Hellenistic-Roman times. Dius' version is as follows:

> They say farther, that Solomon, when he was king of Jerusalem, sent problems to Hirom to be solved, and desired he would send others back to him

---

[1] For W. G. Dever's opposition to my characterization of archaeological remains as "silent" see especially W. G. Dever, "Unresolved Issues: Toward a Synthesis of Textual and Archaeological Reconstructions?" *American Academy of Religion/Society of Biblical Literature: Abstracts* (Atlanta: Scholars, 1987) 309-310; and *idem.*, "The Silence of the Text: An Archaeological Commentary on 2 Kings 23," *Scripture and Other Artifacts: Essays on the Bible and Archaeology in Honor of Philip J. King* (ed. M. D. Coogan, J. C. Exum, and L. E. Stager; Philadelphia: Westminster/John Knox, 1994) 143-68. For my response see J. M. Miller, "Is It Possible to Write a History of Israel Without Relying on the Hebrew Bible?" *The Fabric of History: Text, Artifact and Israel's Past* (ed. D. V. Edelman; JSOTSup 127; Sheffield: Sheffield Academic, 1991) 93-102.

[2] Josephus, *Ant.* 8.146-49; and *idem., Against Apion* 1.106-115.

> to solve, and that he who could not solve the problems proposed to him, should pay money to him that solved them; and when Hirom had agreed to the proposals, but was not able to solve the problems, he was obliged to pay a great deal of money, as a penalty for the same. As also they relate, that one Abdemon, a man of Tyre, did solve the problems, and proposed others which Solomon could not solve, upon which he was obliged to repay a great deal of money to Hirom.[3]

The Hebrew Bible offers two accounts of Solomon's reign: 1 Kgs 3-11 and 2 Chr 1-9. The 1 Kgs 3-11 account is part of a longer composition (Gen-2 Kgs) which recounts events from Creation to the Babylonian destruction of Jerusalem. Likewise, 2 Chr 1-9 is part of the so-called Chronicler's History (1-2 Chr-Ezra-Neh) which begins with Adam and concludes with the careers of Ezra and Nehemiah. Scholars trained in literary-critical analysis recognize that the two accounts and the longer compositions to which they belong did not reach the final stages of compilation and editing until approximately a half millennium after Solomon would have lived. The same is true of the Book of Proverbs, segments of which are attributed to Solomon (Prov 10-24, 25-30), as well as Ecclesiastes and Song of Songs both of which are associated with Solomon in an ill-defined fashion.

Even a casual reading of the 1 Kgs 3-11 and 2 Chr 1-9 accounts of Solomon's reign gives the impression of a legendary figure larger than life. Moreover, by comparing the two accounts, it is possible to observe the Solomonic legend at two stages of its growth. Already in 1 Kings, Solomon's reign is depicted as the golden age of Israel's past when a man after God's own heart was on the throne and God showered blessings on the land through him. God blessed Solomon with renowned wisdom, we are informed, along with amazing wealth and an empire which stretched from the Egyptian frontier to the Euphrates. Admittedly, the narrator seems to concede, there were some less than glorious aspects of Solomon's reign. Once on the throne, for example, he executed his older brother who apparently had a stronger claim to it than did Solomon. One of Solomon's officials in charge of forced labor chose exile rather than to administer Solomon's oppressive policies. Also, Solomon encountered some problems along his frontier with Damascus and Edom. However these less than glorious matters are all presented in a fashion which hardly detracts from the overall thrust of Solomon's wisdom and

---

[3] Josephus, *Against Apion* 1.114-15; W. Whiston, tr., *The Works of Josephus Complete and Unabridged* (new updaded ed.; Peabody, Maryland: Hendrickson, 1987).

the grandeur of his empire. The older brother had designs on the throne, the reader is led to understand; and as for the other troubles, these all happened at the end of Solomon's reign after he had been led astray by foreign wives.

The Chronicler's rendition of Israel's past apparently was produced later than the Genesis-2 Kings composition and reproduces large segments of the latter almost verbatim. However, there are some noticeable new twists and the Chronicler's Solomon is even more ideal than the one presented in 1 Kings. Rather than explaining away the questionable circumstances surrounding Solomon's accession to the throne and the execution of his older brother, for example, all of this is simply dropped from the Chronicler's account. David designated Solomon as his successor early on, we are informed, and later turned the throne over to him in a public ceremony at which everyone pledged their allegiance (1 Chr 29:22b-24). Similarly, the Chronicler omits or recasts all other items which might suggest that Solomon was less than an ideal ruler over a less than fabulous empire. There is only silence about the forced labor problem. Nothing is said about the conflict with Damascus and Edom. While deleting these incidents from the story, the Chronicler expands Solomon's cultic role and occassionally introduces supernatural elements into the ceremonies over which Solomon presided. It is reported, for example, that following Solomon's public prayer at the dedication of the Temple,

> Fire came down from heaven and consumed the burnt offering and the sacrifices, and the glory of Yahweh filled the temple. And the priests could not enter the house of Yahweh, because the glory of Yahweh filled Yahweh's house. When all the children of Israel saw the fire come down and the glory of Yahweh upon the temple, they bowed down.[4]

2. Twentieth-Century Scholarship and the Solomonic "Age of Enlightenment"

Biblical scholars often have commented on the long time gap between when Solomon would have lived and the final composition of the biblical accounts of his reign as well as on the larger-than-life fashion in which the biblical accounts depict him and his reign. Since they are composite documents, however, apparently based on pre-existing written and

[4] 2 Chr 7:1-3.

oral sources, Genesis-2 Kings and the Chronicler's history may include elements which date back very early, possibly even as early as Solomon's time. Moreover, embedded in the idealized depictions of Solomon are elements which give the impression of authenticity, such as the lists of Solomon's officials (1 Kgs 4:1-19). Indeed, the very fact that the compilers of Genesis-2 Kings reported circumstances which reflect negatively on Solomon's image as an ideal ruler suggests that these were remembered circumstances which could not be ignored. Thus, modern scholars have been inclined to place rather high trust in the biblical accounts of Solomon's reign. In fact, it is perhaps fair to say that the Solomon legend has grown as much during the twentieth century at the hands of critical biblical scholars and Palestinian archaeologists as it grew between the 1 Kings account and the Chronicler's account.

What happened, in effect, was that literary critics and archaeologists, beginning with the traditional notion of a Solomonic golden age and reinforced in this thinking by each other's work, made some very compelling cases (or so it seemed at the time) for dating certain elements in the biblical materials and certain archaeological features to the Solomonic period. These "discoveries" in turn, by seeming to confirm in a general way the prior assumption of a great Solomonic golden age, encouraged less than critical thinking about all other aspects of the biblical presentations of Solomon. For example, having "confirmed" that the Solomonic era was one of brilliant literary activity, an age of enlightenment, and that he truly did fortify the very cities reported in 1 Kgs 9:15-19, scholars have been inclined to pass quickly over uncertainties regarding the historicity of other items reported, such as his marriage to the pharaoh's daughter and the Queen of Sheba's visit. Instead, their research energies have been directed toward determining which pharaoh would have given his daughter in marriage to Solomon and spelling out the implications of the Queen of Sheba's visit for Solomon's interntional trade connections. Similarly, speculation regarding the location of Solomon's mines has tended to obscure the fact that even the Hebrew Bible seems unaware that he had mines.

Thus an interesting phenomenon occured. While biblical scholars and archaeologists engaged in heated debate during the mid-twentieth century about the historicity and dating of the biblical patriarchs, the exodus from Egypt, and the conquest of Canaan, and many had reached largely negative conclusions on these issues by the mid-1970's, the same scholars were busy enhancing Solomon's reputation.[5] First among the literary-critical studies that deserve special mention in this regard was A. Alt's "Israels Gaue unter Salomo" (1913)[6] in which he argued that the 1 Kgs 4:7-19 list of *nissabim* "who provided food for the king and his household" is an authentic fragment from Solomon's administrative records. According to Alt, this text shows that Solomon, attentive on the one hand to the inherited tribal structure and on the other to new population elements in his empire, divided Israel into twelve administrative districts. W. F. Albright confirmed and expanded upon Alt's interpretation of the passage in 1925;[7] so Solomon's administrative districts became firmly entrenched in academia on both sides of the Atlantic.[8] The following year, 1926, L. Rost published *Die Überlieferung von der Thronnachfolge Davids*, which made the case that the "Succession Narrative" (2 Sam 9-20 and 1 Kgs 1-2) was written not long after Solomon's accession to the throne.[9] Soon this narrative was being touted as an example of objective history writing unique to the ancient world, a theme which was developed especially by Gerhard von Rad. Von Rad also associated the "Yahwist" and the Joseph narrative with the time of Solomon and probably deserves more credit than any other scholar for advancing the concept of a Solomonic "Age of Enlightenment."[10] According to this notion, Solomon's vast empire and extensive

[5] Martin Noth and John Bright, for example, who treat Israel's origins in radically different fashions in their respective histories from the 1950s, could have written their chapters on Solomon from the same set of notes. Compare M. Noth, *Geschichte Israels* (Göttingen: Vandenhoeck & Ruprecht, 1950) 187-205, with J. Bright, *A History of Israel* (Philadelphia: Westminster, 1959) 190-208.

[6] A. Alt, "Israels Gaue unter Salomo," *Alttestamentliche Studiem Rudolf Kittel zum 60. Geburtstag dargebracht* (BWANT 13; Leipzig: J. C. Hinrichs, 1913) 1-19 = *idem.*, *Kleine Schriften zur Geschichte des Volkes Israel* (Munich: C. H. Beck, 1953) 2.76-89.

[7] W. F. Albright, "The Administrative Divisions of Israel and Judah," *JPOS* 5 (1925) 17-54.

[8] The idea of Solomon's administrative divisions received a further boost as recently as 1972 from Donald Redford who examined Egyptian sources and concluded that "the parallel between Sheshonq's and Solomon's provisioning systems is striking." D. B. Redford, "Studies in Relations between Palestine and Egypt during the First Millennium BC: I, The Taxation System of Solomon," *Studies on the Ancient Palestinian World* (ed. J. W. Wevers and D. B. Redford; Toronto: University of Toronto, 1972) 141-56.

[9] L. Rost, *Die Überlieferung von der Thronnachfolge Davids* (BWANT 3.6; Stuttgart: W. Kohlhammer, 1926) = *The Succession to the Throne of David* (tr. M. D. Rutter and D. M. Gunn; HTIBS 1; Sheffield: Almond, 1982).

[10] G. von Rad, *Das formgeschichtliche Problem des Hexateuch* (BWANT 26.4; Stuttgart: W. Kohlhammer, 1938); *idem.*, "Der Anfang der Geschichtsschreibung im Israel," *Archiv für Kulturgeschichte* 32 (1944) 1-42; *idem.*, "Josephs Geschichte und

international involvements thrust Israel into contact with the international world and all of its influences. Soon Solomon's court became an enlightened center of international learning and literary activity.

Although few scholars wished to take literally the claim in 1 Kgs 4:32 that Solomon "uttered three thousand proverbs; and his songs were a thousand and five," the idea emerged that Solomon's connection with the "Wisdom" literature in the Hebrew Bible had to do with his royal patronage of international learning under Egyptian influence. W. Baumgartner expressed this view in his 1951 survey of research pertaining to the biblical Wisdom books,[11] for example, the same year that Alt published another of his seminal papers, "Die Weisheit Salomos."[12] Alt observed that the subject matter of the proverbs attributed to Solomon in 1 Kings is indeed more reminiscent of the encyclopedic nature-wisdom of Egypt and Mesopotamia than the subject matter of the book of Proverbs. This suggested that the editors of Kings were drawing on reliable sources and reinforced the notion that Solomon's court included a strong "international wisdom" component.

While biblical scholars engaged in literary-critical analysis were isolating sources indicative of the Solomonic Age of Enlightenment, archaeologists were uncovering physical remains of Solomonic architecture. P. L. O. Guy directed the excavations at Tell el-Mutesellim (Megiddo) during 1927-1929 and uncovered what he interpreted to be the Solomonic phase of that city (Stratum IV) with a complex of stables.[13] This seemed an obvious "fit" with 1 Kgs 9:15-19 which mentions Megiddo in connection with Solomon's building activities and 1 Kgs 10:26-29 which reports that Solomon had 1,400 chariots and 12,000 horsemen whom he stationed at chariot cities. Beyond doubt, it seemed, Guy had discovered one of Solomon's chariot cities. Equally dramatic discoveries were made by Nelson Glueck during his archaeological surveys in the southern Transjordan during the 1930's and excavations at

---

'altere Chokma,'" *Congress Volume: Copenhagen 1953* (VTSup 1; Leiden: E. J. Brill, 1953) 120-127. All three studies are translated by E. W. Trueman Dicken in G. von Rad, *The Form-Critical Problem of the Hexateuch and Other Essays* (New York: McGraw-Hill, 1966).

[11] W. Baumgartner, "The Wisdom Literature," *The Old Testament and Modern Study: A Generation of Discovery and Research* (ed. H. H. Rowley; Oxford: Clarendon, 1951) 210-237.

[12] A. Alt, "Die Weisheit Salomos," *TLZ* 76 (1951) 139-144 = *idem.*, *Kleine Schriften zur Geschicte des Volkes Israel* (Munich: C. H. Beck, 1953) 2.90-99.

[13] P. L. O. Guy, *New Light from Armageddon* (Oriental Institute Communications 9; Chicago: University of Chicago, 1931).

Tell Kheleifeh during 1938-1940.[14] In the eastern Arabah south of the Dead Sea, Glueck reported an area of copper mining and smelting sites, one of which was known locally by the name Khirbet Nahas ("Copper Ruin"). Some of these sites presented pottery which, by Glueck's reckoning, placed the mining operation in the time of King Solomon.

> The exploitation of the mines was undoubtedly intensified during the reign of Solomon. Indeed it may be said that he was the first one who placed the mining industry in the Wadi Arabah upon a really national scale...
>
> Solomon's mines added great wealth to his growing riches. Quantities of copper must have been used in construction of the temple and the palace in Jerusalem, but most of it must have served as Solomon's main export and his merchants' main stock in trade.[15]

At Tell Kheleifeh, which had been identified earlier as Ezion-Geber,[16] Glueck reported an elaborate smelter-refinery from Solomon's reign.

> Hundreds of laborers had to be assembled, housed, fed, and protected at the chosen building site. As a matter of fact, most of them were probably slaves who had to be guarded and goaded to work. Skilled technicians of all kinds had to be recruited. Great caravans had to be called into existence to transport materials and food. An effective business organization had to be called into existence to regulate the profitable flow of raw materials and finished or semi-finished products. There was, so far as we know, only one man who possessed the strength, wealth and wisdom capable of initiating and carrying out such a highly complex and specialized undertaking. He was Solomon...
>
> The wise ruler of Israel was a copper king, a shipping magnate, a merchant prince, and a great builder.[17]

The dramatic archaeological discoveries described above fade from the scene during the 1960's. Solomon's stables turned out not to be Solomonic, and probably not stables.[18] Glueck himself would later concede that Tell Kheleifeh was not a copper smelter,[19] and few scholars

---

[14] N. Glueck, *The Other Side of the Jordan* (Cambridge, Mass.: American Schools of Oriental Research, 1970) 59-137.

[15] *Ibid.*, p. 100.

[16] F. Frank, "Aus der Arabah," *ZDPV* 57 (1934) 208-278, especially p. 244.

[17] Glueck, *Other Side*, p. 118.

[18] See especially Y. Yadin, "New Light on Solomon's Megiddo," *BA* 22 (1960) 62-68; and J. B. Pritchard, "The Megiddo Stables: A Reassessment," *Near Eastern Archaeology and the Twentieth Century* (ed. J. A. Sanders; Garden City, NY: Doubleday, 1970) 268-76.

[19] See especially N. Glueck, "Further Exploration in the Negeb," *BASOR* 179 (1965) 6-29, especially pp. 15-17. Glueck's initial interpretation had been overturned by B.

today would equate the site with Ezion-Geber.[20] While Solomon's stables and smelter faded from the picture, however, they were replaced by another dramatic discovery, Solomonic fortifications at Megiddo, Hazor and Gezer.[21] In 1957, excavations at Tell Qadi (Hazor) directed by Y. Yadin revealed a phase of the city which he dated to the tenth century and which had been protected by an impressive six-chambered gate with a casemate wall. According to Yadin's preliminary report,

> This gate, discovered in the northern part of the excavation, consists of six chambers, three on either side, with square towers on the outside walk. Its plan and measurements (it is some 20 m. long) are identical with the Solomonic gate found at Megiddo (strtum IV B). This fact not only confirms quite clearly the biblical narrative (I Kings, ix, 15) that Megiddo and Hazor were both rebuilt by Solomon, but even suggests that both were built by the same architect.[22]

In a follow-up study, Yadin proposed that what Macalister had interpreted as a Maccabean Castle at Tell Jezer (Gezer) was in fact another six-chambered Solomonic gate.[23] Subsequent excavations at Gezer directed by William G. Dever during 1966-1971 confirmed quickly (by 1967) that Yadin was correct.[24] Establishing that these gates were Solomonic was important not only because they supported the historicity of 1 Kgs 9:15, but also because the gates and their stratigraphical contexts, dated now precisely to the mid-10th century with biblical chronology, could serve in turn as benchmarks for more exact dating in ceramic typology.[25]

Rothenberg, "Ancient Copper Industries in the Western Arabah," *PEQ* 94 (1962) 5-71, especially pp. 44-56.

[20] The Tell el-Kheleifeh/Ezion-Geber identification seems especially unlikely in view of G. D. Pratico's reexamination of Glueck's materials, "Where Is Ezion-geber? A Reapprisal of the Site Archaeologist Nelson Glueck Identified as King Solomon's Red Sea Port," *BAR* 12 (Sept.-Oct. 1986) 24-35. Pratico concluded that the settlement probably is post-Solomonic.

[21] Retreating from his interpretation of Tell el-Kheleifeh as a Solomonic smelter-refinery, for example, Glueck reinterpreted the site to fit this newest discovery: "The excavator believes now that his structure was designed as a citadel, and was also employed, as others have suggested, as a storehouse and/or granary, and that indeed Solomon's Ezion-Geber served in a comparatively modest way as the southernmost of the fortified district and chariot cities that Solomon built in elaborate fashion at Hazor, Megiddo, and Gezer (I Kings ix. 15-17, 19)." N. Glueck, "Transjordan," *Archaeology and Old Testament Study* (ed. D. W. Thomas; Oxford: Clarendon, 1967) 329-453, especially p. 439.

[22] Y. Yadin, "Excavations at Hazor, 1957: Preliminary Communiqué," *IEJ* 8 (1958) 1-14, especially pp. 2-3.

[23] Y. Yadin, "Solomon's City Wall and Gate at Gezer," *IEJ* 8 (1958) 80-86.

[24] W. G. Dever, "Excavations at Gezer," *BA* 30 (1967) 34-47, especially pp. 39-42.

[25] See especially, J. S. Holladay, Jr., "Red Slip, Burnish, and the Solomonic Gateway at Gezer," *BASOR* 277-277 (1990) 23-70.

Dever provided a comprehensive overview of what he and others had come to regard as extensive archaeological evidence for the Davidic-Solomonic era at a 1979 symposium on the United Monarchy. Solomon's stables and mines were out of the picture by then, but Dever was confident that archaeology had verified the United Monarchy and progressed to a point that remains from the time of David and Solomon could be identified with a high degree of certainty and separated out from remains of the periods immediately preceding and following.

> Whether we designate the United Monarchy as late Iron I or early Iron II in archaeological parlance, there can be no question that (1) in absolute chronology it is set in the 10th century B.C.; and (2) in the relative course of actual political and cultural developments in ancient Israel, this brief period is a distinct entity, set off from the tumultuous, formative centuries of the period of the Judges preceding it, as well as from the larger separate histories of the states of Israel and Judah flowing from it in the 9th-7th centuries B.C.[26]

3. Reconsidering Solomon

Thus the Solomonic golden age/Age of Enlightenment remained intact through the 1970's and even increased in grandeur at the hands of biblical scholars and Palestinian archaeologists. By the end of the decade, however, new trends had begun to set in which would undercut the confidence of both biblical scholars and archaeologists on the matter. At the same 1979 symposium where Dever catalogued the archaeological remains from the time of David and Solomon, R. M. Whybray observed and documented that there was no longer consensus among critical biblical scholars that anything in the Hebrew Bible could be attributed with confidence to the Davidic-Solomonic era.[27] Whybray focused then in his presentation to the symposium on the idea of Solomonic court wisdom and demonstrated that, while something of that sort was of course possible, no strong case can be made for it. Before the symposium papers were published in 1982, the underpinnings had begun to slip also for the

[26] W. G. Dever, "Monumental Architecture in Ancient Israel in the Period of the United Monarchy," *Studies in the Period of David and Solomon and Other Essays* (ed. T. Ishida; Winona Lake, Ind.: Eisenbrauns, 1982) 269-306.

[27] R. N. Whybray, "Wisdom and Literature in the Reigns of David and Solomon," *Studies in the Period of David and Solomon and Other Essays* (ed. T. Ishida; Winona Lake, Ind.: Eisenbrauns, 1982) 13-26.

line of reasoning by which specific archaeological remains were being attributed to the time of David and Solomon. Specifically, David Ussishkin pointed out serious weaknesses in Yadin's attribution of the six-chambered gate at Megiddo to Solomon, while Israel Finkelstein challenged Dever's dating of the "Outer Wall" and supposed "Solomonic gate" at Gezer.[28] Ussishkin's and Finkelstein's challenges were serious not only because of the potential loss of architectural examples from the time of Solomon; as observed above, there were significant implications as well for ceramic typology. Just as biblical scholars could no longer with confidence attribute any specific parts of the Hebrew Bible to the time of David and Solomon, now it became questionable whether archaeologists could date any specific architectural or artifactual remains to their reigns.[29]

By the mid-1980's, therefore, both the literary-critical and archaeological supports for Solomon's golden age were in trouble and it remained only to raise the prior question whether there had been a Solomonic empire and golden age at all. I pressed this question in the Miller-Hayes history[30] and concluded that there probably had not been, at least

---

[28] D. Ussishkin, "Was the 'Solomonic' City Gate at Megiddo Built by King Solomon?" *BASOR* 239 (1980) 1-18. I. Finkelstein, "The Date of Gezer's Outer Wall," *Tell Aviv* 8 (1981) 136-45.

[29] After the Solomonic gates, the next benchmark of consequence for establishing the ceramic typology for the 11th-9th century horizon is Sheshonq's Asiatic campaign to which destruction levels at Gezer, Megiddo and Tanaach have been attributed. But this benchmark is problematic as well. Sheshonq did not include Gezer among the cities which he claimed to have conquered; the fact that he left a stele at Megiddo suggests that his destruction of that city was only partial at best; and of course the attribution of the late 10th century destructions at these three sites to Sheshonq depended somewhat to begin with on what was understood to be Solomonic period pottery. See an important collection of essays on this and related topics by G. J. Wightman, J. S. Holladay, D. Ussishkin, L. E. Stager, I. Finkelstein and W. G. Dever in the special issue on the 10th and 9th centuries ed. by W. Rast, *BASOR* 277-278 (1990) 1-130. W. G. Dever, "Of Myths and Methods," *BASOR* 277-278 (1990) 121-130, especially 127, responding to Ussishkin and Finkelstein and apparently still championing the cause for Solomonic dating of the six-chambered gates, expresses dismay: "How can we know *anything* [italics his] with certainty about the past (in this case, ancient Palestine and Israel), if we cannot even date the major phases of historical and cultural development within a margin of a century or less?" See, more recently, in response to Dever, I Finkelstein, "Penelope's Shroud Unravelled: Iron II Date of Gezer's Outer Wall Established," *Tel Aviv* 21 (1994) 276-82.

[30] J. M. Miller and J. H. Hayes, *A History of Ancient Israel and Judah* (Philadelphia: Westminster, 1986) 189-217. While I took final responsibility for chapters 1-9 and Hayes took responsibility of chapters 10-14, this whole volume resulted from active exchange of ideas between the two of us. Note also that *A History of Ancient Israel and Judah* is a separate work entirely from the Hayes-Miller, *Israelite and Judean History* (OTL; Philadelphia: Westminster, 1977) for which J.A. Soggin wrote the chapter on Solomon.

not an empire of the extent and grandeur claimed by the biblical writers and depicted in contemporary (i.e., mid-1980's) treatments of ancient Israelite history.[31] Specifically, I argued that the historical Solomon probably was a local ruler whose teritorial domain would have been limited to Palestine west of the Jordan (excluding the coastal zone) and some of the northern Transjordan. This is what he would have inherited from David in my estimation, and I found no reason to suppose that Solomon himself expanded this realm appreciably. The notion that Solomon presided over an extensive commercial empire seemed unlikely to me as well. The Phoenicians, whose merchant ships were already exploring the western Mediterranean at the time, would have desired access to the Red Sea Gulf in order to open other trading markets along the Arabian and African coasts. "Thus they apparently allowed Solomon some participation in the Red Sea trade in return for transit permission through his kingdom and access to the gulf."[32] Regarding 1 Kgs 10:28-29, usually interpreted (at considerable effort)[33] to mean that Solomon was the middleman in overland trade of horses and chariots, I observed that this passage is ambiguous at best and may have been intended as nothing more than another example of Solomon's wealth. The point of the passage, in other words, is to impress the reader that Solomon could afford to buy horses and chariots at regular market prices, not explain how Solomon gained his wealth.[34] "Any attempt to identify the pharaoh who gave his daughter to Solomon in marriage or speculation on the political and commercial implications of the queen of Sheba's visit sim-

[31] Compare, for example, H. Donner, *Geschichte des Volkes Israel und seiner Nachbarn in Grundzügen I: Von den Anfängen bis zur Staatenbildungszeit* (Göttingen: Vandenhoeck & Ruprecht, 1984) 215-232; J. A. Soggin, *A History of Ancient Israel: From the Beginnings to the Bar Kochba Revolt, A.D. 135* (tr. J. Bowden; Philadelphia: Westminster. London: SCM, 1984) 69-85; A. Lemaire, "The United Monarchy," *Ancient Israel: A Short History from Abraham to the Roman Destruction of the Temple* (ed. H. Shanks; Washington, DC: Biblical Archaeology Society, 1988); and G. W. Ahlström, *The History of Ancient Palestine from the Paleolithic Period to Alexander's Conquest* (ed. D. V. Edelman; JSOTSup 146; Sheffield: JSOT, 1993) 501-542. Although not published until 1993, Ahlström's history was prepared during the mid-1980's. Even N. P. Lemche, *Ancient Israel: A New History of Israelite Society* (Biblical Seminar 5; Sheffield: Sheffield Academic, 1988) 124-25, seemed to assume a fairly traditional Solomonic era

[32] Miller and Hayes, *History*, pp. 212-13.

[33] See, for example, Y. Ikeda, "Solomon's Trade in Horses and Chariots in Its International Setting," *Studies in the Period of David and Solomon and Other Essays* (ed. T. Ishida; Winona Lake, Ind.: Eisenbrauns, 1982) 215-38. For the problems with this interpretation, see D. G. Schley, Jr., "I Kings 10:26-29: A Reconstruction," *JBL* 106 (1987) 595-601.

[34] Miller and Hayes, *History*, p. 212.

ply misunderstands the fanciful nature of the material."[35] As for Solomon's renowned wisdom, "Whether he was a wise ruler would have been a matter of opinion even in his own day. Most of his constituency apparently thought not, since they chose to rebel at his death rather than to continue under his policies."[36]

Giovanni Garbini, whose *Storia e Ideologia nell'Israele Antico* appeared the same year (1986) as the Miller-Hayes history, called for an even more radical demolition of the traditional Solomon.[37] Others (notably E.A. Knauf,[38] Donald Redford,[39] and Thomas Thompson[40]) have since reinforced the call for a reevaluation of Solomon, and an increasing number of short studies indicate that such a movement is well underway.[41] Indeed, the whole tenor of the academic discussion pertaining to Solomon has shifted over the past decade, as is illustrated by the shifting reactions to my treatment of his reign. When it first appeared a decade ago, my treatment of Solomon generally seems to have been regarded as overly skeptical, especially in view of what was believed to be strong archaeological evidence in Solomon's behalf. Alan Millard and William Dever were particularly outspoken on this matter.[42] Nowadays, my treatment seems to be viewed as rather traditional and

---

[35] *Ibid.*, p. 196; see also p. 216.

[36] *Ibid.*, p. 199.

[37] G. Garbini, *Storia e Ideologia nell'Israele Antico* (Rome: Paideia, 1986) = *History and Ideology in Ancient Israel* (tr. J. Bowden; New York: Crossroad, 1988) especially pp. 21-32.

[38] E.A. Knauf, "King Solomon's Copper Supply," *Studia Phoenicia, 11: Phoenicia and the Bible* (ed. E. Lipinski; Orientalia Lovaniensia Analecta 44; Leuven: Department Oriëntalistiek, 1991) 167-86.

[39] D. B. Redford, *Egypt, Canaan, and Israel in Ancient Times* (Princeton: Princeton University, 1992) 283-311.

[40] T. L. Thompson, *Early History of the Israelite People: From the Written and Archaeological Sources* (SHANE 4; Leiden: E. J. Brill, 1992).

[41] Noteworthy among these are P. S. Ash, "Solomon's? District? List" *JSOT* 67 (1995) 67-86; and D. V. Edelman, "Solomon's Adversaries Hadad, Rezon and Jeroboam: A Trio of 'Bad Guy' Characters Illustrating the Theology of Immediate Retribution," *The Pitcher Is Broken: Memorial Essays for Gösta W. Ahlström* (ed. S. W. Holloway and L. K. Handy; JSOTSup 190; Sheffield: Sheffield Academic, 1995) 166-91. Also indicative of the current movement to reassess Solomon was a 1995 symposium in Jerusalem sponsored by the Deutsches Evangelisches Institut für Altertumswissenschaft des Heiligen Landes, and of course the collection of papers in this volume.

[42] A. R. Millard, "Texts and Archaeology: Weighing the Evidence, the Case for King Solomon," *PEQ* 123 (1991) 19-27. See also my response, "Solomon: International Potentate or Local King?" *PEQ* 123 (1991) 28-31. W. G. Dever, "Archaeology and the Early Monarchical Period," *The Fabric of History: Text, Artifact and Israel's Past* (ed. D. V. Edelman; JSOTSup 127; Sheffield: JSOT, 1991) 108, n. 2.

conservative; Margaret Galinas recently characterized it as a mere paraphrase of the Bible stories.[43]

4. THE CASE FOR A SOLOMONIC ERA OF MORE MODEST PROPORTIONS

Realizing that the discussion has rushed on ahead, that for some scholars the more appropriate question to be asked now is whether there was a historical Solomon at all, it will perhaps be useful to summarize the case for a less extensive and fabulous Solomonic realm than was generally envisioned until a decade ago. The case reduces to four interrelated but essentially independent arguments: A) The emergence of such an empire during the early Iron Age would have been out of keeping with the general circumstances of the times. B) An empire of such magnitude and renown as envisioned in the biblical accounts surely would have left some epigraphic traces. C) While it is possible that the two biblical accounts of Solomon's reign preserve literary elements which hark back to Solomonic times, this can no longer be maintained with any degree of certainty. Moreover, close examination of the passages which show even some promise of having derived from Solomonic times suggests a territorial realm and royal operation of relatively modest proportions. D) The archaeological evidence also seems to argue against the existence of an empire and golden age centered in the Palestinian hill-country during the 10th century BCE. Taken by itself, no one of these arguments is decisive. Together they constitute a strong case.

A) *The general circumstances of the times*

The opening centuries of the Iron Age (from approximately the beginning of the 12th century well into the 9th century BCE) seems to have been a kind of "dark age" throughout the ancient world. The Bronze Age empires had collapsed, peoples were on the move, and localized sociopolitical structures apparently were the order of the day. A 10th century, Palestinian-based empire of the territorial extent, opulence and international influence envisioned by the biblical writers would have been out

---

[43] M. M. Gelinas, "United Monarchy-Divided Monarchy: Fact or Fiction?" *The Pitcher Is Broken: Memorial Essays for Gösta W. Ahlström* (ed. S. W. Holloway and L. K. Handy; JSOTSup 190; Sheffield: Sheffield Academic, 1995) 225-37, especially p. 226, n. 2.

of keeping with these general circumstances of the times. One can argue that it was precisely the lack of political and commercial competition during the 10th century, the power vacuum which characterized the day, which enabled David and Solomon to create such an empire. The other possibility, however, which seems more likely when the other three arguments are taken into account, is that the Solomonic empire envisioned by the biblical writers was anachronistic as well as idealized. Influenced by what would have been for them the more recent memory of the Assyrian, Babylonian and Persian empires, they imagined an empire of equal magnitude for Solomon, the builder of the Jerusalem temple.

B) *Absence of epigraphic evidence*

While it is conceivable that an empire emerged in Palestine during the early Iron Age, expanded to include territories from the Egyptian frontier to the Euphrates, lasted for almost a half century, and then disappeared without a single epigraphical trace; while this is conceivable, it does stretch the imagination. Sheshonq's single campaign into Palestine left an epigraphical trail,[44] and the recently discovered Tell Dan inscription apparently records a campaign into Palestine by a neighboring Aramaean king (probably one of the kings of Damascus) a half century or so later.[45] Thus to explain the absence of epigraphical evidence for Solomon on the grounds that there is a general absence of epigraphical evidence of any sort from Palestine during his period in not entirely true. Furthermore, this explanation begs the question. If Solomon truly presided over a golden age anything on the order of that described in 1 Kgs 3-11 and 2 Chr 1-9, then why is there so little epigraphical evidence

[44] C. S. Fisher, *The Excavation of Armageddon* (Oriental Institute Communications 4; Chicago: University of Chicago, 1929). See especially the preface by J. H. Breasted, pp. vii-xiii, and fig. 7b. See also R. Penchas' drawing of the inscription fragment in D. Ussishkin, "Notes on Megiddo, Gezer, Ashdod, and Tel Batash in the Tenth to Ninth Centuries B.C.," *BASOR* 277-278 (1990) 72.

[45] A. Biran and J. Naveh, "An Aramaic Fragment from Dan," *IEJ* 43 (1993) 81-98; B. Halpern, "The Stela from Dan: Epigraphic and Historical Considertions," *BASOR* 296 (1994) 63-80. Assuming the accuracy of the "house of David" translation, the new inscription from Tell Dan verifies the existence of a Davidic dynasty during the 9th century BCE and accordingly provides strong circumstantial evidence in support of the biblical materials which place the founding of that dynasty in 10th century Jerusalem. This is rather distant circumstantial evidence, however, and does not necessarily support all the the specifics of the biblical account regarding how the dynasty came to be founded. It is a far cry from supporting the biblical visions of a Solomonic golden age.

of any sort and why are the exceptions occasioned by outside encroachments on the land rather than from Solomon's empire itself?

C) *The biblical accounts of Solomon's reign*

Since my treatment of Solomon in the Miller-Hayes history involved a detailed examination of the biblical materials, it is necessary here only to review several basic points. First, any attempt to extract historical information about Solomon from the Hebrew Bible must focus on the account of his reign in 1 Kgs 3-11; the difficulties which a historian encounters with the Genesis-2 Kings composition are only compounded in the Chronicler's history. Moreover, the larger-than-life image of Solomon which emerges from 1 Kgs 3-11 rests largely on certain passages (especially 1 Kgs 4:20-34) which make broad, sweeping and rather fantastic claims in his behalf. These passages almost certainly were authored by the late Judean compilers of Genesis-2 Kings and represent their idealized and anachronistic image of an era long past. It is difficult to avoid the impression, further, that some of the episodes reported in the 1 Kgs 3-11 account of Solomon's reign are folk legends: e.g., Solomon's arbitration between the two prostitutes, the exotic Queen of Sheba's visit, and his marriage to the anonymous daughter of the anonymous pharaoh. These are the kind of stories one expects to read in the *Thousand and One Nights*.

As observed early on in this essay, literary-critics are no longer confident about attributing any particular sections, sources or passages in the Hebrew Bible to Solomonic times. Moreover, it is not just a question of whether early materials have been preserved, but also whether they have been preserved in proper historical context and intact, i.e., early materials which actually pertained to other kings may have been associated incorrectly with Solomon, or authentic Solomonic materials may have been intentionally revised or unintentionally "muddled" during the process of transmission.[46] Clearly the 1 Kings account of Solomon's reign

[46] Suppose, for example, that we had only the Chronicler's account of Solomon's reign and were considering whether the statement in 2 Chr 8:1-2 that "Solomon rebuilt the cities which Hiram had given to him, and settled the people of Israel in them" represented authentic historical information. Because we do have the 1 Kings account, we know that the Chronicler did in fact derive his information from an earlier source (compare 1 Kgs 9:10-14), but recast the information in such a way as to reverse its meaning. Why should we assume that the compilers of 1 Kgs 3-11 utilized their sources any differently, or for that matter that the 1 Kings rendition of the incident in question is to be trusted over that of 2 Chronicles?

exhibits schematic notions of history which must distort to some degree whatever authenitc historical memory is preserved. This is especially obvious with the chronological data provided: work on the temple was begun in the fourth year of Solomon's forty-year reign which was also the four hundred and eightieth year after the exodus from Egypt; all of Solomon's building projects required exactly half of his reign, twenty years, seven years of which was devoted to building the temple (1 Kgs 6:1,37-38; 7:1; 11:42). Four, forty, multiples of forty, and seven; these are symbolic numbers. Note also that, as with David, Solomon's reign is presented in two segments. 1 Kgs 3-11 presents Solomon the faithful ruler who achieved the golden age, then 1 Kgs 11 presents a later Solomon led astray by foreign wives and struggling to maintain the security of his kingdom. This is an artificial arrangement; the compilers separated out and placed at the end of Solomon's reign the items which conflicted with their notion of an ideal Solomonic era. Donald Redford has warned recently that Solomon may be a thoroughly composit character, such a mixture of quasi-historical memories that we can never hope to get it all disentangled.

> The fashioning of Solomon's figure from such ingredients as imperial hegemony, prowess in building, foreign trade (especially up the Red Sea), wealth, wisdom, and marriage to a great king's daughter suggests the obvious parallel of the semi-legendary emperor of the remote past who took shape in the sixth century B.E. in the person of "Sesostris." Sesostris, an amalgam of the historical Tuthmoses III and Rameses II, is certainly no figment of the imagination; but the tales told of him in Herodotus, Diodorus, and others are quite unreliable. For his part, Solomon, as he appears in I Kings, has assumed the guise of the "Sesostris of Israel."[47]

Similarly, Diana Edelman has raised the possibility that Hadad the Edomite and Rezon of Damascus were composite "type characters."[48]

Among the passages mentioned most often as possibly having derived from genuine early records are 1 Kgs 4:1-6 (the list of Solomon's high officials), 1 Kgs 4:7-19 (the list of Solomon's *nissabim* "who provided food for the king and his household"), and the occasiaonal references to Solomon's commercial ventures such as 1 Kgs 10:11,22 and 28-29. Also largely on the grounds that they go against the grain of the idealized picture of Solomon developed in the editorial passages, confidence has been placed in the brief note about Solomon's forced labor in 1 Kgs 5:13-17

---

[47] Redford, *Egypt, Canaan, and Israel*, p. 309.

[48] Edelman, "Solomon's Adversaries," pp. 166-91.

(although the numbers seem excessive) and the reports in 1 Kgs 11 about Solomon's troubles with Hadad the Edomite, Rezon of Damascus and Jeroboam. Close examination of these passages which seem to offer the most promise of having preserved authentic information from Solomon's time suggests a considerably smaller territorial realm and much less impressive royal operation than the sweeping editorial passages proclaim.

Consider, for example, the matter of Solomon's territorial realm. Whether or not the twelve *nissabim* listed in 1 Kgs 4:7-19 represented twelve districts,[49] the cities and regions involved are all fairly close to the Palestinian hill country and Gilead. Solomon's building activities reported in 1 Kgs 9:15-19 were all well within the limits of western Palestine. Similarly, whether one concludes that Solomon extracted forced labor from "all Israel" or only from the surviving descendants of non-Israelites, both 1 Kgs 5:13-16 and 9:20-22 seem to assume that his labor force came from close to home, i.e., rather than from other peoples who presumably would have been subject to Jerusalem if Solomon actually ruled from the Egyptian frontier to the Euphrates (Aramaeans, Phoenicians, Philistines, Ammonites, Moabites, Edomites). With Rezon entrenched in Damascus and harassing Solomon's frontier (1 Kgs 11:23-25), Solomon could hardly have held much Aramaean territory. The report that Solomon handed over twenty cities in Galilee to Hiram as payment for building materials and gold (1 Kgs 9:11-14) seems to rule out the possibility that Solomon exercised any degree of dominion over Phoenicia. While it is often assumed that David and Solomon ruled Philistia, this is not at all self-evident from the biblical materials. Neither is it clear that David's (and consequently Solomon's) rule over the Edomites and Moabites involved greater Edom and Moab (as often depicted in Bible atlases).[50]

In short, when examined closely, even the biblical materials argue against the notion that Solomon "had dominion over all the region west of the Euphrates from Tiphsah to Gaza." The one outstanding exception is 2 Chr 8:1-6, the Chronicler's parallel to 1 Kgs 9:10-19. Whereas the 1 Kgs 9 context implies that "Tamar (var. Tadmor) in the wilderness" was located somewhere in the Judean wilderness, the Chronicler's version

---

[49] On this problem see Miller and Hayes, *History*, pp. 205-207; and Ash, "Solomon's? District? List," pp. 67-86.

[50] See J. M. Miller, "Early Monarchy in Moab?" *Early Edom and Moab: The Beginning of the Iron Age in Southern Jordan* (ed. P. Bienkowski; SAM 7; Sheffield: J. R. Collis, 1992) 77-92.

clearly takes this to be the Tadmor in the Syrian desert (i.e., Palmyra) and also has Solomon conquering Hamath-zobah and building store cities in that vicinity. This same Chronicles passage has Huram (Hiram) giving Solomon the twenty cities rather than the other way around, however, so simply harmonizing the two passages is not a viable solution. Obviously this is another example of the Chronicler's tendency to adjust information which he found in his sources in order to enhance Solomon's image.

D) *Palestinian archaeology*

Archaeology, by providing parallels and visual examples, illustrates and enlivens the biblical accounts of Solomon's reign. It has long been observed, for example, that the plan of Solomon's temple as described in 1 Kings has parallels in excavated temples from the Iron Age and that its furnishings and decorative motifs were typical of the Iron Age as well.[51] Such parallels and illustrations, besides clarifying and enliving the biblical accounts with visual images, verify that the accounts have their setting in the real world of the Iron Age and are narrated by persons generally familiar with that setting. They may also be drawn upon to argue for the plausibility of certain aspects of the biblical accounts. For example, Alan Millard and Kenneth Kitchen have gone to great lengths to document that the large amount of wealth ascribed to Solomon is paralleled in the case of certain Egyptian pharaohs and therefore plausible.[52] However plausibility does not necessarily imply probability and all of the archaeological parallels and illustrations combined do not verify historicity. The late Judean compilers of the biblical accounts of Solomon's reign would have been familiar with the Iron Age world (it was their own world) and naturally they would have assumed it as the setting for Solomon. Moreover, the Jerusalem temple itself was there to be seen as late as the 6th century. Thus a historian seeking to verify that the biblical writers were transmitting authentic information about Solomon's

---

[51] See most recently E. Bloch-Smith, "'Who Is the King of Glory?' Solomon's Temple and Its Symbolism," and A. R. Millard, "King Solomon's Shields," *Scripture and Other Artifacts: Essays on the Bible and Archaeology in Honor of Philip J. King* (ed. M. D. Coogan, J. C. Exum and L. E. Stager; Louisville, Ken.: Westminster/John Knox, 1994) 18-31 and 286-95, respectively.

[52] A. R. Millard, "Does the Bible Exaggerate King Solomon's Golden Wealth?" *BAR* 15 (1989) 20-29, 31, 34; and K. A. Kitchen, "Where Did Solomon's Gold Go?" *BAR* 15 (1989) 30, 32-33.

day, rather than fantasizing about a legendary king of the distant past, will want to inquire whether any of the archaeological parallels and illustrations would have obtained *only* in the early Iron Age and thus would have been known to the late Judean compilers only if they had access to early Iron Age sources.

If archaeology is to be of much help in the search for the historical Solomon beyond clarifying the general Iron Age setting and verifying the plausibility of the biblical accounts of his reign, we also need to pose three further questions. First, is it possible to connect any particular archaeological remains specifically with Solomon? The fortification systems at Megiddo, Hazor and Gezer are the most likely candidates at the moment and their Solomonic pedigree is in serious trouble.[53] Second, a closely related but broader question, is it possible at this stage of research in Palestinian archaeology to distinquish specifically 10th century remains (i.e., the century within which Solomon would have lived according to biblical chronology) from the archaeological remains of the centuries immediately preceding and following? This is an "in house" question for the archaeologists to work out *unless* the benchmarks and absolute dates which they use to anchor their "archaeological chronology" (and work out the details of 11th-10th-9th ceramic typology) are derived from the Hebrew Bible and/or based on widely accepted dates which themselves are derived ultimately from biblical chronology. In that case, it is no longer a purely archaeological matter, biblical scholars have both a voice and a stake in the discussion. My impression is that archaeologists are not yet to the point where they can date architectural features and related occupational phases specifically to the 10th century with a high degree of certainty, much less narrow the focus to the forty (?) years of that century when Solomon would have been on the throne. Those who claim to be able to do so, such as William Dever and John Holladay, depend heavily on a rather non-critical reading of the Hebrew Bible.[54]

Finally, a third question: Whether or not Palestinian archaeology is sufficiently fine tuned to date architectural and artifactual remains to specifically the reign of Solomon, or even to the 10th century, what can be said about the general archaeological picture of the 11th-10th-9th century horizon? Does the emerging archaeological picture of that

---

[53] I am less confident on this matter now than a decade ago; Miller and Hayes, *History*, p. 189.

[54] See especially the references in nn. 25, 26, and 29 above.

broader time frame seem to represent a good "fit" with the biblical account of the emergence of the Jerusalem monarchy? To pose the question another way, is the emerging archaeological picture such that, even if there were no Hebrew Bible and archaeologists had no prior knowledge of Solomon, would they likely have hypothesized by now something on the order of a Solomonic empire and golden age to explain their findings? I think not. Clearly urban centers were beginning to reemerge throughout the Middle East during the late 11th, 10th, and early 9th centuries BCE. The appearance of stronger fortifications and more impressive building remains during approximately that time period at sites such as Hazor, Megiddo and Gezer suggest the emergence of stronger centralized government(s) in Palestine as well. Yet it does not seem to me that the archaeological picture suggests, or even fits easily, with the biblical claim that there appeared rather suddenly during approximately the 10th century, and then disappeared just as suddenly, a powerful empire centered in Jerusalem whose monarch enjoyed far-reaching international influence and imported expensive goods from distant lands. If nothing else, the fact that surprisingly few international trade items have turned up among the Iron Age I ruins argues otherwise.[55]

5. Some Observations for the Continued Discussion

Anticipating that the debate regarding Solomon will continue for a time, I wish to reemphasize three basic points made above and spell out more explicitly some of my methodological assumptions. A) While the Hebrew Bible obviously is not an ideal source for historical information, it is the only source available to us from pre-Roman times that mentions Solomon. We can hope that future epigraphical and archaeological discoveries will shed further light on the Solomon issue. For the moment, however, even to talk about a historical Solomon implies some degree of reliance on the Hebrew Bible. B) The Hebrew Bible is literature and should be examined with methods and tools appropriate to literature. This is not to promise that literary-critical analysis will produce a trustworthy glimpse of the historical Solomon. My contention is rather that

[55] Observed by K. M. Kenyon, *Archaeology in the Holy Land* (London: Ernest Benn, 1960) 256; and by J. B. Pritchard, "The Age of Solomon," *Solomon and Sheba* (ed. J. B. Pritchard; London: Phaidon, 1974) 17-39.

we have no choice; regardless of how disappointing and uncertain the results, any competent search for the historical Solomon must be firmly grounded in careful literary-critical analysis of Genesis-2 Kings and the Chronicler's history. C) While the literary stratigraphy of these two compositions is easily as difficult to disentangle and interpret as the archaeological stratigraphy of Megiddo and Gezer, and every bit as resistant to firm dates, it seems to me that two important conclusions cannot be avoided. First, both compositions, especially the Chronicler's history and passages such as 1 Kgs 4:20-34, reflect an idealized and legendary Solomon, Solomon as he came to be envisioned in Judean circles approximately a half millennium after he would have lived. Second, close examination of the passages which show the most promise of dating back to Solomonic times suggests a territorial domain, royal operation and national economy of much more modest proportions than the late Judean compilers of Genesis-2 Kings and the Chronicler's history imagined for him.

Emphasizing that any proper search for the historical Solomon must be firmly grounded in the Hebrew Bible and take seriously its literary-critical complexities does not mean that other kinds of evidence are to be ignored. Quite the contrary. My contention is that archaeology, sociology, and other such disciplines, should be allowed to speak first with their own voice, without prompting from the Hebrew Bible, before we jump ahead to "biblical archaeology" and "biblical sociology" kinds of arguments. What we really need from archaeologists, in my opinion, is a fair assessment of what the archaeological evidence in and of itself tells us about Palestine during the early Iron Age. Is it possible at this stage of archaeological research in Palestine, without factoring in information or assumptions derived from the Hebrew Bible, to recognize a distinctive 10th century phase which differs appreciably from the phases preceding and following? What sort of socio-political situation do the material remains from this phase suggest?

For a final assessment of Solomon, of course, it is necessary to move beyond the narrowly defined question of what can be learned from archaeology in and of itself and explore what can be learned when the archaeological evidence and biblical materials are cross-examined in relation to each other. At that point, Dever's "balance of probability" question becomes appropriate: whether the available archaeological evidence viewed alongside a biblical passage "tips the scales of the balance of probability" in favor of confidence in the historicity of the latter.[56] If one begins with that question, however, it is very easy to slip into an "archaeological parallels=plausibility=probability" kind of argument which is deceptive and not at all the same thing as determining "balance of probability." Indeed, Dever himself illustrates the problem in his recent attempt to verify the historicity of Josiah's reform by demonstrating that the sorts of practices which the Hebrew Bible credits Josiah with reforming actually existed in ancient Palestine.[57] This is comparable to verfying the historicity of Agatha Christie's *Murder on the Orient Express* by demonstrating that there really were passenger trains similar to the Orient Express and that the furnishings and characters mentioned in the novel were indeed typical of the era. Starting with the "balance of probability" question also tends to ignore the composite character of the biblical materials. It is not a simple question of whether archaeology tips the scales in favor of confidence in the biblical account of Solomon's reign. Which passages does the archaeological evidence seem to support; those such as 1 Kgs 4:20-34 which make the amazing claims regarding the extent and wealth of Solomon's empire, or the possibly older texts such as 1 Kgs 4:7-19 which seem to imply a more modest Solomonic kingdom?

The same goes for sociology, anthropology and other disciplines. First we need to establish what these disciplines can tell us relevant to circumstances in early Iron Age Palestine without biblical prompting, or at least we need to approach these disciplines in such a fashion that their voices can be heard separately from that of the Hebrew Bible. It begs the historicity question, for example, simply to assume from the Bible that an Israelite empire emerged in the 10th century and then set about to explain "scientifically" with jargon derived from sociology, anthropology, economics and other disciplines how this might have happened.[58] A more appropriate question to ask is whether sociologists and anthropologists, on the basis of their studies of normal societal patterns, might have predicted this sort of thing to happen. Would professional sociolo-

---

[56] See, e.g., W. G. Dever, "'Will the Real Israel Please Stand Up?' Archaeology and Israelite Historiography: Part I," *BASOR* 297 (1995) 61-80, especially p. 72.

[57] W. G. Dever, "The Silence of the Text: An Archaeological Commentary on 2 Kings 23," *Scripture and Other Artifacts: Essays on the Bible and Archaeology in Honor of Philip J. King* (ed. M. D. Coogan, J. C. Exum and L. E. Stager; Louisville, Ken.: Westminster/John Knox, 1994) 143-68, especially p. 158.

[58] As, for example, R. B. Coote and K. W. Whitelam, *The Emergence of Early Israel in Historical Perspective* (SWBA 5; Sheffield: Almond, 1987). See Miller, "Is It Possible to Write," pp. 93-102.

gists regard it as normal for a population group in early Iron Age Palestine to have made two relatively sudden transitions, first from a threatened hill-country tribal society to an internationally prominent empire, and then from an empire back to two relatively insignificant hill-country kingdoms?[59]

Given the ambivalence of our evidence, biblical and otherwise, the most we can hope to achieve is an informed guess about the historical Solomon. My "best guess," spelled out more fully in the Miller-Hayes history, is that Solomon probably was a historical figure, but of more local stature than the biblical writers envisioned.[60] While my approach cannot claim methodological purity and the resulting picture of Solomon offers little in the way of firm historical facts, I nevertheless find this approach more appealing and my Solomon more historically convincing than the two leading options. One option, championed by Alan Millard and Kenneth Kitchen, is to take the Hebrew Bible essentially at face value and depend heavily on the parallels=plausibility=probability line of argument. Consequently, their Solomon is all that the most extravagant biblical passages claim him to be and the grandeur of his empire is richly illustrated by epigraphical and archaeological parallels from other empires of the ancient world. My objections to their approach will be obvious from the discussion above. The opposite extreme, championed by Thomas Thompson,[61] is to dismiss the Hebrew Bible as a source for historical information and declare as non-historical everything it says about Israelite history (including Solomon) before the mid-9th century BCE when Israel begins to turn up for certain in epigraphical sources.[62] I find Thompson's approach no more convincing or methodologically acceptable than that of Millard and Kitchen. If nothing else, the fact that the compilers of Genesis-2 Kings were aware of Sheshonq's Asiatic campaign and placed it well within the ballpark chronologically,[63] suggests to me that they were not operating totally in the dark about political circumstances during the 10th century BCE. The Tell Dan inscription

[59] See, e.g., Lemche, *Ancient Israel*, p. 125.

[60] Miller and Hayes, *History*, p. 160.

[61] Thompson, *Early History of the Israelite People*.

[62] Taking into account that "house of David" is not the only possible translation of *byt-dwd* in line 9 of the Tell Dan Inscription, although it seems the most natural one. See P. R. Davies, "House of David Built on Sand," *BAR* 20 (1994) 54-55.

[63] I am aware of Garbini's suggestion that Sheshonq's Asiatic campaign may have occurred during Solomon's reign rather than in Rehoboam's. By "well within the ballpark" I mean even within the right century. See Garbini, *Storia e Ideologia* = *History and Ideology*, pp. 29-30.

adds further strong circumstantial evidence for an early founding of the Davidic dynasty.[64] I am encouraged still further by the fact that, when the Israelite and Judean kings do begin to turn up in epigraphical records, they appear in the same time frame and chronological sequence as presupposed by the Hebrew Bible.[65] Also there are incidents reported (such as the Assyrian destruction of Samaria and siege of Jerusalem) which "fit," even if not always precisely, with the biblical accounts. Since there is a reasonable degree of "fit" for the later period when we do have some epigraphic evidence against which to check the biblical accounts, it seems methodologically unsound to dismiss the earlier part of the accounts for lack of epigraphical support.

Everything we know, or think we know, about the historical Solomon rests ultimately on the Hebrew Bible. Yet the biblical materials have a long and complex history of their own and the Solomon which they present is a largely legendary figure. I reject the short-cut approaches of Millard (brush aside the Bible's literary complexities and take its account of Solomon essentially at face value) and Thompson (dismiss the biblical account of Solomon as useless for the historian's purposes and declare Solomon unhistorical), and favor a middle course (attempt with the tools of literary-critical analysis to extract from the Bible at least some bits of authentic information about the historical Solomon). I am aware that the literary-critical analysis has its own problems and that this middle course is likely to produce very little in the way of undisputed conclusions. Yet I see this as our only option. While archaeology, sociology and related disciplines have voices to be heard, they do not provide other routes to the historical Solomon which by-pass the complexities and uncertainties in the biblical account.

---

[64] Of course Thompson and his colleagues challenge the "House of David" translation. See nn. 45 and 62 above.

[65] John Hayes made this observation in an oral conversation.

ASSESSING SOLOMON: HISTORY OR LEGEND?

ALAN MILLARD

By the title of his paper "Separating the Solomon of History from the Solomon of Legend" Maxwell Miller begs a question. There is undoubtedly a Solomon of legend, the Solomon known from many stories outside the Bible in Jewish, Arab and other traditions, reaching down to Rudyard Kipling's *Just So Stories*. Whether the biblical accounts of Solomon are legends or contain legends, or not, has to be considered with care and without preconceptions. Alexander the Great is a figure of legend, but there are sufficient contemporary sources, written and artefactual, to assure us he was a magnificent young conqueror. The lack of such sources for Solomon does not permit anyone to treat the narratives about him as legend *simpliciter*. Miller avoids doing that to a large extent, then lets himself down by saying the biblical texts "reflect an idealized and legendary Solomon" [p. 21] and by characterizing some episodes as "the kind of stories one expects to read in the *Thousand and One Nights*" [p. 15]. Those episodes are thereby marked for the reader as unhistorical, without argument or evidence, by a subjective judgment based on comparison with literature from the Middle Ages. And the preceding sentences in Miller's essay share the same attitude, adding supposition about authorship which is, again, unsubstantiated. The ancient Near East does have fantasy stories, such as Gilgamesh and the Garden of Jewels (Tablet IX) or the Egyptian Tale of the Magicians.[1] By contrast, the Solomon Narrative is prosaic, not comparable with those and similar pieces of ancient literature.

In common with many writers, Miller gives the impression there is a lot of historical knowledge available about the 10th century BC, although he begins by noting the absence of contemporary Hebrew and Phoenician records, citing Josephus' version of one Greek reporter of Phoenician history. The period is apparently so well known, however, that, partly quoting from an earlier study, he can assert, "The Phoe-

[1] See K. A. Kitchen, "Israel Seen from Egypt: Understanding the Biblical Text from Visuals and Methodology," *TynBul* 42 (1991) 113-26, especially pp. 118-21.

nicians...would have desired access to the Red Sea Gulf..."Thus they apparently allowed Solomon some participation in the Red Sea trade in return for transit permission through his kingdom and some access to the gulf" [p. 7]. Yet this is speculation in the absence of evidence. If perception of the Phoenicians as thrusting traders in the 10th century is correct, as it is for later times for which there is evidence, that does not prove they dominated Solomon in the manner indicated; it is just as possible they treated him on terms of equality, as in the Hebrew account, and the venture they shared with him contributed to the growth of their mercantile power. Here the biblical text is discounted in favour of speculation.

The tendency to minimize the value of biblical reports and maximize the significance of other sources is exemplified in the work of G. Garbini to whom Miller refers as even more radical than himself [p. 12]. Garbini states, for example, that the pharaoh Siamun "led an expedition against Palestine"[2] as a matter of historical fact, linking the campaign with the capture of Gezer then given to Solomon as a dowry with the Pharaoh's daughter (1 Kgs 9:16). Information about Siamun's campaign comes from a single fragment of relief from Tanis which shows Siamun killing an enemy. The pharaoh is identified by a broken cartouche, the only text present, and the enemy holds an object which has been recognized as an axe of Aegean style. The axe led the discoverer, P. Montet, to suggest Siamun attacked Philistines of the Palestinian coast, an attack which might be linked with the unnamed pharaoh's capture of Gezer.[3] Although this is an acceptable proposal, turning it into a factual statement exceeds the bounds of legitimate scientific interpretation. The qualified phrasing of the eminent Egyptologist J. Černý is more apt: "It seems...that the relief commemorates a real invasion by the Egyptian in this direction [Palestine] and Gezer would be an obvious target. Solomon's father-in-law would, if this were the case, be Siamun."[4] Garbini proceded to argue on general historical grounds against the marriage between a pharaoh's daughter and Solomon, "From whatever point of view we look at it, the marriage of Solomon to the daughter of pharaoh seems improbable," a conclusion which would be true in the

[2] G. Garbini, *History and Ideology in Ancient Israel* (London: SCM, 1988) 28.

[3] P. Montet, *L'Egypte et la Bible* (Neuchatel: Delachaux et Niestlé, 1959) 39-40.

[4] J. Černý "Egypt from the Death of Ramesses III to the End of the Twenty-First Dynasty," *CAH*[2] 3.1.606-57, quotation, p. 657.

heyday of Egyptian power but which, for the time of Solomon, historical reality contradicts.[5]

The extent of Solomon's realm is brought into question for various reasons. One is the imposition of the corvée on the area of Israel, "rather than...other peoples... (Aramaeans, Phoenicians, Philistines, Moabites, Edomites)," as is implied would be expected if they were subjected groups [p. 17]. Logistics contribute to this, for foreign workers would have to be herded into the country, housed and fed, marshalled and controlled, demanding a considerable organisation and body of guards, whereas local workmen, even if reluctant, had their homes in the land and demanded no extra provender. There is no hint of deportation or resettlement such as the Assyrians practiced. Another limitation on Solomon's realm is deduced from the revolt of Rezon of Damascus (1 Kgs 11:23-25). Rezon's rule means "Solomon could hardly have held much Aramaean territory" [p. 17]. Rezon's role is easily magnified. A rebel leader in Damascus would not necessarily exclude Solomon from areas further north at a time when there were several small principalities in the area, nothing indicates Rezon was an equal to the later Ben-Hadad or Hazael. It was the king of Zobah who had some form of control up to the Euphrates which David took over, not a king of Damascus (cf. 2 Sam 8:3-10; 10:6, 15-19). The history of Damascus in the 10th century is known solely from biblical references, so to picture it as a powerful centre controlling all routes from Israel to the north is a greater assumption than to picture it as a centre of hostility to Solomon, perhaps impeding the flow of some trade and tribute, but not cutting him off from other areas of Aramaean occupation. When examined closely, I maintain, the biblical narratives present Solomon as a wealthy, powerful king, though flawed. Neither they nor external evidence offer anything to contradict the claim that he "had dominion over all the region west of the Euphrates from Tiphsah to Gaza" (1 Kgs 4:24 [Hebrew 5:1]), ruling as suzerain over vassal states outside Israel, allied to Tyre.

There is welcome recognition on Miller's part, however, of "the fact that the compilers of Genesis-2 Kings...were not operating totally in the dark about political circumstances during the 10th century BCE...when the Israelite and Judaean kings do begin to turn up in epigraphical records, they appear in the same time frame and chronological sequence as presupposed by the Hebrew Bible" and, given the correlations

[5] See K. A. Kitchen, "Sheba and Arabia," pp. 127-53. [this volume]

between biblical and extra-biblical sources for the 8th and 7th centuries BC, "it seems methodologically unsound to dismiss the earlier part of the accounts for lack of epigraphical support" [p. 24]. (Earlier in his essay Miller used the absence of epigraphical support as a pointer to the unimportance of Solomon's realm.) It is alarming to receive the impression that Maxwell Miller was unaware until recently, when a colleague drew it to his attention [n. 65], how closely the Hebrew and Assyrian texts correlate on regnal names and sequences, both for the names of Israelite and Judaean kings and for the Assyrian emperors. The data are easily accessible in the standard translation of Assyrian royal inscriptions, in the excerpts in *ANET* and now in the volumes edited by W. W. Hallo.[6] Baruch Halpern recently prepared a summary table for a popular magazine to bring home the point.[7] The difference between Miller's approach and mine lies in determining how much information in the books of Kings (for the present study) can be deemed historical, over and above those simple chronological points. Where there is nothing to give written help, recourse to circumstantial evidence is appropriate and demonstrating that is the aim of my essay. The results can never resolve questions of the historic or legendary nature of any biblical statement. By showing some of those statements actually reflect attested ancient practices, they do give plausibility to the Hebrew text, a plausibility which has usually been ignored or denied, as the few quotations included in my paper, taken from a variety of commentators, reveal.

Maxwell Miller contends that "any competent search for the historical Solomon must be firmly grounded in careful literary-critical analysis" of the biblical texts, admitting the results may be "disappointing and uncertain" [p. 21]. My brief comments on literary-criticism were intended to show the precarious basis of certain "results." They dealt with one detail as an example because the whole literary-critical edifice is founded on details and falls if those "results" are undermined. Other literary approaches Miller mentioned see reports about some figures as describing 'composite "type characters,"' so they are concoctions of the writers rather than real biographies, Solomon, Hadad and Rezon being cited [pp. 15-16]. Here human nature is involved! A story of a man whose behav-

[6] D. D. Luckenbill, *Ancient Records of Assyria* (Chicago: University of Chicago, 1926); and W. W. Hallo, ed., *The Context of Scripture* (Leiden: E. J. Brill, 1997).

[7] B. Halpern, "Erasing History: The Minimalist Assault on Ancient Israel," *BibRev* 11 (December 1995) 26-35, 47, table on p. 30; cf. my paper, "Israelite and Aramean History in the Light of Inscriptions," *TynBul* 41 (1990) 261-75.

ior had certain consequences in a certain place at a particular time is open to doubt, in the absence of corroboration, because a comparable story exists elsewhere, variations may enter through separate traditions or by author's preferences. On this premise much of history could be discounted; two thousand years hence a biography of Adolf Hitler focusing on his aim to exterminate the Jewish people could be treated as an account of "a thoroughly composite character" drawn from the figure of Haman. The literary-critical analysis applied to the Hebrew Bible has no sound basis in the ancient Near East and does not work when applied to ancient near eastern texts. Methods of ancient authors, editors, compilers and copyists are only now beginning to be understood and much more investigation is required in order to produce adequate models for discerning the stages in the creation of the Old Testament books. In this situation, literary-critical analysis, established in a late 19th century intellectual milieu, does not deserve the priority it is habitually accorded, the biblical texts need to be viewed in the light of the realities of the ancient Near East, to be examined in their ancient context and assessed within its parameters.

KING SOLOMON IN HIS ANCIENT CONTEXT

ALAN MILLARD

A book known from fragmentary copies to be at least two thousand years old reports the history of kings of Israel whose rule began one thousand years earlier. Although the Book of Kings was certainly written before *ca.* 200 BC, when it was translated into Greek, its actual age cannot be determined. The last event recorded, the elevation of Jehoiachin of Judah from prison to the table of King Awel-Marduk in Babylon, can be set soon after that king's accession in 562 BC. Whether the work was completed shortly after that time or during the following two or three centuries, the historian needs to know what reliance he can place on those reports since there are no other accounts of most of the events they portray from elsewhere in the ancient Near East. In particular, do the chapters about Solomon, 1 Kgs 1-11, which we shall call the Solomon Narrative, reflect situations of the 10th century BC or do they represent concepts about that era which only became current hundreds of years later? Was there a splendid ruler in Jerusalem about 950 BC? Do the reports embroider a more modest kernel, or are they the fables of folklore, or the wistful concoctions of exiled Jews who imagined their past in the light of Nebuchadnezzar's magnificence, or the fictions of theological propagandists? Although the texts are literary compositions, they plainly have a theological purpose and are part of a religious compilation, the Hebrew Bible, they are not thereby rendered worthless as factual sources, for the most artistic literary composition and the most tendentious concoction may portray circumstances and events with great accuracy while arranging them or interpreting them for aesthetic ends or according to a philosophy the reader recognizes as unacceptably biased. While the literary and theological aspects of the Solomon Narrative and their analyses may have value in themselves, the first purpose of this essay is to examine the Narrative in the light of knowledge about the ancient Near East to discover whether it may tell of a 10th century BC king ruling magnificently in Jerusalem or not. Were the Solomon Narrative a hitherto unknown writing embodied in a recently excavated manuscript some two thousand years old, a primary mode of evaluation would be contextual, so that will occupy the major part of this essay.

Historical errors, provable anachronisms, inconsistencies with other records and material remains from the ancient Near East would obviously count against the text. Superficial comparisons with completely different writings from other ages and cultures, such as the Arabian Nights and their fantasies of fabulous monarchs, are disallowed, for they mislead by forcing the Hebrew writing into an alien mould.

1. The Cultural Context

The Solomon Narrative describes a greater range of material culture than other parts of Kings. It therefore allows greater possibility for assessment in the context of the ancient world: can the creations attributed to Solomon's craftsmen be set comfortably in the 10th century, or do they belong only to later years? Arguments brought against a 10th century reality often rest on what modern scholars think likely and need to be balanced against the evidence from ancient times.

A. *The Use of Gold*

1) *The Temple*

Although absence of certain details precludes definitive reconstruction, it is clear that Solomon's temple pattern followed a long-established plan of porch, main hall and sanctuary, with store-rooms built against the outside walls[1] and a surrounding courtyard, and could well belong to the 10th century or earlier or slightly later periods.[2] The majority of commentators are prepared to admit archival documents or specifications lie behind sections of the descriptions of the Temple, as of Solomon's palace, his court and his foreign relations. With regard to the Temple, while details of its structure, dimensions and arrangements gain ready acceptance, when it comes to the lavish embellishment of the interior with gold, almost all shift their ground and try to minimize or reject the relevant phrases, sometimes on text-critical grounds. While the designs

[1] K. A. Kitchen, "Two Notes on the Subsidiary Rooms of Solomon's Temple," *ErIsr* 20 (1989) 107*-12*.

[2] W. G. Dever on the Temple of Solomon in Jerusalem in his "Palaces and Temples in Canaan and Ancient Israel," *Civilizations of the Ancient Near East* (ed. J. Sasson; New York: Scribner's, 1995) 1.608-609, concludes "the biblical texts, at least the vivid descriptions in 1 Kings, would appear to be based on early, authentic eyewitness accounts," p. 609.

of gourds, flowers and cherubim carved in the wood paneling have plentiful analogies in the Late Bronze Age and Iron Age of the Levant, although woodwork from those periods is hardly known,[3] the overlaying of the panelling, the ceiling and the floor of the whole temple is rejected. One modern author has written: "Forceful arguments have been put forward for deleting all references to gold plating in the Temple; some of these references are absent from LXX, and later descriptions of the Temple and its treasures lack references to gold plating (cf. 2 Kg. 14:14; 16:17; 18:16); Ezekiel knew of no gold plating. . . . [verse 20] is suspect because of its claim that the whole of the inner sanctuary was gilded." "The claim that he overlaid the inside of the house with pure gold is an exaggeration that probably originated from a later tradition about the splendor of Solomon's Temple."[4]

Leaving the textual questions for later attention, the objection raised from the absence of references to the gold plating in subsequent parts of Kings can be dismissed, for we can hardly suppose that the final compiler(s) of the book would have been so unintelligent as to narrate the removal of the treasures of the Temple by Shishak in the reign of Rehoboam (1 Kgs 14:26) and then assume a considerable and obvious part remained in position over the next two hundred years! That Hezekiah stripped off the gold he had put on the Temple doors (2 Kgs 18:16) does not mean that such adornment had never been there before. For the writer(s) of Kings, Hezekiah's embellishment went the same way as Solomon's, loot for a powerful enemy. "Suspicious" or "gross exaggeration" are the judgments passed on the claim of a complete gold overlay for the interior (1 Kgs 6:20-22, 30). Whereas for some it is wholly unacceptable, others allow thin or partial gilding, one even suggests "liguid gold sprayed on," in the light of Proverbs 26:23 where the same Hebrew verb (*ṣāpâ*) applies to glaze on a potsherd.[5] Now while a piece of pottery can receive a coating of liquefied metal without harm, it is difficult to conceive of wooden panelling so treated. In every other passage a rendering "to coat, to plate" seems most appropriate and the cognate words

[3] For fragmentary examples from Jerusalem, apparently burnt in a Babylonian attack, see Y. Shiloh, *Excavations at the City of David I* (Qedem 19; Jerusalem: Hebrew University, 1984) 19, pl. 34.1.

[4] G. H. Jones, *1 and 2 Kings* (NCB; Basingstoke, England: Marshall, Morgan and Scott; Grand Rapids: Eerdmans, 1984) 1.169; these comments repeat observations set out by C. F. Burney, *Notes on the Hebrew Text of the Books of Kings* (Oxford: Clarendon, 1903) 73, in the wake of previous commentators and repeated by others.

[5] J. Gray, *I & II Kings* (2nd ed.; OTL; London: SCM, 1970) 168, following Burney.

in Hebrew and Ugaritic lend their support. Interestingly, the Assyrian and Babylonian accounts of gold decoration for temple walls mostly use a verb meaning "to dress, to clad." Even those commentators who show some awareness of the uses of precious metal in the ancient world are prone to dismiss the gold overlay of Solomon's Temple, yet surely no critical attitude can be taken without a thorough scrutiny of the ways gold was used to decorate temples in antiquity; judgments made from the ways society views gold in 20th century Europe or North America are inappropriate for a document from ancient Israel. Moreover, for a century or more travellers have told of gold plated buildings in India and Burma, which should alert everyone to the differences which may exist between cultures. An ancient report of the burial of Egyptian pharaohs in solid gold coffins might have evoked scepticism had not Tutankhamun's tomb been found with its treasures almost intact!

Gold overlay to enhance temples is attested in antiquity in Mesopotamia and in Egypt by contemporary texts and also by physical remains in Egypt. In Assyria, in the 7th century BC, Esarhaddon restored the shrine of Ashur, plated its doors with gold and "coated the walls with gold as if with plaster." His son Ashurbanipal did much the same, "I clad its walls with gold and silver."[6] In Babylon a century later Nebuchadnezzar recorded his enrichment of the shrines of the gods, "I clad (them) in gold and made them as bright as day" and Nabonidus (555-539 BC) followed him, "I clad its walls with gold and silver and made them shine like the sun."[7] The tradition stemmed from much earlier epochs in Babylonia, for Enmetena (also read Entemena) of Lagash built a temple for his god "and covered it with gold and silver" about 2400 BC.[8]

Egypt supplies more extensive evidence. After many years of labour, a French scholar, Pierre Lacau, wrote an essay on the meaning of certain holes and channels in various ancient Egyptian stone monuments.[9] Relating his observations to the statements in contemporary texts, he was

[6] R. Borger, *Die Inschriften Asarhaddons* (*AfO* 9; Graz: Selbstverlage des Herausgebers, 1956) 87; R.C. Thompson, *The Prisms of Esarhaddon and Ashurbanipal* (London: British Museum, 1931) 29.

[7] S. Langdon, *Die Neubabylonische Königsinschriften* (Leipzig: Heinrichs, 1912) 178, 222.

[8] The Enmetena text is translated in E. Sollberger and J.-R. Kupper, *Inscriptions royales sumériennes et akkadiennes* (Paris: Cerf, 1971) IC 7b; and J. S. Cooper, *Sumerian and Akkadian Royal Inscriptions* (New Haven: American Oriental Society, 1986) 67 La 5.27, cf. 60 La 5.6.

[9] P. Lacau, "L'or dans l'architecture égyptienne," *Annales du Service des Antiquités de l'Egypte* 53 (1956) 221-50.

able to show that pillars, doorways, and sections of walls were covered with gold sheets. The holes and channels had been cut to enable the metal to be affixed to the stone surfaces. In the Temple of the Sacred Boat at Karnak stood twelve columns erected by Tuthmosis III, *ca.* 1450 BC, each about 3.5 metres high, designed to represent bundles of papyrus. Each was entirely covered with gold, fastened in slits cut at suitable points in the pattern, vertically in the body of the column and the capital, horizontally in the base. In another hall at Karnak fourteen columns rose to the roof. Their design was similar, a papyrus stem, and they, too, were plated with gold from top to bottom. These pillars were larger; an inscription states that they were 31 cubits, that is 16.25 metres high (53 feet). Other pillars erected in Egypt commemorated royal piety. These are obelisks exemplified in Cleopatra's Needle.[10] Some had gold plating in the very top only, others over the upper half, and others all over their surface. One pair is recorded to have been 108 cubits high (about 56 metres, 180 feet). Like the columns, the stone blocks of doorways and the carved slabs in temple walls show how metal sheets were fastened to them: the plating was attached by means of nails. Plating was apparently the richest form of decoration. Evidence exists that the Egyptians were also in the habit of plastering stone surfaces, then applying a thin gold foil to the plaster. The inscriptions do not make clear which method was used when they catalogue the royal achievements, they use a term that means literally "worked," but which Lacau argued can be rendered "plated" in these contexts.

The prosperous centuries of the New Kingdom (*ca.* 1550-1070 BC) provide most of the records of this type of embellishment in Egypt, and some examples will make the royal activities clear.[11] Tuthmosis III (*ca.* 1490-1436 BC) built a shrine for Amun at Deir el-Bahri "plated with gold and silver," with a floor similarly adorned. Amenophis III, in the next century, decorated several structures in this way. Of one temple in honour of Amun at Thebes, he claimed it was "plated with gold throughout, its floor is adorned with silver, all its portals with electrum," while the temple at Soleb had the same treatment, except that "all its portals are of gold." Ramesses II (*ca.* 1279-1213 BC) provided his mortuary temple at

---

[10] The obelisks are discussed in R. Engelbach, *The Problem of the Obelisks* (London: Fisher Unwin, 1923); and L. Habachi, *The Obelisks of Egypt: Skyscrapers of the Past* (London: Dent, 1978).

[11] Translations of Egyptian texts are found in J. H. Breasted, *Ancient Records of Egypt* (Chicago: University of Chicago, 1906-1907); those cited are taken from vol. 2 §§ 375, 883, 890, cf. 886, 889; vol. 3 § 528; vol. 4 §§ 7, 9, 195, 209; cf. 197.23.

Abydos with doors "mounted with copper and gilded with electrum." Later in this period, Ramesses III (*ca.* 1183-1152 BC) ornamented temples in exactly the same way. At Medinet Habu he constructed a shrine of gold with a pavement of silver and doorposts of fine gold. His Karnak temple was supplied with "great doors of fine gold." Another of his works may be noted here: Ramesses III made a sacred barge for the god to travel along the Nile. It was 130 cubits long (68 metres, 224 feet; long enough to carry two obelisks 30 metres or 100 feet high); its timbers were cedar and it was overlaid with gold to the water-line.

The doors of Solomon's Temple turned on golden sockets (assuming that is the meaning of *pōṯôṯ*, 1 Kgs 7:50). "It seems impracticable that the hinge sockets in the floor and lintel should be of gold,"[12] said one commentator, yet ancient practice actually supports the biblical text. Stone sockets to hold the lower end of hinge posts are common throughout the Near East from the Early Bronze Age onwards. In Mesopotamia kings used to inscribe those they set in important temples and a number survive. In a least one case the rim of the stone was covered with gold foil pressed hard over the engraving so that the inscription was visible on the surface of the gold.[13] That, surely, shows how the golden sockets of Solomon's Temple should be understood; the surface of the stone was plated with gold, not reaching into the socket itself.

"Overlaying the floor [of the Temple] with gold is unlikely" according to one writer, "absurd" according to another. Martin Noth was willing to accept the gold overlay of the walls, but not the floor.[14] Among the Egyptian texts cited were mentioned a floor "wrought with gold and silver," another "adorned with silver," a third "its floor is of silver." These records differ in mostly having silver for the floors, not gold, and it is objected that gold would be impracticable because of its softness. That objection may have some force, although it may be slightly lessened by observing that the priests probably entered Solomon's Temple barefoot.

In presenting his material, the Egyptologist Lacau spoke of the "astonishing way the Egyptians were prepared to make use of gold" to decorate their monuments and added that the majority of Egyptian statues of

[12] Gray, *I & II Kings* (see above, n. 5), p. 202.

[13] Inscription of Shar-kali-sharri, *ca.* 2200 BC; T. Jacobsen, *Cuneiform Texts in the National Museum, Copenhagen* (Leiden: E. J. Brill, 1939) no. 80, pl. 68; text in I. J. Gelb and B. Kienast, *Die altakkadischen Königsinschriften des dritten Jahrtausends v. Chr.* (Stuttgart: Steiner, 1990) 114-15, with a duplicate from a hinge socket stone, Sollberger and Kupper, *Inscriptions royales*, IIA5a.

[14] M. Noth, *Könige* (BKAT; Neukirchen: Vandenhoeck & Ruprecht, 1968) 126.

deities in stone and bronze to be seen in our museums were originally enhanced in the same way, with a golden overlay, something that is visible on certain figures from Ugarit and other sites in the Levant. The gold plating on the wooden shrines that housed Tutankhamun's sarcophagus and coffins and other Egyptian objects is not the fine gold leaf of to-day, 0.0002 mm thick or less, but foil with a thickness varying between 0.01 and 0.09 mm.[15] Gold foil brightened the carved ivory work of Iron Age furniture. Much thinner gold was applied to stucco moulded scenes in Egyptian tombs, where the moulding could not support any weighty attechment. However, plating on temple walls and obelisks may have been at least as substantial as that on Tutankhamun's shrines.

Outside Egypt and the Near East a similar attitude to gold was prominent among the founders of western culture, the Greeks of Athens. In the Parthenon stood a masterpiece of the sculptor Pheidias, the 10.5 metre (35 feet) high statue of Athene. It was made of wood with ivory additions and a plating of gold which could be removed if required.

None of these records or examples can prove there was a gold-plated temple in Jerusalem at any time, but their testimony is sufficient to confute all the objections to the biblical descriptions as exaggeration or fantasy. The enhancement of the Temple ascribed to Solomon is entirely compatible with ancient practice.

2. The Palace Furnishings

a) Tableware. "All Solomon's drinking vessels were of gold and all the plate of the House of the Forest of Lebanon was of red gold" (1 Kgs 10:21). Scattered specimens of gold plate from all parts of the ancient Near East and Egypt imply there is no need to see exaggeration here. The pieces prized in modern museums are the few survivors of great quantities which were fabricated, re-modelled, looted, melted down and turned into other objects. That there were golden utensils of all sorts in considerable numbers is plain from ancient texts which there are no grounds for discrediting, for example, the golden vessels enumerated in the Mari letters of the 18th century BC, or the many bowls and dishes of gold listed as gifts in the El-Amarna letters of the 14th century BC.[16] Vessels from

---

[15] A. Lucas, *Ancient Egyptian Materials and Industries* (ed. J. R. Harris; 4th revised ed.; London: Arnold, 1962) 231-33.

[16] S. Dalley, *Mari and Karana: Two Old Babylonian Cities* (London: Longman, 1984)

the Royal Cemetery at Ur of the 3rd millennium BC and from various hoards of the 2nd millennium found in Egypt, the dishes from Late Bronze Age Ugarit and from a tomb somewhere in the Levant, those in the tombs of Assyrian royal ladies at Nimrud and from various Persian sites of the first millennium illustrate the continuing fashion for gold plate among the wealthy, a means of display which continues to the present day. Golden tableware would be expected in the palace of a wealthy monarch.

b) Shields. Five hundred golden shields in two sizes adorned Solomon's palace (1 Kgs 10:16-17) and David had earlier taken gold shields from the officials of Hadad-ezer of Zobah (2 Sam 8:7). At first sight this might seem to be an example of "the extravagant details . . . the imagination which writers about the Age of Solomon had allowed full rein."[17] Examination of ancient records and artefacts indicates that, like the tableware, the golden shields fall within the scope of royal display. The closest parallel is given by Sargon II of Assyria in rehearsing the booty he took from the temple of Haldi, chief god of Urartu, in Musasir, near Lake Urmia, in 714 BC. His men removed "6 shields of gold which hung to right and left of his shrine, gleaming brightly, with heads of fierce dogs protruding from the centres, by weight 5 talents and 12 minas of red gold." In addition, a sculptured slab in Sargon's palace at Khorsabad depicts soldiers ransacking the temple, some carrying a large shield in each hand, while some shields still hang upon the walls. Although no golden shields have been found and the earliest references, apart from Solomon, belong to the late 8th century BC, the concepts of ancient cultures allow no case for rejecting them.[18]

c) The Throne. "The king also made a great throne of ivory and overlaid it with fine gold" (1 Kgs 10:18). A throne of ivory was not, of course, made of solid ivory, any more than was Ahab's "ivory house" (2 Kgs 22:39), or the Jewel Tower in the Tower of London was made from a gem. In the last case, it contained the Crown Jewels, in the other two, the

57-62; W. L. Moran, *The Amarna Letters* (Baltimore: Johns Hopkins, 1982) nos. 14, 22.

[17] J. B. Pritchard, "The Age of Solomon," *Solomon and Sheba* (ed. J. B. Pritchard; London: Phaidon, 1974) 32.

[18] See A. Millard, "King Solomon's Shields," *Scripture and Other Artefacts: Essays on the Bible and Archaeology in Honor of Philip J. King* (ed. M. D. Coogan, J. C. Exum, and L. E. Stager; Louisville, Ken.: Westminster/John Knox, 1994) 286-95. From a later date may be noted the "gold shield valued at a thousand minas" sent by Simon the Maccabee to Rome, 1 Macc 14:24; 15:18.

ivory was an extensive decoration. There are no grounds for rendering "inlaid with ivory" (REB), nor for supposing that surfaces other than those veneered with ivory were covered with gold.[19] Discoveries at many sites have made ivory veneered furniture a familiar product of the ancient Near East. The manufacture was well-established by the Late Bronze Age (e.g. at Megiddo) and flourished in the Assyrian period, as the hoards from Nimrud, Khorsabad, Arslan Tash and Samaria demonstrate.[20] Thrones and couches were made of wood with ivory covering them entirely, as seen in a tomb at Salamis where a chair and a couch could be reconstructed from the crushed ivory fragments. To modern eyes, the creamy white ivory, expertly carved, is attractive in itself, but to ancient eyes it was something precious to be enriched further by inlay of semi-precious stones or coloured glass and by gold foil overlay. Little of that survives to-day, yet there is sufficient to prove it was the case and the black stains of the bituminous glue used to hold it in place are widespread among the ivories from Nimrud. Describing one piece retaining some gold foil, the modern excavator of Nimrud wrote, "There is little doubt that the majority of the ivories found in Fort Shalmaneser had been similarly covered with gold."[21] The ivories from the Israelite palace at Samaria retain minute traces of comparable covering.[22] In the context of these finds and set beside the golden thrones of Tutankhamun, an ivory-veneered throne, plated with gold, is certainly a conceivable product of ancient Near Eastern furniture maker's art.

B. *Amounts of Gold*

If Solomon's use of gold can be given credence in the light of practices known from antiquity, what can be said of the enormous quantities the Solomon Narrative records? The king of Tyre and the queen of Sheba each brought him 120 talents, 420 talents came from Ophir, while "in one year the weight of gold came to Solomon was 666 talents" (1 Kgs 9:14, 28; 10:10, 14). Taking the talent as about 33 kg or 73 lbs, the first two amounts equate approximately to 3,960 kg or 3.9 tons, the third to 13,860

[19] As does, for example, Jones, *1 and 2 Kings* (see above, n. 4), 1.169.

[20] See R. D. Barnett, *Ancient Ivories in the Middle East* (Qedem 14; Jerusalem: Hebrew University, 1982); G. Herrmann, ed., *The Furniture of Western Asia: Ancient and Traditional* (Mainz: von Zabern, 1996).

[21] M. E. L. Mallowan, *Nimrud and Its Remains* (London: Collins, 1966) 576.

[22] J. W. Crowfoot and G. M. Crowfoot, *Early Ivories from Samaria* (London: Palestine Exploration Fund, 1938) 9-12.

kg or 13.6 tons and the fourth to 21,800 kg or 21 tons of gold. The modern reader's initial reaction is incredulity; these are the figures of legend, of Ali Baba's cave or Grendel's hoard! (In 1979 the gold reserve of Great Britain was about 68,000 tons.) Yet Solomon's gold demands to be treated in the same way in respect of its quantities as for its uses; the amounts of his gold should be set beside amounts claimed for other ancient kings if a fair assessment is to be made.

Before surveying other texts, the matter of the figures themselves deserves notice. It is easy to dismiss large numbers in ancient documents as erroneous. A king might inflate his wealth to impress other kings or his subjects, or scribes might make mistakes, as apparently with the number of Solomon's horses between 1 Kgs 4:26 (40,000) and 2 Chr 9:25 (4,000). Until Hellenistic times Hebrew scribes wrote numbers in words; they did not use ciphers, except in business documents when they borrowed the Egyptian hieratic system, or perhaps occassionally the Phoenician ciphers, so any errors have to be explained in the light of that knowledge.[23] Accountancy was an activity imposing accuracy and thousands of cuneiform documents exhibit it. Some documents provide both the total and the figures of each constituent, showing that a large total could be a sum of many parts. Round totals could be used where fractions were a needless detail. When only the totals are available, they should be treated as accurate unless there are good grounds for thinking otherwise. In dealing with amounts of gold in ancient texts another aspect to be kept in mind is the quality of the gold. Not every amount was of 24 carat standard. Unfortunately, the exact significance of Hebrew words describing gold is unclear (*sāgûr*, "pure," or "red," *pāz*, "fine").

Most records of gold in royal inscriptions are of lesser amounts. Shalmaneser III of Assyria, campaigning in Syria in the mid-9th century BC, received three talents of gold and other precious things from the king of Carchemish who was ordered to pay 1 mana (0.5 kg or 1 lb) with other materials annually thereafter. Half a century later, Adad-nirari III received twenty talents of gold when Damascus surrendered to him (*ca.* 600 kg; 1,320 lbs) with 2,300 talents of silver (*ca.* 69,000 kg; 68 tons). These are typical figures. There are larger ones. When Hoshea was made king in Samaria, he paid to his overlord, Tiglath-pileser III, 10 talents of gold, but when the same emperor accepted the submission of Tyre he

[23] A. Millard, "Strangers from Egypt and Greece: The Signs for Numbers in Early Hebrew," *Immigration and Emigration within the Ancient Near East* (ed. K. van Lerberghe and A. Schoors; OLA 65; Leuven: Peeters, 1995) 189-94.

received 150 talents of gold (4,500 kg or 4.4 tons), more than the earlier king of Tyre reputedly gave to Solomon. A few decades later, Sargon II of Assyria took Babylon. He ensured his generosity to the conquered city's gods was remembered by having inscribed upon his palace wall at Khorsabad, "I gave as a present to Bel ... and the gods of the cities of Sumer and Akkad, from the year of accession [as king of Babylon, 708 BC] until my third year, 154 talents, 26 mana, 10 shekels of bright gold, 1,604 talents, 20 mana of bright silver, incalculable amounts of bronze and iron, precious stones in heaps ..." In modern terms, the gold was about 5,100 kg or 5 tons, the silver 53,000 kg or 52 tons.

Egypt was a famous source of gold. An Assyrian king, who, like his Babylonian contemporaries, wrote to the pharaoh asking for gold, about 1340 BC, "Gold in your land is like dust, one simply gathers it up."[24] Egyptian texts list some amounts obtained from mines in various regions and others received as tribute.[25] Great quantities were stored in the palaces and presented to the temples. Amenophis III boasts he presented to the temple of Montu in Karnak 25,182 deben (=2,290 kg; 2.24 tons) of refined gold; Tuthmosis III donated to the temple of Amun in Karnak 152,10[7] deben in lumps and rings (13,837 kg; 13.6 tons), and other figures could be added. Most astounding of all are the gifts Osorkon I (*ca.* 924-889 BC) claims he devoted to the gods of Heliopolis: 594,300 deben of gold, silver and lapis lazuli, 2,300,000 deben of silver and gold (respectively 54,063 kg; 53 tons and 209,231 kg; 205 tons). These figures are engraved upon disjointed fragments of a monument and the larger may include the smaller, so their full purport is uncertain.[26] Nevertheless, even if exaggerated, when taken with the figures for earlier kings, they exemplify the ways the pharaohs thought it proper to use great quantities of treasure.

Meagre beside those figures, yet still noteworthy, is the amount of gold applied to the statue of Athene Parthenos in the small Greek city-state of Athens. When it was dedicated in 438 BC, the weight of the gold plating

---

[24] El Amarna Letter 16, cf. 19, 20; Moran, *Amarna Letters* (see above, n. 16), 39, 44, 48.

[25] The basic study of the Egyptian gold-fields is J. Vercoutter, "The Gold of Kush," *Kush* 7 (1959) 120-53.

[26] Osorkon's inscriptions are translated in J. H. Breasted, *Ancient Records of Egypt*, vol. 5.§§729-37; and studied in K. A. Kitchen, *The Third Intermediate Period in Egypt* (3rd ed.; Warminster: Aris & Phillips, 1996) 300-304; see also, *idem.*, *The Bible in Its World* (Exeter: Paternoster, 1977; Chicago: Inter-Varsity, 1978) 102; and *idem.*, "Egypt and Israel During the First Millennium B.C.," *Congress Volume: Jerusalem, 1986* (ed. J. A. Emerton; VTSup 40; Leiden: E. J. Brill, 1988) 107-23, especially pp. 117-19.

was said to be forty talents (1,030 kg; almost 1 ton). "This gold was put on it in such a way that it could be quickly removed, doubtless in case of financial stringency."[27]

C. *Sources of Gold*

Egypt had her native gold supply, Israel had none. Could a 10th century king accumulate great amounts of gold in Jerusalem? 1 Kings notes the various sources of Solomon's gold, Tyre, Sheba, Ophir, trade and gifts (1 Kgs 9:26-28; 10:10-12,14-15,22-29). Sheba lay far from Israel in the modern Yemen and her early history is unknown. Her prized products were frankincense and myrrh, a source of great wealth through trade.[28] In addition, there are gold mines in the area which have been worked intermittently since ancient times. Some near Taif are of pre-Islamic date, although how early they are is not yet determined. In 1987 a press report told of samples taken at ancient workings near Riyadh in Saudi Arabia which "indicated one of two veins ... might contain up to one million tonnes of ore grading at a very rich 20 to 30 grams of gold per tonne."[29] We may speculate that such a "lucky strike" enriched the queen of Sheba.

The location of Ophir remains a mystery; if it was the goal of a three-year return voyage, it was obviously a distant place. The Red Sea coasts, Yemen, Somaliland, India have all been canvassed as its location, but no answer can be given. Wherever Ophir lay, its gold was known in the 8th century BC, for a receipt scratched on a potsherd found at Tel Qasile, north of Tel Aviv, acknowledges, "Gold of Ophir for Beth-Horon: 30 shekels."[30] At that time the name could have become a term for a quality of gold rather than pointing to its place of origin, just as damask no longer comes from Damascus exclusively, nor muslin from Mosul, while it could point to the place of origin. The fact that no other sources describe the exotic products of Ophir, or how to find it, need not be a cause for wonder, or for declaring Ophir a mythical place. In Egypt the marvels of the distant land of Punt are described and illustrated in the temple of Queen Hatshepsut built at Deir el-Bahri. Wood and incense were known as products of Punt long before and for long afterwards, but

[27] C. H. V. Sutherland, *Gold* (London: Thames and Hudson, 1959) 73.

[28] See K. A. Kitchen, "Sheba and Arabia," pp. 126-53 [this volume].

[29] *The Daily Telegraph* (London and Manchester, 25:v:1987); cf. K. S. Twitchell, *Saudi Arabia* (Princeton, NJ: Princeton University, 1953).

[30] J. Renz and W. Röllig, *Handbuch der althebräischen Epigraphik* (Darmstadt: Wissenschaftliche Buchgesellschaft, 1995) 229-31.

the strange animals and precious metals brought from the country appear only in Hatshepsut's reliefs. After the end of the New Kingdom, Egypt's links with Punt were broken until the era of the Ptolemies.[31] To speculate again, Solomon may have taken advantage of a "lucky strike" in Ophir. Gold-mining history is well acquainted with major finds which enrich their discoverers, then are rapidly exhausted.

D. *Palace Provisions*

The system for provisioning Solomon's court involved dividing Israel into twelve districts, each to supply the requirements for one month. Vaguely similar forms of regional organisation for feeding the court can be observed in 6th century Babylonian documents.[32] From an earlier time, a large collection of cuneiform tablets stored in jars in the city of Ashur tallies the regular offerings the provinces of the kingdom sent for the temple of the god Ashur in the reign of Tiglath-pileser I (*ca.* 1114-1076 BC).[33] The system is so simple there is no need to seek outside influence for its application in Israel.

The quantities supplied for the sustenance of Solomon's court are large: 30 cattle, 100 sheep, 30 *kor* of fine flour (*ca.* 6,600 litres), 60 *kor* of meal (*ca.* 13,200 litres) daily. They win acceptance from some modern scholars,[34] and others doubt or discount them.[35] No verdict should be passed without attention to figures of other ancient courts. The number of people dependent upon an ancient royal household was very high. The

[31] K. A. Kitchen, "Punt and How to Get There," *Or* 40 (1971) 184-207; and *idem.*, "The Land of Punt," *The Archaeology of Africa: Food, Metals, Towns* (ed. T. Shaw; London: Routledge, 1993) 587-608.

[32] R. P. Dougherty, "Cuneiform Parallels to Solomon's Provisioning System," *Annual of the American Schools of Oriental Research for 1923-1924* (ed. B. W. Bacon; AASOR 5; New Haven: Yale University, 1925) 23-33, 40-46. Note that an Egyptian comparison made by D. B. Redford, "Studies in Relations between Palestine and Egypt during the First Millennium B.C., I: The Taxation System of Solomon," *Studies on the Ancient Palestinian World Presented to F. V. Winnett* (ed. J. W. Wevers and D. B. Redford; Toronto: Toronto University, 1972) 141-56, is discounted by K. A. Kitchen, "Egypt and Israel in the First Millennium" (see above, n. 26), p. 116.

[33] See J. N. Postgate review in *BO* 37 (1980) 68-70; and O. Pedersén, *Archives and Libraries in the City of Assur* (Uppsala: Almqvist & Wiksell, 1985) 1.46.

[34] J. A. Montgomery and H. S. Gehman, *Kings* (ICC; Edinburgh: T. & T. Clark; New York: Scribner's, 1951) 127-28; and Gray, *I & II Kings* (see above, n. 5), p. 142.

[35] Jones, *1 and 2 Kings* (see above, n. 4), 1.147, "may have originated from a later attempt to glorify king Solomon;" J. M. Miller and J. H. Hayes, *A History of Ancient Israel and Judah* (Philadelphia: Westminster; London: SCM, 1986) 195, "belongs to the idealized Solomon of legend."

5,400 men who, Sargon of Akkad boasted in the 3rd millennium BC, ate at his table would have demanded no small provision. The king of Mari's entourage in the 18th century BC and that of Seti I and a successor in Egypt in the 13th century BC consumed big amounts, too (720 litres of flour for bread daily while Seti's court was on a progress).[36] The Ashur temple's supplies from the provinces, mentioned above, included 1,000 homers of grain *per annum*, which may be about 100,000 litres; Solomon's court, naturally a much larger establishment, took about six times as much. Upon the inauguration of his new palace in Nimrud (ancient Kalhu) Ashurnasirpal II of Assyria held a ten-day festival for 69,574 people and proudly listed the produce collected for it. Heading the list are 100 fat oxen, 1,000 calves and sheep, 14,000 sheep of a certain type, 200 more oxen, 1,000 more sheep, 1,000 spring lambs, followed by numerous other animals and fowl, 10,000 loaves of bread, 10,000 jugs of beer, 10,000 skins of wine and much else.[37] While no text displays an exact parallel to this part of the Solomon Narrative, those quoted, with others, indicate comparable systems of collection and amounts supplied.

3. The Archaeological Context

Physical remains may be expected of the works erected by a king who was reputed to be a great builder in his capital, principally, and at many other places, yet excavations of 10th century levels have disclosed "buildings were simple and modestly constructed from materials locally available," according to J. B. Pritchard.[38] Absence of any building certainly Solomonic in Jerusalem should not cause surprise, given the city's history of frequent destructions and rebuildings. At the northern end of the hill of the "City of David," running across it, Kathleen Kenyon

[36] For most of these and other figures, see K. A. Kitchen, "Food," *NBD*, p. 431-32 (2nd ed., 386-87); and *idem.*, "Food," *The Illustrated Bible Dictionary* (Leicester: Inter-Varsity; Wheaton, Ill.: Tyndale House, 1980) 516; more recently in *idem.*, "Egypt and Israel in the First Millennium" (see above, n. 26), p. 117. The text for Seti I is now treated in *idem., Ramesside Inscriptions Translated and Annotated: Notes and Comments* (Oxford: Blackwell, 1993) 159-76, with general discussion on pp. 174-76.

[37] D. J. Wiseman, "A New Stele of Assur-nasir-pal," *Iraq* 14 (1952) 24-44; translation in A. L. Oppenheim, "Babylonian and Assyrian Historical Texts, *ANET*, pp. 558-60; and in A. K. Grayson, *Assyrian Royal Inscriptions* (Records of the Ancient Near East; Wiesbaden: Harrassowitz, 1976) 2.172-76; revised text in *idem., Assyrian Rulers of the First Millennium B.C., I: The Royal Inscriptions of Mesopotamia, Assyrian Periods* (RIMA 2; Toronto: Toronto University, 1991) 292.

[38] Pritchard, "Age of Solomon" (see above, n. 17), pp. 17-39, quote p. 35.

uncovered a part of a wall of massive blocks which she assigned to Iron Age I and also part of a wall which she compared with "Solomonic" casemate walls at Gezer, Hazor and Megiddo, although she could not date it with certainty.[39] The citadel at Samaria makes an instructive comparison. There parts of the Israelite palace of the 9th-8th centuries were discovered, very badly damaged by later construction, especially by the work on Herod's temple for Augustus, while some of the area was inaccessible to the spade. Although that site has been subject to far less upheaval than Jerusalem, a glance at the excavators' plan will show how fragmentary the remains of the Israelite palace really are.[40] Moreover, at Jerusalem, where Solomon's Temple stood, the returning exiles did their reconstruction after 538 BC, Herod rebuilt it almost entirely, then Roman, Christian and Muslim rulers re-arranged the site and erected new buildings, culminating in the Dome of the Rock and the el-Aqsa Mosque. Herod's enormous extension of the Temple platform to the south may have swept away any surviving parts of Solomon's palace which had adjoined the Temple. Excavation within the sacred enclosure is impossible and, as bed-rock is near the surface in much of it, no substantial elements from the 10th century BC could be expected to exist still.

Elsewhere, the widely publicised city gates at Gezer, Hazor and Megiddo have been commonly attributed to Solomon and stratigraphic evidence is adduced especially for Gezer.[41] Without any confirmatory inscription, this attribution cannot be considered final. If accepted and associated with buildings at Megiddo in Stratum VA/IVB, they attest to not inconsiderable construction work of good quality.[42]

Observing "the relative mediocrity of 10th century archaeological remains in Palestine," J. M. Miller, with others, assumes that implies a

---

[39] K. M. Kenyon, "Excavations in Jerusalem, 1962," *PEQ* 95 (1963) 7-21, see p. 17.

[40] J. W. Crowfoot, K. M. Kenyon, and E. L. Sukenik, *Samaria-Sebaste I: The Buildings* (London: Palestine Exploration Fund, 1942) pl. 2. Note that the plan is sometimes reproduced as if complete, without making the restorations, as in Z. Herzog, "Cities," *ABD*, 1.1040, fig.

[41] J. S. Holladay, "Red Slip, Burnish and the Solomonic Gateway at Gezer," *BASOR* 277-278 (1990) 23-70; *idem.*, "The Use of Pottery and Other Diagnostic Criteria from the Solomonic Era to the Divided Kingdom," *Biblical Archaeology Today: Proceedings of the Second International Congress on Biblical Archaeology, Jerusalem, June 1990* (eds. J. Aviram and A. Biran; Jerusalem: Israel Exploration Society, 1993) 86-101.

[42] See A. R. Millard, "Texts and Archaeology: Weighing the Evidence: The Case for King Solomon," *PEQ* 123 (1991) 19-27, especially pp. 24-25. Notice the recent proposal of I. Finkelstein to lower the dates for Megiddo IVA/VB and related levels to the 9th century, "The Archaeology of the United Monarchy: An Alternative View," *Levant* 28 (1996) 177-87.

lesser potentate than the Solomon Narrative portrays.[43] Yet we should ask what material an extravagant forty year reign might leave. Outside the capital, which would naturally enjoy some "trickle down" effect from the monarch's wealth, how far would the royal income spread, taking "silver...was reckoned of no value" (1 Kgs 10:21) as a hyberbolic expression on a par with "gold is like dust in your land" (see n. 24)? Important towns might receive new defences and official residences, which the gateways, casemate walls and certain buildings in Megiddo may represent; smaller places might not see any of that. The material benefit for the majority of the people would be in the peaceful conditions and so better food supply and general prosperity. It is hard to know what clues that would leave for the archaeologist except perhaps through skeletal studies, but regrettably few 10th century burials have been excavated. House plans and building methods would not be likely to change: improved plastering, woodwork or furniture do not endure ruin and envelopment in damp soil. Imported luxury goods will only be detectable if they were themselves durable or transported in foreign containers of pottery or glass; perishable goods carried in wooden containers or sacks or bags of leather or cloth will be invisible.

If the 10th century is elusive in Palestinian archaeology, the conclusion that it was relatively poor is not inevitable. A common archaeological phenomenon has to be taken into account: only the final phase of occupation before a major destruction or desertion will leave rich archaeological deposits, for the last inhabitants will have discarded almost everything more than three generations old. This universal phenomenon is demonstrated most clearly in Assyria. At Nimrud Ashurnasirpal II (*ca.* 883-859 BC) built a large palace. Various modern museums treasure its carved stone wall panels bearing his names and scenes of his exploits. Until Layard revealed them in 1845, they stood undisturbed because later kings built new palaces on other sites in the city and Ashurnasirpal's palace was relatively little used. While the inscriptions on the walls and other monuments attest the activity of the scribes, the number of cuneiform documents on clay actually dated in Ashurnasirpal's reign is one! That does not mean the scribes were few, or lazy, or writing in ink on papyrus, rather it tells us that later generations had no need to keep most of the documents their ancestors wrote. By contrast, from the last century of the Assyrian empire, there are hundreds of tablets of all

[43] J. M. Miller, "Solomon: International Potentate or Local King?" *PEQ* 123 (1991) 28-31.

types.[44] The area of Jerusalem was too small for successive kings to found palaces in new sites, so the Nimrud situation could not arise, and instead, we may assume, the kings of Judah occupied and renovated Solomon's palace. To our disadvantage, the common writing material in Israel was perishable papyrus, so no documents comparable to the cuneiform tablets are available.

Now the failure to find any inscriptions of Solomon is also noted as a counter-indication to the biblical portrayal of him. "Why has there not been found a single inscription, not even a fragment from Solomon himself?"[45] The answer lies in the circumstances just outlined, which are part of the accidental element in archaeology, and in the ancient practice of re-using old building blocks, irrespective of their previous role, very evident at Megiddo.[46] When a rapid calculation reveals that only 16 out of 113 kings ruling in the Levant between 1000 and 600 BC, including the kings of Israel and Judah, are known from their own inscriptions, the absence of Solomon becomes less remarkable. It is less significant still when we recall that there has yet to be found in Palestine a monument inscribed with the name of another powerful and wealthy ruler of the land, many of whose buildings are still visible, King Herod, who reigned one thousand years nearer to our day than Solomon.[47] The lack of physical remains in not an insurmountable objection to accepting the statements of the Hebrew historians.

4. The Historical Context

The assumption that a king of the stature of Solomon would perforce appear in the records of contemporary states has also led to a negative view of the claims the Solomon Narrative makes when it is learned that there are no extra-biblical references to him. Yet again, the ancient context deserves careful examination before any deductions are made.

---

[44] See A. R. Millard, "Observations from the Eponym Lists," *Assyria 1995: 10th Anniversary Symposium of the Neo-Assyrian Text Corpus Project* (Helsinki: Helsinki University, forthcoming).

[45] Miller, "Solomon" (see above, n. 43), p. 30.

[46] The three stelae of Nabonidus found at Haran exemplify this well. They were found re-used as paving and steps in the mediaeval mosque there; see C. J. Gadd, "The Harran Inscriptions of Nabonidus," *AnSt* 8 (1958) 35-92.

[47] See further, A. R. Millard, "Solomon: Text and Archaeology," *PEQ* 123 (1991) 117-18.

The absence of Solomon's name from ancient texts is not peculiar, it is a symptom of our poverty; very few documents relate to that time in ancient Near Eastern history. The events that took place in Syria and Palestine during the 10th century BC are largely unknown to us. This is the position:

A. There are no Assyrian or Babylonian records of the 10th century BC which could be expected to name the king of Jerusalem. Both kingdoms were in decline for most of the century, Assyria beginning to recover from about 925, and neither had contacts so far to the west and south because they were harassed by Aramean tribes moving east from the Euphrates. There are Assyrian royal inscriptions, but they are concerned with internal affairs until the last quarter of the century, while from Babylonia "except for [one stela], no original text is more than four lines long."[48] It was not until 876 BC that Assyrian forces reached the Mediterranean. Shalmaneser III, shortly afterwards, tells of the re-capture of a town near the Euphrates which had been in Assyrian hands long before but had fallen to an Aramean prince about 1000 BC. The Aramean, it has been suggested, was the Hadad-ezer who carried his rule to the Euphrates or beyond and whom David overthrew (2 Sam 8:3; 10:16).[49]

B. The Arameans were becoming powerful in Syria, the Assyrian sources make clear, but from them there are no documents written before the middle of the 9th century BC and their later writings do not look back so far as the 10th century.

C. The realm of Solomon's ally, Hiram of Tyre, is archaeologically almost wholly unknown and there are no texts from the city or related to it older than the 8th century BC. Josephus reproduces information he gleaned from the Menander of Ephesus' *Annals of Tyre*, and another author's *Phoenician History*, with reference to Solomon's ally, Hiram, but how old or how reliable they were cannot be established.[50] The other Phoenician cities are equally silent; their archives would, of course, have been on papyrus scrolls.

D. Egypt supplies no more than a handful of inscriptions relating to Palestine in any way from 1000 BC onwards, the outstanding one being

---

[48] See A. K. Grayson, *Assyrian Rulers* (see above, n. 37); and J. A. Brinkman, "Babylonia *c.* 1000-748 B.C.," *CAH* [2] 3.1.296.

[49] A. Malamat, "The Aramaeans," *Peoples of Old Testament Times* (ed. D. J. Wiseman; Oxford: Clarendon, 1973) 134-55, see p. 142.

[50] G. Bunnens, "L'histoire événementielle partim Orient," *La civilisation phénicienne et punique* (ed. V. Krings; Handbuch der Orientalistik 1.20; Leiden: E. J. Brill, 1995) 222-36, especially pp. 222-25.

Shishak's list of places his forces visited, carved on the Bubastite Portal at Karnak. None of these inscriptions name any king of Israel or Judah. Shishak's campaign was commemorated by a triumphal stele he set up at Megiddo, of which a fragment survives, and there were certainly other contacts, betokened by a vase inscribed with the name of Osorkon II (*ca.* 874-850 BC) which once graced the palace at Samaria where the excavators found it smashed. It was probably a gift to a king of Israel from the pharaoh. Later, pharaoh Necho marched north and killed king Josiah at Megiddo (2 Kgs 23:29-35). So far the only record of this triumph from the Levant is a fragment proclaiming Necho's control of Sidon. This scanty harvest from Egypt results from her generally weak state from the 11th century onwards; Shishak's sally into Palestine was an isolated enterprise. It is debated whether a scrap of triumphal relief of Siamun celebrates a victory in the Levant, or somewhere else (see p. 26). Not a single administrative record relates to external affairs, so the absence of Solomon's name from Egyptian texts carries no weight at all. His marriage to a daughter of a pharaoh is consistent with what is known of Egyptian policy at the time.[51]

The situation with regard to Solomon is not unusual. Many ancient kings and events are known to us from single accounts, sometimes contemporary, sometimes later, and many more kings and events are unknown to us because they are not documented. In reality more written documents of ancient times have perished than we shall ever recover, in Egypt, in Mesopotamia and in Palestine. There is no justification for overlooking these facts and propagating a sceptical stance as one journalist did: "Even more disconcerting [than the lack of Hebrew inscriptions from Solomon's day] is the fact that there is not a single contemporary reference to David or Solomon in the many neighboring countries which certainly were keeping records during the tenth century. At a time when the Bible tells us that Solomon created a major empire in the Middle East, none of his contemporaries, not even the Phoenicians, apparently noticed the fact."[52] How far removed from the evidence that assertion is should be evident, especially inasmuch as no appropriate Phoenician writings of the time are extant.

Admitting the cultural and historical contexts could allow a king to

---

[51] For the Egyptian contribution see Kitchen, *Third Intermediate Period*, and *idem.*, "Egypt and Israel During the First Millennium."

[52] M. Magnusson, *BC: The Archaeology of the Bible Lands* (London: Bodley Head, 1977) 155.

reign in Solomonic spendour, objections are voiced on the grounds of Jerusalem's minor importance and the limited size of the Davidic realm. Yet the rise of small states to great glory, then their rapid or gradual decline is a feature of world history, an able leader turning circumstances to his advantage. Herod the Great is a parade example, having an annual income at the end of his reign which Josephus reported as 1,050 talents, ruling a kingdom which was partitioned immediately after his death and erecting magnificent buildings which had lost their glory within 75 years.

As suzerain over Palestine from the Mediterranean eastwards across the Jordan and from the Red Sea to the Euphrates, Solomon could control major trade routes outside Israel, including the northern parts of those that brought incense from the Yemen (we may imagine a mutually beneficial agreement between the king of Israel and the queen of Sheba) all contributing substantially to his revenue.

5. The Nature of the Hebrew History Book

A. *Content*

The Solomon Narrative is part of the Book of Kings, an account of the history of Israel and Judah from David's death until the fall of each kingdom. No other people of the ancient Near East has left a comparable narrative history, written in the third person, relating frankly royal and national failure beside triumphs, spanning several centuries. It is interpretative narrative, without pretence to be otherwise, its presupposition being Israel's God was in charge of her career through a covenant relationship, ordering affairs to make the impact he wished upon kings and the people. In that respect, the writers had common ground with their neighbors who also proclaimed their gods gave victory or punished their devotees by military defeat, although nowhere else is the covenant idea spelt out. Completed in or after the Exile, is the work a satisfactory historical source for a time four hundred years before?

Scribes in Assyria and Babylonia kept some sort of running records of noteworthy happenings on which they based the Babylonian Chronicles and Assyrian Eponym Chronicles. Wooden tablets covered with wax were the most likely materials for those log-books (Hebrew *lūaḥ*), but they have perished. By analogy, we may surmise, the Hebrew scribes compiling Kings had similar sources, on wax or on papyrus, and, also by analogy, those texts could be many generations old.[53] Were the whole of Kings to be demonstrably folk-lore or highly embroidered stories, there would be a case for dismissing all or parts of the Solomon Narrative as on par with the Arabian Nights, but wherever the book can be checked against adequate records from other states, it can be seen to be a reliable record, keeping its own purpose and view in mind. The absence of those records for Solomon's reign, which has been taken as licence for wholesale scepticism, should not lead to that part of the book being treated so differently from the remainder.

The theological cast of Kings, running through the book, may have already coloured its sources, it need belong only to the time of the final compilation; indeed, it could reach back to the time of Solomon. The theology and style are usually termed Deuteronomistic because they have much in common with the book of Deuteronomy, which is associated with the outcome of Josiah's reform in 622 BC, and also with the book of Jeremiah, whose prophecies began a little earlier. All examples of that doctrine and style are thought to come from the same period, late in the 7th and in the 6th centuries BC. Yet the similarity need not require contemporaneity. The Deuteronomic style has many parallels in the Assyrian royal inscriptions and in them the same style can be followed over many centuries. For example, phrases in "annals" of king Tiglath-pileser I, who ruled *ca.* 1100 BC, recur, with minor variations, in monuments of Sargon II, four hundred years later, or in the "annals" of his successors Sennacherib and Ashurbanipal.[54] Concepts continuing across the centuries in Assyrian records include, in particular, evaluation of a foreign king's conduct in terms of keeping a treaty or covenant. That appears in an "epic" poem about Tukulti-Ninurta I (*ca.* 1244-1208) and recurs for five hundred years. The Assyrian literature echoes concepts typical of the Hebrew, "Deuteronomic," literature, which there is no need to place entirely within a short span of time. It is attractive, now, to argue that Kings may embody material from much earlier written records with little

[53] This topic deserves extended treatment in another study.

[54] A collection of scores of phrases and concepts repeated in this way over many hundreds of years has been made by J. J. Niehaus (unpublished). Three instances make the point, two being stock descriptions, the third having theological significance: "I burnt their towns with fire, devastated and destroyed them" occurs from Shalmaneser I (*ca.* 1250 BCE) to Ashurbanipal (*ca.* 650 BCE); "I made the gulleys and heights of the hills run with blood" in Tiglath-pileser I's prism (iii.25-27 etcetera) and Sargon II's 8th Campaign (line 135); "the fearful splendour of Ashur my lord overwhelmed them" in Tiglath-pileser I's prism (iii.69-70), Sennacherib's annals (ii.39) and Ashurbanipal's annals (B.vi.4-5).

editorial alteration, so its accounts of events in Israel and Judah from David and Solomon onwards may be taken as satisfactory historical sources. That is not proof that they are true, but it does require those who argue their value is small to offer a much stronger case grounded in knowledge of ancient practices.

Various specific criticisms are made of the Solomonic Narrative implying a lack of historical verity, beside those already treated. There is a supposed contrast between Solomon's quantities of gold and the allegedly small amount of gold David received, the Ammonite crown, weighing one talent, is cited (2 Sam 12:30), but 2 Samuel does report other, unspecified amounts, which were probably larger, in the gold shields taken from Hadad-ezer of Zobah, the gift from Toi of Hamath and spoils from other nations, all listed in 2 Sam 8:7-12. The apparently vague references to Solomon's contemporaries, the Queen of Sheba and the Pharaoh, are brought into contrast with the naming of Shishak and other rulers in later chapters. This is another weak argument. 1 Kgs 11:14-22 presents the episode of Hadad, the Edomite nationalist, who had as wife Tahpenes, sister-in-law of Pharaoh; she is named, but not her important relative, the king of Egypt. The absence of the royal name implies no more than that it was unnecessary for the narration. Where one name is present, Hiram of Tyre, it is contrarily taken as a sign of "folk-loristic character" because Hiram is a common Phoenician name, as if a king could not share a current name![55] The assertion that Solomon's rule extended from the Egyptian frontier to the Euphrates has to be balanced, it is averred, against the reference to the troublesome trio, Hadad of Edom, Rezon of Damascus and Jeroboam of Ephraim (1 Kgs 11:14-40).[56] That argument might be reversed, too, for the very presence of the reports about these three can be taken as a testimony to the record's authenticity, as they could hardly be the inventions of a writer trying to magnify Solomon. Moreover, if the records about the first two can be trusted as "post-deuteronomistic insertions...probably derived from archival sources,"[57] then they testify to the availability at a late period of old documents not entirely favourable to Solomon. Threats posed to an emperor by opponents or nationalists do not deny his rule, they challenge it, and they may be successful or they may not, as history frequently reveals. Lastly, for this purpose, we note the assumption that God appear-

[55] Pritchard, "Age of Solomon" (see above, n. 17), p. 32.
[56] Miller, "Solomon" (see above, n. 43), p. 28.
[57] Jones, *1 and 2 Kings* (see above, n. 4), 1.237.

ing in a dream to Solomon sleeping at the shrine in Gibeon and the marriage to pharaoh's daughter are reckoned doubtful because similar stories occur in other languages.[58] That is as unsatisfactory an argument as one that says John F. Kennedy was not assassinated because stories of assassinated presidents exist independently in the same country and others!

B. *Text*

The Hebrew text can be traced as far back as the Dead Sea Scrolls, which include fragments of Kings and there are allusions to the narrative of Kings in Ben Sira 47:12-22, from the 2nd century BC. The Hebrew Bible was translated into Greek during the 3rd and 2nd centuries BC, so the text existed in some form prior to that date. Variations between the Greek version, the Septuagint, and the traditional Hebrew text within Kings suggest that there may have been some fluidity in its contents at that time and have been made into a tool for disentangling editorial additions and revisions to the book. This is a complex topic, suitable only for passing remarks here. One particular is significant, the Septuagint has nothing to correspond with verses about overlaying the Temple with gold (MT 1 Kgs 6:18, 21a, 22b), and so has been used to support the view that this concept is the product of exaggeration over time.[59] However, the Septuagint is not consistent, for it does have a rendering of verse 21, "he overlaid it with gold," and verse 22a which gives the most extravagant description of all, "he overlaid the whole house with gold." D. W. Gooding has examined the Greek text of 1 Kings beside the Hebrew and shown lucidly that, far from reflecting a Hebrew text more primitive than the traditional, the omissions from the Greek can be put down to scribal errors at an early stage in its history; only when the Greek is read in the light of the Hebrew does it make sense. From this and other studies, it appears little reliance should be placed upon the Septuagint as a guide to the history of the Hebrew text of Kings.[60]

---

[58] Miller and Hayes, *History* (see above, n. 35), p. 195.

[59] Montgomery and Gehman, *Kings* (see above, n. 34), p. 150; and other commentators.

[60] D. W. Gooding, "An Impossible Shrine," *VT* 15 (1965) 405-20; *idem.*, "Temple Specifications: A Dispute in Logical Arrangement between the MT and the LXX," *VT* 17 (1967) 143-72; *idem.*, *Relics of Ancient Exegesis: A Study of the Miscellanies in 3 Reigns 2* (Cambridge: Cambridge University, 1976); cf. J. W. Wevers, "Exegetical Principles Underlying the Septuagint Text of I Kings ii.12-xxi.43," *OTS* 8 (1950) 300-22. Notice, for example, that the Greek version of 1 Kgs 10:16 has "300 spears of beaten gold; 300 shekels of gold to each spear" instead of "200 shields...each of 600 talents."

CONCLUSION

This essay has argued for a positive approach to the Solomon Narrative, urging its treatment in the light of knowledge about the ancient Near East, and for a shedding of the presuppositions which biblical scholars have brought to its study. In every ascertainable way Solomon acted in the manner of the kings around him, if we follow the biblical text (and more evidence can be added to that which has been set out here). His enomous wealth and the lack of any external corroboration for his reïgn are the principal bases for modern scepticism; neither is an insuperable obstacle to crediting the Hebrew reports, there is no external or objective evidence negating them. The possibility that those reports do reflect reliably the reign of king Solomon has to be admitted, even if, at present, there is nothing to prove that they do.

RESPONSE TO MILLARD

J. MAXWELL MILLER

Professor Millard's case for confidence in the historicity of the biblical account of King Solomon is clear and to the point. While we reach different conclusions in the end, moreover, we are in agreement on at least three fundamental points: 1) We agree that the Hebrew Bible, specifically 1 Kgs 1-11, is the basic source of information. Archaeology, sociology and all other such disciplines combined cannot even get Solomon on the page without some prompting from the Hebrew Bible. 2) We agree that this 1 Kings presentation of his reign was composed long after Solomon would have lived (Millard places it within two or three centuries after 562 BCE) and that the text remained somewhat fluid at least into the 3rd century BCE. 3) We both are confident, nevertheless, that this 1 Kings account is not entirely a product of the 6th century and later. Both of us agree that those who compiled it had access to pre-exilic materials, some of which possibly dated back to Solomon's time, and we both give reasons for believing that these compilers "were not operating totally in the dark about political circumstances during the 10th century BCE."

Our disagreements cluster around three questions: 1) Recognizing that the compilers of 1 Kings possibly had access to materials dating back to Solomon's time, how confidant should we be that these materials were transmitted over the post-Solomonic centuries without becoming significantly modified or garbled in the process? 2) Is there a considerable amount of authentic Solomonic material embedded in the 1 Kings account of his reign and did this authentic material actually determine the shape of the account, or should we think in terms of only occassional "fossils" from the Solomonic era embedded in what is essentially a late Judean revisionist account of his reign? 3) How far will comparative evidence from epigraphy and archaeology take us toward resolving the preceding questions?

Regarding the Book of Kings, Millard observes that "No other people of the ancient Near East has left a comparative narrative history ..." and then begins to speak of Assyrian and Babylonian record keeping. The implication seems to be that official Assyrian and Babylonian annalistic records are the appropriate literary genera for comparing and understanding the literary composition of 1 Kings. Before looking to other peoples of the ancient Near East, however, it should at least be mentioned that the Chronicler's history is available for comparison. The Chronicler's history illustrates the extent to which Judean scribes of the post-exilic era were prepared to modify and "enhance" the materials which they received and passed on. When we do look to other peoples of the ancient world for comparative examples, moreover, it turns out that there are other "comparable narrative histor[ies], written in the third person, relating frankly royal and national failure beside triumphs, spanning several centuries." The writings of Herodotus, Berossus, Manetho and other Greek historians meet Millard's specifications and also fall roughly within the time frame which he specifies for the final compilation of 1 Kings (i.e., within two or three centuries after 562 BCE).[1] These Greek historians also wrote about real people and events; they also had access to earlier written sources; and contemporary historians also take their works very seriously as sources of historical information. At the same time, contemporary historicans recognize the necessity of reading their accounts critically and of maintaining some objective distance.

As for Millard's extensive catalogue of examples which document that the wealth attributed to Solomon would not have been without parallel in the ancient world, along with his explanations as to how Solomon's empire could have lasted forty years without leaving any epigraphical traces or clearly identifiable archaeological remains, let me first simply repeat that all of these examples and explanations combined take us only so far as the realm of "plausibility." It is a cardinal rule of historiography, however, and one which applies rather specifically to the biblical account of Solomon's reign, that plausibility and probability are two quite different things. Second, Millard does document quite adequately that there were other ancient Near Eastern potentates whose wealth compared to that which the Hebrew Bible attributes to Solomon, note the scarcity of examples from the opening centuries of the Iron Age in contrast to the many which he gleaned from the Late Bronze Age and from the Neo-Assyrian and Neo-Babylonian empires of the latter half of

[1] Van Seter's arguments *on this point* are compelling in my opinion; J. Van Seters, *In Search of History: Historiography in the Ancient World and the Origins of Biblical History* (New Haven: Yale University, 1983).

the Iron Age.[2] Indeed Millard's own review of the meager epigraphical evidence available for the opening of the Iron Age demonstrates that this is not a time of world-class empires and emperors, but rather a "dark age" throughout the Middle East; and the archaeological evidence from Palestine verifies that the scene there was no different. Thus if we fine-tune the question a bit and inquire whether Millard's catalogue of parallel examples suggests the plausibility of such a powerful and wealthy potentate existing *in Palestine during the 10th century BCE*, the answer is at least ambivalent if not negative.

True, archaeologists find traces of only a small percentage of the hundreds of thousands of buildings and documents which were produced in ancient times. Yet it is reasonable to suppose that, on the whole, there is some degree of correspondence between the wealth and grandeur of ancient empires and the extent to which they have left archaeological and epigraphical traces. It is not entirely by accident, in other words, that the Late Bronze Age and Late Iron Age empires are well documented by interlocking epigraphical and archaeological evidence. It is because their rulers were so powerful and commanded such great wealth that they were able to build many monumental structures which they graced with inscriptions and because they required sophisticated administrations which produced mountains of additional records. Accordingly, it is not just the absence of any epigraphical references to Solomon that should give us pause, but the absence of any inscriptions or records of any sort from his supposedly expansive empire, an empire moreover which seems out of keeping with the general circumstances of the early Iron Age.

[2] The notable exception is the record of gifts from Osorkon I to the gods of Heliopolis (205 tons of gold, silver and lapis lazuli) which even Millard characterized as "astounding."

SOURCES AND COMPOSITION IN THE HISTORY OF SOLOMON

NADAV NA'AMAN

1. THE ADVENT OF WRITING IN THE COURT OF JERUSALEM

The histories of David and Solomon as delineated in the books of Samuel and Kings were regarded for many years as evidence for extensive writing in the tenth century court of Jerusalem. Numerous details seemingly support this assumption. For example:
a) the office of scribe, who must have been a state scribe and a personal secretary of the king, among the officials of David and Solomon (2 Sam 8:17; 20:25; 1 Kgs 4:3); b) the establishment of a state, with its foreign, political and commercial connections requiring a system of administration where writing had a prominent place; c) the references to Solomon's wisdom, which were interpreted as evidence of a foundation of a school of scribes and learning in Jerusalem; d) "the book of the acts of Solomon" (1 Kgs 11:41), which was regarded as an official text written in the court of Jerusalem. Many scholars accepted a tenth century date for the beginning of historical writing in Israel.[1]

[1] See, for example, L. Rost, *Die Überlieferung von der Thronnachfolge Davids* (Stuttgart: Kohlhammer, 1926); G. von Rad, "Der Anfang der Geschichtsschreibung im alten Israel," *Archiv für Kulturgeschichte* 32 (1944) 1-42 [English trans., *The Problem of the Hexateuch and Other Essays* (New York: McGraw-Hill, 1966) 166-204]; idem, "Josephsgeschichte und ältere Chokma," *Congress Volume: Copenhagen, 1953* (VTSup 1; Leiden: E. J. Brill, 1953) 120-127 [English trans., *The Problem of the Hexateuch*, pp. 292-300]; S. Mowinckel, "Israelite Historiography," *ASTI* 2 (1967) 75-101; J. Liver, "The Book of the Acts of Solomon," *Bib* 48 (1967) 75-101; J. Gray, *I & II Kings: A Commentary* (OTL; 2nd ed.; Philadelphia: Westminster, 1970) 14-22; T. N. D. Mettinger, *King and Messiah: The Civil and Sacral Legitimation of the Israelite Kings* (ConBOT 8; Lund: CWK Gleerup, 1976); F. Langlamet, "Pour ou contre Salomon? La rédaction prosalomonienne de I Rois, I-II," *RB* 83 (1976) 518-528; P. K. McCarter, *I Samuel: A New Translation with Introduction and Commentary* (AB 8; Garden City: Doubleday, 1980) 23-30; idem, *II Samuel: A New Translation with Introduction and Commentary* (AB 9; Garden City: Doubleday, 1984) 9-16; W. H. Schmidt, "A Theologian of the Solomonic Era? A Plea for the Yahwist," *Studies in the Period of David and Solomon and Other Essays* (ed. T. Ishida; Tokyo: Yamakawa-Shuppansha, 1982) 55-73; T. Ishida, "Solomon's Succession to the Throne of David – A Political Analysis," *Studies in the Period of David and Solomon and Other Essays* (ed. T. Ishida; Tokyo: Yamakawa-Shuppansha, 1982) 175-187.

However, these claims of extensive writing in the courts of David and Solomon, and of an early development of historiography in Israel, have been dismissed in recent research and can no longer be upheld. It is widely accepted today that the Deuteronomistic history was composed either in the late seventh century BCE, or immediately after the destruction and exile of 587/586; and that the development of historical writing in Israel did not antedate the eighth century BCE.

So when was writing introduced into the court of Jerusalem? Determining this date is essential for the evaluation of our sources on the history of Solomon. Several lists that might have been drawn from original documents are usually regarded as indications of writing in Israel as early as the tenth century. Many scholars assume that these sources suggest that the biblical historians had before them original documents of the time of the United Monarchy. Recently, however, some scholars have questioned these assumptions. They suggest that Jerusalem did not become the centre of a state before the 8th century, and that writing in Jerusalem did not antedate the establishment of the state. In their opinion, the history of the United Monarchy was composed purely on the basis of oral traditions, and is devoid of historical foundation.[2]

No extra-biblical sources mention either David or Solomon. This is not surprising. There are no detailed accounts of historical events in the first millennium before the 9th century BCE. All Syro-Palestinian inscriptions of the 10th century refer to local affairs and shed no light on international relations. Even if David and Solomon accomplished the deeds attributed to them in the Bible, no source would have mentioned their names. The silence of 10th century sources neither proves nor disproves the biblical account of the United Monarchy.[3]

---

[2] The fundamental study of the emergence of the Judean state is D. W. Jamieson-Drake, *Scribes and Schools in Monarchic Judah: A Socio-Archaeological Approach* (Sheffield: Sheffield Academic, 1991) esp. pp. 138-145. See also, E. A. Knauf, "From History to Interpretation," in *The Fabric of History: Text, Artifact and Israel's Past* (ed. D. V. Edelman; Sheffield: Sheffield Academic, 1991) 39; idem., "King Solomon's Copper Supply," in *Phoenicia and the Bible* (ed. E. Lipiński; Leuven: Peeters, 1991) 172; P. R. Davies, *In Search of 'Ancient Israel'* (JSOTSupp 148; Sheffield: Sheffield Academic, 1992) 67-70; T. L. Thompson, *Early History of the Israelite People: From the Written and the Archaeological Sources* (Leiden: E. J. Brill, 1992) 409-410; idem, "'House of David': An Eponymic Referent to Yahweh as Godfather," *JSOT* 9 (1995) 59-74; N. P. Lemche, "Is It Still Possible to Write a History of Israel?" *JSOT* 8 (1994) 183-89; N. P. Lemche and T. L. Thompson, "Did Biran Kill David? The Bible in the Light of Archaeology, *JSOT* 64 (1994) 3-23.

[3] *Contra* G. Garbini, *History and Ideology in Ancient Israel* (London: SCM, 1988) 16; see Knauf, "From History to Interpretation," pp. 171-172.

There is one exception to the local nature of 10th century documents: the topographical list of Shishak. The Egyptian king left a long list of places conquered in the course of his Asiatic campaign. An Analysis of the list indicates that the campaign was directed against the Northern Kingdom (Israel) and the non-Judahite Negevite areas, avoiding almost entirely the kingdom of Judah.[4]

Shishak's campaign is referred to in 1 Kgs 14:25-28. The text clearly deals chiefly with the handing over of Solomon's golden shields to Shishak, and their replacement by copper shields. Details of the Egyptian campaign are minimal and its description is schematic. What could have been the source the author drew on for his description? In my opinion, it must have been a chronicle (composed on the basis of earlier sources) which mentioned that in the fifth year of Rehoboam's reign golden shields were delivered to Shishak, king of Egypt, and were replaced by copper shields. The Deuteronomist (henceforth Dtr) logically interpreted this statement to mean that Shishak's campaign, about which he had no other source, was directed against Jerusalem, and that the treasures of the palace and the temple were then delivered to Egypt. He wrote long after the conclusion of the campaign he described and was entirely dependent on his sources. His interpretation of Shishak's campaign may look incomplete and even misleading, but it illuminates part of the historical reality; the campaign did indeed reach the environs of Jerusalem and a heavy tribute was paid to Egypt on that occasion.[5]

The account of Shishak's campaign in the Book of Kings indicates that there was some kind of scribal activity in the court of Jerusalem in the late 10th century BCE. One would naturally assume that it was not introduced by a petty king like Rehoboam, but rather by one of his ancestors, either David or Solomon. The installation of the office of scribe in the courts of David and Solomon, as related in three official lists (2 Sam. 8:17; 20:25; 1 Kgs 4:3) supports this conclusion. It also

[4] N. Na'aman, "Israel, Edom and Egypt in the 10th Century B.C.E.," *Tel Aviv* 19 (1992) 79-86, with earlier literature.

[5] Some scholars have recently suggested that, contrary to the text of Kings, Shishak's campaign should be dated to the late years of Solomon. See Garbini, *History and Ideology*, pp. 29-30; Knauf, "King Solomon's Copper Supply," pp. 181-182; D. B. Redford, *Egypt, Canaan, and Israel in Ancient Times* (Princeton: Princeton University, 1992) 315. They did not, however, attempt to analyze the text of Kings or to discuss the problem of sources and composition in the history of Rehoboam. In my opinion, the suggestion is arbitrary and lacks a concrete foundation. The date of the campaign as recorded in the Book of Kings must have been drawn from a written source and can be used as a safe point of departure for dating the division of the monarchy.

accords with some records which are included in the history of Solomon, and may have been drawn from late copies of old documents. For example:

a) The list of Solomon's high officials (1 Kgs 4:2-6)
b) The list of Solomon's district officers (1 Kgs 4:9-19)[6]
c) Details of Solomon's building activity in his kingdom (1 Kgs 9:15, 17-18).

The evidence presented so far for scribal activity in the 10th century court of Jerusalem may be supported further by epigraphic evidence. Goldwasser has suggested that the hieratic numerals and signs, common in epigraphic documents of Israel and Judah in the 8th-7th centuries BCE, that do not appear in documents of Israel's neighbors, entered the Hebrew script before the 9th century BCE. It passed from Egyptian scribes in the 12th century to local Canaanite scribes, who in their turn passed on their knowledge to the new court of Israel.[7] Egyptian influence on the Hebrew script supports the above conclusions that scribal activity was already introduced into the court of Jerusalem at the time of the United Monarchy.

We may conclude that writing began in the court of Jerusalem in the 10th century, in the reign of either David or Solomon. Scribal activity was first limited to administrative records and the scribes were personal secretaries of the kings rather than state's functionaries. This situation lasted for many decades, and only in the 8th century BCE did writing spread beyond the bounds of the royal and temple courts. Until that time,

---

[6] For a recent discussion, see P. S. Ash, "Solomon's? District? List," *JSOT* 67 (1995) 67-86, with earlier literature. It must be noted that Ash's textual analysis does not differ from the analysis of many other scholars who observed that the text in its present form includes numerous interpolations and glosses. That the data in the text is pre-Dtr is also common knowledge. The new element in the article is the outcome of the observation made recently by scholars, that writing in the 10th century court of Jerusalem was quite limited, and could hardly have produced the records necessary for this kind of document. It is from this observation that Ash draws his conclusions, namely, that the district list was drawn from oral transmission, and that no early source was available for the Dtr historian. However, it is unlikely that the kind of information immersed in the district list was transmitted orally; the historian must have drawn it from a written source. Morevover, the original geographical list is reasonably coherent, and Ash's claim of confusion of names and places in the list is greatly exaggerated. The nature of the source used by the historian, its date and original function, remain unknown. See V. Fritz, "Die Verwaltungsgebiete Salomos nach 1 Kön. 4,7-19," in *Meilenstein: Festgabe für Herbert Donner* (ed. M. Görg; Ägypten und Altes Testament 30; Wiesbaden: Otto Harrassowitz, 1995) 19-26.

[7] O. Goldwasser, "An Egyptian Scribe from Lachish and the Hieratic Tradition of the Hebrew Kingdoms," *Tel Aviv* 18 (1991) 248-253.

learning and scribal activity were confined to the courts of Israel and Judah. Only there were texts produced, partly for the training and educating of pupils. We may further assume that even in later times scribal training in the kingdom of Judah took place primarily, if not exclusively, in Jerusalem, and that all professional administrators were trained there.[8]

Elsewhere I have suggested that the corpus of texts in the Jerusalemite "high school" was the main source used by the Dtr for his composition of the history of Israel.[9] This corpus, which formed the "library" of the Jerusalem palace and temple, included all that was essential for the education and function of royal and temple Judean scribes. It reflected the continuity of Jerusalem as the capital of Judah for four centuries, and some of the texts in the corpus could have been very old, copied by the scribes from generation to generation. Other texts might have been composed relatively late and attributed to prominent past figures. They were then transferred with these attributions into the stream of scribal learning. Analyzing the source material of the Dtr historian is, therefore, an extremely complicated problem. Each and every text must be examined separately, in an effort to trace its possible source, and only then can we decide whether it may be used for the historical reconstruction.

In what follows I will try to analyze the text of 1 Kgs 3-11 in an effort to determine the sources which could have reached the historian, and the way in which he integrated them into his work.

2. The Rebellions against Solomon (1 Kgs 11:14-28, 40)

From the text of 1 Kgs 11 it is evident that the revolts of Hadad the Edomite and Rezon the Aramean took place early in Solomon's reign, whereas Jeroboam's revolt took place in the latter half of his reign. But in their present place the three revolts form a coherent unit, which serves as a divine retribution for the sins of Solomon. God's wrath with Solomon is expressed by external and internal enemies. As suggested by

---

[8] Jamieson-Drake, *Scribes and Schools*, pp. 148-49, 151. For a different opinion, see A. Lemaire, *Les écoles et la formation de la Bible dans l'Ancien Israël* (OBO 39; Fribourg: Éditions Universitaires; Göttingen: Vandenhoeck & Ruprecht, 1981) 46-54.

[9] N. Na'aman, "Sources and Composition in the History of David," in *The Origins of the Ancient Israelite States* (eds. V. Fritz and P.R. Davies; JSOTSup 228; Sheffield: Sheffield Academic, 1996) 180-83; see Lemaire, *Les écoles*, pp. 72-82, with earlier literature.

Knoppers, the Dtr develops parallels between Jeroboam's rise to power and the revolts of Hadad and Rezon.[10] They all shared a common sequence of events: being forced to flee from their homeland, they stay for a while in a foreign land, and with the death of the king of Jerusalem are able to return home and rise to power as adversaries of the new king. This suggestion supports the claim that verse 25a$^{\beta}$b is the original conclusion of the story of Hadad. On the basis of the MT and LXX, we may reconstruct it thus: "and this is (זאת) the evil which Hadad (did). And he abhorred (ויקץ) Israel, and he reigned over Edom.[11]

In a recent article I suggest that a "chronicle of early Israelite kings" was composed in the 8th century BCE and that it was the major source from which the Dtr derived details for the reconstruction of the chain of events in the time of the United Monarchy.[12] The brief description of Saul's kingship (1 Sam 14:47-48), the reign of Ishbaal (2 Sam 2:8-9), the conquest of Jebus, the wars with the Philistines, and the wars with Israel's other neighbors, all could have originated in the chronicle. It seems to me that the three uprisings against Solomon episodes were drawn from this source and, moreover, that the given sequence of the three revolts reflects their original order in the chronicle. By adopting this sequence of events, the historian established a meaningful background for the next episode of Jeroboam's rise to power and the division of the monarchy.

Reconstructing the Hadad and Jeroboam episodes is complicated since both were transmitted in an incomplete form. The story of Hadad is cut after 11:22, and the conclusion (11:25a$^{\beta}$-b) was taken out of its original context and placed erroneously after the Rezon episode. The Rehoboam episode is cut after 11:28, and only its conclusion appears in 11:40. Between, the Dtr inserted the episode of the prophetic prediction of Ahijah (11:29-39), which is part of his theological explanation of the division of the monarchy. Evidently the historian made use of an old written source, which he partly reworked (the Hadad episode was probably expanded in 11:18,20,22) and from which he omitted certain

[10] G. N. Knoppers, *Two Nations Under God: The Deuteronomistic History of Solomon and the Dual Monarchies, 1: The Reign of Solomon and the Rise of Jeroboam* (HSM 52; Atlanta: Scholars, 1993) 164.

[11] D. Barthélemy, *Critique textuelle de l'Ancien Testament, 1: Josué, Juges, Ruth, Samuel, Rois, Chroniques, Esdras, Néhémie, Esther* (OBO 50-51; Fribourg: Éditions Universitaires; Göttingen: Vandenhoeck & Ruprecht, 1982) 361-62; Na'aman, "Edom and Egypt," pp. 76-77; Knoppers, *Two Nations Under God*, pp. 160-61.

[12] Na'aman, "Sources and Composition in the History of David," pp. 173-79.

details, possibly because they did not fit his view of Solomon's reign.
The episodes of Rezon and Hadad are explicitly connected to David's wars against Hadadezer of Zobah (2 Sam 8:3-4) and the slaying of the troops of Aram Damascus (2 Sam 8:5); and 1 Kgs 11:15 refers directly to 2 Sam 8:13, as is evident from comparison of the two texts:

> When he returned from smiting Aram [*sic*] <he smote Edom> in the Valley of Salt eighteen thousand (people) [2 Sam 8:13].[13]
> For when David was in Aram [*sic*], when Joab the commander of the army went to bury the slain, he slew every male in Edom [1 Kgs 11:15].

We may further note that the revolts of Rezon and Hadad took place in the same territories where it is explicitly stated that David stationed governors after conquering them (2 Sam 8:6,14). This is not accidental. It may be explained by the way that the Dtr manipulated his sources. He found in the chronicle that early in Solomon's reign Aram and Edom revolted against Israel, drew the reasonable conclusion that governors and garrisons must have been stationed there before the revolt, and filled in these details within the history of David. Filling in the gaps of his sources by logical inferences is typical of the Dtr's historical work and will be noted in the discussion below.

3. Solomon and Pharaoh's Daughter

Another episode that may have been derived from the "chronicle of early Israelite kings" is Solomon's marriage to the daughter of Pharaoh.[14] The record of Solomon's Egyptian wife is now dislocated in five different places (1 Kgs 3:1; 7:8; 9:16,24; 11:1), but the original source from which the author derived his data may be tentatively restored thus (RSV):

> Pharaoh king of Egypt had gone up and captured Gezer and burnt it with fire, and had slain the Canaanites who dwelt in the city, and

[13] Barthélemy, *Critique textuelle*, pp. 251-52.
[14] See A. Malamat, "A Political Look at the Kingdom of David and Solomon and Its Relations with Egypt," in *Studies in the Period of David and Solomon and Other Essays* (ed. T. Ishida; Tokyo: Yamakawa-Shuppansha, 1982) 198-204, with earlier literature; A. R. Schulman, "The Curious Case of Hadad the Edomite," in *Egyptological Studies in Honor of Richard A. Parker* (ed. L. H. Lesko; Hanover: Brown University, 1986) 122-35, with earlier literature; K. A. Kitchen, "Egypt and Israel During the First Millennium B.C.," in *Congress Volume: Jerusalem, 1986* (VTSup 40; ed. J. Emerton; Leiden: E. J. Brill, 1988) 110-11; Redford, *Egypt, Canaan, and Israel*, p. 311 and nn. 117-18.

> had given it as dowry to his daughter (9:16abα). Solomon made a marriage alliance with Pharaoh king of Egypt; he took Pharaoh's daughter, and brought her into the city of David, until he had finished building his own house (3:1aba). Then Pharaoh's daughter went up from the city of David to her own house which Solomon had built for her (9:24a).

The passage refers to a background episode of the marriage (the capture of Gezer and its transfer to Solomon as dowry), the matrimony, and the temporary stay of the Egyptian princess in the City of David until the completion of her house. The Dtr dislocated the account and separated it into three isolated notes, which he placed carefully in his history of Solomon. One note opens the history of Solomon's reign (1 Kgs 3:1), and is part of the negative slant on Solomon in this introduction (1 Kgs 3:1-3). A second note appears as a gloss after the name of Gezer, one of the cities built by Solomon (1 Kgs 9:16); and a third note was inserted after the end of Solomon's building in Jerusalem (Kgs 9:24). He further worked the episode and wrote a new note, in which he described the building of the princess' house (Kgs 7:8). Finally, her name was inserted into the list of Solomon's foreign wives (Kgs 11:1) as part of an anti-Solomonic critical passage.[15]

The motif of a marriage with an Egyptian princess appears for a second time in the episode of Hadad the Edomite which, as suggested above, was also derived from the "chronicle of early Israelite kings". The interest of the author of the chronicle in the relations with Egypt is evident from the note about Jeroboam's flight to Shishak (Kgs 11:40),[16] and the account of Shishak's campaign against Jeroboam (from which the historian drew the details of the campaign). Contacts between Egypt and Israel in the period of the late XXIth-early XXIIth Egyptian dynasties must have been quite extensive and the chronicler collected several episodes of this time and included them in his work.[17]

---

[15] S. J. D. Cohen, "Solomon and the Daughter of Pharaoh: Intermarriage, Conversion, and the Impurity of Women," *JANES* 16-17 (1984-1985) 23-37, with earlier literature, p. 26 n. 8.

[16] According to the LXX (3 Kgs 12e), Jeroboam also married an Egyptian princess. However, the story in 3 Kgs 12a-z is apparently a late midrashic text; the episode of Jeroboam's marriage is a reworking of the Hadad episode in 1 Kgs 11:19b-22. See Z. Talshir, *The Duplicate Story of the Division of the Kingdom (LXX 3 Kingdoms XII 24a-z)* (Jerusalem Biblical Studies; Jerusalem: Simor, 1989), with earlier literature (Hebrew); S. L. McKenzie, *The Trouble with Kings: The Composition of the Book of Kings in the Deuteronomistic History* (VTSup 42; Leiden: E. J. Brill, 1991) 21-40.

[17] For the relations of Egypt and Israel in the tenth century, see K. A. Kitchen, *The*

4. The Exchange of Letters between Hiram and Solomon

The passage of 1 Kgs 5:15-26 (English 5:1-11) relates the diplomatic exchange between Solomon and Hiram on the building of the temple and the conclusion of a commercial agreement. From an early stage of modern biblical research scholars noted that the passage contains several Deuteronomic expressions (in particular the references to the house for the name of YHWH, and the rest all around from the enemies in 5:17-19). Opinions were divided on the question of whether Dtr contributed the entire pericope, only these expressions, or the verses in which these expressions appear.[18] A close analysis of the passage seems to confirm the suggestion that it is a combination of a pre-Dtr source with a Dtr redaction.

The extent of the source-material is not easily determined. Tentatively, I would suggest that the introduction (1 Kgs 5:15a,16), the end of Solomon's letter (5:20), Hiram's letter to Solomon (5:22-24), and the agreed commercial terms (5:25) were copied from an earlier source. The original words of Solomon in 5:17-19 were entirely reworked by the Dtr in accordance with his theological ideas and cannot be restored. The Dtr additions include a reference to the relations of Hiram and David (5:15b), the motif of divine wisdom (5:21,26a), and the conclusion of a peace treaty between Solomon and Hiram (5:26b), which also served as a bridge for the next pericope (5:27-32).[19]

Assuming that the historian reworked a written source, what might have been its form? Some scholars suppose that an original letter from the time of Solomon had survived in the palace archive of Jerusalem and was used by the Dtr. Thus they reconstruct the Israelite-Tyrian relations

---

Third Intermediate Period in Egypt (1100-650 BC) (Warminster: Aris & Phillips, 1973) passim; Redford, *Egypt, Canaan and Israel*, pp. 309-15, with earlier literature.

[18] See the commentaries; also M. A. O'Brien, *The Deuteronomistic History Hypothesis: A Reassessment* (OBO 92; Freiburg: Universitätsverlag; Göttingen: Vandenhoeck & Rupprecht, 1989) 148-51; V. Hurowitz, *I Have Built You an Exalted House: Temple Building in the Bible in Light of Mesopotamian and Northwest Semitic Writings* (JSOTSup 115; Sheffield: Sheffield Academic, 1992) 171-73; C. Schäfer-Lichtenberger, *Josua und Salomo: Eine Studie zu Autorität und Legitimität des Nachfolgers im Alten Testament* (VTSup 58; Leiden: E. J. Brill, 1995) 287-92, with earlier literature.

[19] For the interpretation of verse 26, see F. C. Fensham, "The Treaty between the Israelites and the Tyrians," *Congress Volume: Rome, 1968* (VTSup 17; ed. J A. Emerton; Leiden: E. J. Brill, 1969) 71-87; Mettinger, *King and Messiah*, pp. 226-27; Hurowitz, *I Have Built You*, pp. 175-79, with earlier literature; F. Briquel-Chattonet, *Les relations entre les cités de la côte phénicienne et les royaumes d'Israël et de Juda* (OLA 46; Leuven: Uitgeverij Peeters, 1992) 40-47.

in the time of Solomon on the basis of this source.[20] But this assumption is fraught with many difficulties. First, alphabetic writing was introduced into the court of Jerusalem only in the 10th century, and it is questionable whether diplomatic letters were exchanged at this early time between Tyre and Israel. Second, the words of the text have no archaic features and it is doubtful whether they reflect the language of the 10th century BCE. Third, as far as we know, historians of the ancient world did not consult archives when they wrote their histories.[21] The assumption that the Dtr had systematically searched in archives for old documents connot be sustained. The source worked by the historian could hardly have been an original 10th century diplomatic letter.

It seems to me that the historian reworked a literary letter formerly used for training scribes in the "high school" of Jerusalem. Literary letters (often called "model letters" by Egyptologists as some of them were used as school texts) are known from Egypt where the majority date from the New Kingdom.[22] Some might have been genuine letters selected by Egyptian scholars, but the majority were artificial writings, either imitating real administrative letters, or using the letter as a new frame for various subjects. The model letters were designed to introduce the pupils to different kinds of letters with their formulae, structures and polite espressions, and thereby develop their epistolary style. Literary letters are also known from Mesopotamia and were composed by scribes in the second and first millennia BCE.[23] Like 1 Kgs 5:15-25, the sending side and the addressee are sometimes kings (e.g., the letters seemingly exchanged between Assyrian and Babylonian kings).[24] The place of these letters in the Mesopotamian scribal education system is not always clear,

[20] See, for example, Fensham, "The Treaty," pp. 71-79; H. J. Katzenstein, *The History of Tyre from the Beginning of the Second Millennium B.C.E. until the Fall of the Neo-Babylonian Empire in 538 B.C.E.* (Jerusalem: Goldberg's, 1973) 96-101; G. Bunnens, "Commerce et diplomatie phéniciens au temps de Hiram Ier de Tyr," *JESHO* 19 (1976) 1-31; Briquel-Chattonet, *Les relations*, pp. 40-47. For a more balanced position, see Hurowitz, *I Have Built You*, pp. 134, 220-23.

[21] J. Van Seters, *In Search of History: Historiography in the Ancient World and the Origins of Biblical History* (New Haven: Yale Univeristy, 1983) 40-51, 195-99.

[22] R. A. Caminos, *Late Egyptian Miscellanies* (London: Oxford University, 1954); idem, "Musterbriefe," in *Lexikon der Ägyptologie* (eds. W. Helck and E. Otto; Wiesbaden: Otto Harrossowitz, 1982) 4.243-44, with earlier literature.

[23] R. Borger, *Handbuch der Keilschriftliteratur* (Berlin: Walter de Gruyter, 1975) 3.57-58; P. Michalowski, "Königsbriefe," *RLA* 6.51-59, with earlier literature; W. Röllig, "Literatur," *RLA* 7.57-58.

[24] Röllig, "Literatur," p. 58a, with earlier literature.

but they must have been composed for purposes similar to those of the Egyptian literary letters.

The literary letters are fictious compositions, although certain elements, such as names, political situations and social/cultural background, may be authentic. The authors might have collected variegated elements and used them in composing their works. I would suggest that the pre-Dtr author of the letter under discussion worked in a similar manner. He was apparently a master scribe in the "high school" of Jerusalem and composed a literary letter in which he described the exchange of letters between the courts of Israel and Tyre. The epistolary language, the diplomatic and legal terminology and the commercial details, were all borrowed from the the reality of his time and outwardly look authentic.[25] Yet the letter is non-historical, and save for a few details (e.g., the contemporaneity of Hiram and Solomon and their possible commercial relations), mainly illustrates the outlines of negotiation and the conclusion of commercial agreements in the author's time.

It seems that this literary letter entered the stream of scribal learning (possibly as part of a larger composition) in the "high school" of Jerusalem, and was thus known to the Dtr. When writing his historical composition, he reworked it according to his theological ideas and used it as a source for the history of Solomon. The attribution of the letter to Solomon may reflect his trust in his source and his dependence on old texts for the reconstruction of the history of the monarchy.

5. Solomon's Land Sale to Hiram

According to 1 Kgs 9:10-14, Hiram supplied Solomon with timber and gold for twenty years. Then Solomon ceded to Hiram twenty cities in the land of Galilee and in return Hiram sent him 120 talents of gold.[26]

Verse 11, which opens the account of the transaction, links it with the

---

[25] For a detailed analysis of the letter in light of ancient Near Eastern texts, see Hurowitz, *I Have Built You*, pp. 174-220.

[26] Some scholars suggest that verse 14 (Hiram's repayment for the cities) is a late gloss inspired by the mention of "gold" in verse 11a. See, for example, I. Benzinger, *Die Bücher der Könige* (KHC 9; Freiburg: J.C. B. Mohr, 1899) 67; B. Stade and F. Schwally, *The Books of Kings: Critical Edition of the Hebrew Text* (SBOT 9; Leipzig: J. C. Hinrichs, 1904) 111; E. Würthwein, *Die Bücher der Könige: 1 Könige 1-16* (ATD 11/1; Göttingen: Vandenhoeck & Ruprecht, 1977) 106-107. However, not only does the suggestion lack textual support, it seems that the opposite is true, and that "gold" was added to verse 11a because of the text of verse 14 (see discussion below).

commercial agreement between Solomon and Hiram (1 Kgs 5:24), except for the mention of "gold," which refers forward. Verse 12 opens with an introductory time-phrase (*'az* = "then") and relates the ceding of towns "in the land of Galilee." Verses 12-13 are a name aetiology which combines Hiram's displeasure when he sees the towns with the etymology of the toponym Cabul. Verse 14 relates Hiram's payment of 120 talents of gold for the twenty cities.

The core of the episode is a land sale: twenty towns with their territories for 120 talents (about 3.6 tons) of gold. In the wider context of the history of Solomon it illustrates his commercial ability: he obtained an enormous amount of gold in exchange for a poor, hilly territory. Cabul has recently been identified at Khirbet Ras ez-Zeitun, 1.5 km northeast of the Arab village of Kabul.[27] The land of Cabul is apparently the peripheral hilly region of western Galilee bordering on the west with the Acco plain.

What could have been the source used by the Dtr? It seems to me that the episode was "borrowed" from the so-called "book of the acts of Solomon" (1 Kgs 11:41). The "Acts" must have been a school text that described Solomon's success in consolidating his kingdom and making it flourish. By way of a name etymology, combined with the dissatisfaction of Hiram with the deal, and by exaggerating the sum paid by the Tyrian king, the author of this pre-Dtr composition portrayed Solomon as an able merchant, who made a good profit from the sale of a peripheral hilly area (hence the emphasis on the regional description "land of Galilee"). The Dtr must have derived the main outlines of the deal (a sale of twenty cities in the area of Cabul for an enormous amount of gold), and the name aetiology, from this source.[28]

The "Acts" might also have been the source of the literary letter discussed above. When composing his history, the Dtr attached the letter to the preparations for the building of the temple, thereby explaining how Solomon was able to secure the needed material for the operation. He then integrated the land sale after the completion of the temple and palace, thereby explaining how Solomon was able to finance his enormous building projects. He introduced the land sale by a chronological

[27] Z. Gal, "Cabul, Jiphtah-El and the Boundary between Asher and Zebulun in the Light of Archaeological Evidence," *ZDPV* 101 (1985) 114-27.

[28] *Contra* M. Noth, *Könige* (BKAT 9/1; Neukirchen-Vluyn: Neukirchener Verlag, 1968) 211-12, who assumes that the aetiology of the name "land of Cabul" is a post-Dtr addition. Noth's opinion was accepted by Würthwein, *Bücher der Könige*, p. 107; and Schäfer-Lichtenberger, *Josua und Salomo*, pp. 330-32.

note (1 Kgs 9:10), which is an artificial combination of the time it took to build the temple (7 years) and palace (13 years), and added a note (9:11) which combines the early (1 Kgs 5:24) and new (1 Kgs 9:14) agreements. The combination of the cedar and juniper timber with the gold in the introductory sentence (9:11) was made by the Dtr in order to emphasize Solomon's ability to obtain all he needed for his building projects.

Some scholars interpreted the episode as reflecting an imbalance in the commercial relations between Solomon and Hiram, and the former's inability to pay for the timber and gold.[29] The interpretation takes for granted the Dtr's dating of the land sale and the authenticity of the episode and, in my opinion, rests on tenuous foundations. The background of the sale (provided it really took place, which, of course, is uncertain) remains unknown and no historical conclusion regarding Solomon's economic situation should be drawn from the episode. Equally unconvincing is the suggestion that 1 Kgs 9 marks the beginning of Dtr's criticism of Solomon and hence his decline.[30] Part of the arguments rests on the erroneous assumption that Solomon is portrayed in this episode as the troubled partner, who is obliged to sell land in order to obtain the needed gold. Rather, the text describes Solomon's commercial ability and his achievement in the transaction with Hiram of Tyre.

---

[29] See, for example, J. Bright, *A History of Israel* (OTL; London: SCM, 1960) 201; Y. Aharoni, *The Land of the Bible: A Historical Geography* (Philadelphia: Westminster, 1967) 275; J. A. Soggin, "The Davidic-Solomonic Kingdom," in *Israelite and Judaean History* (eds. J. H. Hayes and J. M. Miller; OTL; Philadelphia: Westminster, 1977) 375-376; J. M. Miller and J. H. Hayes, *A History of Ancient Israel and Judah* (Philadelphia: Westminster, 1986) 216.

[30] M. Noth, *The Deuternomistic History* (JSOTSup 15; Sheffield: Sheffield Academic, 1981; first published in German in 1943) 60-61; K. I. Parker, "Repetition as a Structuring Device in 1 Kings 1-11," *JSOT* 42 (1988) 23-25. For the suggestion that the critique of Solomon in 1 Kgs 9:10-10:29 is implied and not explicit, see A. Frisch, "Structure and Its Significance: The Narrative of Solomon's Reign (1 Kings 1-12.24)," *JSOT* 51 (1991) 6-12; Schäfer-Lichtenberger, *Joshua und Solomo*, pp. 330-341, 363, 373. For the suggestion that the criticism opens in 9:26, see M. Brettler, "The Structure of 1 Kings 1-11," *JSOT* 49 (1991) 87-97. See also M. A. Sweeney, "The Critique of Solomon in the Josianic Edition of the Deuteronomistic History," *JBL* 114 (1995) 607-22; J. T. Wallis, "The Characterization of Solomon in First Kings 1-5," *CBQ* 57 (1995) 471-93. For criticism of these suggestions, see D. Jobling, "'Forced Labor': Solomon's Golden Age and the Question of Literary Representation," *Semeia* 54 (1991) 57-76, and Knoppers, *Two Nations Under God*, pp. 124-27.

6. The Conscription of Laborers for Building Operations

It seems to me that the records of the mobilization of thousands of workers for Solomon's building projects were derived from the "Acts," and that the original text encompassed 5:27-29 + 9:15,17b-18,23a + 5:30. The Dtr integrated part of this pericope before the temple's foundation and the other part after the temple's dedication. The original sequence of 9:15,17b-18,23a is interrupted twice in the MT: once by a note about the history of Gezer (9:16, with resumptive repetition in verse 17a), and second by post-Dtr notes (9:19-22) whose purpose is to clear Solomon of the offence of mobilizing his Israelite subjects for state labour.[31]

The account of the "Acts" seems to have opened with notes of the conscription of 30,000 laborers for service in Lebanon and the levy of 10,000 laborers to hew stones and carry them to Jerusalem and other building sites (Kgs 5:27-29). It was followed by a list of Solomon's major building projects in his capital and elsewhere (9:15,17b-18) and concludes by describing the organization of overseers who supervised the workers (9:23a + 5:30). This closing part may originally have run thus (RSV):

> These were the chief officers who were over Solomon's work: five hundred and fifty; besides Solomon's chief officers who were over the work: three thousand three hundred who had charge of the people who carried on the work.

We may further suggest that this reconstructed text originally followed the list of Solomon's twelve officers and their districts (4:7-19, 5:7). If this is the case, the account of the "Acts" opened with Solomon's list of high officials (4:1-6), his twelve district officers (4:7-19, 5:7), the mobilization of people for work, the main building projects, and the organization in charge of the workers.

7. Solomon's Trade in Horses and Chariots

The text of 1 Kgs 10:28-29 describes Solomon's central role in the trade in horses between Egypt and southern Anatolia: on the one hand, he

---

[31] See W. Dietrich, "Das harte Joch (1 Kön 12,4). Fronarbeit in der Salomo-Überlieferung," *BN* 34 (1986) 7-16. Verse 19 is a redactional expansion of Solomon's building operations enumerated in verses 15-18. It is written with the post-Dtr image of Solomon as ruler of an empire that extended from the Euphrates to the Nile. See part 11, below.

imported horses and chariots into his country and on the other, exported them to the "Hittite" and Aramean kingdoms.[32] Some scholars regarded this as an authentic description of Solomon's overland commercial activity. They debated whether Solomon had a monopoly on the Syrian trade or acted as a middleman in the commerce between southern Anatolia and Egypt; they have even tried to reconstruct the mechanism by which he gained his central position in the international trade of his time.[33] However, the entire picture of Solomon's involvement with overland trade, and his role as middleman, is nonhistorical. The passage under discussion is not applicable to the time of Solomon.

Solomon's role in the trade as depicted in 1 Kgs 10:28-29 is part of his portrait as an economically-successful ruler who was able to obtain supplies through international connections. Egypt and Que were two export centers of horses and chariots in the eighth-seventh centuries BCE.[34] The role of Solomon's traders as middlemen in the international trade in horses is "borrowed" from those of the *tamkāru* in the Neo-Assyrian empire.[35] It is evident that the author depicted Solomon's trade in terms of the overland trade in horses and chariots in his own time. Like many other descriptions written long after the period in question, it reflects the reality of the author's time and has little in common with the period to which it is attributed.

---

[32] D. G. Schley, "1 Kings 10:26-29: A Reconsideration," *JBL* 106 (1987) 595-601, suggests a poetic form for 1 Kgs 10:28 and 2 Chr 1:16b that is not convincing. The massoretic accents in these verses are the result of misunderstanding the meaning of the toponym "Que," and cannot support the assumed poetic structure; see Barthélemy, *Critique textuelle*, pp. 359-360. The literary quality of certain parts of the text (10:23-25,27) is not applicable to verses 28-29. The cited passage is written in a dry factual manner, as assumed by all commentators.

[33] M. Elat, *Economic Relations in the Lands of the Bible c. 1000-539 B.C.* (Jerusalem: Mosad Bialik, 1977) 198-203 (Hebrew); idem, "The Monarchy and the Development of Trade in Ancient Israel," in *State and Temple Economy in the Ancient Near East* (ed. E. Lipiński; OLA 6; Leuven: Department Oriëntalistiek, 1979) 2.540-541; Y. Ikeda, "Solomon's Trade in Horses and Chariots in Its International Setting," in *Studies in the Period of David and Solomon and Other Essays* (ed. T. Ishida; Tokyo: Yamakawa-Shuppansha, 1982) 215-38, with earlier literature; H. Donner, *Geschichte des Volkes Israel und seiner Nachbarn in Grundzügen* (ATD Ergänzungsreihe 4/1; Göttingen: Vandenhoeck & Ruprecht, 1984) 219.

[34] J. N. Postgate, *Taxation and Conscription in the Assyrian Empire* (Studia Pohl, Series Maior 3; Rome: Biblical Institute, 1974) 11; N. Na'aman, "Two Notes on the Monolith Inscription of Shalmaneser III from Kurkh," *Tel Aviv* 3 (1976) 100-101, n. 24.

[35] See J. N. Postgate, "The Economic Structure of the Assyrian Empire," in *Power and Propaganda: A Symposium on Ancient Empires* (ed. M. T. Larsen; Mesopotamia 7; Copenhagen: Akademisk, 1979) 206-07; K. Deller, "*Tamkāru*-Kredite in neuassyrischer Zeit," *JESHO* 30 (1987) 1-29; M. Elat, "Der *Tamkāru* im neuassyrischen Reich," *JESHO* 30 (1987) 233-54.

It seems to me that the passage dealing with Solomon's trade in horses and chariots was originally part of a larger pericope that described the building of the Israelite chariotry. It was broken by the Dtr and its parts integrated before and after the building of the temple. Possibly the original episode encompassed 1 Kgs 10:26,28-29 + 5:6,8abα, and may be reconstructed as follows (RSV with some changes indicated by an asterisk*):

> And Solomon gathered together chariots and chariot horses*; he had fourteen hundred chariots and twelve thousand chariot horses*, whom he stationed in the chariot cities and with the king in Jerusalem (10:26). And Solomon's import of horses was from Egypt and Que, and the king's traders received them from Que at a price (10:28). A chariot could be imported from Egypt for six hundred shekels of silver and a horse for a hundred and fifty; and so through the king's traders they were exported to all the kings of the Hittites and the kings of Aram* (10:29). And* Solomon had forty thousand teams of horses*[36] for his chariots, and twelve thousand chariot horses* (5:6). Barley also and straw for the horses and teams of horses* they brought to the place where it was required (5:8aba).

8. Solomon and the Queen of Sheba

A new inscription of the governor of Suḫu (a middle Euphrates kingdom), written in the mid-8th century BCE, has recently been published.[37] It relates the plunder by the troops of Suḫu of a large caravan of 200 camels coming "from Teyma and Sheba" to the district of Ḫindanu.[38] The trade goods listed include purple-dyed textiles, iron and alabaster. By analysing the Assyrian royal inscriptions of the 9th century BCE, Liverani has demonstrated that since the early 9th century BCE Ḫindanu's rulers delivered products imported from south Arabia (myrrh, antimony, *musukkannu*-wood) as tribute to Assyria.[39] It is evident that no later than the early 9th century BCE, Ḫindanu was the outlet for the main caravan road leading from Arabia to Mesopotamia.[40]

---

[36] G. I. Davies, "*ʾUrwôt* in 1 Kings 5:6 (EVV 4:26) and the Assyrian Horse Lists," *JSS* 34 (1989) 25-37.

[37] A. Cavigneaux and B. K. Ismail, "Die Statthalter von Suḫu und Mari im 8. Jh. v. Chr.," *Baghdader Mitteilungen* 21 (1990) 343-57.

[38] Cavigneaux and Ismail, "Die Statthalter," pp. 346-47, lines 26-38; 351, 357.

[39] M. Liverani, "Early Caravan Trade between South-Arabia and Mesopotamia," *Yemen: Studi atcheologici, storici e filologici sull'Arabia meridionale* 1 (1992) 111-15.

[40] Before the publication of the Suḫu inscriptions, scholars assumed that the south-

Liverani characterized the biblical story of Solomon and the Queen of Sheba (1 Kgs 10:1-10,13) as a "true and proper 'foundation legend' for the south-Arabic trade in the north." He concludes that "A starting phase of the South-Arabian trade in the second half of the 10th century would perfectly agree, both with the Old Testament traditions and with the Assyrian royal inscriptions."[41]

The early date of the south Arabian trade indicates that commercial relations between the courts of Jerusalem and Sheba may (or may not) have taken place already in the second half of the 10th century BCE. However, the south Arabian trade continued to flourish in later periods and reached its zenith in the 7th-6th centuries BCE, when Assyria and Babylonia established their respective empires over all the Fertile Crescent and secured the caravan routes leading therein.[42] The biblical description of the Queen of Sheba reflects the reality of the developed stages of the commerce rather than its incipience.

Which author is responsible for the composition of the story? Most commentators attribute it to a pre-Dtr source which the Dtr has reworked and integrated into his history.[43] It is more likely, however, that the story was composed by a post-Dtr redactor.[44] This late redactor tried to magnify the figure of Solomon and by inserting the legend of the queen's visit to Jerusalem managed to portray Solomon as a great king who enjoyed an outstanding prestige among the rulers of his time.

The episode of Solomon and the Queen of Sheba (1 Kgs 10:1-10,13) is closely related to the description of Solomon's wisdom (1 Kgs 5:9-14), which should also be attributed to the same post-Dtr redactor.[45]

The account of the Israelite-Tyrian naval expeditions sent to Ophir originally comprised 1 Kgs 9:26-28 and 10:11-12 and was cut by the

Arabian trade with Syria and Mesopotamia began no earlier than the second half of the 8th century BCE. See, for example, I. Eph'al, *The Ancient Arabs, Nomads on the Border of the Fertile Crescent 9th-5th Centuries B.C.* (Jerusalem: Magnes, 1982) 88-89; E. A. Knauf, *Midian: Untersuchungen zur Geschichte Palästinas und Nordarabiens am Ende des 2. Jahrtausends v. Chr.* (Wiesbaden: Otto Harrassowitz, 1988) 29-31.

[41] Liverani, "Early Caravan Trade," pp. 112-14.

[42] For a detailed survey, see Eph'al, *The Ancient Arabs*, pp. 75-169.

[43] See the literature cited by Schäfer-Lichtenberger, *Josua und Salomo*, p. 337, n. 627.

[44] R. B. Y. Scott, "Solomon and the Beginnings of Wisdom in Israel," *Wisdom in Israel and in the Ancient Near East: Presented to Professor Harold Henry Rowley* (VTSup 3; ed. M. Noth and D. Winton Thomas; Leiden: E. J. Brill, 1955) 266-72; Würthwein, *Bücher der Könige*, pp. 115, 120; Schäfer-Lichtenberger, *Josua und Salomo*, pp. 337-38.

[45] Scott, "Solomon and Wisdom," pp. 266-69; see the literature cited by Schäfer-Lichtenberger, *Josua und Salomo*, p. 337, n. 633.

interpolation of the Queen of Sheba episode. The text originally continued in verses 16-22, but was again cut by the insertion of verses 13-15. The original pericope in the Dtr composition (9:26-28 + 10:11-12,16-22) relates how Solomon obtained much gold and exotic trees, and lists the artifacts made from the goods brought from Ophir.

The coherence of the original Dtr pericope of the Red Sea trade seems to indicate that it was the Dtr who wrote this episode. No sign of an early source can be detected in the account.

9. The Description of Solomon's Temple

Many scholars have noted the centrality of the building of the temple and its dedication (1 Kgs 6-8) in the history of Solomon. We have already noted that the Dtr split various episodes that he derived from his sources and integrated them before and after this central episode. What might have been the source from which he drew the details of the building of the temple (and palace)?

It has been sometimes suggested that the Dtr made use of either an old building inscription or archival records from which he drew some details of the Solomonic temple.[46] However, Van Seters has convincingly argued that the kind of details recorded in 1 Kgs 6-7 never appear in ancient Near Eastern documents.[47] The assumption of Solomonic source(s) for the detailed description in 1 Kgs 6-7 is refuted by the following considerations:

a) Syro-Palestinian building inscriptions of the 10th-9th centuries BCE describe the dedicated buildings in a short and schematic manner. They are altogether different from the detailed account in the history of Solomon. 10th century building inscriptions could not have been the source from which the author drew details of Solomon's temple.

b) Royal building inscriptions include some general phrases about the building and its decorations, but not precise details of the kind given in 1 Kgs 6-7. Details of the outlook of any particular building were redundant, since the inscription was erected within its confines. It is only the comprehensive historical composition that is detached from any specific location for which such a detailed description is needed.

c) No ancient Western Asiatic archive produced a document similar to

[46] Hurowitz, *I Have Built You*, pp. 224-59, 311-21, with earlier literature.

[47] *In Search of History*, pp. 301, 309-10.

the account of the temple of Solomon. Temple inventories list various objects and are fundamentally different from the description of 1 Kgs 6-7. Some Neo-Babylonian and Hellenistic descriptions of Babylon and its sacred buildings have certain features in common with the Solomonic temple.[48] But these are literary works, not archival sources. Moreover, these compositions were produced hundreds of years after the construction of the Solomonic temple, in a scribal center that had nothing in common with Solomon's court. These late descriptions are hardly relevant for the study of scribal activity in Jerusalem in the early monarchical period.

As noted in the introduction, literacy spread in Judah no earlier than the eighth century BCE, about two centuries after the time of Solomon. Moreover, the detailed description of the temple with all its appurtenances and vessels might have been written only as part of a comprehensive historical work and no comprehensive work antedated the Dtr history. It is evident that the details of the temple (and the palace) were written by the Dtr and reflect the reality of his time.

What might have been the idea that led the Dtr to reconstruct the original Solomonic temple on the basis of the temple in his own time? I believe that the answer lies in the concept of an uninterrupted continuity between the temples of Solomon and Josiah. In the Book of Kings, the historian never ascribes changes in the temple of Jerusalem to reformer kings. Rather, the kings who carried out extensive reforms in the temple were Ahaz and Manasseh, the two major apostate kings of Judah; and it is the righteous King Josiah who purged the temple and restored everything to its original purity. In the Book of Kings this "original purity" pertains to the time of Solomon when the temple was built and all the sacred objects and vessels were fixed therein.[49] Having the concept of continuity in mind, no wonder that the historian (who apparently lived in the time of King Josiah) felt free to depict the Solomonic temple according to the temple of his own time. His description is so accurate and full of details because he was an eye witness to what he depicted.

Van Seters has noted the great similarity between the list of temple objects taken by the Babylonians as booty (2 Kgs 25:13-17; Jer 52:17-23) and the furnishings of Solomon's temple.[50] It is clear that the temple

---

[48] Hurowitz, *I Have Built You*, pp. 251-53.

[49] N. Na'aman, "The Deuteronomist and Voluntary Servitude to Foreign Powers," *JSOT* 65 (1995) 46-47.

[50] *In Search of History*, p. 310, n. 68.

described in 1 Kgs 6-7 is the same temple that, according to the second Deuteronomistic historian (Dtr^2), the author of 2 Kgs 24-25, was despoiled by the Babylonians in 587/6 BCE.

10. The Sources Available for the Dtr Historian

A systematic analysis of the biblical text and the isolation of the original sources are necessary for the historical evaluation of the material. In the past many scholars were overly optimistic concerning the antiquity of large parts of the history of Solomon. They assumed that the author had before him contemporaneous old sources that he integrated into his work and that could easily be isolated and used for the historical reconstruction. As a result, they wrote descriptions that sometimes were no more than paraphrases of the history as delineated in the Book of Kings. At the other end stand scholars of what might be called the "revisionist" school of thought. They skip over the stage of detailed analysis of the problem of sources and composition and immediately conclude that Solomon's history is fictive and cannot be used for historical reconstruction.[51] It goes without saying that avoiding the complexity of a text is hardly the proper way to handle it, certainly not with a composite and multi-layered text such as the history of Solomon.

As suggested above, already in the tenth century BCE writing for administrative purposes had been introduced into the court of Jerusalem. The Dtr, who apparently wrote before the destruction of the temple, might have seen either a dedication inscription or late copies of a few lists of the time of Solomon. Yet, even if such sources were available to him (which is far from certain), their number was very small and the information included was too little for any historical reconstruction.

Noth claimed to have recovered a pre-Dtr Solomonic history that can be isolated by a systematic analysis of 1 Kgs 1-11.[52] However, his reconstruction of this hypothetical historical work is not convincing and was

[51] Garbini, *History and Ideology*, pp. 21-32; Jamieson-Drake, *Scribes and Schools*, pp. 136-45; Knauf, "From History to Interpretation," p. 39; idem, "King Solomon's Copper Supply," pp. 170-80; Davies, *In Search of "Early Israel"*, pp. 67-70; Thompson, *Early History*, pp. 331-34, 409-12; idem, "House of David," pp. 59-74; Lemche, "Is It Still Possible," pp. 183-89; Lemche and Thompason, "Did Biran Kill David," pp. 3-23.

[52] Noth, *Könige*, pp. 48, 208-09, 263. For other reconstructions of a pre-Dtr Solomonic history see the literature cited in O'Brien, *Deuteronomistic History Hypothesis*, pp. 143-45, nn. 48, 51.

not followed by other scholars.[53] It seems that the Dtr wrote his composition on the basis of sources that he revised, edited, and integrated into his history of Israel.[54] His main sources for the history of Solomon seem to have been the "chronicle of early Israelite kings" and the "Acts of Solomon."

Clearly, the decision on the nature, scope, and contents of any pre-Dtr source depends on the evaluation of a non-existing document. Such details will always remain hypothetical and there will never be concrete data to establish them with certainty. The criteria suggested in this paper for the attribution of the origin of certain episodes, either to the chronicle or to the "Acts," are: a) their splitting in the Dtr history and the joining of several isolated notes to a coherent unit; and b) their incomplete state and the internal evidence that they were cut short by the Dtr. A few additional accounts are also attributed to one of these sources on the basis of an analysis of their form and contents and their relations to the other episodes in the reconstructed sources.

It seems to me that the three episodes of the rebellions against Solomon in 1 Kgs 11, and the episode of Solomon's marriage with the daughter of Pharaoh (and the account of Shishak's campaign to Jerusalem as well) were derived from the "chronicle of early Israelite kings." The work may have been composed in the 8th century BCE by a Judean author.[55]

The most detailed source for the Dtr must have been the "Acts of Solomon." The "Acts" was apparently a school text written in the "high school" of Jerusalem and used for educational and tutorial purposes. The central theme of the work was Solomon's mobilization of the people and the building of the capital city and peripheral towns, the lists of officials and district officers, the building of a chariot force, the sale of the land of Cabul, and possibly also Solomon's negotiations with Hiram (1 Kgs 5:15-26).

---

53 For criticism of Noth's suggestion see O'Brien, *Deuteronomistic History Hypothesis*, pp. 143-45.

54 This was already suggested by Van Seters, *In Search of History*, pp. 301-02, 307-12.

55 Na'aman, "Sources and Composition in the History of David," pp. 173-79.

11. The Age of Solomon as the Golden Age of Monarchial Israel

The "Acts of Solomon" depicted him as a successful king who built and consolidated his kingdom. The Dtr adopted the figure of the king as it was portrayed in his main source, reworked, reorganized, and expanded it wherever he felt it necessary for his composition. The description of the building of the temple and palace, and the temple's dedication (1 Kgs 6-8), is one of the Dtr's major contributions to the history of Solomon. He wrote this whole section and made it the focal unit of Solomon's history, organizing the rest of the material around this central core.[56] Sometimes he interpreted his source material in its complete original form and sometimes broke episodes to pieces and inserted them before and after the building of the temple.

The Dtr "borrowed" the figure of Solomon from the image of successful rulers in his time. Among the achievements that he attributed to him (partly derived from his sources) were the building of a magnificent capital, at the center of which were the seats of the national god and the king; the building of cities all around his kingdom, and the mobilization of the people for the building projects; the building of an enormous chariotry; the development of commercial relations with neighboring and distant kingdoms, and the building of a fleet and the expeditions to faraway lands.

The second major contribution of the Dtr to the history of Solomon is the division of his reign into two parts: the period of flourishing and the period of decline when the king was old. To this end he first attributed to Solomon religious sins to which YHWH reacted with a speech that prophesied the division of the monarchy as punishment for his apostasy. He then integrated the three episodes of the rebellions against Solomon, derived from the chronicle, these, in their new context, appear as punishment for religious sins. Following these episodes he wrote the passages of the meeting of Jeroboam and the prophet Ahijah (1 Kgs 11:29-

---

[56] B. Porten, "The Structure and Theme of the Solomon Narrative (1 Kings 3-11))," *HUCA* 38 (1967) 93-128; Parker, "Repetition as a Structural Device," pp. 19-27; idem, "The Limits to Solomon's Reign: A Response to Amos Frisch," *JSOT* 51 (1991) 15-21; Frisch, "Structure and Its Significance," pp. 3-14; idem, "A Narrative of Solomon's Reign: A Rejoinder," *JSOT* 51 (1991) 21-24; Brettler, "The Structure of 1 Kings 1-11," pp. 87-97.

[57] For 1 Kgs 10:23-25 see Scott, "Solomon and Wisdom," pp. 266-69; and the literature cited by Schäfer-Lichtenberger, *Josua und Salomo*, p. 340, n. 653.

39) in which he repeated the message of the division of the monarchy after Solomon's death.

The motif of wisdom as the key for rendering true justice and for a successful rule is the third major contribution of the Dtr. He wrote the episodes of the dream in Gibeon and the judgment of the two women, integrating them at the beginning of Solomon's reign. He inserted the motif of wisdom to his source of the correspondence between Hiram and Solomon (1 Kgs 5:21,26). Finally, he added it to the reference of his main source (1 Kgs 11:41) in order to create the impression that the episodes in which the motif of wisdom appears also stem from an old source.

Plainly, most of the material in the Dtr history of Solomon has nothing to do with his time. Rather, it reflects the reality either of the time of the author of the "Acts," or the time of the Dtr historian. The figure of the king mainly reflects the image of successful rulers of the time, and the Dtr's ideology of worthy and unworthy kingship. Solomon's deeds were written and shaped in order to portray the glory of Israel in the early monarchical days and his misdeeds serve as a warning against apostasy and its disastrous consequences.

At a later time numerous episodes were inserted into the Dtr Solomonic history. One late text is the passage 1 Kgs 4:20-5:5 (English 4:20-25), according to which Solomon's kingdom extended from the Euphrates to the Nile. Solomon was thus depicted as the ruler of an enormous kingdom, whose extent was equal to the Assyrian, Babylonian and Persian territory of *eber nāri* ("Beyond the River"). Other related post-Dtr texts claim that his building operations extended to Syria and Lebanon (1 Kgs 9:19), that all the kings who lived in this vast area were his tributaries and that rulers who lived on its periphery treated him with great respect and sent him gifts (1 Kgs 10:15,23-25).[57] Another post-Dtr text is 1 Kgs 5:9-14 and 10:1-10,13-15.[58] It developed the motif of wisdom and described Solomon as a supreme sage of mankind.[59] Still another interpolation is 1 Kgs 9:20-22 that contrasts the texts of 1 Kgs 5:27-30 and 9:15-18, 23, and was written in order to clear Solomon of the offence of laying corvee work on his Israelite subjects.[60] Finally, 1 Kgs 9:1-9 was written and interpolated in order to account for the exile and the destruction of the temple.

---

[58] See Part 8, above.
[59] See Scott, "Solomon and Wisdom," p. 271.
[60] See n. 31, above.

The extensive redaction of the Solomonic history develops motifs that appear in the Dtr history of Solomon, but went much further than the original composition. It is only in the redaction that Solomon is presented as the ruler of an empire and as a supreme sage. The image of Solomon as a kind of emperor whose capital was the center of power and learning for all kings of his time was first born in this late redaction.[61] A similar image of Solomon is presented in Ps 72:8-10, both reflecting the image of the king in the Persian period.[62] It is evident that Solomon's figure was gradually transformed in the course of time. Only an analysis of sources, composition, and redaction makes it possible to trace the development of the figure of the king. But we must keep in mind that even the earliest sources available to us were written long after the age of Solomon and thus were far removed from the reality of his time.

---

[61] For the image of Solomon in 1 Kgs 3-10, see K. L. Younger, "The Figurative Aspect and the Contextual Method in the Evolution of the Solomonic Empire (1 Kings 1-11)," in *The Bible in Three Dimentions* (eds. D. J. A. Clines, S. E. Fowl, and S. E. Porter; JSOTSup 87; Sheffield: Sheffield Academic, 1990) 157-75; Jobling, "Forced Labor," pp. 57-76. However, the two scholars treated the text as a coherent unit and did not address the problem of composition and redaction. For a criticism of Younger's historical interpretation, see J. M. Miller, "Solomon: International Potentate or Local King?" *PEQ* 123 (1991) 29-31.

[62] See M. Saebø, "Vom Grossreich zum Weltreich," *VT* 28 (1978) 83-91; T. Veijola, "Davidverheissung und Staatsvertrag," *ZAW* 95 (1983) 22-31.

LE ROI EST MORT, VIVE LE ROI! A BIBLICAL ARGUMENT FOR THE HISTORICITY OF SOLOMON*

Ernst Axel Knauf

1. Introduction

Solomon, as we used to know him: the gold-plated incarnation of Israel's Golden Age, this Solomon is thoroughly dead and the regicides are among us.[1] But what after all, did the Puritan zealots get for beheading Charles I? Charles II, and finally, some day, Charles III. As good monarchists know quite well, a king may die, but *the* king never dies. Exits Solomon the Traditional, enters Solomon the Historical.

This is to say: All the arguments forwarded by the exegetical regicides are to be acknowledged. There was no chapter on Solomon in the annals of the kings of Israel and Judah. No biblical author had a precise idea of how long he actually ruled, a fact clearly indicated by the fictitious number of 40 regnal years; coincidentally (too much of a coincidence!) also the extension of David's reign.[2] In the world of the 10th century as represented in the archaeological record there is no room for a Solomonic

---

* A preliminary version of this contribution was read at the "Colloquium on the Periods of David and Solomon" at the German Protestant Institute for the Archaeology of the Holy Land at Jerusalem in June 1995; cf. now V. Fritz and P. R. Davies, eds., *The Origins of the Ancient Israelite States* (Sheffield: Sheffield Academic, 1996). My sincere thanks are due to all participants for their constructive criticism, though Solomonic maximalists and Solomonic nihilists alike failed to convince me of the higher merits of their approaches. In addition, I have to thank J. Bösenecker and H.-P. Mathys for their valuable remarks and critical questions.

[1] Due credit should be given to B. J. Diebner, who already voted for the abolition of Solomon (e.g., "The problems begin as soon as we subject the text to a closer examination...," *DBAT* 20 [1984] 192-208, especially 197-99), when nearly everybody else did not doubt the "central state" of the 10th century; e.g., N. P. Lemche, *Ancient Israel: A New History of Israelite Society* (Biblical Seminar 5; Shefield: JSOT, 1988) 125, 139-43.

[2] J. H. Hayes and J. M. Miller, *Israelite and Judaean History* (London: SCM, 1977) 679; G. W. Ahlström, *The History of Ancient Palestine from the Palaeolithic Period to Alexander's Conquest* (ed. D. V. Edelman; JSOTSup 146; Sheffield: Sheffield Academic, 1993) 501, n. 2; E. A. Knauf, "King Solomon's Copper Supply," *Phoenicia and the Bible* (ed. E. Lipinski; Studia Phoenicia 11; Leuven: Peeters, 1991) 172-74; and *idem*, *Die Umwelt des Alten Testaments* (NSK-AT 29; Stuttgart: Katholisches Bibelwerk, 1994) 22.

empire, not even a state of Judah[3] of Israel.[4] But these arguments only indicate that the biblical Solomon did not exist in history, they do not imply that no historical Solomon existed at all. On the contrary, more careful reading of 1 Kgs 1-11 provides a number of arguments for the existence of a Jerusalemite king called Solomon, his politics, and his territory.

A careful reading of the biblical text reveals a number of discrepancies which hint at a perception of Solomon quite different from the image intended by the text in its final form. There are basically three texts which constitute "that other Solomon," notably 1 Kgs 8:12b-13 within the context of 1 Kgs 8, 1 Kgs 1-2 as opposed to 1 Kgs 3:4-15, and 1 Kgs 9:16-18 as opposed to 1 Kgs 9:15.

2. SOLOMON AND THE TEMPLE OF JERUSALEM

Let us first regard 1 Kgs 8:12b-13: "Yahweh intended to dwell in the obscurity of a cloud // I, however, verily built you [YHWH] a princely palace / a place for your dwelling, for ever and ever." This proud royal proclamation has nothing to do with the deuteronomistic humility of Solomon's three prayers in 1 Kgs 8:15-21, 23-53, 56-61. Contrariwise, 12b-13 is not a prayer; it is a royal building inscription (or dedication) in poetic verse.[5] In the Hebrew Bible the text is incomplete: 12b consists of an isolated hemistich only. For a more complete text we have to turn to the Septuagint (3 Kingdoms 8:53a) where the proclamation commences: "The sun he recognised in the sky, the Lord, he spoke to dwell in the cloud." It is to be conceeded that Ἥλιον ἐγνώρισεν ἐν οὐρανῷ does not make much sense. It leads, however, to (ה)שמש הבין בשמים in Hebrew,[6]

[3] D. W. Jamieson-Drake, *Scribes and Schools in Monarchic Judah: A Socio-Archaeological Approach* (SWBA 9; Sheffield: Almond, 1991) 138-145.

[4] H. M. Niemann, *Herrschaft, Königtum und Staat: Skizzen zur soziokulturellen Entwicklung im monarchischen Israel* (FAT 6; Tübingen: Mohr, 1993) especially 281-82.

[5] M. Görg, "Die Gattung des sogenannten Tempelweihespruchs (1 Kg 8,12f.)" *UF* 6 (1974) 55-63 = *idem*, *Studien zur biblisch-ägyptischen Religionsgeschichte* (SBAB 14; Stuttgart: Katholisches Bibelwerk, 1992) 32-46, cites a number of pertinent Egyptian examples for the genre.

[6] Already J. Wellhausen, *Die Composition des Hexateuchs und der historischen Bücher des Alten Testaments* (4th ed.; Berlin: Walter de Gruyter, 1963) 269. It is to be conceded that the LXX never renders בין by γνωρίζειν, but by συνίειν; cf. E. Hatch and H. A. Redpath, *A Concordance to the Septuagint* (Oxford: Oxford University, 1897) 273, 1316f; συνίεν, however, may also represent ידע (Exod 36:1), the usual equivalent of

which is easily corrected[7] to שמש הכין בשמים, "The sun he placed in the sky."[8] The transmission of the LXX concerning 1 Kgs 8:12b is too complicated and too problematic to allow the reconstruction of an indisputable original text;[9] but it allows a reasonable conjecture where the MT badly needs one. After reconstruction, v. 12 presents a clear antithetic parallelism: "The sun he placed in the sky / whereas YHWH intended to dwell in the thick of a cloud."

The question remains of who placed the sun in the sky. For the LXX (and subsequent biblical translations), the creator was undoubtedly YHWH himself.[10] Equally undoubtedly, YHWH did not become creator

---

γνωρίζειν. The parallelism of בין \\ ידע being well established (Isa 6:9; 44:18; Hos 14:10; Ps 82:5), Wellhausen's proposal remains the best solution of the textual problem hitherto proffered; unless one accepts O. Keel's most recent interpretation of the verse (see *infra*), which elegantly bypasses the usual philological and/or historical problems of the text.

[7] F. Delitzsch, *Die Lese- und Schreibfehler im Alten Testament nebst den dem Schrifttexte einverleibten Randnoten klassifiziert: Ein Hilfsbuch für Lexikon und Grammatik, Exegese und Lektüre* (Berlin: Walter de Gruyter, 1920) 110 Ā 107, especially Jer 40:13 and Prov 21:29.

[8] Note Ps 74:16: אתה הכינות מאור ושמש.

[9] As my doctoral student J. Bösenecker pointed out to me.

[10] According to O. Keel and C. Uehlinger, "Jahwe und die Sonnengottheit von Jerusalem," *Ein Gott allein? JHWH-Verehrung und biblischer Monotheismus im Kontext der israelitischen und altorientalischen Religionsgeschichte* (ed. W. Dietrich and M. A. Klopfenstein; OBO 139; Fribourg: Universitätsverlag; Göttingen: Vandenhoeck & Ruprecht, 1994) 287, YHWH did not act as creator-god when he exiled the Sun-God(dess) from the temple of Jerusalem, previously dedicated to him/her, and occupied his/her place in the adyton. That the temple had been a temple of the Sun is indeed possible (regarding its orientation and the arguments from the LB period adduced by the authors), even if one prefers an 8th/7th centuries date for the main period of "solarization" in the history of YHWH; thus H. Niehr, "Jhwh in der Rolle des Baalšamem," *Ein Gott allein? JHWH-Verehrung und biblischer Monotheismus im Kontext der israelitischen und altorientalischen Religionsgeschichte* (ed. W. Dietrich and M. A. Klopfenstein; OBO 139; Fribourg: Universitätsverlag; Göttingen: Vandenhoeck & Rupprecht, 1994) 316f. It is, however, highly unlikely that the Judaean YHWH could dispose of the Jerusalemite Sun in such a manner during the reign of Solomon (cf. 1 Kgs 1 and its discussion *infra*), and it is impossible that El was unknown to the theology of Jerusalem previous to Solomon (*pace* Keel and Uelinger, "Jahwe und die Sonnengottheit," p. 296 with n. 55; cf. *infra*). If there was indeed competition between YHWH and the Sun at 10th century Jerusalem, an integrative authority like El Elyon would have had to have been invented. Fortunately, he did already exist. These objections do not apply to the most recent proposition of O. Keel concerning 1 Kgs 8:12-13, notably "Eine Kurzbiographie der Frühzeit des Gottes Israels—im Ausgang von Ausgrabungsbefunden im syro-palästinischen Raum," *Bulletin: Europäische Gesellschaft für Katholische Theologie* 5 (1994) 168, who now reconstructs "The Sun-God(dess) has proclaimed from Heaven: 'YHWH did say he would dwell in obscurity'. (Thus) I (Solomon or the Sun? E.A.K.) have built you (YHWH) a princely house, a dwelling for ever and ever." Historically, it is perfectly understandable that the newcomer YHWH had to be received at Jerusalem by the established God-in-Residence. Two objections may still be raised: was the Sun indeed YHWH's predecessor at Jerusalem, or

of heaven and earth before the end of the 7th century,[11] or even before the middle of the 6th century.[12] Previously, creation was the domain of El (notably under his appearance as Elqōnē'arṣ), epigraphically attested for Jerusalem by Ostracon Jer(8):30.[13] One has to conclude that even in the LXX Solomon's dedicatory poem remains a fragment; the text must originally have been preceeded by one or several lines in praise of the supreme god, the god of creation. This reconstruction is corroborated by metric observations: the two poetic verses are characterized by 4 + 4 accents, each hemistich by 2 + 2:[14]

2 + 2 ‖ 2 + 2	שמש הכין ׀ בשמים אל ‖ יהוה אמר ׀ לשכן בערפל
2 + 2 ‖ 2 + 2	בניתי ׀ בית זבל לך ‖ מכון לשכתך ׀ עלמים

Verse 13 forms another antithesis to 12b: the wild and unruly deity amidst the thickness of the cloud, YHWH, the weather-god (and warrior), who had managed to withdraw from the bright daylight of creation and, up to a certain degree, to resist the intentions of El for an orderly world, is now domesticated, confined within a stately palace provided by Solomon. El, the supreme deity of the Canaanite pantheon and, thus, also of the pantheon of Jerusalem,[15] has finally integrated even YHWH, the

was it rather Shalim, an attendant of the Sun, who may have adopted some traits of his master/mistress under the impact of Egyptian political and cultural influence during the LB period? And, is YHWH's intention to dwell in the obscurity of a cloud really met by his confinement within a princely palace?

[11] A conservative estimate, assuming that Jer 5:22; 27:5; 31:35 represent the view of the prophet and not that of his exilic and post-exilic editors; H. Weippert, *Schöpfer des Himmels und der Erde: Ein Beitrag zur Theologie des Jermiabuches* (SBS 102; Stuttgart: Katholisches Bibelwerk, 1981) against the mainstream of present Jeremianic research as exhibited by, e.g., C. Levin, *Die Verheißung des neuen Bundes in ihrem theologiegeschichtlichem Zusammenhang ausgelegt* (FRLANT 137; Göttingen: Vandenhoeck & Ruprecht, 1985) 153, n. 22; 199.

[12] Isa 44:24-28; 45:7, and R. Albertz, *Relgionsgeschichte Israels in alttestamentlicher Zeit* (ATD 8.2; Göttingen: Vandenhoeck & Ruprecht, 1992) 1.434.

[13] J. Renz and W. Röllig, *Handbuch der alhebräischen Epigraphik I: Die althebräischen Inschriften, 1: Text und Kommentar* (Darmstadt: Wissenschaftliche Buchgesellschaft, 1995) 197-198. Renz tries to avoid reading the divine name *coûte que coûte*, but the alternatives are either impossible (like **zaqin 'arṣ*, which is not a title which could be spelled in one word) or improbable (like *wa=yiqn* "he purchased"). The ostacon may contain the receipt for an offering by several persons, enumerated in lines 1-2, to Elqōnē'arṣ, line 3 (*[l-']⌈l⌉qn'rṣ*). Cf. also Keel and Uehlinger, "Jahwe und die Sonnengottheit," pp. 296-98.

[14] Cf. for the 2 + 2 | 2 + 2 structure the Song of Deborah, Judg 5:2, 3a,4b, 5,6a*,b, 11a,12a,13,14a*,b,15a*,17a,18,19a,b,20,21*,22,23a,b,25,27a,28b,29,30a,b. I hope to present a philological analysis of this 10th century text in the not too distant future; preliminarily Knauf, *Umwelt*, pp. 188, 205, 229.

[15] El may not have been venerated in Jerusalem prior to Solomon (Keel and Uelinger,

tribal deity of Israel, and then of Davidic Judah.[16] The city of Jerusalem has won predominance over the tribe of Judah. The Hebrew verb does by no means imply that Solomon erected a temple *de novo*; some constructional changes to allow the reception of YHWH in the pre-existant main temple of Jerusalem would suffice for the use of the verb.[17] This, then, is what Solomon (or his Privy Counsellor in Theology) really did: integrate the Judean tribal deity YHWH as a minor deity in the pantheon of Jerusalem, subservient to the supreme god El. In this case, Solomon established the theological system of pre-exilic Jeruslaem as attested by Deut 32:8-9 (txt.em.): "When Elyon alloted the peoples in fief (נחל H)[18] | when he distributed the earthlings (בני אדם) || he fixed the territories of the hosts (עמים)[19] | according to the number of the sons of El ||. Thus it

"Jahwe und die Sonnengottheit," p. 296 with n. 55), but by no means could he have been unknown, being the father of Šalim, the tutelary deity of *Yurūšalimum; S. B. Parker, "Shahar," *DDD* 1425. El as head of the pantheon was not peculiar to Ugarit, where he was rather marginalized in the dominant myths. He survived, socially and geographically, at the fringes of Canaanite society, cf. Sinai 378; E. A. Knauf, *Midian: Untersuchungen zur Geschichte Palästinas und Nordarabiens am Ende des 2. Jahrtausends v. Chr.* (ADPV; Wiesbaden: Harrassowitz, 1988) 117; אל אלהי ישראל Gen 33:20 (*ibid.*, p. 140 and n. 595); and the enthroned deity on southern Palestinian seals of the 10th century; O. Keel and C. Uehlinger, *Göttinnen, Götter und Gottessymbole: Neue Erkenntnisse zur Religionsgeschichte Kanaana und Israels aufgrund bislang unerschossener ikonographischer Quellen* (QD 134; Freiburg: Herder, 1992) 155, nos. 158a-60. Still H.-P. Müller, "Religionsgeschichtliche Beobachtungen zu den Texten von Ebla," *ZDPV* 96 (1980) 1-19, especially 5-6 and now F. Stolz, *Einführung in den biblischen Monotheismus* (Darmstadt: Wissenschaftliche Buchgesellschaft, 1996) 106f, 114f. Some sort of competition between El and YHWH still is attested for the 7th century, cf. Hos 12:1 and preliminarily A. de Pury, "Las dos leyendas sobre el origen de Israel (Jacob y Moisés) y la elaboración del Pentateuco," *EstBib* 52 (1994) 95-131, 101 n. 15; E. Bons, *Das Buch Hosea* (NSK-AT 23.1; Stuttgart: Katholisches Bibelwerk, 1996) 147.

[16] For David as the founder of the tribe of Judah, cf. preliminarily Ahlström, *History*, pp. 460-62, who denies the designation of "tribe" to David's political creation without sufficient reason, and A. Lemaire, "Cycle primitif d'Abraham et contexte géographico-historique," *History and Traditions of Early Israel: Studies Presented to Eduard Nielsen May 8th 1993* (eds. A. Lemaire and B. Otzen; VTSup 50; Leiden: E. J. Brill, 1993) 65-66.

[17] Josh 6:26; 1 Kgs 9:17; Amos 9:14; Ps 69:36; 102:17; 147:2; Prov 14:1. It is well established by now that Solomon did not build the temple of Jerusalem; he rather redecorated it, suffice it to recall 2 Sam 12:20 (and 2 Sam 5:9?); K. Rupprecht, *Der Tempel von Jerusalem: Gründung Salomos oder jebusitisches Erbe?* (BZAW 144; Berlin: Walter de Gruyter, 1977); H. Donner, *Geschichte des Volkes Israel und seiner Nachbarn in Grundzügen I* (ATD 4.1; Göttingen: Vandenhoeck & Ruprecht, 1984) 222, n. 28; Keel and Uehlinger, "Jahwe und die Sonnengottheit," p. 286.

[18] Ugaritic *nḥlt* "fief," Sabaic *nḥl* "grant lease," causative stem "hire out."

[19] For עם "levy, militia;" T. Willi, "Kirche als Gottesvolk? Überlegungen zu einem Verständnis von Kirche im Kontext alttestamentlich-frühjüdischer Konzeptionen von Gottesvolk, Gebot und Gottesrecht," *ThZ* 49 (1993) 289-310, 291f.

came to be that YHWH's share is his levy | Jacob the estate of his fief."[20]

One may now understand how Solomon became the builder of the temple in the deuteronomistic narrative midrash of 1 Kgs 8:12-13* in 1 Kgs 8:1-11.[21] Because the notion that the Israelite/Judaean God YHWH once shared rooms with a Canaanite deity in the latter's ancestral mansion was simply insupportable to the deuteronomistic mind, he who established YHWH's cult at Jerusalem must necessarily have been the founder of the temple which housed YHWH alone.

At the end of 3 Kingdoms 8:53a the LXX adds a reference which is also missing in the MT: "Behold, is that not written in the Book of Song?" One can easily correct this ספר השיר, otherwise unattested, to the well-known ספר הישר, "the Book of the Valiant,"[22] a collection of martial poetry from the court of warlords as the kings of Israel and Judah before Solomon probably were.[23] Whoever included 1 Kgs 8:12-13* in this collection either knew a much more violent Solomon than the final redaction of the Biblical text would allow (but there rests 1 Kings 1!), or he wanted to tribalize and to militarize a king who might have been as urbane as the 10th century could suffer: a quest for legitimacy *extra Hierosolymae muros*, then? Both the origin of 1 Kgs 8:12-13* in the 10th century and the transmission of the text between the 10th and the 6/5th centuries are within the limits of reasonable speculation.

---

[20] M. Weippert, "Synkretismus und Monotheismus: Religionsinterne Konfliktbewältigung im Alten Israel," *Kultur und Konflikt* (ed. J. Assmann and D. Harth; Edition Suhrkamp NF 612; Frankfurt am Main: Surkamp, 1990) 146f. Regardless of the date of the final composition of Deut 32:1-43, the fragment v. 8f must have been conceived prior to Josiah, under whom YHWH, in all probability, became "the supreme god;" Ps 82 and L. K. Handy, "A Realignment in Heaven: An Investigation into the Ideology of the Josianic Reform" (Ph.D. dissertation, University of Chicago, 1987); on the other hand, "Jacob" for "Israel" in a Jerusalemite tradition indicates a date after Hezekiah; E. A. Knauf, "Stämme Israels," *EKL* 4.479-83.

[21] The relative independence of the two textual strata is further highlighted by the positioning of 1 Kgs 8:12-13 in the LXX.

[22] Cf. again Wellhausen, *Composition*, p. 269; Keel and Uehlinger, "Jahwe und die Sonnengottheit," p. 287.

[23] Also the source for Josh 10:12-13 (*ibid.*, pp. 283-85); 2 Sam 1:19-27 (S. Schroer and T. Staubli, Saul, David und Jonathan — eine Dreiecksgeschichte? Ein Beitrag zum Thema "Homosexualität im Ersten Testament," *Bibel und Kirche* 51 [1996] 15-22); for the genre Knauf, *Umwelt*, pp. 229f.

3. The Accession of Solomon

We saw that 1 Kgs 8:12f, a text which in all likelihood originated during the 10th century, presents Solomon as a king of Jerusalem who integrated the tribe of Judah into the political and ideological framework of the State of Jerusalem. This political constellation is matched by the distribution of power in the story of Solomon's accession to the throne, 1 Kgs 1-2. Here Solomon is the puppet of the Jerusalemite élite at David's court[24] who becomes king by a veritable *coup d'état* resulting in the physical elimination of the Judaean élite. One is thus forced to concede that even the "story of David's succession" contains some glimpses of real history.

This does not imply that one must necessarily defend the character of the "succession story" as a historical record by some eyewitness. This text is neither historiographical[25] in character, nor does it date from the 10th century; it rather is a sophisticated novel from the 7th century,[26] more precisely and most probably from the reign of Manasseh, when Judah's transition from chiefdom to state, which commenced under Uzziah and Hezekiah, was finally completed and the monarchy indeed "firmly established" and, at the same time, Judah's narrow escape in 701 BCE was still preserved in collective memory, which renders the bitter irony of 1 Kgs 2:46 even more biting. As "historical novel," the David story draws nevertheless on historical memory, not so much in the guise of the notoriously unverifiable "oral tradition" of past exegesis, but rather on the traditions of Jerusalem's great families.[27] Family tradition

---

[24] This goes without saying for Zadok and Benajah; for Nathan, G. H. Jones, *The Nathan Narratives* (JSOTSup 80; Sheffield: Sheffield Academic, 1990); S. Schroer, *Die Samuelbücher* (NSK-AT 7; Stuttgart: Katholisches Bibelwerk, 1992) 157f. Cf. also Ahlström, *History*, p. 503. I. Willi-Plein, "Frauen um David: Beobachtungen zur Davidshausgeschichte," *Meilenstein: Festgabe für Herbert Donner* (eds. M. Weippert and S. Timm; ÄAT 30; Wiesbaden: Harrassowitz in Kommission, 1995) 355f.

[25] Ancient Near Eastern historiography (as a literary genre) is best represented within the Hebrew Bible by the P-complex in the Pentateuch and by Chronicles; that this historiography does not bear much resemblance to factual history as we understand and happen to know it is quite evident.

[26] O. Kaiser, *Grundriss der Einleitung in die kanonischen und deuterokanonischen Schriften des Alten Testaments 1: Die erzählenden Werke* (Güttersloh: Mohn, 1992) 119; W. Dietrich and T. Naumann, *Die Samuelbücher* (ErFor 287; Darmstadt: Wissenschaftliche Buchgesellschaft, 1995) 213-15.

[27] The author(s) may have left their "signature" in 1 Kgs 1:8 by mentioning two supporters of Solomon who have otherwise no function in the narrative: Reï (otherwise unattested) and Shimëi; this Shimëi can hardly be equated with the official in 1 Kgs 4:18, the list in question being Israelite, dating from the reign of Omri (Knauf, "Solomon's Copper

can easily preserve historical facts in a partially correct way for some 500 years.

The David story antedates the (early deuteronomistic)[28] "chronicle of Solomon" (as cited in 1 Kgs 11:41) and has no idea yet that Solomon built the temple (cf. again 2 Sam 12:20). It attests, however, to the Jerusalemite background of Solomon in 1 Kings 1-2 by yet another feature. There is only one reason conceivable why the outrageous story of how David met Solomon's mother was not entirely suppressed: to silence an even more scandalous version of the relationship between the first two kings which may have annihilated the legitimacy of the Dynasty of Jerusalem in the eyes of Judeans.[29] This is to say that in all

---

Supply," p. 178), but may well be identical with the Jerusalemite "Benjaminite" in 1 Chr 8:21 (cf. 8:28; one should not too quickly harmonize this Shimëi with Shema in v. 13, an equation which may agree well with the intentions of the list's compiler, but not at all with his sources).

[28] Probably from the time of Josiah, who wanted (or was wanted by his counsellors) to be the king Solomon was imagined to have been; Knauf, "Solomon's Copper Supply," pp. 174-76; for the Josianic roots of deuteronism: N. Lohfink, "Gab es eine deuteronomistische Bewegung?" *Jeremia und die deuteronomistiche Bewegung* (ed. W. Groß; BBB 98; Weinheim: Beltz Athenäum, 1995) 352-58 = *idem*, *Studien zum Deuteronomium und zur deuteronomistischen Literatur III* (SBAB 20; Stuttgart: Katholisches Bibelwerk, 1995) 65-142, 111-17.

[29] With T. Veijola, "Salomo — der Erstgeborene Bathsebas," *Studies in the Historical Books of the Old Testament* (ed. J. A. Emerton; VTSup 40; Leiden: E. J. Brill, 1979) 230-50 = *idem*, *David: Gesammelte Studien zu den Davidüberlieferungen des Alten Testaments* (Schriften der Finnischen Exegetischen Gesellschaft 52; Helsinki: Finnische Exegetische Gesellschaft; Göttingen: Vandenhoeck & Ruprecht, 1990) 84-105; and also Schroer, *Samuelbücher*, p. 169. The nameless first-born of Bathsheba has to be discarded as an apologetic (not redactional!) addition for the reason made obvious in the text *supra*, especially if the name of Solomon could be understood as an *Ersatzname* (in this case refering to Bathsheba's husband Urijah, but see *infra*). It is, however, inconceivable that the story could ever have circulated without the "addition" 12:15b-24a, which is characterized by the same "dramatic irony" which highlights the work of the "succession story's" author. In this case, it was the author himself who created the chronological and biological discrepancies between the tradition (as known to him) and his own embellishment, for those who had eyes to read and a brain to think. The Judean view which denied David legitimacy to the kings of Jerusalem may have been expressed, at the end of the 8th century, by Mic 5:1-4 (v. 4a is damaged beyond repair; 5 is a redactional addition as evidenced by the repetition of 4b, and certainly not pre-Josianic). It is quite *à la mode* to deny that the voice of Micah can be heard after the end of chapter 3; O. Kaiser, *Grundriss der Einleitung in die kanonischen und deuterokanonischen Schriften des Alten Testaments 2: Die prophetischen Werke* (Gütersloh: Mohn, 1994) 132: "Auch wenn es bis heute nicht an Stimmen fehlt, die ... die messianische Weissagung in 5,1-5* für den Propheten des 8. Jh.s reklamieren, ist dieser Ansicht im Zusammenhang mit der exilisch-nachexilischen Einordnung der auf die Restitution der Königsherrschaft in Juda und Israel gerichteten Erwartungen der Boden entzogen." Mic 5:1 does not, however, talk about the restitution of Jerusalemite kingship, but rather opposes the Bethlehemite-Judaean hero David to the

likelihood Solomon's mother was indeed the Jerusalemite Bathsheba, but as is the case quite often in history (one may recall the cases of James I and Louis XIV), we do not really know who his father was. Altogether, this is a constellation not easily invented under the conditions of fully dynastic ancient oriental statehood as prevailing in the 7th century, and less likely in exilic and post-exilic times when the glorification of David reached hitherto unrivalled degrees.

Solomon's name was given by the mother.[30] As Solomon was Bathsheba's first born, his name cannot be explained as *Ersatzname*.[31] It rather is an hypocoristic name; if it is the theoporic element that is suppressed, one can only think of Shelumiël "El (or: the Deity) is (my) peace" (attested in Num 1:6, e.g.); Bathsheba was neither Israelite nor Judean. It is not, however, unlikely that the predicative element was suppressed (as is the case with the name of Jehu). Then, the name of Solomon basically consists of the name of the tutelary deity of Bathsheba's city of origin, Šalim/Shalem.[32] One should expect **Šəlēmō*, then, and it remains the mute question of whether the traditional vocalisation has been influenced by the king's literary promotion to a "Prince of Peace" or vice-versa. In any case, the non-Judaean ideological affiliation of Solomon is also well expressed by his name.

At Jerusalem and *vis-à-vis* the tribe of Judah, Solomon presented himself (or was presented by his entourage) as David's legitimate successor. In an attempt to renew David's claim to the kingdom of Israel, Solomon sought another patronage, indicating that his links to David were ideo-

---

corruption of Jerusalem, ch. 3. The social, political and ideological cleavage between the tribe of Judah and the city of Jerusalem, which persisted at least through the reign of Manasseh, explains the double foundation of Biblical Israelite kingship, by David on the one hand and by Solomon on the other.

[30] 2 Sam 12:24 Qerê; Schroer, *Samuelbücher*, p. 169.

[31] As proposed by J. J. Stamm, "Der Name des Königs Salomo," *ThZ* 16 (1960) 285-97 = *idem*, *Beiträge zur hebräischen und altorientalischen Namenkunde* (OBO 30; Fribourg: Universitätsverlag; Göttingen: Vandenhoeck & Ruprecht, 1980) 45-57. If one agrees with Veijola, "Salomo," p. 90, the child replaces Urijah. It remains, however, improbable that *-ō* represents the suffix of the 3rd masc. sing. in a personal name rather than the well-attested hypocoristic ending; M. Noth, *Die israelitischen Personennamen im Rahmen der gemeinsemitischen Namengebung* (BWANT 3.10; Stuttgart: Kohlhammer, 1928; Hildesheim: Olms, 1980) 38.

[32] Thus F. Stolz, *Strukturen und Figuren im Kult von Jerusalem* (BZAW 118; Berlin: Walter de Gruyter, 1970) 204; also Ahlström, *History*, pp. 500, 504, though it is highly unlikely that Solomon was called Jedidjah prior to his accession to the throne as 2 Sam 12:24b-25 clearly is (Veijola, "Salomo," pp. 90f), in all probability, responding to the "pagan" connotation that the name שלמה had for a pre-exilic audience.

logical (and utilitarian) rather than natural.[33] The original version of Solomon's sacrifice, incubation and divine endowment with regnal skills at Gibeon in 1 Kgs 3:4-15; 4:1 is hard to reconcile with the deuteronomistic perception of the One place chosen by YHWH to have his name dwell there,[34] ends with "Thus King Solomon became King over all Israel."[35] This, then, is the story's *raison d'être*; but why Gibeon? In all probability, Gibeon was the capital of Saul insofar as he had any.[36] In claiming the throne of Israel, Solomon bypassed David and took recourse to Saul:[37] another facet that renders Solomon's relationship to David more ambiguous than presented by tradition.

He could still be regarded, though, as Rehoboam's predecessor. Starting with Jeroboam/Rehoboam, the sequence of Israelite and Judean kings and their regnal years seems to derive from annalistic sources.[38] Fitting these data into Ancient Near Eastern general chronology does not pose greater difficulties than any comparative sequence of kings. The name of Rehoboam's mother was obviously preserved;[39] it would be rather difficult to suppose that his dynastic father's name was not.

---

[33] Also indicating that David's rule over Israel was less firmly established, and Sheba's revolt more than a non-consequential episode, than 2 Sam 20 is allowed to express.

[34] The deuteronomistic addition to v. 15 only transfers the final sacrifices to the ark at Jerusalem, but fails to remove the initial offerings, v. 4; the task half done was finalized by Chronicles (2 Chr 1:3,13 → 1 Chr 16:39; 21:29).

[35] E. Würthwein, *Die Bücher der Könige: 1 Könige 1-16* (ATD 11.1; Göttingen: Vandenhoek & Ruprecht, 1977) 28-35.

[36] J. Blenkinsopp, *Gibeon and Israel* (Cambridge: Cambridge University, 1972) 86; D. V. Edelman, "Saul," *ABD* 5.989-99, especially 993-94, 998; for a more restrained view of Saul's kingship, which does not, however, cast the role of Gibeon in doubt, see now *idem*, "Saul ben Kish in History and Tradition," *The Origins of the Ancient Israelite States* (ed. V. Fritz and P. R. Davies; Sheffield: Sheffield Academic, 1996) 142-59.

[37] H. M. Niemann, "The Socio-Political Shadow Cast by the Biblical Solomon," *The Origins of the Ancient Israelite States* (ed. V. Fritz and P. R. Davies; Sheffield: Sheffield Academic, 1996).

[38] The assertion to the negative by F. H. Cryer, "To the One of Fictive Music: OT Chronology and History," *SJOT* 2 (1987) 1-27, goes too far. The Book of Kings was composed by descendants of those families who had steered the policy of Judah under Josiah and his successors and who were intimately linked to the royal court, thus having (had) access to the royal annals; Albertz, *Religionsgeschichte*, 2.398f; Lohfink, "Gab es eine deuteronomistische Bewegung?" pp. 358-67 = *Studien III*, pp. 117-27. Even if the archives of Jerusalem did not survive the Babylonian-induced conflageration, and even if none of the exiles had manuscripts in his donkey-pack (but some obviously had: Knauf, *Umwelt*, pp. 159f), there were still the archives of Bethel and its school, where no destruction ocurred during the 7th and 6th centuries.

[39] U. Hübner, *Die Ammoniter: Untersuchungen zur Geschichte, Kultur und Religion eines transjordanischen Volkes im 1. Jahrtausend v. Chr.* (ADPV 16; Wiesbaden: Harrassowitz, 1992) 181.

4. SOLOMON'S FORTRESSES

The best case for Solomon the Historical that can be made on the basis of the biblical tradition is provided by 1 Kgs 8:12f; to this *pièce de résistance*, 1 Kgs 1-2*; 2 Sam 11:1-12:25*; 1 Kgs 3:4-15; 4:1* can be attached and thus essentially be claimed for history. The weakest case within the present context is furnished by the building activities of Solomon, 1 Kgs 9:16-18.

The basic relation between 1 Kgs 8:12f (source) and the rest of chapter 8 (midrash) applies also to the two occurences of Gezer in 1 Kgs 9:15 and 17. Between the *incipit* v. 15 "This is the story of the corvée which imposed the king Solomon in order to build ..." and the story of the corvée, vv. 20ff, a miscellany of building activities has been inserted: the temple, the palace, the Millo, the wall of Jerusalem, Hazor, Megiddo, Gezer[40] and all the ערי המסכנות and the chariotry-fortresses and the calvary-fortresses and what else he pleased to build (vv. 15,19). Inserted

[40] The LXX transfers 1 Kgs 9:15,17-19 to 3 Kingdoms 10:22a. The names of the three cities are rendered Ασσουρ, Μαγδαλ (var. Μαδιαν; Rahlfs proposes *Μαγδαν), Γαζερ instead of Ασωρ, Μεγιδ(δ)ω(ν), Γαζερ. Did even the translator know that Solomon did not build at Hazor and Megiddo? The alleged "Solomonic City Gates" claimed to have been unearthed at the three sites have successfully been removed from the scholarly discussion (rather against the author's intentions) by Z. Herzog, *Das Stadttor in Israel und in den Nachbarländern* (Mainz: Philipp von Zabern, 1986) 127 fig. 8: if there was a "common design," the gates of Megiddo, Hazor and Ashdod were erected by the same ruler, whereas the gate of Gezer is much smaller and abutts into the city wall in quite a different way. The correlation of 1 Kgs 9:15 and the three gates thus destroyed, archaeology lost its chronological benchmark for the 10th century; G. J. Wightman, "The Myth of Solomon," *BASOR* 277-278 (1990) 5-22; D. Ussishkin, "Notes on Megiddo, Gezer, Ashdod, and Tel Batash in the Tenth to Ninth Centuries B.C.," *BASOR* 277-278 (1990) 71-91, especially 82 with n. 5; Niemann, *Herrschaft, Königtum und Staat*, p. 97, n. 435. The archaeological picture which now emerges from the debris of its predecessor is even less favorable to the assumption of a Davidic-Solomonic "empire;" I. Finkelstein, "The Archaeology of the United Monarchy: An Alternative View," *Levant* 28 (1996) 177-187. There is not a single piece of excavated monumental architecture which can be attributed to Solomon, nor can the so-called "Negev fortresses" which are neither fortresses (and clearly not monumental!) nor Solomonic; Knauf, *Midian*, p. 94; D. V. Edelmann, "Solomon's Adversaries Hadad, Rezon and Jeroboam: A Trio of "Bad Guy" Characters Illustrating the Theology of Immediate Retribution," *The Pitcher Is Broken: Memorial Essays for Gösta W. Ahlström* (ed. S. W. Holloway and L. K. Handy; JSOTSup 190; Sheffield: Sheffield Academic, 1995) 176f. Solomon's Judah did not include the population south of the Judean hills (see *infra*), nor was there "Arabian trade" in the 10th century to be controlled (*pace* I. Finkelstein, "Arabian Trade and Socio-Political Conditions in the Negev in the Twelfth-Eleventh Centuries BCE," *JNES* 47 (1988) 241-52, not to speak of a queen in Sheba (Knauf, *Midian*, pp. 26-31).

into this insertion, induced by the catchword "Gezer," we find vv. 16-18: "Pharaoh, the king of Egypt, had ascended and taken Gezer and burnt it and the Canaanite who inhabited the city he had slain and he had given it to his daughter, the wife of Solomon, as dowry.[41] Solomon built Gezer and lower[42] Beth Horon and Baalath[43] and Thamar[44] in the desert, in the land."[45] The two lists of building activities which include Gezer are of rather different geographical scope. They read as if one would state "Ivan the Terrible built Moscow and Nowgorod and Astrachan and Wladiwostok and Sebastopol and Moscow." Only one of the two lists can be historical, if any. In all probability, the one which claims the more restricted territory should be the more ancient. The larger list 15, 19 presupposes "Solomon the Traditional" and attributes various items to his activities which he did not build, like the temple. Containing cavalry, this list cannot antedate the end of the 9th century,[46] containing an Assyrian loanword (מסכנות),[47] it cannot even antedate the end of the 8th century.

In 1 Kgs 9:15-19, literary stratigraphy has inversed the historical sequence of the texts involved: it is the smaller list of fortresses (vv. 17-18) which should come closest to historical reality, and from which originated the elaboration 9:15,19-23. From the point of view of literary his-

---

[41] The LXX places this note after 5:13 MT (3 Kingdoms 5:14a = 3:1 MT; 3 Kingdoms 5:14b = 9:16 MT). A redactional-critical study of 1 Kgs 1-11 which gives due attention to the LXX is to be desired.

[42] LXX: upper, and omits Baalath; for the question of the territorial scope of Solomon's realm, this textual problem may be disregarded.

[43] Either the unidentified place in the vicinity of Ekron (Josh 19:44) or identical with Baalath Yehudah (Josh 15:9f; 1 Chr 13:6); or even Bealoth (Josh 15:24). All that one may reasonably assume is that the town in question was situated in Judah.

[44] To be located at *ʿAin al-ʿArūs*, 10 km SSE of the Dead Sea; S. Mittmann, "Ri. 1,16f und das Siedlungsgebiet der kenitischen Sippe Hobab," *ZDPV* 93 (1977) 213-35, 228-32. This outpost in the desert was strategically located to guard the road between Jerusalem and the Moabite Plateau, especially against raids by the Negebite tribes. The installation at ʿEn Ḥaṣeva / *ʿAin al-Ḥuṣb*, presented by R. Cohen and Y. Yisrael, "The Iron Age Fortresses at ʿEn Ḥaṣeva," *BA* 58 (1995) 229-32, as Solomon's Thamar could not apply, being a small structure of evidently local origin like the "Negev fortresses" mentioned *supra*.

[45] The text is not necessarily damaged, provided that the specification of the "land" was suppressed as evident: ארץ יהדה or maybe even ארץ ירשלם (cf. ארץ חפוח, or ארץ עטרת in the Mesha inscription)? Interestingly enough, the "desert" is not regarded as part of the "land."

[46] One does not need "fortresses" for horses, which in pre-19th century CE armies were kept on pasture; E. A. Knauf, A. de Pury and T. Römer, "*BaytDawīd ou BaytDōd? Une relecture de la nouvelle inscription de Tel Dan," *BN* 72 (1994) 60-69, 64 n. 10.

[47] Knauf, *Midian*, p. 104 and n. 473.

tory, however, the source has been secondarily inserted into the midrash.[48]

Even if the list 9:17f is pre-Assyrian in date, it is not necessarily Solomonic. There is, however, hardly another historical constellation which would match its scope: the Beth-Horons formed part of the kingdom of Israel, but Solomon, having himself proclaimed king of Israel at Gibeon, may indeed have controlled its southernmost districts. Gezer was not yet Israelite at the time of David (2 Sam 5:25) and in any case not Judaean in 734/733 BCE when Tiglath-pileser, who never fought Judah, depicted the siege of *Gazru*.[49] The possibility exists that the list reflects Omride activities in the South of the kind that have led to the traditions concerning "Solomon the Sealord,"[50] a date more in accord, perhaps, with the most recent archaeological chronology of Gezer.[51]

The source-value of the note in v. 16 concerning Pharaoh and his daughter should not be dismissed too easily, although the way of its transmission to the rather late author/redactor remains enigmatic.[52] To evaluate this note we would have to leave the domain of biblical criticism and must turn to the external evidence, which consists of the list of Shosheng's conquests. G. Garbini is probably right in his proposal that Shoshenq came to Palestine during the reign of Solomon.[53] He did not receive tribute from Jerusalem, because otherwise he would have mentioned the city in his list.[54] It is not only Jerusalem and its immediate

---

[48] The case is by no means unique; within their respective contexts, Judg 5:1-31b; 8:4-21 are literarily secondary, but historically more relevant that the basic narrative.

[49] H. Tadmor, *The Inscriptions of Tiglath-Pileser III, King of Assyria: Critical Edition, with Introductions, Translations and Commentary* (Jerusalem: Israel Academy of Sciences and Humanities, 1994) 210f, Misc. II.3.

[50] Knauf, "Solomon's Copper Supply," pp. 177f.

[51] Finkelstein, "Archaeology of the United Monarchy," p. 183.

[52] One could easily assume a folkloristic background. Needless to say that royal blood was not necessarily involved.

[53] G. Garbini, *History and Ideology in Ancient Israel* (New York: Crossroad, 1988) 29f. This is one of the most brilliant observations in a book which is, though aberrant in parts, always placing old problems in a new perspective; now also H. Donner, *Geschichte des Volkes Israel* (2nd ed., 1995) 2.321f, n. 14.

[54] The silence from which this argument is drawn is rather talkative. There are several minor lacunae in the list, but none where the geographical context suggests Jerusalem or any other Judaean town. The list comes closest to Jerusalem with nos. 23-26 (Gibeon, Beth Horon, Kiriathaim, Aijalon), where it arrives from Mahanaim (no. 22) and from where it leaves for Megiddo (no. 27). 1 Kgs 14:25-28 serves as a transition between the Glorious Empire of Solomon the Traditional and historical reality. The hard data core consists of "year 5—Sheshonq came to Palestine." Whose fifth year remains an open question. Perhaps Jeroboam's? In this case the biblical redactor could have calculated "Jeroboam 5 = Rehoboam 5."

vicinity that is spared by Sheshonq, but also Shechem and its environs. Sheshonq thus attests to the territorial nuclei of the later states of Israel and Judah, or the territories that were effectively controlled by Jeroboam[55] and Solomon. Either Sheshonq did not dare to touch these emerging states, which is rather unlikely given the imbalance of power between an imperial army on the one side and a kingdom of 5000-8000 inhabitants[56] on the other; or he did not want to touch them because he regarded them as loyal vassals and campaigned to support them rather than to reduce them.[57] In this case an Egyptian diplomatic marriage of Solomon becomes perfectly understandable.[58] It is highly unlikely that Pharaoh Siamun, an Egyptian traditionalist, became Solomon's father-in-law, but it is not impossible that Sheshonq, the Libyan parvenu, did so. It is dubious whether Siamum conquered Gezer,[59] whereas Sheshonq's conquest of the city is not too badly attested.[60]

If Shosheng campaigned in the interest of Solomon, another disturbing feature of his list of conquests might be explained: he did not touch

---

[55] Who, even according to the biblical narrative, came to power during the lifetime of Solomon; 1 Kgs 11:31, and H. Weippert, "Die Ätiologie des Nordreiches und seines Königshauses," *ZAW* 95 (1983) 244-275. Solomon's persecution of Jeroboam 11:40 presupposes that he did not only receive divine designation, but made it also known, i.e., declared himself king of Israel.

[56] Judah may have had slightly more than 2000 inhabitants, Jerusalem as many; I. Finkelstein, *The Archaeology of the Israelite Settlement* (Jerusalem: Israel Exploration Society, 1988) 332; Keel and Uehlinger, "Jahwe und die Sonnengottheit," p. 281. The estimate *supra* takes the possibly Solomonic districts of Israel (Gibeon, Beth Horon, destroyed Gezer) into account.

[57] For the impact of Sheshonq's campaign on the kingdom of Jeroboam, this has already been assumed by T. H. Robinson, *A History of Israel* (Oxford; Oxford University, 1948) 1.275; see n. 55.

[58] Incidentally, a parallel Egyptian marriage is reported for Jeroboam: LXX 3 Kingdoms 12:24e. It is easy to dismiss the LXX version of Jeroboam's career as wholly midrashic in nature; Ahlström, *History*, p. 545 n. 1. A pre-masoretic date of the narrative has recently been defended by A. Schenker, "Jéroboam et la division du royaume dans la Septante ancienne: LXX 1 R 12,24a-z, TM 11-12; 14 et l'histoire deutéronomiste," *Israël construit son histoire: L'historiographie deutéronomiste à la lumière des recherches* (ed. A. de Pury, T. Römer and D. Macchi; Geneva: Labor et Fides, 1996) 193-236.

[59] That he had himself represented fighting Philistines (J. v. Beckerath, LÄ 5.921) does not necessarily mean that he actually fought any and even if he did, Gezer would not have been the first objective in the Egyptian army's way.

[60] B. Mazar, "Pharaoh Shishak's Campaign to the Land of Israel," *The Early Biblical Period: Historical Studies* (ed. S Aḥituv and B. A. Levine; Jerusalem: Israel Exploration Society, 1986) 144; G. W. Ahlström, "Pharaoh Shoshenq's Campaign to Palestine," *History and Traditions of Early Israel: Studies Presented to Eduard Nielsen May 8th 1993* (eds. A. Lemaire and B. Otzen; VTSup 50; Leiden: E. J. Brill, 1993) 8, who correctly dismisses Siamun but unnecessarily also Solomon from Gezer's historical record; Finkelstein, "Archaeology of the United Monarchy," p. 183.

Jerusalem and its immediate vicinity, but he ravaged the Negeb, the very power-base of David.[61] The cleavage between Solomon's kingdom of Jerusalem and David's chiefdom of Judah is thus elucidated once more.

5. Conclusions

A double conclusion is now called for. Methodologically, the historian's hope for source material even embedded in literary compositions like the Bible is not necessarily always in vain. It requires, however, a critical reading which may not be to everybody's liking and it does not lead further than to reasonable speculation, which all history writing is and which I, for my part, prefer to willful ignorance.

On the factual level, it can be stated that Solomon was the son of a Jerusalemite mother, but not necessarily the son of a Judaean father.[62] He became king of Jerusalem by means of a *coup d'état*, ousting the Judaean elite from power. He was not a monotheist. He introduced the Judaean tribal deity YHWH into the pantheon of Jerusalem as a subordinate god only. With and under Solomon, Jerusalem started to subjugate Judah.[63] He did not rule from the Euphrates to the Brook of Egypt, but rather from Gezer to Thamar, if not from Gibeon to Hebron. But he did exist, after all.

---

[61] Note the (historically reliable) "story of David's rise to power" 1 Sam 22:1-5*; 25:2-43*; 27:4-12*; 30*; 2 Sam 2:1-4 (minimal extant) and my forthcoming article "Jerusalem in the 10th Century," *Jerusalem Before Islam* (ed. M. Abu Taleb; Amman: Royal Academy for Islamic Civilisation).

[62] Veijola, "Salomo," p. 103: "würde bedeuten, daß Bathseba in Wirklichkeit Urias Sohn auf den Thron der Doppelmonarchie gebracht hätte. Diese Möglichkeit ist nicht ganz von der Hand zu weisen, aber ebensowenig auch zu beweisen."

[63] T. L. Thompson, *The Early History of the Israelite People From the Written and Archaeological Sources* (SHANE 4; Leiden: E. J. Brill, 1992) 291f, rightly states "The state of Judah was created as the highlands were subjected to the extensions of Jerusalem's power;" the process started, however, 200 years before Manasseh.

ON THE DATING AND DATES OF SOLOMON'S REIGN

LOWELL K. HANDY

The biblical narratives relating the reign of Solomon provide few chronological notes by which his reign might be dated. The length of time given for his rule in Jerusalem is recorded as having been forty years.[1] The foundation of the temple is reported to have been established in the fourth year of Solomon's kingship and this event is said to correspond to the four hundred eightieth year of the Israelites having left Egypt.[2] The length of time it took to build the palace complex, including the temple, on Mount Zion is said to have been twenty years, or exactly half the time Solomon is recorded as having ruled. Seven of these twenty years were spent building the temple and the other thirteen years were devoted to building his palace.[3] There are no contemporary datable events from the surrounding cultures cited in either biblical narrative (Kings or Chronicles) by which the reign of Solomon might be situated chronologically in its larger world. This allows for a great deal of freedom in attempting to date Solomon's reign.

Among the earliest extant attempts to date Solomon with regard to the chronologies of the surrounding world are the references by Josephus to Tyrian records. While Josephus dates the founding of the temple in Jerusalem, in *Ant.* 8.3.1, with reference to the founding of Tyre, the date of the founding of Tyre is unknown. An event purported to be 240 years afterward is not helpful. However, Josephus, in the same passage, also insists that the Solomonic temple was founded in the eleventh year of the reign of Hiram of Tyre.[4] Perhaps of equal interest is the statement, in the same *Antiquities* passage, that the temple was founded 592 years after the Exodus, rather than the MT 480, which suggests that the Hebrew bib-

---

[1] 1 Kgs 11:42; 2 Chr 9:30; parallel, but not identical passages.

[2] 1 Kgs 6:1, 37-38; 2 Chr 3:2; though in the LXX and Targums, it is 440 years.

[3] 1 Kgs 6:37-38; 9:10.

[4] Josephus' *Contra Apionen* 1.126, states that it was the 12th year of Hiram; neither date may be correct, though 12 has been suggested as a "conventional number," which doesn't actually explain the discrepency in a date taken from a supposedly written source, see E. H. Merrill, 'The "Accession Year" and Davidic Chronolgy,' *JANES* 19 (1989) 101-112.

lical data was either different in Josephus' sources, or that he did not believe the biblical dates. Josephus went on to explain that the Temple was begun 1020 years after Abraham had left Mesopotamia, 1440 years after the flood, and 3102 years after Adam. Needless to say, modern historians do not use these chronologies in order to date Solomon. However, Josephus, in *Against Apion* provided a date for the building of the temple which was not explicitly dependent on the biblical narrative; in 1.17 Josephus reports that the Tyrian records contain references showing that Solomon's temple was built 143 years and eight months before the Tyrians founded Carthage. Using the records from Tyre, as they are presented in *Against Apion* 1.18, Josephus noted that these chronologies showed a complete list of the reigns from Hiram to Pygmalion, whose sister founded Carthage in his seventh year on the throne. If the reference to Hiram's eleventh year being the year of the founding of the temple by Solomon is correct, then that year of Hiram's reign was the fourth year of Solomon's. Assuming that the Tyrian records cited by Josephus existed and were accurate, this provides a set date for the founding of the temple in the 11th year of Hiram of Tyre.[5] Were one to take the date of 814 (± a year) for the founding of Carthage, this would produce a temple founding date of ± 957 BCE and a beginning date for the reign of Solomon of roughly 961 BCE.[6] However, despite it once enjoying a

[5] While it might be questioned whether Josephus would make up sources, there is ample reason to doubt that he or anyone writing Hellenistic histories saw original letters between Solomon and Hiram, or any original Tyrian records from a millennium earlier at all. If records in Tyre were kept on papyrus, or even parchment, they would not have survived the thousand years of sea climate to be read by Josephus or anyone else. If they were copied, they could well have been full of copy errors, since nothing about these mundane records would have insured any care in reproduction. And there is serious reason to doubt whether Josephus or his contemporaries could have read whatever ancient script was being used by Solomon and Hiram in whatever language they might have been writing a millennium earlier. The whole question of pseudonymous documents, popular in the Greco-Roman, world adds yet another question about documents at Tyre from Solomon and Hiram or their time. What Josephus actually was ultimately citing is unknown.

[6] M. Vogelstein, *Biblical Chronolgy, Pt. 1: The Chronology of Hezekiah* (Cincinnati: n.p., 1944) 22, though Vogelstein uses the founding of Tyre date to arrive at the temple founding in 969/8 BCE, p. 1; On the founding of Carthage, W. F. Albright, *Yahweh and the Gods of Canaan: A Historical Analysis of Two Contrasting Faiths* (Anchor Books; Garden City, NY: Doubleday, 1968) 233. By the time one figures in questions concerning the numbering systems of regnal years and the meaning of "year one" of a reign in both Tyre and Judah, it is possible to have a variance of at least three years either side of any proposed date for the enthronement of Solomon. Moreover, there have been other attempts to use the Carthage foundation to determine the reigning dates of Solomon with varying results; see summary in K. Van Wyk, *Archaeology in the Bible and Text in the Tel* (Berrien Springs, Mich.: Louis Hester, 1996) 207-211. There are, however, serious

period of popularity, Josephus' dating is generally not accepted in modern scholarship for arriving at an accurate date for the beginning of the reign of Solomon.[7]

Early Christian chronologists attempted to align biblical events with other historical traditions. Flavius Magnus Cassiodorus in his *Chronicon* places Solomon as a contemporary of the Latin King Latinas Silvius, before the founding of Rome. Eusebius posited that Solomon came to the throne in the 28th year of Eupalmes, making his reign begin in the 1037th year before Christ; forty years later (since the early Church historian had no doubt about the accuracy of the text) was 997 years before Christ.[8] The chronological approach to dating Solomon remained popular in the Church into the 19th century. The most influential such chronology in modern times has been that of Bishop James Ussher.[9] Major dates for the life of Solomon extracted from Ussher's chronology include these:

Event	Date of World	BCE
Solomon's birth	2971	1033
Rehoboam born to Solomon	2988	1016
Solomon anointed King	2989	1015
Adonijah executed, Pharaoh's daughter	2990	1014
Contract with Hiram for building temple	2991	1013

problems with using the founding of Carthage as a secure date in itself; see W. Barnes, *Studies in the Chronology of the Divided Monarchy of Israel* (HSM 48; Atlanta: Scholars, 1991) 51.

[7] Why, it should be asked, would the Tyrians have been interested in recording the construction of a minor temple in a foreign land in the first place, even if they did supply both labor and materials? More to the point, why would they have kept these frivolous documents for a millennium; G. Garbini, *History and Ideology in Ancient Israel* (New York: Crossroad, 1988) 23-25, notes these improbabilities. The pseudonymous composition of these sources in the Hellenistic period appears more rational an explanation than that they reflect accurate file copies and, therefore, all the supposed Tyrian sources for Solomon cited by Josephus should probably be noted more as curiosities of the Hellenistic world than source documents for the age of Solomon.

[8] Eusebius, *Die Griechischen christlichen Schriftsteller der ersten drie Jahrhunderte* (Leipzig: JC Hinrichs, 1913) 69-70; see, also, J. Finegan, *Handbook of Biblical Chronology: Principles of Time Reckoning in the Ancient World and Problems of Chronology in the Bible* (Princeton, NJ: Princeton University, 1964) 184-85.

[9] J. Ussher, *The Annals of the World* (London: E. Taylor for J. Crook & G. Bedell, 1658) 37-40; Bishop Ussher's chronology, however, was not the only one in use in his own time, Sir Walter Raleigh (*ca.* 1552-1618) posited the reign of Solomon as having begun in the year 2991 of the world, the date Ussher uses for the preparation of the temple; *History of the World* (Works of Sir Walter Ralegh, 8 vols.; Oxford: University, 1829) 4:538.

Temple foundation laid (May 21)	2992	1012
Temple finished (jubilee year)	3000	1005
Temple dedicated	3001	1004
Palace finished	3012	992
Shishak begins reign, Jeroboam flees	3026	978
Solomon dies	3029	975

While one occasionally still finds reference made to the dates developed by Ussher, the Solomonic chronology from his work is generally no longer used in scholarly studies. Since the end of the nineteenth century the dates for Solomon's reign have tended to move slowly lower.[10] More recent attempts to date Solomon's reign tend to begin by pointing out that the Bible does not provide the detailed regnal data for Solomon that is supplied for the rulers of the divided kingdoms. This is why Solomon's reign usually becomes dated backward from the reconstructed beginning of Rehoboam's kingship.

This latter approach makes the most important biblical date provided for Solomon's reign the reference in 1 Kgs 14:25 to the fifth year of Rehoboam as the date of the offensive by Shishak.[11] The date for

---

[10] An unscientific survey of biblical references from the mid 19th century to the mid-20th century shows a decided shift from the dates of Ussher [Solomon's reign = 1015-975 BCE] into the tenth century BCE. C. Taylor, "Solomon," *Calmet's Dictionary of the Holy Bible* (9th ed.; London: Henry G. Bohn, 1847) 2.638, and H. Lesétre, "Salomon," *Dictionnaire de la Bible* (Paris: Letouzey et Ané, 1912) 5.1382, both use Ussher's dates. While L. Coleman, *An Historical Text Book and Atlas of Biblical Geography* (New revised ed.; Philadelphia: E. Claxton, 1881) 122, argues Solomon came to the throne two years earlier, in 1017 (at the age of 18 or 20, a popular notion among the 19th century authors), most references from more modern scholars moved Solomon close to the theoretical extreme numbers to be suggested herein: R. Flint, "Solomon," *A Dictionary of the Bible* (ed. J. Hastings; New York: Charles Scribner's Sons, 1902) 4.562, has *ca.* 970-*ca.* 930 BCE; M. Thilo, *Die Chronologie des Alten Testamentes* (Barmen: Hugo Klein, 1917) 36, has reign = 970-931 BCE; N. M. Powell, *Time Was: A New Chronology* (Oklahoma City: Modern Publishers, 1955) 146, founding of temple = 969 BCE = 4th year of Solomon; J. E. Steinmueller and K. Sullivan, *Catholic Biblical Encyclopedia: Old Testament* (New York: Joseph F Wagner, 1956) 1025, reign from 972 to 932 BCE; J. González Echegaray, "Salomón," *Enciclopedia de la Biblia* (2nd ed.; Barcelona: Garriga, 1969) 6.388, reign from 970 to 931 BCE. However, later dates have been proposed: J. M. Myers, "Solomon," *IDB* (1962), 4.399, reign from 962-922 BCE.

[11] For the purpose of this article it will be assumed that biblical Shishak refers to the Egyptian king Sheshonk I (also appearing as Shosenq I). An attempt by P. James to argue that Shishak's invasion recorded in the Bible was actually related to Ramesses III entails a great deal of speculation and creative reconstruction, *Centuries of Darkness: A Challenge to the Conventional Chronology of Old World Archaeology* (London: Jonathan Cape, 1991) 257, 385-86, n. 135. R. Wallenfels, "Redating the Byblian Inscriptions," *JANES* 15 (1983) 87-89, had earlier questioned the correlation between these two names. In addition, the Egyptian military movement was probably not seen by the Egyptians in

Shishak's incursion into Palestine is not exactly known since it is not provided with a dateable context in any Egyptian record.[12] Indeed, the various dates suggested for the military campaign derive from an inscriptional comment to the effect that the construction of the large Karnak monument describing the pharaoh's attacks upon the cities in Israel (and to a lesser extent, Judah) was begun in Shishak's 21st year.[13] One could argue that the monument needed to have been erected during the king's reign, but it need not have been started immediately after the victorious return from "Asia." This being the case, a discrepancy of some fifteen years exists among the suggestions for the incursion itself, giving an early date in the middle of the 930's and a late date around 920. Some Egyptologists and biblical scholars have tended to accept a date within a year of the summer of 925 BCE as the most likely.[14] If the

terms of conquest, but as an internal matter since the divine right to rule over this area of Asia had been a part of the religious/political tradition at least from the 12th dynasty; H. Goedicke, "An Egyptian Claim to Asia," *JARCE* 8 (1969-1970) 12. Garbini, *History and Ideology*, pp.29-30, merely wishes to move the event backward in time such that Shishak invaded Solomon's kingdom and not his son's; this reconstruction has more to commend it than does that of James, but not enough to be acceptable.

[12] The dating of the 22nd dynasty has a number of problems which affect the chronology into the dynasties on either side: E. Young, "Some Notes on the Chronology and Genealogy of the Twenty-First Dynasty," *JARCE* 1 (1962) 109; E. F. Wente, "On the Chronology of the 21st Dynasty," *JNES* 26 (1967) 155-76; J. Goldberg, "The 23rd Dynasty Problem Revisited: Where, When and Who?" *Discussions in Egyptology* 29 (1994) 55-58.

[13] See N. Grimal, *A History of Ancient Egypt* (Oxford: Blackwell, 1994) 323; and G. W. Ahlström, "Pharaoh Shoshenq's Campaign to Palestine," *History and Traditions of Early Israel: Studies Presented to Eduard Nielsen, May 8th 1993* (ed. A. Lemaire and Benedikt Otzen; VTSup 50; Leiden: E. J. Brill, 1993) 3. On problems with dating this event, see Barnes, *Studies*, pp. 57-71, and F. H. Cryer, "Chronology: Issues and Problems," *Civilizations of the Ancient Near East* (ed. J. M. Sasson; New York: Charles Scribner's Sons, 1995) 2.662.

[14] See K. A. Kitchen, *The Third Intermediate Period in Egypt (1100-650 B.C.)* (2nd ed.; Warminster, England: Aris & Phillips, 1986) 295, who accepts the summer of 925 BCE as the date of the invasion; also, A. R. Green, "Solomon and Siamun: A Synchronism between Early Dynastic Israel and the Twenty-First Dynasty of Egypt," *JBL* 93 (1978) 354; Grimal, *History*, p. 322; P. A. Clayton, *Chronicles of the Pharaohs: The Reign-by-Reign Record of the Rulers and Dynasties of Ancient Egypt* (London: Thames & Hudson, 1994) 185; and G. Galil, *The Chronology of the Kings of Israel and Judah* (SHCANE 9; Leiden: E. J. Brill, 1996) 15-16. While D. Ussishkin, "Notes on Megiddo, Gezer, Ashdod, and Tel Batash in the Tenth to Ninth Centuries B.C." *BASOR* 277-78 (February-May 1990) 72, accepts the date as close; and Ahlström, "Pharaoh Shoshenq's Campaign," p. 3, assumes the attack was shortly before the inscription which he dates to 926; which would conform to the 927 BCE date proposed by E. Vogt, "Expeditio Paraonis Soseng in Palasetinam a. 927 A.C.," *Biblica* 38 (1957) 234. Even James, *Centuries*, p. 230, accepts the date of 925 BCE for Shishak's invasion. Note, also that P. van der Meer, *The Ancient Chronology of Western Asia and Egypt* (2nd ed.; Leiden: E. J. Brill, 1955) 70, 83,

summer of 925 was the fifth year of Rehoboam's reign, then Rehoboam would have come to the throne sometime in the three years 931-929.[15] On the other hand, the date of Shishak's invasion need not have been so late, or so close to the time that the Karnak monument was constructed; a date in the last half of the 930's has been proposed.[16] Yet others find the evidence for the military maneuvers as late as 920.[17] The possibility remains that the invasion on the Karnak inscription is not the one referred to in Kings, a situation that would make the date by correlation irrelevant.[18] In the end, one can date the beginning of Rehoboam's reign anywhere from 937 to 924 by using the Shishak invasion as an anchor date.[19] Yet, even having a date for Rehoboam's first year, would not tell us whether Solomon had died that year, or the year before.[20]

Turning to the problem of the length of Solomon's reign. The forty years ascribed to Solomon's rule in Jerusalem has long been understood by many scholars as an appoximate number and neither a reflection of the actual length of the reign nor of material retrieved from court records.[21] The forty years reflect a round number suitable for marking

---

has Shishak destroying Tell Beit Mirsim in 926 BCE in one place, but dating the pharaoh's campaign by Rehoboam's fifth year in 927 BCE in another.

[15] The questions concerning how much of a year constituted a year and how the first "portion" of a year of a reign was counted at the beginning of a reign comes into play; see J. Hughes, *Secrets of the Times: Myth and History in Biblical Chronology* (JSOTSup 66; Sheffield: Sheffield Academia, 1990) 85.

[16] D. B. Redford, *Egypt, Canaan, and Israel in Ancient Times* (Princeton, New Jersey: Princeton University, 1992), 312; Hughes, *Secrets of the Times*, pp. 191-193, discusses the debate over the date of Shishak's Palestine campaign; he himself accepts a date of 933 for the campaign.

[17] J. M. Miller and J. H. Hayes, *A History of Ancient Israel and Judah* (Philadelphia: Westminster, 1986) 238, table, which would fit with the suggested date for the beginning of Rhehoboam's reign, J. M. Miller, "Another Look at the Chronology of the Early Divided Monarchy," *JBL* 86 (1967) 288. W. F. Albright, *Archaeology and the Religion of Israel: The Ayer Lectures of the Colgate-Rochester Divinity School 1941* (Baltimore: Johns Hopkins, 1956) 130, ascribes dates to Shishak which would allow the invasion even after 920 BCE (reign of the pharaoh: 935-915 BCE).

[18] Redford, *Egypt, Canaan and Israel*, p. 314; Cryer, "Chronology," p. 662..

[19] These are Hughes, *Secrets of the Times*, p. 275, appendix D, and Miller and Hayes, *History*, p. 220, chart ix, respectively.

[20] A Question raised by V. Pavlovsky; and E. Vogt, "Die Jahre der Könige von Juda und Israel," *Biblica* 45 (1964) 321-47.

[21] This has been a standard commentary position: J. A. Montgomery, *A Critical and Exegetical Commentary on the Books of Kings* (ICC; Edinburgh: T. & T. Clark, 1951) 244, 267; J. Gray, *I & II Kings: A Commentary* (OTL; 2nd revised ed.; Philadelphia: Westminster, 1970) 298; J. Robinson, *The First Book of Kings* (CBC; Cambridge: Cambridge University Press, 1972) 147. Chronicles simply follows the length of Solomon's reign found in Kings; J. M. Myers, *II Chronicles* (AB 13; Garden City, NY: 1965) 60; S. Japhet, *I & II Chronicles: A Commentary* (OTL; Louisville: Westminster/John Knox, 1993) 644.

off a generation; it was the same number of years used by the authors to designate the length of David's reign (1 Kgs 2:11; 1 Chr 29:27), thereby producing a numerical pattern of sorts for the rulers of the kingdoms of Israel and Judah as a mini-Empire (the "United Monarchy").[22] The actual length of Solomon's kingship is unknown; there is no reason to assume that the symbolic forty years was derived from an approximation to that length of time in the reign itself. Even so, if it could be assumed that the recorded number approximated the actual length of the king's rule, it would leave the possibility of deriving the exact date of Solomon's accession at nil.

The author of Kings provides the information that the temple was founded in the 480th year after the Israelites came out of Egypt. The unknown date of the Exodus (if any) leaves this chronology unhelpful.[23] Moreover, the 480 years bear more theological than chronological weight, displaying the orderliness and symmetry of a supposed divine plan rather than a reflection of actual passing time.[24]

The chronology for building the temple itself presents problems. Begun, according to the biblical narratives, in the fourth year of Solomon's reign, the temple-palace complex is described as two separate building activities. It is hard not to assume that the temple is presented as having been built first, and alone, more for the theological reasons of the author than from historical recollections. The entire palace complex included the much smaller chapel such that it is more rational to assume that the construction project was developed to cover both the king's dwelling and the king's chapel for the patron deity of his reign. The twenty years for the whole building project is a round number, reflecting

---

[22] Miller and Hayes, *History,* p. 196; Hughes, *Secrets of the Times*, pp. 37 (nt. 23), 56; D. N. Freedman, "The Chronology of Israel and the Ancient Near East: Section A. Old Testament Chronology," *The Bible and the Ancient Near East: Essays in Honor of William Foxwell Albright* (ed. G. E. Wright; Garden City, NY: Doubleday, 1961) 208. There are also numerous literary parallels to the two reigns as told both in Samuel-Kings and in Chronicles, supporting the notion of a stylized historiography rather than an accurate record.

[23] Problems with the Exodus narrative as a whole and the possibility of dating anything concerning it are discussed in numerous histories; see, for example: Miller and Hayes, *History*, pp. 64-79; S. Herrmann, *A History of Israel in Old Testament Times* (Philadelphia: Fortress, 1975) 56-85; for a possitive assessment for dating the event, K. A. Kitchen,"Ancient Egypt and the Old Testament," *Bulletin of the Anglo-Israel Archaeological Society* 11 (1991-1992) 48-51, and for a dismissal of the Exodus event as unhistorical see G. W. Ahlström, *The History of Ancient Palestine from the Palaeolithic Period to Alexander's Conquest* (JSOTSup 146; Sheffield: Sheffield Academic, 1993) 28.

[24] On schematic dating throughout Jewish and Christian history, see Hughes, *Secrets of the Times*, pp. 232-263.

half of Solomon's reign; making this project the most important of the king's life as ruler. For the author of Kings the establishment of the proper royal house and, more importantly, the correct religious center bears more weight than the figure of Solomon himself and anchors the central themes of the rest of the book.

The seven years which, according to the texts, were entailed in building the temple reflect the various symbolic meanings attached to the number seven. Notions of completeness, goodness, sacrality, power, and quality were attributed to the number in the ancient Near East, as well as its use as a round number for items on a more modest scale than using forty.[25] All of these associations with the number seven apply to the temple in the palace complex of Jerusalem. Depending on the antiquity of the importance of the number seven in Jerusalem circles, its use by the author of Kings may reflect either a historiographical numbering system, or the possibility that temple construction may in fact have been designed to take seven years simply to reflect in its building all these connotations. As there is no evidence for the latter, the former seems more likely. There is, in short, nothing in these dates which can be taken as historical rather than as symbolic.

The problems with the calendar dates (months of Ziv as the second month and of Bul as the 8th month) demonstrate the question of whether the text is attempting to reflect the calendar of the reign of Solomon or that of the author.[26] Though the annual chronology cannot be established, the month notations may reflect a tradition different from the years or even reflect earlier narratives concerning the founding of the temple, but they cannot be assumed to reflect accurate calendar dates from truswoṛthy sources without having a similar faith in the years attributed to the building and the latter is not reasonably established from the texts. It should be noted, however, that in the numerical dating patterns which have been observed for the biblical citations, the beginning of Solomon's Temple construction does not follow a regular pattern, but

---

[25] On the symbolic use of "seven" in the ancient world, see A. S. Kapelrud, "The Number Seven in Ugaritic Texts," *VT* 18 (1968) 496-97; E. Otto, "שֶׁבַע," *TWAT* 7:1013-15; and, more generally, Z. Giora, "The Magical Number Seven," *Occident and Orient: A Tribute to the Memory of Alexander Scheiber* (ed. R. Dán; Budapest: Akadémiai Kiadó, 1988) 171-73.

[26] G. Larsson, "The Documentary Hypothesis and the Chronological Structure of the Old Testament," *ZAW* 97 (1985) 331-32, argues that the dating system needs to be later than 238 BCE. One need not go that far, however, to see that there is a problem with the months and the recording of the years for this early period; Hughes, *Secrets of the Times*, pp. 159-82.

is unique unto itself as a Sabbath of the second day of the second month.[27]

The lack of any solid dates for the reign of Solomon as well as the schematic numbering system which has been employed in providing years for the narrative says nothing about the historicity (or lack thereof) of the ruler Solomon. It does, however, suggest that the reign of Solomon itself was being related in these extant narratives without the use of dated documents from the time of Solomon. Or, perhaps, the symbolism of the reign's dates were more important to the author, dealing here with the foundation of the cult of Jerusalem and the succession of the dynasty of David, than was actual chronology.[28] In either case, modern historians are left without useable data for dating Solomon's reign in any exact fashion.

It can with some logic be conjectured that King Solomon died sometime between 938 and 924 BCE; taking into account the possible dates for the first year of Rehoboam and the need to be wary of assuming that the last year of one king was taken as the first of the next. Since the length of Solomon's reign cannot be reconstructed, we are left without even an approximate date for the first year of Solomon's rule. If his was the period in which the palace and temple were constructed, it is safe to assume that his was not a passing moment, but a reign of some (indeterminable) years. However, ten years would have been enough for both the construction and the upheaval reported in the texts, just as easily as forty. If ancient court records were available to the author(s), it is no doubt safe to say that Solomon did not, in any case, reign *longer* than forty years. Had that been the case his actual longer reign would probably have been held up as an example of the rewards of good statescraft; no, it is fairly

[27] B. Z. Wacholder and S. Wacholder, "Patterns of Biblical Dates and Qumran's Calendar: The Fallacy of Jaubert's Hypothesis," *HUCA* 66 (1995) 12-14.

[28] As far as the authors of Kings and Chronicles are concerned, Solomon was the son of David and was designated heir apparent even in infancy. This position has been the standard notion for positing a coregency of David and Solomon; see, for example, E. Ball, "The Co-Regency of David and Solomon (I Kings 1)," *VT* 27 (1977) 268-79; Robinson, *First Book of Kings*, p. 33; Ahlström, *History*, p. 500; and Galil, *Chronology*, p. 7. The problems with this theory are mainly two: 1) there is no solid evidence for co-regencies [Galil's "explicit" evidence is at best "implicit"]; see J. Hughes, *Secrets of the Times*, pp. 100-107, and 2) the historical reliability of the designation of Solomon as king by David in his own lifetime is "story" and not "history," as has been noted for some time; see B. O. Long, *1 Kings with an Introduction to Historical Literature* (FOTL 9; Grand Rapids: Eerdmans, 1984) 39; and the story may have nothing to do with an actual historical event, see E. A. Knauf, "Le roi est mort, vive le roi! A Biblical Argument for the Historicity of Solomon," pp. 88-90 [this volume].

safe to say Solomon had died before he saw his fortieth year on the throne, but how long before cannot now be recovered.

Assuming the possibility of Shishak's expedition having come as early as 933 BCE and that this event was in fact the incursion reported for the fifth year of Rehoboam (*and* that this dating reflects a real historical date), the earliest possible date for the beginning of the reign of Solomon would be 973 BCE. Yet, all things considered, it is most likely that the latest possible date for the death of Solomon was in fact 930 BCE, which would be six years prior to the construction of the Karnak monument to Shishak. The earliest corresponding possible date for his having come to the throne from that date would have been 39 years before it, or 969 BCE. Nonetheless, both dates are insubstantial and, moreover, unlikely.

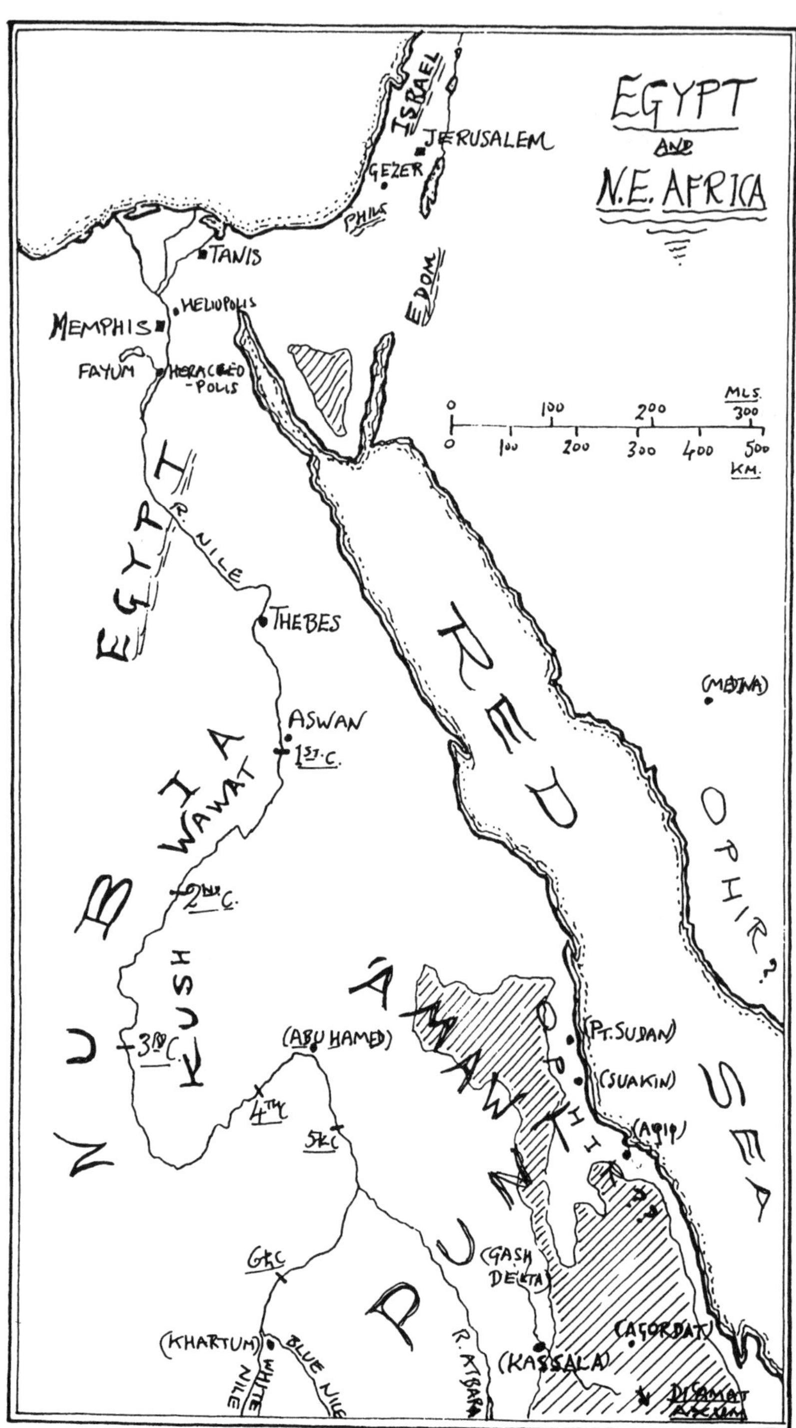
EGYPT
AND
N.E. AFRICA
ISRAEL
JERUSALEM
GEZER
PHILS
EDOM
TANIS
HELIOPOLIS
MEMPHIS
FAYUM
HERACLEO-POLIS
MLS.
0 100 200 300
0 100 200 300 400 500
KM.
EGYPT
R. NILE
THEBES
RED SEA
(MEDINA)
ASWAN
1ST C.
WAWAT
NUBIA
2ND C.
KUSH
3RD C.
OPHIR?
(ABU HAMED)
4TH
5TH C
6TH C
(PT. SUDAN)
(SUAKIN)
(AQIQ)
(GASH DELTA)
(KHARTUM)
BLUE NILE
WHITE NILE
R. ATBARA
(KASSALA)
(AGORDAT)

Map 1.

EGYPT AND EAST AFRICA

Kenneth A. Kitchen

1. Background

Throughout most of the history of Palestine, from antiquity to recent times, Egypt has always been the major political power nearest to that land. Such was certainly also the case in the 10th century BC, the period in which Solomon belongs, if the clear evidence available is to be heeded.[1] South of Egypt, East Africa divides in practice into several zones extending inland westwards from the coast of the Red Sea. First is *Nubia*, an area of hot, barren desert whose heart and lifeline (like Egypt's) is the long thin river Nile, flowing mainly northward and annually fertilising a usually narrow strip of land on each bank. Lower Nubia (ancient *Wawat*) is the stretch from the 2nd Cataract north to the 1st Cataract at Aswan, southernmost town of Egypt proper. Upper Nubia (ancient *Kush*) extends south from the 2nd Cataract to the 4th, and to the great river-bend at Abu Hamed. Second, and further south, we have a *Middle Nile/Red Sea zone*. This embraces A) the Nile valley south from Abu Hamed, and its tributary the Atbara; B) the steppe areas east and west of the Nile from Abu Hamed to the confluence with the Atbara; C) the Red Sea coastal strip (roughly from the Egypto-Sudanese border to that with Eritrea), the mountains behind that strip. Thirdly, we have a vast *Sudan/Ethiopia/Somalia zone*, flanking the Red Sea to the horn of E. Africa. Direct Levantine contact with all three of these great zones south of Egypt was very limited at most periods, by contrast with the long-running relations of Egypt and her northeast neighbors.

[1] Close dating for the Hebrew kings from Ahab to Jehu through the Assyrian sources, plus the closely-synchronised years and rulers in Judah and Israel before them back to Rehoboam and Jeroboam would set an optimum date for Solomon's death in *ca*. 931/930 BC; see, long since, the demonstration by E. R. Thiele, *The Mysterious Numbers of the Hebrew Kings* (Chicago: University of Chicago, 1951) 53-54, 55ff [2nd ed., Exeter: Paternoster; Grand Rapids: Eerdmans, 1965, pp. 50-52, 53ff] which has not been bettered by any of the very unsatisfactory studies of Hebrew royal chronology published since. As Solomon was a younger son of David, there is nothing amiss in allowing him the full 40 years stated for him, to begin his rule in *ca*. 971/970 BC. These dates will be used here. See also the previous chapter of this volume.

2. Egypt in the 10th Century BC

By about 970 BC; Egypt had lived through a century of tacit dyarchy. Late in the reign of Ramesses XI Khaemwaset II (last ruler of the Ramesside Empire), sweeping political changes took place. His 19th year was declared also to be year 1 of a new era, *wehem-mesut*, of "Renaissance." In effect, it was a triumvirate. One man Nesibanebdjed (in Greek: "Smendes") was set up as governor of the north: the Delta with Tanis (Hebrew: Zoʿan) replacing the moribund royal town Pi-Ramesse (Hebrew: Raamses) in the east; Memphis the real administrative capital where the last Ramesside kings had lived; and a little south towards Heracleopolis and the entry to the Fayum lake-province. A second, older man Herihor (possibly a relative of Smendes) was installed as supreme governor of *everything* to the south of Smendes' realm, holding therewith an unprecedented constellation of titles and powers: Generalissimo as military governor of Upper Egypt, High Priest of Amun as titular religious head in Thebes (capital of the south), Vizier as civil governor, and additionally even Viceroy of Nubia, to replace in that region a rebel viceroy who had sought to make himself an independent potentate there. These two men were now in practice the twin rulers of Egypt (hence our term, dyarchy), with only the pharaoh Ramesses XI as their titular superior over all Egypt while he yet lived. Being older, Herihor died soon, to be replaced by one Piankh (perhaps his son-in-law), then by the latter's son Pinudjem I, in each case, as both military governor and high priest of Amun.[2]

At this juncture (*ca.* 1170 BC), Ramesses XI died, leaving the throne vacant. In Egypt the law was "he who buries inherits." The old king was never buried in his unfinished royal tomb in Western Thebes (in Herihor's domain). Thus, instead, he would most likely have been buried where he had died, at Memphis the capital, and hence buried somewhere in the vast desert cemetery of Memphis, now Saqqara; and by Smendes who had ruled there for him. Hence, it was Smendes who became the next formal king of all Egypt, founding what was to be the 21st Dynasty, reigning in Memphis and the family seat at Tanis. But, to maintain his

[2] For this whole epoch of Egyptian history in the 11th-10th centuries BC, see K. A. Kitchen, *The Third Intermediate Period in Egypt (1100-650 B.C.* (2nd ed. with 1995 supplement; Warminster: Aris & Phillips, 1996). The attempt made by K. Jansen-Winkeln, "Das Ende des Neuen Reiches," *Zeitschrift für Ägyptische Sprache* 119 (1992) 22-37, to reverse the order of Herihor and Piankh is totally devoid of any factual foundation. See, for the real situation, Kitchen, *Third Intermediate*, pp. xiv-xvii, §§A-K.

claim to supremacy over all Egypt (at least in name), he had undoubtedly to leave the family of Pinudjem I in place as the real rulers of Upper Egypt, so that Egypt had indeed a dual regime of military governors over the south (who were also high priests of Amun of Thebes), and of titular kings over the north, but recognised as official rulers over the whole, by whose regnal years official documents were dated. So, in effect, we have two parallel dynasties at this period of the 21st Dynasty (*ca.* 1070-945 BC), of kings in the north and over all, and of generals/high priests in the south. This was the basic political situation in Egypt during the entire reigns of Saul and David, and for just over half the reign of Solomon.

Economically, we have only limited data for 11th/10th century Egypt. Essentially, this irrigation-agriculture-based realm slumbered on year by year; we have no surviving reports of great events or of any specific disasters.[3] Before the time of the 6th (and last-but-one) king, Siamun, we have in our possession absolutely nothing from Egyptian soil about relationships abroad, other than one blue lapis bead from the burial of Psusennes I (*ca.* 1040-992 BC), inscribed in cuneiform for the daughter of an Assyrian vizier. However, this piece was almost certainly an heirloom from the end of the previous (20th) Dynasty, when Ramesses XI or Smendes may have received it among gifts, when "the king of Musri" (Egypt) sent gifts including a crocodile to Assur-bel-kala campaigning in Syria around 1070 BC. It therefore tells us nothing about the foreign relations of the 21st Dynasty subsequent to that date.[4] Even in the reign of Siamun it is only the chance find (in excavations at Tanis) of part of a triumphal scene of his that hints at activity by him in the Levant. The seemingly great silence of Egyptian sources at this period (also true for several centuries that followed!) has often been badly misinterpreted by Old Testament scholars to the detriment of mentions of Egypto-Levantine relations in Kings and Chronicles: no Egyptian mention = non-historical. However, the underlying fact is that the sites of the Egyptian Delta have been so thoroughly robbed of their "softer-stone" monuments and inscriptions again and again, and these destroyed by recycling, that 95% at least of the possible data have long since been destroyed. In

[3] There were occasional rumblings of inner-political discontent; when the new high priest and commander Menkheperre was appointed, he had to beat down some opposition at Thebes, exiling some miscreants to the desert oases (Maunier stela); J. von Beckerath, "Die Stele der Verbannten im Museum des Louvre," *REg* 20 (1968) 7-36, pl. I; see Kitchen, *Third Intermediate*, p. 260.

[4] See conveniently, Kitchen, *Third Intermediate*, p. 252, n. 46, and p. 267 and nn. 139-40, with full references.

Upper Egypt several great temples and many rock-cut tombs have survived (along with a multitude of stone-based inscriptions, etcetera) because quarry-facilities have always been more immediate (for new stone), hence these works have in part survived. Also, for more perishable records of wood or on papyrus, the dry valley-edges in Upper Egypt offer a chance of survival, whereas the humidity and sopping wet mud and soil of the Delta are fatal to such materials (unless carbonised by fire, making them almost useless for decipherment). These facts must always be borne in mind. Furthermore, the inscriptional data from Thebes in the 21st Dynasty boil down essentially to the interminable funerary formulae for the afterlife on gaily-painted coffins or Book of the Dead spells in funerary papyri, and to a limited series of "family" inscriptions about purely local, Theban matters (oracles from the god Amun, matters of inheritance), and the linen-makers' and undertakers' datelines on mummy-bandages and dockets. Nobody should expect light on Egypt's international relations from these sources! Any more than one would consult (for example) the Hollywood film *Gone with the Wind* (an inner-American epic) to learn anything about American involvement in war and peace in the Europe of the 1940s.

In the religious sphere, the god Amun of Thebes was recognised still as supreme deity in Egypt, but with new emphases. There was a more pronounced trend (in Thebes, at least) to settle disputes and claims at even a high level by means of the oracle of Amun, including appointments to priestly offices. The very high local political profile gained by the god Amun in the 21st-22nd Dynasties led Eduard Meyer to write of a "theocracy" in Egypt (or, at least in Thebes) at this epoch;[5] he may have overstated the case, but the situation was certainly different from New Kingdom times immediately preceding. Also, the kings resident in Tanis and Memphis adopted the title of High Priest of Amun alongside their normal royal titulary, as if to offest the prestige of their southern contemporaries in bearing such a title. However, the fact is that the god Amun's temporal domains (holdings of fields) were to be found throughout Egypt. And the old East-Delta residence of Pi-Ramesse was largely in holdings of Amun's domain. In the great Papyrus Harris I, for example, Ramesses III deals with this location in the section devoted to Amun

[5] E. Meyer, "Gottesstadt, Militärherrschaft und Ständewesen in Ägypten: Zur Geschichte der 21. und 22. Dynastie," *Sitzungsberichte der Preussischen Akademie der Wissenschaften* (Phil.-hist. Kl. 1928; Berlin: Akademie der Wissenschaften, 1928) 495-532.

and his property. Thus, Tanis (only a few miles north) seems also to have lain within the temporal domains of Amun. And the new temples built at Tanis by the 21st Dynasty kings were indubitably dedicated to Amun, Mut and Khons, the Theban triad. Hence, as their supreme pontiff locally, the Tanite kings could, in fact, very properly adopt the title of high priest of Amun, for they could exercise that office in Tanis if they so wished; Pharaoh was *ex-officio* high priest of all Egypt's gods, and those mortals that bore such titles were in essence his deputies.[6]

Midway through Solomon's reign, in *ca.* 945 BC, the last, heirless Tanite king, Psusennes II, passed the throne to Shoshenq, Great Chief of the Ma (short for Meshwesh), of Libyan origin, resident and commander in Bubastis, itself halfway between Memphis and Tanis, Egypt's twin capitals. Shoshenq had already become the most powerful man in the state. He had earlier made alliance with the outgoing royal house, in that his son Osorkon (the future Osorkon I) had been married to the lady Maatkare, daughter of Psusennes II, while he himself was the nephew of Osorkon the Elder (two kings before Psusennes II), through links already established between his own forebears and the 21st Dynasty.[7] Thus, he was the "obvious" man in the kingdom to succeed Psusennes II in due course, founding thereby the Libyan-origin 22nd Dynasty as Shoshenq I, and reigning 21 years down to *ca.* 924 BC. As regards his dating, one point needs to be made very clear indeed. Namely, that the date of Shoshenq I does *not* depend on the Hebrew chronology of Kings and the Assyrian synchronisms therewith, as some have wrongly assumed. In Egypt we have a firm date of 664 BC for the beginning of the 26th Dynasty and a very narrow margin of error between 715 and 713/12 BC for the start of the 25th Dynasty in Egypt. Before that point we have now 10 kings of the 22nd Dynasty whose *known* reigns from first-hand sources total 224 years minimally and 230 years overall; this brings the accession of Shoshenq I back absolutely minimally to 939/36 BC, but in fact to 945/42 BC, most likely 945 BC.[8] Which happens to agree well with the Near Eastern data.

---

[6] See Excursus D, "Notes on the Cults of Tanis and Thebes," with references, in Kitchen, *Third Intermediate*, pp. 426-30.

[7] See, for full discussion, *ibid.*, pp. 60-61, 111-16, 534-35, 541 end, 573-74; Identification of Osochor as Osorkon the Elder, see J. Yoyotte, "Osorkon fils de Mehytouskhé, un pharaon oublié?" *Bulletin de la Société Française d'Egyptologie* 77-78 (1977) 39-54.

[8] For the relevant data and calculations, see K. A. Kitchen, "The Historical Chronology of Ancient Egypt, a Current Assessment," *Acta Archaeologia* 67 (1996, in press); and *ditto*, in *The Synchronization of Civilizations in the Eastern Mediterranean during the Second Millennium B.C.* (ed. M. Bietak; Vienna, in press). For a critique of recent erro-

Shoshenq I was a determined man of very different stamp from most of the rulers of the preceding century or so. He appointed his own son Iuput as high priest in Thebes, through whom marriage-alliances were made with some of the ruling Theban families. There was to be no dyarchy in *his* time; one supreme ruler of Egypt only! He opened up trade-relations with Byblos and its ruler Abibaal, who inscribed his own name and dedication on a royal statue that Shoshenq I sent to Byblos.[9] He is, of course, the Shishak of Kings and Chronicles, and pursued a radically different policy towards ancient Israel from that of his predecessors, culminating in his invasion of the twin rump-kingdoms of Judah and Israel whose division after Solomon's death he had materially helped to engineer.

3. The Situation in Ancient East Africa

Here our data are more fleeting, less informative, and the state of exploration and research is far less advanced than in Egypt and the Levant. The greatest accessions to knowledge here still lie firmly in the future. We must look in turn at each of our main zones, as defined in Section 1 above.

A. *Nubia, from 1st to 4th Cataracts of the Nile*

In the mid-second millennium BC (before *ca.* 1540 BC), when Egypt's rulers lost control south of Aswan and the Hyksos made themselves supreme for a time in Egypt proper, the Nubians themselves restored their own local chiefdoms and kingdoms, most especially the kingdom of Kush in Upper Nubia. But when the 18th Dynasty pharaohs expelled the Hyksos, reunited Egypt, and expanded their rule into both the Levant and Nubia, then within 60 years (Ahmose I to Tuthmosis I, *ca.* 1540-1480 at latest) all of Nubia was subjected to Egyptian colonial rule to the 4th Cataract of the Nile, and intermittent rebellions firmly crushed. During the next three centuries or more down to *ca.* 1180 BC the New-

neous treatments of the 22nd-23rd Dynasties, see Kitchen, *Third Intermediate*, pp. xxii-xlii, §§U-KK, with full references.

[9] First published by R. Dussaud, "Les inscriptions phéniciennes du tombeau d'Ahiram, roi de Byblos," *Syria* 5 (1924) 145-47, §5 with pl. 42 and fig. 5; for the main subsequent literature, see Kitchen, *Third Intermediate*, pp. 292f, n. 283.

Kingdom pharaohs exploited Nubia to the full. Top prize was the gold in the Eastern Desert between the Nile and the Red Sea, worked largely by Nubians and exiled Egyptians with criminal records, in very harsh conditions. The Nile was also a channel for trade with inner Africa, for products from the deep South. But more fatally, Nubians were exiled into Egypt to become slave-labour there, and those that remained to cultivate the Nile-flood land had to bear ever-increasing taxation. When revolts failed to remove the Egyptian burden from the Nubians' backs, they took the only other alternative. They voted with their feet, by emigrating further southward, out of Egyptian-controlled territory: no more slavery, hard labour or taxes for pharaoh then. The archaeological record (imperfect as it is) seems to show a growing depopulation in Nubia during the 18th Dynasty, culminating under the Ramesside 19th and 20th Dynasties. The various temples built so spectacularly by Ramesses II in Nubia (such as Abu Simbel) were supported by quite limited communities (partly of Egyptian personnel) on local land. There was a shortage of labour for building them; the viceroy Setau had to raid the nearby oases to round up the local south-Libyans there and press-gang them into the labour of building Wadi es-Sebua temple, for example.[10]

As a result, Lower Nubia became almost totally depopulated by *ca.* 1100 BC,[11] while many of the gold-mines were also becoming exhausted. Finally, under Ramesses XI, the viceroy Panehsy rebelled, holding this skeletal realm for himself; neither Herihor nor Piankh (the new rulers of Upper Egypt until 1070 BC) could dislodge him. With his and their eclipse, Egypt's rule ended southward at Aswan, while Lower Nubia below the 2nd Cataract remained an empty land. In Upper Nubia, Egyptian rule may have been less crushing, but here too there is no flourishing culture to benefit from Egyptian withdrawal after 1100 BC. In this first zone, history went to sleep for several centuries, until at last it again became a regular link-route between Egypt and Upper Nubia (and beyond) under the 25th Dynasty (originating from Kush) in the late 8th and early 7th centuries BC. So, Nubia itself was a blank cypher during the 10th century BC, which is our main concern.

---

[10] See J. Yoyotte, "Un document relatif aux rapports de la Libye et de la Nubie," *Bulletin de la Société Française d'Egyptologie* 6 (April 1951) 9-14, pls. 1-2; more accessible in K. A. Kitchen, *Pharaoh Triumphant: Life and Times of Ramesses II* (Warminster: Aris & Phillips; Missisauga: Benben Books, 1982) 136-38.

[11] On the archaeology and cultural history of ancient Nubia, the most comprehensive account is still that of W. Y. Adams, *Nubia: Corridor to Africa* (London: Allen Lane, Penguin, 1977, for this period (New Kingdom), see pp. 229-45, especially pp. 235ff.

B. *Middle Nile / Red Sea Zone*

Here the documentation is more tantalising, but marginally closer to the 10th century Levant. Within this large region, we may now safely place two important entities from just before our period, Punt and ʿAmaw (as well as others much later); Punt being the more famous. Egypt's pharaohs sent expeditions to Punt for many centuries, from *ca.* 2500 BC until *ca.* 1170 BC, in quest of myrrh, incense, gold and exotica (e.g., panther skins). These went via the Red Sea down to the latitude of Port Sudan and Suakin, before striking inland to reach the aromatics growing in an area near the modern Sudan/Ethiopia border southwest towards Kassala and Roseires. The location of Punt is now reasonably fixed by the following factors.[12] 1) Queen Hatshepsut's ships sail to Punt over a sea inhabited by marine life typical of the Red Sea and the Indian Ocean, *not* of the Nile. 2) The fauna of Punt is East African (e.g., giraffes, rhinos, hamadryas baboons). 3) Rains that fell on the mountains of Punt drained into the Nile; they must therefore have fallen on some part of the east and/or north sides of the Ethiopian mountain massif for this to happen. 4) With this ties in the facts about ʿAmaw. Gold of ʿAmaw reached Egypt both via her southernmost Nubian borders (4th Cataract region) and through trade with Punt. If ʿAmaw occupied the area directly east of the Abu Hamed bend of the Nile, and southward between the Nile and the Red Sea mountains, being directly north of the terrain of Punt, then the gold (known in this particular area even today) could readily have been traded west/north into Egyptian-held Kush and south/east via Punt to Egyptian traders there.[13]

Before our period, Egypt's major expeditions to Punt are known under Queen Hatshepsut (*ca.* 1471 BC), just possibly under Sethos I (*ca.* 1290 BC) and Ramesses II (13th century BC), and finally under Ramesses III (*ca.* 1170 BC). In reverse, the Puntites ran their own missions by boat to

[12] For fuller studies of the location, see R. Herzog, *Punt* (Glückstadt: Augustin, 1968), confirmed and corrected by K. A. Kitchen, "Punt and How to Get There," *Or* ns 41 (1971) 184-207; R. Fattovich, "The Problem of Punt in the Light of Recent Field Work in the Eastern Sudan," *Akten des vierten Internationalen Ägyptologen Kongresses, München 1985* (Hamburg: Buske, 1993) 4.257-72; K. A. Kitchen, "The Land of Punt," *The Archaeology of Africa* (eds. T. Shaw and others; London: Routledge, 1993) 587-608, especially pp. 603-04.

[13] Some would place ʿAmaw inside the desert bend of the Nile between the 3rd and 4th Cataracts; references, see K. Zibelius, *Afrikanische Orts- und Völkernamen in hieroglyphischen und hieratischen Texten* (Wiesbaden: Reichert, 1972) 99, with references. But this does not accord either with the independent status of ʿAmaw as a gold-source or with its contiguity with Punt.

Egypt up the Red Sea (and possibly also down the Nile[14]) under Tuthmosis III and Amenophis II and III, Akhenaten and Haremhab (globally *ca.* 1360-1300 BC), and quite possibly in the 13th century BC. But after *ca.* 1170 BC, Punt disappears from history and is never again either the aim or the source of aromatics expeditions from or to Egypt. Some 200 years later, in Solomon's time, we have mention of his and Hiram's expeditions down the Red Sea to Ophir (see following chapter). Some centuries later still we have evidence in Northern Eritrea/Northeastern Ethiopia for a kingdom of Di'amat, dependency of the Sabaeans of southwest Arabia, founded not later than the 5th century BC (and possibly in the 7th) and in turn disappearing from sight (and history?) not earlier than *ca.* 340 BC. During the Hellenistic Period (in Mediterranean terms) is another historical gap, until the rise of the kingdom of Axum, *ca.* 50-700 AD.[15]

However, the seeming historical gaps in this zone during *ca.* 1170-600/500 BC and *ca.* 340 BC-50 AD are *not* real cultural gaps (like that in Lower Nubia, *ca.* 1100-700 BC). Archaeology is beginning to paint in a picture of material cultures in this zone, during these periods which are historically opaque solely because we lack written documentation for them there. The beginnings of extensive work in (e.g.) the Gash Delta region in Sudan (northwest, west and southwest of Kassala) in parts of North Eritrea and through to the Red Sea coast (e.g., at Aqiq) show a long sequence of cultures from the 5th millennium BC into medieval times. Thus, the late Butana, later Gash and Agordat groups come down in time towards *ca.* 1000 BC, while the Jebel Mokram group runs through from *ca.* 1400 BC down to *ca.* 500 BC, well spanning our 10th century BC period. The eclipse of Punt in the 12th century BC may be partly due to climatic factors (some dessication then), as well as the inability of the Egyptian rulers to mount state expeditions to Punt after Ramesses III. However, in Eritrea, the Ona Culture A persisted through from the late 2nd millennium BC well into the 1st millennium BC, easily spanning our period. Thus, there were tribal groups in the Punt/ 'Amaw area whose way of life (alongside foreign trade) embraced basically both pastoral and agricultural modes of life, but in varying propor-

---

[14] On which option, see L. Bradbury, "*Kpn*-boats, Punt Trade and a Lost Emporium," *JARCE* 33 (1996) 37-60.

[15] For discussion of dates of rulers of Di'amat and Axum respectively (with references to primary data) and lists of kings, see K. A. Kitchen, *Documentation for Ancient Arabia* (Liverpool: University of Liverpool, 1994) 1.115-17, 39-41, and lists 10A, 10B.

tions depending on locations and climatic variations through time.[16]

C. *Sudan / Ethiopia / Somalia*

Here we reach the outermost zone of relevance to our main subject. The inland areas of Southern Sudan (south of the confluence of the White and Blue Niles) lie beyond Levantine, Egyptian or Old-Arabian contacts, as does much of Ethiopia;[17] Somalia is largely *terra incognita*, archaeologically.[18]

4. Egypt and East Africa in Relation to Solomon's Reign

Here we must see what may be learned from bringing together the available data from Egypt and East Africa and from our biblical texts for an integrated overview. In regard to Egypt, this falls under two heads: explicit, and possible implicit features. The former covers the clear examples of relations with Egypt offered by the biblical texts; the latter deals with features in those texts in which modern scholars have thought to detect Egyptian impact.

A. *Explicit Links*

The chronologically earliest direct reference is a multiple one. In 1 Kgs 9:16, a mere aside remarks that a pharaoh of Egypt had attacked Gezer and burnt it (in part, at least) and given this fief as a present (or dowry) to Solomon along with his daughter in marriage. From an earlier, "mainline" reference (1 Kgs 3:1), we are told that in fact Solomon and this

[16] See in particular, R. Fattovich, "Problem of Punt," (note 12 above), and his papers, "The Peopling of the Northern Ethiopian-Sudanese Borderland between 7000 and 1000 BP: A Preliminary Model," *Nubica* 1-2 (1990) 3-45; and "Punt: The Archaeological Perspective," *Sesto Congresso Internazionale di Egittologia, Atti* (Turin: Turin Egyptian Museum, 1993) 2.399-405; plus that of K. Sadr and S. Vitagliano, "Society and Territory in the Gash Delta (Kassala, Eastern Sudan) 3000 BC—AD 300/400," *Origini* 14 (1988-1989) 329-57. These papers contain a wealth of further bibliography.

[17] Some Egyptian pieces here, see J. Phillips, "Egyptian and Nubian Material from Ethiopia and Eritrea," *Sudan Archaeological Research Society Newsletter* 9 (November 1995) 2-10.

[18] See, for example, summary presentations for East Africa by D. W. Phillipson in *The Archaeology of Africa* (eds. T. Shaw and others; London: Routledge, 1993) 344-57; and *idem*, *African Archaeology* (2nd ed.; Cambridge: Cambridge University, 1994).

generous pharaoh had made an alliance, such that this marriage was clearly a political one of a kind long familiar in the ancient Near East. This all occurred before Solomon had finished building either his own palace or the Temple of YHWH, or Jerusalem's walls. As the Temple's building took up the 7 years from Solomon's 4th to 11th years (1 Kgs 6:1, 37-38), then on the dates used here, this alliance and scuffle over Gezer would have fallen within *ca.* 967-960 BC, at a median estimate either side of about 965/964 BC. As there is no rational reason[19] to deny a 14/15-year reign to Psusennes II (at *ca.* 960/959-945 BC) immediately prior to the reign of Shoshenq I, it is all but certain that these oft-remarked events fell in fact into the reign of the previous ruler Siamun (*ca.* 979/978-960/959 BC). It is significant that the *only* trace of bellicose activity so far bequeathed to us by the kings of the 21st Dynasty is, precisely, the fragment of a triumph-scene from a monument of Siamun. Alongside Psusennes I (who reigned twice as long), Siamun in any case was the most active ruler of his line, with buildings of some importance at both Tanis and Memphis for example. That scene shows the ritual dispatch of a foe seemingly clutching an Aegean-type "double-axe," which (not unnaturally) has been associated with the Philistines, as having come from that general area. This is not certain, but is reasonable.[20]

It stands to reason that no pharaoh ever invaded Palestine with the sole purpose of reducing the town of Gezer; this episode has to be simply the end-point of a larger enterprise. Between Northeast Sinai (Egypt's extreme northeastern frontier) and Gezer there was then to be found the "pentapolis" of the Philistines. They were a thorn in the side of the Hebrew kingdom and may have been rivals in sea-trade (or adept at charging transit-tolls, overland?) to the disapproval of Egypt. Thus, Egypt and Israel may have combined to humble the Philistine pentarchy to their own mutual profit. A treaty was drawn up; Siamun then invaded Philistia (on whatever pretext) up to Gezer; Solomon might even have staged a "feint" action in that quarter to distract the Philistine commanders, caught between two seeming "fronts." At any rate, the allies had

[19] Spurious earlier attempts to overlap Psusennes II with Shoshenq I were factually refuted in Kitchen, *Third Intermediate*, pp. xix-xxii, §§O-S; G. Hagens's attempt to repeat this error is equally ill-founded, on the same data; "A Critical Review of Dead-Reckoning from the 21st Dynasty," *JARCE* 33 (1996) 153-65.

[20] No convincing alternative has been produced. The scene was published by P. Montet, *Les constructions et le tombeau d'Osorkon II à Tanis* (Paris: Jourde et Allard, 1947) pl. 9A; for other references see Kitchen, *Third Intermediate*, pp. 280, n. 222 and p. 574 §506.

success; the pact was sealed by an inter-dynastic marriage and Gezer passed to Solomon.

The matter of such a marriage has also attracted much comment, if only because in the New Kingdom (*ca.* 1430-1230 BC) it was common enough for the great imperial pharaohs to accept foreign ladies in this way, but never to reciprocate. Amenophis III was very clear and firm on this matter and the example of Ankhesenamun (Tutankhamun's widow) endeavouring to gain a Hittite prince for her second royal husband and new king in Egypt shows why: marriage to the heiress did give claim to that throne. But that was almost 300 years before Siamun and Solomon. Times had changed, as well as dynasties. Seemingly, the 21st and 22nd/23rd Dynasties had (by their practice) a different attitude. Far from shunning commoners and foreigners, these kings married-off their spare daughters quite freely, from Maatkare, daughter of Psusennes II, to the Libyan prince Osorkon, and onwards.[21] So Siamun's marriage-alliance with the Hebrew monarchy is not so suprising at this later epoch. Given the inner weakness of Egypt's political structure (a *de facto* dyarchy), a limited "police-action" type of conflict not too far from home was probably as much as even the shrewd Siamun was prepared to undertake.

Also in Siamun's reign would have fallen the return to Edom of its heir-apparent, Hadad (following the death of David by 970 BC; 1 Kgs 11:14-22). Here the pharaoh, again, is portrayed as having a friendly relationship with West-Semitic royalty, embodied also in a royal marriage with a sister of the then Egyptian queen. So there is consistency in the Egyptian policy of the period.[22]

The remaining explicit political relationship was of a very different colour, in the latter half of Solomon's reign. At that time Shoshenq I (*ca.* 945 BC) established his own fresh regime in Egypt and things changed considerably (see section 2). He clearly saw Solomon's realm as an obstacle and rival to his own ambitions (not an ally) and acted accordingly. Thus we learn that he harboured Jeroboam when the latter fled into Egypt from Solomon's wrath (1 Kgs 11:40). But we read of no more marriage-alliances, not even with this intended opponent to Solomon. The climax came within 5 years of Solomon's death, when Shoshenq I finally invaded the two rump-kingdoms and brought them both to heel (1 Kgs 14:25-26; 2 Chr 12:1-9).

If one scrutinises both the Egyptian data and the biblical texts, there is

[21] Full list of 15/16 examples, see *Ibid.*, p. 282, and table 12, pp. 479, 594.

[22] For further details, *ibid.*, pp. 273-75, 280.

the outline of a consistency in this profile of changing relations in our two groups of sources. In the biblical books, we first see the unnamed pharaoh who was prepared to take circumscribed military action in a zone closest to home and saw advantages in an alliance with his strongest Levantine neighbor; he was very loth to lose the company of an Edomite prince at his court. A generation later, an entirely different and named king (Shishak) viewed Israel as a rival, welcomed an important dissident thereform and (by readily sending him back the moment Solomon died, to head opposition to his successor) helped engineer the break-up of that kingdom into two fragments that he could readily dominate militarily. Turning to the Egyptian data, Siamun's triumph-scene was executed on a modest scale, being incorporated in his overall building-work at the great temple of Amun at Tanis, without any special emphasis laid on it. No other such traces of triumphal scenes by Siamun have so far been found, as at once-imperial Thebes or in the scattered wreckage of Memphis. In strong contrast, Shoshenq I and his flying columns clearly swept through almost the whole length and width of Palestine (even penetrating beyond the Jordan) and he left at least one victory-monument on Israelite soil (at Megiddo).[23] Back in Egypt, he swiftly arranged to maximise the impact of his campaign. *His* triumphal relief at Amun's Karnak temple is a vast tableau of truly imperial dimensions that more than bears comparison with those nearby of the Empire pharaohs themselves of 300 years before. It was part of an entire architectural scheme, for a great forecourt to Amun's temple (with long lateral colonnades) which was half as big again in area[24] as the famed Hypostyle Hall of Sethos I and Ramesses II, no less. And with it, as an integral part of this vast scheme, went the so-called Bubastite Gate and the adjoining triumphal relief.[25] This needs to be emphasised for reasons of dating. The great Stela 100 at Gebel Silsila dates to Year 21 of Shoshenq I (*ca*. 925 BC) and commemorates the quarrying for, and com-

[23] For convenience, see concerning most details, discussion, maps and references, *ibid*, pp. 294-302, fig. 2; 432-47, figs. 8-9; p. xlvi end. Very recent discussion of the list, J. Currid, *Ancient Egypt and the Old Testament* (Grand Rapids: Baker Book House, 1997) chapter 10.

[24] See any good plan of Karnak; for example, B. Porter and R. L. B. Moss, eds., *Topographical Bibliography of Ancient Egyptian Hieroglyphic Texts, Reliefs and Paintings* (2nd ed.; Oxford: Clarendon, 1970) 2.plan 4 at end

[25] This is very clear from the layout of the court, of which the Bubastite Gate with its two columns is an integral part, as is the masonry of the relief indivisible from that of the Gate. See the key-plan in the Epigraphic Survey, *Reliefs and Inscriptions at Karnak, III: The Bubastite Portal* (Chicago: University of Chicago, 1954) sheet before plates.

mencement of, these great works at Karnak (see Excursus §A). Thus the basic building of the court's sidewalls and colonnades, of the Bubastite Gate and continguous masonry that bears the triumph-scene were *not* begun before Year 21. These works are all more or less unfinished: the great court's colonnades are all left in rough masonry to this day, Shoshenq I never finished decorating the Bubastite Gate (nor did his successors) and only the great relief was left virtually complete. This is clear evidence of his death soon after Year 21 (probably well into Year 22). And there is no reason whatsoever to imagine that he waited very long after his victory in Palestine to celebrate it monumentally; no other pharaoh did! Thus, Year 20 is still the earliest-likely date for his campaign; the Silsila stela's date (in 2nd month of Shomu) would fall about February, probably only 8 or 9 months after the Palestine campaign of the summer just past. A separate stela reported the genesis of the conflict, while a new temple at El-Hibeh up north also had a once-splendid triumphal scene of the highest level of workmanship. Thus the contrast in actions and attitudes of the two successive Egyptian regimes can be seen mirrored in both the Egyptian and biblical records; this is the product of first-hand monumental evidence in Egypt and of genuine and original (and detailed) historical data transmitted in the written sources used by Kings and Chronicles, not a dream-world invented by novelists in the Persian epoch.

B. *Possible Implicit Links*

Here we shall be brief on already well-aired matters simply to round off the Egyptian angle. First, much has sometimes been made of possible links between Egyptian and Hebrew instructional wisdom literature, the most acute instance being that of a possible link between the Egyptian Instruction of Amenemope and Proverbs, two sections of which (being books in themselves) bear titles linking them to Solomon, the first (Prov 1-24) indicating contemporaneity and the second (Prov 25-29) classed as a posthumous collection. In terms of date, a 21st-Dynasty ostracon, plus other aspects of the work, would date Amenemope to not later than *ca.* 1000 BC and more likely the early 12th century BC. So, chronologically, in any case, his work could in principle be one of any number of precursors on whom a 10th century (or later) Hebrew writer might have drawn; note the allusions to "words of the wise" (Prov 22:17) and "these also are words of the wise" (Prov 24:23), explicitly drawing upon antecedent observations by others. When thoroughly analysed along with those of the other 40 or so such works from Egypt, Mesopotamia, Hatti and West Semitic sources, the basic literary structures of Proverbs 1-24 ("Solomon 1") indicate clearly that it is a transitional work, standing between the typical productions of the 2nd millennium BC and those clearly of the early to mid 1st millennium BC; that is, a 10th-century date would be optimum.[26]

Quite a different sphere is that of royal administration. It has been fashionable to compare Solomon's arrangements for 12 district-governors to provide supplies for the royal palace on a monthly rota from their respective districts (1 Kgs 4:7-19, 27-28) with superficially similar phenomena in Egypt.[27] However, the fact remains that use of the month as a convenient unit for financial arrangements was well-nigh universal in antiquity (and many still look for their monthy salary-statements even today!). So, a borrowing here between Egypt and Israel in either direction cannot be argued merely on periodicity. And, in fact, there is nothing else in common between the monthly offering of a bull in a subsidiary cult in Heracleopolis in distant middle Egypt and running an entire Levantine palace/government administration under Solomon. One may as well derive the US Federal tax system from the budgeting-methods of some minor church in an out-of-the-way English country town (or vice-versa)! In fact, the best sources for Solomon's system come from the Levant itself, visible at Ugarit and still earlier at Ebla.[28] On the other hand, both Egypt and the Near East provide illuminating comparative data for assessing the scale of Solomon's daily palace/government sup-

---

[26] The basic factual evidence for this was clearly set out by K. A. Kitchen, "Proverbs and Wisdom Books of the Ancient Near East: The Factual History of a Literary Form," *TynBul* 28 (1977-1978) 69-114, and *Idem*, "The Basic Literary Forms and Formulations of Ancient Instructional Writings in Egypt and Western Asia," *Studien zu altägyptischen Lebenslehren* (eds. E. Hornung and O. Keel; OBO 28; Freiburg: Universitätsverlag; Göttingen: Vandenhoeck & Rupprecht, 1979) 235-82. The attempted critique of the Near-Eastern material in an otherwise attractive book by S. Weeks, *Early Israelite Wisdom* (Oxford: Clarendon, 1994), is wholly vitiated by its author's lack of knowledge of the original data; see K. A. Kitchen, "Biblical Instructional Wisdom: The Decisive Voice of the Ancient Near East," *Studies Gordon* (in press).

[27] Borrowing from Egypt to Solomon, credit first goes to D. B. Redford, "Studies in Relations between Palestine and Egypt during the First Millennium B.C.: The Taxation System of Solomon," *Studies on the Ancient Palestinian World Presented to F. V. Winnett* (eds. J. W. Weavers and D. B. Redford; Toronto: Toronoto University, 1972) 141-56, especially 153-56; borrowing from Solomon to Egypt proposed by A. R. Green, "Israelite Influence at Shishak's Court?" *BASOR* 233 (1979) 59-62, especially 61.

[28] Fuller discussion and detailed references in K. A. Kitchen, "Egypt and Israel During the First Millennium B.C.," *Congress Volume: Jerusalem, 1986* (ed. J. Emerton; VTSup 40; Leiden: E. J. Brill, 1988) 116-17.

plies (1 Kgs 4:22-23), well rivalling him in expenditures.[29] And intermittently attempts have been made to equate official ranks and posts in the Hebrew court with those known in Egypt, but here again closer scrutiny tends to show that these comparisons are largely illusory.[30] Much more striking is the case of a Hebrew scribe in the Sinai/Negev area incorporating high-value Egyptian hieratic numeral-signs into his practice-accounts on an ostracon.[31] This at least shows a limited cross-cultural contact for practical purposes in administrative matters.

C. *East Africa*

Here we have an altogether more limited sphere of reference. The term Kush is well-attested in the Old Testament for the Nile-lands in Northeast Africa south from Egypt proper, being in practice the Kush of the Egyptian sources, covering both Wawat and Kush proper, the northern and southern halves of "Nubia." But none of the Hebrew mentions refer specifically to the 10th century BC.

A matter for debate is the location of the land of Ophir, whence gold came to Solomon in his Red Sea maritime enterprises with Hiram of Tyre (1 Kgs 10:11). The likeliest locations would be either in Western Arabia (south of Medina to north of Hawlan) or in East Africa (East Sudan, area of former ʿAmaw and Punt).[32] An Ophir in Western Arabia would have been close to the camel-caravan route that mattered so much to Sheba; so Tyrian/Hebrew intervention there might well have stimulated the kind of Sabaean response that is exemplified by the episode of the queen of Sheba. But Tyrian/Hebrew exploration in East Sudan on the other side of the Red Sea would hardly have had any impact, unless the Sabaeans themselves had already penetrated that area. Such penetration is not so far proven for the 10th century BC (lack of historical sources), although it would have been possible. It is more economical in hypotheses, at present, not to assume such Sabaean penetration until we have some worthwhile data from this barely-explored region.

[29] For details see, for example, M. Heltzer, *The Rural Community in Ancient Ugarit* (Wiesbaden: Reichert, 1976) 39-40; K. A. Kitchen, "Food," *NBD*, pp. 431-32; and *idem*, *Ramesside Inscriptions, Translated and Annotated: Notes and Comments* (Oxford: Blackwell, 1993) 1.162-76, especially p. 175; with translations, *idem*, *Ramesside Inscriptions, Translated and Annotated: Translations* (Oxford: Blackwell, 1993) 1.208-19.

[30] Full discussion in Kitchen, " Egypt and Israel," pp. 111-15 (n. 28 above).

[31] R. Cohen, "Did I Excavate Kadesh Barnea?" *BAR* 7 (May-June 1981) 20-33, especially 26-28, with good illustrations.

[32] For the arguments *pro* and *con*, see the following chapter on Arabia.

The other remaining possibility is that the further destination reached by ships of Hiram and Solomon (beyond Ophir) was African, or included African ports-of-call *en route*, going or returning (see chapter following). Thence came gold, silver, ivory, apes and baboons. Except for the silver, all of these could well have come from East Africa; the silver may bespeak a more remote final port-of-call. Further, in the present state of knowledge, we cannot profitably go.

EXCURSUS

TEXTS OF SHOSHENQ I AT KARNAK

A. *Main Part of Text of Silsilah Stela 100*

After the full titulary of Shoshenq I, we may read:

I. Royal and Princely Introductions

[34]He has undertaken opening-up the quarry anew, for beginning works, made by the Son of Re, Shoshenq I Beloved-of-Amun, who has made monuments for his father Amen-Re, Lord of the Thrones of the Two Lands, that he [=king] might achieve the jubilees of Re [35]and the years of Atum, and living forever. (The King says): "My good Lord, may you grant that people who shall come for millions of years (hence) will say, "It is worthwhile to serve Amun!' May you be agreeable to accord me a great reign!"

[36]He has undertaken opening-up the quarry anew, for beginning works, made by the High Priest of Amen-Re King of the Gods, Generalissimo and Army-leader, Iuput, justified, [37]who is leader of the great army of all Upper Egypt, the King's Son of the Lord of the Two Lands Shoshenq I Beloved-of-Amun, for his lord, for Amen-Re King of the Gods, who has wrought for him life, prosperity and health, a long lifespan, valour [38]and victory, and a high old age in dominion. (Iuput says:) "My good Lord, may you grant that people who shall come for a million years (hence) will say, 'It is worthwhile to serve Amun!' May you be agreeable to accord me valour and victory!"

II. Dated Commission of the Architect

[39]Year 21, 2nd month of Shomu <Day 1>. On this day, His majesty was (at) the Residence of [40]Pi-Ese, the great Spirit of Re-Horakhti. His Majesty commanded to [41]give a charge to the God's Father of Amen-Re King of the Gods, Chief of Secrets of [42]the Temple of Re-Horakhti and Superintendent of all monuments of the Lord of the Two Lands, (even) Haremsaf, [43]justified, to exempt and protect any work south of Sobek, of the [44]choice quarry of Silsila, in order to make great and mighty monuments for the temple of his august [45]father, Amen-Re, Lord of the Thrones of the Two Lands.

It was His Majesty who gave directives, to build great and mighty pylon-towers ⌜of stone⌝ (?), to illumine the City [=Thebes], [47]in setting up for him doors of a million cubits; to make a festival court [48]for the temple of his father, Amen-Re King of the Gods; and to surround it with statues and a colonnade.

[49]Returning in peace from the Southern City [=Thebes, to where His Majesty was, by the God's Father of Amen-Re [50]King of the Gods, Chief of Secrets of the Temple of Re-Horakhti and Superintendent of Works in the Foundation of Hedjkheperre [=Shoshenq I] in Thebes, [51]greatly loved in the presence of his master who performs the ritual (even) the Lord of the Two Lands, Haremsaf, [52]justified. He says (i.e., to the king):

"All things that you have spoken of, they are coming to pass, O my [53]good Lord, with no sleeping by night and no [54]dozing by day, but they build eternal work [55]unwearingly!"

Favours were given by the King—he [=Haremsaf] was rewarded with goods of [56]silver and gold; his able offspring, the priest Paheqanufer who (also) makes monuments for Amun; [57]may he rival him!

B. *Part of the Main Address by Amun to Shoshenq I, Over the Great Topographical List at Karnak*

After a poetic welcoming praise of the king's valour in fairly conventional terms, the deity is made to say:

[11]"My heart is gladdened, (for) I have seen your victories, [12]my son Shoshenq, my beloved, [13]who came forth [14]from me, [15]to be my champion!

I perceive that your plans are beneficial, and you have produced benefactions for my temple. You have established my Theban [shrine?], and the Great Seat whereon my heart dwells.

[16]You have begun to make monuments in Southern On [=Thebes] and in Northern On [=Heliopolis], and (in) every city likewise, for (each) god in his province. You have made my Mansion of Millions of Years, and the [?furnishing]s in it of electrum for my [image?] [17]therein."

The rest of this text returns to a poetical and highly rhetorical celebration of the king's valour and victory. These two texts are Shoshenq I's own statement about his great enterprise at Karnak.

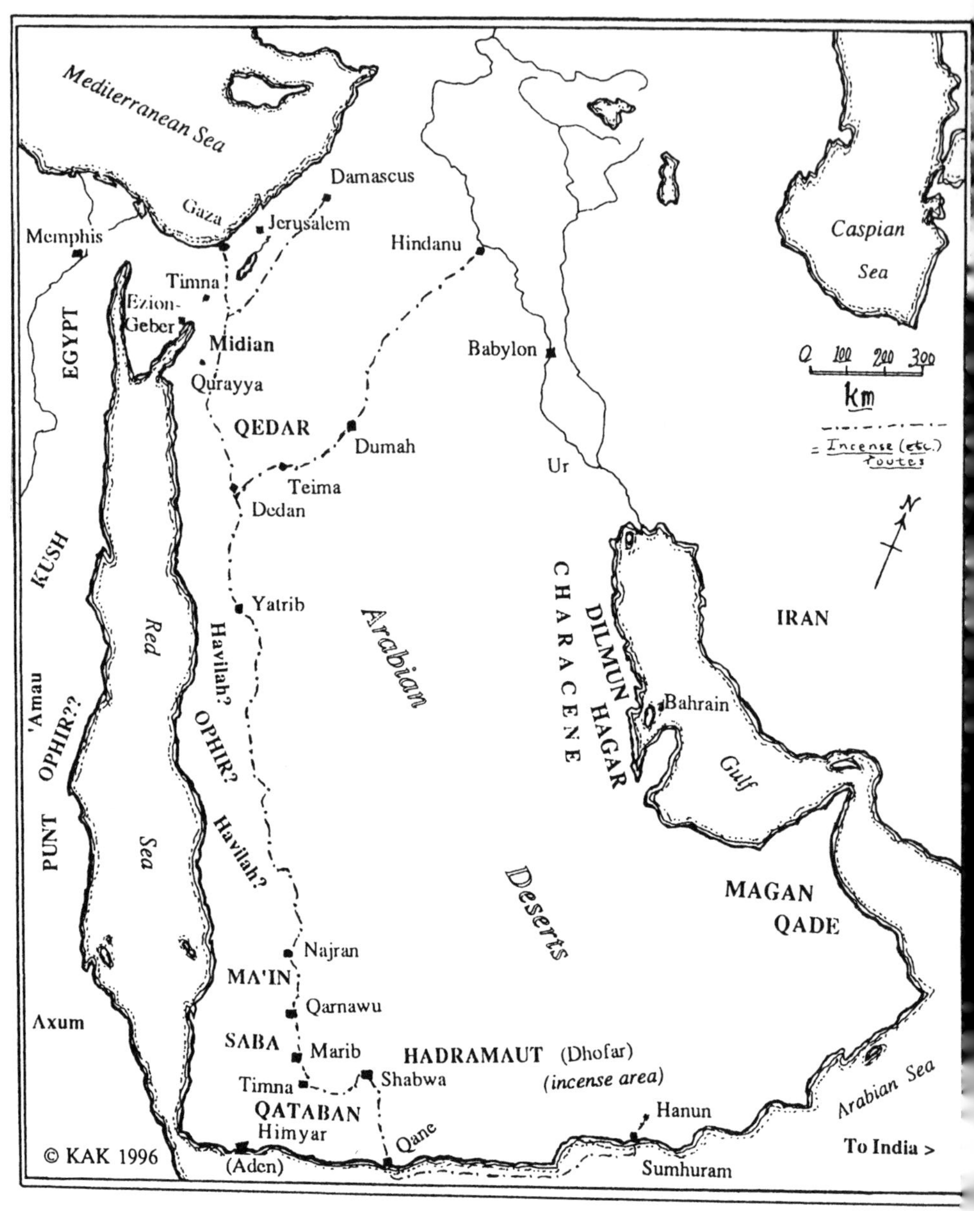

ANCIENT ARABIA *and* ENVIRONS

Map 2.

SHEBA AND ARABIA

Kenneth A. Kitchen

1. The Setting

The vast rectangle of Arabia is bounded sharply on three sides by seas: Red Sea (west), the Persian Gulf (east), and Arabian Sea/Indian Ocean (south). Only on the north does it merge into Syria-Palestine and Mesopotamia. Many people imagine this great rectangle to be simply desert, and most of it is. But both in the south-west (Yemen) and south-east corners (Oman), there are rugged mountains and (in SW) upland plateaus which receive monsoon-related rainfall. This creates a luxuriant vegetation, and permits a settled way of life. An ancient water-table under the Arabian massif supplies the basic resource for oases and wells in more desertic regions.

In preislamic antiquity, there were in practice two Arabias, culturally and historically: East and West, divided from each other by the vast sweep of stony desert and dunes, from the Nafud in the north down to the Rub al-Khali in the south. Eastern Arabia saw the rise and fall of a series of kingdoms along the west side of the Gulf: Dilmun (E. Arabia and Bahrain) and Magan (UAE and NW Oman) from the 3rd to early 1st millennium BC, followed by Hagar and Qade (later 1st millennium), then by Characene (Hellenistic to later Roman times). These do not further concern us here. In the present work, it is the cultures and kingdoms of the west side of Arabia, from southern Jordan to Yemen inclusive, upon which we must focus.

2. The Physical and Economic Basis

a) *Who was who*

During the latter part of the 19th century to the present, intrepid early explorers and modern archaeologists alike have discovered a considerable number of Old Semitic inscriptions in a distinctive form of the alphabet, ranging in broad terms (as we now know) from about 1000 BC to about 570 AD, in and around Yemen. These exhibit four main dialects, from the ancient states of Saba, Maʾin, Qataban and Hadramaut, then from the dual monarchy of Saba and Dhu-Raydan (1st to 3rd centuries AD), then from the all-inclusive Himyarite "empire" (3rd to 6th centuries AD). The overwhelming majority of these texts are Sabean. The term "Saba" corresponds to the "Sheba" mentioned as an Arabian entity in the Hebrew Old Testament: i) in technically undated contexts ("Table of Nations", Gen. 10:7,28 = 1 Chron. 1:9,22; Job 6:19) and brief patriarchal reference (Gen. 25:3 = 1 Chron. 1:32); ii) a realm whence came a "queen of Sheba" to Solomon (1 Kings 10 = 2 Chron. 9; reflex, Ps. 72:10-15); iii) a land whence came merchants (incense, gold, etc.) in the traditionally 7th-6th century prophets (Isaiah 60:6; Jer. 6:20; Ezek. 27:22,23, 38:13).

The identity of Hebrew Sheba and SW Arabian Saba is paralleled by the identity of Itamru the Sabean mentioned by Sargon II in 715 BC and of Karibi-ilu, king of Saba, listed by Sennacherib in 685 BC, with rulers of Saba in the Yemenite texts called Yithaʾamar and Karibil (though which ones of several Yithaʾamars and Karibils is a matter of opinion). Hence, the distant realm of Sheba in the Hebrew record is to be understood as the Saba of Yemen. That there was ever another Saba up in NW Arabia is excluded: i) positively by the existence of a totally-different series of kingdoms there, leaving no room for a theoretical northern Saba, and ii) negatively by the *total absence* of any clearly Sabean inscriptions, in stark contrast with (*e.g.*) Minean texts and local Qedarite, Dedanite, Taymanite, Lihyanite and other inscriptions. So, our understanding of the nature and workings of ancient Sheba is tied to that of Saba in Yemen.

b) *Home-based economics*

In modern literature, Yemeni Saba is above all famous for the trade in incense, other aromatics and suchlike exotic products. But this was never the real basis of the lifestyle of the ancient Sabean state and its communities, nor of the related kingdoms, as recent work has amply shown.

By the 10th century BC, Western Arabia had already had a long development; a fact only revealed in the last decade or so. Work on the Yemeni plateau west from Marib has produced a SW Arabian "Neolithic Age" of small settlements, at least of pastoralists, succeeded by a

"Bronze Age" of the 3rd and 2nd millennia BC (using pottery; some metal as well as stone tools), parallel in time with the Early/Middle/Late Bronze Ages of the Levant further north. By then, agriculture was well developed, with settlements along the sides of wadis (valleys), each with its extent of fields and satellite hamlets, as an economic, social and local-political unit; a world of largely independent "tribal" communities, probably each under a local chief, as is clear in later centuries, when texts are available to tell us explicitly.[1] Meantime, at Marib, something much more ambitious arose. The Wadi Dhana debouched out of the local mountain (Jabal Balaq) eastwards, with its twice-annual water-floods (the *sayl*), bringing water and sediment on which food-crops might be grown. By the late 3rd millennum BC (it appears), the rulers of the local settlement at Marib had already learned to divert the waters regularly onto areas of field adjoining the north and south banks of the wadi and then began to build distributive structures of massive stone ashlar blocks to direct the floods into canals and lesser channels over the two areas of fields. As the sediments rose, new "deflectors" had to be built in the early and then the mid 2nd millennium BC, and then in about the 10th century BC, again in the 6th to 4th centuries BC, and by the turn of the era.[2] The sophistication of the hydraulic planning, massiveness of the stone structures, and very large scope of the irrigated area thus created and maintained show clearly that in Marib from *ca.* 2300 down to *ca.* 940 BC (Schmidt's dates), we are dealing with a highly-organised poli-

[1] For the "Neolithic" and Bronze ages, cf. for simple summaries (with references), F. G. Fedele, "North Yemen: The Neolithic," and A. de Maigret, "The Yemeni Bronze Age,"*Yemen, 3000 Years of Art and Civilisation in Arabia Felix* (ed. W. Daum; Innsbruck: Pinguin; Frankfurt am-Main: Umschau, 1987) 34-37, 38-40 respectively, and 41-43 pls. In fuller detail, cf. A. de Maigret and others, *The Bronze Age Culture of Hawlan at-Tiyal and Al-Hada* (Rome: IsMEO, 1990).

[2] Summary, J. Schmidt, "The Sabaean Irrigation Economy of Mārib," *Yemen, 3000 Years of Art and Civilisation in Arabia Felix* (ed. W. Daum; Innsbruck: Pinguin; Frankfurt am-Main: Umschau, 1987) 55-62, and cf. K. A. Kitchen, *Documentation for Ancient Arabia,* I (Liverpool: Liverpool University, 1994) 128-32, for a critical summary. Full reports, see U. Brunner, *Archäologische Berichte aus dem Yemen* (Mainz: Philipp von Zabern, 1983), 2.1-134, pls. 1-19; I. Hehmeyer & J. Schmidt, W. Wagner, and M. Schaloske (respectively), in *ibid.,* 5(1991), 1-112, pls. 1-12, *ibid.,* 6(1993), 1-99, pls. 1-10, and *ibid.,* 7(1995), 1-177, pls. 1-19. Good summary of ancient agricultural techniques at Marib, and their archaeological traces, cf. I. Hehmeyer, "Irrigation Farming in the Ancient Oasis of Mārib," *Proceedings of the Seminar for Arabian Studies* 19 (1989) 33-44. First serious account of Old-South-Arabian irrigation-agriculture, see R. LeBaron Bowen, "Irrigation in Ancient Qatabân (Beiḥan)," *Archaeological Discoveries in South Arabia,* (ed. R. LeBaron Bowen and others; American Foundation for the Study of Man 2; Baltimore: Johns Hopkins University, 1958) 43-131 (including illustrations).

ty, masters of agricultural engineering, not with some primitive village chiefdom. In short, by the end of the 2nd millennium BC, we have at least a modest-scale state centred on Marib well before the 10th century BC, and probably already to be considered "Sabean," in view of the clear technical continuity in its irrigational engineering. It was probably the most advanced of such irrigation-based polities in SW Arabia, and was thus able to take the lead in new developments when they came.

Before tackling those developments, what was happening up in NW Arabia? Here, the picture before the 13th century BC is far less clear, mainly because intensive archaeological work remains to be done, to follow up the the great preliminary surveys. Life must largely have centred on the artesian oases of Al-ʿUla (ancient Dedan), Tabuk, Teima, Jawf (ancient Dumah) and others, and upon seasonal pasturage heavily dependent on the vagaries of climate; some traces of "Chalcolithic" and Early Bronze Age (down to early 2nd millennium BC) can be established,[3] but only modestly, and very little until *ca.* 1300 BC, when new developments brought a stimulus.

c) *New horizons*

The 13th and 12th centuries BC witnessed many changes in the Ancient Near East. The new 19th (or Ramesside) Dynasty gave fresh impetus to Egypt's involvement in the Levant. Thus, Sethos I (*ca.* 1294-1279 BC) reaffirmed Egypt's control over Canaan and much of Phoenicia and south Syria, beyond which the Hittite Empire ultimately stood firm. On the fringes of north Sinai and south Canaan, he repelled and subdued the semi-nomadic and restless groups covered in his inscriptions by the broad term *Shasu* or *Shosu*, having no ethnic significance.[4] More important here, on the clear evidence of inscribed monuments and small objects of faience and the like, this king, his father and his successors renewed Egypt's turquoise-mining activity in south-central Sinai, and

[3] See (with references) J. Zarins, "Archaeological and Chronological Problems within the Greater Southwest Asian Arid Zone, 8500-1850 B.C.," *Chronologies in Old World Archaeology*, (ed. R. W. Ehrich; 3rd ed.; Chicago: University of Chicago, 1992) 1.42-62 (cf. 46, 48, 49, 58-59), and 2.61-76.

[4] In outline, cf. K. A. Kitchen, *Pharaoh Triumphant: Life & Times of Ramesses II* (Warminster: Aris & Phillips, 1982), 20-25, 247; full translations of texts, *idem.*, *Ramesside Inscriptions, Historical & Biographical: Translations,* I-II (Oxford: Basil Blackwell, 1993, 1996) with explanatory data, *idem.*, *Ramesside Inscriptions, Historical & Biographical: Notes & Comments,* I-II (Oxford: Basil Blackwell, 1994, 1997).

opened-up copper-mining work at Timna, on the east (Arabah) edge of Sinai, there in conjunction with the local population of NW Arabia. These activities were to last until the reigns of Ramesses V (*ca.* 1147-1143 BC) at Timna and VI (*ca.* 1143-36 BC) in Sinai proper,[5] when the Egyptians withdrew, leaving the locals to continue the copper-exploitation briefly at least (perhaps to about 1100 BC, with the rock-fall that destroyed their tent-shrine).[6]

Working with the emissaries of a cosmopolitan power like Egypt seems to have been a cultural stimulus to the NW Arabians. Probably inspired by the lotus-bloom and other Egyptian/East-Mediterranean motifs on Egyptian faience-work,[7] they began to produce, use and circulate their own cheerful, polychrome-painted pottery, firmly associated with the Ramesside mining-temple context. The place-of-manufacture of this attractive ware was not at Timna, but roughly 100 miles/160 km south-east, at a site Qurayya. Hence its archaeological name, "Qurayya ware." Here, the NW Arabians established a major settlement, with a citadel upon a great rock, kilns for making their special pottery, and undertook an irrigation system of cultivation.[8] From Qurayya, their realm of influence and contact (measured by that pottery) reached not only north-west to Timna and beyond, but also nearly 200 miles /320 km south-east to Teima oasis, as well as west of south to the wadis leading onto the Red Sea coast.[9] In biblical tradition, we find people termed

---

[5] For the Timna materials, see B. Rothenberg and others, *The Egyptian Mining Temple at Timna* (Researches in the Arabah 1959-1984 1; London: Thames & Hudson, 1988); Sethos I there, 125:83*a*, 275, pl. 125:3, fig. 31:7.

[6] On the limited time-frame of Qurayya/'Midianite' pottery (13th-12th centuries BC), see P. J. Parr, "Pottery of the Late Second Millennium B.C. from Northwest Arabia and Its Historical Implications," *Araby the Blest: Studies in Arabian Archaeology*, (CNI Publications 7; ed. D. T. Potts; Copenhagen: University of Copenhagen, Museum Tusculanum, 1988, 73-90, esp. 74-83; more briefly, in T. Fahd (ed.), *L'Arabie Préislamique et son environment historique et culturel: Actes du Colloque de Strasbourg 24-27 juin 1987* (Travaux, Centre de Recherche sur le Proche-Orient, Grèce antiques 10; Leiden: E. J. Brill, 1989) 39-66, esp. 40-43; and in *Arabian Archaeology & Epigraphy* 4(1993), 48-58, plus notes by Rothenberg and Glass (note 9 below), 100-1.

[7] On this, cf. P.J. Parr, *Bulletin, Institute of Archaeology, Univ. London* 8/9(1970), 238-240, and J.E. Dayton, *PSAS* 2(1972), [5th Seminar], 25-33.

[8] See P. J. Parr, G. L. Harding, J. E. Dayton, "Preliminary Survey in N. W. Arabia, 1968," *Bulletin of the Institute of Archaeology, University of London* 8/9 (1970), 219-41, plans in figs. 10-11; M. L. Ingraham, T. D. Johnson, B. Rihani, I. Shatla, "Saudi Arabian Comprehensive Survey Program: C. Preliminary Report on a Reconnaissance Survey of the Northwestern Province (with a note on a brief Survey of the Northern Province)," *ATLAL* 5(1981), 71-74, pls. 68 (map), 78-80.

[9] For its distribution, cf. Ingraham, and others, "Saudi Arabian Comprehensive" (see above n. 8), pp. 71-75, esp. pp. 74-75; and B. Rothenberg, J. Glass, "The Midianite Pot-

Midianites in that NW-most corner of Arabia, south of Edom, and sometimes intervening north and west of it, in the Exodus-period (13th century BC, bottom date),[10] and under the Judges (12/11th centuries BC).[11] In the main narratives, they appear as ruled by five princes or four, and as camel-borne raiders. After *ca.* 1100 BC at latest, they disappear from the record; "Midian" is merely a geographical expression in 1 Kgs 11:18, for example, and thereafter occurs almost solely in retrospective references, as in the major prophets.[12] In short, the area and main period of operations of the NW Arabians who produced Qurayya ware and of the Midianites in our literary sources substantially coincide. Hence it is reasonable to accept the suggestion that these two entities are largely one and the same; Qurayya ware is then also Midianite pottery, as some have already dubbed it.

During the period of the later 11th to early 8th centuries, neither modern archaeology nor surviving ancient written sources know anything much of affairs in NW Arabia, probably then given over to camel-nomads and pastoralists; we have only Gindibu of "Arabia" who participated in the Battle of Qarqar in 853 BC; his precise home area is not stated. Then, during 738-690 BC, Assyrian sources name four successive queens in North Arabia and a Hazail, King of Qedar (*ca.* 690-676 BC), followed by three more such rulers. Qedar occurs earlier, under Tiglath-pileser III, as a political entity,[13] and remained the principal north-Arabian power until the 4th century BC.[14]

---

tery," *Midian, Moab and Edom, The History and Archaeology of Late Bronze and Iron Age Jordan and North-West Arabia* (ed. J. F. A. Sawyer and D. J. A. Clines; JSOTSup 24; Sheffield: JSOT, 1983) 65-124.

[10] Cf. Num 22, 25, 31.

[11] Judg 6-8, *passim.*

[12] As in Isa 9:4, 10:26, 60:6; Hab 3:7, cf. Ps 83:7, etc., all retrospective usages.

[13] Iran stela of Tiglath-pileser III, col. IIIA, 2 (plus Arabian Queen Zabibe in 19); latest edition, H. Tadmor, *The Inscriptions of Tiglath-pileser III, King of Assyria* (Fontes ad res Judaicas spectantes; Jerusalem: Israel Academy of Sciences and Humanities, 1994) 106-9.

[14] Principal sources for Qedar, general survey, cf. I. Eph'al, *The Ancient Arabs: Nomads on the Border of the Fertile Crescent 9th-5th Centuries BC* (Jerusalem: Magnes, 1982); chronology of rulers, cf. Kitchen, *Documentation for Ancient Arabia,* I, Liverpool, 1994, 117-9, 49-51, and lists 167-9, 237; two additional rulers before Shahru I and Gashmu I, add Mahlai and Iyas, studied by A. Lemaire, "Histoire et administration de la Palestine à l'epoque perse," *La Palestine à l'Époque Perse* (ed. E.-M. Laperrousaz, A. Lemaire; Paris: Cerf, 1994) 26-27.

d) *Links Further South*

The date of origin of the ancient South-Arabian script has been considered anew in recent years. Some 30 to 40 years ago, Cross suggested its emergence in the 14th/13th centuries BC, while very recently, Sass has argued for the 11th/10th centuries BC.[15] For more than one reason, a 'middle date' may be wiser, *i.e.* about the 13th/12th centuries BC. In the first place, we have the remarkable case of the tablet from Beth-Shemesh inscribed with letters in Ugaritic script, but in the order of the Old-South-Arabian alphabet![16] Clearly, for this even to happen, *somebody* had already invented that very characteristic letter-order by *ca.* 1200 BC and as that order has no place whatsoever in the Mediterranean Semitic world, it is far more likely to have been someone from Arabia.

In the second place, the earliest examples of Old-South-Arabian script go back earlier than generally realised. The original stratigraphic dig at Hajar bin Humeid has now proved to have been fully valid in terms of stratigraphy and overall dating, especially in the light of comparable recent work in Yemen (French, Italian, German and American).[17] Thus, the famous KHLM monogram on a vessel found in level S at Hajar bin Humeid is two strata deeper (and earlier) than a wooden beam from stratum Q whose CRD Carbon-14 date has to come within 1135-805 BC and more narrowly within 905-785 BC. Thus, stratum S has to be clearly earlier still, and the monogram about 900 BC or earlier. After it, there runs a series of informal epigraphs from stratum Q (9th century BC) down through the 1st millennium BC. At As-Sawda (ancient Nashan), the archaic, ornate brief texts of a local ruler Abamar Sadiq may date to *ca.* 788 BC (so, Breton), although there may be grounds for dropping this date by 130 years or so.[18] On the absolutely minimal dates for early

[15] F.M. Cross, "The Evolution of the Proto-Canaanite Alphabet," *BASOR* 134 (1954) 22; *idem.*, "A Ugaritic Abecedary and the Origins of the Proto-Canaanite Alphabet," *BASOR* 160 (1960) 22. B. Sass, *Studia Alphabetica: On the Origin and Early History of the Northwest Semitic, South Semitic and Greek Alphabets* (OBO 102; Freiburg: Universitätsverlag, 1991) 87.

[16] See A. G. Lundin, "L'abécédaire de Beth Shemesh," *Le Muséon* 100 (1987) 243-50, and supplementary presentation, J. Ryckmans, "A. G. Lundin's Interpretation of the Beth Shemesh Abecedary: A Presentation and Commentary," *Proceedings, Seminar for Arabian Studies* 18 (1988) 123-29.

[17] For a summary of the facts, see K. A. Kitchen, *Documentation for Ancient Arabia,* 1.120-132; the criticisms of Pirenne rested on misconceptions, now clearly invalid. Russian work in Hadramaut also runs in parallel, with inscriptions going back to the 8th century BC at least.

[18] Cf. discussion, *ibid.*, 114-15, 134, with references.

rulers of Saba set forth by this writer, our oldest known texts by Sabaean rulers and officials would be those under Karibil A, min. date *ca.* 820-810 BC and Yada'il Yanuf, min. date *ca.* 810-790 BC. But if any credit be given to the very popular (but unproven!) identification of the Karibilu of Assyrian records of 685 BC with the formidable Karibil Watar I (*ca.* 525 BC on my minimal dates), then *automatically* the 300 years' worth of Sabaean rulers *before* Karibil Watar I would have to be dated 160 years earlier to *ca.* 985-685 BC at latest, and probably in fact to *ca.* 1000-685 BC, as that year (685) would *not* needfully have been the year of accession of Karibil Watar I, and some reigns may have been longer than I have (minimally) allowed. Thus, our known rulers would go back beyond Solomon as far as David's time, in biblical terms, and the queen of Sheba would have been the active consort of an early ruler somewhere between Yada'il Yanuf and Yada'il Bayyin I. But, currently, I still regard it as safer and wiser to stay with minimal dates until we know better; there is no final proof (as yet) that the Assyrian Karibilu is Karibil Watar rather than (*e.g.*) Karibil B or another Karibil. Our oldest writing from Western Arabia is Sabaean, and the oldest organised proto-state in Western Arabia was Saba (cf. also on irrigation, etc., above). So, about 1200 BC is perhaps the likeliest minimum date for invention of that alphabet as well as its order.

The impulse to adopt the use of writing would undoubtedly have been a practical one, in service of the state and its communities. And if normal irrigation-agriculture (already up and running in Saba for about a millennium, without writing) was no stimulus, then something else was. In the light of subsequent Assyrian references and the biblical data, that something was the quite rapid emergence of a new international trade, involving Saba/Sheba with the Near East far north of it. The explicit "bottom date" for trade by caravan between Saba through Teima with Mesopotamia is *ca.* 750 BC, as has been demonstrated by publication of tablets from Hindanu (on the Middle Euphrates), in which the local ruler boasts of pillaging a Sabaean caravan of 200 camels that had not announced its arrival in his bailiwick.[19] As Liverani was able to demonstrate, people were trading in the same range of products via Suhu and

---

[19] Published by A. Cavigneaux and B.K. Ismail, "Die Statthalter von Suḫu und Mari im 8. Jh. v. Chr.: Anhand neuer Texte aus den irakischen Grabungen im Staugebiet des Qadissiya-Damms (Taf. 35-38)," *Baghdader Mitteilungen* 21 (1990) 321-456, cf. Text 2, IV:26-39; critical evaluation (in English), M. Liverani, "Early Caravan Trade between South-Arabia and Mesopotamia,"*Yemen* 1(1992), 111-15.

Hindanu under previous Assyrian kings, going back to Tukulti-Ninurta II (891-884 BC) and the logic of the situation requires (as Liverani observed)[20] that this identical trade had the same source, *i.e.* caravan-traffic from Saba, from *ca.* 890 BC, barely 40 years after the death of Solomon in biblical terms. So, chronologically, at least, we are very close indeed (within *ca.* 60 years?) to the episode of the queen of Sheba.

The sudden viability of such a trade (whether with Assyria or Palestine) must also have had its cause; after all, from what we now know, Assyria, Palestine and Saba had already been the foyers of well-organised communities long before 890 BC. Within the timespan bracketed by the seeming invention of the Old-South-Arabian alphabet (evidenced by its order), *ca.* 1200 BC and Tukulti-Ninurta II by 890 BC, one other phenomenon has to be admitted: the rapid rise of the camel to prominence for relatively long-distance travel, be it in peace or war. Besides the 200 camels from Saba in *ca.* 750 BC, we have Gindibu of "Arabia" contributing a fighting-force with 1,000 camels to the allies that confronted Shalmaneser III at the Battle of Qarqar in 853 BC.[21] There is limited but sufficient evidence taking back the knowledge of camels and *restricted* use of them a long way back beyond the 9th century BC, a much-discussed topic which cannot be ventilated at length here. Suffice it to mention Old-Babylonian attestation (early 2nd millennium BC), and the late 19th-Dynasty model from a Ramesside tomb at Rifeh in Egypt, for example.[22] In ancient Arabia (not too surprisingly), knowledge and use of the camel go back earlier than these.[23] In this

---

[20] Liverani, *ibid.*, 112, 114.

[21] D. D. Luckenbill, *Ancient Records of Assyria and Babylonia* (Chicago: University of Chicago, 1926) 1.223, no. 611; A. L. Oppenheim, "Babylonian and Assyrian Historical Texts," *ANET*, p. 279, top left.

[22] The Rifeh example is of a beast with two jars, *i.e.* domesticated; this does *not* imply wide use in Egypt then, but certainly knowledge of that use; the grudging attitude by B. Midant-Reynes and F. Braunstein-Silvestre, "Le chameau en Égypte," *Orientalia* 46 (1977) 337-62 (Rifeh, 350-1) is wholly unjustified, in both this case and several others, and at times borders on special pleading, as does the work of I. Köhler, *Zur Domestikation des Kamels* (Hannover: , 1981). Camels remained marginal to Egypt until very much later; cf. my compact statement of the better-quality evidence long since in K. A. Kitchen, "Camel," *NBD*, pp. 162-63 (now, *Illustrated Bible Dictionary*, 1980, 1.228-30). In Nubia, recent evidence shows clear knowledge of the camel, with dung-specimens dated (CRD) at 95% confidence to 1040-770 BC from Napatan strata; cf. P. Rowley-Conwy, "The Camel in the Nile Valley: New Radiocarbon Accelerator (AMS) Dates from Qaṣr Ibrîm," *Journal of Egyptian Archaeology* 74 (1988) 245-48.

[23] In eastern Arabia (Gulf region), from the 3rd millennium BC; cf. references, D. T. Potts, *The Arabian Gulf in Antiquity* (Oxford: Clarendon, 1990) 1.81-82 and n.93, 129-30 with discussion.

overall context, from the 13th to 9th centuries BC, the clear use of camels for raiding in the 12th century BC by the Midianites (Judg 6-8) has long been recognised as symptomatic of a more extensive use of these animals for desert travel. With this may be appropriately cited the representation of the camel on the Qurayya or "Midianite" ware of the 13th/12th centuries BC.[24] Finally, there is the probability that after the first half of the 12th century BC, Egypt finally lost contact with Punt, her traditional supplier of aromatics and other exotica; Ramesses III was the last-known pharaoh to commission a sea-going expedition to Punt, and the old resource of using intermediaries via the Middle Nile may by now have begun to fail.[25]

So, the 12th-11th centuries BC would see the convergence of several factors. 1) The camel began to be used much more extensively in Western Arabia, after long use in Eastern Arabia. 2) Supplies of aromatics and other exotica that had once been a trickle of marginal trade, often from one hand to another, could now be turned into a more successful long-distance trade, possibly to expanding markets (*e.g.*, Egypt, after her loss of contact with Punt as a source). 3) The nucleus-kingdom of Saba (already a highly-organised polity with its large-scale state irrigation-works and schemes) took the lead, heading a federation of groups,[26] in conducting this trade, which is why we find it in full swing four centuries later in 9th/8th-century Assyrian records. 4) This incipient trade led speedily to the need to keep records, hence the birth of the Sabaean script by *ca.* 1200 BC. So, by about 1100 BC, the whole situation was probably already crystallised and beginning quietly to expand, and was fully regular by the 9th century BC. *That* scenario, in the light of everything outlined so far, is the background against which the episode narrated in 1 Kgs 10:1-13 and 2 Chr 9:1-12 *has* to be viewed, regardless of what

---

[24] Drawing of pot, published by M. Ingraham and others, "Saudi Arabian Comprehensive" (see n. 8 above), pl. 79:14, and already noted by Parr, "Pottery of the Late Second Millennium" (see n. 6 above), p. 86. There and in Fahd (ed.), *L'Arabie préislamique,* pp. 43, 46, Parr would correlate the more extensive use of camels in the 12th to 8th centuries BC with the eclipse of the Qurayya settled culture, and rise of a more nomadic/pastoral regime.

[25] For Punt and sources thereon, cf. K. A. Kitchen, "The Land of Punt," *The Archaeology of Africa* (ed. T. Shaw; London: Routledge, 1993) Ch. 35, pp. 587-608 (with illustrations); earlier, *idem.*, "Punt," *Lexikon der Ägyptologie* (ed. W. Helck and W. Westendorf; Wiesbaden: Otto Harrassowitz, 1982) 4.1198-201.

[26] Marked by the Sabaean rulers' adoption of the title *Mkrb*, '*mukarrib*', "uniter" or paramount ruler. The title was already held by Yada'il Yanuf (*ca.* 820 BC, minimal dates; *ca.* 980 BC, maximal dates), hence the Sabaean federation was in being already by his time, and could have begun earlier.

one's response to that narrative may be, in terms of history, legend or any other category.

3. The Structure and Content of our Base-Text

Following on from the accounts of the inauguration of Solomon's reign and of his concern with the Jerusalem temple, palaces and other building-projects, we find in 1 Kgs 9:26-10:22, a section of text remarkable not only for its oft-remarked "exotic" content but also for its "interleaved" format.[27] This segment of text shows the following structure in terms of content.

§1. [9:26-28]. *Trade abroad (Ophir) part I.* Solomon builds a fleet, jointly manned by Hebrews and Tyrians in a common venture with Hiram of Tyre; gold is the commodity imported.

§2. [10:1-10]. *Queen of Sheba, part I.* A queen from Sheba visits Solomon, by camel-caravan, with rich gifts (spices, gold, gems) for a friendly summit-meeting.

§3. [10:11-12]. *Trade abroad (Ophir) part II.* At this point, an "insert" has "Hiram's ships" return with gold from Ophir (as before), plus almug-wood and gems; use of the wood is noted.

§4. [10:13]. *Queen of Sheba, part II.* The queen receives gifts from Solomon and departs home.

§5. [10:14-21]. *Regular revenues & Conspicuous consumption.* Brief notice of annual gold-revenue, and fleeting reference to other regular trade.

§6. [10:22]. *Trade abroad part III.* **Not** stated to be with Ophir. Two fleets (one for each king) operate on a "3-year" cycle, importing gold, silver, ivory, plus apes and baboons.

Any of us, today, would have opted for a "tidier" narrative. That is to say, we might have kept together everything on Trade abroad (§§1, 3, 6), then on General revenues (§5) and then on the Queen of Sheba (§§2, 4), in whatever order, rather than interleaving these topics as the ancient writer has done. But our Hebrew writer is *not* one of us moderns; he belongs to his own world, that of the preclassical Ancient Near East. His

---

[27] Repeated with only minute variations in 2 Chr 8:17-9:21; the import of those minutiae is all too easily exaggerated by modern commentators not sufficiently *au fait* with such phenomena in ancient Near-Eastern texts; cf., *e.g.,* J. B. Pritchard "Introduction," *Solomon & Sheba* (ed. J. B. Pritchard; London: Phaidon, 1974) 10-11.

mind operated by its rules, not ours. The sequence he uses may in fact be meaningful, not mere accident or theoretical editorial jumbling (as some of the more academically or informationally challenged Old Testament scholars might be tempted to suppose). Let us examine the sequence as we have it, regardless of whether it be fact, fiction or whatever at this stage.

The starting-point is Solomon and Hiram's joint sea-venture to Ophir (be it in Arabia or Africa), starting from the vicinity of Eloth and Ezion Geber (Gulf of Aqaba), and hence somewhere down the Red Sea (§1). From the second mention of the Ophir-trade (§3), it is clear that it became a regular activity so long as these two kings acted in concert.

The next thing we learn is that a queen of Sheba is on her way to see Solomon, ostensibly to compliment him on his fame, piety and fortune. But just as today, rulers of antiquity were a hard-nosed lot, and did not undertake long journeys simply to exchange a few flattering pleasantries. Therefore, in the light of the rise of a new overland trade between SW Arabia and the Near East to her far north, during the 12th to 9th centuries BC (cf. end of previous section, above), the real reason for any such visit is more likely to have had an economic motive. *I.e.*, the Sabaeans saw this new sea-venture between the Levant and Arabia as a potential threat to their overland camel-borne trade north to that same quarter, and sought to sort matters out at first hand.[28]

Then, in the midst of the Sheba narrative, we find mention of Hiram's ships arriving with more gold, etc. (§3). Solomon had been shown as the recipient of wealth from the queen of Sheba; after this argosy's arrival is noted (treated as parenthetical by most translators and others), he in turn bestows a rich bounty (no details) on the queen, prior to her departure (§4). There may well be a deliberate connection of these two themes here. First, explicitly, Solomon did not become wealthy simply by the generosity of a visiting female ruler,[29] he had his own, independent sources of wealth (the Ophir and other trade). Second, implicit in the

[28] A point made by others, *e.g.*, G.W. van Beek, "The Land of Sheba," *Solomon & Sheba* (ed. J.B. Pritchard; London: Phaidon, 1974) 47-48.

[29] This would not trouble us today, in a world of ardent femininism, or of all the humbug of "political correctness" and suchlike claptrap. But the Ancient Near East (while allowing very major roles to women, and rightly so) had its sensitivities in these matters. Cf. the Hittite queen Pudukhepa's reproaches to Ramesses II, when he cheekily suggested to her that the Hittites send a dowry even if a princess was not to be had as a wife! Text, W. Helck, "Urḫi-Tešup in Ägypten," *JCS* 17 (1963) 87-97. In popular English form, cf. Kitchen, *Pharaoh Triumphant*, p. 84.

underlying economic situation suggested just above, such an arrival during the Sheban's sojourn at Jerusalem would have underlined the apparent permanency of the Tyre-Israel sea-venture, at least in bulky goods like timber or heavy metals like gold, while, in theory, she could have pressed upon a Solomon the superiority of the camel-route for lightweight, high-value goods such as aromatics and spices. With nothing more to be gained in such a case, she is shown going back home (§4).

The whole episode of the Queen of Sheba was clearly viewed by our narrator as a "one-off" event; no further such direct relations with Sheba recur. So, by contrast (§5), he deemed it appropriate and politic briefly to highlight Solomon's regular revenues and wider ongoing contacts (10:14-15), and then to illustrate Solomon's use of some of this wealth (just like most Near-Eastern kings) for conspicuous display.

Finally (§6), the narrator rounds off the whole topic of exotic trade. When exploration and enterprise of this kind prove successful, then, throughout the history of commerce, the well-nigh universal response is to go still further, and seek yet more gain. This final pericope illustrates that axiom. Apart from gold, all the details here (10:22) are different from those on Ophir, and there is no justification for seeing the distant destination of 10:22 as yet again Ophir, it is elsewhere, and unnamed. We find not a joint fleet, but two fleets (one of each king), there are fresh commodities imported (silver and ivory; exotic animals), and there is a long time-cycle, "3 years" (perhaps part of one year, all of a second, and part of a third, in the way these matters were often reckoned in antiquity).

Seen in this light, regardless of whether it be viewed as fact, fiction, or whatever, this narrative's format makes good sense. Levantine economic entry into western Arabia (close to a SW Arabian trade route) sparks off a SW Arabian visit to the Levant. The solidity of the sea-trade at that time could not be altered, so a *modus vivendi* (heavy stuff by sea; light stuff overland) could be implied as having been reached between SW Arabia and the Levantine partners (who proceed to trade still further away).

4. Application of the Geo-political, Geographical and Economic Backgrounds

a) *The Queen of Sheba herself*

The foregoing has concentrated on the essential build-up in western Arabia and its neighbours down to the late 2nd millennium BC, and on the changes that occurred at the change from the 2nd to the 1st millennium, setting new patterns for the early 1st millennium. And then we have examined compactly the format/content of the narrative whose existence has given rise to this chapter in the first instance. But we need finally to set the content of that narrative against other Arabian and allied factors, if we are to gain the best understanding and assessment of the biblical texts, in order to complete our survey.

Perhaps the first feature in our biblical texts that is so striking is the *nature* of Solomon's Arabian visitor: a *queen*, not a king. Regardless of whether one prefers the minimal chronology suggested here, or a more maximal dating of rulers exemplified above, the long series of early rulers of Sheba (Saba) down to the 4th century BC in each case bore the title *MKRB*, "*mukarrib*," "uniter" (or paramount ruler)[30] of a federation of groups around Saba, including the progenitors of the eventual kingdoms of Main, Qataban and Hadramaut that claimed their full independence by the 4th century BC. And we have (so far) no queen-regnant in that series. It is, therefore, logical to suggest that the queen of Sheba was in fact the consort of a reigning *mukarrib* of Saba and involved in her land's government, but was not herself sole ruler. From Sheba itself, we have no other data on active queens, although it is clear that women did serve alongside men in various capacities; for example, even as beaters on a royal hunt by the *mukarrib* Yithaʾamar Bayyin I (min. *ca.* 540 BC/max. *ca.* 720 BC).[31] But in NW Arabia, when Assyrian texts are first available to inform us during the 8th to early 7th centuries BC, a clear pattern emerges, of *queens* wielding political, executive powers, rather than just emirs or kings. So, we have Zabibe as "queen of Arabia" (in Qedar) in 738 BC, then Queen Samsi of Arabia in 733 BC, Queen Iatiʾe

[30] *Not* "priest-king," as is often stated in the older literature.

[31] Text Yala AQ 17 (Iryani 43), in A. de Maigret, G. Garbini, M.A. al-Iryani, *The Sabaean Archaeological Complex in the Wadi Yala (Eastern Ḫawlān at-Ṭiyāl, Yemen Arab Republic) Preliminary Report* (Reports and Memoirs 21; Rome: IsMEO, 1988) 30-31 (Arabic, 57-58), cf. re-edition, by A. Jamme, *Miscellanées d'ancient arabe,* XVII, (Washington: personal publication, 1989) 78.

of Arabia in 703 BC, and finally Teʾelkhunu in 691 BC[32] (with whom was associated a king Hazail in Qedar). But it is especially important to notice that Teʾelkhunu was the last of her ilk. After her, from 690 BC, *we never again find any Arabian queen playing an active political role* and, in fact (in Arabia proper) practically *no mention whatever* of Arabian queens at all in the preislamic period right up to the 570s AD. Alone, in 225 AD, do we hear of just one Sabaean princess who was married-off as queen to a king of Hadramaut, and then solely because (later) her brother the next Sabaean king hijacked her back home to Marib in Saba![33] Otherwise, after Teʾelkhunu, the record currently is a total blank, while kings abound in plenty. Thus, the phenomenon of a *queen* of Sheba playing an active political role is entirely realistic *before* 690 BC for most of two centuries back in our known records, and conceivably earlier still if we had any other record. *After* 690 BC, any mention of such a person as active in Arabian affairs would be a glaring anachronism. In old-fashioned Old-Testamentarian terminology, she is rigorously pre-Deuteronomic (pre-621 BC). There cannot be a Persian-period spoof here, just to suit current prejudices; all Arabian rulers then were kings. Given this situation, that she is an early socio-cultural phenomenon, the queen of Sheba deserves to be treated as historical, on strictly factual, not dogmatic, grounds.

Of course, it is easy for anyone to suggest (as some do), "she's a figure of legend, so historicity is out." And, of course, her appearance in Kings and Chronicles has indeed generated a luxuriant flowering of legendary tale-telling, theological allegorising and what-not.[34] But whatever literary *floraisons* arise long after a character's decease have, of course, no bearing whatsoever on the historicity of the character concerned. Suffice it here to allude to the various forms of "Alexander

---

[32] For handiest references to these ladies, cf. A. L. Oppenheim, "Babylonian and Assyrian" (see n. 21 above), pp. 283-86, 301; plus Luckenbill, *Ancient Records*, 2.130, §259 (Iati'e).

[33] The text Iryani 13; summary translation in English, A.F.L. Beeston, "Warfare in Ancient South Arabia (2nd—3rd Centuries AD)," *Qahtan* 3 (1976) 47-48.

[34] For handy and entertaining accounts of the legends, etc., see chapters 3-6 in *Solomon & Sheba* (ed. J. B. Pritchard; London: Phaidon, 1974) 65-145: L. H. Silberman, "The Queen of Sheba in Judaic Tradition," pp. 65-84; W. M. Watt, "The Queen of Sheba in Islamic Tradition," pp. 85-103; E. Ullendorff, "The Queen of Sheba in Ethiopian Tradition," pp. 104-14; P. F. Watson, "The Queen of Sheba in Christian Tradition," pp. 115-45. Also, H. St. J. Philby, *The Queen of Sheba* (London: Quartet Books, 1981); those with a good sense of humour may enjoy the legend's last(?) avatar in P. A. Crutch, *The Queen of Sheba, her Life and Times* (New York: G. P. Putnam's, 1922).

Romance" that grew up around Alexander the Great, or even a "Cambyses Romance" inspired by the history of Cambyses, in Egypt at least.[35] Nobody in their senses would (I trust) doubt the historical existence of either Alexander or Cambyses (given the first-hand data available), merely because each gave rise to later lush legends. So, why be perverse about this queen? The excuse that (outside the Old Testament) we as yet have no document for her proves nothing. The full and precise chronology of the earlier rulers of Saba remains to be definitively established, and nobody knows what may be hidden deep in the almost totally undug mounds of the site of Marib. So, prejudgment must remain premature, especially as (in our sole source) she fits her general era.

Saba, moreover, is a long way from the Levant; as Pritchard pithily put it on behalf of the doubters, "the vast distance that separates the capital of Sheba ... from Jerusalem, 1,400 miles of rugged desert, lends an air of improbability to the story."[36] However, such doubters (as is their wont) never go to the trouble of comparing like with like, to form an objective judgement. Did ancient royalty travel such distances, and through rough terrain? Some examples may set the queen in context here, too. It is known that the Hittite prince Hishmi-Sharruma (the future Hittite king Tudkhalia IV) visited Egypt in the 13th century BC, and Ramesses II at that time issued pressing invitations to the prince's father Hattusil III, to come and visit him, that they might get better acquainted personally[37] for far less reason, so to speak, than the Sheban queen's curiosity about Solomon's shrewdness and wealth (and more likely, economic matters also). From Hattusas to Egypt was most of 900 miles to Pi-Ramesse, most of 1,000 miles to Memphis, Egypt's greatest capital; and the Hittite visitors had also mountains to cross. In the New Kingdom, it was customary for Egyptian pharaohs to conduct armed expeditions far into desert Nubia (into N. Sudan), up the Nile to the 4th Cataract and well beyond in some cases (so, Tuthmosis I and III to Kanisa Kurgus; Amenophis III), for up to 1,300 or 1,400 miles from Memphis. Conversely, in 702/1 BC, prince Taharqa brought a whole army-force from Kush (N. Sudan) down to Memphis for his brother king Shebitku's disastrous intervention against Sennacherib of Assyria,

---

[35] Compare the work in Coptic of perhaps a thousand years after Cambyses, published by H. L. Jansen, *The Coptic Story of Cambyses' Invasion of Egypt* (Oslo: I kommisjon hos J. Dybwad, 1950).

[36] Pritchard, "Introduction," *Solomon & Sheba*, p. 12.

[37] For convenience, see Kitchen, *Pharaoh Triumphant*, pp. 89-91, 251 (sources); and, of course, two Hittite princesses made the same journey (but on one-way tickets!)

again, up to 1,800 miles before seeing Palestine at all.[38] Over 13 centuries before Solomon and Sheba, the redoubtable Sargon of Akkad campaigned westward to the "Silver Mountains" over 900 miles from home, and possibly further.[39] Closer to Sheba, there is the wholly bizarre episode of Nabonidus king of Babylon marching west into Western Arabia to set himself up in Teima, 600 miles from home for a decade, and moving even further down W. Arabia then, to Dedan, Khaybar, etc., even to Yathrib (Medina), up to 1,000 miles from "home" in Babylon.[40] If Nabonidus's acts were not known to us from first-hand records (as they are), but only, say, from the Old Testament, what would the critics say about him, it is worth asking! And finally, the Old-South-Arabian alphabetic order had reached the sphere of the Ugaritic script two centuries before Solomon and the queen, and perhaps many miles further north. As for the rugged route, many others of non-royal stock had already travelled it, and it does have a long series of wells and some oases, of course. So, the queen's journey was remarkable but certainly not "out of this world" in ancient terms.

b) *The Quest for Ophir*

In our sole descriptive source (the Old Testament), Ophir was clearly somewhere best reached by sea-travel from the Gulf of Aqaba, hence in some relation to the present-day Red Sea.[41] Nothing more is told us. Gold, almug-wood and gemstones were shipped-in, either as its products or traded-on from beyond. As pointed out by von Wissmann,[42] Ophir should not be confused (as is commonly done) with the unnamed destination (yielding other products) for whose visit the Tyrian-Hebrew fleets

---

[38] Data, K. A. Kitchen, *Third Intermediate Period in Egypt* (2nd ed.; Warminster: Aris & Phillips, 1986, and augmented reprint, 1996) 157-58, 383-85, 553-54, 557, etc.

[39] Cf. convenient summary and map, M. Roaf, *Cultural Atlas of Mesopotamia and the Ancient Near East* (New York: Facts on File, 1990) 96-97 and map.

[40] Published and annotated by C.J. Gadd, "The Harran Inscriptions of Nabonidus," *Anatolian Studies* 8 (1958) 35-92 (places, 80ff.); recent translation also Oppenheim, p. 562 (= *ANET, Supplement*, p. 126).

[41] For previous theories about the location of Ophir, cf. (*e.g.*) the writers and views cited by G. Ryckmans, "Ophir," *Supplément au Dictionnaire de la Bible* (Paris: Lotouzey, 1960) 6.744-51; by H. von Wissmann, "Ophir," *Pauly's Realencycopädie der classischen Altertumswissenschaft, neue Bearbeitung, Supplementband XII*, (ed. K. Ziegler; Stuttgart: Alfred Druckenmüller, 1970) col. 969, and by F. Briquel-Chatonnet, *Les relations entre les cités de la côte phénicienne et les royaumes d'Israël et de Juda* (Orientalia Lovaniensia Analecta 46; Louvain: Peeters, 1992) 277-83.

[42] H. von Wissmann, "Ophir" (see n. 41 above), col. 975.

needed a "3-year" cycle (1 Kgs 9:22). As no distance-indicator is given, Ophir was probably closer to the Gulf of Aqaba than was the "3-year cycle" destination. That it was in fact a reputed source of gold in real life is proven by the well-known Tell Qasile ostracon (8th century BC), recording "Gold of Ophir to/for Beth-Horon, [...]: 30 shekels."[43]

On the foregoing basis, along with most modern commentators such as Ryckmans, von Wissmann and Briquel-Chatonnet, it is safest not to seek Ophir beyond the Red Sea and its southern limit at Bab el-Mandeb. If so, our options are immediately limited to East Africa (Sudan, Eritrea, Ethiopia) or Western Arabia. Gold exists and was long exploited in both areas. In East Africa, behind the mountains that extend behind the Red Sea coastland north from Port Sudan, is an area (stretching towards the Nile at its bend below the 5th cataract) that is gold-bearing. In antiquity, this was almost certainly the land of ʿAmau that produced gold of ʿAmau, just as did Ophir "gold of Ophir." The position of ʿAmau explains how it was that the Egyptians obtained "gold of ʿAmau": 1) by trade into the southern part of their Nubian empire (4th cataract northwards) and 2) via Punt (which lay immediately south of ʿAmau). If Ophir were in this general area of north-east Africa, Ophir could have been an 11th-10th century successor to Punt and ʿAmau, and therefore a source of gold for possible Tyrian-Hebrew expeditions. In our second notice about Ophir (1 Kgs 10:11), almug wood is recorded as a product.[44] Von Wissmann had argued at length that this wood was juniper,[45] but it is more likely to have been tree-aloe; this is attested in eastern Africa, as well as in western Arabia.[46] While Briquel-Chatonnet and oth-

---

[43] B. Maisler, "Two Hebrew Ostraca from Tell Qasîle" *JNES* 10 (1951) 266-67, pl. 11:2. The phrase "gold of Ophir" (even if it means a quality) must go back to an initial reality for its origin; cf. exactly analogous uses, such as "gold of Koptos" and "of desert of Koptos," and "gold of Kush" (refs., A. Erman, H. Grapow, *Wörterbuch der Aegyptischen Sprache* (Leipzig, 1928) 2.237:14, 238:1; with *Belegstellen* (Leipzig, 1938) 2.341; and "gold of ʿAmau," refs., K. A. Kitchen, "Land of Punt," (see n. 25 above), p. 597 (twice). There is no valid excuse for treating Ophir any differently.

[44] The attempt to eliminate the MT mentions of Ophir and almug from this verse (on the basis of inferior LXX-readings) by Briquel-Chatonnet, *Les Relations* (see n. 41 above), p. 272, is unfounded, especially as 2 Chr 9:10 should be read as a whole, not artificially sliced up. In 1 Kgs 10:11, the structure in MT regarding Ophir and products is virtually chiastic: "Now also, the fleet of Hiram that brought gold from Ophir, it brought from Ophir almug-timbers in very great amount, and gemstones." Omitting (with LXX) the second "from Ophir" makes no difference: the fleet that brought gold from Ophir was the one that brought almug-wood, obviously, by sailing the same sea, not by an unstated miraculous transfer to the Mediterranean. The LXX name-form Suphir is also corrupt.

[45] Von Wissmann, "Ophir" (see n. 41 above), cols. 971-75.

[46] Cf. Briquel-Chatonnet, *Les Relations* (see n. 41 above), pp. 271-87, esp. 257-58,

ers have insisted that almug wood was also available in Lebanon (citing 2 Chr 2:8, and external sources from Mesopotamia), this does not exclude its import from elsewhere, especially if large quantities could be got more cheaply from open Arabian hillsides than from the terrain of money-jealous Levantine local rulers.[47] Thus, Ophir could be East-African (as preferred by (*e.g.*) Ryckmans and Briquel-Chatonnet). But the two principal products, gold and tree-aloe, are equally well attested in West-Arabia, which destroys any attempt to prove that Ophir is African on these grounds. On products, Africa and Arabia are equally possible. Is there any other factor? The very visit by the queen from Sheba probably indicates so. As noted above, the account of her is "interleaved" with the notices on Ophir. An Ophir in Western Arabia would adjoin or straddle the vital "incense-route," and so intervention by a fleet from the Levant would risk touching fatally the vital trade-interests of Sheba up north; hence her intervention with Solomon. By contrast, such activities far away and out-of-sight behind the Sudanese mountains 300 miles west from Arabia's gold lands would not have been of direct interest to an early ruler of Saba.[48] Hence, the balance of probability inclines more realistically towards a W. Arabian location for Ophir. Gold-bearing areas in W. Arabia are well attested, and traces of extensive mining in mediaeval and much earlier periods, from inland south of Medina (Mahd adh-Dhahab) to around Wadi Baysh and N. Hawlan (part of 'Havilah'), a zone of some 600 km/370 miles in length.[49]

---

272. For tree-aloe in East Africa, cf. R. Germer, *Flora des pharaonischen Ägypten* (Mainz: P. von Zabern, 1985) 197 (in Egypt from further south), and H. Edlin, *Atlas of Plant Life* (London: Heinemann, 1973) 57 (tree-aloe symbol in Eritrea on map). In W. Arabia, cf. (*e.g.*) M. McKinnon, *Arabia — Sand, Sea, Sky* (London, 1990) 62 end, 65; F.N. Hepper, I. Friis, *The Plants of Pehr Forsskal's Flora Aegyptiaco-Arabica* (Kew/ Copenhagen, 1994) 283.

[47] One thinks of Egypt's luckless Wenamun trying to buy timber at Byblos, *ca.* 1075 BC; translations, many; *e.g.*, M. Lichtheim, *Ancient Egyptian Literature* (Berkeley: University of California, 1976) 226-28.

[48] At present, we simply lack evidence for or against Albright's and von Wissmann's view that Saba already ruled an area in E. Africa as early as the 10th century BC.

[49] Cf. modern map, *The Kingdom of Saudi Arabia* (4th ed.; London: Stacey International, 1979) 25, which refutes Briquel-Chatonnet, *Les Relations* (see n. 41 above), p. 280, end, putting gold only in central Arabia. Also, papers by R.J. Roberts and H. Sabir (ancient gold-mining in this region), in *Arabia Antiqua Roma 1991*, in press, besides von Wissmann (note 41 above), cols. 907-8, 911-13, 916, 918-21, 940, 969-71, with map, Ophir: Abb. 2.

c) *Beyond Ophir*

Here, we return to 1 Kgs 10:22. As pointed out above, the "3-year cycle" remark may point to somewhere well beyond an Ophir either in E. Sudan or in W. Arabia, and (apart from the ubiquitous gold) the products brought thence are different (silver, ivory, exotic animals), and there are twin fleets, not one joint fleet. It is, therefore, unjustified 1) to confuse the data of this verse with Ophir, 2) to treat it as a gloss, and 3) to dismiss the "3 years" as merely a symbolic round number.[50] It is not Ophir (as von Wissmann indicated), the differences noted exclude a mere gloss, and the "3 years" should indeed be treated more seriously, as minimally part of one civil year, all of a second, and part of a third. Precisely as when the Egyptians sailed down the west side of the Red Sea to reach Punt (landing along the Port Sudan/Suakin coast), using the summer winds that blew from NW to SE down that sea, and parallel currents,[51] so a Tyrian-Hebrew expedition either to Ophir or to the south end of the Red Sea could have used these selfsame phenomena, especially in June-September, to aid their voyage southward.[52] In the 15th century BC (and probably also in earlier times), Egyptian ships could have reached the Suakin area in 4 to 6 weeks (overnight stops, sailing at as little as 3 knots, barely 4 mph).[53] In the 10th century BC, with better ships, and the probability of fewer practicable stops along the east coast, the Levantine fleet could have made Bab el-Mandeb in some 8 to 10 weeks, by sometime in August. From that point, their explorations could have taken them round and southward, along the E. African coast past present-day Somalia, but in the teeth of opposing winds of the SW monsoon. Africa might yield ivory on this route, but not silver. Or they could have gone on eastward, either along the south coast of Arabia, and on by the Iranian coast to the west coast of India, if not directly from Aden or beyond it on the monsoon wind to western India. India certainly had silver, ivory and exotic animals, although ivory could have been picked up on a return journey along the African side of the Red Sea, along with apes and

[50] As is mistakenly done by Briquel-Chatonnet, *Les Relations* (see n. 41 above), pp. 272-77 and n. 10; any whole number can too easily be dismissed as "round," without good reason. Her comparison with Punt and its products (pp. 275-76) is in part also mistaken; Punt yielded primarily aromatics (not in 1 Kgs 10:22) and did not yield silver (included in 1 Kgs 10:22).

[51] Cf. K. A. Kitchen, "Punt and How to Get There," *Orientalia* 40 (1971) 194-95.

[52] See, for example, *Red Sea & Gulf of Aden Pilot* (11th edition, London: Hydrographer of the Navy, 1967) 18-22 (currents), 30-32 (winds).

[53] Cf. Kitchen, "Punt and How to Get There" (see n. 51 above), p. 196.

baboons. Hugging the coasts to such a "further African" or Indian destination (at up to 2,400 miles) might conceivably have taken 80 days at 30 miles a day, for example, or almost three months, to add to 1,400 miles from Ezion-Geber to Aden, (two months or so, above). Allowing for delays and occasional longer stops, a relatively coast-hugging run might have taken from July through to November or December, to reach significant ports on the west coast of India. A quick turn-round might then have permitted a similar journey back, especially from the south Iranian coast westward, when (during January-March), the north-east winter monsoon winds would propel returning vessels along the south-Arabian coast, and related south-east winds take such ships north up the Red Sea to 20° latitude.[54] Thereafter, oars rather than sails would work the ships (against north winds) back the last 700 miles up to Ezion-Geber. This might mean a return trip of 5 or 6 months, to reach home port by May or June. A year's interval might then be needed to fit out the next expedition. The allusion to 'once in 3 years' may bear either of two meanings: (i) the fleet took (part of) 3 years for the round trip, or (ii) intervals for turn-round and refit at home port may have spread outbound and return trips over such intervals. Either way, we sail increasingly into the realms of hypothesis at present, so we now must return to *terra firma*.

d) *Economics and Poetry of Conspicuous Consumption*

And what of the wealth recounted in 1 Kings 10? It is very easy to run the eye over such figures as 666 talents from Ophir, 420 (var. 450) talents from Ophir, and the gift of 120 talents from the Queen of Sheba, all of gold, and then dismiss them as fantasy without any attempt at imposing some kind of external and objective factual control. If we do do this, then these figures take on a different perspective. The Queen's gift to Solomon (120 talents; almost 4 tons) is less than the 150 talents of gold (almost 4 1/2 tons) extracted from Metten II of Tyre by Tiglath-pileser III of Assyria.[55] With the apparently "steep" figures of 420 and 666 talents (some 13 1/2 and 21 1/2 tons), one may compare, for example, the annual revenue of "India" (the Indus basin) of 360 talents (10 1/2 tons) under the Persian Empire.[56] And nothing has ever so far surpassed the

[54] Cf. the July and January wind-charts in *The Red Sea & Gulf of Aden Pilot*, figs. 3-4.

[55] Text, Oppenheim, "Babylonian and Assyrian" (see n. 21 above), p. 282 (66), now in Tadmor, *Inscriptions of Tiglath-pileser III*, p. 170/1:16'.

[56] Cf. long since, A. R. Millard, "Solomon in All His Glory," *Vox Evangelica* 12

2,000,000 deben weight of silver and 2,300,000 deben weight of silver and gold (some *400 tons*, all told, equal to some 14,000 talents), donated to the gods and temples of Egypt by Osorkon I in the first four years of his reign, barely a year or so after his father Shoshenq I (Shishak) had stripped Rehoboam of Judah of the Solomonic wealth of Jerusalem.[57] Given the close coincidence in time, it is difficult not to see some link here, unless one prefers blind obscurantism to first-hand original data. Solomon's wealth, of course, was concentrated in his capital city, Jerusalem. It then in large measure disappeared into Egypt's coffers and temples, and from there was dissipated into Kushite, Assyrian, Persian and other coffers by conquest, annexation or tribute, and from those coffers into the general stream of Hellenistic and Roman antiquity, to be seen no more. Archaeologists digging in Israel (and especially in Jerusalem, ravaged and rebuilt so often) need never expect to find any of this gold, barring a few accidental grains perhaps!

So much for figures at present—what about "poetry?" Alongside prosaic listings of revenues (1 Kgs 10:14) and of palace furnishings (1 Kgs 10:18-21), the Hebrew narrator proudly includes rhetorical flourishes to emphasise Solomon's fame and fortune, as in 1 Kgs 10:21 (silver, of no account) and 10:23-24 (unequalled wealth and repute). Such asides *are* poetical rhetoric, and should be understood as such, in contrast to specifics. Being unfamiliar with the internationally valid conventions of the biblical world, Old Testament scholars have sometimes tended to reason: 1) that such poetic flourishes are legendary, hence 2) so is all the rest, and Solomon was ultimately a nobody. However, again, *no* valid judgment can be made without employing external (and objective) standards of comparison. Then we may better see the relationship between rhetoric and reality.

A few examples may illustrate the point. Thus, in the rhetorical introduction to the Nauri Decree in favour of his great temple at Abydos (holy city of Osiris), Sethos I vaunts the opulence of the temple whose interests the strictly legal paragraphs of the decree are intended to safeguard: "You have built (Osiris's) temple like the horizon of heaven, ... A palace

---

(1981), 5-18, and K. A. Kitchen, *The Bible in Its World* (Exeter: Paternoster, 1977) 101-102 and references.

[57] First pointed out, Kitchen, *Bible in Its World*, p. 102; cf. A.R. Millard, "Does the Bible Exaggerate King Solomon's Golden Wealth?" *BAR* 15 (May-June 1989) 20-31, 34; and K. A. Kitchen, "Where Did Solomon's Gold Go?," in *BAR* 15 (May-June 1989) 30; and *idem*., "Shishak's Military Campaign in Israel Confirmed," *BAR* 15 (May-June 1989) 32-33.

is within it, richly adorned with real electrum from the best of the desert (mines). The terrace(?) in it is a surface of silver... The treasuries are full of valuables, silver and gold in heaps on the floor, ... millions of measures of oil, incense, wine and honey, limitless in reckoning their abundance."[58] At his neighboring temple in Abydos, Ramesses II rhapsodises that "the granaries are filled to bursting, the grain-heaps reach the sky... (the) treasury is festooned with every (kind of) precious stone, and silver and gold in ingots, ... filled with the tribute of all foreign countries."[59] Above this text, a calendar of feasts once gave full details of some of those revenues in practice. And over a century later (*ca.* 1153 BC) Ramesses III at death left through his son Ramesses IV a statement of wealth given to Egypt's temples during his reign, in the Great Harris Papyrus. He speaks of dispatching "my emissaries to the land of Atika, to the great copper-mines which are there ..... yielding copper, loaded by the tens of thousands into their [=the Egyptians'] ships." To temples, he gave offering-altars of gold and silver, and says to the god Amun: "I made for you great tablets of hammered gold, ... bearing my (hymns of) worship, ... I made for you other tablets of hammered silver, ... with the regulations of the temple, ... [with] decrees and inventories of the temples and chapels made in Egypt in my reign,"[60] and much, much more besides.

So much for poetry and related fact. To end this topic, one may briefly point to some relevant background for Solomon's palace-furnishings that impressed such as the Queen of Sheba. In 1 Kgs 10:18-21, we read of a throne inlaid with ivory and overlaid with gold, gold goblets, etc. This sort of thing was (so to speak) "standard issue" at royal courts long before Solomon. In the 14th century BC, the king of Babylon sent (among wedding-gifts) 4 gold-plated beds of ebony (one also with

---

[58] Nauri Decree, lines 7-9, 14-15 (extracts); full English translation of these, Kitchen, *Ramesside Inscriptions: Translations*, 1.40-41. Unlike Solomon's temple in Jerusalem, Sethos I's great shrine was never destroyed (except the roof in parts), but sanded up, so, at least its walls of superb sculpture, often glowing with colour, give us a hint of what has been lost. Among "popular" books, cf. in colour K. Lange and M. Hirmer, *Egypt* (3rd ed.; London: Phaidon, 1961) pls. 220-21.

[59] Citation, Kitchen, *Ramesside Inscriptions: Translations*, 2.330.

[60] Great Papyrus Harris I, 78:1ff. (Atika), and 6:5-8 (tablets; with these, cf. Solomon's shields of "hammered gold," 1 Kings 10:16-17). Also translated by J.H. Breasted, *Ancient Records of Egypt*, (Chicago: University of Chicago, 1906) 4.204, no. 408, and 118, no. 202, respectively; for a full study of this document, see now P. Grandet, *Le Papyrus Harris I* (Cairo: Institut français d'archéologie orientale du Caire, 1994) vols. 1-2. The expeditions to Atika correspond to known Egyptian mining involvement at Timnah, on the eastern edge of the Arabah rift valley.

ivory), and 10 ebony chairs with gold overlay, plus matching footstools.[61] And from Tutankhamun's tomb come actual examples of such beds, thrones and footstools, embodying such gold, silver and ivory overlays . And gold goblets, basins, drinking-rhytons, etc., all appear in sets of gifts for the wedding of a Mitannian princess to Akhenaten of Egypt (El Amarna letters 22, 25), a grand occasion that cost the proud father (in gold alone) somewhere about a half-million dollars/quarter of a million pounds in modern terms.[62] And such weddings (and costs!) happened every so often; this one was not unique. So, Solomon's gold goblets and a throne decorated with gold and ivory was customary usage in his position. With the fleeting reference to his palace-staff, admired by the Arabian queen (1 Kgs 10:4), we may compare remarks made by Ramesses III of about 150 years earlier, that he "organised Egypt in numerous groups: cupbearers of the palace, great chiefs, infantry and chariotry, abounding by the hundred-thousand, and .... minions by ten-thousands."[63] Rhetorical, but the intent is clear. Anything but rhetorical are the actual accounts for grain, thousands of loaves, etc., for the palace of Sethos I at Memphis a century earlier still.[64] The wealth of the ancients (like so much other wealth) may have been ephemeral and largely limited to capital-city palaces and main temples, but it was real enough at the times that it was flaunted.

5. General Conclusions

a) *Geographical/ecological Basis*

The biblical term "Sheba" is to be identified with the "Saba" of numerous inscriptions of SW Arabia (Yemen), linked with Assyrian data. There, we have pastoralism down into the 3rd millennium BC, and regular agricultural communities from 3rd millennium BC onwards, utilising seasonal flash-flood irrigation. At Marib, from 2nd millennium BC

[61] El Amarna letter 5; cf. W.L. Moran, *The Amarna Letters* (Baltimore: Johns Hopkins University, 1992) 11.

[62] Cf. Kitchen in E. Cline (ed.), *Studies in the Reign of Amenophis III* (Madison, Wis.: University of Wisconsin, in press) Ch. 12.

[63] Great Papyrus Harris I, 76:5-6.

[64] In English, Kitchen, *Ramesside Inscriptions: Translations*, 1.208ff. with notes on quantities of bread, numbers of people, etc., Kitchen, *Ramesside Inscriptions: Notes & Comments*, 1.162-66, 174-76.

(and perhaps late 3rd), sophisticated techniques of water-diversion irrigation were developed, to found a basic Sabaean state. That kind of agriculture remained its economic basis thenceforth.

b) *Late 2nd/early 1st Millennia BC: Epoch of change and growing intercommunications*

In NW Arabia, the brief prosperity of a "Midianite" culture (and polity?), in 13th/12th centuries BC, was stimulated in part by cooperative mining with Egypt for Timna copper. Its remarkable Qurayya pottery is found all the way from Timna to Teima. Meantime, the unique Old-South-Arabian letter-order is attested in Ugaritic script at *ca.* 1200 BC (Beth Shemesh tablet), implying OSA contact in the Levant by that time. Also, during 13th/12th centuries BC, came the genesis of use of camel-based long-distance transport in W. Arabia (Rifeh statuette, Egypt; Qurayya pot-painting), enabling a rapid rise in trade in lightweight, high value commodities such as aromatics, up to the Levant and Mesopotamia. In SW Arabia, Saba was best placed to exploit this phenomenon with the emergence of her paramount rulers (*mukarribs*) not later than *ca.* 820 BC (absolute bottom date) on texts known so far, and probably from rather earlier (and inevitably from 1000 BC minimum on 685 BC date for Karibil Watar I). By 750 BC, explicitly Sabaean camel caravans were reaching the Middle Euphrates, while records of identical trade earlier would take this phenomenon back to *ca.* 890 BC, within 40 years of Solomon and 60 years of the "queen of Sheba." That episode is thus bracketed (at *ca.* 950 BC?) between the emergence of the new trade-modes from the 12th century BC, and their already customary use by the 9th-8th centuries BC. This period is thus the backcloth against which any objective study of the data in 1 Kgs 10 *has* to be set, regardless of any modern observer's opinions about that pericope.

c) *Results of Comparison of 1 Kings 10 with External Data*

For the present, our sole record of the acts of Solomon and the queen from Sheba is that in 1 Kings, simply because the relevant classes of external documents have never yet been recovered that would enable us to assess their reality or roles directly. Instead, we are obliged to set the content and format of the Kings narrative against the backcloth of the 12th-9th centuries BC, to see what data it may provide, relevant to an assessment of 1 Kgs 10.

First, it is remarkable that a *queen*, not a king, of Sheba visits Solomon. In NW Arabia, queens (from Zabibe to Te'elkhunu) have an active political role down to 690 BC *and never again*. In S. Arabia, our minute amount of evidence shows women having a minor role in the royal hunt of Yitha'amar Bayyin I, but nothing like this later. Queens disappear from Arabian politics from 690 BC. Thus, the *queen* of Sheba is a "pre-Deuteronomic" phenomenon (621 BC), and would be an anachronism any later than 690 BC. Second, the mass of later legend about the Queen of Sheba is totally irrelevant to the question of her historicity. In SW Arabia, we have no data, because nothing relevant has as yet been dug! Marib is almost untouched by serious excavation, and material of the 10th century BC is probably 70 ft or more under the "tell" of old Marib. Third, long-distance travel by potentates in the biblical Near East is well-attested, in all directions, from as early as Sargon of Akkad via Tuthmosis I and Hishmi-Sharruma (if not also Hattusil III) down to the bizarre pilgrimage of Nabonidus; the queen from Sheba is no different. Fourth, Ophir as a geographical source of gold is no different to Koptos, ʿAmau or Kush, in identical expressions (gold of Koptos, of ʿAmau, of Kush, etc.), and its location is either in Africa west of the Red Sea (E. Sudan) or in W. Arabia east of the Red Sea; the Queen of Sheba episode favours the latter solution. Fifth, the quite different products (aside from gold) traded-in on the 3-year cycle of fleets come from further away than Ophir. Sixth, external data on royal wealth in the preclassical Near East set a standard by which we may judge the statistics in 1 Kgs 10 (and *not* merely from our own uninformed and subjective impressions). Against that standard, Solomonic wealth finds a reasonable context, in a world where intermittent, international royal weddings cost over $500,000 or up to £250,000 in gold alone, besides silver and much other cost, for example, with not just one gold/ivory adorned chair or throne, but ten at a time. And rhetorical flourishes cannot of themselves imply legendary status for accompanying statistics (Egyptian data cited above, to which Mesopotamian could be added).

In short, lack (so far...) of explicit mentions of either the Queen of Sheba or of Solomon (or any link between the two) proves nothing so far. We have no data in either proof or disproof of the Levant-Arabia relations of 1 Kgs 10; thus, we can neither affirm nor deny categorically these relations in terms of direct evidence. We have (so far) no Hebrew texts from the ofttimes destroyed site of Jerusalem (much of which cannot be dug, anyway), and no Egyptian inscriptions of the 21st Dynasty that give any running historical account whatsoever of relations abroad; Tanis is but a ruin-field of brick and granite, with most limestone inscriptions long since removed and reused. Assyria had no military or imperial pretensions in the westlands after Tiglath-pileser I (died 1077 BC) until the 880s BC under Assurnasirpal II at earliest. So neither Solomon nor Sheba *could* be mentioned in these sources from east and west till things changed. When they did, then Itamru and Karibil of Arabia do duly appear, as does Ahab of Israel. Marib will yield nothing unless it is very extensively (and deeply) dug. But until we do find fresh information in these categories, we must be content with intelligent use of the wider background charted above. That background cannot deliver proof either way, but it does provide an intelligible framework for what is found in 1 Kgs 10.

PHOENICIANS IN THE TENTH CENTURY BCE: A SKETCH OF AN OUTLINE[1]

LOWELL K. HANDY

1. INTRODUCTION

The "Phoenicians" were defined by the Greeks, who gave them this name by which the European world has come to know them. Debate still revolves around what φοινῖκικός was exactly supposed to describe about these particular people; usually it is explained as related to the dark-red/purple dye these people traded.[2] The "Phoenicians" themselves appear to have called themselves by the name of the particular city from whence they came, or, as an aggregate, "Canaanites."[3]

The term "Phoenician" was used by the Greeks to refer to those people who lived in a series of city-states along the east Mediterranean coast extending, at its largest, from Arwad to Acre.[4] Though the three major cities in the ancient world were Byblos, Sidon and Tyre, there were other

[1] An apology is due the reader. The chapter on the Phoenicians for this volume was contracted with two Phoenician scholars who were jointly to produce the article. A series of problems precluded their completing the manuscript by the deadline. It is hoped that the chapter will yet appear in another venue. This short overview is intended only to round out the series on surrounding areas and provide the introductory student with a basis on which to continue research. The secondary and tertiary sources used are primarily from the author's own library; time constrants being as they were.

[2] See, for example, G. Markoe, "Phoenicians," *The Oxford Encyclopedia of Archaeology in the Near East* (ed. E. M. Meyers; Oxford University, 1997) 4.324; B. Peckham, "Phoenicia, History of," *ABD* 5.349; D. R. Ap-Thomas, "The Phoenicians," *Peoples of Old Testament Times* (ed. D. J. Wiseman; Oxford: Clarendon, 1973) 263-64; and F. W. Danker, "Purple," *ABD* 5.558; L. Casson, *The Ancient Mariners: Seafarers and Sea Fighters of the Mediterranean in Ancient Times* (2nd ed.; Princeton, NJ: Princeton University, 1991) 62.

[3] Ap-Thomas, "Phoenicians," pp. 262-64, and G. W. Ahlström, *The History of Ancient Palestine from the Palaeolitic Period to Alexander's Conquest* (ed. D. V. Edelman; JSOTSup 146; Sheffield: JSOT, 1993) 59-60, both attempt to connect "Phoenician" and "Canaanite" as descriptive terms.

[4] Debate continues as to which locations, at which times, should be considered "Phoenician." This conforms to Markoe, "Phoenicians," p. 325. The largest extent and smallest extent are given in Ap-Thomas, "Phoenicians," p. 259 as (large) the entire eastern Mediterranean coast to (small) a 200 mile strip centered on ancient Byblos.

cities and several smaller "daughter" towns within the cultural and territorial sphere. The common denominator for these locations was a Syro-Palestinian population which had taken to the sea as prolific traders. At no time did these city-states form a single governmental body; that is, there was never a nation of Phoenicia.

The origin of these people is somewhat murky. The major cities were well established long before the 10th century BCE.[5] However, the definition of the region as bring "Phoenician" is generally understood to begin after the invasions during the 12th century BCE by the Sea Peoples who destroyed Ugarit, may have damaged Byblos, and certainly affected the other cities on the Syro-Palestinian coast.[6] Tyre appears to have come through the Sea Peoples invasion fairly intact and quickly became the major trading city of the area in its wake. The Syro-Palestinian population took up trade with the invading peoples now in their new territory, Philistia, as well as continued to trade with the home countries in the Aegean. It was the trading cities which properly became known as Phoenicia.

2. Sources

The 10th century evidence for the Phoenician cities leaves much to be desired. Archaeologically, for a long time the major sites had been excavated extensively only for the Hellenistic and Roman periods, with some work done in selected Bronze Age locations.[7] The Iron Age was reflected in some strata excavations and in the pottery dating charts, but extensive knowledge of the cities themselves from the sites for the 10th century remained beyond the data. Recent excavations have uncovered Iron

---

[5] Byblos was occupied in some form or another from *ca.* 6000 BCE, with housing units from *ca.* 4500 BCE, M. S. Joukowsky, "Byblos," *The Oxford Encyclopedia of Archaeology in the Near East* (ed. E. M. Meyers; Oxford University, 1997) 1.391; Sidon has been shown to have been inhabited since *ca.* 2700 BCE with a possible gap during the first half of the 2nd millennium, W. A. Ward, "Tyre," *The Oxford Encyclopedia of Archaeology in the Near East* (ed. E. M. Meyers; Oxford University, 1997) 5.247; and Sidon, which, while ascribed as the founding mother of Tyre by the Greek Seleucids, first appears in texts in the 14th century BCE, P. C. Schmitz, "Sidon (Place)," *ABD* 6.17.

[6] W. Röllig, "On the Origin of the Phoenicians," *Berytus* 31 (1983) 79-93; Markoe, "Phoenicians," p. 326.

[7] Ap-Thomas, "Phoenicians," pp. 265-266; aside from some scattered finds, there is a gap in the strata at Byblos from *ca.* 1200 to *ca.* 600 BCE, N. Jidejian, *Byblos Through the Ages* (Beirut: Dar el-Machreq, 1971) 57.

Age levels, but the data remains in the process of publication at this time.

There are very few contemporary inscriptions from which to extract data. Three inscriptions concerning rulers of Byblos form the entire collection.[8] Abibaal, during the reign of Sheshonq of Egypt, received a gift from the Egyptians to the Mistress of Byblos and expressed the hope that he should have a long reign. Yehimilk dedicated a temple to the Mistress of Byblos (*gbl*) declaring himself the legitimate ruler and expecting long days of life for this action. Elibaal established a statue for the Mistress of Byblos, again a gift from Egypt; though this last may come just after the 10th century. These supply a series of rulers' names, a modicum of knowledge about state religion, and a vague notion of a connection between Egypt and Byblos. It is not much.

The Bible has long been the primary source of information concerning Tyre in the 10th century BCE. Both David and Solomon are said to have had cordial relations with the city's ruler, King Hiram I.[9] 2 Sam. 5:11; 1 Kgs 5, 9-10; and 2 Chr 1:18-2:15 [English 2:1-16] set out the diplomatic and economic relations of the two rulers. A short survey of this material discloses a number of differences in the presentation of the relationships of the kings of Tyre and Jerusalem and a variety of manners to reconstruct the political balance of power have been proposed.[10] The extent to which the biblical narratives retain accurate remembrances of the period has been questioned due to the admitedly late date for the present version of the Bible texts referring to Hiram.[11] Nonetheless, the biblical accounts *can* be read as reflecting *possible* 10th century conditions in Tyrian foreign policy.

---

[8] They may be conveniently found in *TSSI*, pp. 17-22.

[9] There are a variety of ways of spelling the king's name in the Bible and in Josephus [Hiram, Hirom, Huram, Eiromoš, all of which may be shortened forms of ʾAhiram, a royal name attested at Byblos, from another time period; see K. W. Whitelam, "Hiram," *ABD* 3.203. "Hiram" has been the standardized English spelling and so will be consistently used here regardless of the source's spelling.

[10] See *ibid*., p. 204.

[11] From positive acceptance of the texts to negative rejection of them, see: E. W. Heaton, *Solomon's New Men: The Emergence of Ancient Israel as a National State* (New York: Pica, 1974) 28, 64-65; H. Donner, "The Interdependence of Internal Affairs and Foreign Policy during the Davidic-Solomonic Period (with Special Regard to the Phoenician Coast)," *Studies in the Period of David and Solomon and Other Essays* (ed. T. Ishida; Winona Lake, Ind.: Eisenbrauns, 1982) 205-14; G. Garbini, *History and Ideology in Ancient Israel* (New York: Crossroad, 1988) 22-24. On the question of usable material for the time of Solomon, see chapters by N. Naʾaman, "Sources and Composition in the History of Solomon," pp. 57-80, and E. A. Knauf, "Le roi est mort, vive le roi! A Biblical Argument for the Historicity of Solomon," pp. 81-95 [this volume].

Josephus provides the largest amount of information about Tyre in the 10th century.[12] In that he uses the biblical texts (adapting them slightly with some of his own interpretation) as well as a pair of citations from historians of Tyre, he produces a view of King Hiram I of Tyre contemporary with David and Solomon. This material appears in *Ant.* 7.3.2; 8.2.1; 8.6.4; and *Against Apion* 1.17-18. The last citation (*Against Apion* 1.18) provides a list of Tyrian kings which covers the time from Hiram I to the founding of Carthage, giving a list of the kings of Tyre for the majority of the 10th century. While the names of the rulers have generally been accepted as reflecting accurate records of kings of Tyre, the dates provided for the length of their lives and reigns have serious problems, these have tended to be "corrected" before being used.[13] The clear instance of inaccurate copying of these materials might also caution against too quickly accepting the list of names as totally correct as well.[14] References to dating the building of the Temple in Jerusaelm by events in Tyre's history also should be treated with some caution: what exactly is meant by the founding of Tyre (*Ant.* 8.2.1) is unclear, since 240 years before Solomon's temple clearly is not anywhere near the founding date for Tyre; whether Hiram was in his 11th year on the throne (*Ant.* 8.2.1) or his 12th (*Against Apion* 1.18) when the temple was started is a minor slip, but one worth noting; and the chronological problems of dating the beginning of construction on the Temple to 143 years before the founding of Carthage (*Against Apion* 1.17) compound questions of accurate records properly copied and historical recollection.

Josephus provides us with our only surviving material from two ancient historians who dealt with Hiram I. Menander of Ephesus appears to be among the numerous far-flung Greek historians who set out to write histories of the many peoples known in the Hellenistic era; he chose Phoenicians.[15] What Josephus cites from his work (*Against Apion* 1.18) is fairly much the same material as he had already cited from the Phoenician historian Dius, with the addition of noting that Hiram crushed a revolt by the Tityans when they failed to pay tribute and that

---

[12] See L. Feldman, "Josephus' View of Solomon," this volume, pp. 348-74.

[13] See discussion in J. Van Seters, *In Search of History: Historiography in the Ancient World and the Origins of Biblical History* (New Haven, Conn.: Yale University, 1983) 196-98

[14] At least one king appears to have been left out (on and beyond the problem of year numbers not adding up), Garbini, *History and Ideology*, p. 24.

[15] A. Lesky, *A History of Greek Literature* (2nd ed.; New York: Thomas Y. Crowell, 1963) 770-71.

he tore down old temples to build new ones. As for Dius, nothing else is known about him beyond what Josephus had to say, which was that he was a trustworthy historian (*Against Apion* 1.17) and that he made his history from the highly accurate and very ancient records kept at Tyre, which were still kept in the city's archives in the days of Josephus.

The only other source that might be cited for Phoenician culture of the 10th century is the "Phoenician History" of Philo of Byblos, which is purported to contain ancient information from a variety of Phoenician temples in assorted Phoenician cities.[16] While the work is known now only in disjointed narratives cited mostly in Eusebius of Caesarea, its reliability as a genuinely antiquarian Phoenician text has been popular in this century.[17] However, there are far too many questions about the text to use it as a source for the beliefs of the Phoenicians in the 10th century BCE.[18]

A few other classical references may be mentioned. Homer (*ca.* 800 BCE?), describing events of the 12th century, has a couple offhand comments to make concerning the Phoenicians generally.[19] Herodotus, of course, begins his *History* by noting that the whole problem of conflict among peoples began with the Phoenicians, who came out of the Red Sea, settling on the eastern Mediterranean coast and trading Egyptian and Assyrian goods to the temptation of young Greek women; whom they then kidnapped (1.1). Several other comments are made about Phoenicians, but not about the 10th century. Pliny, of course, mentions the Phoenicians sporodically throughout his natural history, but not with any 10th century information; which is the case for the numerous other classical references to Phoenicians, both Roman and Greek.

[16] H. W. Attridge and R. A. Oden, Jr., *Philo of Byblos, The Phoenician History: Introduction, Critical Text, Translation, Notes* (CBQMS 9; Washington, DC: Catholic Biblical Association, 1981); and A. I. Baumgarten, *The "Phoenician History" of Phio of Byblos: A Commentary* (Études préliminaires aux religions orientales dans l'Empire Romain 89; Leiden: E. J. Brill, 1981)

[17] See short discussion in Attridge and Oden, *Philo of Byblos*, pp.1-9.

[18] L. K. Handy, *Among the Host of Heaven: The Syro-Palestinian Pantheon as Bureaucracy* (Winona Lake, Ind.: Eisenbrauns, 1994) 44-48.

[19] E. Lipiński, "The Phoenicians," *The Oxford Encyclopedia of Archaeology in the Near East* (ed. E. M. Meyers; Oxford University, 1997) 1322, citing *Iliad* 23.742-43 and *Odyssey* 15.415-16.

3. Trade

Since Phoenicia was most noted by Greeks and Egyptians for trade both before the 10th century and afterward, this aspect of the cities of Sidon, Tyre and Byblos deserves the most attention from the little data extant. Already by the early 2nd millennium these cities had been trading with the Aegean area, the latter's pottery appearing in the major cities of the northeast Mediterranean coast and inland, including Alalakh, and Byblos, as well as Gezer and Lachish. From Mesopotamia came cylinder seals traded eastward at least as far as Crete.[20] The Phoenician control of sea trade, however, came after *ca.* 1200.[21]

For regional economics, nothing could match wood. Egyptian lumber trade with the port of Byblos clearly precedes the time of the "Phoenicians;" the use of cedar wood, especially the highly prized Lebanon cedar, in temple and palace construction is recorded in both Egyptian and Assyrian annals.[22] It is a certainty that the trade in this home-grown commodity remained the main large-scale export objective, at least among those doing the purchasing through the 10th century. The wood was taken by ship to Egypt, to Cyprus, and points west, while it had to be maneuvered overland to the Mesopotamian kingdoms to the east.[23] Other forms of wood, taken from the forested hillsides were good sources of trade items to those nations where wood of any kind was scarce, which included both Egypt and Assyria. This supply of readily available wood for building their ships also gave them the distinct

---

[20] N. Jidejian, *Tyre Through the Ages* (Beirut: Dar el-Machreq, 1969) 33; *idem*, *Sidon Through the Ages* (Beirut: Dar el-Machreq, 1971) 29. Though Byblos is the only city noted in the Egyptian documents for the earliest period for its trade with the area; D. Harden, *The Phoenicians* (Ancient Peoples and Places; revised ed.; London: Thames & Hudson, 1963) 44.

[21] G. Bunnens *L'expansion phénicienne en Méditerranée: Essai d'interprétation fondé sur une analyse des traditions littéraires* (Études de Philologie, d'Archéologie et d'Histoire Anciennes 17; Brussels: Institut Historique Belge de Rome, 1979) 15; Casson, *Ancient Mariners*, pp. 60-63; J. Elgavish, "Ships and Boats," *The Oxford Encyclopedia of Archaeology in the Near East* (ed. E. M. Meyers; Oxford University, 1997) 5.32.

[22] On the trade in Lebanon's wood in general and with respect to the biblical passages in particular, see F. Briquel-Chatonnet, *Les relations entre les cités de la côte phénicienne et les royaumes d'Israël et de Juda* (OLA 46; Louvain: Peeters, 1992) 250-58.

[23] While the report of Wenamun comes from about a century before the 10th century BCE itself, this document about the frustrations of obtaining the desired Lebanon wood for use in Egyptian temples (in this case the god Amun-Re's official boat) also demonstrates that the wood was transported by ship and needed diplomacy to obtain; H. Goedicke, The Report of Wenamun (JHNES; Baltimore, Md.: Johns Hopkins University, 1975) 17-129, text with notes.

advantage over Egypt in the ship building and trading business.[24]

Luxury items were also popular trade materials derived from Phoenican ports. The hand carving of ivory for export from the Phoenician cities can be documented from the 13th to the 7th centuries BCE.[25] These works appear originally to have been carved in local hippopotamus tusk ivory, until the animal became scarce and then extinct in the region; then the carvers extended their use of elephant tusk ivory imported from Africa, through Egypt, from India, through Mesopotamia, and perhaps from as close as inland Syria (along with imported hippo tusk ivory from Egypt).[26] The motifs included local designs as well as Egyptian art forms.

The production of dark-red/purple dye and cloth in the Phoenician cities continued to produce luxury trading goods. Purple, used for royal and priestly attire (not to mention just the general social elite and the spendthrift populace), was highly prized, especially in the deep shades which could be obtained from the murex snails (*murex brandaris*) abundant along the Phoenician coast. Not alone in making purple goods, the Phoenicians had a superior product and made use of it in what was already then a highly competitive luxury goods market.[27] Egyptians, Greeks, Romans, and even the Judean Solomon (if there is any historical value to 2 Chr 2:3,7) valued the Tyrian purple wear.

Like other recognizable groups of people, the Phoenicians had their own pottery.[28] This too, they traded. The flasks and jugs distinctive to the Phoenicians were made both in the home cities and in Phoenican cities on Cyprus.[29] In the 11th century bi-chrome ware from their industrial output could be found not only in Phoenica and Cyprus, but also among the Philistine cities, the northern Negev and in Egypt; by the 9th century, the pottery decoration most commonly found was red ware.[30]

---

[24] Jidejian, *Tyre*, p. 26. Earlier Phoenician ships were depicted in paintings and models in Egypt (mid 2nd millennium) and the cargo of one has been sea-excavated near Uluburun, Turkey; later ship depictions by Assyrians provide pictoral representations of more recent Phoenician ships, but not from the 10th century; G. F. Bass, "Sea and River Craft in the Ancient Near East," *Civilizations of the Ancient Near East* (ed. J. M. Sasson; New York: Charles Scribner's Sons, 1995) 3.1426-30

[25] M. L. Uberti, "Ivory and Bone Carving," *The Phoenicians* (ed. S. Moscati; Milan: Bompiani, 1988) 404.

[26] Briquel-Chatonnet, *Les relations*, pp.262-264.

[27] Danker, "Purple," p. 558, cites Pliny the Elder as declaring Tyrian purple the most expensive of garments.

[28] P. M. Bika, *The Pottery of Tyre* (Warminster: Aris & Phillips, 1978).

[29] Briquel-Chatonnet, *Les relations*," p. 258.

[30] Lipiński, *Phoenicians*, p. 1324.

Pottery, therefore, also continued to be a constant in the trade relations of the Phoencians and their clients and just as certainly many of these pottery pieces were shipped with wine, olive (or other) oil or other commodities inside.

Metals were imported into the Phoenician cities and also traded among other peoples. Copper, gold, silver, tin and iron are all reported to have been part of their merchandise and all could well have been in trade by the 10th century.[31] The Phoenicians appear to have worked and then exported some of the metal as finished products (especially as decorated bowls) along with furniture, glass, and the other luxury items mentioned above.

The Phoenicians also transported items from other areas farther along its trade routes. Such items as ivory, silk, and spice from India, coming through Mesopotamia, as well as papyrus and linen from Egypt that was conveyed westward from Phoenician ports.[32] As traders they appear to have had no real rivals in the eastern Mediterranean for the first quarter of the 1st millennium BCE.

4. Government

Only the city of Tyre has sufficient information concerning the 10th century to make any serious comments about it based on material supposed to derive from the century. It is probable that the earlier city-state structure discernable at Ugarit was similar to the Phoenician city states of two centuries earlier, but a couple hundred years, the change of political and cultural alignments left in the wake of the Sea Peoples, and the explosion of trade westward with its accompanying colonization, make it unlikely that the system had remained quite the same.[33]

The city-states were ruled by monarchies. The head of the local organization was the king. It appears to be the case that the throne was inher-

---

[31] J. D. Muhly, "Mining and Metalwork in Ancient Western Asia," *Civilizations of the Ancient Near East* (ed. J. M. Sasson; New York: Charles Scribner's Sons, 1995) 3.1501-21, provides a thorough overview. On tin, see M. McKay, "The Problem of Tin from Byblos," *Berytus* 31 (1983) 143-45, who clearly points out that there was no tin in Byblos, so it did not come from there, but was shipped in and out from elsewhere.

[32] Casson, *Ancient Mariners*, p. 64.

[33] For Ugarit, see M. Heltzer, *The Internal Organization of the Kingdom of Ugarit* (Wiesbaden: Reichert, 1982); and *idem*, "Royal Economy in Ancient Ugarit," *State and Temple Economy in the Ancient Near East* (ed. E. Lipinski; OLA 6; Louvain: Department Oriëntalistiek, 1979) 2.459-96

ited from father to son on the death of the parent.[34] From the evidence of Wenamun's report, a century earlier than our period, it would appear that the Phoenician bureaucracy, at least at Byblos, allowed for foreign traders to seek audience with the king directly; however, the whims of the ruler could be less than gracious.[35] The same material, as well as the portrait of Hiram in the biblical accounts, suggests that the kings of the cities of Byblos and Tyre had effective control of the economic sector of these cities including the collection of raw materials, the manufacture of trade goods, the skilled labor, and the merchant fleet. The territory of the surrounding countryside would also be at the disposal of the ruler (if 1 Kgs 9:11-14 reflects actual practice).

The rulers were also central figures in the religious world of their cities. The inscriptions from Byblos suggest that the king was understood to have been placed on the throne by the patron deity of the city and that his tenure as monarch depended on the will of the divine world.[36] To this end the king made certain that the gods' temples were in good repair and that proper ritual was maintained.[37] It is not possible to determine, for the 10th century, whether or not the king was simultaneously the city's high priest.

Reconstructions of the king-lists of Phoenicia have been made so that the 10th century rulers of the cities of Byblos and Tyre can be approximated. This list from Brian Peckham is admittedly conjectural:[38]

TYRE		BYBLOS	
ʾAbibaʿal	(1000)	ʾAḥirām	(1000)
Ḥiram I	(980)	ʾIttôbaʿal	(975)
Baʿalʿazor I	(950)	Yaḥimilk	(950)
ʿAbdʿaštart	(930)	ʾAbibaʿal	(930)
ʿAštart	(920-900)	ʾElibaʿal	(920-?)

Aside from the note that he died leaving his son Hiram on the throne (*Agianst Apion* 1.17-18), we know nothing about Abibaal of Tyre. This

[34] Josephus, *Against Apion* 1.18, has sons following fathers upon their deaths; except for the palace coup, of course.

[35] Goedicke, *Report of Wenamun*, pp. 45-52

[36] *TSSI*, pp. 17-19; B. Pekham, "Phoenicia and the Religion of Israel: The Epigraphic Evidence," *AIR*, p. 82.

[37] Josephus' references in *Against Apion* 1.17-18 to Hiram's cultic behavior; also the rituals performed by Zekerbaʿal during the visit of Wenamun, Goedicke, Report of Wenamun, p.53.

[38] Peckham, "Phoenicia, History of," pp. 355-56, note sources for the names, p. 355.

may indeed be said about the son of Hiram as well. The Kings of Byblos leave behind some religious artifacts and a clear sense of a continuing relationship to Egypt as both Abibaal and Elibaal make donations to the patron goddess of the city on behalf of the Egyptians. This leaves Hiram as a study for the time period.

Hiram, if the numbers in Josephus were correct (which they are probably not), came to the throne at the age of ca. 19 and reigned for 34 years. The power of Egypt was in relapse at the beginning of his reign and Assyria had disappeared from the region for some hundred years. He is credited with uniting two islands to form the city of Tyre by bringing the town and its temple together on one island mound while they had previously been two. This he then fortified. His trade arrangements expanded and colonies bagan to be established in the western Mediterranean, perhaps as far as Cadiz.[39] A naval colonization and tributary arrangement had apparently been devised as Hiram is reported to have successfully forced a tributary state into submission (*Against Apion* 1.17-18).

The treaties between David and Solomon in Samuel and Kings have been taken both as accurate historical reflection and as creative historiographical invention.[40] The treaty itself is not improbable, though whether there was one with David depends on a chronology that cannot be reconstructed with any certainty. The material aid presented in the Bible as being offerred to Solomon for his palace and Temple are not inconsistent with what might be expected from a friendly and generous neighboring kingdom, allied and at peace. Certainly craftsmen, metalworkers, metals, and timber are all items which Phoenicia could have supplied; all being classic Phoenician items in the trade market. Whether Tyre did supply them however, is another concern.

Hiram left a stable throne which was occupied by his son Baalazor, who is recorded as having reigned only 7 years, leaving the throne, in

---

[39] Whether the Tyrians' colonies reached as far west in the 10th century as Spain or not until the 9th is open to debate; respectively: H.J. Katzenstein, *The History of Tyre: From the Beginnings of the Second Millennium B.C.E. until the Fall of the Neo-Babylonian Empire in 538 B.C.E.* (Jerusalem: Schocken Institute for Jewish Research, 1973) 75; Lipiński, *Phoenicians*, p. 1322. However, Cadiz appears to have already been settled; *ibid.* p. 1327.

[40] Katzenstein, *History of Tyre*, pp. 77-115, accepts almost everything in the biblical narrative and in Josephus as accurate historical data; Ahlstöm, *History*, pp. 515-18, accepts the biblical material as essentially accurate; and Garbini, *History and Ideology*, pp. 22-25, assumes the biblical material is largely late legendary material and he mistrusts Josephus' accounts.

turn, to his son, Hiram's grandson, Abdashtart, who then reigned for 9 years. The ensuing coup may have had something to do with international events; both Egypt and Assyria began to make moves toward reestablishing themselves as empires in the late 10th century. That Assyria would succeed and Egypt did not does not tell us anything about the perceptions of the world in Tyre itself.[41] Then, again, it may have been simply a grab for power or a personal hatred for the king and/or the royal family. In any case, Abdashtart was assassinated by palace retainers who placed one of their own on the throne. The usurper, we are told, reigned 12 years.

5. Religion

Each of the Phoenician cities had a patron deity, or at least one that was deemed superior to the others of their pantheon by Greeks, Romans, and Jewish commentators. For Tyre it was the god called Melqart. Though nothing is actually known about the deity until the 9th century, it is assumed that the worship of the deity extended backward through the 10th century.[42] The "Mistress of Byblos" was the reigning deity in Byblos. The inscriptions of all three kings found from the 10th century BCE are devoted to her. The Greeks called her Aphrodite and from this some scholars assume the city worshiped Astarte, but the evidence is slight and inconclusive.[43] The inigmatic healing deity Eshmun was the central deity at Berytos, but he had a sanctuary at Sidon as well, though Sidon's central deity is uncertain.[44] It has been argued that the Phoenicians worshipped their deities in triads, but this is less clear in the data than in the theory; what can be said is that they did like their deities in couples.[45]

---

[41] Certainly Byblos was continuing to maintain its international ties to Egypt through the end of the century; *TSSI*, pp. 19-22.

[42] S. Ribichini, "Beliefs and Religious Life," *The Phoenicians* (ed. S. Moscati; Milan: Bompiami, 1988) 108; Röllig, "On the Origin," p. 88.

[43] Ribichini, "Beliefs," p. 107; though note that the rulers' names tend to be compounded with "Baʿal" while those of Tyre do contain "Astarte" as a divine aspect and even as the whole name.

[44] Röllig, "On the Origin," p. 88; 1Kgs 11:5 has Ashtoreth (biblically tampered form of Astarte) as the "goddess of the Sidonians" (2 Kgs 23:13 has her as the "abomination" of the Sidonians); however, Hebrew (like Greek at times) uses "Sidonian" to mean Phoenicians in general..

[45] On this aspect of Phoenician religions see: S. Moscati, *The World of the Phoenicians* (New York: Praeger, 1968) 36-37; A. van den Branden, "La Triade phénicienne," *BeO* 23 (1981) 35-63; R. J. Clifford, "Phoenician Religion," *BASOR* 279 (1990) 62; and P. C. Schmitz, "Phoenician Religion," *ABD* 5.362.

Little is known about regular worship of these gods, but it can be safely asserted that there were daily rituals as well as cyclical ceremonies.[46] The city temple was the site of royal, official, state respect for what the deities did for the ruler and the city; however, no temples from this period survive in ruins or otherwise. From some two centuries later, the temple at Sarepta dedicated to Tanit, had a first phase which had a *langraum* structure with the doorway at one end and the altar at the far wall;[47] whether this reflected temple construction of centuries earlier cannot be determined.

There were clearly professional priests of various levels, but little is known about them. There were sacrifices of many types as throughout the ancient Near East, but the most notorious Phoenician sacrifice was clearly that which entailed the ritual slaying of small children. Both biblical and classical writers condemned this practice as evil.[48] However, the Phoenicians and their colonial descendents maintained the practice so it must have been an important part of their relgious world view. In addition the Phoenician deities could communicate with their subjects by way of prophets; there may have been professional court/temple prophets on the state payroll, but it is clear that the gods could seize any person and use them as an ecstatic prophet.[49]

---

[46] Note the ritual in Wenamun's account; Goedicke, *Report of Wenamun*, p. 53; otherwise there is not much known, at least for this early period, Schmitz, "Phoenician Religion," p. 361.

[47] J. B. Pritchard, *Recovering Sarepta, a Phoenician City: Excavations at Sarafand, Lebanon, 1969-1974, by the University Museum of the University of Pennsylvania* (Princeton, Conn.: Princeton University, 1978) 134-36, fig. 127. It might be worth noting, that if the דבר in Solomon's temple was a cedar wood cube, the temple itself might have had a stone outline not unlike that of the Sarepta temple foundation; J. Ouellette, "The Solomonic *Debir* According to the Hebrew Text of 1 Kings 6," *JBL* 89 (1970) 338-43. For other possible cultic sites, without enough remains to reconstruct them as temples, see: T. A. Busink, *Der Tempel von Jerusalem von Salomo bis Herodes* (Leiden: E. J. Brill, 1970) 461-62 (remains of the Sidon temple to Eshmun); N. Avigad, "Excavations at Makmish," *IEJ* 10 (1960) 91-92; and Moscati, *World of the Phoenicians*, pp. 39-40, 46.

[48] The evidence has recently been thoroughly examined in a pair of studies: G. C. Heider, *The Cult of Molek: A Reassessment* (JSOTSup 43; Sheffield: Sheffield Academic, 1985); and J. Day, *Molech: A God of Human Sacrifice* (University of Cambridge Oriental Publications 41; Cambridge: Cambridge University, 1989).

[49] If the references to prophets of Baal and Asherah eating at Jezebel's table reflect professional temple-employed prophets, this would appear to be an import with the queen from Phoenicia, or at least the author wants the reader to so believe (the numbers may be exaggerated) 1 Kgs 18:19. As for ecstatic prophets, note the use by the god of the page in Wenamun's report; Goedicke, *Report of Wenamun*, pp. 53-55, a message which is accepted as being the word of the god even by the King of Byblos who has been delaying for days. See note in Schmitz, "Phoenician Religion," pp. 361-62

It is clear that Phoencian religion developed on a straight trajectory from the Syro-Palestinian religion of the 2nd millennium BCE.[50] Behind the titles given to the patron deities of the Phoenician cities stand the pantheon familiar from both the Bible and the Ugaritic texts; however, the exact correlations cannot be made with certainty with such small extant data.[51] The continual contact with Egypt did have its effect on these cities' religious beliefs and practices. One influence was the religious artistic representations of the Phoenician deities which included aspects of Egyptian sacred art.[52] The Phoenicians also introduced Egyptian deities into their religious sphere and religious iconography.[53]

6. Conclusion

It would appear that in the 10th century BCE the major force in the eastern Mediterranean was an economic one. Though Tyre appears to have had colonies paying tribute, it was the Phoenician sailing trade which allowed them to become major forces in their world. The lack of a powerful Egypt until after mid-century and the absence of Assyria as a real threat to the coast until after the century left Tyre and its neighboring cities to ply their trade without serious restraints. The relations of Hiram and Solomon (maybe David) portrayed in the Bible all seem to reflect a superior city-state aiding a lesser city-state, perhaps as a buffer for the inevitable rise of Egypt as a power to the south.[54] It appears clear, however, that Tyre saw its future on the seas and not in conquest of inland territories.

---

[50] Röllig, "On the Origin," p. 90.

[51] Several attempts have been made to equate the titles with known Semitic deities, but aside from Resheph, who had his own temple at Byblos (and more on Cyprus), it is pretty much guesswork; Ribichini, "Beliefs," p. 107, on Resheph in Byblos. However, do note the names of gods in the royal families: Ba'al, Astarte, and (possibly) Molech/MLK.

[52] *Ibid.*, pp. 107-108.

[53] Bes appears in Phoenician artwork as late as the 6th century BCE; S. Moscati, "Arts and Crafts," *The Phoenicians* (ed. S. Moscati; Milan: Bompiami, 1988) 144-47. A presumably 10th century Phoenician bowl dedicated to Amun has been found on Cyprus; Lipiński, *Phoenicians*, p. 1324.

[54] It appears unlikely that Hiram owed his importance to his dealings with Solomon, as has sometimes been suggested; M. E. Aubet, *Tiro y las colonias fenicias de occidente* (Barcelona: Bellaterra, 1987) 36. Tyre was well established and trade had made it a powerful city with an essentially impregnable defensive location; Jerusalem was a minor town of no particular location or importance, only lately out from under Egyptian control. It was in Solomon's interest to deal with Tyre; it was not particularly of importance for Tyre to deal with Solomon, save that there was trade to be had here.

INLAND SYRIA AND THE EAST-OF-JORDAN REGION IN THE FIRST MILLENNIUM BCE BEFORE THE ASSYRIAN INTRUSIONS

Mark W. Chavalas

Introduction

The focus of this essay will be a historical and cultural description of the territory of inland Syria and the northeast Jordan region in the 10th century BCE until the accelerated intrusions of Assyria during the reign of Ashurbanipal II (883-859 BCE). Syria had been under the control of the Hittite kingdom until its fragmentation and relocation at the beginning of the 12th century BCE.[1] Neo-Hittite successor states gradually formed in the following three centuries, as attested in sources primarily from the 9th to 7th centuries BCE. These states spoke an Anatolian dialect known as Luwian (attested in the Hittite cuneiform texts from Hattusha) and wrote in a hieroglyphic script.[2] These Luwian polities recognized their debt to the Hittite political and cultural tradition.

Also in this region there are contemporary Assyrian accounts of Aramean intrusions into Syria east of the Euphrates and northern Iraq during the reign of Tiglath-Pileser I (reigned 1114-1076 BCE), the first Assyrian king to mention the Arameans.[3] The Arameans also caused problems in the Khabur triangle during the reign of Ashur-Bel-kala (reigned 1073-1056 BCE).[4] The Assyrian texts describe the Arameans in

---

[1] For the relocation of Hittite power, see H. Hoffner, "The Last Days of Khattusha," *The Crisis Years: The 12th Century B.C. from Beyond the Danube to the Tigris* (ed. W. Ward and M. Joukowsky; Dubuque: Kendall/Hunt, 1992) 46-52.

[2] See J. D. Hawkins, "The Neo-Hittite States in Syria and Anatolia," *CAH* (1982) 3.372-75. For a recent survey of the Neo-Hittite states, see *idem*, "The Political Geography of North Syria and South-east Anatolia in the Neo-Assyrian Period," *Neo-Assyrian Geography* (ed. M. Liverani; Rome: Università di Roma, 1995) 69-85.

[3] See *ARI* 2.n. 363. and *AR* 239, 287; for a discussion of Arameans in Syria, see G. Schwartz, "The Origins of the Arameans in Syria and Northern Mesopotamia: Research Problems and Potential Strategies," *To the Euphrates and Beyond: Archaeological Studies in Honour of Maurits van Loon* (eds. O. Haex and others; Rotterdam: Balkema, 1989) 281-86.

[4] *ARI* nn. 235-47, and J. Brinkman, *A Political History of Post-Kassite Babylonia 1158-722 B.C.* (AnOr 43; Rome: Pontifical Biblical Institute, 1968) 383-89.

this period as pastoral and partly rural, with no political centralization, at least in relation to the Assyrians.

By the beginning of the 10th century BCE the extension of Aramean tribes inland disturbed the Luwian dynasties. Most argue that these two people groups remained distinct for a short period, but gradually fused together somewhat to create what has been called the Syro-Hittite culture.[5] The writer of 1 Kings records that Solomon traded with "all the kings of the Hittites and the kings of Aram," a phrase that showed that the Israelites recognized a distinctness of the two groups, at least in their perception of the political configurations of the 10th century BCE.[6] In addition, both Phoenician and especially Hurrian influences can also be seen in Syria in this period. In sum, these city-states in Syria were part of a broader cultural continuum stretching to Cilicia in southeast Anatolia.

1. Textual and Archaeological Sources

At the beginning of the 10th century BCE local use of the cuneiform writing system in Syria was discontinued.[7] However, memorial royal stone inscriptions appear to have increased primarily as a result of the Neo-Hittite polities. These texts were written in the aforementioned hieroglyphic Luwian, a script which continued in use until the 7th century BCE.[8] Moreover, the Luwians also employed the alphabetic Phoenician script for specific purposes. The existing hieroglyphic Luwian texts, whole and fragmentary, have been found at the sites of Carchemish,[9] Til-Barsip (modern Tell Ahmar),[10] and small amounts

---

[5] Hawkins, "Neo-Hittite States," 373-74.

[6] 1 Kgs 10:29; for the relationship of Israel to the Aramean states, see B. Mazar, "The Aramean Empire and Its Relation to Israel," *BA* 25 (1962) 98-120; and G. Reinhold, *Die Beziehungen Altisraels zu den aramäischen Staaten in der israelitisch-judäischen Königzeit* (Europäische Hochschulschriften 23, Theologie 268; Frankfort: Lang, 1989).

[7] For the supplanting of cuneiform by the simpler alphabetic scripts, see A. Millard, "Assyrians and Arameans," *Iraq* 45 (1983) 101-108.

[8] E. Larouche, *Les hiéroglyphs hittites I: L'écriture* (Paris: Centre national de la recherche scientifique, 1960); J. D. Hawkins, *The Hieroglyphic Luwian Inscriptions of the Iron Age* (3 vols.; forthcoming); and *idem.* and others, *Hittite Hieroglyphs and Luwian: New Evidence for the Connection* (Göttingen: Vandenhoeck & Ruprecht, 1973).

[9] There are at least forty texts; see J. D. Hawkins, "Building Inscriptions at Carchemish: The Long Wall of Sculpture and the Great Staircase," *AnSt* 22 (1972) 87-114; and C. L. Woolley, R. D. Barnett, "The Inscriptions," *Carchemish: Report on the Excavations at Jerablus on Behalf of the British Museum* (London: British Museum, 1952) 3.259-68.

[10] G. Bunnens, ed., *Tell Ahmar: 1988 Season* (Leiden: E. J. Brill, 1990); and F. Thureau-Dangin and others, *Til-Barsib* (BAH 23; Paris: Paul Geuthner, 1936).

from the regions of Aleppo, Hama, and the Amuq plain (El-Mina and Tell Tayinat). There are royal autobiographies in hieroglyphic texts in which the rulers (including a few queens) stress their piety and their dynastic histories.[11] Apparently these rulers considered themselves monarchs.[12] A few letters have survived from what must have been a very large corpus, although they are from periods after the Assyrian involvement in the area.[13]

The Arameans wrote their own language in the alphabetic script developed by Semitic speaking peoples in Syro-Palestine (especially the Phoenicians) in the late second millennium BCE.[14] The earliest attested texts in Aramaic, however, date to the 9th century BCE.[15] The main body of existing texts in Aramaic (as well as Luwian) are seals and monumental stone inscriptions made for dedicatory purposes.[16] These can be categorized as cultic, royal, and personal (some of which are autobiographical in nature). There are a few deeds of land sales and short treaties. For the most part, however, the literary tradition has not survived for either group, as most writing was apparently done on perishable material. Aramaic inscriptions have been found at Afis,[17] Hama,[18] Zinjirli,[19] Arslan Tash,[20] and Tell Fekheriyah,[21] but are primarily from

---

[11] E.g., the Suihis and Yairis of Carchemish, Hawkins, "Building Inscriptions," pp. 88-114.

[12] See, Laroche, *Les hiéroglyphs*, nn. 10, 17, 18, 21.

[13] See W. Andrae, *Hethitische Inschriften auf Bleistriefen aus Assur* (WVDOG 46; Leipzig: J. C. Hinrichs, 1924); J. D. Hawkins, "The Negatives in Hieroglyphic Luwian," *AnSt* 25 (1975) 119-56; and T. Özgüc, *Kültepe and Its Vicinity in the Iron Age* (Türk Tarih Kurumu Yayinlarindan 5.29; Ankara: Turk Tarih Basimevi, 1971) pls. xlvii, l-lii.

[14] See *KAI* and *TSSI* 2.1-76. For the Aramean script, see J. Naveh, *The Development of the Aramaic Script* (Jerusalem: Israel Academy of Sciences and Humanities, 1970). For a survey of the Aramean states, see A. Dupont-Sommer, *Les araméens* (Collection l'orient ancien illustré 2; Paris: Maisonneuve, 1949); and H. Sader, *Les états araméens de Syrie depuis leur fondations jusqu'a leur transformation en provinces assyriennes* (Beirut: Orient-Institut der Deutschen Morganländischen Gesellschaft, 1987).

[15] See survey in S. Layton, "Old Aramaic Inscriptions," *BA* 51 (1988) 172-89. The recently discovered Tel Dan inscription may date to the early 9th century; see A. Biran and J. Naveh, "An Aramaic Stele Fragment from Tel Dan," *IEJ* 43 (1993) 81-98.

[16] Hawkins, "Neo-Hittite States," pp. 437-39; and Laroche, "Liste des documents hiéroglyphiques," *RHA* 27 (1969) 110-31

[17] *KAI* 202.

[18] *KAI* 203-13.

[19] *KAI* 214.

[20] See F. Thureau-Dangin, P. Bordreuil, and A. R. Millard, *Arslan Tash* (2 vols.; BAH 16; Paris: Paul Geuthner, 1931).

[21] A. Abou-Assaf and others, *La statue de Tell Fekheriye et son inscription bilingue assyrio-araméenne* (Études assyriologiques 7; Paris: Recherche sur Les Civilisations, 1982).

the period after the early 9th century BCE Assyrian encroachment into the area. They, however, likely reflect conditions of the previous century. The Aramaic inscriptions are modelled on the hieroglyphic Luwian type, especially in terms of royal autobiographies, showing that the rulers, like the Neo-Hittites, considered themselves kings. For example, the local Aramean ruler in the bilingual Tell Fekheriyah inscription fashions himself a king in Aramaic, but in the subsequent Akkadian translation is called a "governor." The two corpora show similar features in terms of formulas, but little of a historiographic nature, unlike the contemporary Assyrian texts.[22]

Assyrian royal inscriptions from the 9th century BCE and later likewise probably mirror conditions in the 10th century in Syria, as do excerpts from the Assyrian Eponym Canon,[23] as well as chronicles of military campaigns to the regions of Arpad, Uqni, Amanus, Hatarikka, Damascus, and elsewhere.[24] There are, of course, a number of biblical references to Syria (and the Syro-Hittite states in particular) during the reigns of Saul, David, Solomon and later kings in 2 Sam-1 Kgs, and 1-2 Chr.

Extensive archaeological remains for this period have been uncovered at Carchemish,[25] Tell Ahmar,[26] Arslan Tash (Bit-Adini),[27] Zinjirli,[28] on the plains of Antioch,[29] ʿAin Dara,[30] Hama(th),[31] and Tell Halaf.[32]

---

[22] Hawkins, "Neo-Hittite States," pp. 437-39.

[23] A. K. Grayson, *Assyrian and Babylonian Chronicles* (TCS 5; Locust Valley, NY: J. J. Augustin, 1975).

[24] For the Assyrian inscriptions, see H. Tadmor, "Assyria and the West: The Ninth Century and Its Aftermath," *Unity and Diversity: Essays in the History, Literature, and Religion of the Ancient Near East* (eds. H. Goedicke and J. J. M. Roberts; JHNES; Baltimore: Johns Hopkins University, 1975) 336-48.

[25] D. G. Hogarth, *Carchemish I: Introductory* (London: Trustees of the British Museum, 1914); and C. L. Woolley, *Carchemish II: The Town Defenses* (London: Trustees of the British Museum, 1921). For a general survey, see H. Güterbock, "Carchemish," *JNES* 13 (1954) 102-14.

[26] See Thureau-Dangin and others, *Til-Barsib.*

[27] See Thureau-Dangin and others, *Arslan-Tash.*

[28] F. von Luschan, *Ausgrabungen im Sendschirli I-V* (Berlin: Walter de Gruyter, 1893-1943).

[29] R. Haines, *Excavations on the Plain of Antioch II: The Structural Remains of the Later Phases* (Chicago: Oriental Institute, 1971).

[30] F. Seirafi and A. Kirichian, "Recherches archéologiques à Ayin-Dara," *Annales Archéologiques Arabes Syriennes* 15/2 (1961) 3-20; and A. Abou-Assaf, *Der Tempel von ʿAin Dara* (Mainz am Rhein: Philipp von Zabern, 1990).

[31] J. D. Hawkins, "Hamath," *RLA* 4.67-70.

[32] M. von Oppenheim, *Tell Halaf I-IV* (Berlin: Walter de Gruyter, 1943-1962).

2. Geographic and Historical Context

Based upon the fragmented textual and material remains, it is possible to make a geographic and historical survey of the various Syro-Hittite states in the 9th-7th centuries BCE, and by way of analogy reconstruct the socio-political horizon in the 10th century BCE. The Aramean states appear to have been ruled by members of a dominant tribe, many of which were named after the putative ancestor of the dynasty. The Neo-Hittite states were, of course, culturally related to the earlier Hittite kingdom, but on a much smaller scale. The Neo-Hittite states beyond historic Syria and the Taurus mountain range are beyond the scope of this present essay.[33]

Large scale population movements occurred at the end of the Late Bronze Age (*ca.* 1200 BCE) with the destruction of most of the major urban centers in Anatolia and Syria. The Hittite culture survived and expanded into the region of Syria. Arguably the most important of these states was centered at Carchemish along the northernmost part of the Euphrates.[34] This principality was the seat of a Luwian dynasty with intimate connections to Hittite traditions. The polity of Carchemish is evidenced by a number of sculptural and architectural forms. Only a few fragmentary inscriptions give scant evidence of its political history. However, it is fairly certain that the monarchs used the Hittite title of Great King.[35] The material remains at Carchemish give strong evidence of a long standing dynasty before the advent of Ashurbanipal II.[36]

Northwest of Carchemish near the Mediterranean coast was the Aramean state of Samʾal (modern Zinjirli). It appears to have been an autonomous dynasty that was created sometime later in the 10th century.[37] The earliest mention of the state is in the annals of Shalmaneser III

---

[33] See Hawkins, "Neo-Hittite States," pp. 372-441.

[34] J. D. Hawkins, "Assyrians and Hittites," *Iraq* 36 (1974) 69-83; *idem.*, "Karkamis," *RLA* 5.426-46; *idem.* "Kuz-Teshub and the 'Great Kings' of Karkamish," *AnSt* 38 (1988) 100-108; and *idem.*, "'Great Kings' and 'Country Lords' at Malatya and Karkamish," *Studio Historiae Ardens: Ancient Near Eastern Studies Presented to Philo H. J. Houwink ten Cate on the Occassion of the 65th Birthday* (eds. Th. P. J. van den Hout and J. de Roos; Istanbul: Nederlands Historisch-Archaeologisch Instituut, 1995) 73-85.

[35] See J. D. Hawkins, "Kuz-Teshub and the 'Great Kings' of Karkamish," pp. 100-108.

[36] M. E. L. Mallowan, "Carchemish," *AnSt* 22 (1972) 63-85; contra D. Ussishkin, "The Monuments of the Lower Palace Area in Carchemish: A Rejoinder," *AnSt* 26 (1976) 105-12.

[37] Hawkins, "Neo-Hittite States," pp. 386-87.

(858-824 BCE).[38] The artistic style of Sam'al betrays a Phoenician influence.

South of Sam'al along the north Syrian coast on the Amuq plain was the Luwian state of Uqni, with its capital at Kunulua (possibly Tell Tayʿinat).[39] Material remains at ʿAin Dara, including a large temple complex with Hittite artistic conventions, a palace complex with the *ḫilāni* style, and many examples of sculpture, attest to the importance of this polity.[40]

To the south of Carchemish on the Euphrates was the large Aramean tribal state of Bit-Adini (biblical Beth-Aden[41]) centered at Til Barsip, dominating the Euphrates to the confluence of the Khabur River.[42] Although Bit-Adini was not actually referred to until the reigns of Adad-nirari II in 899 BCE[43] and Ashurbanipal II,[44] it can be assumed that it existed in the previous century.

To the west was Bit-Agusi (also known as Yahan), another large Aramean state centered at Arpad.[45] The earliest mention of the state is in the annals of Ashurnasirpal II (884-859 BCE),[46] although there are biblical references later than the 10th century.[47]

On the Syrian coast in the Baqʿa Valley was the large kingdom of

[38] *KAI* 24, ll. 2-3, and B. Landsberger, *Sam'al: Studien zur Entdeckung der Ruinenstaette Karatepe* (Ankara: Drukerei der turkishen historischen Gesellschaft, 1948) 37, n. 82.

[39] J. D. Hawkins, "Hattin," *RLA* 4.160-62; and *idem*., "Assyrians and Hittites," pp. 81-83. A recent survey of Uqni and the Amur Region is by T. Wilkinson, "The History of the Lake of Antioch," *Crossing Boundaries and Linking Horizons: Studies in Honor of Michael C. Astour Celebrating His 80th Birthday* (eds. R. Averbeck and others; Bethesda, Md: CDL, forthcoming).

[40] W. Orthmann, *Untersuchungen zur späthethitischen Kunst* (SBAlt 8; Bonn: R. Habelt, 1971) 56-59, 136-38; and H. Genge, *Nordsyrisch-südanatolisch Reliefs: Eine archäologische-historische Untersuchung: Datierung und Bestimmung* (Copenhagen: Munksgaard, 1979) 184-86.

[41] Amos 1:5.

[42] D. Ussishkin, "Was Bit-Adini a Neo-Hittite or Aramean State?" *Or* 40 (1971) 431-37; and A. Lemaire, "Le pays d'Eden et le Bit-Adini aux origines d'un mythes," *Syria* 58 (1981) 313-30.

[43] *ARI* 426.

[44] *ARI* 547, 582, 83; *AR* 559-561, 599-601.

[45] J. D. Hawkins, "Jahan," *RLA* 5.238-39; K. Elliger, "Sam'al und Hamat in ihrem Verhältnis zu Hattina, Uqni, und Arpad," *Festschrift Otto Eissfeldt* (ed. J. Fück; Halle: M. Niemeyer, 1947) 69ff.; and J. Matthers, "The Iron Age (1200-700 B.C.)," *The River Qoueiq, Northern Syria and Its Catchment: Studies Arising from the Tell Rifaat Survey, 1977,79* (ed. J. Matthers; Oxford: British Archaeological Reports, 1981) 415-37.

[46] Hawkins, "Jahan," pp. 238-39.

[47] 2 Kgs 18:34; 19:13.

Hamath.[48] The rulers of this kingdom in the 10th-9th centuries had a mix of Anatolian and some Aramaic names. By the 8th century, the names of the rulers became almost exclusively Aramaic. The Bible preserves some information about Toi, King of Hamath,[49] who was a contemporary of David. The name Toi has been argued to be Hurrian, showing another ethnic element in Hamath.[50] Toi's sons, however, had Semitic names, showing the ethnic complexity of the area. A royal altar, towered gate, and temple (possibly dedicated to Baʿalat), a small city gate, and a palace have been found at Hamath. A Luwian inscription of Urhilla (contemporary of Shalmaneser III) has also been found. Hamath was allied to the kingdom of Israel, and Solomon built fortresses and grain storage units in Hamath's territory.[51]

Aram-Zobah was along the upper Orontes River in the Baqʿa Valley and was mentioned among the enemies of Saul of Israel. Hadad-ezer was its king (by a union with Bit-Rehob) during the reign of David (*ca.* 1010-971 BCE).[52] This Aramean king ruled over a vast territory in the Damascus area and had vassals in the north Transjordan,[53] and was influential as far as Ammon in the south and Hamath in the north,[54] expanding beyond the Euphrates.[55] He was ultimately defeated by David of Israel.[56] It has been argued that the King of Aram who seized the two Euphrates cities from Assyria at the beginning of the 10th century may well have been Hadad-ezer of Aram-Zobah.[57]

---

48 J. D. Hawkins, "Hamath," *RLA* 4.67-70.

49 2 Sam 8:9-10; 1 Chr 18:9-10; see E. Fugmann, *Hama: fouilles et recherches 1931-1938*, Vol. 2/1: *L'Architecture dės périodes pré-hellénistique* (Copenhagen: Nationalmuseet, 1958); and P. Riis, *Hama*, Vol. 2/2: *Les objects de la période dite Syro-Hittite (Age du Fer)* (Copenhagen: Nationalmuseet, 1938).

50 See M. Liverani, "Antecedenti dell'onomastica aramaica antica," *RSO* 37 (1962) 65-76.

51 2 Chr 8:4.

52 A. Malamat, "The Kingdom of David and Solomon in Its Contact with Egypt and Aram-Naharaim," *BA* 21 (1958) 96-102; see also G. Buccellati, *Cities and Nations of Ancient Syria: An Essay on Political Institutions with Special Reference to the Israelite Kingdoms* (Studi Semitici 26; Rome: Istituto di Studi del Vicino Oriente, 1967) 143-45.

53 2 Sam 10:6; 1 Chr 19:6-7.

54 2 Sam 8:9-10.

55 2 Sam 8:3; 10:16; 1 Chr 19:16.

56 A. Malamat, "Aspects of Foreign Policies of David and Solomon," *JNES* 22 (1963) 1-6.

57 *AR* 603; R. Borger and W. Schramm, *Einleitlung in die assyrischen Königsinschriften: Zweiter Teil: 934-722 V. Chr* (HOE 5; Leiden: E. J. Brill, 1973); and A. Malamat, "The Arameans," *Peoples of Old Testament Times* (ed. D. J. Wiseman; Oxford: Clarendon, 1973) 142, nn. 20-21.

The Arameans of Damascus apparently supported Aram-Zobah but were defeated by David. Soon thereafter, Aram-Zobah was replaced by a dynasty from Damascus,[58] which became the largest of the Aramean states.[59] During the reign of Solomon, a certain Rezon (former servant of Hadadezer of Zobah) took the city of Damascus and was proclaimed king.[60] Solomon could not regain the territory and it became a dominant power in southern Syria. In the next century Damascus became a leader of the twelve state coalition against the Assyrian monarch Shalmaneser III.[61] A later Damascene monarch mentioned in the Bible was Ben-Hadad I, son of a certain Tab-Rimmon.[62] He was involved in a boundary dispute between Israel and Judah, aligning with Asa of Judah.

Further east in Syria the Arameans formed large tribal states of Bit-Bakhiani on the Khabur River at Guzanu (Tell Halaf),[63] Bit-Khalupe on the lower Khabur north of Sirqu (the name of Tell Ashara/Terqa in the Late Assyrian period), and Laqe to its south.[64] Adad-Nirari II (911-891 BCE) fought in the Khabur region and mentioned Dur-Katlimu (Tell Sheikh Hamad) and Sirqu.[65] His successor Tukulti-Ninurta II (890-884 BCE) received tribute from Sirqu, as evidenced by a memorial stela.[66] The Arameans were able to move into northern Mesopotamia in the 10th century until checked by Ashur-Dan (reigned 934-912 BCE),[67] and formed the large tribal state of Bit-Zamani on the upper Tigris.

The Bible mentions the Aramean states of Beth-Rehob (on the upper Jordan River), Maacah, and Geshur, all of which were apparently minor states. Geshur was a semi-independent Aramean kingdom in the south-

---

[58] 2 Sam 8:5; 10:16-19; see A. Malamat, "Arameans," pp. 141-46; and *idem*., "Aspects of Foreign Policies," p. 5.

[59] See W. Pitard, *Ancient Damascus: A Historical Study of the Syrian City-State from Earliest Times Until Its Fall to the Assyrians in 732 B.C.E.* (Winona Lake, Ind.: Eisenbrauns, 1987); and M. Unger, *Israel and the Arameans of Damascus: A Study in Archaeological Illumination of Bible History* (Grand Rapids: Zondervan, 1957).

[60] 1 Kgs 11:23-25; see A. Jepsen, "Israel und Damaskus," *AfO* 14 (1941-1945) 153-72.

[61] A. L. Oppenheim, "Babylonian and Assyrian Historical Texts," *ANET*, pp. 278-79.

[62] 1 Kgs 15:16-22 = 2 Chr 16:1-6.

[63] Grayson, *Assyrian and Babylonian Chronicles*, no. 5:189; annals of Tiglath-pileser III.

[64] *ARI* 434, 773; and J. N. Postgate, "Laqe," *RLA* 6.492-94.

[65] *ARI* 421, 424-34.

[66] R. Tournay and S. Saouf, "Stèle de Tukulti-Ninurta," *Annales Archéologiques Syriennes* 2 (1952) 169-90; and *ARI* 520.

[67] J. N. Postgate, "Some Remarks on Conditions in the Assyrian Countryside," *JESHO* 17 (1974) 233-40.

ern part of the Golan Heights.[68] The royal names of the kingdom reflect a Hurrian element (e.g., Talmai, grandfather of Absalom; Absalom's mother was from Geshur).[69] Along with Maacah in the north, Geshur joined with Damascus against David.[70] During Solomon's time it was subject to Israel, but during the Divided Kingdom it joined with Aram Damascus against Israel, but was later incorporated into that kingdom. The kingdom of Maacah was south of Mt. Hermon in the Transjordan. The city of Abel Beth-Maacah is mentioned in the annals of Tiglath-pileser III.[71] Beth-Rehob was along the southern border of Hamath and was mentioned in close connection with Aram-Zobah. Hadad-ezer of Aram-Zobah was probably native to this area. Beth-Rehob supplied the Ammonites with mercenaries in their war against David.[72]

3. Cultural Forms

Much of our knowledge of Syria in the 10th century BCE is derived from the surviving art and architecture. It has been argued that when the Arameans settled amongst the Neo-Hittite peoples they borrowed a variety of artisitic forms, creating, however, a somewhat autonomous style. By the end of the century there appears to have been a blending of the two groups, in what is known as the Syro-Hittite style. The art of southern Syria in the Damascus area is even less known, since only some ivory pieces and a stone relief have survived. These few pieces betray a Phoenician influence.[73]

The Syro-Hittite cities were characterized by an upper citadel and lower town.[74] We also know of these cities by representations on

[68] Deut 3:14; and B. Mazar, "Geshur and Maacha," *The Early Biblical Period: Historical Studies by Benjamin Mazar* (ed. S. Ahituv and B. Levine; Jerusalem: Israel Exploration Society, 1986) 113-25.

[69] 2 Sam 3:3.

[70] 2 Sam 10:6; 13:37; 14:23; 1 Chr 19:7.

[71] *KAI* 265.

[72] 2 Sam 10:6-8

[73] See I. Winter, "Phoenician and North Syrian Ivory Carving in Historical Context," *Iraq* 39 (1976) 1-22; *idem*., "Is There a South Syrian Style of Ivory Carving in the First Millennium B.C.?" *Iraq* 43 (1981) 101-30; and E. Akurgal, "Aramean and Phoenician Stylistic and Iconographic Elements in Neo-Hittite Art," *Temples and High Places in Biblical Times* (ed. A. Biran; Jerusalem: Nelson Gleuck School of Biblical Archaeology, 1981) 131-39.

[74] R. Naumann, *Architectur Kleinasians von ihren Anfängen bis zum Ende der hetitischen Zeit* (2nd ed.; Tübingen: E. Wasmuth, 1971) 204-235; and S. Lloyd, *Early Highland Peoples of Anatolia* (New York: McGraw-Hill, 1967) 88.

Assyrian wall reliefs, such as those at Balawat built by Shalmaneser III.[75] Temples have been found at Carchemish, Zinjirli, Tell Taʿyinat and Hama.[76] Few private houses, however, have been excavated in this period (except for Carchemish). The monumental architecture is represented by the widespread Bit-Ḫilāni style (a columned portico), found at Halaf and Zinjirli.[77]

Sculpture has also been found, primarily at Carchemish and Zinjirli,[78] with subjects in a religious, royal, or individual context.[79] It has been assumed that the Neo-Hittite material dates to at least 1000 BCE based on a study of the sculptural forms therein.[80] Thus far, over one hundred inscriptions and fragments have been found in a sculptural context. The Phoenician/Aramean tradition has not been attested earlier than the beginning of the 9th century. Neo-Hittite style figures with inscriptions dated to Shalmaneser III have been found at Zinjirli which provide local dynastic information.[81] One text gives the names of rulers dated to the late ninth century BCE, with Neo-Hittite and Aramaic forms. The large assemblage of sculpture from Zinjirli has helped in the understanding of the relationship of Neo-Hittite and Aramean art. Some argue that the Hittite style was adopted by Aramaic dynasts, possibly at the end of the 10th century BCE,[82] about the same time of the Aramean adoption of the Phoenician script.

The Syro-Hittite states were known for ivory carving (possibly in imi-

---

[75] L. W. King, *Bronze Reliefs from the Gates of Shalmaneser, King of Assyria B.C. 860-825* (London: Trustees of the British Museum, 1915); Naumann, *Architectur*, 316-17, fig. 433; and A. T. Olmstead, "Shalmaneser III and the Establishment of Assyrian Power," *JAOS* 41 (1921) 345-82. R. Jacoby has argued that the Assyrian depictions of cities were not accurate, "The Representation of Cities on Assyrian Reliefs," *IEJ* 41 (1991) 112-31. For an opposing view, see D. J. Tucker, "Representations of Imgur-Enlil on the Balawat Gates," *Iraq* 56 (1994) 107-16.

[76] Naumann, *Architectur*, 411-30, 470-72; Haines, *Antioch*, pp. 36ff., and Fugmann, *Hama*, pp. 150-269.

[77] E.g., I. Singer, "Hittite hilammar and Hieroglyphic Luwian ḫilāna," *ZA* 64 (1975) 69-103.

[78] Orthmann, *Späthethitischen Kunst*, pp. 30-50, 136-47; and Genge, *Nordsyrisch-südanatolische Reliefs*, pp. 78-83, 184-86.

[79] M. Wäfler, *Nicht-Assyrer neuassyrischer Darstellung* (AOAT 26; Kevelaer: Butzen & Bercker, 1975).

[80] See the general discussion in Orthmann, *Späthethitischen Kunst*; and Genge, *Nordsyrisch-südanatolische Reliefs*.

[81] *Ibid.*, pp. 86-90; *KAI* 24; Liverani, "Antecedenti," p. 72; B. Landsberger, *Samʾal*, pp. 8-82; and Orthmann, *Späthethitischen Kunst*; pp. 199-205.

[82] Orthmann, *Späthethitischen Kunst*; pp. 133-36; Genge, *Nordsyrisch-südanatolische Reliefs*, pp. 43-50, 84-86.

tation of Assyrian styles)[83] and metallurgy.[84] Little glyptic art, however, has been found.[85]

Neo-Hittite religion is not well known, but some general statements can be made from artistic forms and from the inscriptions.[86] Their religion was certainly derived from Hittite Anatolian traditions of the previous millennium. The Neo-Hittites worshiped the Storm God, Tartkhunzas, as the head of the pantheon, which also included the Moon God from Haran.[87] The Neo-Hittite style is uniform, with renderings of the Storm God and ruler.[88] Occassionally there is an example of syncretism of Neo-Hittite and Aramean forms.[89] For example, the Syro-Hittite dynasty in Hamath worshipped the Semitic goddess Baʿalat.[90]

Aramean religion probably originated from West Semitic forms in the second millennium BCE.[91] It is known only from various inscriptions, occasional references in the biblical and cuneiform sources, and evidence from personal names which often reveal popular attitudes towards religion.[92] It appears that each city had its own patron deity, although the primary god appears to have been Hadad, the Storm God, who is featured in the Tell Fekheriyah inscription.[93] Hadad-Rimmon was worshiped in Aram-Damascus.[94] In the north, however, the Moon God (Aramaic Siʾ) was preeminent, centered at Haran. Other deities were

---

[83] Again, Winter, "Phoenician and North Syrian Ivory Carving," 1-22; and *idem.*, "Is There a South Syrian Style," pp. 101-30.

[84] M. van Loon, "The Place of Urartu in First-Millennium B.C. Trade," *Iraq* 39 (1977) 229-31; J. Birmingham, "The Overland Trade Route Across Anatolia in the Eighth and Seventh Centuries B.C.," *AnSt* 11 (1961) 185-95; and O. Muscarella, "Near Eastern Bronzes in the West: The Question of Origin," *Art and Technology: A Symposium on Classical Bronzes* (ed. S. Doeringer and others; Cambridge, Mass.: MIT, 1970) 109ff.

[85] Larouche, *Les hiéroglyphs*, pp. xxxi-xxxv. Most seals are from the Late Bronze Age.

[86] See O. R. Gurney, *Some Aspects of Hittite Religion* (Schweich Lectures 1976; Oxford: Oxford University, 1977).

[87] Larouche, *Les hiéroglyphs*, #199; and M. Kalaç, "Das Pantheon der hieroglyphenluwischen Inschriften," *Or* 34 (1965) 401-27.

[88] Orthmann, *Späthethitischen Kunst*; pp. 233-44, 287-97.

[89] *KAI* 41.

[90] P. Meriggi, *Hieroglyphisch-hethitisches Glossar* (2nd ed.; Wiesbaden: Otto Harrassowitz, 1962) s.v. d pahalati.

[91] See J. Greenfield, "Aspects of Aramean Religion," *AIR*, pp. 67-78.

[92] See J. Fowler, *Theophoric Personal Names in Ancient Hebrew: A Comparative Study* (JSOTSup 49; Sheffield: Sheffield Academic, 1988).

[93] See A. Abou-Assaf and others, *La statue de Tell Fekherye*; and A. Millard and P. Boudreuil, "A Statue from Syria with Assyrian and Aramaic Inscriptions," *BA* 45 (1892) 135-41.

[94] 2 Kgs 5:18.

either local Syrian or Mesopotamian deities that the Arameans, like other West Semitic peoples, may have also worshiped at high places. Prayers, vows, and festivals are all mentioned in later Aramaic texts, but it is unclear whether they apply to earlier periods.

SUMMARY

Although politically decentralized and not as well documented as other periods, it should be apparent that Syria in the early years of the first millennium BCE was a rich and diverse region which merged the varying traditions of the Hittites, Hurrians, Arameans, Phoenicians, Assyrians, and even Israelites into a Syro-Hittite civilization which survived for five hundred years.

"HOW THE MIGHTY ARE FALLEN": THE PHILISTINES IN THEIR TENTH CENTURY CONTEXT*

CARL S. EHRLICH

Philistia and the Philistines have been the object of an ever increasing amount of scholarly attention over the course of the past few decades. Although textual sources for Philistine history remain scarce,[1] the archaeologist's spade has uncovered a wealth of information relating to the material culture of the southern coastal plain of Canaan, in particular for the Iron Age I and IIC periods. The region of Philistia is bordered in the north by the Yarkon or Sorek Rivers (depending on the period), in the south by the Wadi el-Arish (the "Brook of Egypt"), on the east by the Judean Hills or Judah, and on the west by the Mediterranean Sea. Included within this geographical framework are the cities of the Philistine Pentapolis of biblical fame: Ashdod, Ashkelon, Gaza, Ekron (Tel Miqne[2]), and Gath (Tell es-Safi?[3]),[4] as well as a number of sec-

* This article was researched and written during my stay as guest professor at the Kirchliche Hochshule of Wuppertal, Germany. I am most grateful to the librarians of the institute for their ready help in securing needed materials. As the astute reader, however, will note, the search was not always successful. I assume any and all responsibility for lacking bibliographic information.

[1] See the general surveys in T. Dothan, *The Philistines and Their Material Culture* (Jerusalem: Israel Exploration Society, 1982) 1-24; J. Brug, *A Literary and Archaeological Study of the Philistines* (BAR International Series 265; Oxford: BAR, 1985) 5-50; H. J. Katzenstein, "Philistines: History," *ABD* 5.326-28; E. Noort, *Die Seevölker in Palästina* (Palaestina Antiqua 8; Kampen: Kok Pharos, 1994) 27-112. More limited in scope are H. Tadmor, "Philistia Under Assyrian Rule," *BA* 29 (1966) 86-102; and C. S. Ehrlich, *The Philistines in Transition: A History from ca. 1000-730 B.C.E.* (SHCANE 10; Leiden: E. J. Brill, 1996) passim.

[2] This identification was established by J. Naveh, "Khirbet al-Muqannaʿ-Ekron: An Archaeological Survey," *IEJ* 8 (1958) 87-100, 165-70.

[3] On this identification, viewed as most probable by a majority of scholars, see A. F. Rainey, "The Identification of Philistine Gath: A Problem in Source Analysis for Historical Geography," *ErIsr* 12 (1975) 63*-76*; and J. D. Seger, "Gath," *ABD* 2.908-909. Following Stager, B. J. Stone has tentatively proposed Tel Haror as the site of Gath, "The Philistines and Acculturation: Culture Change and Ethnic Continuity in the Iron Age," *BASOR* 298 (1995) 22.

[4] The first three cities on this list are situated along the coast from north to south, the latter two are inland sites. Their geographical location was a determining factor in their changing fortunes over the course of time.

ondary settlements. The results of the excavations of Ashdod,[5] Ashkelon,[6] Tel Batash-Timnah,[7] Tel Miqne-Ekron,[8] and Tell Qasile,[9] as well as of a number of smaller sites and regional surveys (both in Philistia proper and at which evidence of Philistine material culture has been adduced) are still being analyzed and debated.[10] The fact that a number of these projects are yet to be completed or published does not simplify the analysis. However, a number of general tendencies, directions, and controversies in the scholarly discussion have become evident.

---

[5] On this and the other sites see the relevant articles in *The New Encyclopedia of Archaeological Excavations in the Holy Land* (ed. E. Stern; 4 vol.; Jerusalem: Israel Exploration Society; New York: Simon & Schuster, 1993); in addition to M. Dothan and D. N. Freedman, *Ashdod I: The First Season of Excavations, 1962* (ʿAtiqot 7; Jerusalem: Israel Department of Antiquities and Museums, 1967); M. Dothan, *Ashdod II-III: The Second and Third Seasons of Excavation, 1963, 1965, Soundings in 1967* (ʿAtiqot 9-10; Jerusalem: Israel Department of Antiquities and Museums, 1971); M. Dothan and Y. Porath, *Ashdod IV: Excavation of Area M, The Fortifications of the Lower City* (ʿAtiqot 15; Jerusalem: Israel Department of Antiquities and Museums, 1982).

[6] L. E. Stager, *Ashkelon Discovered: From Canaanites and Philistines to Romans and Moslems* (Washington, D.C.: Biblical Archaeology Society, 1991); B. L. Johnson and L. E. Stager, "Ashkelon: Wine Emporium of the Holy Land," *Recent Excavations in Israel: A View to the West: Reports on Kabri, Nami, Miqne-Ekron, Dor, and Ashkelon* (ed. S. Gitin; AIA Colloquia and Conference Papers 1; Dubuque, Iowa: Kendall/Hunt, 1995) 95-109.

[7] G. L. Kelm and A. Mazar, *Timnah: A Biblical City in the Sorek Valley* (Winona Lake, Ind.: Eisenbrauns, 1995).

[8] T. Dothan, "Tel Miqne-Ekron: The Aegean Affinities of the Sea Peoples' (Philistines') Settlement in Iron Age I," *Recent Excavations in Israel: A View to the West: Reports on Kabri, Nami, Miqne-Ekron, Dor, and Ashkelon* (ed. S. Gitin; AIA Colloquia and Conference Papers 1; Dubuque, Iowa: Kendall/Hunt, 1995) 41-59; S. Gitin, "Seventh Century B.C.E. Cultic Elements at Ekron," *Biblical Archaeology Today, 1990: Proceedings of the Second International Congress on Biblical Archaeology, Jerusalem, June-July 1990* (ed. A. Biran and J. Aviram; Jerusalem: Israel Exploration Society, 1993) 248-59; *idem.*, "Tel Miqne-Ekron in the 7th Century B.C.E.: The Impact of Economic Innovation and Foreign Cultural Influences on a Neo-Assyrian Vassal City-State," *Recent Excavations in Israel: A View to the West: Reports on Kabri, Nami, Miqne-Ekron, Dor, and Ashkelon* (ed. S. Gitin; AIA Colloquia and Conference Papers 1; Dubuque, Iowa: Kendall/Hunt, 1995) 61-79; *idem.*, "Tel Miqne-Ekron: A Type-Site for the Inner Coastal Plain in the Iron Age II Period," *Recent Excavations in Israel: Studies in Iron Age Archaeology* (ed. S. Gitin and W. G. Dever; AASOR 49; Winona Lake, Ind.: Eisenbrauns, 1989) 23-58; S. Gitin and T. Dothan, "The Rise and Fall of Ekron of the Philistines: Recent Excavations at an Urban Border Site," *BA* 50 (1987) 197-222.

[9] A. Mazar, *Excavations at Tell Qasile, Part One, The Philistine Sanctuary: Architecture and Objects* (Qedem 12; Jerusalem: Hebrew University, 1980); *idem.*, *Excavations at Tell Qasile, Part Two, The Philistine Sanctuary: Various Finds, the Pottery, Conclusions, Appendixes* (Qedem 20; Jerusalem: Hebrew University, 1985).

[10] See list of sites and their remains in T. Dothan, *Philistines*, pp. 25-93. Also useful in this regard is Brug, *Philistines*, pp. 66-106, in which the discussion centers on the ceramic evidence.

Most of the attention devoted to the Philistines has focused on the period of their settlement and on the distinctive material culture traditionally associated with them in Iron Age I.[11] The material basic to all theories is the distinctive bichrome ware of that period, which has been found at sites traditionally associated with the Philistines, as well as at a number of other sites throughout the land. It is mainly on Trude Dothan's ground-breaking synthesis that all subsequent work rests, irrespective of whether it is supportive or critical of individual aspects of her reconstruction; therefore, her synthesis may serve as the basis of discussion.[12]

The association of the Philistines with the bichrome ware of the early Iron Age is one which goes back to the turn of the century.[13] It is an assemblage of white-slipped ware which is decorated with red and black paint. The decoration consists of various bands and oftentimes intricate geometric forms, in addition to metopes with depictions of animals, in particular birds looking backward. As Dothan points out, the identification as "Philistine" pottery is based on its "typology, stratigraphy, and geographical distribution."[14]

Dothan has distinguished five major typological groups within the Philistine ceramic repertoire. Group I ceramic forms, derived from Mycenean prototypes, include bell-shaped bowls (Type 1) and kraters (Type 2), stirrup jars (Type 3), pyxides and amphoriskoi (Type 4), three-handled jars (Type 5), strainer-spout or "beer" jugs[15] (Type 6), basket-

---

[11] The major exception to this can be found in the work of S. Gitin, who, in a series of studies, has been attempting to trace the development of the regional material culture of the southern coastal plain in Iron Age II (see n. 8).

[12] Dothan, *Philistines* (see n. 1). She has presented a number of shorter syntheses of her conclusions, many reached in conjunction with her husband, Moshe: T. Dothan, "Philistines: Archaeology," *ABD* 5.328-33; "Philistines: Material Culture," *Encyclopaedia Biblica* (Hebrew) 6.500-508; "What We Know About the Philistines," *BAR* 8 no. 4 (1982) 20-44. See also T. Dothan and M. Dothan, *People of the Sea: The Search for the Philistines* (New York: Macmillan, 1992).

[13] For a summary of the history of interpretation of this ware, see T. Dothan, *Philistines*, p. 94, n. 1.

[14] *Ibid.*, p. 94. It is particularly in the area of typology Dothan has made her greatest contribution; *ibid.*, pp. 94-218. See also H. Weippert, *Palästina in vorhellenistischer Zeit* (Handbuch der Archäologie, Vorderasien 2.1; Munich: C. H. Beck, 1988) 373-82; and the critical discussion in Brug, *Philistines*, pp. 53-144; and Noort, *Seevölker*, pp. 113-28.

[15] In reaction to Johnson and Stager's conclusion that wine and not beer was the Philistines' beverage of choice (B. L. Johnson and L. E. Stager, "Ashkelon: Wine Emporium," p. 95), W. G. Dever has commended them for gentrifying the Philistines and for turning them from "loutish beer-guzzlers to genteel sippers of white wine – no doubt, properly chilled and accompanied by just the right brie," "Orienting the Study of Trade in Near Eastern Archaeology," *Recent Excavations in Israel: A View to the West: Reports on*

handled jugs with spout (Type 7), and juglets with pinched-in girth (Type 8). Group II types, derived from Cypriote prototypes, include cylindrical bottles (Type 9), horn-shaped vessels (Type 10), and gourd-shaped jars (Type 11). Group III consists of one vessel, a jug with an elongated and oftentimes bulging neck, which evidences Egyptian influence in both shape and design (Type 12). Group IV consists of forms derived from local Canaanite traditions, yet decorated in the Philistine style. These include small bowls with bar handles (Type 13), jugs (Type 14), juglets (Type 15), and juglets with trefoil mouths (Type 16). Group V, which Dothan dates to the late 11th and early 10th centuries BCE, includes forms derived from Group I, namely jugs with strainer spouts and basket handles (Type 17, derived from Types 6 and 7), and deep kraters (Type 18, derived from Type 2).

In her discussion of Philistine ceramics Dothan also made reference to a style of pottery found at Ashdod as of Stratum XIIIb, which appeared to be antecedent to the Philistine bichrome ware and in its later stages partially overlapped with the latter.[16] This she designated monochrome ware, on account of its monochrome dark brown painted designs. It has since been found in abundance at Ekron and Ashkelon,[17] and appears to be a locally produced assemblage derived from the Myc(enean) IIIB import ware of the Late Bronze Age. Owing to its similarity to contemporaneous examples from Cyprus it has been given the name Myc IIIC:1b. Emphasizing the differences between the earlier monochrome Myc IIIC:1b and the later bichrome "Philistine" pottery, the Dothans have concluded that they are representative of two waves of immigration to Canaan in the 12th century BCE.[18] Most other scholars, however,

---

Kabri, Nami, Miqne-Ekron, Dor, and Ashkelon (ed. S. Gitin; AIA Colloquia and Conference Papers 1; Dubuque, Iowa: Kendall/Hunt, 1995) 116.

[16] T. Dothan, *Philistines*, p. 96.

[17] J. Gunneweg, I. Perlman, T. Dothan, and S. Gitin, "On the Origin of Pottery from Tel Miqne-Ekron," *BASOR* 264 (1986) 3-16; Stager, *Ashkelon*, p. 13.

[18] See M. Dothan, "Archaeological Evidence for Movements of the Early 'Sea Peoples' in Canaan," *Recent Excavations in Israel: Studies in Iron Age Archaeology* (ed. S. Gitin and W. G. Dever; AASOR 49; Winona Lake, Ind.: Eisenbrauns, 1989) 59-70, especially 65-68; and *idem.*, "Ethnicity and Archaeology: Some Observations on the Sea Peoples at Ashdod," *Biblical Archaeology Today, 1990: Proceedings of the Second International Congress on Biblical Archaeology, Jerusalem, June-July 1990* (ed. A. Biran and J. Aviram; Jerusalem: Israel Exploration Society, 1993) 53-55, in which Dothan attempts to identify this presumed pre-Philistine Sea People population at Ashdod with the biblical Anakim. See also, M. Dothan, *Ashdod II-III*, p. 20; Dothan and Dothan, *People of the Sea*, pp. 165-70, 258; T. Dothan, "The Arrival of the Sea Peoples: Cultural Diversity in Early Iron Age Canaan," *Recent Excavations in Israel: Studies in Iron Age*

view the bichrome pottery as a direct outgrowth of the earlier monochrome. The latter thus posit an initial monochrome phase which lasted about one generation and is indicative of the initial Philistine settlement in Canaan. This was followed by a more eclectic assemblage which developed from it *ca.* 1150 BCE and reflected the diverse cultural influences acting on the southern coastal strip of Canaan.[19] Tied in with these analyses are fundamental questions concerning the origins and initial settlement of the Philistines.[20]

The question of Philistine origins is closely linked with the question of the transition from the Bronze Age to the Iron Age throughout the world of the eastern Mediterranean. The phenomenon of the seemingly simultaneous collapse of the great Bronze Age civilizations of the eastern Mediterranean world is still the subject of intense speculation. This also holds true for the possible relationship of the legends of the Trojan War and the subsequent wanderings of the Achaeans as related in the Homeric epics to that collapse.[21] There is a growing body of evidence which indicates that groups of Aegean/Mycenean background were on the move in the eastern Mediterranean world during the period of transition between the Bronze and Iron Ages *ca.* 1200 BCE. The phenomenon of pirates of Aegean origin was well known in the Late Bronze Age.[22] At quite a number of sites remains of the so-called "Sea Peoples"[23] were found in levels following those related to the destruction of the Late Bronze. Yet the question arises, whether their presence was indicative of

---

Archaeology (ed. S. Gitin and W. G. Dever; AASOR 49; Winona Lake, Ind.: Eisenbrauns, 1989) 1-14, especially 1-7; T. Dothan, *Philistines*, pp. 294-95; and B. Mazar, *Biblical Israel: State and People* (ed. S. Ahituv; Jerusalem: Magnes, 1992) 14.

[19] W. G. Dever, "The Chronology of Syria-Palestine in the Second Millennium B.C.E.: A Review of Current Issues," *BASOR* 288 (1992) 18-19; A. Mazar, *Archaeology of the Land of the Bible 10,000-586 B.C.E.* (ABRL; New York: Doubleday, 1990) 307-308, 327; D. B. Redford, *Egypt, Canaan, and Israel in Ancient Times* (Princeton: Princeton University, 1992) 291 (in which Redford argues against postulating two immigration waves on the basis of destruction levels); Stager, *Ashkelon*, p. 13; and H. Weippert, *Palästina*, pp. 380-82.

[20] See the discussion in Stone, "Acculturation," pp. 14-16, especially the comparative stratigraphic chart on p. 15, fig. 1.

[21] See, for example, Redford, *Egypt*, p. 254; and Stager, *Ashkelon*, pp. 15-18. Both deduce a direct relationship.

[22] See Redford, *Egypt*, pp. 225, 243, 250; Noort, *Seevölker*, pp. 84-85 (regarding the Sherden).

[23] This is a general term for the peoples of a supposedly Aegean/Anatolian origin who were on the move in the transitional period between the Bronze and Iron Ages. On the genesis of the term "Sea Peoples" see Noort, *Seevölker*, pp. 54-55.

a cause or of a result of the collapse of the Bronze Age civilizations, or of an unrelated phenomenon.

Egyptian texts of the 19th and 20th Dynasties are central to the debate. In the account of Ramses II's campaign against the Hittites, which ended in a stalemate at the battle of Kadesh on the Orontes, mention is found of one of the Sea Peoples, namely the Sherden, among the Egyptian mercenary troops.[24] Merneptah listed five Sea Peoples as enemies of Egypt in an account of a war against the Libyans.[25] The Onomasticon of Amenope lists the coastal Philistine cities and three of the Sea Peoples, including the Philistines.[26] The account of the journey of Wen-Amon to Phoenicia in *ca.* 1100 BCE refers to Dor on the Canaanite coast as a city of the Tjeker.[27]

However, the most important among the texts for understanding the putative settlement of the Sea Peoples in Canaan are those dated to the reign of Ramses III, among which the pride of place undoubtedly belongs to the Medinet Habu inscriptions and their associated reliefs.[28] They relate an egyptocentric account of Ramses III's battle against the Sea Peoples. In this account, dated to Ramses' eighth year (*ca.* 1175 BCE), Egypt was threatened with a massive invasion by land and sea by a large coalition of Sea Peoples including the Philistines,[29] the Tjeker, the Shekelesh, the Denyen,[30] and the Weshesh, as well as the Teresh and

[24] J. A. Wilson, "Egyptian Historical Texts," *ANET*, pp. 255-56. The Sherden may also be mentioned in three letters from Byblos (Gubla) found among the Amarna correspondence (EA 81, 122, 123) and dating to the mid 14th century BCE. See Noort, *Seevölker*, p. 85; D. M. Rohl, "Review of William L. Moran, *The Amarna Letters* (Baltimore-London: Johns Hopkins University, 1992)," *PEQ* 127 (1995) 78-79; but see Moran, *Amarna Letters*, p. 393. The Sherden are thought by some (e.g. Dothan and Dothan, *People of the Sea*, p. 214) to have given their name to the island of Sardinia. They also have been linked with the region of Sardis on the Ionian coast. See Redford, *Egypt*, p. 243 and n. 13.

[25] Noort, *Seevölker*, p. 84; Redford, *Egypt*, pp. 247-49.

[26] T. Dothan, *Philistines*, pp. 3-4; Redford, *Egypt*, pp. 292-93.

[27] J. A. Wilson, "Egyptian Myths, Tales, and Mortuary Texts," *ANET*, pp. 25-29. The Tjeker have been identified both with the Teukrians (Redford, *Egypt*, pp. 252, 292) and with the Sikeloi or Sikilayu, the latter designation of which is known from Ugaritic texts; see E. Edel, "Die Sikeloi in den ägyptischen Seevölkertexten und in Keilschrifturkunden," *BN* 23 (1984) 7-8; Stager, *Ashkelon*, p. 19 n. 23; E. Stern, *Dor: Ruler of the Seas* (Jerusalem: Israel Exploration Society, 1994) 20, 85-101. Assuming that the second identification is indeed correct, they both settled in the region of Dor and gave their name to the island of Sicily.

[28] Wilson, "Egyptian Historical Texts," pp. 262-63.

[29] Egyptian *prst*. The name Palestine is their indirect legacy.

[30] In cuneiform inscriptions they are referred to as Danuna. Many scholars connect them with the Danaoi of Greek fame. Y. Yadin theorized that the Israelite tribe of Dan

the Sherden. The pharaoh met them in Djahi[31] and at the mouth of the rivers[32] and inflicted an annihilating defeat upon them. The associated reliefs depict both the land and sea battles as well as details concerning the personal appearance and family structure of the various defeated groups. The defeat of Egypt's enemies is thorough. The Sea Peoples' fleet is surrounded, their sails furled.[33] Also depicted are a number of Sea Peoples, both combatants and civilians, including the Philistines, Denyen, and Tjeker with their distinctive "feathered" headdresses.[34] Papyrus Harris I summarizes Ramses III's war against the Sea Peoples.[35] The defeat of the Denyen, Tjeker, Philistines, Sherden, and Weshesh is recapitulated, with the additional information that the foes who were slain, turned to ashes and made non-existent, were brought in captivity to Egypt and settled in fortresses.[36]

Among the major indicators of the transition from the Bronze Age to the Iron Age in Canaan are the lessening of Egyptian control and the replacement at many sites of Egyptian material culture with the classic

---

was descended from the Denyen, who had settled on the coast between the Tjeker to the north and the Philistines to the south; "And Dan, Why Did He Remain in Ships?" *AJBA* 1 (1968) 9-23. There is, however, no external evidence that the Denyen settled on the coast of Canaan. In addition, Niemann has adduced no archaeological connection between the material culture of the region originally assigned to the tribe of Dan in the biblical texts (Josh 19:40-48) and the remains from Tel Dan to which the tribe supposedly migrated (Judg 17-18). He thus rejects Yadin's effort to link the Danites and the Denyen/Danuna/Danaoi, as well as those of Cyrus H. Gordon and Michael C. Astour; H. M. Niemann, *Die Daniten: Studien zur Geschichte eines altisraelitischen Stammes* (FRLANT 135; Göttingen: Vandenhoeck & Ruprecht, 1985) 273-91.

[31] This term refers in a general sense to the eastern Mediterranean coastal regions.

[32] The reference here is most likely to the Nile delta region.

[33] This is one of the pieces of evidence presumably adduced by A. Raban and R. R. Stieglitz in their argument that the Egyptians attacked the Sea Peoples by surprise, "The Sea Peoples and Their Contributions to Civilization," *BAR* 17 no 6 (1991) 35-36.

[34] For discussions and interpretations of the reliefs see T. Dothan, *Philistines*, p. 13; Noort, *Seevölker*, pp. 56-83.

[35] Wilson, "Egyptian Historial Texts," pp. 260-62; B.G. Wood, "The Philistines Enter Canaan: Were They Egyptian Lackeys or Invading Conquerers?" *BAR* 17 no 6 (1991) 49.

[36] Whether the last two clauses are to be understood sequentially or as independent statements has occassioned debate. In a sequential understanding, the captives were settled in Egypt, while the rest of the Philistines or Sea Peoples carved out a territory for themselves in Canaan. See, for example, Wood, "Philistines," pp. 44-52, 89-92. To this reconstruction Redford adds the observation that if Ramses III claims to have allowed the Philistines to settle as mercenaries in Canaan, it would have been "*post eventum*;" *Egypt*, p. 289. The paratactic nature of the text also allows an interpretation as evidence that Ramses III settled captive Sea Peoples (mainly the Philistines) as mercenaries in Canaan. See, for example, I Singer, "The Beginning of Philistine Settlement in Canaan and the Northern Boundary of Philistia," *Tel Aviv* 12 (1985) 109-14.

Philistine ware.[37] Since the first literary mention of the Philistines places them among the Sea Peoples in the texts dating to the eighth year of the reign of Ramses III, a connection has been sought between their arrival in Canaan and Ramses' war against the Sea Peoples. Among the various reconstructions of the historical sequence of events, one may identify both maximal and minimal positions, in addition to a myriad of variations on them.

A maximal position would hold that at the collapse of Mycenean civilization hordes of refugees invaded the eastern Mediterranean in search of a new land to settle. During the course of their long journey by land and sea toward the fertile Nile Valley, they destroyed the Hittite empire and the coastal Phoenician/Canaanite city-states. Ramses III was able to prevent them from invading Egyptian soil and settled the Sea Peoples, among whom the Philistines played a leading role, as mercenaries on the southwestern coastal strip of Canaan. However, the weakened Egyptian New Kingdom, already in decline, never recovered from the exertion and eventually lost its holdings in Canaan to the Philistines.[38]

This reconstruction, with modifications including the question of the location of the two(-pronged) battle(s)[39] and of whether the Philistines were settled by the Egyptians as mercenaries[40] or seized the land for themselves,[41] has become the dominant model in the field. Although there is some discussion of whether the eighth year of Ramses III repre-

[37] Other characteristics adduced for the transition from the LB to the IA include the breakdown of international trade and the change in settlement patterns.

[38] For recent variations of such a reconstruction see Redford, *Egypt*, pp. 241-56, on pp. 253-54 he refers to a major coalition of groups centered in Caria, who had fought in the Trojan war; Stager, *Ashkelon*, pp. 9-18; and Wood, "Philistines," pp. 44-52.

[39] In essence there have been three models of the relationship of the land and sea battles to each other: 1) both in Syria or northern Palestine; see Singer, "Philistine Settlement," p. 109 and n. 1; 2) the land battle in Syria and the sea battle in the eastern delta region of Egypt; see R. D. Barnett, "The Sea Peoples," *CAH*[3] 2.2.374; 3) both in the eastern Nile delta, thus postulating an attack on Egypt from Philistines/Sea Peoples already in Canaan as settlers or as sojourners; see M. Bietak, "The Sea Peoples and the End of the Egyptian Administration in Canaan," *Biblical Archaeology Today, 1990: Proceedings of the Second International Congress on Biblical Archaeology, Jerusalem, June-July 1990* (ed. A. Biran and J. Aviram; Jerusalem: Israel Exploration Society, 1993) 299-300.

[40] T. Dothan has referred to the Egyptians' granting permission to the Philistines to settle in Canaan, "Philistines: Archaeology," p. 329; while I. Singer has referred to the Egyptians' "[s]ettling Philistines in Egyptian bases along the coast after Ramses III's eight year," "Merneptah's Campaign to Canaan and the Egyptian Occupation of the Southern Coastal Plain of Palestine in the Ramesside Period," *BASOR* 269 (1988) 6. See also B. Mazar, *Biblical Israel*, p. 28.

[41] Bietak, "Sea Peoples," p. 300; Wood, "Philistines," pp. 46-48.

sents the first Philistine incursion into the Near East or not, a direct correlation is sought between the settlement of the Philistines and the bichrome pottery which made its appearance in the 12th century BCE. Those who find a direct progression from the monochrome Myc IIIC:1b ware to the bichrome ware date the appearance of the former to Ramses' eighth year and the latter to *ca.* one generation later, i.e. *ca.* 1150 BCE.[42]

The position labeled minimalist takes a much more critical stance vis-à-vis the historical credibility of the Medinet Habu inscriptions and their association with the settlement of the Philistines in Canaan.[43] The texts are viewed as standardized literary texts, which may contain a historical kernel. However, the reference to a grand coalition of "Sea Peoples" is interpreted in typological terms, and the engagement between them and Ramses is understood as the conflation of a gradual process of tension between Canaan and Egypt or as the reinterpretation of a local conflict in the Nile Delta into a battle of quasi mythic proportions in order to glorify the pharaoh.[44] Butressing these interpretations are the literary structure of the inscriptions and the ideological ordering of the reliefs, in which two of the reported wars of Ramses III appear to have no basis in historical reality.[45]

The difficulty of associating pots with peoples or ethnic groups has often been commented on.[46] Nonetheless, the association of the Philistines with the Iron Age I bichrome pottery bearing their name is most often taken for granted. Although most scholars have backed off from postulating that every site with bichrome pottery was under Philistine control, the ethnic association remains. Wherever the distinctive early Iron Age bichrome is found, Philistine ethnic presence is assumed. Indeed, Singer has recently argued that the Myc IIIC:1b ware be designated "Monochrome (or early) Philistine pottery."[47] A cautionary note

---

42 See, for example, A. Mazar, *Archaeology*, pp. 307-308; Stager, *Ashkelon*, p. 13.

43 For sceptical attitudes towards Ramses III's claims in his Medinet Habu inscriptions see, in addition to those listed below, Bietak, "Sea Peoples;" Brug, *Philistines*, pp. 27-28; and especially B. Cifola, "Ramses III and the Sea Peoples: A Structural Analysis of the Medinet Habu Inscriptions," *Or* ns 57 (1988) 275-306.

44 *Ibid.*, p. 303; and Noort, *Seevölker*, pp. 54-55, 104-12, who follows Helck among others in this interpretation. In Noort's opinion, Ramses III's battle against the Sea Peoples was nothing more than a revolt of Egyptian mercenaries against their overlord.

45 These would be the campaigns against the Nubians and the Asiatics; see Noort, *Seevölker*, p. 108, and literature there.

46 G. London, "A Comparison of Two Contemporaneous Lifestyles of the Late Second Millennium B.C.," *BASOR* 273 (1989) 37-55, and literature there.

47 Singer, "Philistine Settlement," p. 112.

has, however, been sounded in particular by Brug, Bunimovitz, H. Weippert, and Noort, among others.[48]

In essence their theories rest on the fact that even among sites in the Philistine heartland, the supposed Philistine pottery does not represent the major portion of the finds.[49] Although Brug's statistical analysis of the proportion of bichrome pottery to other forms is flawed by his reliance on samples not gathered to be analyzed in this manner, the cumulative thrust of his argument is probably valid, namely that the bichrome ware represents a small proportion of the total assemblage from supposedly Philistine sites.[50] For example, at Tell Qasile, the only city thought to have been *founded* by the Philistines, the bichrome pottery represents just 20% of the total assemblage.[51] It is thus conjectured that the bichrome ware and its antecedent monochrome ware were the fine china or luxury ware of their time. The fact that both the monochrome and the bichrome wares were locally produced (along with pottery which continued the Bronze Age Canaanite traditions) after the cessation of trade contracts with Cyprus and the Aegean leads to the con-

---

[48] Brug, *Philistines*, pp. 53-144; Bunimovitz, "Problems," pp. 212-13; Noort, *Seevölker*, pp. 113-28; *idem.*, "Seevölker, materielle Kultur und Pantheon: Bemerkungen zur Benutzung archäologischer Daten – ein kritischer Bericht," *Religionsgeschichtliche Beziehungen zwischen Kleinasien, Nordsyrien und dem Alten Testament* (eds. B. Janowski, K. Koch and G. Wilhelm; OBO 129; Freiburg: Universitätsverlag; Göttingen: Vandenhoeck & Ruprecht, 1993) 373-79; H. Weippert, *Palästina*, pp. 380-82.

[49] See also M. Weippert, "Review of Trude Dothan, *The Philistines and Their Material Culture* (Hebrew; Jerusalem: Israel Exploration Society, 1967)," *Göttingische Gelehrte Anzeigen* 223 (1971) 16-18.

[50] Brug is aware of the problems associated with his sample, yet he assumes that the results would more likely be skewed to overemphasize the presence of the decorated bichrome ware; *Philistines*, 53-144. Stone has attacked Brug's overly heavy reliance on statistical analysis. While he agrees that the Mycenean origin of isolated pieces of evidence could be questioned, the cumulative force of the evidence has to point in the direction of an invasion theory; "Acculturation," p. 13.

[51] A. Mazar, *Archaeology*, p. 316. The one exception to this general trend would appear to be Tel Miqne-Ekron Stratum VII, in which Myc IIIC:1b ware accounts for over half of the pottery excavated. See T. Dothan, "Aegean Affinities," p. 46; T. Dothan and S. Gitin, "Miqne, Tel (Ekron)," *The New Encyclopedia of Archaeological Excavations in the Holy Land* (ed. E. Stern; Jerusalem: Israel Exploration Society; New York: Simon & Schuster, 1993) 3.1053. The large amounts of Myc IIIC:1b pottery combined with the expansion of the city from 10 to 50 acres lead Mazar to see at Iron Age IA Ekron clear evidence of the settlement of a large group of Aegeans; "The Northern Shephelah in the Iron Age: Some Issues in Biblical History and Archaeology," *Scripture and Other Artifacts: Essays on the Bible and Archaeology in Honor of Philip J. King* (ed. M. D. Coogan, J. C. Exum, and L. E. Stager; Louisville, Ken.: Westminster/John Knox, 1994) 250. See also Stone, "Acculturation," p. 18, who following Stager has claimed that the Myc IIIC:1b ware made up 30%-50% of the ceramic repertoire of the cities of the Philistine Pentapolis.

clusion that, rather than being evidence of a massive foreign incursion into Canaan *ca.* 1175, these wares were local replacements for the now unavailable Late Bronze Age luxury import wares. While not denying Cypriote and/or Aegean/Mycenean influence in the material cultural traditions of coastal Canaan in the early Iron Age, in addition to that of Egyptian and local Canaanite traditions, the above named "minimalist" scholars emphasize the continuities between the ages and not the differences. As H. Weippert has stated, "Könige kommen, Könige gehen, aber die Kochtöpfe bleiben."[52] In regard to the bichrome pottery she follows Galling[53] and speculates that it was produced by a family or families of Cypriote potters who followed their markets and immigrated to Canaan once the preexisting trade connections had been severed. The find at Tell Qasile of both bichrome and Canaanite types originating in the same pottery workship[54] would appear to indicate that the ethnic identification of the potters is at best an open question. At any rate it cannot be facilely assumed that all bichrome ware was produced by "ethnic" Philistines.[55] Thus Bunimovitz's suggestion to refer to "Philistia pottery" rather than to "Philistine" must be given serious consideration.[56]

What holds true for the pottery of Philistia holds true for other aspects of the regional material culture. Whereas Aegean cultural influence cannot be denied, the continuity with the Late Bronze traditions in Philistia has increasingly come to attention. A number of Iron Age I features which were thought to be imported by the Philistines have been shown to have Late Bronze Age antecedents.[57] It would hence appear that the Philistines of foreign (or "Philistine") origin were the minority in Philistia.[58] Just as the origins of Israel in Iron Age I are shrouded in mys-

---

[52] H. Weippert, *Palästina*, p. 352.

[53] K. Galling, "Review of Kathleen M. Kenyon, *Archäologie im Heiligen Land* (Neukirchen: Neukirchener, 1967)," *ZAW* 86 (1970) 91-92.

[54] A. Mazar, "The Iron Age I," *The Archaeology of Ancient Israel* (ed. A. Ben-Tor; tr. R. Greenberg; New Haven: Yale University, 1992) 271.

[55] Mazar, "Archaeology," p. 317.

[56] Bunimovitz, "Problems," pp. 212-13. H. Weippert has suggested the name "*palästinische submykenische Keramik*" in order to draw attention both to the place of production of this style of pottery and to its foreign antecedents; *Palästina*, p. 382.

[57] These features will be discussed in the following pages; however, it should be noted that a number of scholars now propose that certain material cultural features, thought to be native to Canaan, are in reality Sea People imports. Raban and Stieglitz argue that among other innovations the Sea Peoples introduced ashlar masonary, composite anchors, and collared rim jars to the ancient Near East; "Sea Peoples," pp. 34-42, 92-93. Dever also attributes the introduction of ashlar masonry to the Sea Peoples, in addition to the dromos bench-tomb and possibly also some types of four-room houses; "Orienting," p. 115.

[58] Thus Kelm and Mazar have speculated that the Philistines were the "overlords and

tery and we are unable to pinpoint the changeover from a "Canaanite" consciousness to an "Israelite" one on the basis of isolated cultural phenomena, so, too, in the case of the contemporaneous inhabitants of the coastal regions of Canaan. Many cultural influences were at work in a variegated population[59] to which the name "Philistine" was given (similarly to Israel) *pars pro toto*, possibly by the late 11th century BCE, ironically a time at which the distinctive material culture traditionally associated with the Philistines was waning.[60]

Drawing on the evidence of remains spanning a number of centuries, a picture of the culture and society of Philistia emerges. The emergence of a new cultural tradition in Canaan is most evident in a distinct change of diet identified at some Philistine sites. Faunal remains at Tel Miqne-Ekron indicate that in the change from the Bronze Age to the Iron Age the diet changed from one in which mutton and goat were the meats most often consumed to one in which pork and beef were preferred.[61] The phenomenon of a shift in domesticated species, indicative of change both in consumption patterns and in the general pastoral economy, from

aristocrats" at Tel Batash-Timnah, which was populated in the main by the "descendents of the earlier Canaanite inhabitants;" *Timnah*, p. 93. Mazar has also argued that Egyptian domination of cities in Canaan was replaced by Philistine domination. Thus the local Canaanite population continued in existence as vassals to their new overlords; *Archaeology*, pp. 313, 327.

[59] Noort refers to the Philistines as a mixture of *plst* and Canaanites; *Seevölker*, pp. 179, 183. H. Weippert has referred to an ethnic mixture consisting of Canaanites, Sea Peoples, Syrians, Phoenicians, and Cypriots in various proportions at various sites; *Palästina*, p. 392. On the difficulties associated with the ethnic identification of the Philistines see Gitin, "Type-Site," p. 54 n. 22; Stone, "Acculturation," pp. 16-17.

[60] As pointed out by Stone in his important article on "The Philistines and Acculturation," it has been traditional in the scholarly community to speak of the "assimilation" of Philistine culture to Canaanite models. This is due to the fact that most scholars have focused their attention solely on the earliest phases of Philistine history and, hence, viewed the disappearance of the bichrome ware and associated Aegean influence styles as evidence of this alleged assimilation. However, Stone argues persuasively that it is more proper to speak of the *acculturation* of the Philistines to life in the Levant, in which they were but a tiny minority; see M. Broshi and I. Finkelstein, "The Population of Palestine in Iron Age II," *BASOR* 287 (1992) 53. As is only now coming to be appreciated, the region of Philistia retained an independent existence and a distinct material culture throughout the Iron Age II period.

[61] See in particular B. Hesse, "Animal Use at Tel Miqne-Ekron in the Bronze Age and Iron Age," *BASOR* 264 (1986) 17-27; and T. Dothan, "Aegean Affinities," p. 46; Dothan and Dothan, *People of the Sea*, p. 248; P. Wapnish, "Archaeozoology: The Integration of Faunal Data with Biblical Archaeology," *Biblical Archaeology Today, 1990: Proceedings of the Second International Congress on Biblical Archaeology, Jerusalem, June-July 1990* (ed. A. Biran and J. Aviram; Jerusalem: Israel Exploration Society, 1993) 426-42, especially 439.

sheep and goats to pigs and cattle as sources of meat in the diet is also attested at Ashkelon.[62] The latter site has also presented evidence concerning the importance of fish in the diet in Iron Age II.[63]

The attempt has been made to identify at least the later large clay sarcophagoi found in Canaan with the Philistines.[64] However, a direct correlation has been shown to be doubtful.[65] The large anthropoid coffins are evidence of the presence of Egyptians and their mercenaries, some of whom may have been of Sea People descent. In essence, very little evidence can be adduced for Philistine burial practices and beliefs, other than to claim that they appear to have been eclectic.[66]

Philistine sanctuaries have been excavated at Ashdod, Tell Qasile, and Tel Miqne-Ekron. Although a number of the cultic implements, such as lion-headed rhyta and kernoi, evidence Aegean connections, in these specific cases the claim can be made that these forms were already known and employed in Bronze Age Canaan and, hence, cannot be used as indicators of newly imported cultures.[67] The cult stands found at Ashdod and Tell Qasile would also be carryovers of the Late Bronze Canaanite traditions.[68] In fact a large portion of the cultic finds at

---

[62] Stager, *Ashkelon*, p. 9; *idem.*, "Ashkelon," *The New Encyclopedia of Archaeological Excavations in the Holy Land* (ed. E. Stern; Jerusalem: Israel Exploration Society; New York: Simon & Schuster, 1993) 1.107. The emphasis on pork in the diet at these Philistine sites stands in contrast to the eating habits at presumably Israelite sites such as Ai and Raddanah. Compare the dietary patterns at presumably Israelite Tel Kinneret in Iron Age II. Pork played a marginal role in the diet (2% of total meat consumption), in spite of the fact that it was native to the Kinneret region; R. Ziegler and J. Boessneck, "Tierreste der Eisenzeit II," *Kinneret: Ergebnisse der Ausgrabungen auf dem* Tell el-ʿOreme *am See Gennesaret 1982-1985* (ADPV 15; Wiesbaden: Otto Harrassowitz, 1990). U. Hübner has argued that the Iron Age Israelite consumption of pork did not differ that greatly from the Bronze Age Canaanite habits; "Schweine, Schweineknochen und ein Speiseverbot im alten Israel," *VT* 39 (1989) 225-36. Pork always played a minor role in the Canaanite diet, yet it is continuously attested.

[63] Stager, "Ashkelon," 1.107.

[64] T. Dothan, *Philistines*, pp. 252-88.

[65] Noort, *Seevölker*, pp. 128-33; H. Weippert, *Palästina*, pp. 366-73.

[66] Bunimovitz, "Problems," pp. 216-17; A. Mazar, *Archaeology*, pp. 326-27.

[67] Bunimovitz, "Problems," pp. 213-16; Noort, *Seevölker*, p. 160; H. Weippert, *Palästina*, pp. 389-90. On the rhyta see also A. Mazar, *Qasile II*, p. 126.

[68] On the "Musician Stand" from Ashdod see M. Dothan, *Ashdod II-III*, pp. 20-21, 125-35; *idem.*, "The Musicians of Asdod," *Archaeology* 23 (1970) 301-11; and Dothan and Dothan, *People of the Sea*, pl. 7. A. Mazar, *Qasile I*, pp. 87-96, pls. 32-33 (34); see also T. Dothan, *Philistines*, pp. 249-51. Some of the Qasile examples were topped by bird-shaped bowls in an Egyptian or Canaanite style; A. Mazar, *Qasile I*, pp. 99-100. It must be added that the bird motif played an important role in Philistine art; it is found as a frequent decoration on both monochrome and in particular on bichrome pottery. Both the prows and sterns of the Sea Peoples' ships in the Medinet Habu reliefs are bird-shaped. See Dothan and Dothan, *People of the Sea*, p. 229.

Philistine sites would not be out of place in a Canaanite cultural context.[69]

Clearer Aegean or Cypriot influences may, however, be identified in a number of distinctive finds of a cultic nature in Philistia. Bovine scapulae, which were incised on their edges, have been found at Philistine Tel Miqne-Ekron and at Tel Dor,[70] the latter of which was inhabited by another of the Sea Peoples, namely the Tjeker. These scapulae, which may have been used as cultic instruments, have also been found in large numbers on Cyprus.

That the Philistines at least initially worshipped a mother goddess in the Aegean mold may be indicated by the find of an almost complete figurine of a sitting woman at Ashdod and parts of similar figurines there as well as at Tell Qasile and Tel Miqne-Ekron.[71] In the complete figurine, nicknamed "Ashdoda,"[72] the woman merges with the chair. Thus the back of the chair is the woman's torso and the seat her lap. Parallels have been adduced in Mycenean figurines of seated goddesses, in which, however, the figure of the goddess is generally molded in the round and is more or less distinct from the chair upon which she sits. The Mycenean models also have arms and make a somewhat more naturalistic impression. The decoration of the Philistine models evidences Egyptian influence, particularly in the stylized lotus pattern on the torso. Later examples of the Ashdoda-type have lost their applied breasts and are interpreted as masculine deities.[73] This has been viewed as an example of the assimilation of the Philistine religion to the male-dominated pantheon of Canaan.

Philistine worship of a goddess at a later date is, however, indicated

---

[69] H. Weippert, *Palästina*, pp. 386-92.

[70] On Tel Miqne-Ekron: T. Dothan, "Aegean Affinities," p. 48; and *idem.*, "Arrival," p. 9. On Tel Dor: Stern, *Dor*, pp. 96, 99; *idem.*, "The Renewal of Trade in the Eastern Mediterranean in Iron Age I," *Biblical Archaeology Today, 1990: Proceedings of the Second International Congress on Biblical Archaeology, Jerusalem, June-July 1990* (ed. A. Biran and J. Aviram; Jerusalem: Israel Exploration Society, 1993) 330; and *idem.*, "Tel Dor: A Phoenician-Israelite Trading Center," *Recent Excavations in Israel: A View to the West: Reports on Kabri, Nami, Miqne-Ekron, Dor, and Ashkelon* (ed. S. Gitin; AIA Colloquia and Conference Papers 1; Dubuque, Iowa: Kendall/Hunt, 1995) 84.

[71] T. Dothan, "Philistines: Archaeology," p. 330.

[72] Concerning the discovery and significance of "Ashdoda" see Dothan and Dothan, *People of the Sea*, pp. 153-57.

[73] T. Dothan and R. L. Cohn, "The Philistine as Other: Biblical Rhetoric and Archaeological Reality," *The Other in Jewish Thought and History: Constructions of Jewish Culture and Identity* (eds. L. J. Silberstein and R. L. Cohn; New York: New York University, 1994) 69.

by a number of inscriptions found at Tel Miqne-Ekron from a 7th century context, in which the Canaanite-Phoenician-Israelite(?) goddess *'šrt* is mentioned, as well as by the find of petal chalices which are associated with her worship.[74] On the basis of these and related finds Gitin observes that there were both centralized and individual Philistine cult places, the former of which were served by a priestly support system.[75] The presence of large numbers of limestone altars at Ekron, on the other hand, would bear witness to the influx of (northern) Israelites after the fall of Samaria in 720 BCE.[76]

Female figurines molded in the round also play a role in the case of the "mourning women" found at Ashdod, Azor, Tell Jemmeh, Tell Jerishe, and (probably) Tell ʿAitun (Tel Eton).[77] These latter figurines hold one or both of their hands to their head in a gesture of mourning. Although artistically in the Canaanite tradition, they were originally attached to the rim of a krater and, hence, reflect a local expression of a type of figurine known from the Aegean world and attached to vessels associated with the burial cult known as *lekanai*. Among the additional artifacts found in cultic contexts at Philistine sites are bi-metallic knives with ivory handles (Tell Qasile, Tel Miqne-Ekron),[78] parts of a miniature bronze wheeled cult stand (Tel Miqne-Ekron),[79] and a gynamorphic vessel whose breasts served as spouts (Tell Qasile).

In the public architecture of Philistine sites both Aegean and Canaanite architectural features have been identified. To the former belong the hearths found at Tels Qasile and Miqne-Ekron.[80] To the latter belong the *bamot* found at the latter site. The hearth is an architectural feature known from sites in Cyprus and the Aegean. It played a central role in the life of the community. The hearths found at Tell Qasile and Tel Miqne-Ekron belong to the earliest Iron Age levels at these sites. At Tell Qasile it was found in the public building southeast of the temple

---

[74] Gitin, "Cultic Elements," pp. 253-54.

[75] *Ibid.*, p. 253.

[76] *Ibid.*, p. 250; see also *idem.*, "Incense Altars from Ekron, Israel and Judah: Context and Typology," *ErIsr* 20 (1989) 52*-67*.

[77] T. Dothan, *Philistines*, pp. 237-49.

[78] T. Dothan, "Aegean Affinities," p. 48; Dothan and Dothan, *People of the Sea*, p. 225.

[79] T. Dothan, "Aegean Affinities," pp. 49-50.

[80] A. Mazar, "Qasile, Tell: Excavations in Area C," *The New Encyclopedia of Archaeological Excavations in the Holy Land* (ed. E. Stern; Jerusalem: Israel Exploration Society; New York: Simon & Schuster, 1993) 4.1207-208; and *idem.*, *Archaeology*, pp. 317-19. For Tel Miqne-Ekron: T. Dothan, "Aegean Affinities," pp. 42-45; T. Dothan and Gitin, "Miqne, Tel," pp. 1054-55; and Dothan and Dothan, *People of the Sea*, pp. 242-45.

precinct. In the hall of the building an elliptical raised mud-brick platform was found, in which a round plastered depression served as a hearth. It was founded in Stratum XI (second half of 12th century BCE) and probably continued in use through Stratum XII (first half of 11th century BCE). At Tel Miqne a round hearth set in the plastered floor and measuring 2.5 meters in diameter (somewhat smaller than parallels from the Cypro-Mycenean world) was found as the central feature in the "hearth sanctuary" of Stratum VII (early 12th century BCE). It was subsequently incorporated into the large public building 351 of Stratum VI, dating to the latter two-thirds of the 12th century BCE. By the turn of the century, building 351 had been replaced by the monumental building 350, which spanned Strata V-IV. Here a hearth was still in evidence at less than half its original size and constructed of pebbles. By the final phase of Stratum IV (late 11th-early 10th century BCE) the hearth had ceased to exist. This has been understood as a graphic example of the loss of the Philistine's Aegean heritage and of their gradual assimilation to indigenous culture.[81] A parallel cultural development may be observed in the contemporaneous disappearance of the bichrome ware.

Northwest of the building with the hearth at Tell Qasile was a sacred precinct. Three superimposed and increasingly larger temples were found there dating to the 12th through 10th centuries BCE. Although the temples' irregular plan and lack of uniformity in design from one level to the next led some to speculate that the Philistines brought with them an amorphous Aegean sacred building tradition, more recent work has indicated that the Tell Qasile temples stood in a Late Bronze and early Iron Age Canaanite architectural tradition.[82] Since some parallels to this

[81] See, however, Noort, who is willing to go no farther than to recognize an affinity between the Ekronite and Cypriote (not Aegean!) hearths; *Seevölker*, p. 147.

[82] A. Mazar has classified the Qasile temples as among those "with indirect entrances and irregular plans;" "Temples of the Middle and Late Bronze Ages and the Iron Age," *The Architecture of Ancient Israel from the Prehistoric to the Persian Periods* (ed. A. Kempinski and R. Reich; Jerusalem: Israel Exploration Society, 1992) 177. Other Canaanite examples include the Lachish Fosse Temples, the temple at Tel Mevorakh, and the temples of Bet Shean Strata IX and V (as well as those of VII-VI). Mazar also includes two buildings whose function as temples is unclear: Tell Abu Hawam Building 30 and the "Lion Temple" at Jaffa. In spite of the fact that they form a diverse group, the features thay have in common are: "their size; in several cases they are not freestanding buildings; they have a corner or indirect entrance which does not allow the holy-of-holies to be seen from the doorway; benches are built along the walls; the ceiling is supported by columns; the holy-of-holies is in the form of a raised platform; and the temples contain back rooms which served as treasure rooms or storerooms for offerings;" *ibid.*, pp. 181-82. See also Bunimovitz, "Problems," pp. 213-16.

type of architecture have been adduced in the Aegean and Cypriote world, the question of direction of influence has been raised. In this case Bunimovitz and A. Mazar agree that the influence would have had to have been from Canaan westwards.[83]

Information has also been uncovered relating to the economy of Philistia in the Iron Age. Surprisingly enough, maritime trade does not appear to have played all that great a role in the Philistine economy.[84] Oded speculates that this was due to the Phoenicians driving them out of that market.[85] However, this would not have applied to the period of Philistine settlement. Agriculture appears to have been a major focus of production at Philistine sites. Both Tell Qasile, which was founded in the mid 12th century BCE, and Tel Mor, the port of Ashdod, which became Philistine about a century later, bear witness to this phenomenon, in spite of the fact that they were both port cities. The importance of textiles to the Philistine economy had already been deduced from Assyrian inscriptions.[86] The discovery of biconical loomweights at both Ashkelon and Tel Miqne-Ekron from the 12th century levels substantiates this deduction.[87] Under Assyrian rule, 7th century Tel Miqne-Ekron together with its satellite Tel Batash-Timnah became the major olive oil producing center in the entire ancient Near East.[88] However, oil production was limited to only four months of the year. The industrial zones could not be allowed to lie fallow and the workers employed there could not be allowed to remain inactive for the rest of the year. Evidence was uncovered that the industrial complexes which were employed in the production of olive oil for one third of the year were converted into textile

---

[83] *Ibid.*, p. 214; A. Mazar, "Temples," p. 182; however, Mazar does speculate that the clustering of temples at Qasile XI-X may be evidence of Aegean influence; p. 182 n. 78.

[84] Dothan and Dothan, *People of the Sea*, p. 125.

[85] B. Oded, "Neighbors on the West," *The Age of the Monarchies: Political History* (World of the Jewish People, First Series 4.1; Jerusalem: Magnes, 1979) 236.

[86] *Ibid.*, p. 236; Tadmor, "Philistia Under Assyrian Rule," p. 93.

[87] Stager, *Ashkelon*, pp. 14-15; and *idem.*, "Ashkelon," p. 107. This style of unbaked cylinder had not previously been identified in Canaan. Its identification as a loomweight is dependent on parallels in Cyprus and in the Mycenean world, as well as on the high concentration of textile fibers which was found in the surrounding fill and was isolated by water sieving. The typical Canaanite loomweight is pyramidal and has a perforation at the upper end. For Tel Miqne-Ekron, T. Dothan, "Aegean Affinities," pp. 46-47.

[88] Kelm and Mazar, *Timnah*, pp. 150-64; A. Mazar, "Northern Shephelah," pp. 260-63. Gitin, "7th Century," pp. 63-69; *idem.*, "Ekron of the Philistines, Part II: Olive Oil Suppliers to the World," *BAR* 16 no 2 (1990) 36-39; and *idem.*, "Type-Site," pp. 48-50. See the former article in its entirety for an exemplary discussion of the place of Ekron within the context of Assyrian imperial economic policy.

production facilities for the remainder of the year. Textile dyeing seems to have been a facet of Tell Qasile's economy.[89] Finds at Ashdod indicate that it was a major hub for international trade. Concurrent with the expansion and specialization of the olive oil trade at Tels Miqne and Batash during the 7th century *pax assyriaca*, Ashdod served as a major producer of pottery, as is indicated by a potters' quarter found in Stratum VII.[90] Evidence has been found at Ashkelon for a flourishing wine industry in the destruction layer of 604 BCE.[91] In later periods the production of wine was a major factor in the city's economic life. Working backwards on the basis of archaeological finds and the regional ecology, Johnson and Stager have concluded that wine making was a major industry at Ashkelon throughout its history.

The picture that has emerged of Philistine city planning is one of carefully conceived and executed settlements, with well defined zones: public, private, industrial, and cultic.[92] Tell Qasile Stratum X (late 11th to early 10th century BCE) was carefully laid out in an orthogonal pattern. The rarity of this concept in Canaan has led the excavator, A. Mazar, to conclude that this may be another indication of the relationship between the settlers of Qasile and the island of Cyprus, specifically Enkomi.[93]

Stratum VII at Tel Miqne-Ekron (first third of 12th Century BCE), which followed upon the last level of the Late Bronze Age city, was a well planned urban area, which was protected by a mud-brick wall and which had a distinct industrial area in which a number of kilns were found.[94] In Stratum VI (last two thirds of the 12th century BCE) the city, which had been restricted to the ten acre acropolis of the tell during the Late Bronze Age, expanded into the area of the lower city and grew to the size of fifty acres.[95] It was in the elite area of the lower city, which spanned Strata VI-IV (12th to early 10th centuries BCE), that the "hearth sanctuary" was found. The high point of the early Iron Age city was

---

[89] T. Dothan and Cohn, "Philistine as Other," p. 67.

[90] M. Dothan, "Ashdod," *The New Encyclopedia of Archaeological Excavations in the Holy Land* (ed. E. Stern; Jerusalem: Israel Exploration Society; New York: Simon & Schuster, 1993) 1.100; Oded, "Neighbors," p. 237.

[91] Johnson and Stager, "Wine Emporium," especially p. 92.

[92] T. Dothan and Cohn, "Philistine as Other," p. 66.

[93] A. Mazar, *Qasile I*, pp. 76-77.

[94] Concerning the Iron Age I city see T. Dothan, "Arrival;" *idem*., "Aegean Affinities," pl. 4 on p. 59 following the article has the most recent stratigraphic and chronological chart of Tel Miqne; and T. Dothan and Gitin, "Miqne (Tel)," pp. 1053-56.

[95] This part of the tell had been abandoned since the close of the close of the Middle Bronze Age; T. Dothan, "Aegean Affinities," p. 42.

reached in Stratum IV, during which the distinctive material culture associated with the Philistines waned.

A destruction level associated with the end of the Late Bronze Age at Ashkelon has not yet been identified throughout the site.[96] The last Bronze Age levels were followed in Iron Age I by an enormous fortified port city which expanded to a size of 150 acres. The excavation of the site is ongoing.

The story of Ashdod in Iron Age I is one of continual expansion.[97] Founded on the widespread destruction layer of the Late Bronze Age city, the first phase of the Iron Age city (Stratum XIII), which was characterized by the presence of Myc IIIC:1b pottery, was poorly inhabited. Parts of the Late Bronze Age "stronghold palace" were reused as an industrial area, including a pottery making workshop. Throughout the following strata the city continued expanding until it reached its greatest extension in Stratum X (late 11th or early 10th century BCE[98]), when it expanded outside of the acropolis into the lower city. A major feature of the fortification of the lower city was a massive two (i.e. four) chambered gate.[99]

A Philistine town has been identified at Tel Batash-Timnah (Stratum V).[100] It followed upon a Late Bronze Age Canaanite city which had been in decline for some time.[101] The early "Philistine" inhabitants in part reused some of the remaining Late Bronze walls. Yet, two *tabuns* were constructed over some of the remaining Late Bronze walls. The city appears to have been well planned and densely settled. Although evidencing some classic Philistine characteristics in material culture (bichrome pottery as luxury ware and a pyramidal limestone seal depicting a lyre player[102]), the continuity with Late Bronze Age traditions in

---

[96] Stager, "Ashkelon," p. 107.

[97] See the reports of M. Dothan and others, *Ashdod I, II-III, IV*; as well as M. Dothan, "Ashdod" (Encyclopedia) 1.93-102 and "Ashdod,"*ABD* 1.477-82.

[98] Mazar, "Northern Shephelah," p. 254, who sees a direct correlation between the decline of Ekron and the expansion of Ashdod in the early 10th century.

[99] In the first phases of the Iron Age defensive issues seemed not to play as major an issue as during the latter part of Iron Age I, since a number of extra-mural buildings have been discovered at Philistine sites dating to these earlier phases; T. Dothan and Cohn, "Philistine as Other," p. 65. See also Dothan and Dothan, who attribute the need for protective fortifications to the burgeoning conflict with Israel in the latter half of the 11th century BCE; *People of the Sea*, p. 173.

[100] The latest treatment is in Kelm and Mazar, *Timnah*, pp. 91-104.

[101] The excavators are undecided whether there was an occupation gap between the LB and IA levels; *ibid.*, p. 92.

[102] *Ibid.*, p. 98. However, in his study of the group of seals to which the example from

most aspects of the material culture leads to the aforementioned theory that the Philistines were overlords of a mainly Canaanite population.[103]

A. Mazar views Beth Shemesh, east of Tel Batash-Timnah along the Sorek Brook, as a problem.[104] In essence, Beth Shemesh's material culture in Iron Age I is indistinguishable from that of Tel Batash-Timnah. However, the Bible claims that it was an Israelite town during the period of the Judges, in contrast to Philistine Timnah. On the one hand this underlines the difficulty of relying on the witness of the biblical text. On the other hand, this tension also evidences the problems associated with the ethnic identification of pots and other isolated aspects of material culture.[105] Although there are many other sites with "Philistine" remains, the question of their identification as Philistine is at best an open issue.[106]

The picture that emerges of Philistia at the turn of the 10th century BCE is that of a flourishing urban culture. It stands in marked contrast to the highland culture of central Canaan in the same period. In her thorough survey of the archaeology of ancient Palestine, H. Weippert distinquishes not between "Israelite" and "Philistine" culture, but between the *Dorfkultur* in the inland regions and the *Stadtkultur* of the Canaanite coast.[107] As she has noted, the successors to the urban culture of Late Bronze Age Canaan were to be found in the coastal plain, specifically in Philistia.[108] While retaining and developing many aspects of Canaanite culture, the coastal plain was, owing to its mixture of cultural influnces, a creative cauldron during the early Iron Age. However, the 10th century brought with it a change in the material culture and settlement patterns of Philistia.

The disppearance of the bichrome ware, hearths, and other "Aegean"

Tel Batash-Timnah belongs, O. Keel has concluded that the group as a whole develops Late Bronze Age traditions, although some may be of Egyptian origin; it is only the seal from Tel Batash which evidences a *decoration* which can be considered new/Philistine; "Philistine 'Anchor' Seals," *IEJ* 44 (1994) 21-35.

[103] Kelm and Mazar, *Timnah*, p. 93. This tempers their claim on the previous page that the expulsion of the Canaanite population of Timnah was "almost inevitable."

[104] Mazar, "Iron Age I," p. 273. See also *idem.*, "Northern Shephelah," pp. 251-53, where he speculates that the Samson stories in Judg 13-16 may reflect tensions between two groups of Sea Peoples.

[105] Brug, *Phistines*, pp. 135-44; and Noort, *Seevölker*, pp. 113-28.

[106] T. Dothan, *Philistines*, pp. 25-91; Bunimovitz views Philistine culture as a subgroup of the regional culture of the coastal plain.

[107] H. Weippert, *Palästina*, pp. 383 ff., 393 ff.

[108] *Ibid.*, p. 353. The city-state system of government was also retained in Phoenicia, in distinction to the system of national states which arose thoughout the rest of Palestine.

aspects of Philistine culture has been alluded to above. A number of Philistine sites evidence a development from the bichrome ware to a red-slipped ware which was to take its place in the regional assemblage.[109] However, the regional culture of Philistia was never again to have as wide a distribution as it had until the end of the 11th century BCE.

Thus the 10th century was a transitional period in Philistine history and culture. A number of sites in Philistia show evidence either of destruction, of abandonment, or of cultural change which has been dated to the first part of the 10th century BCE. However, there also exists a lively debate in the archaeological community regarding the exact dating and, hence, ascription to historical events and characters of the various strata. There are generally three candidates to whom the major upheavals at sites in Philistia during this period are ascribed: David, King of Israel and Judah, as well as the Pharaohs Siamun and Shoshenq (biblical Shishak).

Among the major Philistine sites, Tel Batash-Timnah V ended without destruction around 1000 BCE. Since it lay between Philistine Tel Miqne-Ekron and possibly Israelite Beth Shemesh,[110] it has been theorized that the site was abandoned by the Philistines as a consequence of the hostilities between Philistia and Israel during David's reign.[111] After a short uninhabited period, Tel Batash IV was in existence until destroyed near the end of the 10th century, probably by Shoshenq. Although the gate at Tel Batash IV has its closest parallel in the gate at Ashdod X, the pottery assemblage and other material culture remains find their closest parallels in the assemblages from sites in the Judean hills, the Shephelah, and the central coastal plains. Thus it is deduced that Tel Batash became an Israelite holding during the 10th century (i.e., during the united monarchy).[112]

Tel Miqne-Ekron Stratum IV-A suffered a violent destruction in the first part of the 10th century, which has been attributed either to David or to Siamun.[113] Subsequently the city was in decline for over two and a

---

[109] On Tel Miqne-Ekron see T. Dothan, "Arrival," p. 12; on Ashdod and its "Ashdod ware" see Dothan and Dothan, *People of the Sea*, pp. 178, 252; A. Mazar, *Archaeology*, p. 533.

[110] See W. G. Dever, "Monumental Architecture in Ancient Israel in the Period of the United Monarchy," *Studies in the Period of David and Solomon and Other Essays* (ed. T. Ishida; Winona Lake, Ind.: Eisenbrauns, 1982) 278-80.

[111] Kelm and Mazar, *Timnah*, pp. 105-14.

[112] But see D. Ussishkin, "Notes on Megiddo, Gezer, Ashdod, and Tel Batash in the 10th to 9th Centuries B.C.," *BASOR* 277-78 (1990) 82-88.

[113] T. Dothan, "The Rise and Fall of Ekron of the Philistines: Recent Excavations at

half centuries, until it experienced a dramatic economic revival under Assyrian hegemony. During this time of decline Ekron was restricted to the ten acre northeast acropolis. It was in the latter part of the 10th century or early 9th century that a mud-brick tower faced with ashlar masonry in a header-stretcher pattern was constructed. It was part of a fortification system that included a mud-brick wall. Gitin speculates that this was the wall depicted in the reliefs of Sargon II at Khorsabad.[114] Since Tel Miqne lay on the border with Judah, tensions between the city-state of Ekron and the national state of Judah were probably the cause of Tel Miqne's 270 year long period of decline, during which it became a political and economic backwater. When the restoration came following Hezekiah's failed revolt against Assyria, the upswing in Ekron's economic situation was dramatic. Tel Miqne grew to such an extent that for the first time in its history it sprung the bounds of the fifty acre Middle Bronze Age fortifications and grew to its greatest extent, namely 85 acres.[115]

Tel Mor (Ashdod-Yam, i.e., the port of Ashdod) Stratum III was also destroyed in the early 10th century. The destruction is generally ascribed to either David or Siamun.[116]

At Ashdod itself, Stratum X was destroyed about a third of the way into the 10th century.[117] Since this is the period to which Siamun's supposed capture of Gezer is dated, the excavators of Ashdod have attributed this destruction to him.[118] It would follow that this would also influence the dating of Tel Mor III to the same time.[119] Some theorize that Solomon conquered or at least controlled Ashdod on the basis of the "Solomonic" or three (i.e. six) chambered gate found there.[120] However,

an Urban Border Site, Part I: The Late Bronze and Early Iron Age," *BA* 50 (1987) 205; and *idem.*, "Arrival," p. 9.

[114] Gitin, "Type-Site," pp. 25-26.

[115] Gitin, "7th Century," p. 62.

[116] M. Dothan, "Mor, Tel," *The New Encyclopedia of Archaeological Excavations in the Holy Land* (ed. E. Stern; Jerusalem: Israel Exploration Society; New York: Simon & Schuster, 1993) 3.890; T. Dothan, *Philistines*, p. 43.

[117] Since Dever dates Stratum IX at Ashdod to the 11th century, it follows that he would not agree with a dating of Stratum X in the 10th; "Monumental Architecture," pp. 289-90.

[118] M. Dothan and Porath, *Ashdod IV*, p. 54.

[119] A. Malamat, "Aspects of the Foreign Policies of David and Solomon," *JNES* 22 (1963) 12; see also Ussishkin, "Notes," pp. 77-82.

[120] See, for example, A. Malamat, "A Political Look at the Kingdom of David and Solomon and Its Relation with Egypt," *Studies in the Period of David and Solomon and Other Essays* (ed. T. Ishida; Winona Lake, Ind.: Eisenbrauns, 1982) 203 and n. 45.

the date of the gate and its conceptual provenance are yet to be determined, although it would appear to be a development from the earlier two chambered one.[121] On the basis of recent work, it would appear that a Solomonic ascription of the gate and all that it would imply are at best questionable.

Three 10th century destruction layers have been identified at Tell Qasile. The excavator A. Mazar attributes the destruction of Stratum X to David in about 980 BCE.[122] The destruction of Stratum VIII and possibly of Stratum IX is attributed to Shoshenq in the second half of the century.[123] At any rate, as of the early 10th century Tell Qasile belonged to a different sphere of influence.[124] The northern border of Philistia was now more likely to be determined by the Sorek Brook than by the Yarkon River.

It can be assumed that during the course of the 10th century Philistia came under at least nominal Egyptian hegemony. Its period of expansion was over. A period of consolidation had begun. Owing to pressures from Israel, the inland cities, Ekron and presumably Gath, declined in importance. At the former site a radical reduction in size and hence population is graphically evident. Beneficieries of Ekron's and presumably also Gath's decline were the coastal Philistine cities, which reached their greatest extent during this period. The flourishing of sites along the Besor Brook, far removed from Israel and Judah, during the 10th century may also be indicative of the political situation.[125] The leading Philistine cities until the time of the Assyrian conquest were to be the coastal sites, which served as vital outlets for both land based and maritime international trade.[126]

---

[121] M. Dothan and Porath, *Ashdod IV*, pp. 54-55; Ussishkin, "Notes," pp. 77-82.

[122] A. Mazar, *Qasile I*, pp. 10-11.

[123] See also Dever, "Monumental Architecture," pp. 278-80.

[124] In spite of this, there is evidence that the "Philistine" sanctuary was rebuilt and continued in use through Strata IX-VIII (first and second half of the 10th century BCE). See A. Mazar, *Qasile I*, pp. 50-57; as well as Dothan and Dothan, *People of the Sea*, pp. 228-29.

[125] A. Mazar, *Archaeology*, p. 533.

[126] For a mainly text-based discussion of the relationship between the Philistines and the united monarchy of Israel in the 10th century BCE see Ehrlich, *Philistines*, Chapter Two; and *idem.*, "Sklavenauslieferung in der Bibel und im alten Orient," *Trumah* 4 (1994) 111-18.

ASSYRIA AND BABYLONIA IN THE TENTH CENTURY BCE

STEVEN W. HOLLOWAY

1. PRIMARY SOURCES

The extreme political and economic contraction experienced by the ancient urban centers of Mesopotamia during this century translates, for us, into one of the bleakest archaeological records of this region in recorded history. After 150 years of exploration on the major urban tells of the Assyrian and Babylonian heartlands, it is scarcely possible to date any building activity to the "dark age" of the 10th century BCE;[1] there are no known examples of royal or private correspondence, economic[2] or administrative documents from these years.[3] A handful of inscribed bronze objects,[4] Babylonian *kudurru* (boundary) stones,[5] Assyrian steles

---

[1] Mesopotamian specialists wax eloquent when describing the 10th century: "general chaos and anarchy," A. Kuhrt, *The Ancient Near East* c. *3000-330 BC* (Routledge History of the Ancient World; London: Routledge, 1995) 1:379; "a nadir even within the obscurity of Babylonian history," J. A. Brinkman, "Babylonia *c.* 1000-748 B.C.," in *CAH* 3.1.296; "obscurity of the tenth century," A. K. Grayson, "Assyria: Ashur-dan II to Ashur-nirari V (934-745 B.C.)," *CAH* 3.1.247.

[2] An as-yet unpublished economic text may date from the reign of the Babylonian king Nabû-mukīn-apli (987-943); see E. Sollberger, "The Cuneiform Collection in Geneva," *JCS* 5 (1951) 19 no. 2.9.

[3] J. A. Brinkman, "Settlement Surveys and Documentary Evidence: Regional Variation and Secular Trend in Mesopotamian Demography," *JNES* 43 (1984) 177 n. 18.

[4] P. Calmeyer, *Datierbare Bronzen aus Luristan und Kirmanshah* (Untersuchungen zur Assyriologie und Vorderasiatischen Archäologie 5; Berlin: Walter de Gruyter, 1969); idem, "Luristan Bronzen," *RLA* 7:174b-79a; O. W. Muscarella and E. Williams-Forte, "Surkh Dum at the Metropolitan Museum of Art: A Mini-Report," *Journal of Field Archaeology* 8 (1981) 327-59. Grant Frame unequivocally states that the provenance of the inscribed "Luristan bronzes" are unknown, as all of the examples published in *RIMB* 2 come from unscientific excavations and the antiquities market. Some may have been created in Babylonia and later smuggled into Iran; some may be ancient copies that reproduce the royal inscriptions of earlier kings. See Frame's remarks in *RIMB* 2, pp. 3-4. An excellent edition of the inscriptions with duplicates and other pertinent data are to be found in *RIMB* 2 B.4.1.1, 2 (reign of Eulmaš-šākin-šumi [1004-988]); 4.2.1 (reign of Ninurta-kudurrī-uṣur I [987-985]); B.5.1.1 (reign of Mār-bīti-apla-uṣur [984-979]); B.6.1.1 (reign of Nabû-mukīn-apli [978-943]). All regnal dates in this essay are those of the *RIMA*/*RIMB* publications; all dates are BCE unless otherwise noted.

[5] BM 90835 (reign of Nabû-mukīn-apli, 978-943); CBS 13873, also from the reign of Nabû-mukīn-apli, in J. A. and M. E. Brinkman, "A Tenth-Century Kudurru Fragment,"

from Assur,[6] and, toward the end on the century, Assyrian royal annals,[7] are the only datable contemporary texts. A series of non-contemporary royal and religious chronicles,[8] and perhaps one literary work, the Erra Epic,[9] establish the royal succession and confirm the precarious state of social and political order, but disclose little else. In the end, illumination of the darkness of this period is largely a matter of contrast with the relative richness of the preceding Middle Assyrian and Middle Babylonian periods, and the resurgent Neo-Assyrian and Neo-Babylonian civilizations that follow. Accordingly, the discerning reader will bear in mind the tentative nature of the following historical reconstruction.

Two keys are frequently used in the scholarly literature to unlock the mysterious decline of Assyria and Babylonia at this time: climatic change and nomadic incursion. On the basis of textual and archaeological evidence, a serious case can be argued that urban Mesopotamia *circa*

ZA 62 (1972) 91-98. BM 90835 describes in happily fulsome detail efforts by one Buruša, a craftsman, to obtain a clear title to real estate and to have its back taxes paid by Arad-Sibitti, a financially-strapped Kassite chieftain and Babylonian governor who accidentally slew a valuable slave belonging to Buruša and thus began a legal saga spanning the years 986-954.

[6] VA Ass 1202, Ass 15549, Ass Ph 4526 = *RIMA* 2 A.0.96 (Aššur-rēša-iši II [971-967]; Ass 15550 = *RIMA* 2 A.0.97.1 (Tiglath-pileser II [966-935]). These objects that collectively span some 750 years of Assyrian rule are part of the "Stelenreihen" found during the German excavations of Assur (modern Qalʿat Širqāt), 98 rough-hewn aniconic stone pillars with laconic inscriptions identifying them as the property or image (*ṣalmu*) of a king, high official, or occasionally a queen. Patterns of weathering reveal that some were exposed to the elements for many years in antiquity before (re)burial. For the *editio princeps* with full details of the excavation, see W. Andrae, *Die Stelenreihen in Assur* (WVDOG 24; Leipzig: J. C. Hinrichs, 1913).

[7] *RIMA* 2 A.0.96-99.

[8] A. K. Grayson, *Assyrian and Babylonian Chronicles* (TCS 5; Locust Valley, NY: J. J. Augustin, 1975), Religious Chronicle, pp. 136-38 ii 26-iv 6 (BM 35968); ibid., Dynastic Chronicle, p. 143 v 9-15 (K 8532+8533+8534); ibid., Synchronistic Chronicle, pp. 166-67 iii 1-21 (K 4401a+Rm 854); ibid., Eclectic Chronicle, p. 181 obv. 14-rev. 2 (BM 27859 [98-7-11,124]); idem, "Königslisten und Chroniken. B. Akkadisch," *RLA* 6:86-135. J. Neumann and S. Parpola, "Climatic Change and the Eleventh-Tenth-Century Eclipse of Assyria and Babylonia," *JNES* 46 (1987) 179, maintain that isolated examples from the astrological omen corpus that contain references to nomadic incursions, e.g., "If (the crescent of) the moon is sighted on the thirtieth of Sivan, the *aḫlamû* will eat up the abundance of Amurru (Syria); if the moon is sighted on the thirtieth of Tebet, the *aḫlamû* will eat up Subartu (Assyria), and a foreign tongue will rule over Amurru," can be dated to the disasters of the 11th and 10th centuries.

[9] The most recent English language translations of the Erra Epic are those of S. Dalley, *Myths from Mesopotamia: Creation, the Flood, Gilgamesh and Others* (New York: Oxford University Press, 1989) 282-315; and B. R. Foster, *Before the Muses: An Anthology of Akkadian Literature, vol. II: Mature, Late* (2nd ed.; Bethesda, Md: CDL, 1996) 757-89.

1200-900 experienced sustained drought conditions. The Tigris and the Euphrates streamflow was greatly reduced, causing water shortages in the south and shifting stream beds, with disastrous effects upon the local riverine economies.[10] Surface surveys of lower Mesopotamia reveal a significant reduction in numbers of settlements during this period.[11] Crop failures and famine conditions in both Assyria and Babylonia fueled a spiral of political weakness and social instability. "The political, military, and economic decline of Assyria and Babylonia in the twelfth through tenth centuries appears to coincide with the period of notable warming and aridity which set in about 1200 and lasted till about 900".[12] For the "drought model" to function as a satisfactory explanation of the calamities of the 10th century, it is necessary to accept this corollary phenomenon: institutional safeguards against semi-nomadic tribes and other marginal groups suffered an eclipse as the central governing authority weakened, with the result that the business of normal urban life, including the major public cultic celebrations, became difficult or periodically impossible to observe. The destabilizing effect of repeated crop failure on rural and urban economies can be seen most weeks on the national evening news broadcasts, and requires no elaborate defense. Whether the widespread aridity, inflated grain prices and crop failures recorded in the cuneiform sources of the 13th through the10th centuries were sufficient to trigger the parlous political and economic conditions that contrast markedly with the preceding and following centuries is an educated guess.

The second key to the catalogue of misfortunes that plagued Mesopotamia in the 10th century, nomadic incursion, may be termed the "Aramaean question." Thirty years ago Brinkman summarized his discussion about the Aramaeans in Babylonia during the period 1150–746 by noting that, at present, we do not know the origins of the Aramaeans, where they came from, why they entered Babylonia and, most damning, what they actually did there prior to the middle of the 8th century, when Assyrian and Babylonian sources flow copiously.[13] Reams of analysis but woefully little fresh primary evidence has left the Aramaean question

[10] P. A. Kay and D. L. Johnson, "Estimation of Tigris-Euphrates Streamflow from Regional Paleoenvironmental Proxy Data," *Climatic Change* 3 (1980-1981) 251-63.

[11] Brinkman, "Settlement Surveys and Documentary Evidence," pp. 172-75.

[12] Neumann and Parpola, "Climatic Change and the Eleventh-Tenth-Century Eclipse of Assyria and Babylonia," p. 177.

[13] J. A. Brinkman, *A Political History of Post-Kassite Babylonia, 1158-722 B.C.* (AnOr 43; Rome: Pontifical Biblical Institute, 1968) 280.

much as Brinkman found it. Globally speaking, the Aramaeans appear to have been one of many Semitic-speaking tribal groups living in Syria and upper Mesopotamia through much of the second millennium BCE. The evolution of a new dialect and cultural name are not unusual events among semi-nomadic groups, and cannot be taken in isolation as proof that the Aramaeans formed an intrusive migratory wave in the ancient Near East.[14] By the 10th century at the latest, often adopting Neo-Luwian patterns of cultural expression and political expansion, Aramaean polities began to found cities or fortify older settlements in northern Syria and the territory of Hanigalbat which formed the nuclei of the powerful city-states that would decisively shape Neo-Assyrian *Realpolitik* in the following centuries.[15] Fragmentary 11th-century Assyrian texts suggest that once-prosperous Assyrian cities were abandoned under the pressure of Aramaean hostilities: the populations either retreated to fortified cities like Arbaʾil or Nineveh, or fled to the foothills of Iraqi Kurdistan.[16] Better preserved documents from Babylonia speak of disturbances by semi-nomads (Aramaeans and Sutians), in which the northern and southern cities of Sippar and Nippur were plundered during the reign of Adad-apla-iddina (1069-1048).[17]

---

[14] A point made by G. M. Schwartz, "The Origins of the Arameans in Syria and Northern Mesopotamia: Research Problems and Potential Strategies," *To the Euphrates and Beyond: Archaeological Studies in Honour of Maurits N. van Loon* (ed. O. M. C. Haex, H. H. Curvers, and P. M. M. G. Akkermans; Rotterdam: A. A. Balkema, 1989) 283-84.

[15] See the evidence and discussions in S. Mazzoni, "Aramaean and Luwian New Foundations," *Nuove fondazioni nel Vicino Oriente antico: Realità e ideologia* (ed. S. Mazzoni; Seminari di Orientalistica 4; Pisa: Giardini Editori e Stampatori in Pisa, 1994) 319-40; H. S. Sader, *Les états araméens de Syrie depuis leur fondation jusqu'à leur transformation en provinces assyriennes* (Beiruter Texte und Studien 36; Beirut: Franz Steiner Verlag, 1987) 21-22 (Guzana/Tell Ḥalaf), 88 (Bīt Adini); Schwartz, "The Origins of the Arameans," pp. 278-79 (Tell Aḥmar, Tell Ḥalaf, Tell Rifaʿat, Zinjirli).

[16] The reconstruction of the badly-damaged text of Tiglath-pileser I (1114-1076) used as a major piece of evidence in bolstering this claim in H. Tadmor, "Historical Implications of the Correct Rendering of Akkadian *dâku*," *JNES* 17 (1958) 133-34, and Grayson, *Chronicles*, Assyrian Chronicle Fragment 4, p. 189 1'-13' (VAT 10453+10465 = Ass 3072+3074), has been challenged by W. T. Pitard, "An Historical Overview of Pastoral Nomadism," *"Go to the Land I Will Show You": Studies in Honor of Dwight W. Young* (ed. J. E. Coleson and V. H. Matthews; Winona Lake, Ind: Eisenbrauns, 1996) 299-300. The ambiguity of the textual sources, which Pitard instructively holds up to the light, does not in itself disprove the hypothesis of the dispossession and displacement of Assyrians by Aramaeans in and about the Assyrian heartland, however, and in my opinion Pitard's challenges to the status quo lack teeth in the absence of any serious treatment of the "Aramaean question" in the 10th-century cuneiform sources.

[17] Grayson, *Chronicles*, Eclectic Chronicle, pp. 180-81 obv. 8-11 (BM 27859 [98-7-

Scholarship of the past has tended to represent these disturbances in Cold War discourse as waves of rapacious tribal invaders sweeping in from the desert in order to seize cities of the fertile crescent weakened by famine.[18] Dissenting studies of the 1990s entertain the possibility that the Aramaeans mentioned in the Assyrian and Babylonian texts were primarily a new ethno-linguistic designation for nomadic pastoralists in the Euphrates and Habur regions, comparable to the Sutians and Haneans of earlier times, who posed chronic problems for centralized authorities that were amplified in periods of political and economic distress.[19] That these groups caused widespread difficulties for the sedentary populations of Babylonia in particular in the late 11th and 10th centuries is avowed by contemporary and later sources: the annals of the earliest Neo-Assyrian kings were preoccupied with reclaiming territory lost to Aramaeans, while Babylonian sources tell of cities plundered by nomadic forces and major religious festivals suspended. That Aramaeans attempted the wholesale invasion and occupation of Assyria or Babylonia, however, is not borne out by the gossamer filaments of evidence currently available.[20] What relationship, precisely, existed between the Aramaean groups that troubled the cities of Assyria and Babylonia of the 10th century with Aramaean enclaves and dynasts of the Jezireh and north Syrian cannot be determined at present. Whether increased sophistication in the establishment of pottery typologies and sequences will enable us someday to distinguish between Aramaean, Assyrian and Babylonian occupations during this period is speculation.[21]

11,124]); C. B. F. Walker, "Babylonian Chronicle 25: A Chronicle of the Kassite and Isin II Dynasties," Zikir šumim: *Assyriological Studies Presented to F. R. Krauss on the Occasion of His Seventieth Birthday* (ed. G. van Driel et al.; Leiden: E. J. Brill, 1982) 401 rev. 29-34 and 414-15 (BM 27796 [98-7-11,61]).

[18] Albright's notion that the Aramaeans were camel-nomads, a theory based on unsound analogies with the biblical Midianites, was highly influential in its day, and the spirit of the proposal maintains its hold even if the camel connection has been dropped; see W. F. Albright, "Syria, the Philistines, and Phoeniçia," in *CAH* 2.2, p. 532. On the other hand, Aramaeans were certainly capable of forming large defensive or offensive coalitions, as witness the Battle of Qarqar during the reign of Shalmaneser III (858-824; RIMA 3 A.0.102.2 ii 89b-102; 6 ii 26-33; 8.16'-19'; 10 ii 17b-25; 14.59b-66; 16.32-38a; 28.29-34a; 30.22-28a; 40 i 14-24; 76), and multiple accounts of an invading force of 2,000 Aramaean tribesmen that swept through the land of Laqê on the Middle Euphrates in the mid-8th century, only to be ambushed and slaughtered by the resourceful Ninurta-kudurrī-uṣur, governor of Sūḫu; *RIMB* 2 S.0.1002.1-4, 6-8.

[19] Schwartz, "The Origins of the Arameans," pp. 275-93; Pitard, "An Historical Overview of Pastoral Nomadism," pp. 298-301.

[20] Schwartz, "The Origins of the Arameans," pp. 281-286; Pitard, "An Historical Overview of Pastoral Nomadism," pp. 298-301.

[21] A desideratum voiced by Schwartz, "The Origins of the Arameans," pp. 285-86.

A plausible scenario for the tribulations of the first half of the 10th century, therefore, is that of royal and municipal governments weakened by famine and political isolation, periodically unable to cope with the aggressive tactics taken by mobile nomadic groups opportunistically prepared to ensure their own survival, and urban economies caught in the double bind of internal famine coupled with lost trade arteries either in the hands of semi-nomads or otherwise too dangerous to be practicable in an era when safety could not be guaranteed even within city walls.[22]

2. Population groups

By the 10th century the Assyrian heartland, the thin strip of fertile land that stretched north from Assur (modern Qalʿat Širqāt) along the Tigris to Nineveh, would have been host to the Assyrians, whose ancestors occupied the city of Assur by the mid-3rd millennium; descendants of various Amorite groups; Hurrians, possibly the aboriginal inhabitants of

[22] On the blockage of trade routes in northern Mesopotamia and the Middle Euphrates, see R. Zadok, "Elements of Aramean Pre-History," *Ah, Assyria . . . Studies in Assyrian History and Ancient Near Eastern Historiography Presented to Hayim Tadmor* (ed, M. Cogan and I. Ephʿal; Scripta Hierosolymitana 33; Jerusalem: Magnes, 1991) 114-15; Brinkman, "Babylonia in Eclipse," pp. 296-300. Other factors that might have contributed to the urban decline of this century include, for the Assyrians, systemic flaws in the provincial administrative structure that could not withstand combined stresses of chronic food shortages and semi-nomadic harassment. The interactions between the semi-nomads and the city dwellers of Assyria and Babylonia were undoubtedly more fluid and nuanced than the meager textual evidence (and our theories interpreting them) suggest. To this end, at the risk of indulging in anachronistic parallels, it is instructive to look through a recently published window into Aramaeans and Babylonian interactions two centuries later. S. W. Cole, *Nippur IV: The Early Neo-Babylonian Governor's Archive from Nippur* (OIP 114; Chicago: Oriental Institute of the University of Chicago, 1996), has edited some 113 Babylonian letters recovered from the West Mound of Nippur in 1973; all are dated on internal evidence to 755-732. This archive reveals that the higher echelon of rulers in mid-8th-century Nippur spent much of their energies in dealing with reports of kidnapping and ransom, much of it initiated by Chaldean and Aramaean tribesmen (nos. 2, 4, 18, 19, 24, 26, 28, 30, 40, 72, 74, 75, 77, 79, 80, 81, 84, 85, 86). Although one evidently ran the risk of personal kidnap when dealing with them, Aramaeans had slaves, wool and cattle to sell (nos. 46, 47, 60, 105). The entire Puqūdu tribe was reported to travel to Nippur to participate in municipal cultic celebrations (no. 27). No. 15 describes a letter that had been sent to all the Aramaeans; the addressee is enjoined to write again. A treaty was sworn between the lord of Nippur and the Rubu' tribe (no. 6). Intelligence reports were inserted detailing rumors of shifting alliances among the various Aramaean tribes (nos. 13, 14, 83). Aramaean migrants were part of the available labor force in Nippur (no. 96). Land disputes with an Aramaean shaykh are discussed (no. 98). "There is not an Aḫlamû or a single dog-of-a-crim[inal] around" (no. 109, p. 221 17b-19 [IM 77135 (12 N 158)]).

northern Iraq who spoke a non-Semitic language; and Aramaeans together with other semi-nomadic peoples.[23] Major population groups within Babylonia, the flat alluvial plain lying between the Tigris and Euphrates south of Assyria, would have included the Babylonians themselves;[24] Kassites with their distinctive tribal structure, several of whom held high office during the 10th century;[25] Aramaeans and, if there is a significant distinction, Sutians,[26] who are portrayed as the threatening "other" in contemporary records; and, to the south, the Chaldeans, whose three principal tribes of Bīt Iakīn, Bīt Dakkūri, and Bīt Amukāni are attested by 850, but who played no appreciable role in the political life of the Babylonian cities of the 10th century.[27]

3. Political organization and history

Despite the severe internal trials experienced by both countries, neither lapsed into the earlier political pattern of autonomous city-states, but retained the institutions of kingship and royal bureaucracies through this troubled century. Not surprisingly, the more centralized and militarily aggressive Assyrian government recovered more quickly than its southern counterpart. Maintenance throughout the 10th century of eponym lists at Assur, an ordered roster of high Assyrian officials circulated for the purpose of establishing chronological continuity, meant that, in addition to the organization of palace and temple administrative records, private commercial transactions could also be transcribed and records

[23] The extent to which Aramaeans settled in—as opposed to circulated and marauded through—Assyria at this time is hotly debated. On the question of Aramaean origins see Schwartz, "The Origins of the Arameans," pp. 275-93; Zadok, "Elements of Aramean Pre-History," pp. 104-17; A. R. Millard, "Arameans," *ABD* 1:345-46.

[24] G. Frame, *Babylonia 689-627 B.C.: A Political History* (Uitgaven van het Nederlands Historisch-Archaeologisch Instituut te Istanbul 69; Leiden: Nederlands Instituut voor het Nabije Oosten, 1992) 33-36 prefers the term "Akkadians."

[25] See Brinkman, *Post-Kassite Babylonia*, pp. 247-259; ibid., "Kassiten," *RLA* 5:464b-473b.

[26] See Brinkman, *Post-Kassite Babylonia*, pp. 285-287; M. Heltzer, *The Suteans* (Istituto Universitario Orientale, Seminario di Studi Asiatici, Series Minor 13; Naples: Istituto Universitario Orientale, 1981) 86-94. Neither the Assyrians nor the Babylonians consistently distinguished between the Aramaeans and the *Sutû* in their inscriptions.

[27] See Brinkman, *Post-Kassite Babylonia*, pp. 260-67; Frame, *Babylonia 689-627 B.C.*, pp. 36-43. Chaldeans first occur in cuneiform sources in 878. Although the Aramaeans and the Chaldeans were both West Semitic groups, the Babylonians always treated them as separate entities.

archived.[28] The reigns of five Assyrian monarchs spanned this period, all of whom claimed a single line of descent, in contrast with eight or more Babylonian kings stemming from at least three different "dynasties".[29] Military campaigns beyond the borders of Assyria beginning in the reign of Aššur-dan II reveal that the complex chain of command necessary for the army to function was intact.[30] Witnesses on a *kudurru* stone from the reign of Nabû-mukīn-apli reveal the offices of provincial governor,[31] governor,[32] vizier,[33] temple administrator,[34] and "keeper of the equipment storehouse".[35] An inscription from a Babylonian governor of the Sealands is preserved from the first half of the 10th century,[36] and "Luristan" bronzes exist with inscriptions of *sakrumaš*-officials, a military title.[37]

Virtually nothing is known of the reigns of the Assyrian kings Aššur-rabi II (1012-972), Aššur-rēša-iši II (971-967), and Tiglath-pileser II (966-935). An inscription by a vassal king of Aššur-rabi II and Aššur-rēša-iši II reveals that Assyrian authority in some fashion extended as far west as Šadikanni (modern Tell ʿAjaja) on the Habur river.[38] Texts from the reigns of Aššur-dan II (934-912) and Shalmaneser III (858-824) speak of the reconquest of cities on the Euphrates near Til-Barsip lost to the Aramaeans under Aššur-rabi II.[39] As Grayson observes, while this

---

[28] For Cᵉ (VAT 10670), the heavily damaged eponym list that covers the reigns of Tiglath-pileser I to Aššur-dan II, see the discussion and edition in A. Ungnad, "Eponymen," *RLA* 2:414a; *ARI* 2:70-71, XCV; 74, XCVII.2*; 81, XCVIII.7*; and for Cᵃ1, Cᵃ2 and SU 52/150 that begins with the accession of Adad-nārārī II, see the edition in A. R. Millard, *The Eponyms of the Assyrian Empire 910-612 BC* (SAAS 2; Helsinki: The Neo-Assyrian Text Corpus Project, 1994) 23-24.

[29] It should be noted that the "project" of the Assyrian King List is the legitimation of the king by "proving" the existence of a single line of royal descent. The royal inscriptions of Aššur-dan II and Adad-nārārī II claim a single ancestry; at present, the Assyrian King List is, aside from the titularies of the aforesaid two kings, the only source for the claim of unbroken descent by Aššur-rabi II, Aššur-rēša-iši II, and Tiglath-pileser II.

[30] Governors (*šaknu, šākin māti*): *RIMA* 2 A.0.99.1.rev. 19', 20'; A.0.99.2.61; commander-in-chief (*turtānu*): *RIMA* 2 A.0.99.2.64; other offices mentioned in the annals of Aššur-dan II and Adad-nārārī II include mayor (*ḫazannu*): *RIMA* 2 A.0.99.1.20'; palace prefect (*ša pān ekalli*): *RIMA* 2 A.098.1.87.

[31] *bēl piḫati*: L. W. King, *Babylonian Boundary-Stones and Memorial-Tablets in the British Museum* (London: Trustees of the British Museum, 1912) 58 I .21; p. 68 IVb 5

[32] *šaknu* and *šākin ṭēmi*: ibid., p. 58 I 16, 20; p. 68 IVa 34.

[33] *sukallu*: ibid., p. 58 I 19; p. 68 IVb 2.

[34] *šatam ekurri*: ibid., p. 68 IVa 31.

[35] *šatam bīt unâti*: ibid., p. 68 IVb 6.

[36] *RIMB* 2 B.4.0.2001.

[37] *RIMB* 2 B.6.1.2004, 2005.

[38] *RIMA* 2 A.0.96.2001, a clay cylinder from Assur.

[39] *RIMA* 2 A.0.98.1.24-25; 3 A.0.102.2 ii 35-38.

period in Assyrian history was one of military retrenchment, there is no evidence that Assyria lost its independence.[40] The survival of annals recording the campaigns of Aššur-dan II marks the conventional beginning of the Neo-Assyrian empire. This is misleading from the standpoint of what the early Neo-Assyrian kings claimed they were accomplishing, which was the reclamation of territories lost to their forefathers during the Middle Assyrian period and the "dark age" of the 10th century, over which they expressed themselves fully entitled to rule.[41] Aššur-dan II fought successfully against Aramaeans on two occasions; although his journeys never took him as far west as the Habur river and probably never exceeded two hundred miles from Assur, these campaigns signaled to the world at large that the Assyrians were again a power to be reckoned with. Adad-nārārī II (911-891) moved his line of conquest westward as far as the Aramaean kingdoms of the Middle Euphrates, and received gifts from Bīt-Adini on the west bank of the Euphrates; he also dealt with Aramaeans in the Zagros foothills.[42] Following the reduction or effective containment of Aramaean aggression, for the first time in a century Assyria and Babylonia entered one another's military and political field of vision. At some point between 908 and 902, Adad-nārārī II defeated the Babylonian king Šamaš-mudammiq, extending the borders of greater Assyria southeast to the important cult city of Dēr, and expropriating fortresses on the Middle Euphrates less than 100 miles from Babylon itself.[43] Late in the reign of Adad-nārārī II, the Babylonian king Nabû-šuma-ukīn I pushed the Assyro-Babylonian border back to the basin of the Lesser Zab and apparently won the respect of the Assyrian king, who exchanged daughters in diplomatic marriage with the Babylonian and thus began three-quarters of a century of peaceful relations between the two countries.[44] Assyria had made an auspicious recovery of her former might by the close of the 10th century. However, she had yet to match the imperial ambitions of the most accomplished Middle Assyrian monarchs, and lacked the military strength and provincial infrastructure to menace lands that lay west of the Euphrates on the Levantine coast.

---

[40] Grayson, "Assyria: Ashur-dan II to Ashur-nirari V (934-745 B.C.)," p. 248.

[41] Aššur-dan II is particularly eloquent in his litany of the reversal of the evils wrought by the Aramaeans. This rectification included repatriation of Assyrian refugees who had fled due to "famine, hunger (and) want" (*sunqi bubūte ḫušaḫḫi*); *RIMA* 2 A.0.98.1.60. Tribute withheld from the god Aššur is restored.

[42] *RIMA* 2 A.0.99.2.

[43] *RIMA* 2 A.0.99.2.26-29.

[44] Grayson, *Chronicle*, Synchronistic Chronicle, pp. 166-67 iii 10-21.

4. Social Conditions

During the reign of Adad-apla-iddina (1069-1048), the former Kassite capital Dūr-Kurigalzu, Dēr, Sippar and the southern Babylonian cities of Uruk and Nippur were plundered by Aramaean marauders. During the following century, famine, crop failure, repeated semi-nomadic incursions and the closing of the western Euphrates trade routes resulted in turbulent and even anarchic conditions within Babylonian cities, especially to the northwest. Grain prices are recorded at seven and one-half times the normal rate of exchange in the Bīt-Abi-Rattaš *kudurru* (986-954).[45] In the same document, indications of irregular gathering of taxes signal a weak central authority, together with the protracted financial embarrassment of Arad-Sibitti, who was no less a personage than a Babylonian governor. The Babylonian New Year's Festival, a vital public legitimation of the king's authority and the attendant prosperity of the country, went unobserved fourteen times in the first half of the 10th century, several instances of which were attributed to Aramaean hostilities.[46] Although the text of the Erra Epic was probably composed in the 8th century, the horrific disasters of the 11th and 10th centuries, such as the nomadic plundering of the cities and temples of Sippar and Dēr, are evoked as literary foils in the construction of a cosmic order that dissolves into chaos through the ambitions of a Babylonian god of warfare and pestilence. Ištarān, the outraged goddess of Dēr, addresses a plaintive speech to Erra:

> You turned the city Dēr into a wasteland,
> You fractured her populace like reeds...
> And as for me, you did not spare me but gave me over to the Sutaean nomads!...
> Men forsook truth and took up violence...
> He who did not die in battle will die in the epidemic,
> He who did not die in the epidemic, the enemy will plunder him,
> He whom the enemy has not pl[undered], the bandit will murder him.
> He whom the bandit did not murder, the king's weapon will vanquish him.[47]

---

[45]Brinkman, "Babylonia in Eclipse," p. 298; Neumann and Parpola, "Climatic Change and the Eleventh-Tenth-Century," p. 181 n. 70 provide comparative data suggesting that the 10th-century price was indicative of severe famine conditions.

[46] By holding a key river crossing, the Aramaeans cut off the route used to transport the divine statues of Marduk and Nabû from Borsippa and thus stalled the New Year's celebration; Grayson, *Chronicles*, Religious Chronicle pp. 137-38 iii 4'-15'.

[47] Foster, *Before the Muses*, pp. 782-783, IV: 66-67, 69, 73, 76-79.

The revival of Assyria's fortunes in the second half of the century brought with it the renewal of royal building projects: both Aššur-dan II and Adad-nārārī II refurbished temples and public edifices at Assur and other cities.[48] Royal continuity and military recovery of Assyria bears witness to a social milieu less systemically stressed than that of Babylonia, with its high dynastic turnover and repeated cultic disruptions.

5. Intellectual Life and the Fine Arts

In light of the paucity of datable finds, our best evidence for the persistence of the Sumero-Akkadian literary corpus and fine arts in the 10th century is continuity with what came before and after. For example, Neo-Assyrian city gates retained their Bronze Age names in Assur,[49] an unlikely scenario if the scribal arts had fallen into complete abeyance. Several characteristic genres of Neo-Assyrian art (obelisks, foundation figurines, rock reliefs, and gateway colossi) actually have roots in Middle Assyrian ateliers, and indirectly prove that the bridge of the 10th century remained intact.[50] The representation of the divine pantheon as symbols and not in anthropomorphic guise, the standard mode of visually evoking the gods on Neo-Assyrian royal steles, is clearly seen on the "Broken Obelisk" attributed to Aššur-bēl-kala (1073-1056), and may be a harbinger of the growing reluctance witnessed in Iron Age glyptics to model the gods in human form.[51] In Babylonia the genre, iconography

---

[48] Aššur-dan II: rebuilt the "New Palace" at Assur (*RIMA* 2, A.0.98.1.73-81a), the Craftsman's Gate (*RIMA* 2 A.0.98.3, 5: several clay cones found in and around the gate itself), performed work on the Aššur Temple itself (*RIMA* 2 A.0.98.4: clay cones found in the courtyard of the temple), and carried out construction work of some type at Kalizi (modern Qasr Šemamok), judging from the laconic clay cone found there (*RIMA* 2 A.0.98.6). Both Aššur-dan II and his successor claim to have constructed palaces in the various districts of their land; it is very probable that they built more than the meager archaeological finds reveal.

Adad-nārārī II: rebuilt the quay wall of the temple at Assur (*RIMA* 2 A.0.99.1.rev. 10'-16a'); rebuilt the temple of Gula at Assur (*RIMA* 2 A.0.99.2.128-131a); rebuilt the city and royal palace of ancient Apqu (modern Tell Abū Marya?; *RIMA* 2 A.0.99.2.36-38); performed unknown building operations at Nineveh, as evidenced by numerous inscriptions found there (*RIMA* 2 A.0.99.5, 7, and possibly 1001), and Šibaniba (modern Tell Billa; *RIMA* 2 A.0.99.8).

[49] See the evidence marshalled in A. R. George, *Babylonian Topographical Texts* (OLA 40; Louvain: Departement Oriëntalistiek and Peeters, 1992) 456-58.

[50] D. Stein, "Mittelassyrische Kunstperiode," *RLA* 8:300a.

[51] J. Börker-Klähn, *Altvorderasiatische Bildstelen und vergleichbare Felsreliefs* (Baghdader Forschungen. Deutsches Archäologisches Institut Abteilung Baghdad 4;

and even ductus of the *kudurru* stones bespeak the survival of traditional arts. BM 90835, a *kudurru* with captioned images of king Nabû-mukīn-apli, Arad-Sibitti and his sister, sports decorative motifs on the king's clothing that include rosettes and vignettes of the sacred tree, flanked either by bird-headed genii/*apkallū* holding situla and cones or by scorpion-tailed bird-men, mythological motifs attested in Kassite and Middle Assyrian glyptics, and amply represented in the palace reliefs of the Neo-Assyrian capitals.[52] The technical excellence of the so-called Luristan bronzes also illustrate the continuation of a tradition of metallurgical refinement and artistic accomplishment available to the Babylonian kings in the lowest ebb periods.[53] The near complete lack of datable monumental art from this period, however, bears grim testimony to the harsh realities that consumed the resources of would-be royal patrons of the arts.

One consequence of the renewal of Assyria as a campaigning military machine in the last third of the 10th century meant that, with the flow of exotic luxury objects into the capital city together with the transplanting

---

Mainz am Rhein: Philipp von Zabern, 1982), no. 131 (BM 118898; the dating of the object is disputed). T. Ornan, "The Mesopotamian Influence on West Semitic Inscribed Seals: A Preference for the Depiction of Mortals," *Studies in the Iconography of Northwest Semitic Inscribed Seals* (ed B. Sass and C. Uehlinger; OBO 125; Fribourg: Universitätsverlag Freiburg Schweiz; Göttingen: Vandenhoeck & Ruprecht, 1993) 71-72; *Idem*, "The Transition from Figured to Non-Figured Representations in First Millennium Mesopotamian Glyptic," *Seals and Sealings in the Ancient Near East: Proceedings of the Symposium Held on September 2, 1993, Jerusalem, Israel* (ed. J. G. Westenholz; Bible Lands Museum Publications 1; Jerusalem: Bible Lands Museum Jerusalem, 1995) 39-56; T. N. D. Mettinger, *No Graven Image: Israelite Aniconism in Its Ancient Near Eastern Context* (ConBOT 42; Stockholm: Almqvist & Wiksell International, 1995) 39-48.

[52] King, *Babylonian Boundary-Stones*, pp. 51-69, pl. LXVII-LXXIX = U. Seidl, *Die babylonischen Kudurru-Reliefs: Symbole mesopotamischer Gottheiten* (OBO 87; Fribourg: Universitätsverlag Freiburg Schweiz; Göttingen: Vandenhoeck & Ruprecht, 1989), no. 74/74', pp. 44-45, 54-55, 89. B. Wittmann, "Babylonische Rollsiegel des 11.-7. Jahrhunderts v.Chr.," *Baghdader Mitteilungen* 23 (1992) 169-289, amplifies one's impression of the stock nature of these decorative motifs by the frequency of the "sacred tree" and the presence of familiar mythological monsters in the glyptic art of the period (11th-9th centuries). On the history and cultural significance of these mythological beings, see F. A. M. Wiggermann, *Mesopotamian Protective Spirits: The Ritual Texts* (Cuneiform Monographs 1; Groningen: Styx & PP, 1992) 75-76; A. Green, "Mischwesen. B. Archäologie. Mesopotamien," *RLA* 8:252b §3.9; pp. 254b-255a §3.15.

[53] Unless these objects were manufactured from recycled bronze, sufficient trade activity had to have existed to supply the artisans with the requisite tin from sources far distant from Mesopotamia. For a general discussion of the topic, see J. A. Brinkman, "Textual Evidence for Bronze in Babylonia in the Early Iron Age, 1000-539 BC," *Bronzeworking Centres of Western Asia c. 1000-539 B.C.* (ed. J. Curtis; London: Kegan Paul International, 1988) 135-68.

of captive peoples within the Assyrian heartland, all aspects of Assyrian culture would be exposed to mounting foreign influence, as seen, for instance, in the increasing Aramaicization of the Assyrian language from the 9th century forward.[54]

6. City Cults

The significance of the Babylonian cult of Marduk and the celebration of the New Year's Festival is mirrored in the so-called cultic chronicle, in which the suspension of the New Year's Festival is often the sole event deemed worthy of record in a given year.[55] There are clues that the cult of Nabû of Borsippa, the son of Marduk, was growing increasingly influential in Babylonia during this period; Brinkman attributes this in part to the waning of nearby Babylon's fortunes.[56] In contrast to the 9th century and later, the popularity of Nabû did not spread to Assyria during the "dark age" of the 10th century, judging from the complete absence of the god in royal Assyrian inscriptions of that century. The Šamaš temple at Sippar was destroyed by Aramaeans during the second half of the 11th century; regular offerings were briefly reinstated under Simbar Šipak (1025-1008), only to be suspended during the reign of his successor. Following a plea before the Babylonian king by the priest of Sippar, a very modest daily allotment of wine and flour (one liter each) was siphoned off from the provisions for the Marduk temple in Babylon and dispatched to nearby Sippar, whose resources were apparently unable to supply the demand.[57] Normal provisions for the temple would not be available until more settled times in the reign of Nabû-apla-iddina (890?-851?).[58] Representations of Kassite deities persisted in the tra-

[54] See H. Tadmor, "The Aramaization of Assyria: Aspects of Western Impact," *Mesopotamien und seine Nachbarn: Politische und kulturelle Wechselbeziehungen im Alten Vorderasien vom 4. bis 1. Jahrtausend v. Chr.* (ed. H.-J. Nissen and J. Renger; XXV Rencontre Assyriologique Internationale, Berlin, 3. bis 7. Juli 1978; Berlin: Dietrich Reimer, 1982) 449-70; A. R. Millard, "Assyrians and Babylonians," *Iraq* 45 (1983) 101-108; J. N. Postgate, "Ancient Assyria—A Multi-Racial State," *ARAM* 1/1 (1989) 1-10.

[55] The failure of the New Year's Festival to take place was recorded for the first time in 1015; Brinkman, "Babylonia in Eclipse," p. 293 n. 12.

[56] Ibid., p. 293 n. 13.

[57] King, *Babylonian Boundary Stones*, no. 36, pp. 121-22 I 1-II 17.

[58] Due to the extreme scarcity of inscriptions from this period, it is currently impossible to date Babylonian temple renovations to a particular king. Take, for example, the ancient Ningal temple of Ur in southern Babylonia. The final excavation report is C. L. Woolley, *The Ziggurat and Its Surroundings* (Ur Excavations 5; Philadelphia: University

ditional iconography of the *kudurru* stones.[59] In Assyria, traditional royal support for the patron deity of the capital city and nation, Aššur, continued, as attested in royal inscriptions and the choice of royal names;[60] other major city cults were also patronized by the state.[61] Adad-nārārī II claims to have sacrificed to Adad of Kumme, a site near modern Zāḫo on the western Turkish-Iraqi border. The god is attested at Mari, and the city was a famous Hurrian cult site; by worshipping at his temple, the Assyrian king sought to secure the favor of the ancient god of the land even as he slaughtered, pillaged, and finally claimed to annex the region to Assyria.[62]

Museum; London: British Museum, 1939) 60-67. According to Woolley, Sîn-balāssu-iqbi, governor of Ur during the late Sargonid period, abandoned the temple last built by the Kassite king Kurigalzu I(?) and created "an original work of his own planning" on the same site (p. 60). No comprehensive restoration work seems to have been undertaken between the temple's foundation in the 14th century and its re-establishment under Sîn-balāssu-iqbi. T. Clayden, "The Date of the Foundation Deposit in the Temple of Ningal at Ur," *Iraq* 57 (1995) 61-70, argues on the basis of the altar excavated in the Ningal temple that the foundation offerings were deposited in the 8th or 7th century prior to the work of Sîn-balāssu-iqbi. "It is clear that following the original foundation of the Temple of Ningal in the fourteenth century B.C. until its virtually complete rebuilding in the seventh century B.C., the building was allowed to fall into decay" (p. 63).

[59] Šumalia/Šuqamuna (BM 90835); Seidl, *Die babylonischen Kudurru-Reliefs*, pp. 150-51.

[60] Both Aššur-dan II and Adad-nārārī II claim to have "given" deported gods to Aššur, which presumably meant that the divine images of defeated cities were housed in the Aššur temple at Assur as graphic symbols of the Assyrian state god's supremacy. Judging from chance inscriptional recovery and building sections in royal annals, many Middle and Neo-Assyrian kings made localized modifications and repairs on the Aššur temple, including Aššur-dan II and Adad-nārārī II (see note 48 above). However, regarding major changes to the fabric of the temple that affected overall layout and function, there appears to have been a hiatus between the reigns of Shalmaneser I (1276-1246) and Sennacherib (704-681); see A. Haller and W. Andrae, *Die Heiligtümer des Gottes Assur und der Sîn-Šamaš-Tempel in Assur* (WVDOG 67; Leipzig: J. C. Hinrichs, 1955) 40-73, and G. van Driel, *The Cult of Aššur* (Assen: Van Gorcum, 1969) 15-21.

[61] D. Stronach, "Village to Metropolis: Nineveh and the Beginnings of Urbanism in Northern Mesopotamia," *Nuove fondazioni nel Vicino Oriente antico: Realità e ideologia* (ed. S. Mazzoni; Seminari di Orientalistica 4; Pisa: Giardini Editori e Stampatori in Pisa, 1994) 96 mentions a tablet of Aššur-nāṣir-apli I (1049-1031) found in 1990 in the Maški Gate area that describes the construction of a temple of Adad in Nineveh. Adad-nārārī II built or refurbished a temple for the healing goddess Gula at Assur. The gods that appear in the inscriptions of Aššur-dan II and Adad-nārārī II (Aššur, Enlil, Ninlil, Sîn, Šamaš, Adad, Marduk, Ninurta, Nergal, Nusku, Ištar, Girra and Gula) constitute, with the exception of the missing Nabû, a pantheon that one might encounter at any point in the Neo-Assyrian royal inscriptions of the 9th century or later.

[62] *RIMA* 2, A.0.99.2.91-93 (VAT 8288). Adad-nārārī II would be emulated in his devotions at Kumme by the Urartian emperors Išpuini and Menua, as other nearby Adad-class deities would be revered by succeeding early Neo-Assyrian emperors in their bid to control the lands where Hurrian Tešub was formerly supreme. These observations are elaborated in a manuscript currently in preparation for E. J. Brill Press.

7. Parting Shot

This article was commissioned for the sake of providing historical context for the "age of Solomon." For those biblical specialists who entertain the possibility that the same shadow of the Mesopotamian superpowers that enveloped the kingdoms of Israel and Judah late in their lives extended backwards to the 10th century, I leave you with an image conjured literally from the sands of lower Mesopotamia.

Accumulation of *aparna* (sand-like silt and clay particles) in the courtyard of the Ekur (Enlil) temple of Nippur between the reigns of Nebuchadnezzar I (1125-1104) and Assurbanipal (669-627?) indicates that

> the personnel belonging to the Ekur were in such straitened circumstances at least for part of the interval . . . that they were unable to perform even the elementary maintenance of keeping the temple courtyard swept clean; as a result, the pavement was buried under a forty-centimeter accumulation of naturally laid debris . . . it is tempting to attribute this most difficult period in the life of the Ekur to the tenth century".[63]

It is safe to conclude that the course of 10th-century Palestinian politics was unhampered by the inhabitants of lower Mesopotamia, who could not muster the resources to sweep the blowing desert sands from the courtyard of the preeminent regional temple of yesteryear.

---

[63] J. A. Armstrong, "The Archaeology of Nippur from the Decline of the Kassite Kingdom until the Rise of the Neo-Babylonian Empire," (Ph.D. dissertation, University of Chicago, 1989) 230.

ARCHAEOLOGY AND THE "AGE OF SOLOMON": A CASE-STUDY IN ARCHAEOLOGY AND HISTORIOGRAPHY

William G. Dever

Introduction

Until a decade ago both biblical scholars and Syro-Palestinian archaeologists spoke of a historical "age of Solomon" as a matter of course. Most, however, were sophisticated enough to recognize that some of the stories of First Kings are fictional and that the overall portrait is exaggerated. Today that has all changed. Consider the latest pronouncement of two leading biblicists of the "revisionist" school:

> That is the issue we have today: namely, the question of whether the Bible in its stories is talking about history and the past at all. Our argument is not that the Bible exaggerates the exploits of David, nor is it that Solomon was never as rich as the Bible makes him out to be. We are not dealing with issues of skepticism here. Rather, we are trying to argue that the Bible's stories of Saul, David and Solomon are not about history at all.[1]

Even if we allow for the oversimplification and rhetoric typical of the "revisionist" school's style of discourse, there is a challenge here that must be met, especially since all of the "revisionists" make some sort of appeal to *archaeology*, however inept. As I shall argue, it is not only the archaeological assemblage of the 10th-9th centuries BCE and its absolute date that is at issue here, but also, and fundamentally, a historiographical issue that is now urgent in both biblical studies and archaeology. That is: What is the nature and relationship of the *two* classes of data now available for writing a history of ancient Israel; texts and archaeological evidence? In short, can we any longer write a history of ancient Israel *at all*, and if so, how? That question is implicit in all the recent literature in our several disciplines, especially on the present subject, but in my opinion it has been addressed only obliquely.[2]

---

[1] N. P. Lemche and T. L. Thompson, "Did Biran Kill David? The Bible in the Light of Archaeology," *JSOT* 64 (1994) 18.

[2] W. G. Dever, "Archaeology and the Current Crisis in Israelite Historiography," *ErIsr* 25 (1996), and references there to the wider literature; M. and H. Weippert, "Die

1. Archaeological Evidence for the Emergence of an Israelite "State" in the 10th/9th Century BCE

Before defining what we mean by a "state," then determining whether or not the archaeological data of the 10th-9th centuries BCE allow us so to designate ancient Israel (and Judah), we need to summarize those data. Details cannot be given in this brief presentation, but the basic data and some synthesis may be found in standard reference works on the earlier American Iron IC-IIA or the more common Israeli usage, Iron IIA-B, which we shall use here.[3]

The approach we shall use in analyzing the 10th-9th century BCE archaeological complex is a simplified version of "General Systems Theory," which has provided an interpretive paradigm for many archaeologists around the world since the advent of the New Archaeology thirty years ago. While the literature is enormous, and the theory has been applied to numerous fields, the basis of the "systematic" approach is simply the assumption that social systems, like biological organisms, are dynamically integrated; composed of several closely coordinated "sub-systems;" tend to seek their own equilibrium ("homeostasis"); and may periodically collapse when one or more of the sub-systems malfunctions. The potential application to archaeology is obvious,[4] for even if "General Systems Theory" is not wholely applicable to archaeological data (it is commonly observed that "archaeologists do not dig up social systems"), the overall paradigm provides at least a holistic approach, as well as a practical scheme for organizing the available data. In our usage here, this means that we can readily discuss the sites presented in Fig. 1 in terms of "sub-systems" such as: 1) settlement type and patterns;

Vorgeschichte Israels in neuem Licht," *TRu* 56 (1991) 341-90. See also articles in a dialogue between Dever and N. P. Lemche in *JSOT* (1996); (see n. 27 below), as well as the recent programmatic statement of T. L. Thompson, "A Neo-Albrightean School in History and Biblical Studies?" *JBL* 114 (1995) 683-705. See further nn. 15, 27, 74 below.

[3] The basic archaeological data are discussed and documented fully in H. Weippert, *Palästina in vorhellenistischer Zeit* (Handbuch der Archäologie: Vorderasiaen 2/1; Munich: C. H. Beck, 1988) 417-781; A. Mazar, *Archaeology of the Land of the Bible 10,000-586 B.C.E.* (ABRL; New York: Doubleday, 1992) 368-402; and G. Barkay, "The Iron Age II-III," in *The Archaeology of the Land of Israel* (ed. A. Ben-Tor; New Haven: Yale University, 1992) 325-72.

[4] For an orientation to General Systems Theory and an example of its possible application to Palestinian archaeology, see W. G. Dever, "The Collapse of the Urban Early Bronze Age in Palestine: Toward a Systemic Analysis," *L'urbanisation de la Palestine a l'âge du Bronze ancien* (ed. P. de Miroschedji; Oxford: BAR International, 1989) 225-46.

2) demography; 3) techno-environmental adaptations, subsistence, and the economy; 4) social structure; 5) political organization; 6) ideology, including religion; 7) larger historical-cultural context; and 8) the question of "ethnicity."

Rank	Sites, 10th cent. BCE	Size (ac.)	Population	9th cent. BCE	Source
"Tier 1"	Dan IV	50	5,000	III	
Cities	Hazor X-XI	15	1,500	VIII-VII	
(22,350 total	Megiddo VA/IVB*	13.5 (15-25)	1,300 (500)	IVA	YS
population)	Ta'anach IIA-B	16	1,600	III	
	Beth-shan Upper	10	1,000	IV	
	Tell el-Far'ah N. VIIb	15 (?)	1,500	VIIc-d	
	Shechem X	13	1,300	IX	
	Aphek X_8	15	1,500	X_7	
	Gezer IX-VIII	33	3,300	VII	
	Jerusalem 14	32	2,500	13	YS
	Lachish V	18 (38)	1,800 (500)	IV	YS; H
"Tier 2"	Tel Kinrot V-IV	1.25	1,250	III	
Towns	Tel Amal III	0.75	75		
	Yoqneam XVI-XIV	10	1,000	XIII	
	Tel Qiri VIIA	2.5	2,500	VIIB-C	
	Dothan 4 (?)*	10 (15)	1,000		YS
	Tel Mevorakh VIII-VII	1.5	150		
	Tell Michal XIV-XIII	0.3	30		
	Tell Qasile IX-VIII	4	400	VII	
	Azekah	14 (?)	1,400 (?)		
	Tel Batash IV	6.5	650	III	
	Beth-Shemesh IIa	10	1,000	IIb	
	Tell el-Ful II		?	?	
	Tell Hama		1	100	
	Tell Mazar XII	?	?		
	Tell Beit Mirsim B_3*	7.5	750 (1,300)	A_2	H
	Tel Halif VII		300	VIA	
	Tel Ser'a VII		500	VI	
	Beersheba VI (V?)*	2.5	250 (600)	(?V) IV	H
	Arad XII		?	XI-X	
"Tier 3"	Tell el-Kheleifeh I			II?	
Villages,	Qadesh-Barnea 1			2	
hamlets,	Negev forts				
camps, etc.					

Fig. 1. "Three-tier" hierarchy of major 10th century BCE sites in Palestine with population estimates. Some coastal and Jordan Valley sites are eliminated since they are probably "non-Israelite." YS=Shiloh 1980; H=Herzog 1992.

A. *Settlement Type and Pattern*

If one compares the typical Iron II or 10th-9th century BCE sites listed in Fig. 1 with the Iron I or "Proto-Israelite" sites of the 12th-11th century BCE, several significant changes are apparent in settlement type and overall pattern of distribution.

1) Most of the small Iron I highland villages, based on an agrarian economic system and on kin-based or "acephalous" social relations, are gradually abandoned by the mid-late 10th century BCE. These would include nearly all the most characteristic "Proto-Israelite" sites, i.e., those that had been founded *de novo* in the late 13th-12th century BCE, that have been excavated to date: Ai, Raddanah, Shiloh, Izbet Sartah, and Tel Masos. The same overall pattern of demographic shifts is seen in the many dozens of other Iron I villages known from surface surveys. Only the settlements of Arad and Beersheba are somewhat atypical, both continuing uninterruptedly into Iron II and developing into important towns by the 9th century BCE.[5]

2) The abandonment of the Iron I villages is but one aspect of increasing centralization, i.e., of the advent of the first *urban* era in ancient Israel, perhaps to be designated "proto-urban" in its initial phase. The other aspect of urbanization is, of course, the refounding of the old Bronze Age urban centers now as "central places," or market towns and administrative centers. These newly established urban centres of Iron II, including several of those listed in "tier 1" in Fig. 1, exhibit a pattern of town-planning; the beginnings of monumental architecture, including city walls and gates; and increased population growth. In short, after a long decline in the Late Bronze Age, followed by an "intermediate," non-urban period of resettlement in Iron I, the Israelite cities of the Iron

[5] For the term "Proto-Israelite" and its rationale, see W. G. Dever, "The Late Bronze-Early Iron I Horizon in Syria-Palestine," *The Crisis Years: The 12th Century B.C. From Beyond the Danube to the Tigris* (eds. W. A. Ward and M. S. Joukowsky; Dubuque, Iowa: Kendall/Hunt Publishing Company, 1990) 99-110. For convenient summaries of the archaeological data on the 12th-11th centuries BCE, see I. Finkelstein, *The Archaeology of the Israelite Settlement* (Jerusalem: Israel Exploration Society, 1988); R. B. Coote, *Early Israel: A New Horizon* (Minneapolis: Fortress, 1990); N. K. Gottwald, "Recent Studies of the Social World of Premonarchic Israel," *Currents in Research: Biblical Studies* 1 (1993) 163-89; W. G. Dever, "Cultural Continuity, Ethnicity in the Archaeological Record, and the Question of Israelite Origins," *ErIsr* 24 (1993) 22*-23*; *From Nomadism to Monarchy: Archaeological and Historical Aspects of Early Israel* (eds. I. Finkelstein and N. Na'aman; Jerusalem: Yad Izhak Ben-Zvi, 1988); see also the exchange between Lemche and Dever referred to in n. 2, above, and nn. 15, 27, 30, 74, below, and references there to much other literature.

IIA period witness a revival, so to speak, of the highly urbanized settlement pattern of the Early and Middle Bronze Ages, as Fritz has pointed out.[6]

3) The resultant shifts in settlement type and pattern by early Iron II may best be characterized as a reflection of the "three-tier" hierarchy of sites (Fig. 1) that archaeologists, anthropologists, and economic geographers usually employ to define "urbanism" in cross-cultural comparisons.[7] We shall return below to ask what these changes mean, as well as to ascertain whether the terms "urban" and "city" can be specified so as to apply to them.

B. *Demography*

We have already argued that major demographic shifts were a part of the growth of urbanism, i.e., not simply that the total population is growing, but that a declining rural and village population is offset by a concomitant growth in the urban centers. But can we attach any absolute numbers to these trends? Unfortunately, demography is not yet a science in archaeology. This is especially true when the data come from partially and often badly excavated and published sites, and even more from surface surveys that at best are not always statistically valid. Nevertheless, much recent demographic analysis in Syro-Palestinian archaeology suggests some *relative* figures.

Drawing principally on analyses of Broshi and Gophna, Gonen, Finkelstein, Stager, Shiloh, and Sharon, it may be suggested that the population of Palestine in several successive periods may be estimated as follows:[8]

---

[6] V. Fritz, *The City in Ancient Israel* (Biblical Seminar 29; Sheffield: Sheffield Academic, 1995) 118-20. For more detailed discussions of spacial models, see *Spacial Analysis in Archaeology* (eds. I. Hodder and C. Orton; Cambridge: Cambrige University, 1976) 55-73. See also n. 9.

[7] For orientation to Central Place Theory, "rank-size" anayses and "three-tier" settlement pattern hierarchies, see R. J. Sharer and W. Ashmore, *Fundamentals of Archaeology* (Menlo Park, Calif.: Benjamin/Cummings Publishing, 1974) 426-35; C. Renfrew and P. Bahn, *Archaeology: Theories, Methods, and Practices* (New York: Thames and Hudson, 1991) 159-62, 182-94.

[8] On demography in general in archaeology, see F. A. Hassan, *Demographic Archaeology* (New York: Academic, 1981) 49-103. For the Iron Age of Palestine, see principally Y. Shiloh, "The Population of Iron Age Palestine in the Light of a Sample Analysis of Urban Plans, Areas and Population Density," *BASOR* 239 (1980) 25-35; L. E. Stager, "The Archaeology of the Family in Ancient Israel," *BASOR* 260 (1985) 1-35; M. Broshi and I. Finkelstein, "The Population of Palestine in Iron Age II," *BASOR* 287 (1992) 47-60; I.

Middle Bronze II-III, 18th-16th centuries BCE	=	140,000
Late Bronze II, 14th-13th centuries BCE	=	60,000
Iron IA, 12th century BCE	=	25,000
Iron IB, late 11th century BCE	=	65,000
Iron IIA, late 10th century BCE	=	100,000
Iron IIB-C, 9th-7th centuries BCE	=	150,000

More significant than the estimate of total population (i.e., the evidence of recovery and growth in the early Iron Age) is the concentration of a relatively larger proportion in the urban centers. Regardless of one's judgment concerning the absolute accuracy of the projections in Fig. 1, it is obvious that the growth of the cities listed by the 10th century BCE yields a portrait of the classic "three-tier" site hierarchy noted above as a typical indication of an urbanized society. By "three-tier" we designate a settlement hierarchy that when plotted on a "rank-size" graph yields a distinctive curve. The resultant pattern is characterized by: 1) a few very large "upper-tier" sites, with a significant percentage of the total population, or "central places" in Central Place Theory parlance; 2) a larger number of "middle-tier" sites, or towns widely distributed and related to the centers in a sort of nodal network; and 3) many more "lower-tier" or very small sites, such as villages, hamlets, and farmsteads, farther out in the nodal network.[9]

Finkelstein, "Environmental Archaeology and Social History: Demographic and Economic Aspects of the Monarchic Period," *Biblical Archaeology Today: Proceedings of the Second International Congress on Biblical Archaeology, Jerusalem, June 1990* (eds. J. Aviram and A. Biran; Jerusalem: Israel Exploration Society, 1993) 56-66; Z. Herzog, "Settlement and Fortification Planning in the Iron Age," *The Architecture of Ancient Israel from the Prehistoric to the Persian Periods* (eds. A. Kempinski and R. Reich; Jerusalem: Israel Exploration Society, 1992) 231-74. Despite many differing interpretations of specific data, there is a consensus that an estimate of *ca.* 100 persons per acre of inhabited domestic area gives the best results; I have employed that rule-of-thumb in Fig. 1, with the exception of the few sites with an asterisk, for which the reader can compare the literature cited here. The population estimates in the following table are taken from Broshi, Finkelstein, Gonen, Shiloh, and Stager, except for my estimate of *ca.* 100,000 for the 10th century BCE, which is a projection based on a population growth rate of 1.5 per generation of 25 years, meaning that the population would double every 50 years; cf. I. Sharon, "Demographic Aspects of the Problem of the Israelite Settlements," *Uncovering Ancient Stones: Essays in Memory of H. Neil Richardson* (ed. L. M. Hopfe; Winona Lake, Ind: Eisenbrauns, 1994) 119-301. Assuming a typical figure of *ca.* 50,000-60,000 in the mid-11th century BCE, it would be entirely reasonable to propose a population of *ca.* 100,000 by *ca.* 950 BCE; the usual projections are of 150,000-160,000 by the 9th-8th centuries BCE. Note that some coastal sites like Tell Keisan, Tell Abu Hawam, Ashdod, and Ekron are not included on the assumption that they were ethnically "Philistine," rather than "Israelite."

[9] See the references in n. 7 above. Several scholars divide the Iron II settlements into three or four loosely-defined categories. See Mazar, *Archaeology of the Holy Land* : 1)

C. *Techno-environmental adaptation, subsistence, and the economy*

Assuming that the foregoing assessments of shifts in settlement patterns and population are cogent, it follows that there were accompanying changes in the economy that were both the cause and the effect of urban growth. The agrarian economy that had developed in the 12th-11th centuries BCE had been confined largely to a unique ecological niche, comprising highlands, intermontane valleys, and adjacent steppe-zones, had been based almost exclusively on subsistence farming (often on terraced hillsides), limited stockbreeding, and some pastoralism. This economy I have called, following Sahlins' *Stone Age Economics*, the domestic mode of production.[10] In earliest Israel there is almost no evidence of long-distance trade in the highland villages, only what we might call "cottage industry." The socio-economic structure is family-based.

By the 10th century BCE, however, the emergence of centralized cities, even if few in number, necessitated a shift to more intensive agricultural production in the hinterland, even though the archaeological evidence, by definition, is sparse.[11] One must presume that cities like Megiddo or Gezer cannot have sustained themselves on an ancient version of "truck-gardening." Furthermore, the considerable archaeological evidence for growning specialization and social stratification by the 10th century BCE presupposes the development of certain industries which

---

"Royal Cities," 2) towns, and 3) villages; and Herzog, "Settlement and Fortification Planning": 1) Capital cities, 2) major administration cities, 3) secondary administrative centers, and 4) provincial towns. Only J. S. Holladay, however, makes use of any of the specific models advocated here (n. 5); see his seminal essay "The Kingdoms of Israel and Judah: Political and Economic Centralization in the Iron IIA-B (ca. 1,000-750 BCE)," *The Archaeology of Society in the Holy Land* (ed. T. E. Levy; Leicester: Leicester University, 1995) 372-76, and especially n. 3. Holladay defines a hierarchy of 1) complex/central places, 2) partially differentiated settlements towns, 3) differentiated settlements, 4) dependent villages, and 5) hamlets, farmsteads. Holladay, however, despite mentioning Christaller's basic work on Central Place Theory and listing some other literature, does not actually employ either that theory, "rank-size" analyses, or a "three-tier" model in his otherwise sophisticated discussion. It should also be noted that fundamental reference works such as Mazar, Barkay, Herzog, and Fritz (above, nn. 3, 5) do not even define a "city" by any criteria; see also n. 7 above and further below.

[10] W. G. Dever, "Unresolved Issues in the Early History of Israel: Toward a Synthesis of Archaeological and Historical Reconstructions," *The Bible and the Politics of Exegesis: Essays in Honor of Norman K. Gottwald on His Sixty-Fifth Birthday* (eds. D. Jobling, P. L. Day, and G. T. Sheppard; Cleveland: Pilgrim, 1992) 195-208.

[11] On agriculture generally, see D. C. Hopkins, *The Highlands of Canaan: Agricultural Life in the Early Iron Age* (SWBA 3; Sheffield: Almond, 1985). The most provocative treatment of the 11th-10th century BCE archaeological evidence is that of Holladay, "Kingdoms of Israel and Judah," pp. 372-79, 386, making the rare attempt to quantify some of the data. See also Stager, "Archaeology of the Family."

always accompany urbanization. In this case, they are principally: standardized ceramics; planned monumental construction; and the manufacture of elite goods. Finally, trade, conspicuously absent in the previous period, resumes by the 10th century BCE; as examples one could point to the resumption of trade in Cypriot ceramics, and arts and crafts of Phoenician derivation.

Holladay has argued recently that the "Phoenician connection" was especially significant and probably fueled urban expansion in Iron II Palestine. He also posits that the Arabian spice route, coming through southern Palestine, was a producer of revenue through sizable tariffs.[12] Holladay's novel treatment is somewhat speculative, but the point is that we no longer need to invoke outworn biblical notions of "Solomon's seaport at Ezion-geber" to postulate growing international relations in 10th century BCE Palestine. One may safely characterize the economic shift as one from a small-scale agrarian kin-based society and economy, based on risk-sharing, to one that was increasingly urbanized and "entrepeneurial."[13]

D. *Social structure*

In looking at the evidence for the development of an urbanized economy we have already implied that an accompanying change was the gradual emergence not only of vocational specialization, but also of social stratification, i.e., a "ranked society." The differential access to goods and services typical of urban societies would have produced many inequalities, in particular the emergence of a class of elites whose status and wealth were no longer necessarily inherited (as in earlier kin-based societies), but could now be acquired through individual prowess and could even be passed on to one's heirs. That is why I suggested above the term "entrepeneurial" for the society and economy of the 10th-9th centuries BCE.

The archaeological evidence for this is still scant, due to limited excavation. But one can easily cite such data as the large palaces of Megiddo VA-IVB and Gezer IX-VIII; administrative complexes, including possibly scribes' work areas, at several sites; and a growing *corpus* of luxury goods such as items of personal adornment, seals, ivories, etc. (although

[12] Holladay, "Kingdoms of Israel and Judah," pp. 379-86.

[13] See references in n. 11. These authors, however, do not employ my term "entrepeneurial" for the later urban stages.

not well attested until the 9th century BCE). The most ambitious attempt so far to distinguish a class of elites in the archaeological record is certainly that of Holladay, in characterizing "the social organizational shift from acephalous (lacking hereditary leadership) segmented society to centralized nation-state."[14] Holladay's scenario is somewhat speculative, but highly suggestive, especially for avenues of further archaeological research. In any case, we will not likely find more "elites" in the archaeological record until we start developing research designs that are more deliberate and sophisticated.

A final category should be mentioned here with reference to a stratified society, namely the existence of a system of writing. This would have been a *sine qua non* not only for the functioning of the requisite urban bureaucracy, but also to serve both as a powerful staus-marker and an instrument for maintaining control over an increasingly diversified and perhaps resistant society. Here the archaeological data are limited so far: a 13th/12th century BCE inscribed jarhandle from Raddanah, a 12th century BCE abecedary ("Proto-Canaanite" alphabet) from Izbet Sartah, a group of inscribed 11th century BCE arrowheads, and a probable schoolboy's exercise tablet from the 10th century BCE from Gezer. Yet all these tantalizing remains, it seems to me, suggest the widespread use of the old Canaanite script to write early Hebrew, not only among the upper classes, but among tradesmen, mercenaries, and even perhaps some peasant farmers. If not "scribal schools" in these written remains, we may at least have evidence of a level of practical notation, i.e., "functional literacy."[15]

E. *Political organization*

The social and economic evolution sketched above implies, of course, a system of political organization that was also more centralized, more hierarchical, "politics" (Greek πόλις) being the art of living in and gov-

[14] Holladay, "Kingdoms of Israel and Judah," pp 37-39.

[15] On the difficult problem of writing and the extant of literacy in ancient Israel, see A. R. Millard, "The Question of Israelite Literacy," *Approaches to the Bible: A Multitude of Perspectives* (ed. H. Minkoff; Washington, DC: Biblical Archaeology Society, 1995) 142-53. Cf. Holladay, "Kingdoms of Israel and Judah," p. 381 (although the Izbet Sartah abecedary is certainly not "Solomonic," but 12th or early 11th century BCE at lhe latest). The skepticism of P. R. Davies, typical of the "revisionist" historians, that the population of Iron Age Israel was only 5% literate is entirely unwarranted given the constantly increasing *corpus* of 9th-6th century BCE seals, ostraca, weights, etc.; see P. R. Davies, *In Search of "Ancient Israel"* (JSOTSup 148; Sheffield: JSOT, 1992) 103.

erning cities. The archaeological evidence for increasing political complexity and centralization consists largely of what have been regarded as planned cities with "royal monumental" architecture. These are principally Hazor, Megiddo, and Gezer, all best described as regional administrative centers among the "1st tier" cities listed in Fig. 1. We shall discuss absolute chronology presently, but I would regard the following installations as all roughly contemporary, dating broadly to the mid-late 10th century BCE and constituting archaeological evidence of state-level political organizations.[16]

1. Hazor X	Citadel of upper city, on new plan
	Four-entryway city gate
	Casemate wall
2. Megiddo VA/IVB	New town plan
	Four-entryway city gate
	Casemate wall
	Palaces 6,000 and 1723
	Building 338
3. Gezer VIII	Four-entryway city gate
	Double wall system
	Palace 10,000

Several points are worth stressing because controversy among archaeologists about these "royal cities" tends to obscure their validity as historical evidence for the question of state-formation processes. 1) The cities, particularly Megiddo, represent "new foundations"[17] of the 10th century BCE, in many ways radically different from the Iron I or even the Late Bronze Age towns, no doubt regional administrative centers. 2) What has been revealed of these cities in excavations, however limited the

[16] For the basic archaeological data on these three sites, see Weippert, *Palästina*, pp. 417-781; Mazar, *Archaeology of the Holy Land*, pp. 380-87; Barkay, "Iron II-III," pp. 305-10; Herzog, "Settlement and Fortification," pp. 244-46, 249-53; Holladay, "Kingdoms of Israel and Judah," pp. 371-73; Fritz, *City in Ancient Israel*, pp. 79-83, 87-96; see further below and the references in nn. 32-36 to the protracted controversy of "Tel Aviv-American" schools over the dating of these three sites.

[17] For a critique of the "chiefdom" model as applied by biblical scholars like Frick and Flanagan to Iron I Israel, see W. G. Dever, "From Tribe to Nation: State Formation Processes in Ancient Israel," *Nuove fondazioni nel Vicino Oriente Antico: Realtà e ideologia* (Seminari di Orientalistica 4; ed. S. Mazzoni; Pisa: University of Pisa, 1994) 213-29. For more recent literature, also suggesting that the "chiefdom" model has been over-worked, see N. Yoffee, "Too Many Chiefs? or Safe Texts for the 90's," *Archaeological Theory—Who Sets the Agenda?* (eds. A. Sherratt and N. Yoffee; Cambridge: Cambridge University, 1993) 60-78.

exposure, clearly suggests a sophisticated level of town-planning, with public constructions like defenses, palaces, and administration buildings that are particularly well laid out and are dominant in proportion to residential areas. 3) Certain elements, such as the four-entryway city gates at all three sites, and to some degree the palaces at Megiddo and Gezer, are so similar in plan and details of construction such as ashlar masonry that they point almost certainly to centralized planning emmanating from a single source, as Yadin suggested long ago.[18] 4) At the "middle tier" of site hierarchy (Fig. 1), a number of smaller sites could be regarded as lower-level administrative centers, certainly so by the 9th century BCE: Tel Kinrot V, Tell el-Far᾿ah North VIIb, and Beersheba V. 5) Finally, some 50 enclosed forts in the Neqev, most apparently dated to the 10th century BCE, are best understood as an extension of centralized authority to the borders with Egypt and Edom.[19]

The above observations remain true even if one follows Aharoni, Herzog, and Ussishkin (against the majority) in downdating the Megiddo gate to the early 9th century BCE. As "new Foundations" in the 10th century BCE, Hazor, Megiddo, and Gezer may even be considered "disembedded capitals," i.e., as relatively isolated towns, some quite small, founded or refounded diliberately to serve as administrative centers, typically with impressive public building and installations but relatively few domestic facilities.[20] Such a description would fit Megiddo (and even Hazor) admirably in the 10th century BCE and in particular Samaria and probably Jerusalem by the 9th century BCE. Even allowing for differences in date and interpretation, the above archaeological data in my judgment yield conclusive evidence for defining 10th century BCE Israel as not only "urbanized," but now under *centralized* political authority, call it what you like (or a "state").

---

[18] Y. Yadin, "Solomon's City Wall and Gate of Gezer," *IEJ* 8 (1958) 8-18. On ashlar masonry, see Y. Shiloh, *The Proto-Aeolic Capital and Ashlar Masonry* (Oedem 2; Jerusalem: Israel Exploration Society, 1979).

[19] See also Mazar, *Archaeology of the Holy Land*, pp. 390-96, and references there; Holladay, "Kingdoms of Israel and Judah," p. 395, n. 16. For the alternate interpretation of these walled enclosures as "pastoral encampments," which I think highly unlikely, see N. Na᾿aman, "Israel, Edom and Egypt in the 10th Century B.C.E.," *Tel Aviv* 19 (1992) 71-82, and references there.

[20] See the paper of my student A. H. Joffe, "Disembedded Capitals in Western Asiatic Perspective," *Antiquity*, forthcoming.

F. *Ideology*

The general category of ideology is always somewhat difficult to specify in the material culture record. But in so far as archaeology properly deals with the "material correlates of behavior," it is able at least to infer certain aspects of individual and collective thought.[21]

1. Cult. I would argue that the very foundation of several central cities in the 10th century BCE, with stereotyped defenses and other monumental architecture, is itself a reflection of the beginnings of a homogeneous "national consciousness," not to mention ethnic identification.

2. Religion. One of the most diagnostic aspects of ideology is religion. In the 12th-11th century BCE in Palestine we have only the early "Bull Site" of Mazar (excepting Zertal's Mt. Ebal installation, which few authorities believe is cultic). By the 10th century, however, we can cite possibly the extensive Tel Dan cult installation (although perhaps early 9th century BCE); the "Gate sanctuary" at Tell el Far'ah North; and certainly the "Cult Building" at Ta'anach, with its stunning terra cotta cult-stands and much other explicit paraphernalia; several small cultic installations at Megiddo; Lachish "Cult Room 49;" and possibly the prototype of the Arad tripartite temple.[22] Few of the typical Iron II female figurines have been found (fragments at Tell el-Far'ah North and a mold for making them at Ta'anach) but these seem to indicate continuity with the cult of the old Canaanite Mother Goddess Asherah,[23] whatever "Yahwism" may have meant at this early stage.

---

[21] On the current focus on the possibilities for a "cognitive" archaeology, see I. Hodder, *Reading the Past: Current Approaches to Interpretation in Archaeology* (Cambridge: Cambridge University, 1985); *Ideology, Power and Prehistory* (eds. D. Miller and C. Tilley; Cambridge: Cambridge University, 1984); *The Meaning of Things: Material, Culture and Symbolic Expression* (ed. I. Hodder; London: Unwin Hyman, 1989); M. Shanks, *Experiencing the Past: On the Character of Archaeology* (London: Routledge, 1992). The new, "post-processual" approach, however, is regarded with great skepticism by unrepentent "new archaeologists" (now "old"); L. R. Binford, *Debating Archaeology* (San Diego: Academic, 1989) Chapters 1-6.

[22] On the "Bull Site," see A. Mazar, "The 'Bull Site'—An Iron Age I Open Cult Place," *BASOR* 247 (1982) 27-42; and on Mt. Ebal, see A. Zertal, "An Early Iron Age Cultic Site on Mt. Ebal: Excavation Seasons 1982-1987," *Tel Aviv* 13-14 (1986-1987) 105-65. On the date of the Arad temple, see Mazar, *Archaeology of the Holy Land*, pp. 396-97, and references there; and Holladay, "Kingdoms of Israel and Judah," pp. 385, 394; if Str. XII is late 10th century BCE, destroyed by Shishak, as these scholars argue (contro Herzog), then Str. XI and the sanctuary would be early 9th century BCE.

[23] On the cult of Asherah there is considerable recent literature; see, conveniently, W. G. Dever, "Will the Real Israel Please Stand Up? Archaeology and the Religion of Ancient Israel, Part II," *BASOR* 298 (1995) 27-38, and literature cited there.

One might, of course, cite as evidence of a "national religion" the Solomonic Temple described in the Hebrew Bible. No actual trace of it survives, however, and although its location is known, archaeologists will likely never be permitted to excavate the area. In any case, it is worth noting that virtually every detail of the hitherto enigmatic descriptions of the building and its furnishings in 1 Kgs 5-7 can now be readily illuminated by comparison with a long sequence of Middle Bronze, Late Bronze, and Iron Age Canaanite/Phoenician temples, especially good parallels coming from the 9th-8th century BCE tripartite temple at Tell Tayinat in Syria.[24]

3. Industries. The principle industries that reflect ideology are ceramics, as well as a number of modules and building techniques that relate to both public and private constructions. We cannot go into detail on 10th century BCE pottery, but the significant development in this period is the first standardization of a distinctive and properly "Iron Age" (or Israelite) repertoire, in contrast to the early Iron I pottery, still very much in the Late Bronze Age tradition.[25] The marked homogeneity includes aspects of form, decoration, and technique; and it extends from the extreme north of the country to the south (in contrast to north-south divisions later in Iron II). In architecture the major reflections of what we may call a "national ideal" are the features we noted above in administrative centers like Hazor, Megiddo, and Gezer: standardized four-entryway gates (a revival and adaptation of Middle Bronze Age gate plans); casemate walls; the use of Phoenician-style ashlar or dressed header-stretcher masonry; and the ubiquitous "four-room" or courtyard house, a rural house-style now widely adapted to urban living.[26] It is significant that *all* these aspects of material culture and, of course, the ideology behind their full expression, continue throughout the subsequent Iron II

[24] For recent, archaeologically based reconstructions of an actual 10th century BCE Solomonic temple, see Mazar, *Archaeology of the Holy Land*, pp. 376-80; C. Meyers, "Temple, Jerusalem," *ABD* 5.350-69; Fritz, *City in Ancient Israel*, pp. 123-27.

[25] On the emergence of the *real* "Iron Age" ceramic repertoire in the 10th century BCE, now almost completely freed from Late Bronze Age Canaanite tradition, see Dever, "Ceramic Continuity," pp. 27, 30. On archaeology's growing capability today of recognizing cultural norms (ideology) in the archaeological record, see the references in n. 21 above.

[26] For synthetic discussions of the so-called "four-room house," see Y. Shiloh, "The Four-Room House, Its Situation and Function in the Israelite City," *IEJ* 20 (1970) 180-90; and update by reference to Herzog, "Settlement and Fortification," p. 269; and especially J. S. Holladay, "House, Israelite," *ABD* 3.308-18.

period, *ca*. 900-600 BCE. Those who do not specialize in material culture remains (like biblicists who repeat the old canard that archaeology is "mute") may remain skeptical, but to archaeologists these aspects of cultural homogeneity are not fortuitious. They can only be interpreted as evidence of a growing *national consensus* of what it means to be an "Israelite" (as distinct from "Canaanite"), and what is "appropriate" for a developing self-conscious state.

G. *Language and script*

Language and script constitute a well recognized component of ethnicity, but the evidence from Palestine in Iron I and IIA is thus far limited, as discussed above. One observation, however, may be pertinent. We have 9th century BCE *monumental* inscriptions from the Aramaean city-states to the north, from Moab in Transjordan, and now from northern Israel at Tel Dan (not Hebrew, however). These are all in related Northwest Semitic languages and scripts that are rapidly diverging from old Canaanite on a "national" basis. We also have the 9th century BCE Neo-Assyrian inscriptions that mention Israel for the first time (as the "House of Omri;" cf. the contemporary Dan inscription, "House of David," and "Kings of Israel").[27] It is not unreasonable to assume that these mid-9th century BCE linguistic developments had their predecessors in the mid-late 10th century BCE, even though to date we have little direct archaeological evidence.

H. *The larger cultural context*

One measure of the rise of independent territorial "states" in ancient Western Asia is the evidence of increasing competition among these entities, or political constellations, each vying for hegemony in the area. By the 10th century BCE, to judge from the textual and archaeological data, Israel was at war with the local Philistines, ethnically distinct, as

[27] For these 9th century BCE inscriptions, see conveniently A. L. Oppenheim, "Babylonian and Assyrian Historical Texts," *ANET,* pp. 279, 281, 320. On the recent Tel Dan inscription, see the negative view of Lemche and Thompson, "Did Biran Kill David?" pp. 3-22, and references; but for a much better balanced, positive view, see W. M. Schniedewind, "The Tell Dan Stela: New Light on Aramaic and Jehu's Revolt," *BASOR*, forthcoming, and references there. For an archaeological perspective, see W. G. Dever, "Revisionist Israel Revisited: A Reply to N. P. Lemche," *JSOT* (1996) 4: 35-50.

their decidedly different material culture attests. In addition, the archaeological data demonstrate overlapping but probably adversarial relations with the nascent Neo-Hittite and Aramaean Kingdoms to the north, as well as with the emergent "tribal states" in Transjordan.[28] These increasingly complex international contacts, as well as the defense of the Egyptian border, point to a growning sense of national identity and destiny: the biblical concept of "Israel among the nations."

I. *The questions of "ethnicity"*

Finally, there is the question of interpreting archaeological remains that is most difficult, namely whether we can identify specific ethnic groups in the archaeological record, in this case, "Israelites." This question is more controversial for the Iron I period because most now agree that the "Israel" of the Hebrew Bible is a later concept, and we have no extra-biblical texts except the well known reference to an "Israel" in Canaan in the Merneptah Stele, *ca.* 1207 BCE. Nevertheless, I have argued at some length elsewhere that even in the 12th-11th century BCE the term "Proto-Israelite" is fully justified for the highland settlers discussed above. This is so not only because of the Merneptah reference, but because in material culture remains *alone* we can identify an ethnic group distinct from other known contemporary groups such as Canaanites, Egyptians, and "Sea Peoples."[29]

By the 10th century BCE, the emergent national culture reflected in the archaeological data summarized above demonstrates beyond doubt

---

[28] For the emergent Neo-Hittite and Aramaean territorial states, see the superb resume of H. Sader, "The 12th Century B.C. in Syria: The Problem of the Rise of the Aramaeans," *The Crisis Years: The 12th Century B.C.: From Beyond the Danube to the Tigris* (eds. W. A. Ward and M. S. Joukowsky; Dubuque: Kendall/Hunt Publishing Company, 1992) 37-63. On the early Iron Age Transjordan states in process, see now the excellent collection of essays in *Early Edom and Moab: The Beginning of the Iron Age in Southern Transjordan* (ed. P. Bienkowski; Sheffield Archaeological Monographs 7; Sheffield: J. R. Collins Publishers, 1992).

[29] On ethnicity in the archaeological record, see Dever, "Ceramic Continuity," and the dialogue in I. Finkelstein, "Pots and Peoples Revisited: Ethnic Boundaries in the Iron Age I," *The Archaeology of Israel: Constructing the Past, Interpreting the Present* (eds. N.A. Silberman and D. Small; Sheffield: Sheffield Academic, 1997) 216-37; and W. G. Dever, "Israelite Origins and the 'Nomadic Ideal': Can Archaeology Separate Fact from Fiction?," *Mediterranean Peoples in Transition: Thirteenth to Eleventh Centuries B.C.E.* (eds. S. Gitin and A. Mazar; New York: New York University, 1997). *BA* 58 (1995) features a series of articles on archaeology and ethnicity. See nn. 30, 73.

that the use of the biblical designation "Israel" is justified. The objection of "revisionists" like Davies, Lemche, and Thompson (that this archaeologically defined Israel is not identical to the ideal "Israel" of the final redactors of the Hebrew Bible) is obvious but irrelevant.[30] If we did not happen to find the term "Israel" in texts, we would have to invent it or another term to characterize the Iron IIA archaeological complex that we now have. Of course, only slightly later, in the mid-9th century BCE, we can cite historical references to "Israel" in the Moabite stele, the Neo-Assyrian annals and now the Tel Dan inscription. That the latter also mentions "the House of David" according to most authorities is a considerable embarassment to the "revisionists," who had previously denied that there was an early Israelite state.[31]

II. The Absolute Date of the Iron IIA/B Archaeological Assemblage

Having summarized the pertinent archaeological data that might define "statehood" in early Israel, we must confront the fact that some archaeologists would date part of these materials later, i.e., to the early-mid 9th century BCE or the reigns of Omri and Ahab. The controversy involves the four-entryway city gate at Megiddo and to a lesser degree the "outer Wall" at Gezer.[32]

A. *The Controversy: A Summary of Views*

The literature on the above controversy has burgeoned in the last decade or so, but for purposes of discussion we can group the opinions of various authorities as follows (ignoring the biblicist "revisionists," since their *archaeological* judgments obviously carry no weight):

---

[30] For a refutation of the notion of Davies, Lemche, Thompson, and Whitelam that there was *no* "early Israel" in either the biblical or the archaeological sense, see Dever, "Revisionist Israel Revisited;" and *idem*, "The Identification of Early Israel: A Rejoinder to Keith W. Whitelam," *JSOT* (1996); see also n. 73.

[31] See n. 26 on the Tel Dan inscription.

[32] The literature on this controversy is now extensive, but see the latest publications, with full references to earlier discussion: W. G. Dever, "Further Evidence on the Date of the Outer Wall of Gezer," *BASOR* 289 (1993) 33-54; I. Finkelstein, "Penelope's Shroud Unravelled: Iron II Date of Gezer's Outer Wall Established," *Tel Aviv* 21 (1994) 276-82. See also more specific references to the "Tel Aviv" school below and nn. 32-38.

1. "Maximalist" position (10th century BCE):

Albright	(1943)
Wright	(1950)
Kenyon	(1971)
Yadin	(1958, 1972, 1980)
Shiloh	(1980)
A. Mazar	(1990)
Holladay	(1990, 1995)
Stager	(1990)
Fritz	(1995)
Dever	(1986, 1992)

2. "Minimalist" position (9th century BCE):

Aharoni	(1972, 1974)
Herzog	(1976, 1986, 1996)
Ussishkin	(1980, 1990)
Finkelstein	(1990)
Wightman	(1990)

It might be noteworthy that all the "revisionists" here are Israeli archaeologists connected with Tel Aviv University. On the other hand, all the prominent international archaeologists of the previous generation, all those at Hebrew University of Jerusalem, and all the American archaeologists have held to the traditional phasing and dating. There are, however, some nuances of interpretation within the "Tel Aviv school." Thus on the date of the crucial four-entryway gate at Megiddo, Herzog, Ussishkin, and Wightman move it from Str. VA/IVB to Str. IVA, dating it to the 9th century BCE; Finkelstein raises methodological issues but offers no new opinion, apparently siding somewhat reluctantly with the traditional 10th century BCE date; and Aharoni, followed until recently by Herzog, had assigned the gate, but not Yadin's casemate wall (denying it be such), to Str. IVB, regarding it as "Solomonic."[33] The less con-

[33] See Y. Aharoni, *The Archaeology of the Land of Israel* (Philadelphia: Westminster, 1982) 179-180; Z. Herzog, "Settlement and Fortification," pp. 244-47, 250-58 (see also n. 39 below); idem., *Das Stadttor in Israel und in den Nachbaren Landern* (Mainz: P. von Zabern, 1986) 93-108; D. Ussishkin, "Was the 'Solomonic City' Gate Built by King Solomon?," *BASOR* 239 (1980) 1-18; see reply by Y. Yadin, "A Rejoinder," *BASOR* 239 (1980) 19-23; G. J. Wightman, "The Myth of Solomon," *BASOR* 277/278 (1990) 5-23; I. Finkelstein, "On Archaeological Methods and Historical Considerations: Iron Age II Gezer and Samaria," *BASOR* 277/278 (1990) 109-30; D. Ussishkin, "Notes on Megiddo, Gezer, Ashdod, and Tel Batash in the Tenth to Ninth Centuries B.C.," *BASOR* 277/278 (1990) 71-91. For my own direct response to the latter several articles, see W. G. Dever, "Of Myths and Methods," *BASOR* 277/278 (1990) 121-30; and for other scholars who date the Gezer

troversial Gezer VIII four-entryway gate is thought by Ussishkin to be either 10th or 9th century BCE; Herzog does not defend any position, but apparently would allow for a 10th century BCE date; Wightman argues for a 9th century BCE date; and Finkelstein again raises methodological questions but does not decide on a date (although his 1981 study assumes that the gate goes with the "Outer Wall," dated now by Finkelstein to the 9th century BCE).[34] As for Hazor X, Ussishkin still dates the four-entryway gate there to be 10th century BCE; Herzog and Finkelstein are non-commital, but leave a 10th century date as a possibility; and Wightman dates it, like the other two, to the 9th century BCE.[35]

The recent controversy would probably seem to the non-specialists to have generated much heat, but little light. Yet disagreements have an impact not only on general questions of archaeological and historical method (as well as implications for the proper use of biblical texts in archaeology), but also on the specific question of how much of the foregoing data can be used to elucidate a "Solomonic era," and particularly the emergence then of an "Israelite state."

The main aspect of the controversy that affects the issue at hand has to do with the recent attempt to remove some of the three stereotypical city gates and some of the city walls from the 10th century BCE archaeological assemblage. Accepting that revision would rob us of crucial data for regarding Hazor, Megiddo, and Gezer as Solomonic "regional administrative centers." But how persuasive are the arguments of the "Tel Aviv school?" In an entire issue of *BASOR*, Holladay, Stager, and I have offered what I believe to be an effective rebuttal to Finkelstein, Ussishkin, and Wightman.[36] Fundamental as these several articles are, however, they unfortunately do not resolve the chronological problems, nor can we do so here.

---

and Megiddo gates and defences to the 10th century BCE, see J. S. Holladay, "Red Slip, Burnish, and the Solomonic Gateway at Gezer," *BASOR* 277/278 (1990) 23-70; idem., "Kingdoms of Israel and Judah," pp. 371-73; L. E. Stager, "Shemer's Estate," *BASOR* 277/278 (1990) 93-107; V. Fritz, *The City in Ancient Israel*. For older literature in support of a 10th century BCE date, see n. 34.

[34] On their dates for the Gezer defenses, see Ussishkin, "Notes on Megiddo," pp. 76-77; Herzog, "Settlement and Fortification," p. 268; Wightman, "Myth of Solomon," pp. 15-17; Finkelstein, "Penelope's Shroud." See Dever, "Further Evidence;" Holladay, "Red Slip," idem, "Kingdoms of Israel and Judah," pp. 371-73. For older literature in support of our 10th century or "Solomonic" date, see Yadin, "Solomon's City Wall," pp. 80-86; and K. Kenyon, *Royal Cities of the Old Testament* (New York: Schocken Books, 1971) 69.

[35] On their dating of Hazor X, see Finkelstain, "Archaeological Methods," p. 112; Herzog, "Settlement and Fortifications," p. 250; Wighman, "Myth of Solomon," pp. 10-11.

[36] See n. 33.

We may cut through some of the confusion by isolating the specific issues (as is rarely done). Apart from the underlying, but often unexamined, epistemological dilemma (i.e., how archaeology relates to texts, and both to history-writing) the following are, I think, specifically at issue: 1) comparative stratigraphy and how to use it; 2) the significance of pottery, especially the red-slipped hand-burnished wares, for relative chronology; 3) historical texts as fixed points for absolute chronology; and 4) what constitutes an archaeological "fact." Readers are invited to peruse the opposing articles in the 1990 *BASOR* with these issues in mind and appraise the various arguments in reference to them. I am convinced that if they do so, they will see that certain observations can be made that raise doubts about the validity of the positions set forth by the "Tel Aviv school."

1. Theirs is a decidedly minority view, so their arguments are forced, as well as being highly polemical (especially Finkelstein and Wightman).

2. Some of them (Herzog and Ussishkin) have changed their minds on the dates of Megiddo, whose stratigraphy in any case is too confused to allow it to serve as a type-site.

3. The thinly-veiled attack on American-style "biblical archaeology" is uninformed, often slanderous (Wightman), and as couched is irrelevant to the issues.

4. The absolute date of the hand-burnished wares, recognized since Albright's day as pivotal, is treated cavalierly, with no real attempt to fix it absolutely.

5. There are rarely any hard data presented, mainly assertions, often based on circular arguments.

6. The role of common-sense, so essential in archaeology because it is not a science, is downplayed, even violated.

7. The minimization and even rejection of the evidence supplied by the well-dated Shishak raid *ca.* 930 BCE seems to be part of an Israeli "revisionist" agenda, perhaps in reaction to their own teachers.

B. *A Critique of the "Revisionists"*

Since there is ample agreement on Hazor X and Gezer VIII has been sufficiently defended elsewhere, the dating of Megiddo VA/IVB and IVA becomes the decisive question. Even here, it is really only the four-entryway gate (and perhaps Yadin's "casemate wall") that need concern us here, since revisionists like Herzog and Ussishkin still accept the major elements of the plan of Str. VA/IVB (or at least VA), including palaces 1723 and 6,000, Building 338, and a supposed earlier "simple gate," as 10th century BCE, indeed "Solomonic."

What are their *grounds*, however, for separating the four-entryway gate, reassigning it to Str. IVA, and positing an absolute date in the 9th century BCE? Ussishkin's stratigraphic arguments are intriguing, but certainly unconvincing, since they are based entirely on the excavation and recording ot the Chicago excavators, open to almost any reinterpretation one may propose. Wightman's arguments, as far as I can see, rest entirely on his baseless caricature of "biblical archaeology" and those he thinks espouse it; on an assessment of Samaria that is not only easily refuted,[37] but is completely irrelevant to the question of Megiddo; and otherwise on nothing more than dogmatic asertions (and, in the case of Gezer, several serious errors of fact).[38] Finally, Herzog's latest statement not only reverses his earlier view but offers only two rather flimsy reasons for doing so: 1) the supposed "contrast between the plan of Megiddo IVB and all other cities attributed to Solomon;" and 2) the assertion that "this date [9th century BCE] is supported by the finds of Str. IVB."[39]

No documentation is given for the above statements, which I suggest are presuppositions, not conclusions (i.e., merely opinions). And argument number two is clearly circular. As for Herzog's and Ussishkin's redating scheme, they are left with a "city of Solomon" (Herzog's Str.

[37] See Stager, "Shemer's Estate;" and add now R. E. Tappy, *The Archaeology of Israelite Samaria, Vol. I: Early Iron Age through the Ninth Century B.C.E.* (HSS 44; Atlanta: Scholars, 1992). Stager and Tappy conclude from Kenyon's own unpublished fieldnotes that she, and later G. E. Wright, correctly interpreted the early Samaria stratigraphy, thereby destroying the *foundation* on which nearly all of Wighman's arguments rested. Both Stager and Tappy support our dates for the Gezer defenses, as well as our use of the Shishak datum. Even Finkelstein, "Archaeological Methods," p. 116, criticizes Wightman's use of burnishing in dating.

[38] Wightman, "Myth of Solomon;" cf. however, Dever, "Myths and Methods." Curiously, Wightman concludes that the "Solomonic [*sic*] period witnesses the emergence of a prosperous state with an effective administration system;" "Myth of Solomon," p. 14.

[39] These quotations are from Herzog's forthcoming book, *The Archaeology of the City: Architectural and Social Perspectives on City Planning in Ancient Israel* (1996), the manuscript of which I have seen courtesy of the author. In chapter 5.3, on cities in the 10th century BCE, there is no mention whatsoever of the two *critical* data: the date of the hand-burnished wares and the Shishak destruction. For Herzog's earlier publication, see "Settlement and Fortifications," p. 250, where Gezer is mentioned only once in passing, with the comment that "the archaeological data are insufficient," quoting none of our publications. I hardly consider the above effective counter-arguments. Still, Herzog dates the Gezer gate to the "mid-10th century" on the chart, p. 268, table 2.

VA, Ussishkin's Str. IVB) that has monumental architecture such as palaces 1723 and 6,000; a building (1482) for "royal adminstrative officers" or "scribes;" and elite residences (building 2163) and clear evidence of social stratification. Yet this city is unlike the other "royal cities" in that it has no *city walls* (Yadin's "eastern casemate," they think is simply a row of houses), and only a "*simple gate*." It is not specified what this "gate" consists of, but it is clearly not the four-entryway gate, which Herzog and Ussishkin assign to the 9th century BCE.

Such theoretical reconstructions are what I meant above in speaking of violating the rule of common-sense. The revisionists' scenario may be possible, given Megiddo's notorious stratigraphy, but does it make much *sense*? Are there any *empirical* data to support such radical reworkings of Megiddo? I suggest not.

C. *Hand-burnished Pottery and Historical "Dead-Reckoning"*

This brings us to the two classes of data that are instructive, and I would argue, potentially decisive, namely: 1) the relative 11th-10th century BCE chronology determined by the stratigraphic sequence of red-slipped, red-slipped and hand-burnished, and red-slipped and wheel-burnished pottery; and 2) the fixed point provided by the well-dated Shishak raid, *ca.* 930 BCE. It is worth noting that Wightman belabors the first without sufficient command of the data, and without substantiating his conclusions whatsoever. And Ussishkin simply sets aside the Shishak datum, stating that Megiddo IVB was not really destroyed (despite the fragment of a Shishak stela found there), and further that such textual references as that of Shishak cannot be confidently related to stratigraphy, and thus to an archaeologically-based history.

I would simply observe in passing that acceptance of Ussishkin's latter dictum would seem to put us archaeologists out of business as historians, since *all* our fixed chronologies are based ultimately on independently datable historical (i.e., written) sources. Finkelstein decries my heuristic principle of "historical dead-reckoning," but what *else* does he suppose we have to deal with?

I. *Hand-burnished pottery*

It was Albright, at Tell Beit Mirsim in the 1930's, who first isolated the distinctive red-slipped and *hand*-burnished wares and regarded them as diagnostic for (and exclusive to) the 10th century BCE. To be sure,

Albright's conclusions may have been intuitive and his stratigraphy at Tell Beit Mirsim somewhat faulty. Today, however, it can easily be demonstrated on the basis of comparative stratigraphy of many sites, not just Tell Beit Mirsim, that a pottery sequence does exist, consisting of: 1) red-slipped *unburnished* wares, *ca.* mid-11th-mid 10th centuries; 2) red-slipped *hand*-burnished wares, *ca.* mid-late 10th century BCE; 3) red-slipped *wheel*-burnished wares, *ca.* 9th century BCE.[40] Wightman attempts to blur these distinctions and to date hand-burnishing down to the 10th century BCE; and Finkelstein thinks that there are occassional occurrences of hand-burnished wares as early as the 12th-11th centuries. As Holladay (1990; 1995) has shown, however, there is a *remarkably consistent pattern* in the sequence of the red-slipped wares, wherever sound stratigraphy provides controls, not least of all at Gezer X-VII.[41] A forthcoming paper by A. Mazar,[42] while differing with Holladay's statistics and some of his methodology, provides what I would regard as confirmation of the relative sequence of the hand-burnished wares. Mazar even suggests an absolute date, since the wares in question occur at Beth-shan in well dated stratigraphic contexts immediately before the dramatic late 10th century destruction that surely must be attributed to the raid of Shishak, *ca.* 930 BCE.

While detailed analysis of the stratigraphic context of the diagnostic hand-burnished wares is beyond our scope here, it can be shown that they predominate in at least the following sites, all dated to the 10th century BCE:[43]

---

[40] These ceramic phases overlap, of course, but that does not invalidate the *relative* dates, or their significance. Nowhere do the revisionists offer a detailed, well documented discussion of the comparative stratigraphic context of the diagnostic hand-burnished wares, apparently because they believe that they cannot be well stratified. But they certainly can be at well dug sites, as Holladay's "Red Slip" has shown, the first statistical study (although I do not accept Holladay's down-dating of Tel Qasile IX and Beersheba IX to the 9th century on his burnishing argument; see also the misgivings of Tappy, *Samaria*, p. 239). A. Mazar's even more detailed analysis in his forthcoming paper in *Mediterranean Peoples in Transition: Thirteenth to Eleventh Centuries B.C.E.* (1996), based on much more data than Holladay had and using somewhat different methods, arrives at ressuringly similar results. These studies effectively negate Wightman's arguments on hand-burnishing wares, leaving his conclusions unsupported.

[41] Holladay, "Kingdoms of Israel and Judah," pp. 371-73; *idem.*, "Red Slip," pp. 49-63.

[42] Due in 1996 . On a visit to Beth-shan with Mazar, he showed me a late 10th century BCE destruction of a major wall, which could have been a mirror-image of the outer towers of the Gezer gate, even to the burnt and calcined stones. Mazar rightly takes this to be the destruction of Shishak, on whose stela Beth-shan is listed.

[43] C.f. Mazar, *Archaeology of the Holy Land*, pp. 377-378; Holladay, "Kingdoms of Israel and Judah," pp. 372, 378, 384, 385.

Hazor X	Tell el-Ful
Megiddo VA/IVB	Tell Beit Mirsim B_3
Beth-shan V lower	Lachish V
Gezer VIII	Beersheva IX-VIII
Tel Batash IV	Arad XII
Tel Qasile XI-X	Tel Malhata
Beth-shemesh IIa	Negev forts
In addition, "Proto-Israelite" sites:	
Izbet Sartah II	Tel Masos II

It is just such stratigraphic and cemmic data (as close to archaeological "facts" as we can come) that Wightman and Finkelstein distort, and Ussishkin and Herzog ignore. How, then, can we have any confidence in their pronouncements on the date of the supposedly "Solomonic" construction summarized above? In the absence of effective counter-argument, I think that prudence dictates retaining the traditional view for the present, not in *any* sense on "biblical" grounds (as Wightman and Finkelstein charge), but rather on the recognized fundamentals of sound *archaeological* method, namely: 1) comparative stratigraphy, and 2) ceramic typology and chronology. Meanwhile, the burden of proof would seem to be on the revisionists.

2. *The Shishak raid and absolute dates*

The raid of Pharaoh Sheshonk I, the first king of the XXII Egyptian dynasty (*ca.* 945-924 BCE), the "Shishak" of the Hebrew Bible, has long been a fixed point for both Palestinian archaeology and biblical studies. That is because it provides a rare synchronism with the the relatively well-fixed chronology of Egypt. In 1 Kgs 17:25-29 the raid of Shishak, which can be dated *ca.* 930-925 BCE, is said to have taken place in the 5th year after Solomon's death. This datum would put Solomon's accession, according to the "40 years" of the biblical records, *ca.* 975 BCE. That date, in turn, can be roughly corroborated by a synchronism cited by Josephus between the 4th year of Solomon and the 11th or 12th year of Hiram, King of Tyre, *ca.* 960 BCE, the latter date reckoned back from well established Assyrian dates. Thus the Shishak raid obviously has great significance for fixing the early dates of the biblical king-lists, as well as providing a possibility for dating a series of late 10th century destruction levels toward the end of Iron IIA at archaeological sites.

The Egyptian list of Palestinian towns on the Karnak stele, claimed to have been destroyed by Shishak, is damaged and no doubt incomplete, as Kitchen has shown.[44] The reading of "Gezer" was taken for granted by earlier studies and we had utilized this reading in the early work on the Field III four-entryway gate and related defenses at Gezer.[45] In view of better readings, Finkelstein may be correct in removing the actual *reference* in the Shishak list to a "Gezer" from consideration, although others differ.[46] He is not correct, however, in dismissing either 1) the clear evidence of a major destruction of the Fields II-III gate and wall systems early in their history, or 2) the still-viable possibility that this destruction may have been part of Shishak's campaign in Palestine. In favor of the latter correlation is the fact that Gezer was the most prominent site along this entire stretch of the Via Maris, directly situated so as to overlook the vital junction with the Ayalon Valley. The Egyptian army could scarcely have bypassed it. Indeed, as Mazar and Na'aman have noted, Shishak's battle itinerary after the Negev took him up the Shephelah and

[44] K. A. Kitchen, *The Third Intermediate Period in Egypt (1,110-650 B.C.)* (2nd ed.; Warminster: Aris and Phillips, 1986) 432-37; Holladay, "Kingdoms of Israel and Judah," p. 371; also, N. Na'aman, "Israel, Edom and Egypt in the 10th Century B.C.E.," *Tel Aviv* 19 (1992) 71-93.

[45] For convenient references to the literature and the historiographical issues, see Na'aman, "Israel, Edom and Egypt," pp. 79-86; and n. 46.

[46] Finkelstein, "Penelope's Shroud," p. 279, candidly declares that the use of the Shishak datum by Holladay and myself rest on the "shaky pillar of a literary source;" misreading the *stratigraphic* evidence we have often presented; see n. 47. Note, for instance, his statement, p. 77, regarding our 1990 season in Field XI that "*all* the pottery found in the trenches and accumulations inside the wall dates to Iron II." A glance just above, at Fig. 1, reproduced exactly from my 1993 report (Dever, "Further Evidence," p. 48), will show that our trench never penetrated anywhere *near* the Wall 22002 in question; and it was *we*, of course, who had argued that the excavated upper walls (21000 and 22000) were 10th-9th century BCE. Finkelstein's critiques of the "Gezer method" are, I'm sorry to say, often facile; some are even disegenuous. Note also, p. 279, his citation of Kitchen's doubts about the reading of "Gezer" in the Shishak list, immediately followed in the same sentence by the statement that Na'aman's identification of Gezer with toponym II in the list, instead of toponym 12 (1992:79-80), could not have been known to Dever when he wrote his article" (i.e., "Myths and Methods," 1992). Finkelstein clearly (and deliberately?) implies that Na'aman *agrees* with Kitchen, and that this is a "shaky pillar" in my argument. But, in fact, what Na'aman (an excellent critical historian) actually said ("Israel, Edom and Moab," pp. 79-83) was that "restoring it as Ge[zer], however, is equally possible and fits the context better." Na'aman goes on to point out that this group of names (#12, 13, 24-26) listed *with* "Gêzer]" Rubute, Gittaim, Aijalon, and Beth-Horon are all well identified and in the immediate *vicinity* of Gezer. Furthermore, Na'aman points out that "the Egyptians entered the hill country only by the ascent of Beth-horon," i.e., the main route up from the Shephelah, which Gezer sits astride. Finally, Na'aman concludes that "the Shishak destruction is based on conclusive historical evidence and should be taken as an anchor point for dating contemporaneous sites." The latter was precisely *my* point, before Na'aman wrote. How can Finkelstein be taken as a serious historian when he misquotes Na'aman *against* me?

right past the entrance to the Ayalon Valley, which Gezer guards, on his way to Jerusalem. Furthermore, Gezer had been a critical target of previous Egyptian raids, from the time of Thutmosis III, to Merneptah, to Siamun (?) in the early 10th century BCE, all archaeologically attested. Positing that Shishak was the agent of the destruction of the Field II-III defenses at Gezer is entirely reasonable, on the basis of strategic military considerations *alone*. The absence of the actual name on the damaged stela, even if that could be demonstrated, hardly consitutes overwhelming evidence against our reconstruction; in any case, an argument from silence is not an argument at all.

In our view, critics of this reconstruction of the Gezer defenses have erred in overlooking the detailed stratigraphic and ceramic evidence that we have presented in numerous preliminary reports, especially in the reports of two additional seasons in 1984 and 1990 that we undertook *precisely* to respond to their challenge.[47] The results fully confirmed our earlier conclusions, and the only substantive response since then is that of Finkelstein in 1994, who again accuses us of basing ourselves on biblical and "literary" sources; he misrepresents our published data, makes statements that are full of egregious errors, simply dismisses the possibility of a Shishak destruction, and never once refers to the crucial, diagnostic sequence of hand-to-wheel-burnished pottery. One cannot escape the impression that the "*idée fixe*" here is Finkelstein's, not ours. Finally, it can be easily shown that *his* present reconstruction results in an obvious absurdity. By dating the "Outer Wall" to the 9th-8th cneturies BCE, yet admitting the 10th century BCE date of the gateway complex and casemate wall, he ends up with a massive upper city gate with only a very short, isolated stretch of casemate wall, and a lower gatehouse (integral with the upper four-entryway gate) that has absolutely no wall at all.[48] An attacker could simply make an "end-run" around the "floating" Field II-III defenses. Once again, doctrinaire notions overcome

[47] See principally Holladay, "Red Slip;" *idem.*, "Kingdoms of Israel and Judah," pp. 371-73. Dever, "Further Evidence," and full references there to publications going back to 1970. The final publication will appear as *Gezer VI*.

[48] One has only to glance at *any* of our published plans of Gezer to see that if one dates the Outer Wall post-10th century BCE, there is only a short, isolated casemate wall to go with the Upper Gate, and none at all to go with the outer Gatehouse. A. Zertal, whose 8th century BCE date is even lower, long ago pointed out this problem; see his "The Gates of Gezer," *ErIsr* 15 (1981) 222-28 (Hebrew). Herzog's and Ussishkin's separation of the defense elements in Megiddo VB, VA/IVB, and IVA leaves them with the same problem there.

common sense, not to mention the evidence of stratigraphy and comparative ceramic typology.

The following Fig. 2 sets forth our original Field III phasing in 1967-1971, coordinated with the results of the additional seasons in 1984 and 1990.

In all our reports we have stressed the salient facts. 1) A massive destruction, which literally "melted" the boulders of the outer towers of the Gate and necessitated the addition of internal buttresses in the succeeding phase, took place *after* the third repaving of the Gate roadway and the addition of Palace 100,000, the central drain, and the two-entryway Outer Gatehouse (which is now known to have been connected, after all, to the Outer Wall to the west. 2) The red-slipped and *hand*-burnished wares are confined to this *early* phase and do not occur in later phases (except, of course, in mixed fills), wheel-burnished wares being exceedingly rare and occurring only at the very end.[49] 3) The most likely historical event that may account for the destruction of the defenses is the campaign of Shishak, *ca.* 930 BCE, there being absolutely no other known destructions on this horizon except for the Aramaean incursions and the Neo-Assyrian menaces (only in the north) *ca.* 840-810 BCE. I invite our critics to refute this reconstruction of events and to offer a more satisfactory scenario.

The Shishak destruction at Gezer does not stand alone, of course. Mazar lists at least ten sites where archaeological destructions can be attributed to Shishak, including sites on Fig. 1 here such as Tell Abu Hawam III, Megiddo VA/IVB, Tel Qasile VIII, Tell Mevorakh VII, and Gezer VIII. A number of other sites might be added to this list, including Ta'anach IIA-B; Beth-shan V lower, and in all likelihood many of the 10th century BCE Negev forts (some fifty places are named in the Negev section of the Shishak list.[50]

---

[49] Holladay, "Red Slip," fig. 12:4, has only *one* wheel-burnished sherd among the hundreds and hundreds he has analyzed and this belongs to his "Upper Gate 3A" phase, his *latest* 10th century BCE phase, transitional to the 9th century BCE when all authorities agree that wheel-burnishing comes into use.

[50] Mazar, *Archaeology of the Holy Land*, pp. 395-98; see nn. 43-46 above. For possible Shishak destructions in addition to Mazar's list, see Holladay, "Kingdoms of Israel and Judah," p. 394, n. 8. On the Negev forts, see Mazar, *Archaeology of the Holy Land*, pp. 390-96; and Na'aman, "Israel, Edom and Egypt," pp. 81-83.

Gnl. Str	Holladay 1990	Dever	Date 1986	Features
VIII	Ph.I PG1-2 UG 1	Ph.3	mid-10th century	Pre-Gate fills; red-slip. Upper Gate construction. Streets 1-3, Casemate Wall, and Outer Wall rebuild. Hand burnish begins; no wheel burnish.
	Ph. II: UG2	——	late-10th century	Lower Gatehouse. century Central drain; Streets resurfaced; Palace 10,000. Hand-burnish, rare wheel-burnish. Destruction at end.
VII	Ph. III UG3A-C UG4	——	very late 10th century	Upper Gate buttresed, 10th/9th Reduction to 3-entry-way. Additional streets. Wheel-burnish now.

Fig. 2. Gezer Field III phasing; PG = pre-gate; UG = upper gate.

III. Archaeological Evidence for the Emergence of an Israelite State in the 10th Century BCE

In the foregoing discussion I hope that I have established: 1) that there is a considerable body of archaeological data that reflects the initial growth of urbanism and centralization of administration in the early Iron II period, and 2) that virtually all the disgnostic material can be securely dated to the mid-late 10th century BCE. The remaining questions are whether the archaeological data are sufficient to warrant our designating this phase, or Iron IIA, an emergent "state," and if so whether such an entity or polity can be characterized as "Israelite."

A. *On the definition of terms*

It must be noted at the outset that nearly all standard reference works on Iron Age Palestine neglect to define the key terms "urban" and "state" and thus have few quantifiable criteria for assessing the archaeological data. That is a pity, because such parochialism robs Iron Age Palestine/ Israel of its proper status as an instructive case-study in the wider world of cross-cultural anthropology, archaeology, and much recent study in what are called "state formation processes."

1. *The term "urban."*

It is of critical importance to define the term "urban" first of all in assessing the archaeological data summarized above for the 10th century BCE. Most scholars seem to assume that urban means simply "large" and that therefore in Palestine we are dealing with "cities" and an "urban" society. If, however, we attempt to quantify the demographic estimates now available, we can readily see in Fig. 1 that some dozen or so relatively large sites may account for as much as 20-25% of the total population, despite the proportionately much greater number of "tier two" and "tier three" sites. Thus I would argue (using the most common rule-of-thumb in the broader fields of archaeology, anthropology, and ethnography) that 10th century BCE Palestine had reached a sufficient degree of *centralization* to qualify it as a truly urban society.

The "revisionist" historians of ancient Israel noted above, and even a surprising number of Palestinian archaeologists, seemingly unaware of the wider literature, continue to look at population size alone in defining "city," "urban" and "state," not recognizing that it is not absolute size, not even the character of the sites, but rather the *distribution of population* (the overall settlement pattern) that determines whether a society is urban or not.[51] Apart from theoretical naivete, some commentators simply have all their figures wrong. Thus the biblicists Lemche and Thompson have recently declared:

> In the history of Palestine that we have presented, there is no room for a historical United Monarchy, or for such kings as those presented in the Biblical stories of Saul, David or Solomon. The early period in which the traditions have set their narrativesis an imaginary world of long ago that never existed as such. In the real world of that time, for instance, only a few dozen villagers lived as farmers in all the Judaean highlands.[52]

This statement is absurd to anyone with even a rudimentary knowledge of Palestinian archaeology. Compare it with the carefully researched conclusions of archaeologists that are presented and discussed widely in the scholarly literature, which the "revisionists" rarely cite. It is unfounded assertions like this statement that tend to discredit the "revi-

[51] On "rank-size" and "three-tier hierarchy" models, see above and n. 9.
[52] Lemche and Thompson, "Did Biran Kill David?," p. 19.

sionists" as "historians of ancient Palestine," which they claim to be. It is *their* "Israel" that is imaginary, not ours.[53]

Although I have argued that the overall configuration of sites is more important in characterizing urbanism than the size of any particular site, it is still important to define what we mean by the term "city." Here Syro-Palestinian archaeologists are notoriously imprecise: anything large, especially with defensive walls, is assumed to be a city. But *how* large is large? Childe, one of the first modern archaeologists to address this issue, developed a "trait-list" that he thought might define "urbanized" as well as "civilization" ("citified"), since he thought that the two stages of cultural evolution were virtually identical. Such a list may still be useful. Among several criteria for recognizing urbanism, Childe isolated such variables as 1) size, 2) socio-economic stratification, 3) institutionalized political administration, 4) ability to produce surplus and sustain long-distance trade, 5) monumental art and architecture, and 6) the use of writing.[54] One might note that Palestine in.its largest population agglomeration in the 10th-9th centuries BCE exhibits all these traits in general, based entirely on the *archaeological* evidence now available, not on the admittedly tendentious biblical texts. Nevertheless, some of these variables remain difficult to measure archaeologically, since subjective individual judgments differ.

A more objective, quantifiable model of urbanism for the Southern Levant has been developed by Falconer.[55] He argues basically that a population agglomerate may be defined as "urban" when it outgrows its capacity to feed and sustain itself on resources immediately available. At that stage of growth it must organize and control the surrounding agricultural hinterland, i.e., must become a "market-town" in Central Place parlance. On the rich alluvial plains of southern Mesopotamia, where Falconer developed his model, and where agricultural yields can be calculated more or less accurately, the "threshold" at which the transition to an urban center or city took place can be fixed at about 85 acres, or a population of *ca.* 8,000-9,000, using the most common coefficient.

I have pointed out, however, that Palestine is characterized by a much

---

[53] Cf. Wightman, "Myth of Solomon."

[54] Cf. V. G. Childe, "The Urban Revolution," *Town Planning Journal* 21 (1950) 3-17.

[55] S. E. Falconer, *Heartland of Villages: Reconsidering Early Urbanism in the Southern Levant* (unpublished Ph.D. dissertation, University of Arizona, 1987). Falconer's title is obviously a play on R. McC. Adams, *Heartland of Cities: Surveys of Ancient Settlement and Land Use on the Central Floodplain of the Euphrates* (Chicago: University of Chicago, 1981).

smaller-scale landscape, not only fragmented but also marginally productive because of poor soil and water resources. Thus we have a critical *scaler difference* in comparing the large cities of southern Mesopotamia with those of peripheral areas like Bronze and Iron Age Palestine.[56] Taking the differences into account, it is reasonable to place the "threshold" for truly urban configurations in Palestine at about 15 acres or some 1,500 people. Kolb's seminal work proposes an even smaller criterion, a site of 25 acres but with a population of only 1,000, qualifies as a "city."[57]

In all these projections, of course, the particular coefficient that one chooses will affect the absolute numbers that are obtained. Shiloh, in the first systematic work on Palestinian Iron Age demography, used as a rule-of-thumb the figure of up to 250 persons per hectare (100-120 persons per acre), based on calculations to total site-size, estimates of the proportion of domestic to public buildings, assumed average family size per dwelling (6-10), and ethnographic observations.[58] Stager, however, challenged Shiloh's coefficient, basing himself on New World archaeological calculations of average floor space required in a dwelling by an individual, which Naroll and others had calculated at about ten square meters. Stager nevertheless still came up with a figure of about 100-120 persons per acre (although figuring a lower family size, *ca.* 5-6 persons).[59] The differences cannot be resolved here, but I have suggested above a moderate "threshold" of 15 acres and 1,500 population. In that case, the numbers given in Fig. 1 would indicate that as many as 8-10 sites in Palestine in the 10th century BCE would qualify as "cities" by overall site size and population; and at least 20 as "towns," i.e., 250-1,500 population. Of course, since estimates of both population size and the absolute date of the archaeological strata and materials to be considered differ significantly, an overall assessment of early Israelite "urban-

---

[56] See the elegant development of the model of "scaler difference" in the work of my student A. H. Joffe, *Settlement and Society in the Early Bronze I and II of the Southern Levant: Complementarity and Contradiction in a Small-Scale Complex Society* (Sheffield: Academic, 1993).

[57] F. Kolb, *Die Stadt im Altertum* (Munich: C. H. Beck, 1984).

[58] For the basic bibliography on demography, especially of the Iron Age, see references in n. 8.

[59] Cf. Shiloh, "Population of Iron Age Palestine," pp. 17-21, suggesting an average population density of about 40-50 persons per dunam, or about 100-125 per acre; and Stager, "Archaeology of the Family," pp. 17-21, using the rule-of-thumb of 100-20 per acre. Note also Broshi and Finkelstein, "Population of Palestine," p. 48 (270 persons per hectare, or *ca.* 110 persons per acre).

ism" at this point is admittedly difficult. I shall simply argue here that by generally accepted anthropological and archaeological criteria, a half-dozen or so 10th century BCE Israelite sites would qualify as "cities;" and the overall pattern of a "three-tier hierarchy" of settlement sites enables us to characterize the period as a whole as "urban."

Even "minimalists" such as Herzog and Ussishkin would concede that these developments are fully in place by the early-mid 9th century BCE, as would some biblical "revisionists" (the latter not on archaeological or bibilical grounds, only because of historical references in Neo-Assyrian texts, and excluding Judah from statehood until the 7th century BCE). I see no difficulty whatsoever in projecting the initial development of Iron Age or Israelite urbanism back into the mid-10th century BCE. Indeed, without positing such a "formative" or "Proto-Urban" period, we cannot adequately explain the "flourescent" period that all authorities would acknowledge by the early 9th century BCE (although these terms are mine).

2. *The terms "civilization" and "state"*

In the English-speaking world scholarly interest has focussed on "state formation processes" since Fried's *The Evolution of Political Society: An Essay in Political Anthropology* (1967) and Service's *Origins of the State and Civilization: The Process of Cultural Evolution* (1975). Since then, more than 20 major analyses have been published, many advancing theories of the state, including major works by Sahlins (1968), Carneiro (1970), Renfrew (1972), Wright (1977), Cohen and Service (1978), Haas (1982), and others. A succinct summary and critique of these works on state formation will be found in Tainter's *The Collapse of Complex Societies*, supplemented specifically for the Southern Levant by the essays in Khoury and Kostiner, *Tribes and State Formation in the Middle East*.[60]

The proposed universal cultural evolutionary sequence (from "band" to "tribe" to "chiefdom" to "state" [thus Service]) need not detain us here, although the Iron I period in Israel has been conceived as "tribal," and the Davidic era in Iron IIA as a "chiefdom."[61] What is important

[60] J. A. Tainter, *The Collapse of Complex Societies* (Cambridge: Cambridge University, 1988) 26-38; see also *The Collapse of Ancient States and Civilizations* (eds. N. Yoffee and G. Cowgill; Tucson: University of Arizona, 1989); and *Tribes and State Formation in the Middle East* (eds. P. S. Khoury and J. Kostiner; Los Angeles: University of California, 1990).

[61] See n. 17 above.

here is that all scholars agree that, while definitions of the state may vary, there is a common denominator in the stress on *centralization* of decision-making and administration (which denotes, practically speaking, kingship). Thus Service states that the State is "bureaucratic governance by legal force;"[62] or Sahlins, "the State is a society in which there is an official authority, a set of offices of the society at large, conferring governance over the society at large."[63] Of course, many *types* of primitive states have been described, such as "pristine/precocious" states (usually imposed by force on neighboring peoples), "inchoate early states" (Claeson and Skalnik), "conditional states" (Webb), and "tribal states."[64] I would suggest, as others may also have, another category of "peripheral" states, to which I shall argue early Israel belongs as do most of the other emerging Iron Age territorial states in ancient Western Asia. It is important, however, to keep in mind Tapper's caution that "typologies" of early states may be too rigid, that in fact most early states were "hybrids."[65]

Elsewhere I have reviewed the several works published by biblicists on the question of "Israelite statehood," such as Frick (1985), Coote and Whitelam (1989), and Flanagan (1988). All three are unsatisfactory, not only because of a good deal of social science jargon (especially Flanagan), but principally because of their minimal or inept use of the critical *archaeological* data presented here.[66] The same objection is obviously to be made of all the pretentious statements made more recently by the "revisionists," which it is tempting to dismiss as so much post-modernist piffle.[67]

It is somewhat surprising, however, that so few Syro-Palestinian *archaeologists* have addressed the issue of state-formation processes, perhaps an indication of our general (and deliberate?) theoretical impoverishment. Only Holladay has utilized a deliberate model, and this is borrowed from Service and others. Holladay describes the transition from Iron I to Iron IIA in the 10th century BCE in terms of a shift from an

---

[62] E. R. Service, *Primitive Social Organization: An Evolutionary Perspective* (New York: Random House, 1962) 175.

[63] M. D. Sahlins, *Tribesmen* (Englewood Cliffs, NJ: Prentice-Hall, 1968) 6.

[64] For references, see Tainter, *Complex Societies*, pp. 26-30.

[65] R. Tapper, "Anthropologists, Historians, and Tribespeople on Tribe and State Formation in the Middle East," in *Tribes and State Formation in the Middle East* (eds. P. S. Khoury and J. Kostiner; Los Angeles: University of California, 1990) 68.

[66] See n. 17.

[67] See my critiques referred to in nn. 5, 15, 27, 30 above, together with reference to "revisionists" like Davies, Lemche, Thompson, and Whitelam.

"acephalous . . . segmented society to centralized mature state," based partly on his argument, like mine, that a "new urban society" and "class stratification" are witnessed in the archaeological complex summarized above, especially in the royal cities" discussed there.[68]

Among Service's general criteria for "statehood," as categorized by Holladay, are: 1) a population over 20,000; 2) a hierarchical, urban settlement pattern, often characterized by regional centers; 3) a king, a centralized bureaucracy, and probably a standing army, together with defense works; 4) a class of stratified and craft-specialized society; 5) evidence of palaces and separately distinquishable temples; 6) a redistributive economic system, based on taxes and tribute; and 7) some system of writing. Need one belabor the point? *All* these criteria of "statehood" are met in the archaeological evidence from Iron IIA. The only possible factors in Service's criteria for the rise of the state to be disputed are the existence of kings, a standing army, and a full-fledged temple, the evidence for which still stems largely from the biblical texts. Nevertheless, we have already shown that the Solomonic Temple can scarcely be mythical; and, quite apart from the epic tales of Solomon, kings are attested in non-biblical textual sources by the mid-9th century BCE.

Another model is Childe's "trait-list" for urbanization, already noted, which he thought synonymous with the development of "civilization" and the state. Of Childe's 10 criteria for statehood, Iron IIA Palestine/ Israel meets 8 without doubt, and the other 2 are plausible.[69]

3. *The term "state"*

Having cited Childe on "urbanism," we need at this point to note that he, like Adams, equated "civilization" or urban life (today's more common "complex society") with the state; indeed both argued that urbanization normally precedes the state, that if not actually the "cause," it is at least a major contributing factor in state formation. In short, the state presumes the prior existence of urbanism.[70] Service, however, disagrees; but even he sees urbanization and the development of a state as often

---

[68] Holladay, "Kingdoms of Israel and Judah," pp. 372-73, table I. Service's criteria are not put in the way that Holladay and I list them, but our summary is based on his discussion, as well as on criteria that are generally accepted by archaeologists and anthropologists; see Service, *Primitive Social Organization*, and, for instance, Renfrew and Bahn, *Archaeology*, pp. 417-34.

[69] Cf. Childe, "Urban Revolution."

[70] *Ibid.*; R. M. Adams, *The Evolution of Urban Society* (Chicago: Aldine, 1966) 73.

inextricably linked.[71] I tend to side with Service in the case of ancient Palestine, since Palestine in the Early and Middle Bronze Ages was highly urbanized, yet no one supposes that a true "state" had yet come into existence, only the characteristic pattern of Southern Levantine city-states. Nevertheless, with rare exceptions like the Han Dynasty in China and several of the Mesoamerican states, the process of urbanization does normally precede state-level development and is often a contributing factor. I would argue that was the case with ancient Palestine in the Iron Age.

If the small scale of cultural and political evolution in Palestine is thought to preclude state formation, one need only recall that the entire region of Western Asia in the Iron Age was characterized by regional or what I have called "peripheral states" (in this case with the rise of the Neo-Assyrian empire in mind). No one doubts that the Neo-Hittite and Aramaean Kingdoms were "states;" and even the entities of Ammon, Edom, and Moab in Transjordan are now seen as moving toward statehood early in the Iron Age, even if only of the "tribal state" type.[72] Furthermore, in a very sophisticated recent study, Joffe has shown that the "scalar difference" of the Southern Levant, in comparison with ancient Egypt and Mesopotamia, was an indigenous and determinative factor in cultural development throughout the Bronze and Iron Age,[73] i.e., until the advent of advanced technologies that helped to overcome the natural environment in the Classical era. Finally, we may observe that anthropologists and social theorists have no difficulty in regarding the lowland Maya of Tikal as a "state," with a total population of 25,000-40,000; and several of the multi-valley Inca states had a population of only 75,000-160,000.[74] Thus on the basis of Palestine's gross population size *alone* (100,000-150,000 during the Monarchy) the attempts of "revisionists" like Lemche and Thompson to deny early Israel and Judah statehood are easily dismissed. The biblical data are not decisive, much less their misinterpretation; *archaeological* data are. And

---

[71] E. R. Service, *Origins of the State and Civilization: The Process of Cultural Evolution* (New York: Norton, 1975) 280-82. It should be noted that certain early states, like Han Dynasty China and some of the Mesoamerican states, remained non-urban.

[72] For Transjordan, see the references in n. 28.

[73] See n. 56.

[74] Service, *Origins of the State*, p. 198, citing an unpublished paper of R. P. Schaedel. See also the opinion of Sanders and Price, *Mesoamerica: The Evolution of a Civilization* (eds. W. T. Sanders and B. J. Price; New York: Random House, 1960) 229, based on Mesoamerican case-studies, that at a population of *ca.* 10,000 a society reaches a "critical mass" that requires the socio-economical-political hierarchy characteristic of civilization.

if the 10th century BCE state of the Divided Monarchy, as the material culture remains overwhelmingly attest, was not ethnically "Israelite," then what *was* it? This is a question that biblical "revisionists" and minimalist archaeologists cannot answer.[75]

CONCLUSION

Wightman, the most extreme of the "Tel Aviv school," dismissed the Age of Solomon as a "myth." I and other mainstream Palestinian archaeologists (Israeli, Continental, and American) had "invented" it because of biblical biases.[76] Ostensibly an archaeological argument, this was an anticipation of the same propositions that were soon to be set forth by a small but vocal group of biblical historians calling themselves "revisionists." The careful reader will observe that in the case I have tried to make here for a 10th century "Israelite state," including of course the institution of kingship, I have made no reference to the biblical texts as evidence,[77] nor have I tried to "salvage" Solomon's reputation in the Hebrew Bible. My evidence throughout has been archaeological, and my point simple. We *have* an Israelite state in the Iron IIA period. If we had never heard of a "Solomon" in the biblical texts, we should have to invent a 10th century BCE Israelite king by another name.

---

[75] T. L. Thompson, *Early History of the Israelite People from the Written and Archaeological Sources* (SHANE 4; Leiden: E. J. Brill, 1992), and K. W. Whitelam, "The Identity of Early Israel: The Realignment and Transformation of Late Bronze-Iron Age Palestine," *JSOT* 63 (1994) 57-87, both consistently deny the validity of the term "Israel" (despite Thompson's title), since it is "biblical" and therefore "unhistorical." They speak rather of an anonymous "Iron Age Population of Palestine." For my response to this know-nothingness, see Dever, cited in nn. 5, 27, 29, 30 above.

[76] Wightman, "Myth of Solomon."

[77] For orientation to biblical scholars' views on the "Age of Solomon," beyond our deliberate purview here, cf. *Studies in the Period of David and Solomon and Other Essays* (ed. T. Ishida; Tokyo: Yamakawa-Shuppansha, 1982), and B. Halpern, *The Constitution of the Monarchy in Israel* (Chico, Calif.: Scholars, 1981).

THE SOCIO-POLITICAL SHADOW CAST BY THE BIBLICAL SOLOMON*

HERMANN MICHAEL NIEMANN

Translated by Michael Johnson

For all sceptics, minimalists and nihilists the point must be stressed: the existence of the biblical Solomon is a fact! The same cannot, with absolute certainty, be said of the historical Solomon.

1. FIRST THOUGHTS AND METHODS

To establish something concerning the socio-political situation in the Solomonic epoch[1] is not easy, because there is not one single non-biblical witness to the historical Solomon which can be compared with the biblical data. So it seems that everything concerning the socio-political situation of a character, who himself cannot be historically proven, is destined from the very beginning to have, at the best, the "reality" of a shadow. Although the author considers himself, methodologically, to be near the minimalists (not the nihilists) camp, he does not think it necessary to end the essay at this point. The reason is that, contrary to the usual approach, here the historical accuracy of the biblical account of

* This essay is gratefully dedicated to my colleague Winfried Thiel (Bochum University, Germany). He is a noble example of the fact that diametrically opposed scientific opinions do not inherently have negative implications for personal friendships. My former student, Michael Johnson, has taken care of the translation into English and my friend, Axel Knauf, discussed with me an early draft of this paper, for which I owe Axel and Michael my thanks. [Editor's note: this chapter has been edited to conform to the requirements of the volume.]

[1] What does "socio-political" mean? "Politics/social politics" deal with concepts and measures concerning the organisation of a community. This must not refer to a community which has developed into a "state." The more organised the community is, the more differentiated is the ruling group ("tertiary sector") as well as their tools and activities; in modern terms these would include the executive and legislative. Important factors include: prestige goods, prestige activities, the organisation of rule and the ruling class and attempts to attain a generally accepted ideological/religious basis. For terminology ("chiefdom," "state," "tertiary sector," and others) see below n. 87.

Solomon, either prescribed or deducted, is not a prerequisite. We begin by contemplating the socio-political situation in the "Solomon-epoch" using ecological framework and non-biblical sources (epigraphic and archaeological). Of course it is not possible to work totally free of presuppositions. We have to limit ourselves chronologically in that Solomon is assumed to be a personage at the transition from the Iron Age I (*ca*. 1250-950 BCE) to the Iron Age IIA (*ca*. 1050-850 BCE) and a contemporary of Sheshonq (950/45-929/24 BCE). As far as it is possible to draw an outline of the "Solomonic epoch," this outline should provide the framework for possible behavioral patterns of a personage such as Solomon. These patterns should be checked against the historical facts about a comparable contemporary. Finally the historical framework result thus attained can be compared to the biblical texts concerning Solomon.

A sketch of this brevity does not allow space to deal with all the questions that arise in a detailed manner.[2] It is achievement enough to separate the certain from the uncertain and the non-ascertainable.

2. Background and Sources

A. *Background: The Three-Stepped Stage of Solomon's Appearance*

Ever since the pioneering work of Karl Lamprecht in Germany and the Annales-School in France,[3] no historical analysis can avoid the fact that

---

[2] For Solomon in general, cf. recently J. M. Miller and J. H. Hayes, *A History of Ancient Israel and Judah* (Philadelphia: Westminster, 1986) 189-217; E. A. Knauf, "King Solomon's Copper Supply," *Phoenicia and the Bible: Proceedings of the Conference held at the University of Leuven on the 15th and 16th March 1990* (OLA 44.Phoenicia 11; Leuven: Peeters, 1991) 167-86; J. A. Soggin, *Einführung in die Geschichte Israels und Judas von den Ursprüngen bis zum Aufstand Bar Kochbas* (Darmstadt: Wiss. Buchgesellschaft, 1991) 62-75; G. W. Ahlström, *The History of Ancient Palestine from the Paleolithic Period to Alexander's Conquest* (JSOTSup 146; Sheffield: Sheffield Academic, 1993) 498-542; H. M. Niemann, *Herrschaft, Königtum und Staat: Skizzen zur soziokulturellen Entwicklung im monarchischen Israel* (FAT 6; Tübingen: Mohr, 1993) 17-41, 96-104, 151, 169-73, 192-205, 246-51; P. Särkiö, *Die Weisheit und Macht Salomos in der israelitischen Historiographie* (SESJ 60; Helsinki: Finnish Exegetical Society; Göttingen: Vandenhoeck & Ruprecht, 1994); and H. Donner, *Geschichte des Volkes Israel und seiner Nachbarn in Grundzügen* (ATD Erg. 4.1; Göttingen: Vandenhoeck & Ruprecht, 1995) 242-57.

[3] K. Lamprecht, *Alternative zu Ranke: Schriften zur Geschichtstheorie* (RUB 1256; Leipzig: Reclam, 1988); F. Braudel, *The Mediterranean and the Mediterranean World in the Age of Philip II* (London: Fontana, 1972); for the ANNALES School and their prin-

a responsible portrayal of a historical personage or event can only be reconstructed on the basis of a threefold stepped stage. The constantly changing *political history* must be placed in the context of the longer term *social history*. Both of these must then be seen in light of the very slowly changing *geomorphological-ecological environment*. Additionally, more weight and more explanation than hitherto must given to *behavioral patterns and structures instead of (only) events and personages*.[4]

1) *Geomorphologic/environmental factors to consider*

– Syria-Palestine as a land-bridge between Mesopotamia and Egypt.

– Palestine as a narrow north-south oriented area between the Mediterranean and the Syrian-Arabian desert.

---

ciples and the texts upon which they are based, see M. Middell and S. Sammler, eds., *Alles Gewordene hat Geschichte: Die Schule der ANNALES in ihren Texten 1929-1992* (Leipzig: Reclam, 1994); as for their consequences for archaeologists, see A. Sherratt, "What Can Archaeologists Learn from Annalistes?" *Archaeology, Annales, and Ethnohistory* (ed. A. B. Knapp; Cambridge: Cambridge University, 1992) 135-42; for important anthropological approaches for archaeologists, see L. Binford, "Archaeology as Anthropology," *American Antiquity* 28 (1962) 217-25; I. Hodder, *Symbolic and Structural Archaeology* (Cambridge: Cambridge University, 1982); *idem*, *Reading the Past* (Cambridge: Cambridge University, 1991); and *idem*, ed., *Theory and Practice in Archaeology* (London: Routledge, 1992). See also an overview by C. Renfrew and P. Bahn, *Archaeology: Theories and Practice* (New York: Thames & Hudson, 1993).

[4] Under the same, or only slowly changing, geomorphologic environmental conditions, social processes and action run their course over decades, centuries, even millennia with, in principle, very little change, unless they are affected by a strong impulse for change from without (disturbance, interruption). For ethnological literature as case studies, see n. 98. In the interest of completing the picture and drawing connections concerning the interrelatedness of movements lasting over centuries and millennia (*longue durée*) detailing and quantifying examinations are indispensible; see for example the studies of survey-archaeology, M. Kochavi, ed., *Judaea, Samaria and the Golan: Archaeology Survey 1967-1968* (Jerusalem: Carta, 1972) and more recently A. Ofer, "'All the Hill Country of Judah': From a Settlement Fringe to a Prosperous Monarchy," *From Nomadism to Monarchy: Archaeology and Historical Aspects of Early Israel* (eds. I. Finkelstein and N. Na'aman; Jerusalem: Yad Izhak Ben-Zvi, 1994); for the socio-economic and social structures of Ottoman Palestine, see W. D. Hütteroth and K. Abdulfattah, *Historical Geography of Palestine, Transjordan and Southern Syria in the Late 16th Century* (Erlanger Geographische Arbeiten 5; Erlangen: Fränkische Geographische Gesellschaft, 1977); W. D. Hütteroth, *Palästina und Transjordanien im 16. Jahrhundert: Wirtschaftsstruktur ländlicher Siedlungen nach osmanischen Steuerregistern* (BTAVO B33; Wiesbaden: Harrassowitz, 1992); A. Cohen, *Palestine in the 18th Century: Patterns of Government and Administration* (Jerusalem: Magnes, 1973); as well as detailed economic studies such as C. Zaccagnini, "The Price of the Fields at Nuzi," *JESHO* 22 (1979) 1-31; and M. Liverani, "Reconstructing the Rural Landscape of the Ancient Near East," *JESHO* 39 (1996) 1-41.

– Of importance within Palestine is the east-west division into coastal strip, transitional area, highlands, Jordan Valley and the Transjordan plateau. Prosperity and cultural development are dependent on the rain and wind, which are oriented from the NW to the SE in Palestine. This means that the coastal region in comparison with the highlands, the north(west) with the south(east), Phoenicia/Philistia with Israelite/Judean mountainous country, and the northern kingdom of Israel, rather differentiated in comparison with the smaller, more isolated and more isolationist southern kingdom of Judah, all had advantages in relation to prosperity and development. These natural advantages favoring the north and west could be limited by geopolitical and trade related politics. In times of crisis the secluded position and relative uniformity of the Judean highlands seemed an advantage, whereas the land along the coast and the Northern Kingdom with the international routes seemed to be at a disadvantage. It is interesting to look through the history of Syria-Palestine to see when people from the east and south looked to the west and north for prosperity and development so as to consider when and why colonisation occurred in the opposite direction.

– The frontier between Judah and Israel is the mountainous "saddle" running from east to west in which Jerusalem and Benjamin lie. This "saddle" is an area of climatic transition. South of it the rainfall decreases overproportionally toward the southern desert border.[5]

– The characteristics of the Palestinian landscape: the highland, the plains, the small mountain valleys, each separated from the other, the steppe and the desert with its borders, must all be considered along with their hierarchy of settlements, their impact on cultural, economic and socio-political lifestyle and history of the inhabitants.[6]

---

[5] The main area of the northern kingdom of Israel, between north Galilee and Jerusalem, receiving an average annual rainfall varying from over 900 mm to 550 mm, is much more fertile than the southern area extending from Jerusalem south to the desert border near Beersheba. This southern area is only a third of the size of the north and the precipitation falls drastically from 550 mm to only 200-150 mm; O. Keel, M. Küchler and C. Uehlinger, *Orte und Landschaften der Bibel, Band 1* (Zürich: Benziger; Göttingen: Vandenhoeck & Ruprecht, 1984) 46.

[6] Niemann, *Stadt, Land und Herrschaft: Skizzen und Materialien zur Sozialgeschichte im monarchischen Israel* (Habilitationsschrift; Rostock: Theologische Fakultät der Universität, 1990); and G. Lehmann, *Biblische Landeskunde oder kultur- und sozialgeographische Raumanalyse? Ein Forschungsbericht über aktuelle Entwicklungstendenzen in der historischen Geographie von Palästina* (forthcoming).

2) *Social and economic facts to consider*

The data presented above explain the much more modest and slow economic and cultural development of Judah in comparison with Israel.

– On the basis of the geomorphologic background, the following factors are important for social economic history: The area north of Jerusalem (the Northern Kingdom) is geomorphologically subdivided into the Ephraimite-Samarian highland, the plain of Jezreel and the Galilean highland which itself is further subdivided. The Judean highland with the southern steppe does not show such strong divisions. Due to these small mountain valleys, each being separated from the other, both socio-economic and socio-political differentiation can be seen in the populations of Judah and Israel. The stark contrasts in the landscapes bring with them not only political differentiation among the inhabitants, but also advantageous large economic differentiation and therefore less vulnerability in times of crisis.[7] The emergence of central places ("cities") of various rank with their potential for innovation, is based on the existence and development of differentiated economic units.[8]

– The following are important for the long-term cultural rather than the short-term political history: As is true of the Early and Middle Bronze Ages, a formation period, a main period and a period of decline can, for the most part, be seen and differentiated in the Iron Age as well.

The *political history*, on the basis of the two points mentioned above, requires most detailed information for its presentation. In attempting to shed light on the socio-political situation of the Solomon-epoch, the larger picture of the entire Middle East must be taken into account. All of these factors cannot be dealt with here *in extenso*.

[7] D. C. Hopkins, "The Dynamics of Agriculture in Monarchical Israel," *SBL 1983 Seminar Papers 22* (Chico, Calif.: Scholars, 1983) 177-202; *idem*, *The Highlands of Canaan: Agricultural Life in the Early Iron Age* (SWBA 3; Decatur, Ga.: Almond, 1985); *idem*, "Life on the Land," *BA* 50 (1987) 178-91; B. Rosen, "Subsistence Economy in Iron Age I," *From Nomadism to Monarchy: Archaeology and Historical Aspects of Early Israel* (eds. I. Finkelstein and N. Na'aman; Jerusalem: Yad Izhak Ben-Zvi, 1994) 339-51. For important developing tendencies in cultural and sociogeographical analyses of Syria-Palestine, see Lehmann, *Biblische Landeskunde*.

[8] Niemann, *Stadt, Land und Herrschaft*, 1-62; for a comprehensive definition of the "city" phenomenon, with special consideration of Iron Age Palestine, see *idem*, "Das Ende des Volkes der Perizziter: Über soziale Wandlungen Israels im Spiegel einer Begriffsgruppe," *ZAW* 105 (1993) 233-57, especially n. 4.

B. *Sources*

1) *Epigraphical Sources from Within and from Outside Israel and Judah*

At this time not one documented piece of extrabiblical evidence exists from the Israelite-Judean context or from cultures or societies near or far in time or place for the historical existence of Solomon. This has to be stressed. This observation contrasts sharply with the biblical portrayal (upon which the historical depiction of Solomon has usually been based) of him as an outstanding ruler of a "mighty kingdom."

With what we know today about the political and cultural situation and the stage of the social development of the region and time in which the biblical narrative of Solomon takes place, an abundance of written records should not be expected. At the transition from the Bronze Age to the Iron Age and for some time following, a general state of upheaval ruled![9] That can be interpreted to mean that in a low state of develop-

---

[9] N. K. Sandars, *The Sea Peoples* (Ancient Peoples and Places; London: Thames & Hudson, 1978); L. Marfoe, "The Integretive Transforamtion: Patterns of Sociopolitical Organization in Southern Syria," *BASOR* 234 (1979) 1-42; W. H. Stiebing, "The Mycenean Age," *BA* 43 (1980) 7-21; D. N. Freedman and D. F. Graf, eds., *Palestine in Transition* (SWBA 2; Sheffield: Sheffield Academic, 1983); L. E. Stager, "The Archaeology of the Family in Ancient Israel," *BASOR* 260 (1985) 1-35; N. P. Lemche, *Early Israel: Anthropological and Historical Studies on the Israelite Society Before the Monarchy* (VTSup 37; Leiden: E. J. Brill, 1985); R. B. Coote and K. W. Whitelam, *The Emergence of Israel in Historical Perspective* (SWBA 5; Sheffield: Sheffield Academic, 1987); M. Liverani, "The Collapse of the Near Eastern Regional System at the End of the Bronze Age: The Case of Syria," *Centre and Periphery in the Ancient World* (eds. M. Rowlands, M. Larsen and K. Kristiansen; Cambridge: Cambridge University, 1987) 66-73; H. Weippert, *Palästina in vorhellenistischer Zeit* (Handbuch der Archäologie. Vorderasien 2.1; Munich: Beck, 1988) 340-417; I. Finkelstein, *The Archaeology of the Israelite Settlement* (Jerusalem: IES, 1988); and *idem*, "The Emergence of the Monarchy in Israel: The Environmental and Socio-Economic Aspects," *JSOT* 44 (1989) 43-74; A. Leonard, Jr., "The Late Bronze Age: Archaeological Sources for the History of Palestine," *BA* 52 (1989) 4-39; G. London, "A Comparison of Two Contemporaneous Lifestyles of the Late Second Millennium B.C.," *BASOR* 273 (1989) 37-55; S. Timm, *Moab zwischen den Mächten* (ÄAT 17; Wiesbaden: O. Harassowitz, 1989); A. Mazar, *Archaeology of the Land of the Bible, 10,000-586 B.C.E.* (ABRL; New York: Doubleday, 1990); *idem*, "The Iron Age I," *The Archaeology of Ancient Israel* (ed. A. Ben-Tor; New Haven, Conn.: Yale University, 1992) 258-301; U. Hübner, *Die Ammoniter: Untersuchungen zur Geschichte, Kultur und Religion eines transjordanischen Volkes im 1. Jahrtausend v. Chr.* (ADPV 16; Wiesbaden: Harrassowitz, 1992); P. Bienkowski, ed., *Early Edom and Moab: The Beginning of the Iron Age in Southern Jordan* (SAM 7; Sheffield: Sheffield Academic, 1992); R. Drews, *The End of the Bronze Age: Changes in Warfare and the Catastrophe ca. 1200 B.C.* (Princeton, NJ: Princeton University, 1993); E. Noort, *Die Seevölker in Palästina* (Palaestina Antiqua 8; Kampen: Kok Pharos, 1994); I. Finkelstein and N. Na'aman, eds., *From Nomadism to Monarchy: Archaeological and*

ment the lack of primary sources is normal, so this fact can be used neither as positive proof in favour of Solomon's existence nor against his historicity. However, the total absence of a single source mentioning Solomon "the Great" from within or outside the region of Canaan is suspicious. As far as it is characteristic that not until after a hundred years of excavation in 1993 the first extrabiblical source (from Iron Age IIB) mentioning the "*House* of David" was found.[10] So, too, it is characteristic that not one non-biblical text concerning Solomon has been found. This sheds light on the low state of development at that time and on the modest cultural situation.

As far as it is correct to speak of statehood in Israel beginning with Omri and in Judah with Uzziah, then Solomon is to be placed in the prestate period.[11] In light of the obviously idealized and typical portrayal of Solomon, which possibly reflects Hezekiah and/or Josiah, Solomon perhaps is found in an idealized Judean/Israelite dawn of history.

Historical Aspects of Early Israel (Jerusalem: Biblical Archaeology Society, 1994); K. W. Whitelam, "The Identity of Early Israel: The Realignment and Transformation of Late Bronze-Iron Age Palestine," *JSOT* 63 (1994) 57-87; S. Bunimovitz, "The Problem of Human Resources in Late Bronze Age Palestine and Its Socioeconomic Implications," *UF* 26 (1994) 1-20; *idem*, "On the Edge of Empires: Late Bronze Age (1500-1200 BCE)," *The Archaeology of Society in the Holy Land* (ed. T. E. Levy; London: Leicester University, 1995) 320-31; I. Finkelstein, "The Date of the Settlement of the Philistines in Canaan," *Tel Aviv* 22 (1995) 213-39; *idem*, "The Great Transformation: The 'Conquest' of the Highlands Frontiers and the Rise of the Territorial States," *The Archaeology of Society in the Holy Land* (ed. T. E. Levy; London: Leicester University, 1995) 349-65; *idem*, "The Archaeology of the United Monarchy: An Alternative View," *Levant* 28 (1996) 177-87; L. E. Stager, "The Impact of the Sea Peoples in Canaan (1185-1050 BCE)," *The Archaeology of Society in the Holy Land* (ed. T. E. Levy; London: Leicester University, 1995) 332-48; K. Bartl, "Das Ende der Spätbronzezeit und das 'Dunkle Zeitalter," *Zwischen Euphrat und Indus: Aktuelle Forschungsprobleme in der Vorderasiatischen Archäologie* (Hildesheim: G. Olms, 1995) 175-92; Ø. S. LaBianca and R. W. Younker, "The Kingdoms of Ammon, Moab and Edom: The Archaeology of Society in Late Bronze Age Transjordan (ca. 1400-55 BCE)," *The Archaeology of Society in the Holy Land* (ed. T. E. Levy; London: Leicester University, 1995) 399-415; N. P. Lemche, *Die Vorgeschichte Israels* (BibEnz 1; Stuttgart: Kohlhammer, 1996).

[10] *Editio Princeps*: A. Biran and J. Naveh, "An Aramaic Stela Fragment from Tel Dan," *IEJ* 43 (1993) 81-98; *idem*, "The Tel Dan Inscription: A New Fragment," *IEJ* 45 (1995) 1-18; bibliography concerning the discussion, H. P. Müller, "Die aramäische Inschrift von Tel Dan," *ZAH* 8 (1995) 121-39.

[11] See Niemann, *Herrschaft*; D. W. Jamieson-Drake, *Scribes and Schools in Monarchic Judah: A Socio-Archaeological Approach* (SWABA 9; Sheffield: Sheffield Academic, 1991); E. A. Knauf, "King Solomon's Copper Supply;" and *idem*, "The Archaeology of Literature and the Reality of Fictitious Heroes," forthcoming.

2) *Archaeology*

Despite the remaining uncertainties, today a picture can be drawn of the cultural development in the Palestinian coastal plain as well as in the central highlands during the Iron Age I and the beginning of the Iron Age II. According to this picture Late Bronze Age settlements of the coastal plain survived the disturbances, some of them on a reduced scale. In the central highlands, the number of settlements increased, varying from region to region. However, not all of these new settlements survived.[12]

It seems that in the Iron Age IB there was a cultural innovative expansion from the coastal plain towards the highlands.[13] Traditionally, based on biblical texts, a steep ascent of the highland area, associated with the "mighty kingdoms" or "empires" of David and Solomon, has been assumed during the Iron Age IIA.[14] Monumental architectural works of the Iron Age have also been attributed, by using biblical texts, to David and Solomon.[15]

The example of the 6-chamber-gates. Because no existing finds can be archaeologically traced directly to Solomon, the stately 6-chamber-gate is often given as a concrete illustration of the biblical portrayal of Solomon's kingdom as portrayed in 1 Kgs 9:15, 17-19. Examples of this

---

[12] The varying degrees of intensity and duration of the new settlements in different regions are to be taken into consideration: Kochavi, ed., *Judaea, Samaria and the Golan*; Stager, "Archaeology;" Finkelstein, *Archaeology of the Israelite*; Mazar, *Iron Age I*; Finkelstein and Na'aman, eds., *From Nomadism.*

[13] Noort, *Seevölker*, and n. 20. See also my comments (p. 255) concerning the structural changes caused by the geographic-climatic gradient from the northwest to the southwest.

[14] These or similar terms and ideas related in such exaggerated and misleading dimensions can be found in research literature all over, right up to the present; see, for example, N. P. Lemche, *Ancient Israel: A New History of Israelite Society* (Biblical Seminar 5; Sheffield: Sheffield Academic, 1988) 125, 130, 137ff; M. J. Mulder, "Solomon's Temple and YHWH's Exclusivity," *New Avenues in the Study of the OT: A Collection of OT Studies* (ed. A. S. van der Woude; OTS 25; Leiden: E. J. Brill, 1989) 49-62; Soggin, *Einführung*, pp. 42ff, 62ff; W. E. Rast, *Through the Ages in Palestinian Archaeology* (Philadelphia: Trinity, 1992) 129; Ahlström, *History of Ancient Palestine*, p. 480; A. R. Millard, "Texts and Archaeology: Weighing the Evidence: The Case for King Solomon," *PEQ* 123 (1991) 19-27; *idem*, "King Solomon's Shields," *Scripture and Other Artifacts: Essays on the Bible and Archaeology in Honor of Philip J. King* (eds. M. D. Coogan, J. C. Exum and L. E. Stager; Louisville: Westminster/John Knox, 1994) 286-95; and Donner, *Geschichte des Volkes Israel*, 220ff.

[15] See for example, Y. Yadin, *Hazor* (Schweich Lectures 1970; London: Oxford University, 1972) 147ff; Y. Aharoni, "The Building Activities of David and Solomon," *IEJ* 24 (1974) 13-16; W. G. Dever, "Monumental Architecture in Ancient Israel in the Period of the United Monarchy," *Studies in the Period of David and Solomon and Other Essays* (ed. T. Ishida; Tokyo: Yamakawa-Shuppansha, 1982); B. S. J. Isserlin, "Israelite Architectural Planning and the Question of the Level of Secular Learning in Ancient Israel," *VT* 34 (1984) 169-78. Critical of this with reference to the history of research, Finkelstein, "Archaeology of the United Monarchy," pp. 178f.

type of gate from the Iron Age have been found at Hazor X, Megiddo IVB, Gezer 6, Lachish IV-III, Asdod 9, Tel Ira (*Ḫirbet Ġarra*) and possibly Timna.[16] Their distribution across Palestine fits into the traditional picture of the outstandingly great kingdom of Solomon, who is said to have carried out building projects throughout the land.[17] Further, the argument that the gates are identical in their blueprint and must therefore be the product of central planning in the capital of Solomon's "empire" is not convincing. The gates are not so precisely alike as to be necessarily the product of one builder or one architect.[18] The idea of central planning is dependent on the thesis of a centrally controlled "mighty kingdom," which at this time seems ever more unlikely. The gates can be neither dated to the epoch of Solomon nor be attributed to Solomon, whose rule cannot be dated; the sole clue is 1 Kgs 9:15, 17-19. Such a claim would require proof of Solomon's local control of one of the gate sites or proof of his centralised authority.[19] Is there another plausible explanation for the existence of this element in the Iron Age architecture of Palestine? E. Noort demonstrates that it is unacceptable historically and archaeologically to suddenly in 1200 BCE speak of a homogenous Philistine people living on the coastal plain who subjected the previous inhabitants. The people the Bible lumped together as "Philistines" consisted both of natives from Canaan and "sea peoples" settlers including *plst*. One element of the new Philistocanaanite coastal culture was the so-called submyceenean *monochrome ceramic* (belonging to Myc IIIC 1b) and the so-called *bichrome Philistine ceramic*. However, they developed not only this ceramic, which spread through the highlands, but also,

[16] D. Ussishkin, "Notes on Megiddo, Gezer, Ashdod, and Tel Batash in the Tenth to Ninth Centuries B.C." *BASOR* 277-278 (1990) 82-88; G. L. Kelm and A. Mazar, *Timnah: A Biblical City in Sorek Valley* (Winona Lake, Ind.: Eisenbrauns, 1995) 109f, 122-27.

[17] A critical question can be raised against this interpretation: Why would Solomon have built a 6-chamber-gate in the Philistocanaanite Ashdod and possibly Timna? And who built the gate at Tel Ira (*Ḫirbet Ġarra*) in the 7th century BCE?

[18] Contra Isserlin, "Israelite Architectural Planning," in agreement with Herzog, "Settlement and Fortification Planning in the Iron Age," *The Architecture of Ancient Israel: From Prehistoric to the Persian Periods* (eds. A. Kempinski and R. Reich; Jerusalem: Israel Exploration Society, 1992) 272-74; *idem*, *Das Stadttor in Israel und in den Nachbarländern* (Mainz: Zabern, 1986) 89-128; see also D. Milson, "On the Design of the City Gates at Lachish and Ashdod," *Jahrbuch des Deutschen Evangelischen Instituts für Altertumswissenschaft des Heiligen Landes* 2 (1990) 15-21.

[19] I still consider it convincing that Judah was socio-politically a chiefdom in the 10th century BCE; contra C. Schäfer-Lichtenberger, "Sociological and Biblical Views of the Early State," *The Origins of the Israelite States* (ed. V. Fritz and P. R. Davies; JSOTSup 228; Sheffield: Sheffield Academic, 1996) 78-105.

[20] Noort, *Seevölker*; for architectural impulses from the coastal plain in the inland

according to Noort, the 6-chamber-gate.[20] This is a design originating in the coastal plain, an area more innovative than the highlands. Philistocanaanite craftsmen could be responsible for the various 6-chamber-gates in the highland as well as in their homeland (Ashdod, Timna?).[21] For whom these were built is another question; on the coastal plain, for the Philistocanaanites themselves, in the highlands for local or regional rulers. Whoever looks critically at the allocation of monumental building projects to the Solomon-epoch has even more reason for scepticism when Jerusalem in the early Iron Age (IB-IIA) is considered. There are no architectural finds for this time except for single remains of walls and supporting works.[22] That does not have to mean the biblical reports of Solomon's palace and temple construction are pure fantasy; however, it is important to remember the modest dimensions of Jerusalem in the early Iron Age.[23] The dimensions of Solomon's temple and palace were likewise modest.[24] The main problem lies in the discrepancy between the presentation of Solomon's glorious rule in the biblical-theological report and the very modest archaeological evidence.

---

areas recorded prior to Noort, see H. Weippert, *Palästina*, pp. 440-441; Niemann, *Herrschaft*, pp. 97-98.

[21] A single specialised "house of builders" or two? That could explain the relative similarity in the planning despite the differences.

[22] Y. Shiloh, *Excavations at the City of David I: 1978-1982* (Qedem 19; Jerusalem: Hebrew University of Jerusalem, 1984) 26f; *idem*, "Jerusalem," *The New Encyclopedia of Archaeological Excavations in the Holy Land* (ed. E. Stern; New York: Simon & Schuster, 1993) 702ff; Mazar, *Archaeology*, pp. 347-80; H. Weippert, *Palästina*, pp. 449f. That the few stone remains, dated by Shiloh to the 10th century, possibly belong to the 13th-11th centuries BCE is argued in the new analysis by J. M. Cahill and D. Tarler, "Excavations Directed by Y. Shiloh at the City of David, 1978-1985," *Ancient Jerusalem Revealed* (ed. H. Geva; Jerusalem: Israel Exploration Society, 1994) 34-36. But also see M. L. Steiner, "Redating the Terraces of Jerusalem," *IEJ* 44 (1994) 13-20, who distinguishes between older terraces (13-12th century) and the "stepped stone structure" as an addition from the 10th century, as Shiloh did.

[23] The south-east hill has a length of *ca.* 400 m. and width of *ca.* 60-80 m. Additionally, there is the expansion beyond the cleft to the north of the Ophel with the assumed new palace building and its temple annex, both of which belong to the modern temple mount.

[24] H. Weippert, *Palästina*, pp. 460ff; *idem*, "Der Ausschließlichkeitsanspruch des salomonischen Tempels," *Spuren eines Weges: Freundesgabe für Bernd Janowski zum fünfzigsten Geburtstag am 30. April 1993* (eds. T. Podella and P. Riede; Unpublished manuscript on file, Wissenschaftlich-Theologisches Seminar, Universität Heidelberg, 1993) 265ff; A. Mazar, *Archaeology*, pp. 375ff. For temples see overview by *idem*, "Temples of the Middle and Late Bronze Ages and the Iron Ages," *The Architecture of Ancient Israel: From Prehistoric to the Persian Periods* (eds. A. Kempinski and R. Reich; Jerusalem: Israel Exploration Society, 1992) 161-87; for palaces, R. Reich, "Palaces and Residences in the Iron Age," *The Architecture of Ancient Israel: From Prehistoric to the Persian Periods* (eds. A. Kempinski and R. Reich; Jerusalem: Israel Explorarion Society, 1992) 202-22.

The biblical-theological presentation arouses false expectations for the true historical dimensions of Solomon's building projects. One should also be careful when considering the dimensions of Solomon's "mighty kingdom," in light of the very modest size of Jerusalem and its surrounding communities (as well as the area south to Hebron and the sparse population there) between 1200 and 900/850 BCE. This was a rather remote place and region in no way lying at the intersection of major crossroads.[25]

In general, it has become clearer recently that archaeological finds cannot be dated according to biblical records. At the very latest, since the debate in *BASOR* 277-78, it has no longer been possible to date archaeological finds from the 10th or 9th century BCE more exactly than ± 50 years.[26] That means that archaeological finds cannot be convincingly attributed to a specific ruler of Israel/Judah. For example, whether a find tentatively dated around 900 actually is to be ascribed to Solomon (*ca.* 940 BCE) or to Ahab (*ca.* 860 BCE) cannot at this time be determined with desirable certainty. G. J. Wightman's suggestion of lowering the archaeological dating has already been corrected in *BASOR* 277-78 and by R. Tappy, while the new approach by I. Finkelstein places the discussion on a promising basis even in the case of socio-political thought concerning Solomon.[27]

Because the monumental building projects in Megiddo and Hazor have been dated less according to archaeological arguments than to the biblical records of 1 Kgs 9:15,17-19, Finkelstein has looked for an independent basis for dating archaeological finds. He determined that the Philistocanaanite bichrome ware existed until the middle of the 10th century BCE so that following strata without this ware must be dated after the middle of the 10th century BCE. The consequences are: Beer-sheva

[25] A. Mazar, "Jerusalem and Its Vicinity in Iron Age I," *From Nomadism to Monarchy: Archaeology and Historical Aspects of Early Israel* (eds. I. Finkelstein and N. Na'aman; Jerusalem: Yad Izhak Ben-Zvi, 1994) 70-91; Ofer, "All the Hill," pp. 92-121; A. Alt, "Jerusalems Aufstieg," *Kleine Schriften zur Geschichte des Volkes Israel III* (Munich: Beck, 1968) 243-57; H. Weippert, *Palästina*, p. 451.

[26] G. J. Wightman, "The Myth of Solomon," *BASOR* 277-278 (1990) 5-22; J. S. Holladay, Jr., "Red Slip, Burnish, and the Solomonic Gateway at Gezer," *BASOR* 277-278 (1990) 23-70; Ussishkin, "Notes on Megiddo," pp. 71-91; L. E. Stager, "Shemer's Estate," *BASOR* 277-278 (1990) 93-107; I. Finkelstein, "On Archaeological Methods and Historical Considerations: Iron Age II Gezer and Samaria," *BASOR* 277-278 (1990) 109-19; W. G. Dever, "Of Myths and Methods," *BASOR* 277-278 (1990) 121-30.

[27] R. E. Tappy, *The Archaeology of Israelite Samaria, I: Early Iron Age through the Ninth Century BCE* (HSS 44; Atlanta: Scholars, 1992); Finkelstein, "Archaeology of the United Monarchy," pp. 177-87; and *idem*, "Date of the Settlement," pp. 213-39.

V is 9th century, Arad XII (destroyed by Sheshonq) is 10th, Arad IX is 9th. Megiddo VIA, dated to mid-10th century and possibly destroyed by Sheshonq, contains the last of the degenerated Philistine ceramic. Then Megiddo VB must be *ca.* 900 and VA-IVB (with the palaces 6000+ 1723) in the 9th century. Stratum IVA (6-chamber-gate, water facility and "pillar houses") belongs to the end of the 9th/first half of the 8th century BCE. The one-phase compound of Jezreel (*Ḫirbet Zerʿîn*) contains ceramic from the middle of the 9th century comparable to Megiddo VA-IVB. Further, Finkelstein's method solves the "gap" problem. In the past many excavators noticed a "gap" in the 9th century at many sites. For example, Megiddo IVA (Ahab *and all following kings*) is supposed to be followed directly by the Assyrian Megiddo (III)! Archaeologically speaking, where is the cultural and economic "golden age" of the first half of the 8th century? Finkelstein's solution is very convincing here! Yet another consequence is the dating of Gezer strata. Here bichrome ware appears last in Stratum XI; Strata X-IX were destroyed by the Egyptians in the second half of the 10th century and Stratum VIII, with its 6-chamber-gate, belongs in the 9th century BCE.

It is especially important in Finkelstein's results that Iron Age I stretches into the 10th century and that the 11th and 10th centuries are more closely related to each other in the highlands than previously thought. The 10th century belongs more to Iron Age I than to Iron Age II. A cultural impetus or cultural turning point upwards began in the north during the 9th century, not in the south during the 10th century. Through the lowering of the dates, the difficult problem concerning the missing finds of the 9th century in many places have been solved. The cultural development in Iron Age I and IIA would no longer have to make unexplainable leaps forward, but could orderly unfold from its modest beginnings. The "gaps" in so many finds from the 9th century would no longer exist. Works previously attributed to Solomon without any archaeological evidence belong in the 9th century. Not only through literary criticism, but also on the basis of archaeological finds, Solomon can now be reckoned to Judean pre-state history. The problematic dissonance between the absence of historical knowledge concerning Solomon and the supposedly huge archaeological finds is now past. It is this archaeologically based result of Finkelstein which corresponds to the expected cultural development and critical biblical exegesis.[28]

[28] Jamieson-Drake, *Scribes and Schools*; Niemann, *Herrschaft*.

Finkelstein also calls attention to a significant population difference from the west to the east and from north to south, which can be calculated using the amount of building space (built-up area) in communities with bichrome ceramics in the 10th century BCE.

From West to East:

Philistine south of Jarkon		
including Shefela	160ha × 200 persons/ha =	32000 persons
Central highlands	220ha × 200 persons/ha =	44000 persons

From North to South (central highlands)

from the Plain of Jezreel		
to Jerusalem	210ha	42000 persons
Judah	11ha	2200 persons[29]

When the cultural developments as presented by archaeological research are considered it is clear that the time between the "cave period" and the "village culture" of Iron Age IA and the further development to Iron Age IIB-C (i.e., Iron Age IB-IIA) is the *beginning* and not, as presented in the biblical-literary tradition and research base upon it, the *cultural golden age* of Israel/Judean history! It is a point of departure that belongs to the pre-state history of Israel/Judah. If that is the case, it is possible to suggest a corridor in time in which the Solomon-epoch is to be surmised. Within the cultural evolution, this epoch belongs to the Iron Age *formative period*, not to the later differentiated main Iron Age II. As a biblical clue, it fits that the age of Solomon shouldn't lie far from that of Sheshonq. I therefore see the time frame of the Solomon-epoch running from *ca*. 970-900 BCE.

Archaeologically this time frame does not offer any concrete evidence for Solomon, except the recognition that during the presumed reign of Solomon Judah and Jerusalem were, culturally speaking, very modest. Solomon is truly far from the level of development found at the time of the Omrides or even Uzziah and Jeroboam II. The archaeological quest for the golden "mighty kingdom" of Solomon, which stretched from Egypt's brook to the Euphrates and from Saba to Lebanon, can be called off.[30] Still, the stage for the presumed reign of Solomon is not empty and

---

[29] More extensive information in Ofer, "All the Hill."

[30] J. Van Seters, *In Search of History: Historiography in the Ancient World and the Origins of Biblical History* (New Haven, Conn.: Yale University, 1983) 307ff; J. D. Muhly, "Timna and King Solomon," *BO* 41 (1984) 275-92; E. Würthwein, *Die Bücher der Könige: 1. Könige 1-16* (ATD 11.1; Göttingen: Vandenhoeck & Ruprecht, 1985); G. Garbini, *History and Ideology in Ancient Israel* (New York: Crossroad, 1988) 1ff, 27ff;

some historical structures and the general background for the biblical Solomon can be pieced together.

3) Ethnographic Comparison[31]

Ḍâhir b. ʿUmar, as the youngest (!) son, followed his father as high sheikh of Galilee, with authority from the Sublime Porte and regional representative in Sidon. At that time the Ottoman Empire was in crisis and in order to keep control it turned to native forces. During the first half of the 18th century CE, Ḍâhir put together an armed troop and extended his control from his ancestral seat of Tiberias all the way to the Mediterranean. He gained economic profit by working together with foreign traders. With his increasing political clout, he stood above his Ottoman "superior" in Sidon. He fortified his hometown of Tiberias; enlarged the port of Acco, established law and order in the city and made it his capital. In time Ḍâhir also took on regional politics, taking Sidon in 1771 and in 1772 Ramle, Gaza, Jaffa, and almost capturing Jerusalem. He always tried to induce the Ottoman authority (mostly belatedly) to legitimate his actions. Only after lengthy hesitation, as his independence became too great, did the Ottoman Empire intervene. His capital Acco, as well as other coastal cities, was taken by the Ottoman fleet and Ḍâhir was killed in Acco in 1775.

Politically Ḍâhir dextrously maneuvered among Sublime Porte, his own governor in Sidon and the governors in Damascus. It was a period structurally comparable to the time of El-Amarna: a non-present ruling power from abroad let the reins slip in Palestine. Like the kings of the city-states in the Late Bronze Age, the Ottoman dignitaries barely felt safe enough to leave their bases. In this type of situation a merely formal ruling power uses the services of a local chief. Also typically, with growing power and independence, the chief shows the rulers less respect while his own ambitions rise.

The instruments and methods used by Ḍâhir for gaining and executing power are important. As long as they remained loyal to him, he left

J. B. Pritchard, "The Age of Solomon," *Solomon and Sheba* (ed. J. B. Pritchard; London: Phaidon, 1974) 17-39; Knauf, "King Solomon's Copper Supply;" J. M. Miller, "Solomon: International Potentate or Local King?" *PEQ* 123 (1991) 28-31; Niemann, *Herrschaft*; M. M. Gelinas, "United Monarchy—Divided Monarchy: Fact or Fiction?" *The Pitcher Is Broken: Memorial Essays for G. W. Ahlström* (eds. S.W. Holloway and L. K. Handy; JSOTSup 190; Sheffield, Sheffield Academic, 1995) 227-237; G. Auld, "Re-Reading Samuel (historically): 'Etwas mehr Nichtwissen,'" *The Origins of the Israelite States* (eds. V. Fritz and P. R. Davies; JSOTSup 228; Sheffield: Sheffield Academic, 1996) 167-68.

local and regional rulers in peace. For safety's sake he arranged marriages between his family and local rulers. He posted sons and close relatives at strategically important points. Sometimes his sons rebelled and both singly and in various combinations fought against their father. At one point, with the help of Bedouin, three of his sons held the stronghold at Tiberias. Once Ḍâhir captured a son and thereby kept the rebel in Egypt in check. The sons even sought help from their father's arch rival in Damascus; however, when Ḍâhir was threatened from abroad, all his sons fought on his side.

Ḍâhir is a perfect example of how a member of a Bedouin clan can step by step take control of a region and its population. He enjoyed the support of the Bedouin tribe *Banū Ṣaḥr* for a long time, but this changed as it became clear that Ḍâhir was establishing a strict central authority and they deserted him, joining forces with his opponents. The Ḍâhir epoch shows that even in the Ottomon Empire the north was economically and politically more important than the south and that the west (the coast) more than the east, from whence Ḍâhir led his campaigns as David and Solomon had from the south.

Ḍâhir had roots in the region, paid attention to legitimisation (at least *pro forma*), maintained permanently armed troops and constantly enlarged his urban-based central control. He made up for his lack of authority in certain places through military and economic strength as well as through the dispersal of trusted representatives. His rise to power happened at a time of weak central control!

As a member of a nomadic people, Ḍâhir was accepted by the settled inhabitants of Galilee because he offered security and stability in return for loyalty. As ruler he first relied on independence-oriented relatives (Bedouin). To free himself of their sensitivities regarding independence, he expanded his central control. The Galilean farmers had to pay 1/6 to 1/4 of their income as tax. At the end of his reign it was half! A state and a ruler are expensive! The consequence of this economic pressure was that at the end of his reign many farmers had fled his territory.[32]

Whoever is familiar with the biblical stories of David and Solomon does not need the many structural parallels pointed out. This is how it

---

[31] Cohen, *Palestine in the 18th Century*; the following essay excerpts should be read keeping the biblical stories of David and Solomon constantly in mind!

[32] For structurally related events at the end of the Late Bronze Age, see Bunimovitz, "Problem;" and *idem*, "On the Edge."

could have been in the time of David and Solomon. This is perhaps how it often was in Palestine and similar societies under similar conditions. The biblical portrayal of David and Solomon is, at least in part, structural,[33] but that does not necessarily mean that it is totally non-historical.[34] The structural character of the text makes giving it an exact and exclusive date in the Iron Age IB-IIA difficult. However, with the help of the information concerning Ḍâhir b. ʿUmar and by comparing the typical structures which go beyond individuals and single epochs, it is easier to recognise the stories of David and Solomon as stories or to recognise the structures as such. The contemporary religious-ideological tendency of Solomon can be better understood and picked out from historical background. That is an achievement because this makes it possible to notice structural differences in the future analysis. Historical, non-structural contemporary information might be hidden behind such differences. This might not only reflect information concerning the age in which the Solomon stories were composed, but also perhaps even information from the Solomonic Age itself.

4) Biblical Evidence: A Critical Review

Traditionally Solomon stands at a turning point in the history of Israel.[35] For an accurate portrayal of the Solomonic epoch it is important to have as deep as possible an understanding of the time which led to it.

The Bible portrays Saul's reign as a first socio-political stage of development after which follows a hard fall for religious reasons. Behind the biblical-theological portrayal there are historical reasons to assume that Saul fit into a Late Bronze Age pattern for rulers.[36] He was

---

[33] Therein lies an applicable element in C. Schäfer-Lichtenberger's general thesis, *Josua und Salomo: Eine Studie zur Autorität und Legitimität des Nachfolgers im Alten Testament* (VTSup 58; Leiden: E. J. Brill, 1995); but also see the criticism of T. Veijola, Review of C. Schäfer-Lichtenberger: *Josua und Salomo* (VTSup 58; Leiden: E. J. Brill, 1995) in *TLZ* 121 (1996) 27-29. The biblical-theological portrayal of David and Solomon was intended to be both exemplary and didactic; see the structures "representative building construction," "wealth" and "wisdom of the ruler," "the just king," and others.

[34] On the other hand, when it seems probable that an event occured as portrayed in the biblical text, that does not mean that it, in fact, so happened. The sentence *Potest ergo est* is worthless as scientific proof; Donner, *Geschichte des Volkes Israel*, pp. 30-31.

[35] "Break" in the sense of "the breaking apart of David's empire," the collapse of the "double monarchy," or the "personal union," that is, "break" in the sense of a rapid decline. This assumes, or suggests, that the "kingdom" had stood at a political and cultural high point. It will be shown that Solomon was *more likely at the beginning of a planned ascent*, which, however, broke from the plan after his death.

36 For Saul: K.-D. Schunck, *Benjamin: Untersuchungen zur Entstehung und Ge-*

more successful and talented than shown in the biblical portrayal, which is not historically, but theologically directed. In some ways he was even more successful and innovative than David.[37] He designed and introduced measures for the ruling structure from which both David and Solomon greatly profited.[38]

The biblical portrayal of David's and Solomon's time was told with

---

schichte eines israelitischen Stammes (BZAW 86; Berlin: de Gruyter, 1963); *idem*, "König Saul-Etappen seines Weges zum Aufbau eines israelitischen Staates," *BZ* 36 (1992) 195-206; J. Blenkinsopp, *Gibeon and Israel* (Cambridge: Cambridge University, 1972); *idem*, "Did Saul Make Gibeon His Capital?" *VT* 24 (1974) 1-7; Miller and Hayes, *History*, pp. 120-49; E. A. Knauf, "Das zehnte Jahrhundert: Ein Kapitel Vorgeschichte Israels," *Heidel-Berger Apokryphen: Eine vorzeitige Nikolausgabe zum 50. Geburtstag von Prof. Dr. K. Berger* (Unpublished manuscript on file, Wissenschaftlich-Theologisches Seminar, Universität Heidelberg, 1990) 156-61; N. Na᾽aman, "The Kingdom of Ishbaal," *BN* 54 (1990) 33-37; Ahlström, *History of Ancient Palestine*, pp. 423-54; Niemann, *Herrschaft*, pp. 3-8, 192-93; D. V. Edelman, "Saul's Rescue of Jabesh-Gilead (1 Sam 11,1-11)," *ZAW* 96 (1984) 195-209; *idem*, "The 'Ashurites' of Eshbaal's State (2 Sam 2,9)," *PEQ* 117 (1985) 88-91; *idem*, "Saul," *ABD* 5.989-99; *idem*, "Saul ben Kish in History and Tradition," *The Origins of the Ancient Israelite States* (eds. V. Fritz and P. R. Davies; JSOTSup 228; Sheffield: Sheffield Academic, 1996) 142-59. See below nn. 37-38, 57.

[37] See the map in Edelman, "Saul," p. 997. The area in which Saul held influence (2 Sam 2:9) was economically and politically much more important than Judah; see for Judah the detailed archaeological survey study by Ofer, "All the Hill," pp 92-121, and his demographic conclusions. Both Saul and Solomon were more successful than David in the dynastic continuation of their regimes (Saul only short term), whereas in this David suffered his worst defeat. On the other hand, David, as a leader of mercenaries, had a more difficult starting point than either Saul or Solomon; he had first to build a support base (1 Sam 21ff) and in so doing, establish himself. Saul and Solomon both established themselves using a different, but in both cases, preexisting and merely expanded tribal or urban power base.

[38] The most important factors are: 1. *Securing a functionally important central city for an urban-supported territorial rule* in the Late Bronze Age model (e.g. Lab᾽ayu: EA 237; 244-46; 249-50; 252-53; 255; 263; 280; 287; 289); for *Saul*: from Zela (2 Sam 21:14) to Gibea after his victory (1 Sam 13-14) and then to Gibeon (see Schunck, Blenkinsopp, Knauf, Niemann, and Edelman, in n. 36); for *David*: Hebron and then Jerusalem. 2. *Possessing a traditional and integrated shrine*, for *Saul*: the Great High Place (הבמה הגדלה) near Gibeon (see also n. 57); for *David and Solomon*: Gibeon and Jerusalem. 3. *An ever-ready military corps*: for *Saul*: see 1 Sam 14:50-52; 17:55; for *David*: see 1 Sam 22:1-2; 1 Sam 27 and 2 Sam 23:8-39. 4. *Establishment through fighting against the Philistocanaanites*, who represented the greatest threat to Israel and Judah on the western flank: for *Saul*: see 1 Sam 13-14 with limited, but successful, measures, which seem to have been a signal for further campaigns in the mountains of Ephraim, but which also provoked a response by the Philistocanaanites (1 Sam 29 and 31). For *David*: see also local and regional limited skirmishes and duels: 1 Sam 23:1-5; 2 Sam 5:17-25; 21:15-22; 23:9-10, 11-12 and 13-17. Nothing points to a great battle or victory by the Philistocanaanites over David or by David over the Philistines. Maybe the Philistocanaanites finally gave up (because of the constant skirmishes?) their attempts at colonising the highlands. Normal

theological interests in mind. So it includes few historical details. The lack of historical interest in and the lack of historical information concerning David and Solomon is contrasted with the previous texts dealing with Saul and the later texts telling of Rehoboam, Jeroboam I and their followers where we find more historical information. This is made clear by the fact that, as opposed to their predecessor[39] and successors,[40] especially for the reign of the two greatest (?) kings, David and Solomon, no specific dates are given (or perhaps even known)!

Whoever tries to analyse Solomon using the *biblical-theological* portrayal as the basis of a *historical* analysis without considering the *theological* motives lying behind this tradition, brings the same tendency to the historical analysis as the biblical authors had toward idealised dimensions of the protagonist. The picture of the temple-founding and God-fearing wise ruler arrived at through precisely such flawed analysis has, in the past, led to false interpretations and disappointment when comparing literary results with archaeological research. Its influence has also sometimes led to misreading the archaeological finds themselves.[41] It is very important for a proper analysis to avoid any presumptions concerning the *historical dimensions* of Solomon based on the *theological dimensions* of the biblical portrayal.

---

relations then developed (2 Sam 8:18; 15:18; 1 Kgs 2:39-40). The summary of the successful defence against the Philistocanaanites in 2 Sam 5:25 ("from Gibeon to Gezer") of course, does not geographically fit in the context of David's battles south-west of Jerusalem (2 Sam 5:17-25), but does describe the geographical area from which Saul, in defence of his residence Gibeon, might have driven the Philistines back to their starting point (Gezer). It seems that this success, for which Saul was remembered, was later credited to his more lucky Judean competitor David.

[39] For a long time Saul was, unjustly, assumed to have ruled for only two years: an "Episode," classically, M. Noth, *Geschichte Israels* (Göttingen: Vandenhoeck & Ruprecht, 1966) 163. See against that Schunck, *Benjamin*, pp. 108-24; and Edelman, "Saul," pp. 992-93. One can reckon with more than one decade: 12 or 22 (or 32?) years.

[40] According to 1 Kgs 11:41, annals were begun by Rehoboam, which is in line with the synchronisms from the reigns of Rehoboam and Jeroboam I (see 1 Kgs 14:19-20,29). The keeping of annals begins, traditionally, with the situation of the predecessor, in this case, Solomon. The annals from the time of Rehoboam may, as portrayed in 1 Kgs 11:40f, contain some information concerning the time of Solomon, but they cannot even exactly say when Solomon's reign began (much less that of David) giving just round "40 years" (1 Kgs 11:42 and 2 Sam 2:11, 5:4-5); Ahlström, *History of Ancient Palestine*, pp. 500-501. Knauf, "King Solomon's Copper Supply," pp. 174-76, conjectures with good reason that 1 Kgs 11:41 is from the time of Josiah.

[41] See discussion of 6-chamber-gates above; also history of research in Finkelstein, "Archaeology of the United Monarchy," pp. 178-79.

The biblical Solomon complex consists of:

Story concerning coming to the throne and the beginning of Solomon's reign	1 Kgs 1-2
Exemplary deeds, prestige and large numbers:	
Fame, piety and righteousness	1 Kgs 3
Clever and organised ruler	1 Kgs 4
Prestige, wealth, wisdom and trade policy	1 Kgs 5[42]
Wisdom, prestige and trade in prestige goods	1 Kgs 10[43]

This is a characteristic structured way of acting in the framework of the 1st millennium BCE.

Critical theological conclusion	
Foreign women and idolatry	1 Kgs 11:1-8
Consequences and threats	1 Kgs 11:9-13
"Trio of 'Bad guy' characters"	1 Kgs 11:14-28[44]

---

[42] Despite all the theological-ideological changes and expansions, 1 Kgs 5:15-32 still allows an insight into the relationships of strength and power: The Phoenician-Tyrian coastal trading power ("first world"), supplied the developing lands ("third world": Judean highlands, that is the Philistine/Phoenician backlands) with luxury/prestige goods *in limited quantity* and craftsmen too. The developing land of Judah not only had to supply labourers, but also, as is typical, agricultural and similar raw materials *in almost unlimited quantities*; see also Knauf, "King Solomon's Copper Supply;" and J. K. Kuan, "Third Kingdoms 5.1 and Israelite-Tyrian Relations During the Reign of Solomon," *JSOT* 46 (1990) 31-46. As to prestige and its trade; see n. 43.

[43] Prestige goods and the trade in them is, to a large extent, a *socio-political* factor of rule. *Socio-economically* they carry less weight. That being the case, prestige goods and their trade do belong here (see n. 46). As to the term and to the individual items of prestige, prestige goods and the trade in prestige goods, see S. Morenz, *Prestige-Wirtschaft im Alten Ägypten* (SBAW 4; Munich: Beck, 1969), for Egypt; as well as M. H. Fried, *The Evolution of Political Society: An Essay in Political Anthropology* (New York: Random, 1967) 32f, 73ff, 106ff, 115, 118, 131ff; U. Rüterswörden, *Die Beamten der israelitischen Königszeit* (BWANT 117; Stuttgart: Kohlhammer, 1985) 113f; B. Streck, ed., *Wörterbuch der Ethnologie* (Dumont Taschenbücher 194; Köln: Dumont, 1987) 164-67; S. Breuer, *Der archaische Staat: Zur Soziologie charismatischer Herrschaft* (Berlin: Reimer, 1990) 42, 45ff, 52, 58, 63ff; Kuan, "Third Kingdoms;" A. and S. Sherratt, "From Luxuries to Commodities: The Nature of Mediterranean Bronze Age Trading Systems," *Bronze Age Trade in the Mediterranean: Papers Presented at the Conference Held at Rewley House, Oxford, in December 1989* (Studies in Mediterranean Archaeology 90; Jonsered: P. Alström, 1991) 351-86; Niemann, *Herrschaft*, p. 53, n. 221; N. Crüsemann, B. Feller and M. Heinz, "Prestigegüter und Politik: Aspekte internationaler Politik im 2. Jt. v. Chr.," *Zwischen Euphrat und Indus: Aktuelle Forschungsprobleme in der Vorderasiatischen Archäologie* (eds. K. Bartl and others; Hildesheim: G. Olms, 1995) 175-92; Bartl, "Ende der Spätbronzezeit," p. 203 (exchanging prestige goods). The existence of prestige goods such as "golden shields" in other regions and times says nothing about Solomon; contrary to Millard, "King Solomon's Shields."

[44] See the convincing analysis by D. V. Edelman, "Solomon's Adversaries Hadad, Rezon and Jeroboam: A Trio of 'Bad Guy' Characters Illustrating the Theology of

The successors	1 Kgs 11:29-43[45]

As a central point and not to be overlooked with formal and technical content:

Building of the Temple	1 Kgs 6
Building of the Palace	1 Kgs 7:1-12
Temple ornaments and dedication	1 Kgs 7:13-8:66
Promises and threats	1 Kgs 9:1-9

Standing out from the typical structures and generalised and idealised blocks and therefore worth considering in light of the contemporary socio-political situation:

Concrete historical (?) details	1 Kgs 9:10-28
The area of Kabul	1 Kgs 9:10-14
Forced labour used in *building projects*	1 Kgs 9:15
How Gezer came under Solomon's rule	1 Kgs 9:16,17a
Further *building projects*	1 Kgs 9:17b-19
Forced labour	1 Kgs 9:20-22
Leading functionaries	1 Kgs 9:23
Pharaoh's daughter, Millo	1 Kgs 9:24
Offerings upon completion of Temple	1 Kgs 9:25
Fleet of Hiram/Solomon, gold from Ophir	1 Kgs 9:26-28[46]

The exemplary generalising style of 1 Kgs 3-5 and 10 on the one hand arouses historical sceptisim, but on the other hand draws attention to the obvious theological intentions. Likewise, 1 Kgs 6:1-9:9 does nothing to further the understanding of Solomon's historical situation.

Recently several scholars have emphasised the Solomon tradition as ideological, legitimising, theological and of limited worth as historical evidence.[47] With this came the problem of dating archaeological struc-

---

Immediate Retribution," *The Pitcher Is Broken: Memorial Essays for Gösta W. Ahlström* (eds. S. W. Holloway and L. K. Handy; JSOTSup 190; Sheffield: Sheffield Academic, 1995) 227-37, "sorting story from history."

[45] See H. Weippert, "Die Ätiologie des Nordreiches und seines Königshauses (I Reg 11,29-40)," *ZAW* 95 (1983) 344-75.

[46] Provisionally critical D. G. Schley, Jr., "1 Kings 10:26-29: A Reconsideration," *JBL* 106 (1987) 595-601; Niemann, *Herrschaft*, pp. 25, 169-73. Just as the legendary depiction of the "wisdom of the ruler" following this text in 1 Kgs 10:1-13 is to be understood as a "structure," so too is the further depiction of fairy tale-like riches and trade in prestige goods in 1 Kgs 10:14-29 structural in nature. If I am correct, it is not possible to concretely limit even one single fact from this text in place and time to the Solomonic epoch.

[47] In principle, Van Seters, *In Search of History*, pp. 307ff; Gelinas, "United Monarchy;" Auld, "Re-Reading Samuel," pp. 167-68; more concretely, Garbini, *History and Ideology*, pp. 1ff, 27ff; Knauf, "King Solomon's Copper Supply;" Miller, "Solomon;"

tures and strata as no longer certain. In fact, almost nothing from the 9th or 10th centuries BCE can be attributed with certainty to Solomon (or to any single ruler) at Megiddo, Hazor or Gezer.[48]

That Solomon should be reckoned to the legendary pre-state history of Israel/Judah is not only based on the lack of dates for his reign.[49] Evidently the keeping of royal annals did not begin under the alleged two greatest kings, but under their less important successors. How does that fit in with the precise enumeration of the literally fairy-tale-like representation of the building projects, great deeds and other data concerning Solomon? One need only observe the size of the Temple and the palace in Jerusalem in the 10th century BCE to bring the correct dimensions into focus![50]

It makes sense to place Solomon in the legendary, theologic pre-state of Judah/Israel because the biblical description of Solomon corresponds to the idealisation and perfectness of protagonists in stories concerned with the origin and legitimisation of a constituency. In addition, the introduced verses critical of Solomon can easily be picked out. Thus, I consider the biblical Solomon to be part of the legendary pre(-state) history of Israel. It is possible that a historical figure, of different, more modest dimensions, was the basis of this picture. We have to concentrate on points of departure for socio-political elements behind the biblical Solomon.

I see two groups of structural socio-political factors in the Solomon stories:
1) Building projects as a provision for religious/ideological and representative prestige to legitimate the reign alongside with political marriage and trade to support royal authority. This includes: A) Building projects in Jerusalem and B) Building projects outside Jerusalem, political marriage and trade. 2) Measures taken to expand, organise and stabilise the kingdom. This includes: C) Government functionaries and D) Attempt to expand northward in 1 Kgs 4:7-19.

Würthwein, *Bücher der Könige*; Soggin, *Einführung*, pp. 62-75; and for 1 Kgs 10:1-13, Pritchard, "Age of Solomon," pp.17-39.

[48] See above, pp. 262-64, with nn. 26, 28, 30.

[49] "If 'history' is distinguished from 'pre-history' by the availability of contemporary written narrative source material both David and Solomon still belong to Israel's pre-history;" Knauf, "Archaeology." See Auld, "Re-Reading Samuel," p. 167; however, H. J. Nissen, "History Before Writing" (unpublished paper, Mario Liverani Seminar om Oldtidshistorie, Copenhagen, November 17, 1995).

[50] H. Weippert, *Palästina*, pp. 452, 457-76; *idem*, "Ausschließlichkeitsanspruch," pp. 265ff; Mazar, *Archaeology*, pp. 375ff; above, nn. 22-24.

A) *Building projects in Jerusalem, especially the Temple and Palace.* Only as a subordinate clause does the biblical tradition of 2 Sam 6:17 mention that David placed the Ark of YHWH in a tent. That chapter is interested in other things. The fact that the holy object *from the north* was brought *to Jerusalem* is more important. In his moving prayer of dedication for the Temple (1 Kgs 8:17-21), Solomon states something apparently newly known: David played with the idea of building a YHWH Temple in Jerusalem, but YHWH had turned down the offer, honouring David's good intentions, but giving no concrete reasons why. "Your son, who shall be born to you shall build the house for me" (8:19). Naturally, one can speculate about the reasons why there are no temple building reports from David.[51] That an old, Middle and Late Bronze Age city like Jerusalem did not have any city temple, albeit a modest one, is out of the question. H. Donner recognised an "anti-aetiology" behind 2 Sam 24: the story claims that a temple and even a place for a temple existed for the first time under David.[52] The historical-religious probability of *stabilitas loci* should be sorted out; no temple to a god besides YHWH existed in Jerusalem before David. The creator of this story seems to have seen reason enough to fight against the opposing tradition. For this reason K. Rupprecht's argument makes sense, that Solomon did not build a *new* temple in Jerusalem, but rather *modified or expanded* an older one, while E. A. Knauf saw artisans at work on the temple during Solomon's reign as probable.[53]

If Solomon is justifiably connected with a modification or expansion of the Jerusalem temple, that lies in the interest of the ideological line of deuteronomistic theology.[54] Solomon deals with this historically plausi-

[51] Even the biblical authors had been doing this. 1 Kgs 5:17: no time because of the enemies; 1 Chr 17: YHWH was not interested in a temple at that time, but at a later time David's descendents should build a temple. Every author has his ideas, but no one knows exactly why. However, in 2 Sam 12:20 we find a reference to the old pre-Davidic and pre-Solomonic city temple in Jerusalem.

[52] H. Donner, "Der Felsen und der Tempel," *ZDPV* 93 (1977) 5-6.

[53] K. Rupprecht, "Nachrichten von Erweiterung und Renovierung des Tempels in 1. Könige 6," *ZDPV* 88 (1972) 38-52; *idem*, *Der Tempel von Jerusalem: Gründung Salomos oder jebusitisches Erbe?* (BZAW 144; Berlin: de Gruyter, 1977); and Knauf, "King Solomon's Copper Supply."

[54] See also 1 Kgs 8:12-13 in the Septuagint; and *ibid.*, pp. 183-84; *idem*, "Le roi est mort, vive le roi! A Biblical Argument for the Historicity of Solomon," pp. 81-95 [this volume]; O. Keel, "Fern von Jerusalem: Frühe Jerusalemer Kulttradition und ihre Träger und Trägerinnen," *Zion: Ort der Begegnung: Festschrift L. Klein zur Vollendung des 65. Geburtstags* (eds. F. Hahn, F. L. Hossfeld, H. Jorissen and A. Neuwirth; BBB 90; Bodenheim: Athenäum, 1993) 486ff; and *idem*, "Zur Theologie in Europa: Eine Kurzbiographie

ble measure exactly as is required in the obligatory canon of an ancient oriental (city) ruler. However, if Solomon acted so, why hadn't David before him? Are there different legitimising traditions between David and Solomon? It has been assumed that Solomon, with his Jerusalem city mother (as opposed to the Judean rural David) triumphed in conflict for succession because of support from the Jerusalem city party at the expense of the Judean rural party and the traditional Davidic clan.[55] If true, this turn in lineal descent would have been a sore spot with later listeners from the house of David and the people of Judah. It is striking that in 1 Kgs 8-9 the fact (?) that Solomon was David's son is conspicuously repeated.[56] Was there justifiable doubt? We see in the Solomon tradition that, even after David, Gibeon played an important role for Solomon up to the building of the palace and Temple in Jerusalem. Until this point the sacred precinct of Gibeon seemed to play a decisive role for him. Did the urban ruler of Jerusalem use this to attach himself to or even bypass the rural Judean David? With this he connected himself as a city ruler to the city of Gibeon, to the YHWH cult in Gibeon, to Gibeon as Saul's capital,[57] even to the kingdom of Saul and to Saul himself, who had been the most successful ruler north of Jerusalem! Whereas David had taken advantage of some clever and innovative manoeuvres of the often underestimated Saul, Solomon connected himself even more consistently to

der Frühzeit des Gottes Israels im Ausgang von Ausgrabungsbefunden im Syro-Palästinensischen Raum," *ET Bulletin* 5 (1994) 168.

[55] E. Würthwein, *Die Erzählung von der Thronfolge Davids-theologische oder politische Geschichtsschreibung?* (Zürich: Theologischer, 1974); *idem, Bücher der Könige*, pp. 1-28, 146-49; T. Veijola, "Salomo—der Erstgeborene Bathsebas," *Studies in the Historical Books of the Old Testament* (ed. J. A. Emerton; VTSup 30; Leiden: E. J. Brill, 1979) 230-50; Keel, "Fern von Jerusalem," pp. 470ff; *idem*, "Theologie," p. 166; Knauf, "Le roi est mort."

[56] 1 Kgs 8:15, 17, 18, 20, 24-26; 9:4-5; see 8:19: "Your son who issues from your loins (חלצים)" (or "who shall be born to you") which means that even the thought of adoption is preventively ruled out! See n. 100.

[57] For the connection of Saul to Gibeon, see first Schunck, *Benjamin*, pp. 114f, 131ff; then Blenkinsopp, *Gibeon and Israel*, and *idem.*, "Did Saul;" and finally, Niemann, *Herrschaft*, pp. 4-5; Edelman, "Saul," and *idem*, "Saul ben Kish," pp. 154-59. Also nn. 36, 38 above. It is important to note Saul's far-sighted efforts at establishing legitimising contacts with important shrines: first with Shiloh and with the Eli priesthood (1 Sam 1; 1 Sam 14:3), which continued in Nob but were later destroyed by the struggle between David and Saul (1 Sam 22) and also with the "Great High Place" near Gibeon (as well as with Zadok, the Gibeonite priest; 1 Chr 16:39). The relationships came about after Saul moved from Zela (2 Sam 21:14) to Gibea (after liberating the city from the Philistocanaanite post; 1 Sam 13-14) and then in more important urban Gibeon as his residence.

Saul, although being not always successful and smart enough concerning northern sensitivities.[58]

If these suppositions lead in the right direction, Solomon continued David's attempt to socio-politically integrate the northern groups by means of religion, bringing Gibeon's tradition of a *sacred precinct* to the *temple building* in *Jerusalem* as David had brought the *sacred object* (Ark) of Shiloh to the *temple* of *Jerusalem.* David had taken on what Saul recognised: to be a successful territorial ruler, one must have an integrated shrine! The expansion of the temple and the integration of two sacred traditions as stabilising and religious legitimising factors for a ruling city is a socio-political measure of the first degree. The northern *tribal sacred object* (Ark of Shiloh) and the *city of Gibeon's sacred place tradition* (הבמה הגדלה near Gibeon) were combined with the *city temple* of Jerusalem. The northern tribal deity YHWH and YHWH as the dynastic-god of David were integrated in Jerusalem.[59]

The building of a palace in Jerusalem means a representative symbol of rule.[60] But archaeologically nothing can be proved. According to the biblical report, the palace was comprised of several buildings.[61] That is possible, but what dimensions did the Jerusalem complex have at the time of Solomon? Does the description of the many palace buildings have its origin in the time of Solomon or is it textually a later work (developed over decades or centuries)? Were all these buildings erected

---

[58] For structural and factual similarities between Saul and Solomon on the one hand, and differences between both of them and David, see nn. 37-38.

[59] See among others, J. Jeremias, *Das Königtum Gottes in den Psalmen* (FRLANT 141; Göttingen: Vandenhoeck & Ruprecht, 1987) 167-82; H. Niehr, *Der höchste Gott: Alttestamentlicher JHWH-Glaube im Kontext syrisch-kanaanäischer Religion des 1. Jahrtausends v. Chr.* (BZAW 190; Berlin: de Gruyter, 1990); B. Janowski, "Keruben und Zion: Thesen zur Entstehung der Zionstradition," *Ernten was man sät: Festschrift für Klaus Koch zu seinem 65. Geburtstag* (eds. D. R. Daniels and others; Neukirchen: Neukirchener, 1991) 231-64; Niemann, *Herrschaft*, pp. 203-205. For integrating achievements of Solomon, see O. Keel, "Fern von Jerusalem;" and *idem*, "Theologie," pp. 165ff, especially 168-69. In light of the cultural history, Solomon's achievements in the area of integration are, in respect to the shrine and temple traditions a "fall back," that is, Solomon joined the old *urban temple* tradition of the (Late) Bronze Age with the just emerging rural home-shrine or open-air-shrine tendency outside of cities (epoch of Saul and David); H. Weippert, "Ausschließlichkeitsanspruch," pp. 272-80.

[60] K. W. Whitelam, "The Symbols of Power," *BA* 41 (1986) 166-73; Niemann, *Herrschaft*, pp. 91-96.

[61] 1 Kgs 7:1-11; H. Weippert, *Palästina*, pp. 474-76; A. Mazar, *Archaeology*, pp. 378-80.

simultaneously and all during the reign of Solomon? Many questions, but few substantiated explanations![62]

B) *Further Measures taken for Prestige* (Building Projects outside of Jerusalem, Political Marriage, Trade). Royal building outside of the capital is also socio-politically relevant. It documents royal protection as well as having a representative function. A fortified and recognized border hints at a phase of sociological development with the state emerging. This phase overlaps that of the chiefdom.[63] 1 Kgs 9:15-19 tells of Solomon's building projects outside of Jerusalem.

One has to assume that the narrator wants to express something meaningful when he reports that Solomon built both in *Hazor* and *Megiddo* (1 Kgs 9:15); utilising these places as border fortifications is too punctual.[64] Both are functional places and traditional centres of operation. Hazor plainly represents the centre of operations in the north and guarantees safety in the direction of Aram and Damascus.[65] Megiddo rules the Plain of Jezreel, holds a key position between Galilee and the northern central Palestinian highlands and controls one of the most crucial north-south passes from the coastal plain to the north (Phoenicia) and/or northeast (Syria). Whoever reports that a ruler controls the area is saying that the ruler understands strategy, shows the flag and either defends, raises or announces a claim. But how can we be sure that the historical reality of Solomon's time is behind this theoretical recognition of the importance of both locations and the reason why the author mentions them? Archaeology seems to say the opposite.

With Gezer (1 Kgs 9:16) comes another peculiarity, although the only witness is the Bible: the addition of the key phrase concerning Pharaoh's daughter (see also 1 Kgs 3:1; 9:24) is increasingly mistrusted. Notwithstanding, a seed of truth is not to be ruled out [see excursus]. Gezer's

---

[62] As to the city wall and "Millo," they need not be discussed here, see H. Weippert, *Palästina*, pp. 457-61. Such defensive construction can be rated as part of a ruler's social prestige and therefore of social-politics. However, up to this point there are no archaeological clues; most recently, J. M. Cahill and D. Tarler, "Excavations Directed by Y. Shiloh at the City of David, 1978-1985," *Ancient Jerusalem Revealed* (ed. H. Geva; Jerusalem: Israel Exploration Society, 1994) 31-36.

[63] Fried, *Evolution of Political Society*, p. 175; E. R. Service, *Ursprünge des Staates und der Zivilisation: Der Prozeß der kulturellen Evolution* (Frankfurt am Main: Suhrkamp, 1977) 99.

[64] Not necessarily "new" construction, but rather large or small scale "expansions" or "reconstruction" of existing buildings, that is, changed to fit him and his purposes. Niemann, *Herrschaft*, p. 142, map 2.

[65] Even Joshua 11:10 knew of its country-wide leading function.

location is not as geopolitically strategic as Hazor or Megiddo, but it is important as a stronghold in the middle of the southern half of the coastal plain, between Egypt's brook and the Carmel/Acco. From the east the city does have value for exhibiting influence on the coastal plain to the north and south. From the west it is strategically valuable in exercising influence in the highlands. Gezer lies exactly between the Judean highlands in the south and the middle Palestinian mountains in the north, facilitating the ascent into the mountains from west to east. A strong power in Gezer can be uncomfortable for a ruler in Jerusalem, but he can guard himself against Gezer by placing Judean forces at Baalat/Kirjat-Jearim north-west of Jerusalem at the upper mountain's edge and additionally Lower-Bethoron at the lower mountain's edge,[66] between himself and Gezer. Best of all is when he controls Gezer himself.

Lower Bethoron, Baalath and Tamar appear in 1 Kgs 9:17b-18; while the function of the first two cities has been mentioned, that of Tamar is difficult to state since there is not even a decisive identification.[67] That this was a single remote place serving as a border point or stronghold is unlikely. Assumably it had the function of showing the ruler's presence in and claim to the south. Archaeology does not offer help in the interpretation of these places.

In verse 19 no further cities are mentioned, rather, Solomon's functional locations named in verses 15-18 are meant.[68] The biblical author now describes his ideas concerning the function of these cities as had been handed down in the traditionally glorious and phenomenal portrayal of Solomon. This summarising sentence, sprung from the idealised picture of the king doesn't provide any new details. "Lebanon" could be erroneous (LXX didn't yet know *lbnwn*) being an addition *ad maiorem regis gloriam*, but understandable in light of 1 Kgs 5:1, 4; it does not fit into the geographic framework at all.[69]

The section of verses 20-22 is pure ideological. Various "peoples," some of whom never existed,[70] serve here as the compulsory labourers. Verse 22 rejects the idea that Solomon had forced Israelites into com-

---

[66] For both places, Niemann, *Herrschaft*, pp. 20-22, 97-102, 106, 118-19, 143, 146, 151; for Baala(t) in particular, pp. 192-93.

[67] Rather to be identified with *'Ēn el-'Arûṣ = 'Ēn Tamar*; *ibid.*, p. 97 n. 434; less likely with *'Ēn Ḥaṣb*, most recently, Cohen-Yisrael, "Iron Age Fortresses."

[68] Würthwein, *Bücher der Könige*, pp. 109, 112; Niemann, *Herrschaft*, pp. 99-102.

[69] Würthwein, *Bücher der Könige*, p. 112; G. H. Jones, *1 and 2 Kings* (NCB; Grand Rapids: Eerdmans; London: Marshall, Morgan & Scott 1994) 217.

[70] Niemann, "Ende des Volkes."

pulsory labour, thus removing shame from both him and the Israelites, despite the detailed and realistic reasons given for the "discharge" of the northern groups during their negotiations with Solomon's successor (1 Kgs 12). If what verse 22 states were historic there would have been no reason for the northerners to complain to Rehoboam and distance themselves from the House of David after Solomon's death.

In summary, buildings of unknown art and size are claimed literarily in the biblical texts in all of the locations, but cannot be verified through archaeology. The historical content is not clear and our knowledge of cultural development in the 10th century BCE seems to advise scepticism. Only in Gezer is there a scenario open to discussion; maybe Solomon's possessing the city is more than an ideological claim. Hazor and Megiddo are traditional central cities, but without any recognisable (historical) connection with Judah and Jerusalem or David and Solomon. The naming of them could have functional and structural (ideological and legitimising) meaning.[71] In any case, neither city can be seen as part of a chain of cities created by Solomon for the border security of a "state."[72] At the most they represent a first isolated attempt at royal presence.

Trade in the Solomonic epoch is not the issue here. Solomon's alleged middle-man trade in war-chariots and horses (1 Kgs 10:28-29) can be set aside as this mode of Solomonic trade is most likely neither historic nor provable.[73] However, we hear in the Bible (typical for a "Third-world-country") of the import of luxury goods, prestige goods and craftsmen on the one hand and the export of raw materials (e.g., foodstuff) on the other hand (1 Kgs 5:20ff; 9:26-28; 10:14ff). Luxury goods and prestige goods are means of legitimising rule, so the biblical contention of Solomonic trade in such items must be dealt with here. Whoever wants to depict Solomon in a theological idealising manner as a world famous, wise, immeasurably rich king has to say from whence this wealth in the poor Israelite-Judean highlands at the end of a cultural depression comes.

---

[71] For this functionally typical structural language and manner of portrayal, in which successful kings constructed important buildings, organised armies and were victorious in wars, see P. Welten, *Geschichte und Geschichtsdarstellung in den Chronikbüchern* (WMANT 42; Neukirchen-Vluyn: Neukirchener, 1973); and Whitelam, "Symbols of Power," pp. 166-73.

[72] Until recently I, too, thought too optimistically; Niemann, *Herrschaft*, p. 101.

[73] Würthwein, *Bücher der Könige*, pp. 128-29; Schley, "1 Kings 10:16-29," pp. 595-601; Garbini, *History and Ideology*, p. 31; Knauf, "King Solomon's Copper Supply," pp. 178-79; Niemann, *Herrschaft*, p. 172.

Maybe historically the biblical writers are refering to the (friendly) relations (below in the excursus suspected as vassalage) of Solomon to Tyre as a starting point. An archaeological point of departure cannot be *Tell el-Ḫlēfe* (=Elat) as previously thought since it came into existence in the 8th century as the successor settlement of Ezion Geber.[74] Rothenberg reported settlement remains and ceramics from Iron Age I-II;[75] if this date is correct, maybe we can see in this fact an historical point behind the biblically reported trade and fleet cooperation between Hiram and Solomon. Taking the historicity for granted, the Phoenicians were the dominating part of this cooperation. Solomon as a vassal or subordinate of Tyre may have rendered assistance and partook (adequately?) in the trade profits. This may be a possible scenario, yet it is unproven. The "efficiency" of Solomon's acquired prestige-goods and wealth for legitimising his rule was of such "amount" that it did not prevent the collapse of Solomon's rule after his death.

C) *Government Functionaries*. The existence of full-time functionaries ("tertiary sector") in the service of the government organisation serves as an important characteristic when determining the degree of socio-political development in a given society. During the reign of Saul and David a "tertiary sector" is almost totally missing. Therefore, I have to refer to this time as a "chiefdom," and not yet a "state."

Saul relied almost exclusively on family members to serve as royal functionaries and David made only minimal changes; the vast majority of his dignitaries came from the "House of David," in other words, from his clan.[76] Only twice did their socio-political functions extend beyond the royal court.[77] David did introduce an important new dimension: based on common interests, he made and nursed relationships with local and regional elite in areas of interest to him.[78] The Solomonic epoch left a divided impression on the socio-political aspects of the governmental

[74] Probably *Ğezīret Farʿūn*, Niemann, *Herrschaft*, pp. 169-71 with bibliography.

[75] B. Rothenberg, *Timna: Das Tal der biblischen Kupferminen* (Bergisch-Gladbach: Lübbe, 1973) 201-207; M. Weippert, "Edom: Studien und Materialien zur Geschichte der Edomiter auf Grund schriftlicher und archäologischer Quellen" (Unpublished dissertation, Universität Tübingen, 1971) 433; O. Keel and M. Küchler, *Orte und Landschaften der Bibel, Band 2* (Zürich: Benziger; Göttingen: Vandenhoeck & Ruprecht, 1982) 290.

[76] Niemann, *Herrschaft*, pp. 3-17.

[77] Joab led the *ad hoc* summoned conscription and Ado(ni)ram is responsible for the forced labour (2 Sam 20:24). The existence and the extent of forced labour at the time of David is controversial; *ibid*, pp. 11-12.

[78] 2 Sam 15-19, where the Absalom revolt makes clear how important good (or bad) relations with the local and regional elite were for David. See especially also 2 Sam 19; 2 Sam 20:1-22, and for the interpretation, *ibid*., pp. 14-17.

organisation (1 Kgs 4):[79] on the one hand, there appears to have been little development in comparison to David concerning the functionaries in Solomon's immediate residential situation, as well as their number and range of tasks given to them, aside from the fact that "civilian" in contrast to "military" functionaries did increase under Solomon. On the other hand, there are two areas in which administrative and therefore socio-political development can be seen: forced labour (1 Kgs 4:6; 5:20-32; 9:15-23; 11:28) and Solomon's 12 נצבים (1 Kgs 4:7-19).

Forced labour is a socio-economic factor with possible socio-political consequences. In fact, it is very likely that forced labour did exist at the time of Solomon, because without it the refusal of the northern groups to pass on their allegiance to Rehoboam (1 Kgs 12) would be unexplainable. Because the product of this forced labour (above all Solomon's building projects) is not clear, the amount of forced labour actually used cannot be properly calculated and, hence, I decline to make any speculation.

D) *Attempt at Northern Expansion.* Within the Solomon tradition, with its idealisations, we come upon a section (1 Kgs 4:7-19) which gives the impression of a sober administrative document. This list has long been the basis of a strong argument claiming that Solomon was historically the far-sighted ruler portrayed in the theological and idealising description, who had his sphere of interest outside of Judah under effective control using an all-encompassing administrative system with "governors" at the top of administrative departments.[80] When it is normally presumed that David (and Solomon) controlled the entire northern region (even had influence from the Brook of Egypt to the Euphrates), then it is not amazing to hear of the hypothetical system of administrative organisation mentioned in 1 Kgs 4:7-19. However, in light of the rather modest archaeological finds in the main functional Palestinian cities of the 10th century BCE, one must be amazed by these reports of a thoroughly organised provincial and administrative system. One has to wonder, how did the House of David come to have such complete organisational control over the north as is seemingly the case in 1 Kgs 4:7-19,

---

[79] See provisionally summarised, *ibid.*, pp. 17-41.

[80] The classical/traditional *Opinio communis* was last represented by V. Fritz, "Die Verwaltungsgebiete Salomos nach 1 Kön 4,7-19," *Meilenstein: Festgabe für H. Donner* (ed. M. Weippert and S. Timm; ÄAT 30; Wiesbaden: Harrassowitz, 1995) 19-26; and *idem*, "Monarchy and Re-urbanisation: A New Look at Solomon's Kingdom," *The Origins of the Ancient Israelite States* (eds. V. Fritz and P. R. Davies; JSOTSup 228; Sheffield: Sheffield Academic, 1996) 187-95.

by W. Thiel's interpretation.[81] And why did this alleged highly differenciated administrative system break down so quickly (1 Kgs 12)? A short look at the biblical tradition of David holds some surprises.

David's campaigns that can claim historical probability were confined to a limited radius in the area around Gibeon in the north to the Negev in the south.[82] In the west one can only say David succeeded in defending the highlands against the Philistocanaanites (from Gibeon to Gezer, 2 Sam 5:25). Limited conflicts east of the Jordan are credible.[83] David and his people were conspicuously often to be found near Saul's urban base Gibeon (2 Sam 2:12-17, 18-32; 2 Sam 5:25). Even in the crisis between David and the Benjaminites, Gibeon played an important role (2 Sam 20:1-22). The pursuit of his enemies went non-stop from Gibeon to the northern border, because David enjoyed only sporadic or no influence up to the northern border/Abel Beth-Maacha. David never truly expanded beyond Gibeon to the north! However, David valued good relations with the elite in the north, which seemed to be necessary, but also proved helpful in time of crisis (2 Sam 9; 17:27-29). It seems that his authority wasn't so unlimited as to make it possible for him to give orders everywhere. The often underestimated Saul seems to have been active in at least as expansive an area (2 Sam 2:9) as the often overestimated David! It is worth noticing that David had to fight against his own family and his clan Judah to overcome his worst crisis.[84] The biblical record is correct in that the only basis for David's rule in the north was the voluntary and retractable support for his authority given by the northern groups. He did not lead any military campaigns in the north. The degree to which David or Solomon actually "ruled" in the north, and especially in Syria, must therefore be much more cautiously estimated. This also helps explain 1 Kgs 4:7ff. If the differentiated administrative network, as suggested in and assumed by research literature, the sociopolitical influence and the supposed degree of organisation of David's and Solomon's reign were all exaggerated, how then should 1 Kgs 4:7ff

[81] W. Thiel, "Soziale Auswirkungen der Herrschaft Salomos," *Charisma und Institution* (ed. T. Rendtorff; Gütersloh: Mohn, 1985) 297-314.

[82] 1 Sam 22:1-5; 25:2-43; 27:4-12; 30; 2 Sam 2:1-4, 12-17; 5:17-25 (?); 8:1-2; 10:1-14 (?); 12:26-31; 22:15-22; 23:8-39.

[83] With cities of origin (almost entirely Judah and Benjamin), P. K. McCarter, *II Samuel* (AB 9; Garden City, NY: Doubleday, 1984) 529, map, and the radius of activity of David's most important soldiers, 2 Sam 23:8-39 offers a realistic picture of David's military sphere of operation as opposed to the later theologically determined amplification of far beyond Syria or to the Euphrates.

[84] 2 Sam 15:1-19:16; the parallels with the family of Ḍâhir are evident.

be interpreted, if *not* as the reflex of an intensive administrative organisation?

I have already given details as to proposed new interpretations of the personnel and the geographic aspects of the so-called "list of Solomon's governors."[85] My point of departure entailed a fresh look at the structure (abnormal for a "provincial administrative system"), the personnel and the geographic information concerning Solomon's 12 representatives. A community, location or region is listed after the name of each person in 1 Kgs 4:7-19. The first (or only) location has been accepted as the "residence," in the sense of an administrative centre for the respective "province." However, if the unproved presumption of a pre-existing administrative system is questionable, then I suggest that the first (or only) location describes the family city, or the current place of residence, whereas each regional name represents the native region of the respective representative of Solomon. Also supporting this argument is the fact that two of the communities previously interpreted as provicial *capital* cities, were in reality very small, unimportant and unidentifiable (Makaz, v. 9, Arubbot, v. 10). If Solomon was just *beginning* to put together a corps of representatives for his plans and goals it is understandable that he would not immediately have found persons from the local and regional elite as representatives everywhere or be able immediately to establish his relatives or courtiers everywhere. This explains the uneven distribution of locations and representatives and the uneven size of the regions. These were in no way provinces with exactly defined borderlines. The names of further communities and landscapes might have been added whenever the hometown of the respective representative was little known or traditionally important cities were in his area. The detailed analysis leads to the following conclusion:

The persons mentioned in 1 Kgs 4:7-19 are selected relatives or courtiers of Solomon and the king's allies from the local and regional elite. They are Solomon's representatives spread out in the non-Judean northern areas. Because Solomon's presumed provincial administration, great building projects, and so forth, cannot be assumed to have existed, the above mentioned should not be seen as established functionaries who hold on to and expand Solomon's already existing stable dominion. It would be more accurate, and in better agreement with the archaeological evidence, to say that they are there to help transfer the authority and sovereignty, which had been offered to David on a voluntary basis

[85] Niemann, *Herrschaft*, pp. 27-41, 246-51.

(2 Sam 2:4; 3:12-13; 5:1-3; 16:7-8), to his successor, Solomon. It is no coincidence that the Bible does not report any voluntary pledges of allegiance by the northerners to Solomon as to David. There was obviously no parallel action. Solomon tried to make up for this through the careful construction of a network of representatives for his expansive plans and aims. Therefore 1 Kgs 4:7-19 does not document an existing administrative system, but rather the careful *first attempt* at building such a system.

Whereas Saul relied almost exclusively on his clan for the closest advisors in his dominion, the (relatively small) circle of leaders around David showed a limited, but nonetheless observable extension beyond his family.[86] The tendency shown in the list of Solomon's functionaries represents the evolution of this process, in that he installed as "representatives" (נצבים), alongside members of his family and courtiers, increasingly trustworthy men from the local and regional elite in the non-Judean north. The way he acted in regards to this socio-political question was guided throughout by one basic intention: Solomon distributed his representatives according to their reliable allegiance to him and according to the economic, trade politics and strategic importance of the area. His relatives and sons of his courtiers were stationed at especially important economic and strategic points. As people with their roots in the local and/or regional elite, the other officials could best make use of their own authority for royal purposes. As a matter of practicability, a complete uninterrupted network of officials had to be achieved as best as possible, but the availability of qualified candidates sometimes limited this, so that some geographically problematic "provinces" came into being (vv. 10,12 and 13 in connection with vv. 14 and 19). That one of Solomon's court functionaries in Jerusalem, Asarja b. Nathan (1 Kgs 4:5), played a co-ordinating role, shows that the נצבים were not in Jerusalem, but represented the king's interests in their home regions. That supports the idea of honorary posts, not fully institutionalised professional functionaries. As for the two relatives of courtiers listed as "representatives," here one can speak of institutional functionaries and the same goes for Solomon's sons-in-law. That means that at this time his reign *began* to partially develop from the status of a chiefdom into that of a state. For one of the distinguishing factors of a "state" is the presence of professional functionaries (tertiary sector).[87] What did the representatives do to stabilise

[86] See above, pp. 279-80, with nn. 77-79, and text discussion there.

[87] For details concerning the terms *chiefdom, state, tertiary sector* see Niemann,

royal influence and how did they serve a representative function for Solomon's interests? 1 Kgs 4:7 and 5:7f mention that they provided food for the court as well as for the horses of Solomon's army. The rotational system of supply, each of the 12 men being responsible for one month, was mechanically thought up and does not take into account the reality of the agricultural calendar. In contrast one need only look at the differences in the size and economic capabilites of the various regions. Furthermore, what is the use of the harvests from the Judean-Davidean royal property, from which one would expect the court to be provided? Traditionally, it has been thought probable that the נצבים were held responsible for helping supply the fortifications (1 Kgs 9:15, 17-19) in their areas. One notices, however, that not one of the fortified towns in the north (Hazor) or the west (Megiddo, Gezer, Lower Bethoron) was listed as the residence of נצבים, which would be expected from an administrative-organisational or military-strategic point of view or when considering the assumed job as provider and supplier. That again speaks both for the above mentioned interpretation of the first named communities in verses 9,10,13 and 14 as their hometown and not the "provincial capital." There is also no evidence that they had military enforcement power (troops).[88] In light of falling income from tributes in the sec-

Herrschaft, p. 7 n. 34; pp. 34-35. For now, a brief differentiation might suffice: In a chiefdom, the power is personalised and concentrated, whereas in a state it is institutionalised and organised by the elite and functionaries. A chiefdom is characterised by a society organised into two classes: "the chief and his personal clientele" and the "underclass." A state, on the other hand, has three classes: the ruler along with the ruling apparatus, an upper-class and an underclass. It is important to note that the ruling apparatus ("tertiary sector") is, for the most part, recruited from the upper-class and therefore tends to be a functional and institutional class of full- and part-time dignitaries between the ruler and the underclass/people. It is also characteristic of a chiefdom that the chief must constantly prove his authority. Horizontal forms or ranking systems exist equally alongside the vertical structures. Through further development of the vertical and hierarchic structures (stratification) of the society, the chiefdom gives rise to the state. A state, as opposed to a chiefdom, tends to constantly lay increasing claim to a monopoly of power, and tends to build an enforcement body. Power and rank are distinctly institutionalised. Fried, *Evolution*; Service, *Ursprünge des Staates*; B. Price, "Secondary State Formation: An Explanatory Model," *Origins of the State: The Anthropology of Political Evolution* (eds. R. Cohen and E. R. Service; Philadelphia: ISHI, 1978) 161-86; T. K. Earle, "Chiefdoms in Archaeological and Ethnohistorical Perspective," *Annual Review of Anthropology* 16 (1987) 279-308; Breuer, *Der archaische Staat*; Y. Portugali, "Theoretical Speculations on the Transition from Nomadism to Monarchy," *From Nomadism to Monarchy: Archaeology and Historical Aspects of Early Israel* (eds. I. Finkelstein and N. Na'aman; Jerusalem: Yad Izhak Ben-Zvi, 1994) 203-18; Renfrew and Bahn, *Archaeology*, pp. 153-94.

[88] The voluntary transfer of authority over the northern groups to David (2 Sam 5:1-3) corresponds, realistically and factually, to a denoucement, without the need of a battle for

ond half of Solomon's reign and after the construction of his Temple and palace as well as fortifications and other building projects of unknown size outside Jerusalem, one could expect to see a scale of financial planning and organisation (tax collection) with the implementation of the נצבים (1 Kgs 11:14ff in connection with 2 Sam 8:6). The abandonment of claims against the Phoenicians in Tyre to the rich "Land of Kabul" (1 Kgs 9:10-14)[89] might be a second sign of financial and liquidity problems along with lack of Solomon's political influence in the north.[90] However, nothing is known of tax collection during Solomon's reign. The existence of tax collection at all has become rather improbable in light of U. Rüterswörden's reasoning.[91]

In my view, the people in 1 Kgs 4:7-19 are to be seen as "delegates" or "representatives" who were trusted by the king and who had authori-

---

independence, of further recognition of the Davidic authority in 1 Kgs 12. Although this report is surely Judean tendentious, it shows that not one of the (according to the traditional view) powerful "provincial capitals" and their "governors" and "garrisons" (1 Kgs 4:9ff) stood up to fight for Solomon's successor. They were simply not "provincial capitals," there were no garrisons.

[89] Even if the most accepted (and in my opinion most probable) identification of Kabul with Ḥurbat Rōš Zayit (*Rās ez-Zētūn*; 10 km = 6 mi. east of Acco) is inaccurate, the biblical "Land of Kabul" must lie in the Plain of Acco, which was surely in the Phoenician-Tyrian sphere of influence; R. Frankel, "Upper Galilee in the Late Bronze-Iron I Transition," *From Nomadism to Monarchy: Archaeology and Historical Aspects of Early Israel* (eds. I. Finkelstein and N. Na'aman; Jerusalem: Yad Izhak Ben-Zvi, 1994) 18-34; Z. Gal, "Iron I in Lower Galilee and the Margins of the Jezreel Valley," *From Nomadism to Monarchy: Archaeology and Historical Aspects of Early Israel* (eds. I. Finkelstein and N. Na'aman; Jerusalem: Yad Izhak Ben-Zvi, 1994) 35-46. As to the situation of the Plain of Acco, which, because of its economic and geographic importance, must have been of interest to Solomon; see the thorough archaeological and cultural-historical analysis by G. Lehmann, "Zur Siedlungsgeschichte des Hinterlandes von Akko in der Eisenzeit," forthcoming. As to possible relations between the populations of the Ephraim mountains and the area north of the Plain of Acco; see D. V. Edelman, "The 'Ashurites' of Eshbaal's State;" *idem*, "Asher," *ABD* 1.482-83; and *idem*, "Ashurites," *ABD* 1.494. I suspect that Tyrian pressure on Solomon to renounce any claim as ruler of the plain, lies behind 1 Kgs 9:10-14. Such ambitions on Solomon's part may have been inspired by the relations between the populations of western Ephraim and the western Galilaean Asser region. That the (later) ideal king Solomon gave in to this pressure, or was forced to give in to it, was later theologically qualified through the assertion that the area was worthless anyway.

[90] 1 Kgs 5:1 LXX; Kuan, "Third Kingdoms 5.1;" and excursus at the end of this chapter.

[91] Rüterswörden, *Beamten* pp. 127ff, is correct in his assertion against the whole of previous research, which has not produced a justified counter-argument; see for example, J. Gray, *I and II Kings: A Commentary* (OTL; London: SCM, 1980) 130f, 135f; N. Na'aman, "The District System in the Time of the United Monarchy (1 Kings 4:7-19)," *Borders and Districts in Biblical Historiography* (Jerusalem Biblical Studies 4; Jerusalem: Simor, 1984) 167ff; G. W. Ahlström, *History of Ancient Palestine*, pp. 476, 478, 489, 508 and passim.

ty either through their personal relations with the ruler, or through their position as members of the local or regional elite, in which case they were to use this authority to better integrate the (north) Israelite groups and regions into the Judean-Davidic territory. An administrative-organisational planning intention[92] *could* have been coupled with this command stabilising function, for which the representatives should have prepared the way. All together, this formed a cautious, loose, wide-meshed, socio-political *attempt* at organisation. Later in northern Israel, the aftereffects of this attempt are nowhere to be seen.[93] Indeed, this attempt could only be successful as long as the population voluntarily co-operated with the representatives. And that could be assumed only as long as the requirements made by the king remained tolerable and understandable. That the delegates never came far with this attempt at stabilising the sovereignty in Solomon's interests, can be seen in the rapid retreat of the northern groups from the House of David after Solomon's death.

It can be recognised that through the installation of relatives and courtiers as well as trusted men from the local and regional elite of Israel as stabilising representatives of his claim to sovereignty, Solomon strove towards the better political-ideological and perhaps economic integration of the area north of Jerusalem. That marks the socio-political transition phase, from an organisation based on the ruler's family and courtiers to one taking in the local and regional elite, even if these elite cannot be described as truly professional functionaries ("tertiary sector"). From a cultural sociological point of view, Solomon's reign therefore represents the beginning of the change from a chiefdom to a state. This is only true of the north; corresponding evidence for such a socio-political organisation is not existent for the south (Judah) and the Philistocanaanite coastal area ruled, according to the leading research, by David and Solomon.

It is possible to fit Solomon's suggested presumably socio-political attempt at organisation in the north into a more comprehensive picture of the Solomon epoch and the general Middle Eastern history? If Solomon truly was a vassal to or under the influence of Sheshonq as sus-

---

[92] A much later realisation of a Judean division, might lie behind Josh 15:21-44, 48-62; Niemann, *Herrschaft*, pp. 251ff. When put together with Josh. 13-14; 15:1-20; 16-19; a theological ideal division is depicted. The unrealistic ideal helped to preserve the integrated historical report.

[93] Against Na'aman, "District System" pp. 194-201; T. N. D. Mettinger, *Solomonic State Officials* (ConBOT 5; Lund: CWK Gleerup, 1971) 124, whose arguments are not convincing.

pected below [excursus], is it then impossible that he tentatively expanded northwards tolerated by, supported by, or perhaps even in the interest of, Sheshonq? Maybe he was a kind of viceroy or governor to Pharaoh, rewarded with and authorised by the handing over of the Libyan aristocratic princess or "court-lady" and the city of Gezer as a foothold and instrument of power in the direction of the north. As a ruler of Jerusalem who watched over the north, could he not also, in the interest of Pharaoh, keep an eye on the coastal inhabitants, the Philistocanaanites?

However, is it believable, in light of the lack of sources from the tenth century, that an "administrative organisational document" (1 Kgs 4:7-19) would have been preserved in its original form until after the fall of Judah and Jerusalem?[94] Perhaps the question is not correctly stated. In no way does it have to be an administrative document in its original condition. The unique distribution of names, places and regions, as well as the unbalanced personnel and geographic details do not fit the description of a completed departmental system of government. For that, a more balanced and polished system would be needed (compare Josh 13-19). From the time of Rehoboam up to the fall of the northern kingdom, there was no time any real chance of Judah organising the north in the manner implied in 1 Kgs 4. Therefore, the text, that is the intentions and structures behind it, truly does belong to the time before Rehoboam and Jeroboam I, or it represents a plan for northern expansion after the fall of the northern kingdom.[95] The personal names listed in the text and the

[94] The question has most recently been raised and denied by P. S. Ash, "Solomon's? District? List," *JSOT* 67 (1995) 67-86. He reckons with oral information brought to Judah after the fall of the northern kingdom, "selected, abbreviated and garbled," with which the tradents in the south wanted to legitimise their claims. That is a possible scenario. However, Ash's attempt does not fully explain the specific structure of the information brought from the north. My own suggestion was obviously unknown to Ash; Niemann, *Herrschaft*, pp. 27-41, 246-51.

[95] Was the sphere of retroactively legitimised influence in the north ascribed to Solomon on such a scale as Hezekiah and Josiah planned to achieve? See Knauf, "King Solomon's Copper Supply," pp. 174-76. Another argument put forward by Knauf, *ibid*, pp. 178-79, fits into this consideration: if in 1 Kgs 4:19 according to LXX^{BL} "Gad" instead of "Gilead" (MT) is correct (which I consider at this time less likely, Niemann, *Herrschaft*, pp. 30-31, n. 120), then it can be argued that the names in the list (e.g., "Gad" in v. 19) could at least in part have their roots in the time of Omri because, according to the Mesha-Inscription (ll. 10-11) Gad was not Israelite before Omri's invasion, but rather only through the Israelite occupation. However, in contradiction to Knauf's suggestion, the other possibility must be considered, that the old Gilead area, which in the Omridic and post-Omridic time was expanded to the south, then included Gad (1 Sam 13:7). Maybe this expansion southwards to Gad led to the change from "Gilead" to "Gad" in the LXX text (likewise the unnecessary and geographically improbable addition of "Gad"

make-up of the geographical and local names' structure in 1 Kgs 4:7-19 need not necessarily be of the same mould. It would have been no problem for an informed author to put together the geographic structure for the covered socio-political diagram of the area as a "desktop project" and decide upon the points of interest based on his own knowledge, sometimes detailed and sometimes vague. Within this framework, a third possibility for the origin of the text, or at least its structure, can be seen: It could be the socio-political structure of important regions and places in the northern kingdom according to the knowledge and the intentions of an author from the north.[96] An author from Judah could also be behind this scheme.[97] Once such a geographic portrayal scheme was devised, it could have been filled in at various times with various people's names and fit into various text-complexes and chronological situations (i.e., for legitimasing purposes). With the precondition that 1 Kgs 4:7-19 was not first composed during the reign of Omri or later and then retroactively placed in the time of Solomon (which cannot be ruled out), the text and its structure make sense using the suggested interpretation as a cautious probing, a punctual attempt to gain influence with the help of the local and regional elite within the framework of the cultural and socio-political situation during the Solomon epoch. Together with the comprehensive regional historical and archaeological evidence, the text fits the natural ruling-structure element of a socio-political phase of formation, which began to develop again upwards after a "depression" (Iron Age IA). If 1 Kgs 4:7-19 represents an *attempt* at the stabilisation and expansion of Solomon's power, it sketches the *beginnings and not an already existing system*. It is possible that names now present in the list do not all stem from the Solomon-epoch. The structure could have been filled later with new material and names in comparable situations (Omridian Age?). In any case, whether the basic structure is Solomonian or Omridian, it is still true that it represents a cautious, wide-meshed first phase. It does not document a completed stable and efficient socio-political administrative structure. Such a structure would look different.

---

next to the realistic "Gilead" in 1 Sam 13:7). As a consequence of the change from "Gilead" to "Gad" in 3 Kgs 4:18 LXX, the remark "(in) the land of Sihon [from Heshbon, not far from Gad], the king of the Amorites and the king Og from Bashan" fit Gad. "Gilead" would then be the older name in v. 19 MT and the *lectio difficilior* (see Ash, "Solomons?" p. 75 n. 37; p. 78).

[96] Knauf, "King Solomon's Copper Supply," p. 178 (Omride time). It is possible that this knowledge came to Judah during the reign of Atalja.

[97] Ash, "Solomon's?" pp. 84-85, is thinking, in general, of the time following the fall of the northern kingdom.

3. RESULT: THE SOCIO-POLITICAL SHADOW CAST BY THE BIBLICAL SOLOMON

We can now sketch a shadowy outline of the socio-political situation of the Solomonic epoch. In light of the cultural situation in the central Palestinian highlands during the transition from Iron Age I to II, the non-existence of epigraphical witness to the presumed Solomon epoch is understandable. That fact sheds light on the modest cultural and socio-political situation. Archaeological results further illustrate this. Currently, it is not possible to place finds from the presumed Solomon epoch (traditionally within the last two-thirds of the 10th century) with any degree of certainty within Solomon's reign. It is, however, possible to create a rough sketch of the situation in which Solomon presumably belongs based on the known geomorphologic-environmental facts, the cultural development of Syria-Palestine and the archaeological research. The outline thus achieved could then, to some extent, be filled in by comparing regional as well as typical living conditions and behavioral structures from ethnological research. This is acceptable because the Palestinian ecology remained the same and the economic patterns and structures changed so little between the Late Bronze Age and the Ottoman Empire, that indeed such comparisons are worth while.[98] In light of such ethnological comparisons the critically analysed biblical evidence, differentiated between "story" and "history," can then be more fully appreciated.

When one looks at the socio-political structural elements of his time

---

[98] For good socio-structural comparative material, see among others, H. Kopp, *Al-Qāsim: Wirtschafts- und sozialgeographische Strukturen und Entwicklungsprozesse in einem Dorf des jemenitischen Hochlandes* (BTAVO B31; Wiesbaden: Reichert, 1977); W. Dostal, "The Shihūh of Northern Oman: A Contribution to Cultural Ecology," *Geographical Journal* 138 (1972) 1-7; *idem*, "Sozio-ökonomische Aspekte der Stammesdemokratie in Nordost-Jemen," *Sociologus* 24 (1974) 1-15; and *idem*, *Egalität und Klassengesellschaft in Südarabien: Anthropologische Untersuchungen zur sozialen Evolution* (Wiener Beiträger zur Kulturgeschichte und Linguistik 20; Vienna: Ferdinand Berger & Söhne, 1985) (South Arabia); see also the detailed report of scholarly investigations by Lemche, *Early Israel*, pp. 95-201; C. Kramer, ed., *Ethnoarchaeology: Implications of Ethnography for Archaeology* (New York: Columbia University, 1979); C. Kramer, *Village Ethnoarchaeology: Rural Iran in Archaeological Perspective* (Studies in Archaeology; New York: Academic, 1982); for Palestine see Cohen, *Palestine*; and E. A. Knauf, "Berg und Tal, Staat und Stamm-Grundzüge der Geschichte Palästinas in den letzten fünftausend Jahren," *Pracht und Geheimnis: Kleidung und Schmuck aus Palästina und Jordanien* (eds. G. Völger and others; Köln: Rautenstrauch-Joest-Museum der Stadt Köln, 1987) 26-35.

and reign, Solomon is recognisable, in rough outlines at least, as a typical oriental (small) ruler. He stands in the tradition and the evolutionary line of both Saul and David. Apart from the theological and critical make-over, Saul innovatively joined his two traditional roots: that of a Late Bronze Age city-state ruler and that of his own birth into a rural clan. Without giving up his clan base, he strove towards a territorial domination with an urban centre (Gibeon). His territory may have reached as far as the Plain of Acco. If this territorial claim was truly made by Saul, passed on to David and then to Solomon, it must have been given up at the latest by Solomon (1 Kgs 9:10-14). Although Saul held success and finally defeat at the hands of the Philistocanaanites of the coastal plain in balance, his differentiated and loose regional sovereignty was (even if it only lasted a single decade, with a size not achieved since the rule of Labaʾyu in the Late Bronze Age) as large, if not larger (and in any case economically more potent) than David's Judean homeland.

David was a rural Judean clan *chief*. The power relationships among the elite and the fighting between rural and urban parties upon his death imply this; but he too clearly recognised the value of an urban base. He also realised that every city isn't the same and that Hebron was of lesser functional geographic value than Jerusalem. Jerusalem held many advantages for his reign. David combined this insight with his traditionally tribal oriented organisation. It seems that David formed the tribe of Judah from two parts (1 Sam 21ff): Core-Judah from Bethlehem to Hebron, and various southern groups. Subsequently, he tried to integrate the *city-state* Jerusalem into his *tribal* rule. However, in his *coup d'état*, Solomon ended up doing the opposite. He brought the tribal Judah into the city-state of Jerusalem. But this remained an issue of contention. The tribal Judean elite occasionally made a play for power in Jerusalem (2 Kgs 11; 14:19ff; 21:24). As Knauf recently pointed out (in this volume), Micah 5:1-4 depicts the voice of rural Judah opposed to the possibly non-Judean urban dynasty in Jerusalem at the end of the 8th century BCE. In addition to moving the centre of power from Hebron to Jerusalem, with its long-term consequences, David's main achievement was the continuation of what Saul had only been able to temporarily accomplish: defending the highlands against the Philistocanaanites and expelling them from the area "from Gibeon to Gezer" (2 Sam 5:25). He was not active beyond the region of Benjamin to the north: he was satisfied with the role of recognised protector of the groups north of Jerusalem. This had nothing to do with modesty, but rather the authority was given to a person according to his actual achievements. In any case, it wasn't little that he so attained: a sphere of *influence* of this size was unknown in the preceding age. To his power base, Judah, David added Saul's political inheritance, those areas that transferred authority and duties to him. Peace outside his dominion spared him having to prove his ability as a powerful protector to hold all of Palestine from Dan to Beer-sheba and Tamar. Small campaigns in middle and south Transjordan remained regionally limited. David seemed less far-sighted, despite moving the northern Israelite Ark to Jerusalem, when it came to creating an integrated societal and religious symbolism for his entire dominion.[99] In regards to setting up such a basic symbolism, it looks as if Saul before him (Gibeon) and Solomon after him achieved more.

David's successor (son?[100]) Solomon worked at precisely this deficit. As an urbanite, more specifically a Jerusalemite, he enjoyed inherent advantages over David.[101] When it came to religion, Solomon attached himself to Saul's politics (Gibeon) and continued the religious integration of the north (Shiloh, the Ark) and the urban-Gibeonite tradition with the Jerusalemite tradition. It certainly seems that Solomon, even more than Saul, fits into the tradition of the Late Bronze Age Canaanite city-state ruler. He connected the rulal protoisraelite (Saul) and the rural Judean (David) with urban Jerusalemite traditions. Solomon was, more than David, the one who brought the north, south, and Jerusalem together to the future importance of Jerusalem.[102]

His socio-political goal was a complex, urban-based territorial rule. The duties and instruments traditionally needed for such complex sovereignty placed burdens on the population which surpassed the possibilities of David's economically modest clan area or Solomon's Jerusaelm. Thus Solomon's attempts were to no avail, though the dimensions were measurably more modest than later idealisingly portrayed. The burden

[99] Keel, "Theologie," p. 166. Does David show his rural Judean roots here, tending less towards urban supported territorial rule than the (more) urban oriented Saul and Solomon?

[100] Was Solomon David's son? In an excellent study Veijola, "Salomo," pp. 230-50, raised the possibility that he was more likely Uriah's son. The consequence that after David no other Davidic even sat on David's throne would have been so explosive for later Judean listeners or readers that the existing biblical report of David's scandalous adultary was the less embarrassing of the two and was used to cover the more serious scandal. See also Knauf, "Biblical Argument."

[101] Keel, "Theologie," pp. 167ff.

[102] Against Alt, "Jerusalem," pp. 253ff, in agreement with Keel, "Fern von Jerusalem;" and *idem*, "Theologie."

was enough to provoke the north to revoke the voluntary loyalty[103] they had given, not him, but David. The following concrete socio-political measures were taken:

1. The intensification of the legitimising role of Jerusalem through the reconstruction and expansion of the city temple, itself reclaimed as the temple of YHWH connected to both David and Israel; thereby supporting Jerusalem's claim to Judah *and* the northern groups.

2. The representative building of the palace and fortifications in Jerusalem of unknown dimensions.

The socio-political legitimising elements of rule mentioned above cannot be archaeologically proven. Their assumed existence is based solely on biblical reports. Through the general knowledge of the cultural development in Palestine and comparable ethnographic structures, it can be said that they might have existed.

3. If and what Solomon did, in fulfillment of the ancient oriental ruler's duty, in terms of buildings and fortifications outside of Jerusalem is unknown. Despite claims to the contrary, in the six places mentioned in 1 Kgs 9:15,17-19 nothing can, at this time, be archaeologically traced without a doubt to the Solomon epoch, much less to Solomon himself. If and in what measure Solomon even had influence in Hazor and Megiddo is not known to us. If in both locations archaeological caution is called for the possibility of Solomon having had influence in Gezer is greater. In the case of Lower Bethoron one can only, in general, point to the strategic (and in the case of Baalat, religious) value of the cities as seen from Jerusalem looking northwest toward the coastal plain and, in the case of Tamar, to the value as a foothold and an outermost point of influence in the south-east. A chain of fortresses for defending the border of the Solomonic territory and as such a characteristic of a state-typical border-guarding cannot be seen in these scattered points around Solomon's claimed sphere of influence.

4. If Solomon's marriage to a Libyan-Egyptian princess (or "court-lady") has a historical basis it could be connected with Sheshonq's cam-

[103] Herein possibly lies the key to understanding the *seemingly* incomprehensibly stupid actions on the part of Rehoboam when dealing with the northern groups (1 Kgs 12). I assume that he did not, as is theologically portrayed, place such hard and provoking demands out of youthful wantonness or on poor advice. As son of the (non-Judean, non-tribal) Jerusalemite Solomon, he saw the obvious need for forced labour, and insisted on the normal Late Bronze Age ruler's right of disposal over his subjects; see below n. 114. What one can accuse him of is a lack of sensitivity towards the northern groups, who were as tribal non-urbanites sociologically distanced from him.

paign into Palestine, an Egyptian occupation of Gezer and a transfer of the city to Solomon. That could hint at a vassal relationship giving Solomon the role of an Egyptian viceroy or governor in the direction of the Philistocanaanite coast on the one side and the central Palestinian highland north of Jerusalem on the other. At the same time this Egyptian-Solomonic vassel-relationship might hint at an Egyptian attempt to counterbalance the Phoenician-Tyrian influence on Solomon. The absence of Jerusalem in the Sheshonq list could be thus explained: There already existed such a relationship, or, more likely, a dependent relationship might have been achieved during the Sheshonq campaign. This scenario is neither archaeologically nor Egyptologically certain.

5. Either in connection with the suspected Egyptian supported vassel role "from Dan to Tamar," or as an independent strategy without Egyptian initiative, Solomon might have begun to gain a foothold in the north. He tried to stabilise his influence and authority through the establishment of members of the northern local and regional elite who gained his confidence, as well as relatives and courtiers. This cautious attempt and the failure of similar actions in Judah as well as the Philistocanaanite coastal plain, sheds an interesting light on the socio-politically loose, little structured organisation of Solomon's rule, which was still a *complex chiefdom* at the very most, only just beginning to head towards a state.

Likewise, there exists no epigraphical or archaeological evidence for this socio-political action. It is understandable in light of the general cultural tendency of this epoch not proven but deducted from the interpretation of biblical texts. This interpretation of 1 Kgs 4:7-19 lies consequentially within the tendency towards the development of personnel as socio-political instruments of rule by Saul over David to Solomon.

The presumed socio-cultural scenario is further emphasised through the ethnological comparison with Ḍâhir b. ʿUmar. This makes the pattern of action, which can be seen in the biblical record of David and Solomon structurally believable and historically possible. The comparison does not, however, fix the biblical portrayal of Solomon in the 10th century and therefore cannot be used as evidence to prove historically the 10th century's existence of Solomon as well as his biblical portrayal.

All told, one can say that some of the socio-political beginnings of the ruling organisation and legitimisation in Judah/Israel probably are rooted in the presumed Solomon epoch. Most important among these was the functional strengthening of Jerusalem's role, especially the religious components. This was also the factor with the most lasting consequences, especially because the second measure worth mentioning, the attempt to structurally integrate the northern groups' region through Solomon's "delegates," (if this measure even belongs only in the time of Solomon and not also/only in the time of the Omridic dynasty) failed to achieve its desired effect. The intention behind this measure (stronger governing integration) and the burden of unknown degree, which Solomon's royal building and representative projects caused, hindered each other. So the northern groups ended by withdrawing their loyalty to the House of David precisely because of the burdens caused by prestige measures, which were supposed to stabilise Solomon's reign.

It is especially important to emphasise that, contrary to the previous leading interpretation, the assumed socio-political measures behind 1 Kgs 4:7-19 represent a beginning, a first attempt at socio-political organisation. During Solomon's reign the time was not necessarily unfavorable for a strict socio-political unification of Palestine, because Syria, Mesopotamia and Egypt had little or no imperial expansive tendencies. But such a unification is a difficult task in a geomorphologically differentiated mountainous territory and among a population traditionally living in small groups. The situation was not such that the traditional groups with their regional composition and basis urgently needed strong central rule to guarantee their own survival. After David, a Judean tribesman, had succeeded in transforming the northern Judeans and the groups in the south of Hebron from a regional tribal power (Judah) to an urban-based power (Judah and Jerusalem), the main achievement of Solomon, an urbanite (from Jerusalem), was *attempting* to form a territorial reign combining Judah and Israel around his urban centre of Jerusalem. To do this Solomon first had to repress the Davidic/rural Judean element within his city-state Jerusalem. As soon as he had secured his position, he integrated the fresh Judean tribal powers so firmly into his Jerusalemite rule, that Judah steadfastly remained loyal to the "House of David." However, the feat of integrating the differentiated and separating (centrifugally) forces of the northern Israelite groups as a third party to the urban Jerusalemite and rural Judean basis proved to be too great in the given historical situation.[104] So Solomon's assumed

[104] The prospect of a loosely organised structural union of Judah with the northern groups on a culturally further developed niveau and under favorable foreign-political conditions, existed first during the time of Ahab, then even more so at the time of Jeroboam II and Uzziah. However, Judah and the northern kingdom soon fell into the maelstrom of the rising Assyrian empire. The perspective of profitable co-operation awakened during the Omride time and during the late Nimsidic time (Jeroboam II), was, if not Hezekiah, then under Josiah again intensively strived towards. The latter planned for the integration

attempt at socio-political organisation in the north, if indeed the structures, names, places and regions, handed down in 1 Kgs 4:7-19 truly belong to the Solomonic epoch, proved to be culturally evolutionary merely a first short trial without direct lasting results. The total absence of a corresponding attempt in Judah points in the same direction. The socio-political summit, upon which Solomon today appears to stand according to the contextual portrayal, prove to be ideological and theological, not historical.

of the "lost" northern area. This Greater Israel was projected into a time before the numerous hostile relations between Judah and Israel: into the time of the ideal ancestors David and Solomon.

EXCURSUS

Solomon, Rehoboam and "the Egyptian (Dynastic) Connection"

The following factors are in need of co-ordinated interpretation:
1. An unnamed pharaoh moves on Gezer, occupies it and gives it to "his daughter," who becomes Solomon's wife. The time frame of Solomon's reign is not clear. We can only assume it is to be placed before that of Rehoboam, whose enthronement can be dated by means of synchronisms around 926/5 BCE.[105] But the identity of the pharaoh who conquered Gezer remains a mystery (Siamun? Psusennes II? Sheshonq?).
2. "In the fifth year of King Rehoboam" Sheshonq moved on Palestine (1 Kgs 14:25).
3. The so-called List of Sheshonq[106] dates from his 21st year (929 or 924 BCE).[107] That means that the described military campaign took place before either 929 or 924 BCE. How long before is not at all clear.
4. The list does not mention Jerusalem: accident or intended? If on purpose, why?

Interpretation: The fact that the list dates from the end of Sheshonq's reign could imply that it summarises the achievements of his rule; it may represent the combined results of several campaigns.[108] The campaign(s) took place before 929/924 BCE, but how long before is uncertain. It is therefore likely that Sheshonq's Palestinian campaign(s) took place

[105] J. H. Hayes and P. K. Hooker, *A New Chronology for the Kings of Israel and Judah and Its Implications for the Biblical History and Literature* (Atlanta: John Knox, 1988) 16ff.

[106] Editions and interpretations of the Sheshonq list: J. Simons, *Handbook for the Study of Egyptian Topographical Lists Relating to Western Asia* (Leiden: E. J. Brill, 1937) 178-86, no. XXXIV; A. Jirku, *Die ägyptischen Listen palästinischer und syrischer Ortsnamen in Umschrift und mit historisch-archäologischem Kommentar herausgegeben* (Aalen: Scientia, 1967) 47-50; M. Noth, "Die Wege der Pharaonenheere in Palästina und Syrien: Untersuchungen zu den hieroglyphischen Listen palästinischer und syrischer Städte, IV: Die Schoschenkliste," *ZDPV* 61 (1938) 277-304 (= *idem, Aufsätze zur Biblischen Landes- und Altertumskunde II* (Neukirchen-Vluyn: Neukirchener, 1971) 73-93; B. Mazar, "Pharao Shishak's Campaign to the Land of Israel," *The Early Biblical Period* (eds. S. Ahituv and B. A. Levine; Jerusalem: Israel Exploration Society, 1986) 139-50; G. W. Ahlström, "Pharaoh Shoshenq's Campaign to Palestine," *History and Traditions of Early Israel: Studies Presented to Eduard Nielsen, May 8th 1993* (eds. A. Lemaire and B. Otzen; VTSup 50; Leiden: E. J. Brill, 1993) 1-16; Soggin, *Einführung*, pp. 135-37.

[107] E. Hornung, *Grundzüge der ägyptischen Geschichte* (Darmstadt: Wiss. Buchgesellschaft, 1992) 117; M. L. Bierbrier, "Scheschonq," *LÄ*, p. 585 (Sheshonq I, 945-924 BCE); Garbini, *History and Ideology*, pp. 29f (950-929 BCE).

[108] According to Ahlström, "Pharoah Shosheng," Sheshonq's list consists of combined reports from various parts of the armies under Pharaoh's control.

before Rehoboam's reign (from 926/5) during the time of Solomon. The fact that Sheshonq and Solomon were contemporaries is further supported by 1 Kgs 11:40. Taking into account the vagueness of the dates, in Rehoboam's fifth year (1 Kgs 14:25 = 922/921), Sheshonq was probably no longer living. Is it possible that the original biblical document contained "the fifth year of king Solomon" or "Jeroboam"[109] or "the fifth year of Sheshonq?" There are no facts which help answer this question. We are limited to proposing scenarios which appear reasonable in light of our knowledge of the tendencies in the biblical texts and within the framework of the historical situation. To do the opposite, to reconstruct the historical facts based on the biblical-theological picture, is not an option for a scientific-critical portrayal. Which means that one should distance oneself from vague or unknown dates. The interesting fact that Jerusalem is not explicitly mentioned in the Sheshonq list cannot be fully weighed as an *argumentum e silentio*. Because the missing fragments are so large it is possible that Jerusalem was not touched, but it is also possible simply that the name has not survived.[110]

Since the old argument does not bring us any further, a new way of looking at the problem is desirable. For this it must be clearly stated that the Egyptian king mentioned in 1 Kgs 9:16 might well have been Solomon's contemporary Sheshonq. If Sheshonq did, in fact, occupy the city and thereby (partially) destroy it, it would make sense, despite possible damage, to give it to a local or regional ruler of the hinterland/inland presiding near the important coastal plain as a vassal responsibility, in line with traditional Egyptian colonial practices. The ruler of Jerusalem would be one possibility for such a position. This makes even more sense in light of the fact that the region of Canaan, traditionally claimed by Egypt, had also become of political-economic interest for the aspiring Phoenician coastal power Tyre. 1 Kgs 5:1 LXX clearly supports this idea.[111] It may be that Egyptian diplomacy also used a marriage connection with the ruler of Jerusalem to further limit or end Tyrian influence. That Egyptian princesses were not generally given in marriage abroad may be true,[112] but the "princess" need not necessarily have been

---

[109] Knauf, "King Solomon's Copper Supply," p. 182.

[110] In this regard, *ibid*., pp. 181-82; Ahlström, "Pharaoh Shoshenq," pp. 15f. Knauf, "Biblical Argument," recently gave reasons why Jerusalem and Judah, as well as Shechem and its vicinity were intentionally not mentioned in the list.

[111] Kuan, "Third Kingdoms 5.1."

[112] Considerations and bibliographical references *pro et contra* in Soggin, *Einführung*, pp. 40, 70-71; Garbini, *History and Ideology*, pp. 27ff; Knauf, "King Solomon's Copper Supply," pp. 181-82.

a very high ranking member of the royal court (at least from the Egyptian point of view!). This would naturally have been seen differently in Jerusalem and taken advantage of for propaganda purposes. Additionally, Sheshonq was not a classic Egyptian or traditional Pharaoh, but an assimilated Libyan.[113] So it may be that in the Bubastidic times the ends occasionally justified the non-traditional means. For *Solomon*, Egypt's condescension to such an atypical "dynastic" marriage might have been worth an impressive gift (=tribute in the form of golden shields, 1 Kgs 14:25-26).[114] However, in later portrayals this temple tribute must have appeared a sacrilege or weakness, which could not be attributed to the Temple builder, but better to Rehoboam, he who gambled away the chance to unite Judah and Israel in his time.

The archaeological finds in Gezer do not bring any clarity to the picture.[115] If, according to Finkelstein, bichrome ware last appears in stratum XI and stratum X-IX was destroyed by the Egyptians (2nd half of 10th century), as most accept, then stratum VIII already belongs in the 9th century, which further means that this stratum including the 6-chamber-gate cannot possibly be connected with Solomon.[116] In light of the sparse excavation in Gezer to date, there might still be much left to discover. But for the time being, archaeology does not offer an answer to the questions as to whether Solomon truly built anything in Gezer, and if so what. That he did order some construction remains possible.

If the assumed vassal relationship of Solomon to Egypt (1 Kgs 9:16) as well as the vassal and economically dependent relationship with Tyre (1 Kgs 5:1 LXX and 1 Kgs 5:15ff; 9:10-14) are at least in tendency true, then in the eyes of later Jerusalem-centered thought, these relationships could easily have been mutated into a new constellation in which both

---

[113] E. Otto, *Ägypten: Der Weg des Pharaonenreiches* (Stuttgart: Kohlhammer, 1955) 218-26; Knauf, "King Solomon's Copper Supply," p. 182 n. 59.

[114] W. L. Moran, *The Amarna Letters* (Baltimore: Johns Hopkins, 1992) 366; EA 369; where the Pharaoh demanded both beautiful women and gold from Milkilu of Gezer(!); parallels pointed out to me by E. A. Knauf. We do not know anything about other dynastic marriages of Solomon besides the case of the Egyptian princess. Marriages with daughters of princes or petty rulers around Judah (and Israel) may be plausible (1 Kgs 11:1-8). Yet, not even in the case of Rehoboam's mother, Naama the Ammonite (1 Kgs 14:21,31) can we be sure that she was of royal birth; against Hübner, *Die Ammoniter*, p. 181. David and Solomon knew of the principle importance of close relations to the local and regional elite. In any case it was not necessary for a diplomatic marriage to be of *royal* origin.

[115] Niemann, *Herrschaft*, p. 97 n. 431 with bibliography; W. G. Dever, "Gezer," *The New Encyclopedia of Archaeological Excavations in the Holy Land* (ed. E. Stern; New York: Simon & Schuster, 1993) 502-05.

[116] Contra *ibid;* Finkelstein, "Archaeology of the United Monarchy," p. 183.

powers, Egypt and Tyre, zealously endeavoured to maintain friendly relations with the ruler of Jerusalem through both trade and marriage. From the Jerusalemite point of view, the interests of wisdom-oriented intellectual (1 Kgs 10:1-13), military (trade in arms), and economic (1 Kgs 10:14-29) worlds seemed to come together.[117]

Of course, this cannot be historically proved, but as a possible scenario it is based on historical facts. It integrates biblical tendential theological interpretation, which is, in a theological way, understandably rationed out to the ideal king Solomon (positive: connections to the Egyptian court) and to his imperfect successor (negative: payment of the "golden shields" tribute to Egypt).

[117] When Solomon is credited with making Jerusalem a world centre of importance and riches, this may represent a possibly dangerous oversimplification of itself and a deceiving hopefulness at the time of Hezekiah (2 Kgs 20:12-13), with even more dangerous consequences during the time of Josiah; see also Knauf, "King Solomon's Copper Supply," pp. 174-76.

THE WEIGHT OF THE BRONZE COULD NOT BE CALCULATED: SOLOMON AND ECONOMIC RECONSTRUCTION

DAVID C. HOPKINS

The "Age of Solomon": the phrase conjures the incomparable leader, administrator, builder, sage, and trader. Biblical tradition and scholarly reconstruction join to portray Solomon as the economic commander of his times. Solomon presides over an empire that took full advantage of its strategic geo-position, riding the fulcrum of a political-commercial axis embracing Tyre in the north and Arabia in the south. Solomon contracts with Hiram of Phoenicia, trades with the Queen of Sheba, and brokers horses for the Egyptians. His bureaucracy implements monumental construction, socio-economic reorganization, taxation, and conscription, producing an era of general and unprecedented prosperity. This constellation of claims is familiar from numerous studies touching on the economic basis of Solomon's reign. It encourages a close examination of data and method in reconstructing the economics of the Solomonic era.

1. SOLOMETRICS

In the first half of this chapter's title, the Deuteronomistic historian's assessment (1 Kgs 7:47) of the immeasurable weight of the pots, shovels, forks, and other equipment cast for the temple, calls our attention to the issue of quantification. Are there sufficient data to attempt what we might term "Solometrics," a particular brand of Solomonic cliometrics (the application of economic methods to the study of history)? Lamentably, the answer is "no;" we simply cannot attempt any cliometrics of the Solomonic period. The constraints that confront historians of the economy of ancient Palestine in general grow even more troublesome in Solomon's case. The data, literary or epigraphic, are not available. This reality is foiled by the fact that there are some figures preserved in the Bible. At least one commentator remarks on the exactness of the biblical presentation of Solomon and his achievements.[1] 1 Kgs 10:29 does report

[1] A. R. Millard, "Texts and Archaeology: Weighing the Evidence, The Case for King Solomon," *PEQ* 123 (1991) 23.

the price of imported chariots and horses (600 and 150 silver shekels respectively). But it does us little good to calculate conservatively that Solomon's total chariot force (1,400 chariots and 12,000 horses) demanded an initial investment of nearly 1.5 million silver shekels or, for animal lovers, over 700,000 rams, following Lev 5:15, for chariots alone.[2] Such calculations are nonsensical because we simply lack the data necessary to relate such numbers to the Solomonic gross national product or gross national consumption or any other broad economic context. Moreover, counting on the reliability of such figures on the basis of their exactness confuses precision for accuracy. So we are little better off than the deuteronomistic historian: we cannot calculate the weight of the bronze, the volume of the grain or the olive oil, the number of board feet of cedar, the value of the incense, or the extent of Solomon's chariotry and its impact on the availability of fodder from the fields or manure for the fields.

2. As many economies as wives

The narrative of Kings reports Solomon's seven hundred princesses and three hundred concubines (1 Kgs 11:3) and suggests their influence upon their husband was both considerable and pernicious. Any influence in reverse escapes mention; the disproportionate numbers undoubtedly weighed against Solomon's potential sway. While the balance may not have been tipped so unevenly with respect to Solomon and his economic world, we can naturally ask: How much economic influence did Solomon and the administrative apparatus gathered around him have? As noted, the text highlights Solomon's role as the economic commander of his times: administrator, builder, tribute collector, trader, transit toll-taker, and import-export broker. Yet the realities of ancient economies and the social institutions in which they were embedded suggest some immediate qualifiers.

First, it is crucial to recognize ancient Palestine's economic multiplicity. Solomon would have interacted with a set of economies founded on Palestine's fragmented landscape. This set included economies shaped especially in relation to heterogenous resource bases and varied distances to developed zones and trade corridors. Solomon's territory was

---

[2] C. E. Hauer, "The Economics of National Security in Solomon's Israel," *JSOT* 18 (1980) 65-66.

economically variegated. If Solomon's capacity was stretched in dealing with his thousand wives, it would have been no less tested in dealing with the intersecting economies and societies of his realm.

Solomon belongs, like all his royal cohorts, to the urban zone. How much did he influence life of the hinterlands? A conclave of officers (was it "a well-oiled bureaucracy"?) carried out the king's wishes. The district taxation system, also described in 1 Kgs 4, saw to plenteous provisions for the palace and barley and straw for the stables, implying a significant degree of economic coordination, if not planning. The construction of the temple may have acted as the most tangible unifying agant. As Meyers portrays it, the Davidic-Solomonic temple represented not just the scale of monumental architecture indicative of state-level society, but an integrating project, the creation of the whole society. "The requirements of manpower and materials that are part of the effort to produce monumental architecture contribute to the solidarity of a political unit. . . . The appearance of a temple on the human landscape," Meyers elaborates, "meant that a wide spectrum of the population had participated in some way in the construction process and hence shared in the communal welfare that the temple inaugurated."[3]

Yet the general rules of extremely high transportation costs and poorly developed managerial techniques limit the extent to which imaginations can roam in considering the width of the spectrum (social? geographical?) and breadth of the communal welfare that emanated from the temple. There are practical limits to the extent to which the politically powerful urban world of monumental construction and temple building ever dictated the life of the hinterlands. And beyond the requisitioning reach and grasp of the urban zone lay any ability to fashion integrated regional economies.

For the Solomonic period, there is precious little indication of regional integration in the archaeological record. If a central temple-palace complex struggled to unify the region's economy, perhaps the city building projects pointed to in 1 Kgs 9:15-19 carried the weight of this imposition, enabling and enforcing the administrative agenda, as Ahlström asserts.[4] Solomonic period building projects encompassed the Yadin trinity of Hazor, Megiddo, and Gezer as well as many other sites (almost

---

[3] C. Meyers, "David as Temple Builder," *Ancient Israelite Religion: Essays in Honor of Frank Moore Cross* (ed. P. D. Miller, P. D. Hanson and S. D. McBride; Philadelphia: Fortress, 1987) 366.

[4] G. W. Ahlström, *The History of Ancient Palestine from the Paleolithic Period to Alexander's Conquest* (JSOTSup 146; Sheffield: Sheffield Academic, 1993) 507-508.

exclusively unfortified) in what Mazar terms the "initial renewal of urbanization."[5] This is hardly compelling attestation of a heavy-handed administrative re-casting of the social and economic framework of 10th-century Palestine. Perhaps none should be expected. As Postgate writes of Assyrian imperial rule, "its economic structure . . . consists of the impression of an administrative pattern upon underlying and largely unchanging economic realities."[6]

Yet even the specific modes of administration no longer add up to an unequivocal burst of Solomonic nation building. Many archaeologists contest the dating and question the purported constructional unity of the famous four-entryway gates that bind Hazor, Megiddo, and Gezer into a Solomonic feat in most reconstructions.[7] While there is every reason to continue to note the eruption of these three sites into "new fortified governmental centers," these cities do not exhibit a uniformity implied by centralized planning and construction.[8] Other sites heeding this impetus toward urbanization (such as Lachish, Tell el-Far'ah North, and Tell en-Naṣbeh) receive their fortifications in the 9th century.

"Israel and Judah," editorializes the Kings historian, "were as numerous as the sand by the sea; they ate and drank and were happy." "During Solomon's lifetime," the commentary continues, "Judah and Israel lived in safety, from Dan even to Beersheba, all of them under their vines and fig trees."[9] While some commentators reflect on the "burgeoning economic development" of Solomon's era,[10] Walter Brueggemann has noted the undertone of irony in these two summaries, coming as they do amidst the report of Solomon's bureaucracy, taxation system, daily provisions, and cavalry. If Solomon and his retainers were eating that well, ain't nobody sitting down with their feet up enjoying the fruits of their

---

[5] A. Mazar, *Archaeology of the Land of the Bible 10,000-586 B.C.* (ABRL; New York: Doubleday, 1990) 388.

[6] J. N. Postgate, "The Economic Structure of the Assyrian Empire," *Power and Propaganda: A Symposium on Ancient Empires* (ed. M. T. Larsen; Mesopotamia 7; Copenhagen: Akademisk, 1979) 214.

[7] Z. Herzog, "Settlement and Fortification Planning in the Iron Age," *The Architecture of Ancient Israel from the Prehistoric to the Persian Periods* (ed. A. Kempinski and R. Reich; Jerusalem: Israel Exploration Society, 1992) 231-74.

[8] *Pace* J. S. Holladay, Jr., "The Kingdoms of Israel and Judah: Political and Economic Centralization in the Iron IIA-B (*ca.* 1,000-750 BCE)," *The Archaeology of Society in the Holy Land* (ed. T. E. Levy; New York: Facts on File, 1995) 372.

[9] 1 Kgs 4:20, 25.

[10] C. Meyers, "The Israelite Empire: In Defense of King Solomon," *Backgrounds for the Bible* (ed. M. P. O'Connor and D. N. Freedman; Winona Lake, Ind.: Eisenbrauns, 1987) 183.

own labors.[11] More crucial is the leveling of Israelite and Judahite societies implicit in the assertions: all share in the pax Solomonic and the prosperity of his reign. Yet the social reality of ancient Palestine again offers a fractured portrait. Ancient Israel and Judah were not a society so much as a constellation of "plural societies."

The nature and structure of this constellation were inherited from Bronze Age urban-based polities (the "city-states") with their proportionately tiny aristocracy served by an assortment of townspeople and sustained by a hinterland populated by farmers and nomadic pastoralists. This prevailing social structure had undergone a striking effacement in the highlands during the Late Bronze Age and even in the coastal plains and valley systems during the Late Bronze Age-Early Iron Age transition period. But this society re-surfaced in the increasingly urbanized life of the Iron Age monarchies. However benevolent and prosperous one may wish to imagine Solomon and his era, his rule as depicted in Kings embraced this Bronze Age tradition more than anything else: a centralizing, palace-temple focused, urban-ruled polity. However effective Solomon's role as the economic commander of his capital city, there is no reason to believe that his command sought to spread economic welfare beyond its walls.

Such an assessment of the embeddedness of Iron Age economies and social structures in Bronze Age traditions does not dismiss the new political phenomenon constituted by any Davidic or Solomonic territorial unification or the decisive impact of tribal traditions in the ongoing life of the Highlands. Under the auspices of successor policies, the Highlands did eventually achieve a degree of homogenous material culture. Yet, even Judahite and Israelite nation-states replicated the city-states of the Bronze Age to a far greater extent that they anticipated the nations of the European industrial age. The nationalistic ideology of the biblical literature projects a unity that simply did not exist economically or sociologically. Economic reconstruction (even of the Solomonic period) must not let the potency of this nationalistic ideology skew its portrayal.

---

11 W. Brueggemann, "The Vine and the Fig Tree," *CBQ* 34 (1981) 195-98.

3. SOLOMON LIVED IN A FOREIGN COUNTRY: THEY DID THINGS DIFFERENTLY THERE . . .[12]

Escaping the snare that would cast Solomon's world in terms of the economics that rule the western nations, reconstruction must still confront the foreignness of the economy of ancient Israel and Judah, in a word, its embeddedness in the pre-industrial, agrarian, aristocratic ancient world. This concept of "embeddedness" encapsulates the insight of economic anthropologists that economic relationships have non-economic, social, cultural and political parameters.[13] "Embeddedness" characterizes the modern economy as well; our economic behavior takes place in a non-economic matrix, albeit generally transparent to us. But non-economic parameters had a greater weight in the pre-industrial world. For example, modern "single-stranded," short-lived economic relationships contrast with "multi-stranded," kin-based relationships characteristic of pre-modern economic exchange. Thus, Solomon and his royal administrators were not members of the modern species *homo economicus*. Yet their embeddedness did not preclude their making rational economic choices (just like we moderns always make!). However one characterizes the kind of economy that existed in the pre-capitalist world, it remains crucial to recognize that a variety of economic mechanisms (from gift giving to marketing) stimulated and directed the provisioning of ancient society.

Can anything be said of these mechanisms in the 10th century? Literary traditions of Solomon's trading activities, especially with Sheba (1 Kgs 10), may be taken to represent the gift-giving and sanctions of reciprocal exchange. His taxation and feasting at the temple dedication suggest the surplus accumulation and hierarchical distribution of re-distributive exchange.[14] Does the importation of horses and chariots represent the "economizing" exchange of goods in a price-producing market arena? Whether these traditions actually pertain to the 10th century or not, they are poor informants: the relative weight of each kind of exchange mechanism and the relationship between them remain unknown. Moreover, the examples are confined to the royal house. Nothing is com-

---

[12] "The past is a foreign country, they do things differently there." This opening line of L. P. Hartley's *The Go-Between* is quoted in D. Lowenthal, *The Past Is a Foreign Country* (Cambridge: Cambridge University, 1985) xvi.

[13] See the articles and bibliography gathered in S. Plattner, *Economic Anthropology* (Stanford, Calif.: Stanford University, 1989).

[14] 1 Kgs 3:15, 8:5, 8:62-66.

municated about the operation of private ventures, if such existed. How the society at large was provisioned we hardly learn. The archaeological record offers only indirect help in gauging the assemblage of economic mechanisms that commanded the ebb and flow of goods and services in the10th century.[15] The absence of the realia of market-oriented institutions (money, standardized weights, specialized containers) suggests an underdeveloped economy.

4. Debating a dead horse trader

No treatment of Solomon's era fails to note Palestine's position on a strategically crucial commercial and military crossroads. Major trade routes funneled through Palestine from all four compass points: from Europe through the Phoenician ports, from Egypt along the Mediterranean coast, from Arabia and East Africa through the Gulf of Aqaba/ Eilat, and from Syria and Mesopotamia skirting the Arabian desert. With David securing command of the overland routes, the Solomonic empire took full advantage of this geo-position, notably in creating what Malamat has called "a North-South political-commercial axis embracing Tyre-Israel-Sheba, with branches across the Mediterranean and Red Seas."[16] Solomon's court was an active participant in trade, e.g., with Hiram and Sheba, to the extent of owning, rather than merely taxing, the transit trade through Palestine.

Solomon also served as "a middleman," and, as a horse trader, "opened," in Ikeda's grand eloquence, "a 'window' to the international trade, through which contemporaneous cultural 'trade winds' could breeze in and out, conveying innumerable cargos of costly goods and commodities, together with their cultural tastes, among the royal courts of the day."[17] But there are three economic qualifications to this enthusiastic rendering of Solomon's grand empire.

---

[15] See section 5 below.

[16] A. Malamat, "A Political Look at the Kingdom of David and Solomon and Its Relations with Egypt," *Studies in the Period of David and Solomon and Other Essays* (ed. T. Ishida; Winona Lake, Ind.: Eisenbrauns, 1982) 191.

[17] Y. Ikeda, "Solomon's Trade in Horses and Chariots in Its International Setting," *Studies in the Period of David and Solomon and Other Essays* (ed. T. Ishida; Winona Lake, Ind.: Eisenbrauns, 1982) 238. With respect to Solomon as horse trader, the biblical tradition offers nothing more than an ambiguous reference to equine importance, no sales intermediary at all; J. K. Kuan, "Third Kingdoms 5.1 and Israelite-Tyrian Relations During the Reign of Solomon," *JSOT* 46 (1990) 31-46. Participation in transit trade from

A) The flow of goods along this Phoenicia-East Africa-Arabia route as well as the rest of the international trade network responded to economic forces of supply and demand but more significantly to military-political coercion. Both stimuli remained dampened in the 10th century. In other words, there is a fundamental contradiction in portraying vast wealth gained through control of transit trade as Solomon takes advantage of an interlude in which the traditional coercive forces of Egypt, Mesopotamia, and Anatolia are quiescent. The severe paucity of imported items in the archaeological record of Palestine's 10th century (what was the cumulative value of the trade?) puts teeth in this caution.

B) The relationship between Hiram and Solomon certainly saw Hiram in the ascendancy. Biblical tradition suggests as much in its portrait of Hiram's dictation of the terms of trade with Solomon (1 Kgs 5:6 versus 5:9). Moreover, the exchange of timber, gold, and skilled labor for agricultural products suggests the kind of unbalanced exchange that takes place between a more developed and a less developed society. The facts that Solomon delivered his commodities yearly (*shanah beshanah* 1 Kgs 5:11) and that his payments failed to "please" Hiram (1 Kgs 9:12) both reinforce this picture of Hiram as the superior in the relationship.

C) The imports listed in Kings fit perfectly well among those commodities known archaeologically and epigraphically to have filled the hulls of ships and ornamented the backs of donkeys and camels: precious metals, ivory, bizarre animals, in a word, preciosities with lofty value to weight ratios. The exchange of these commodities did not enhance the life of the country; they were destined for the court and circulated only within the circumscribed range of royal administration. They served to reinforce the legitimacy of royal rule, but had a negligible economic impact outside the palace sector.[18]

The ways in which the monarchy exerted itself to provide items of exchange for these preciosities did register in town and country. Through its taxation, conscription, patronage, and juridical powers, the ruling

---

Arabia and East Africa responded to the same incentives as did Tel Masos in the eleventh century, even discounting the fleet at Ezion-Geber; I. Finkelstein, "The Iron Age 'Fortresses' of the Negev Highlands: Sedentarization of the Nomads," *Tel Aviv* 11 (1984) 189-209.

[18] M. Elat, "The Monarchy and the Development of Trade in Ancient Israel," *State and Temple Economy in the Ancient Near East* (OLA 6; Louvain: Department Oriëntalistiek, 1979) 2.546; see also D. W. Jamieson-Drake, *Sribes and Schools in Monarchic Judah: A Socio-Archaeological Approach* (SWBA 9; Sheffield: Sheffield Academic, 1991) 107-35, on the limited circulation of luxury items.

house encouraged and commanded the production of the most tradeable (i.e., the most liquid) agricultural products: wine, oil, perfume, and spices.[19] Thus monarchical policy could spur the intensification of production, a boon for the elite, though a bust for the rural poor. Again, there are as yet no archaeological indicators that Solomon's reign instituted such policies.

5. The Center That Does Not Hold

Analysts have rightly placed the construction of the temple in the context of Solomon's international aspirations. The key point is often taken to be ideological, that the temple complex legitimated Solomon according to the ancient Near Eastern cultural expectations. But there was an economic reality as well: the temple served to facilitate international contracts, including trading contracts. The temple brokered transactions and served as the institutional context for contracts. The oath before the gods cemented agreements, political treaties as well as the terms of exchange. In economic terms, as Silver has argued, temples lowered the transaction costs of international commerce by providing a sense of shared security between exchange partners.[20]

The temple did offer legitimation of Solomon in the eyes of his neighbors. Such legitimation, we are told, had a hegemonic edge: it symbolized Solomon's right to dominion over even his international subjects. Thus, temple has been associated with empire. Even the size of the temple, grander than known parallels in Syria-Palestine, reflected the extensive nature of Solomon's imperial territory, the greatest in the region's history.[21] Goods flowed from all corners of Solomon's domain as Jerusalem occupied the economic, political, and ideological center of the realm: "every one of [the kings of all the earth] brought a present, objects of silver and gold, garments, weaponry, spices, horses and mules, so much, year by year" (1 Kgs 10:25). Solomon's kingdom was "the major power of its day," according to Malamat.[22] Some would even use the jar-

[19] D. C. Hopkins, "The Dynamics of Agriculture in Monarchical Israel," *Society of Biblical Literature: 1983 Seminar Papers* (ed. K. H. Richards; Chico, Calif.: Scholars, 1983) 177-202.

[20] M. Silver, *Economic Sturctures of Antiquity* (Contributions in Economics and Economic History 159; Westport, Conn.: Greenwood Publishing, 1995) xxi-xxii, 3-38.

[21] Meyers, "Israelite Empire," p. 190.

[22] Malamat, "Political Look," p. 189.

gon of world systems theory to label Jerusalem "the center of an empire and the locus of activities and structures that impinged upon the 'periphery.'"[23] Or again, Solomon's realm was "a highly complex political conglomerate with Judah as its nucleus . . . a supra-national system of political and economic domination of a center over a periphery."[24]

This standard imperial model requires a core that simply does not exist on the ground in 10th-century Palestine. Judean settlement patterns tell the story.[25] In the 10th-century Jerusalem did emerge, once and for all, as the center of its region. Yet the settlement site hierarchy still approximated the rank-size model. Two centuries would have to pass before Jerusalem loomed as a primate site even within its own circumscribed territory. At the same time (the 8th century), Judah's settlement landscape reached its Iron-Age zenith, and Jerusalem itself took on world-class proportions. 10th-century Jerusalem was not the center of an empire when it was just barely the center of its contiguous domain. The 10th century simply continued the Highland socio-political transition (begun in some places at the end of the 13th century, in Judah in the middle of the 11th century) that eventually coalesced in the separate monarchies of Judah and Israel. If there remains something to be said for a Davidic or Solomonic unification of northern and southern highland regions as well as the lowlands, valley systems, and transjordanian highlands, the model will have to involve some sort of "personal union"[26] or supra-tribal kingdom.[27]

---

[23] Meyers, "Israelite Empire," p. 189.

[24] Malamat, "Political Look," p. 196.

[25] A. Ofer, "'All the Hill Country of Judah': From a Settlement Fringe to a Prosperous Monarchy," *From Nomadism to Monarchy: Archaeological and Historical Aspects of Early Israel* (ed. I. Finkelstein and N. Na'aman; Jerusalem: Yad Izhak Ben-Zvi and Israel Exploration Society; Washington, DC: Biblical Archaeological Scoiety, 1994) 102-106; I. Finkelstein, "Environmental Archaeology and Social History: Demographic and Economic Aspects of the Monarchic Period," *Biblical Archaeology Today 1990: Proceedings of the Second International Congress on Biblical Archaeology, Jerusalem June-July 1990* (ed. A. Biran and J. Aviram; Jerusalem: Israel Exploration Society, 1993) 62-63.

[26] A. Alt, "The Formation of the Israelites State," *Essays on Old Testament History and Religion* (Garden City, NY: Doubleday, 1966) 282.

[27] Ø.S. LaBianca and R. Younker, "The Kingdoms of Ammon, Moab and Edom: The Archaeology of Society in Late Bronze/Iron Age Transjordan (*ca.* 1400-500 BCE)," *The Archaeology of Society in the Holy Land* (ed. T. E. Levy; New York: Facts on File, 1995) 403-10.

6. Appealing to Solomon

More cogently than many others, Ian Hodder has called attention to the subjectivity of the pasts we construct in relation to contemporary power strategies: "the past," he writes, "is subjectively constructed in the present and the subjective past is involved in power strategies today."[28] Positing a Solomonic empire may plead some case today, whether one keys on the laudatory aspects of Solomon's diplomatic rather than militaristic maintenance of his hegemony or his fundamental dependence upon surpluses created by the diligence of the people in developing and husbanding the land. It certainly performed such a role for the pre-exilic Deuteronomistic historian. As Knoppers maintains:

> "in the seventh century BCE, the Deuteronomist's presentation of Solomon's success would have special appeal. By this time, the monarchy's appeal had worn thin for many. Judah had already suffered through centuries of foreign threats and domination. In the divided monarchy, tribute usually flowed from Jerusalem elsewhere, not vice versa. . . . Judah and Israel's kings sometimes plundered their own temple treasures to meet foreign demands for tribute. Monarchs found it necessary to embrace vassalship. . . . By constructing a Solomon in the tenth century who enjoys unmitigated success in domestic politics, interntional commerce, and national cult, the Deuteronomist provides ideological justification for monarchical ambitions . . . ."[29]

Josiah's temple refurbishing, cult reforms, and expansionistic national ambitions find a hearty second in the portrait of the Solomonic Age: "in no other period in Israelite history does a leader or king receive such a encomium of material and verbal tribute."[30] And tribute does dominate the final panel of the presentation in Kings: the building of the temple ushers in an era made rich by the tribute of the nations. While not an economic argument *per se* for signing on to Josiah's ambitious program, the emphasis on tribute realistically portrays the chief means by which ancient conquerors enriched themselves. The surest, swiftest form of enrichment was the golden target strategy.[31] Josiah's own aspirations for tribute find a model in the portrait of Solomon.

---

[28] I. Hodder, *Reading the Past: Current Approaches to Interpretation in Archaeology* (2nd ed.; Cambridge: Cambridge University, 1991) 166.

[29] G. N. Knoppers, *Two Nations Under God: The Deuteronomistic History of Solomon and the Dual Monarchies, 1: The Reign of Solomon and the Rise of Jeroboam* (HSM 52; Atlanta: Scholars, 1993) 133.

[30] *Ibid.*, p. 126.

[31] T. F. Carney, *The Shape of the Past: Models and Antiquity* (Lawrence, Kan.: Coronodo, 1975) 172.

7. Ships or not, Solomon was fleeting

"The weight of the bronze could not be calculated." The historians in Kings meant for readers to be impressed, not to get out calculators. "The accruing of bullion, vessels, and other valuable artifacts in Jerusalem is not intended to be credible, but incredible."[32] The historiographer aims to promote the incomparable achievments of Solomon. And the modern audience has been convinced to the extent that it has turned the Kings portrayal of the lifetime of Solomon (*bymy slmh* 1 Kgs 4:21) into the "Age" of Solomon (cf. the title of the 1994 ASOR/SBL Hebrew Bible, History, and Archaeology Section). The rationales for this heightening may lie in an assessment of the "Age's" durability or of its transformative significance or of its uniqueness.

Unfortunately, archaeology and even economic history can prepare themselves for the incomparable, but it runs counter to standard operating procedures. Archaeological data privilege long term trends and structured patterns of behavior over individual variation. The realia unearthed and handled by archaeologists eclipse elements of the organization and the relations of production that can only be "invisible" in the archaeological record. In the absence of data, the models utilized in economic reconstruction may not be astute enough (certainly not endowed with Solomonic sagacity) to recognize the incomparable, even if it is the Age of Solomon.

Solomon's glory, as Meyers notes, was ephemeral: "For a fleeting period of time in millennia of human existence and civilization in the ancient Near East, the narrow strip of land between the Jordan River and the Mediterranean Sea was united under a centralized government and controlled by indigenous rulers." Is it truly conceivable, is it probable, that this "fleeting" rule effected some measure of durable change, least of all in economic structures? Despite all the details of the biblical portrait and the archaeological signals of the Iron Age transformation underway, customary depictions of a trade-tax, and tribute-sustained "Age of Solomon" disintegrate and fade due to deficiencies in data and methods.

---

[32] Knoppers, *Two Nations Under God*, pp. 130-31.

ON DOING SOCIOLOGY WITH "SOLOMON"

Niels Peter Lemche

Recent scholarship has called into jeopardy the very existence of the united Israelite kingdom in the 10th century BCE.[1] The archaeological remains from Judah seem to pre-exclude that a major kingdom could have been established here already in the 10th century, if at all in the Iron Age of Palestine.[2] It goes without saying that should this be the case, then it is just as difficult to retain the biblical picture of Solomon as the great monarch of his time, a king for whose favor even the Pharaohs of once mighty Egypt sued.

To present a sociological analysis of the kingdom of Israel in the time of Solomon would in this way be impossible, as there was no kingdom to study. A scholar interested in presenting a sociological analysis of Solomon's time would necessarily be forced to turn to an analysis of the biblical text, not in order to paraphrase this with the aim of retaining the basic historicity of the text itself as a source for the study of the past, but in order to explain why at all this text was written. What were the sociological motives for composing such a text, and what kind of a kingdom is in fact presented by the author(s) of the tales about Solomon as we find them in 1 Kings. Did this (these) author(s) entertain any idea of the Kingdom of Solomon as a parallel to socio-political aspirations of their

[1] Opening the game: G. Garbini, *History and Ideology in Ancient Israel* (London: SCM, 1988) 21-32. T. L. Thompson, *Early History of the Israelite People from the Written and Archaeological Sources* (SHANE 4; Leiden: E. J. Brill, 1992); N. P. Lemche, "Is It Still Possible to Write a History of Ancient Israel?" *SJOT* 8 (1994) 165-90, especially pp. 183-89; D. J. Jamieson-Drake, *Scribes and Schools in Monarchic Judah: A Socio-Archeological Approach* (SWABA 9; Sheffield: Sheffield Academic, 1991); H. M. Niemann, *Herrschaft, Königtum und Staat* (FAT 6; Tübingen: J. C. B. Mohr, 1993). Closing in: I. Finkelstein, "The Archaeology of the United Monarchy: An Alternative View," *Levant* 28 (1996) 177-87; see also, in relation to the Bet-Dawd inscription from Tel Dan, N. P. Lemche and T. L. Thompson, "Did Biran Kill David? The Bible in the Light of Archaeology," *JSOT* 64 (1994) 3-22.

[2] Both Jamieson-Drake, *Scribes and Schools*, and Finkelstein, "Archaeology of the United Monarchy," agree on this, although they still speak about the kingdom of David and Solomon as having been a small chiefdom in the central highlands of Palestine. However, the rulers of such a chiefdom are not the great kings of the united monarchy of the Old Testament.

own time, or does the narrative simply reflect realities of their own time. A sociological analysis of the narratives about Solomon would thus, in itself, be a valid subject, not because we would know more about Solomon's own time (which probably never was), but because the narratives would reflect the social world of the author(s).

It would thus hardly be difficult to demonstrate that the image of a kingdom as reflected by 1 Kgs 2-11 is to a certain degree a never-never kingdom of a fairy tale, although as is so often the case in the OT, the narrative is not a tale in itself but rather an elaborate literary product which includes a series of fairy tale motifs and plots.[3] This would place the narratives about Solomon not only on line with those about his father, David, but would also line up these narratives with, for example, the patriarchal narratives and other narrative complexes in the OT.[4] The place to look for the milieu of the production of such a narrative (a quest which is truly a historical one) would probably be among a literary elite not only used to writing various sorts of official documents but also interested in written literature; the demand would be that this group would be in possession of the leisure time which enabled it to pursue such utterly non-productive interests. Literature in this sense is certainly a luxury and would reflect a fairly complex society with an extended scribal class. Such a sociological analysis of the narratives would certainly be productive and worth-while, although the historical Solomon would have to go.

This is one way of proceeding with the theme. Another would be to look into the minds of the scholars who have almost senselessly been paraphrasing the biblical text, molding the period of Solomon into a time of greatness in ancient Israel, probably the culturally most productive era of the Israelite people. Also in this case we would have to admit that his

---

[3] This author has on several occassions compared the narrative about David's Rise (1 Sam 16-2 Sam 6) to the Idrimi narrative and similar literature from the ancient Near East; see my *Ancient Israel: A New History of Israelite Society* (Biblical Seminar 5; 2nd repr.; Sheffield: Sheffield Academic, 1996) 53-54. The first to see this connection was G. Buccellati, "La 'carriera' di David e quella di Idrima, re di Alalac," *Bibbia e oriente* 4 (1962) 95-99; cf. also exploiting the literary elaborations on a basic fairy tale, M. Liverani, "Partire sul carro, per il deserto," *Annali dell'Istituto Universitario Orientale di Napoli* n.s. 22 (1972) 403-15.

[4] On the literary applications in the OT of motifs originating in folk-literature see J. Van Seters, *Abraham in History and Tradition* (New Haven: Yale University, 1975); and now also N. P. Lemche, *Die Vorgeschichte Israels: Von den Anfängen bis zum Ausgang des 13. Jahrhunderts v. Chr.* (Biblische Enzyklopädie 1; Stuttgart: W. Kohlhammer, 1996) 1-73.

analysis would have little to say about Solomon, less about the biblical authors, but a lot about the sociological situation of the scholars of the modern world who produced the never-never land of the usual histories of Israel as found in most textbooks of the modern age. Such a study would, of course, also have to include a fair share of psychology and especially an extended understanding of European mental history since the beginning of the 19th century.[5]

None of these venues will be followed here. Instead it is the author's intention to deal more extensively with a kind of sociological analysis which he denounced more than a decade ago but which seems, especially in a North American environment, to blossom, although hardly more realistic than it used to be, the so-called holistic approach to historical studies as found not least in the integration of sociology in archaeological studies in the form of "social archaeology."[6]

When approaching a subject like the Old Testament and the history of Israel from a sociological angle, it is first and foremost important to understand that this will involve an extensive amount of archaeology. It is, however, not indifferent how the integration between archaeology and sociology takes place, as there are as many kinds of sociology as there are of archaeology. In this connection it should be realized that traditionally North American and European archaeology have been very differently organized (although it is true to say that probably the best known social archaeologist at the moment is an European, the British archaeologist Colin Renfrew).[7] In Europe sociology will normally be part of the political sciences whereas the departments of archaeology will traditionally be situated in the faculties of humanistic studies, staffed by scholars who are brought up mainly in the humanistic tradition. The perspective has therefore been from the beginning humanistic, i.e., the human race in its variety has always stood in the center of interest. In North America, on the other hand, archaeology is more often than not placed much closer to the behavioral disciplines such as sociology, social anthropology, and the social sciences and economy. Although it

[5] I will be dealing with this subject in my, *The Ancient Israelites in History and Tradition* (LAI 12; Louisville: Westminster/John Knox, forthcoming).

[6] On social archaeology and Palestine in antiquity see T. E. Levy, ed., *The Archaeology of Society in the Holy Land* (London: Leicester University, 1995).

[7] See already, C. Renfrew, *Social Archaeology: An Inaugural Lecture* (Southampton: University of Southampton, 1973), and more recently his, *Approaches to Social Archaeology* (Edinburgh: Edinburgh University, 1984), and with P. Bahn, *Archaeology: Theories, Methods, and Practice* (2nd ed.; London: Thames and Hudson, 1996).

would certainly be wrong to say that European archaeology is not interested in social affairs (which it very much is), its place next to humanistic studies have without doubt produced a different attitude from the one found among American archaeologists who will arguably be dependent on the methods of the behavioral sciences, which is by and large a kind of scholarship that works with models that are considered to be valid as long as they are not falsified. The correct scientific procedure would in this case probably be Karl Popper's, always aiming at the falsification of a model, rather than a defense of its validity, whereby it one and the same time is both verified and modified, i.e. improved.

In the study of pre-Columbian North American history, an approach along such lines as have been normal among North American archaeologists of the last generation has been both necessary and productive, as no other remains exist except material ones. There are no written sources pre-dating the advent of the Spanish conquistadors saying anything about the history of the Indians on, for example, the great plains or the Pueblo Indians in New Mexico; all they have left are artifacts, remnants of dwellings and settlements, a casual object of art or the like. There is no way a coherent history can be written about these people. A history attached to an archaeology which worked with models would place its trust in sociological models that are construed to explain socio-cultural and socio-economic changes and they will they will demand models that are not falsified and, on the other hand, forceful enough to convince. It goes without saying that such models must be stable; i.e., the models themselves are not allowed to embrace too many exceptions from the rule or they would lose their value as tools for research. A model allowing for, say, ten different explanations to a certain cultural or socio-economic fact would do more harm than no model at all.

In this century in social anthropology (mostly of the variety found in North America) a school of cultural evolutionism arose aiming at general explanations of the development of civilizations. It is not the place to go into a prolonged discussion of its merits and/or fallacies (it has been done before by this writer and he still considers his criticism to be valid in spite of the appearance of ever more refined general models that have appeared over the last twenty years[8]), but it should be stressed that it has

[8] On this N. P. Lemche, *Early Israel: Anthropological and Historical Studies on the Israelite Society Before the Monarchy* (VTSup 37; Leiden: E. J. Brill, 1985) 216-19; and more extensively in *idem.*, "On the Use of 'System Theory,' 'Macro Theories' and Evolutionistic Thinking in Modern OT Research and Biblical Archaeology," *SJOT* 4

produced a number of theories about the origins of states in societies comparable to the Palestinian society in the so-called transitional period between roughly 1300 BCE and 900 BCE (which in some archaeological and historical quarters are increasingly being considered a period best studied as one coherent period) that are in some circles considered satisfying explanations of the formation of the Israelite state(s). It is therefore the opinion of scholars adhering to the results of the school of cultural evolutionism and its by-products in archaeology and history that the history of the emergence of ancient Israel can be studied and described in some detail even during the "dark" centuries of Palestine, the period that has left almost no written sources behind.

In contrast to this, other schools of social anthropology have appeared, including structural functionalism (mostly British or inspired by British anthropologists[9]), structuralism,[10] even a blend of both,[11] and on the basis of both structural functionism and structuralism a kind of processual anthropology which also concentrates on the development of culture but includes a dynamic element allowing for an almost indefinite variety of explanations.[12] It is natural that the adherents of the last mentioned anthropological approach will normally be much less assured of

(1990/2) 73-88, repr. in *Community, Identity, and Ideology: Social Sciences Approaches to the Hebrew Bible* (eds. C. E. Carter and C. L. Meyers; SBTS 6; Winona Lake, Ind.: Eisenbrauns, 1996).

[9] Including such leading anthropologists as A. R. Radcliffe-Brown, E. E. Evans-Pritchard, and M. Fortes.

[10] It should never be forgotten that some of the foremost representatives of structuralism have been social anthropologists, such as C. Lévi-Strauss.

[11] It would probably be most correct to include under this heading the British social anthropologist E. Leach and his students.

[12] Among the best known of such anthropologists we should mention the Norwegian social anthropologist F. Barth (otherwise best known from his work on Middle Eastern nomadism). In order to present an example of the difference of attitude, see the definitions of ethnicity as presented by R. Narroll, "On Ethnic Unit Classification," *Current Anthropology* 5 (1964) 283-91, and by F. Barth, in his introduction to *Ethnic Groups and Boundaries: The Social Organization of Culture Difference* (Oslo: Universitetsforlaget, 1969) 19-38. Whereas Narroll's definition consists of four rather invariable conditions: an ethnic group can be characterized by the following four criteria: 1) is largely biologically self-perpetuating, 2) shares fundamental cultural values, realized in overt unity in cultural forms, 3) makes up a field of communication and interaction, 4) has a membership which identifies itself, and is identified by others, as constituting a category distinguishable from other categories of the same order. By comparison, Barth speaks of the necessity of having at least two opposing groups around in order to create culture differences. For some unknown reason W. B. Dever has attributed Narroll's definition to Barth, see his "Ceramics, Ethnicity, and the Question of Israel's Origins," as presented on his homepage (http://scholar.cc.emory.edu/scripts/ASOR/BA/Dever.html) p. 1 (last revision November 21, 1996).

their historical reconstructions than advocates of cultural evolutionism,[13] since to the last mentioned his model explanation will be considered valid as long as it is not falsified, whereas the processional anthropologist would always have to reckon his explanation to be just one among many possibilities. It is also clear that the first mentioned will be able to produce explanations which outwardly look much more coherent and convincing than his colleague who will never be able to go beyond probabilities.

So, according to a holistic approach it should, when approaching such a subject as the kingdom of Solomon in the 10th century BCE, in spite of the lack of contemporary literary sources, but with the help of the modes and manners of the school of evolution and its tributaries, be possible to reconstruct the history of the formation of the Israelite state. Solomon should so-to-speak be allowed to make his reappearance in the mute, material remains from literally hundreds of excavations executed in the territory attributed to Solomon by the writers of the Old Testament.

The first endeavor in biblical studies to employ the ideas and methods of cultural evolutionism was done in a most idiosyncratic way by George Mendenhall in his study of the Hebrew Conquest of Palestine.[14] We need not pay much attention to the particulars of his explanation, as a major work in his tradition was subsequently published by Norman Gottwald, who made extended use of models from social anthropology in order to explain the origin of statehood among the scattered inhabitants of the central Palestinian mountains in the Early Iron Age.[15] A Few years later the individual elements in Gottwald's model were analyzed and rejected by this author in a work which parted with the idea of producing stable models for the explanation of societal changes which dominated the school of Mendenhall and Gottwald.[16] Instead of a stable model, I advocated, in the manner of European social anthropology, a dynamic explanation which gave up the idea that it could produce without documents an adequate *history* of a certain region and, instead of this, concentrated

---

[13] Thus A. R. Radcliffe-Brown simply gave up his interest in history after his fieldwork among the Andamanes; see his *The Andaman Islanders* (Cambridge: Cambridge University, 1922; repr. New York: Free, 1964).

[14] G. E. Mendenhall, "The Hebrew Conquest of Palestine," *BA* 25 (1962) 66-87.

[15] N. K. Gottwald, *The Tribes of Yahweh: A Sociology of the Religion of Liberated Israel, 1250-1050 B.C.E.* (Maryknoll, NY: Orbis Books, 1979).

[16] Lemche, *Early Israel.*

on describing what seems to have materially happened and to deliniate as many possible explanantions as possible.

It should in this way be understood that the diversities of historical reconstructions have not so much to do with a difference in sources as a difference in how to evaluate the information contained in the sources. Whereas according to the cultural evolutionist and his colleagues in archaeology the explanation is to be looked for in the remains themselves, that are generally stable in so far as they do not change (only the explanations of them will change over time), but are only augmented by the introduction of still more evidence, the ability of the humanistically oriented scholar to explain socio-cultural change will rely on the people who produced the material remains (i.e. in the human factor) which is always different and changeable. The difference between the two approaches can almost be boiled down into one (a kind of a "chicken and egg") formula: what came first: a piece of art, some furniture, a house style, or the people who produced this piece of art, that furniture or the house in question?

In practice this has sometimes led to a curious dismissal of even written sources by members of the evolutionist school, as has been the case in some recent studies on the history of Palestine in the Late Bronze Age and the Early Iron Age in spite of the fact that we are, from exactly this period (i.e. from the middle of the 14th century), in possession of a remarkable collection of documents which come from Palestine (also Syria and Phoenicia), the royal archives from El-Amarna which includes a collection of some hundred letters, most of which are written on behalf of the local princes of Palestine, Phoenicia and Syria.[17] Most often these documents are brushed aside as representing a special situation in the history of Syria and Palestine; a period supposed to be dominated by the heretic Pharaoh, Akhnaton, and because of his religious speculations something special and therefore not representative is presumed for the

[17] The most convenient edition of which is still L. A. Knudtzon, *Die Amarna-Tafeln* (Vorderasiatische Bibliothek 2; Leipzig: Hinrichs, 1915; repr. Aalen: Otto Zeller, 1964) 2 vols.. Recent translation: W. L. Moran, *Les lettres d'el-Amarna: Correspondance diplomatique du pharaon* (Paris: Cerf, 1987); English ed., *The Amarna Letters* (Baltimore: Johns Hopkins University, 1992). The negligence of the testimony of these letters was already a fact in R. B. Coote and K. W. Whitelam, *The Emergence of Early Israel in Historical Perspective* (SWABA 5; Sheffield: Almond, 1987), and they certainly play no role in the historical discourse in more recent studies, such as, for example, the description of the developments in Palestine in the LBA in S. Bunimowitz, "On the Edge of Empires—Late Bronze Age (1500-1200 BCE)," *The Archaeology of Society in the Holy Land* (ed. T. E. Levy; London: Leicester University, 1995) 321-31.

general history of this area. However, it seems likely that this interpretation of the Amarna age and the Amarna letters is based on a misunderstanding of the content of the letters themselves, of the general situation which they reflect and of their importance for a first-hand evaluation of the political situation in Syria during the 18th dynasty.[18] This is also supported and partially confirmed by other documents from Egypt, Syria and Palestine, as well as from Asia Minor (from the Hittite kingdom) and from Mesopotamia showing the Egyptians to be very active in Syria, although not very successful, also during the latter part of the 18th dynasty.[19]

Such texts as the Amarna letters in combination with a more traditional study of the history of Syria and Palestine in the second half of the 2nd millennium BCE will probably tell us that the situation in Palestine with its seemingly anarchical socio-political system (every petty chieftan fighting his colleagues) was hardly as chaotic as a first glimpse at the

[18] The repeated complaints of the Palestinian petty chieftains (so-called "kings") in the Amarna letters have often been understood to be caused by a very special and difficult political situation related to the religious disturbances in Egypt under the heretic Pharaoh Akhnaten. To mention an example of this, we should refer to the description of this period in such classics as, from the point of view of a biblical scholar, J. Bright, *A History of Israel* (London: SCM, 1960) 101-102, and from an Egyptologist's vantage point, A. H. Gardiner, *Egypt of the Pharaohs* (Oxford: Oxford University, 1961) 230-32. It is, however, a highly questionable interpretation of the situation of Palestine during this period which may rather have been witnessing an Egyptian endeavor to tighten up their control of Palestine and Phoenicia in order to be better able to withstand the pressure from the Hittites under Shuppiluliumash I. The complaints of the petty kings of Palestine and Phoenicia (not least Rib-Adda's extensive correspondence with Pharaoh) should not be understood as primarily reflecting a political situation as much as they bear testimony to an ideological crisis which, among other things, had to do with very different understandings of the relation between the ruler and hiis subject in Egypt and Western Asia. On this see M. Liverani, *Antico Oriente: Storia—Società—Economia* (Bari: Laterza, 1988) 563, based on a series of articles including, among others, his "Contrasti e confluenze di concezioni politiche nell'età di El-Amarna," *RA* 61 (1967) 1-18, "Le lettere del Faraone a Rib-Addaʾ," *OrAnt* 10 (1971) 253-68, and "Rib-Adda, giusto sofferente," *Altorientalische Forschungen* 1 (1974) 175-205. On the continuation of the Egyptian control, and in general the Egyptian perception of the situation, see also M. Liverani, "A Seasonal Pattern for the Amarna Letters," *Lingering Over Words: Studies in Ancient Near Eastern Literature in Honor of William L. Moran* (eds. T. Abusch, J. Hühnergard, P. Steinkeller; HSS 37; Atlanta: Scholars, 1990) 337-48. Such ideological reasons, which are extremely difficult to control and to understand for modern scholars of the modern world, are, of course, of little use for social archaeologists working with general models and they are therefore normally disregarded.

[19] For an analysis of the Egyptian relations to Asia in this period see D. B. Redford, *Egypt and Canaan in the New Kingdom* (Beer-Sheva 4; Beer-Sheva: Ben Gurion University of the Negev, 1990), and *idem.*, *Egypt, Canaan, and Israel in Ancient Times* (Princeton: Princeton University, 1992) 192-214.

letters will show. A careful analysis of the letters would probably disclose a kind of code followed by the local chieftains in their reports to the Egyptian court, according to which they tried to influence the Pharaoh to act in their favor against their adversaries (i.e., the neighboring princelets). The province was, however, not in disorder, although the Egyptians were at the time pressed by the Hittites in Syria (not in Palestine, which never left Egyptian control). As a matter of fact, the Amarna letters most likely say that Egyptian rule over Palestine and Syria was extremely limited in purpose during the days of the 18th dynasty. Egyptians were only present at a few selected centers such as Hazor and the power of the empire was established not by permanently residing governors, but mostly by rather low-ranking emissaries coming out of Egypt with special purposes in mind.[20] When the Amarna letters speak about the absence of Egyptian military forces, this was hardly unusual. It is much more likely that this was always the case in that it was not in the interest of the imperial overlords to interfere with the politics of the local vassals as long as they paid their taxes and dues to the royal court.[21] The lack of a permanent Egyptian military presence reflected in the Amarna letters was therefore normal rather than unusual in those days.

The textual remains from this time would, on the other hand, also tell us that at the beginning of the Ramesside period the Egyptian grasp on Palestine and southern Syria was strengthened and that something approaching proper provinces with their own political centers were established at this time in Gaza, Kumidi, and Hazor.[22] It is also now almost an established fact that the Egyptians did not leave Palestine at the end of what is usually called the Late Bronze Age, but their sway over the country continued, according to some authorities, down to a period not so far away from the time of Saul and David. We are at least speaking about a time difference between the disappearance of the Egyptian empire and the emergence of the "Israelite" one of only a few generations, not two centuries or more.[23]

---

[20] On emmissaries from Egypt and their status; *ibid.*, pp. 201-203.

[21] Liverani, "Contrasti e confluenze," pp. 1-18.

[22] On the system of strongholds, see already A. Alt, "Das Stützpunktsystem der Pharaonen an der phönikischen Küste und im syrischen Binneland," *ZDPV* 68 (1950) 97-133 (repr. in *Kleine Schriften zur Geschichte Israels* [Munich: Beck, 1960] 3.107-41). In general for the political organization during the Ramesside period, Redford, *Egypt, Canaan, and Israel*, pp. 203-207.

[23] Redford, *Ibid.*, p. 290, gives a date of *ca.* 15 years after the death of Ramesses III (i.e., around the middle of the 12th century) as the end of the Egyptian empire in Asia. This date is dependent on a view of the crisis of the "sea-people" and the settlement of the

This outline of the history of Palestine in the Late Bronze Age and the beginning of the Iron Age is mostly based on political documentation written down. How is this reflected in the recent "socio-archaeological" analyses of the Palestinian scene during the Late Bronze Age-Early Iron I transition such as the ones published by Shlomo Bunimowitz, Israel Finkelstein, and John S. Holladay in a recent volume on social archaeology?[24] The answer is: In Bunimowitz's article the presence of written sources (the Amarna letters) is mentioned, but they only play an insignificant role in his socio-historical reconstruction.[25] In Finkelstein's studies it plays no role at all although Finkelstein's analysis is less burdened by holistic social theory than other studies in this genre. As such, Finkelstein's model is (as in other recent works by this author) more or less based on a more dynamic understanding of society, sometimes closely resembling processual anthropology.[26] In Holladay's analysis of the emergence of the Hebrew kingdom written documents from Palestine and the neighboring countries play no role, whereas his approach to social archaeology is flawed by his rather commonplace rationalistic paraphrases of the OT narrative.[27]

Philistines which places this in the time of Ramesses III. For an alternative view, see now I. Finkelstein, "The Date of the Settlement of the Philistines in Canaan," *Tel Aviv* 22 (1995) 213-39, who reckons with a later date and a break-down of the Egyptian control that was limited to two phases of reduction, firstly a retreat from Northern and Central Palestine to the coastal plain which occurred in the first half of the 12th century, and secondly, a phase when the control of the coastal plain was lost to the Philistines at the end of the 12th century. It should be mentioned that there are also scholars who reckon the Egyptian rule to have ended almost at the end of Ramesses III's battle against the sea-people in his 8th year (i.e., *ca.* 1180 BCE), in Levy, *Archaeology of Society*, pp. 332-48.

[24] S. Bunimowitz, "On the Edge of Empires," pp. 321-31; I. Finkelstein, "The Great Transformation: The "Conquest" of the Highlands Frontiers and the Rise of the Territorial States," *The Archaeology of Society in the Holy Land* (ed. T. E. Levy; London: Leicester University, 1995) 349-65; and J. S. Holladay, "The Kingdoms of Israel and Judah: Political and Economic Centralization in the Iron Age IIA-B (ca. 1000-750 BCE)," *The Archaeology of Society in the Holy Land* (ed. T. E. Levy; London: Leicester University, 1995) 369-98.

[25] He, however, shows considerable awareness that a proper analysis would include a dialogue between the written and the material sources. It must also be said that he does not consider it his duty in this article to present such a dialogue.

[26] The best example of Finkelstein's approach to social archaeology is delivered by his recent monograph, *Living on the Fringe: The Archaeology and History of the Negev, Sinai and Neighboring Regions in the Bronze and Iron Ages* (Monographs in Mediterranean Archaeology 6; Sheffield: Sheffield Academic, 1995).

[27] It is increasingly becoming a problem that too many scholars may work perfectly rationally until the moment they begin to tackle biblical matters. Then their methodology and approach to textual analysis suddenly changes as does the discourse of their scholarship. An archaeologist like W. G. Dever has in many publications opted for the separa-

Holladay's study is especially important in this connection because it has direct bearing on the subject of this article (i.e., the relevance of social studies to the study of the time of Solomon). In his article Holladay is heavily dependent on holistic social-archaeological studies in general and on analyses of cultural change and the formation of the state as found mostly among anthropologists belonging to the above-mentioned school of cultural evolutionism. He is (and this is strange in a study as methodologically self-conscious as his) however, equally dependent on the biblical narrative and seems to accept most of it at face value, at least as long as it suits his interpretation of the archaeological artifacts. Sometimes this has the opposite effect, as when he interprets archaeological remains in light of biblical narrative, which is the case when he defends the unlikely theory of the presence of stables at Megiddo, Hazor, Beersheba and elsewhere,[28] and in support refers to the presence of a superior force of chariotry in the army of King Ahab of Israel which took part in the battle against the Assyrians at Qarqar in 853 BCE.[29]

However, the crucial point of interest to the historians dealing with the appearance of the states of Israel and Judah in the Iron Age and related to socio-archaeological analysis is the change of settlement habits in the highlands of Palestine at the beginning of the transitional period reflecting a major societal and to some also an ethnic change.[30] To Holladay,

---

tion of archaeology from biblical studies in order that biblical literature should not, in advance, dominate the archaeological interpretation, most recently in his "Revisionist Israel Revisited," *CRBS* 4 (1996) 35-50, or *idem.*, "Archaeology and the Current Crisis in Israelite Historiography," *ErIsr* 25 (1996) 18*-27*. He is absolutely correct, although he may himself not (like so many other scholars) quite live up to his own ideal, see on this T. L. Thompson, "Historiography of Ancient Palestine and Early Jewish Historiography: W. G. Dever and the Not so New Biblical Archaeology," *The Origins of the Ancient Israelite States* (eds. V. Fritz and P. R. Davies; JSOTSup 228; Sheffield, Sheffield Academic, 1996) 26-43.

[28] Holladay, "Kingdoms of Judah and Israel," p. 373. Y. Yadin reckoned the complex at Hazor to his stratum VIII, dating it to the 9th century and accepting it as a store house; Y. Yadin, "Hazor," *The Encyclopedia of Archaeological Excavation in the Holy Land* (ed. E. Stern; London: Oxford University, 1976) 2.485. It is, however, interesting that he describes the exact similar complex at Megiddo stratum IVB (supposed to be in the 10th century BCE) as stables; *idem.*, "Megiddo," *The Encyclopedia of Archaeological Excavation in the Holy Land* (ed. E. Stern; London: Oxford University, 1976) 3.852-53. It is obvious that the biblical discourse has here substituted common sense.

[29] However, Ahab is obviously not the same as Solomon (or is he? see N. P. Lemche, "Is It Still Possible to Write a History of Ancient Israel?" *SJOT* 8 [1994] 183-89). On Qarqar, see the monolith inscription of Shalmaneser III; A. L. Oppenheim, tr., "Babylonian and Assyrian Historical Texts," *ANET*, pp. 278-79.

[30] The major work on this is I. Finkelstein, *The Archaeology of the Israelite Settlement*

as was also the case of Bunimowitz and to some degree also of Finkelstein, the disappearance of village culture in the central highlands of Palestine at the end of the Middle Bronze Age may reflect a change of the socio-economic and socio-political structure in Palestine after the inclusion of this territory in the Egyptian empire in Western Asia. The reappearance and intensification of village culture at the end of the Late Bronze Age may likewise mean that serious societal changes took place. According to Bunimowitz we here have evidence of a development from an urban culture to a more locally oriented, village-based culture (i.e., in fact to a more primitive stage of development). The end of the transitional period is, however, also characterized by a change in the settlement pattern, when more comprehensive urban structures reappeared, according to Holladay in the shape of a first limited number of royal cities such as Megiddo and Beersheba, later a more extensive urbanization of Palestine, present in almost every part of the country.

While it is a pretty safe guess and does not demand a great deal of sociological insight to say that the urbanization of Palestine in Iron II (roughly after 900 BCE) has to do with the establishment of some kind of statehood, the reasons for the disappearance and the reappearance of the villages in the highlands of Palestine may be quite different from the ones imagined by Bunimowitz, Holladay, but also to some degree Finkelstein. I see no reason to doubt the general validity of Finkelstein's analysis of the factual remains, herein included his distribution of the archaeological documentation according to, on one side, a time axis and, on the other, a space axis. His geographical analysis, which made the village culture appear at first at the eastern fringe of the arable land also seems logical and may well be correct.[31] It is also likely that this development, which was probably not limited to Palestine proper but also to some degree felt in other parts of the southern Levant,[32] had little to do with migrations of newcomers such as the ancient Israelites to the

(Jerusalem: Israel Exploration Society, 1988), concentrating on the archaeological surveys conducted mainly in the central highlands of Palestine to the north of Jerusalem. This study should be supplemented by the resumés of this and other surveys in I. Finkelstein and N. Na'aman, *From Nomadism to Monarchy: Archaeological & Historical Aspects of Early Israel* (Yad Izhak Ben-Zvi; Jerusalem: Israel Exploration Society; Washington, DC: Biblical Archaeology Society, 1994).

[31] As an improvement in social relations may first be felt in the periphery; see discussion below.

[32] On a similar case in the Beqa Valley; L. Marfoe, "The Integrative Transformation: Patterns of Sociopolitical Organization in Southern Syria," *BASOR* 234 (1979) 1-42.

Palestinian scene.[33] It was mainly, as far as Palestine is concerned, an inner Palestinian development, thereby reflecting a serious change of habitation habits among the inhabitants of this country.

Why did the settlement system change in this radical way? Should we think of it as reflecting a retribalization of the urbanized population of Palestine in the Late Bronze Age? Or should we look for some other reasons?

It probably seems obvious to a scholar brought up in the tradition of cultural evolutionism that we are here witnessing at the end of the Late Bronze Age a decline in material culture which must be compared to a decline in the living standards of the population of Palestine at large. The cities were no longer in a position to maintain themselves. The more complicated socio-economic system to be found in the cities had to give way to a kind of basis economy where people were mostly engaged in producing primary food stuff. The luxury production of the cities was no longer profitable, and the cities were no longer able to support their citizens.

Although this seems to be a plausible explanation of the demographic movements of Palestine and on line with some general ideas about what produces societal changes, it needs not be correct. A comparable change of settlement patterns occurred (as remarked by, among others, I. Finkelstein) at the end of the Early Bronze Age, however, without leaving any written records which may present us with an inside view of the development, *and again* after the Turkish conquest of Syria and Palestine at the beginning of the 16th century. The consequences of the last one is well documented in Turkish archives (mostly taxation lists)[34] that cover the whole period of Turkish domination over the Middle East in the period from *ca.* 1525 to 1918.

---

[33] Although the old idea of A. Alt, *Die Landnahme der Israeliten in Palästina* (1925), repr. Kleine Schriften zur Geschichte des Volkes Israels (Munich: Beck, 1953) 1.89-125, English tr., "The Settlement of the Israelites in Palestine," *Essays on Old Testament History and Religion* (Oxford: Basil Blackwell, 1966; repr. Biblical Seminar; Sheffield: Sheffield University, 1989) 133-70, of a gradual infiltration of nomads from the desert around Palestine may still occassionally find supporters, such as Redford, *Egypt, Canaan, and Israel*, pp. 257-80.

[34] W. D. Hütteroth, "Schwankungen von Siedlungsdichte und Siedlungsgrenze in Palästina und Transjordanien seit dem 16. Jahrhundert," *Deutscher Geographentag Kiel 1969: Tagungsbericht und wissenshaftliche Adhandlungen: Verhandlung des Deutschen Geographentages*, Bd. 37 (Wiesbaden, 1970) 463-75; and *idem.*, "The Pattern of Settlement in Palestine in the Sixteenth Century: Geographical Research on Turkish *defter-i Mufassal*," *Studies on Palestine During the Ottoman Period* (ed. M. Ma'oz; Jerusalem: Magnes, 1975) 3-10.

Skipping general anthropological models and moving to the well-documented case of the decline of village culture in Palestine, Transjordan and Syria after the Osman occupation, it is quite easy to recognize what happened here. Between 1525 and 1865 we find a catastrophic reduction of settled lifeforms in the Middle East. In Syria between 50 and 75% of the villages disappeared, and also the cities were reduced in size and welfare. Now, we should have expected the opposite because a great imperial power had taken over the control of the area of supposedly incompetent local Arab authorities. This, however, was not the case because the Turks did not care about the welfare of their provinces, but following the tradition of the former Greek, Roman and Arab imperial masters of the Middle East, they sold the taxation rights to local officers without ever controlling their activity, for example through the presence of an imperial army. Every tax collector was so-to-speak on his own and responsible to nobody as long as he paid a predecided amount to the sultan in far-off Istanbul. If he wished, he could raise a private police force to extract as much tax revenues from ordinary people in his area as he wished; in fact, he was absolutely free to do according to his own will, as long as he did not represent a danger to the official rule of the sultan. Nobody, however, protected the local population, and they accordingly had to look for their own salvation, which seems to have involved a new mobile lifestyle, including different kinds of nomadisation, in order to be able to escape the bullies of the tax collectors. In anthropological terms, the population to a large extent, however gradually, chose to exchange settled life for a mobile, nomadic lifestyle, and to invest in livestock instead of agriculture; although agriculture continued to be a part of the life cycle of most nomadic communities in the Middle East.

The major change in the fate of the populations of Syria and Palestine occured when Turkey, after having lost the European part of its empire and after the so-called Young Turkish Revolution" in 1865, decided to reinvest in its oriental provinces (i.e., to assume power for itself and to reduce the importance of the local middlemen). The history is well-known and need not be repeated in extension here.[35] However, the political and military strengthening of the Turkish presence in Syria and Palestine changed the general demographic development and encouraged a resettlement of the territory, a process which continued until WW I, and also after this with the effect that settled village culture, favored

[35] See my *Early Israel*, pp. 134-35, with case examples from Jordan, pp. 175-77, 179-81.

by at first the Turkish state, then the Mandate authorities, and finally, after WW II, the new Arab states of the Middle East, has been re-established, and that in little more than a hundred years.

Now it is a truism that history does not repeat itself as no historical case is identical. Although this is true, history (as well as social anthropology, economical studies, etc.) nevertheless provides us with comparative examples which can be computerized and used to throw light over historical situations not so well recorded in writing. That is the general idea behind a holisitc approach to historical interpretation of archaeological remains. However, when we return to Palestine at the beginning of the LB-EI transition, it is remarkable that the reappearance of the village settlement system comes one or two generations *after* the consolidation of the Egyptian military and political presence under the first Ramessides and in a period where the Egyptians had shown no intention to leave Palestine.[36] The settlement process may therefore, from a historical point of view, but also from a socio-political and economical angle, reflect the more peaceful environment in Palestine due to the active Egyptian interest in this border province during the 19th and early 20th dynasty, which made it possible for at least a part of the mobile (nomadicizing) population to submit themselves to the imperial authorities and become settled in mainly *unfortified* small villages and hamlets,[37] or to leave the fortified cities and move into the countryside, which probably occurred in northern Galilee.[38] It is certainly in accordance with this that such a development may have begun in the peri-

[36] A number of inscriptions may be testimonies of this activity in Palestine from the part of the Egyptian overlords: 1) The major Beth-Shan stele of Seti I (J. A. Wilson, "Egyptian Historical Texts," *ANET*, pp. 253-54) about the garrisoning of an Egyptian corps at Beth-Shan, 2) The smaller Beth-Shan stele of Seti I reporting Egyptian military activity in the vicinity of Beth-Shan (*ibid.*, p. 255; see W. F. Albright, "The Smaller Beth-Shan Stela of Sethos I (1309-1290) B.C.," *BASOR* 125 [1952] 24-32, and 3) The "Israel"-stela of Mernephtah (J. A. Wilson, "Egyptian Hymns and Prayers," *ANET*, pp. 375-78). Although the last mentioned testifies to the presence of a population group in Palestine bearing the name of Israel and important enough to be mentioned alongside the cities of Gezer, Ashkelon and Yanoam, the defiant wording of the inscription shows no intention to leave Palestine to this Israel or to some other local power.

[37] Agreeing with Finkelstein, for example in his "The Great Transformation," that a comprehensive nomadic element was certainly part of this process escpecially on the fringe of the cultivatable land.

[38] See Y. Aharoni's old theory about the relationship between the appearance of unfortified village settlements in the northern Galilean mountains and the decline of the LBA city of Hazor; "Problems of the Israelite Conquest in the Light of Archaeological Discoveries," *Antiquity and Survival* II:2-3 (1957) 225-46. See now also R. Frankel, "Upper Galilee in the Late Bronze-Iron I Transition," *From Nomadism to Monarchy: Archaeo-*

phery of the centralized socio-political system of Palestine in the Late Bronze Age, because the lack of military control and lack of security would have had the severest consequences for the settled population in such remote and badly exploited territories.[39] Only later may the settlement process have moved into the more central parts of the country. A part of the Egyptian political control of the country would have included the pacification not only of various kinds of nomadic groups,[40] but also of the parasocial elements hiding here,[41] but also because the distance between the city centers and the fields to be tilled in such quarters

logical & Historical Aspects of Early Israel (I. Finkelstein and N. Na'aman; Yad Izhak Ben-Zvi; Jerusalem: Israel Exploration Society; Washington, DC: Biblical Archaeology Society, 1994) 18-34.

[39] It is a romantic stereotype (nevertheless a false one) that nomads should live together in peace. On the contrary, the stronger elements among such a population would tend to dominate (even tyranize) the other parts of the population making life miserable for them. An example of this destructive activity of nomadic tribesmen is presented by F. Barth in his often overlooked, *Principles of Social Organization in Southern Kurdistan* (Universitetets etnografiske Museum Bulletin 7; Oslo: N.p., 1953; repr. New York: AMS, 1979). A study of J. Black-Michaud's dissertation, "The Economics of Oppression: Ecology and Stratification in an Iranian Tribal Society" (Ph.D. disseration, University of London, 1976), published as *Sheep and Land: The Economics of Power in a Tribal Society* (Cambridge: Cambridge University, 1986), would also help to understand the processes which may be active in a border zone like the one imagined by Finkelstein.

[40] It is a weakness in Finkelstein's otherwise excellent interpretation of nomadic culture that he (although he follows this writer's idea of a polymorphous society built along a *continuum* line) still sometimes refers (for example in "The Great Transformation," p. 361, speaking of a dimorphic chiefdom) to M. B. Rowton's antiquated idea of the *dimorphic society*; see M. B. Rowton, "Dimorphic Structure and Topology," *OrAnt* 15 (1976) 17-31, "Dimorphic Structure and the Problem of the 'Apirû—'Ibrîm'," *JNES* 35 (1976) 13-20, "Dimorphic Structure and the Tribal Elite," *Al-Bahit: Festschift J. Henninger* (Studi Instituti Anthropos 30; St. Augustine bei Bonn, 1976) 219-257, and "Dimorphic Structure and the Parasocial Element," *JNES* 36 (1977) 181-98. By doing so he also subscribes to Rowton's equally antiquated idea of an *enclosed nomadism* (nomads living in a more or less natural and peaceful symbiosis with settled culture; see M. B. Rowton, "Enclosed Nomadism," *JESHO* 17 [1974] 1-30), which should be substituted with the concept of the *encapsulated nomadism* (nomads in the Middle East are so to speak encapsulated into the political organization of the area; i.e., their freedom to move has normally been curtailed by local authorities normally residing in cities and towns), see Finkelstein, "The Great Transformation," p. 353. On encapsulated nomadism, see F. Barth, "A General Perspective of Nomads-Sedentary Relations in the Middle East," *The Desert and the Sown: Nomads in the Wider Society* (ed. C. Nelson; Berkeley: University of California, 1973) 11-21. On the Middle Eastern nomadism in general I would still refer to the chapter on this in my *Early Israel*, pp. 84-163.

[41] See the smaller Beth-Shan stele of Seti I (n. 36), which expressly mentions Egyptian campaigning against the *habiru*. On the adaptability of Palestinian soil to the pastoral way of living, see M. B. Rowton, "The Topological Factor in the Habiru Problem," *Assyriological Studies* 16 (1965) 375-87, and *idem.*, "The Woodlands of Ancient Western Asia," *JNES* 26 (1967) 261-77.

would have exceeded the distance to be bridged on a daily basis by the peasants.

A theory of village development which goes against the prevailing ideas of social change according to which such change mostly relies on economic and climatic circumstances and therefore to be understood as a kind of response to an impending natural and demographic factor will also have to find an answer to the change from the city culture of the Late Bronze Age. This can hardly be the consequence of an Egyptian conquest supposed to have occurred around 1500 BCE and which may have caused the destruction of several urban centers of Palestine,[42] as the destruction of cities would most likely have been followed by a surge of village culture, partly inhabited by the part of the urbanized population which escaped the destruction. However, nothing of this occurred and no villages were established. To the contrary, the villages of the Middle Bronze Age mostly disappeared, while at the same time the city centers of the Middle Bronze Age continued to exist also in the Late Bronze Age, still heavily fortified. A precise analysis of the settled areas may tell us that the built up area of the Middle Bronze Age was extensively reduced in the Late Bronze Age.[43] This would speak against an idea saying that the villagers may have found a refuge inside the walls of the cities. It looks much more sensible to imagine an extended nomadization of the former settled peasant population. However, the details are unknown to us, as is the occupational distribution of the population of Palestine around, say, 1500 BCE. But let us turn to the cities or townships of Palestine in the Late Bronze Age.

It is a serious drawback for the reconstruction of the historical development in the highlands of Palestine by Finkelstein, Bunimowitz and Holladay and others that they show little understanding of the socio-economic set-up of the Palestinian cities. Somehow scholarship has been beguiled by the very word "city" with all its implications of western cul-

---

[42] On this, for example, A. Mazar, *Archaeology of the Land of the Bible 10,000-586 B.C.E.* (ABRL; New York: Doubleday, 1990) 226-27. However, see Bunimowitz, "On the Edge of Empires," as critic of the prevailing view on the transition from the Middle Bronze Age to the Late Bronze Age.

[43] *Ibid.*, p. 324, and *idem.*, "Social-Political Transformations in the Central Hill Country in the Late Bronze-Iron I Transition," *From Nomadism to Monarchy: Archaeological & Historical Aspects of Early Israel* (I. Finkelstein and N. Na'aman; Yad Izhak Ben-Zvi; Jerusalem: Israel Exploration Society; Washington, DC: Biblical Archaeology Society, 1994) 179-202, especially p. 193, against R. Gonen, "Urban Canaan in the Late Bronze Age," *BASOR* 253 (1984) 61-73. Bunimowitz speaks about a reduction from the MBA of 220 sites to around 20 in the LBA.

ture, stratification, differentiation of occupation, and so forth. As a matter of fact, the word itself is a bad choice. It would be much better to speak about a traditional town, or even a township, when addressing the question of Late Bronze Age walled settlements in Palestine (if we should not call them fortress townships or simply fortresses in the European medieval sense of the word as the center and the same time shelter of embryonic towns and cities). Contrary to the belief of many scholars, the Palestinian cities were in general no more than agrarian settlements which centered around an extremely small elite of rulers and administrators, or as it has been maintained by modern observers, the traditional Middle Eastern city (town) is only a walled village, or an agglomeration of villages, it is not like its European counterpart a sociopolitical unity.[44] As becomes evident when reading the Amarna letters, the elite of the Palestinian society (by all means extremely limited in number) did not command an extensive bureacratic or military apparatus. It is much more likely that very few around were able to write or read (probably not even including the members of the elite), and that hardly more than a few scores of soldiers or police officers were present in any place, at least in Palestine. However, more important is the differentiation of occupation to be found in the Palestinian townships. While it is true that specialization was more extensive than in the previous villages of the Middle Bronze Age and certainly than in the villages of the Early Iron I period, it was never very important in the townships of the central highlands, Shechem included. Although such cities may have housed a couple of thousand inhabitants, it is obvious (and also well-documented) that the primary occupation of traditional urbanized societies like the ones found in Palestine in this period is agriculture, with a large population group directly involved in food production while at the same time another part was engaged in the refining of agricultural products of various kinds. Only a tiny minority would have been engaged in the production of artifacts, including pottery, and even fewer would have handled the production of luxury goods.[45] In short, the town-

[44] On this, see my *Early Israel*, pp. 164-201, including the literature cited there (until 1983).

[45] In Jamieson-Drake, *Scribes and Schools*, pp. 107-35 (chapter 4: "Luxury Items"), one of the subjects investigated is the amount of luxury goods found in the towns of the Iron Age as the surplus of manpower and economic ability to support such a production is seen as an example of statehood. No comparable statistics exist from the LBA, for example from Shechem, saying anything about the kind of statehood, the organization of production and labor, and so forth, which may have existed here. That luxury items were

ships were mostly agricultural strongholds which probably housed the population which tilled the fields around the towns themselves (i.e., the towns were primarily a place of residence and acted as protective fortresses in periods of unsafety). Although the towns of Palestine survived the transition from the Middle Bronze Age to the Late Bronze Age (albeit reduced in scale and welfare) they continued to act as havens of safety to a plagued population mostly consisting of peasants, much in the same way as the fortress cities or towns of Europe in the early Middle Age.

In this light, the improved political climate in the time of the 19th and 20th dynasties favored a resettlement of the countryside, on the one hand by people who formerly either stayed on the fringe as a parasocial or as a nomadic element and on the other people who used to live inside protecting walls. There is no compelling reason to see an increase of tribalization behind this process, as the population was at any time probably always segmented to a fair extent (i.e., including the traditonal kinship units of the family and the lineage with the usual variations). The tribe is in fact a rather unnecessary part of this organization as it contributes nothing which is not already taken care of by state officials, and that in a much more efficient way, and clans were probably totally missing (except of course if the clan should be understood as patronage groups of clients which is, however, not normally a part of the definition of a clan).[46]

This is, of course, only one among many possible explanations of the change of settlement patterns in Palestine at the end of the Late Bronze Age, but as such it illustrates how different such explanations may be.[47] It would, of course, be possible to say that the new distribution of villages and homesteads were a consequence of the reduction of the importance of the cities to the economic life of the inhabitants of this area, following the reduction and break down of international trade around 1300

---

imported (some of it probably also locally made) is however, certain but was that to a scale comparable for example to the situation in Syrian LBA sites like Ugarit or Alalakh, where a kind of industry was set up for the production of such items?

[46] On the clan and tribe, see my *Early Israel*, pp. 231-44.

[47] To follow this up, an interesting article has recently appeared by D. Wengrow, "Egyptian Taskmasters and Heavy Burdens: Highland Exploitation and the Collared-Rim Pithos of the Bronze/Iron Age Levant," *Oxford Journal of Archaeology* 15 (1996) 307-26, who sees this characteristic type of pottery as reflecting Egyptian taxation practice (and who would probably agree to see the establishment of the rural landscape around 1200 BCE to the result of a deliberate Egyptian plan to make use of the territory of the highlands of Palestine for fiscal reasons).

BCE.[48] Although it is certain that such a disruption occurred, it is still relevant to ask how far this situation influenced the life and whereabouts of the small Palestinian walled settlements and townships, especially those in the mountains who were at any rate mostly situated at a solid distance from the international trade routes.

It is obvious that any kind of holistic theory that pays no attention to the human factor, to human sentiments, politics, to values esteemed by the human populations of a certain time, and such aspects, is to be considered a truncated kind of theory, hardly contributing much to the understanding of a societal process *involving human beings*. The problem is, however (as I stressed already many years ago following an input by Edmund Leach[49]) that this human factor is unpredictable in as far as its reactions cannot be foreseen; although different venues of development may always be delineated. Without historical sources in the clasical sense, we only have the models to rely on, but these models can be overturned the moment we are in possession of only a single written source. As we shall see, they may be just as dependable on an ever-changing archaeological hoard of evidence and may have to be given up should the scholarly opinion about this archaeological evidence be modified.

The coming of the so-called Israelite nation-state ("so-called" because this is not part of the socio-archaeological approach, but belongs to the biblical discourse) is, according to Holladay, linked to the appearance of walled urban centers like Megiddo, Hazor, Gezer, and Beersheba, to mention only a few.[50] To a certain degree these centers are characterized by a kind of uniform layout (six-chamber gates,[51] stables,[52] casemate walls or the like) to be linked with the Bible's description of the building activities of Solomon and his military projects. While this is true

---

[48] Which was the general thesis of Coote and Whitelam, *The Emergence of Early Israel*.

[49] Lemche, *Early Israel*, p. 217, quoting E. Leach, "Concluding Address," *The Explanation of Culture Change: Models in Prehistory* (ed. C. Renfrew; London: Duckworth, 1973) 761-71.

[50] Holladay, "Kingdoms of Israel and Judah," p. 373, table 1.

[51] Although it is an often repeated mistake that these gates should represent only one characteristic type of gates. See, for example, the plans of the gates at Gezer, Hazor, Ashdod, Lachish and Megiddo in Mazar, *Archaeology*, p. 384, where the ones from Ashdod, Lachish and Megiddo show some resemblance, while Gezer is different in layout and construction as is also Hazor (which on the other hand is also very different from the one at Gezer).

[52] But see n. 28.

(i.e., that a surge in the settled culture began to be felt already in the 10th century) and (in a Palestinain scale) almost exploded during the late 9th and early 8th centuries BCE, it is only the Bible which allows Holladay to assume that a nation-state has arisen. As no inscription has so far survived from before the 9th century which speaks about an Israel,[53] it is a fair guess that the development in the 10th century may have to do with the emergence of this entity, but it has also to be acknowledged (as does Finkelstein)[54] that the development towards urbanization in the northern part of Palestine was very different from the one found in the southern part, where the urbanization was delayed by at least several generations and probably never reached the scale of the northern one.

As a matter of fact, a proper socio-archaeological analysis of the process that led to statehood in Palestine should leave out of consideration any facile reference to late biblical sources, which are by all means (although, of course, written) secondary and most likely of little help when reconstructing the developments of the 10th century BCE. If the Amarna letters are not believed to provide any adequate answers to the demographic situation of the Late Bronze Age, so much less the biblical sources, and no other written sources exist that date to the 10th century to throw a light over this period.

Furthermore, it is obvious that an approach to the subject like Holladay's, with its contaminated methodology blending Bible with archaeology, is simply running the risk of presenting an argument in favor of something which may never have existed if anything should happen to the archaeological material such as the one he is basing his explanation of the societal shift from tribalized village culture via the embryonic chiefdom to proto-state to the fully developed centralized state. As already mentioned, an archaeological revision such as a change in the ceramic chronology will do the job and destroy his edifice like a house

[53] The first references to Israel are to be found in the Tel Dan inscription, dated by A. Biran and J. Naveh, "An Aramaic Stele Fragment from Tel Dan," *IEJ* 43 (1993) 81-98, to the middle of the 9th century BCE. See, however, F. Cryer, "On the recently-Discovered 'House of David' Inscription," *SJOT* 8 (1994) 3-19, who dates it to the 8th century; and the Mesha inscription, J. C. L. Gibson, *Textbook of Syrian Semitic Inscriptions I: Hebrew and Moabite Inscriptions* (Oxford: Clarendon, 1971) 71-83. The "Israel" of the Mernephtah stele is irrelevant to this discussion (see above, n. 36).

[54] See the graphic presentations in Finkelstein, "The Great Transformation," pp. 355, 358-59, especially fig. 7, p. 358, illustrating the built up area in the Judean hills and in the northern part of the highlands north of Samaria. The scale in the northern part of Palestine is very different from the one in the southern part of the country. On Judah, see also Jamieson-Drake, *Scribes and Schools*, pp. 48-80.

of cards. As a matter of fact, such a revision has recently been published by Israel Finkelstein,[55] and if Finkelstein is correct, Holladay's Solomonic structures will have to be lowered to the 9th century. Then he can, of course, reintroduce his biblical social archaeological procedure, but will not escape the evidence of, by now, both biblical and extra-biblical sources, among which is the fact that the eponymous hero of that kingdom was not "David" or "Israel," but Omri, reckoned already many years ago by Martin Noth as an Arab mercenary in the service of the Israelite king.[56] In fact it may turn out that the eponymous ancestor of the first Israelite *state* was an Arab. That will probably destroy another part of Holladay's argument, that we are witnessing the formation not only of a secondary state,[57] but also of a nation-state.

Any student of the history of European civilization would know that the idea of the nation-state is a romantic stereotype invented by members of the bourgeois class in the post-revolutionary and proto-democratic Europe of the 19th century. I will be dealing extensively with the issue in another place and shall not repeat the argument here,[58] only to say that Holladay has here introduced a kind of bogus term that has no relevance for the situation in the ancient Near East. The prerequisite of this state is the presence of a tribal society which may have developed into a state society, however, this need not be the case as the village culture of the Late Bronze Age-Early Iron transition says nothing about a tribal society which may or may not have existed. Instead of nationality (i.e., an Israelite nationality) Holladay should have referred to the concept of *ethnicity* which would be a more correct term to apply to the situation in the ancient Near East. The introduction of this concept, however, demands

[55] I. Finkelstein, "The Archaeology of the United Monarchy: An Alternative View," *Levant* 28 (1996) 177-87.

[56] M. Noth, *Geschichte Israels* (Göttingen: Vandenhoeck & Ruprecht, 1950) 210, with n. 1; see already, *idem., Die Israelitischen Personennamen im Rahmen der gemeinsemitischen Namengebung* (BWANT 3.10; Stuttgart: W. Kohlhammer, 1928) 63. Noth also reckons the name of Ahab to be Arabic.

[57] This terminology is popular among cultural evolutionists and denotes a state which appears in a territory where states have already before been in existence. We should, however, ask how important the distinction between primary and secondary states is to the situation in the ancient Near East where such states at the beginning of the 1st millennium BCE had already been in existence for at least 2000 years! But the term is probably reflecting the sociological stereotype that states are substituted by tribal societies and vice versa. There were in fact many forms of states and many varieties of tribally organized societies and a kind of continuum line between the extremes of the fully developed state and the absolute segmentarized tribe.

[58] In my forthcoming, *The Israelites in History and Tradition* (n. 2, above).

that this ethnicity can be seen in the cultural remains of the transitional period and, as is now obvious, there are no archaeological remains which point at ethnic differences in the highlands of Palestine in this period.[59] It is, on the other side, probably correct, as maintained by many authors, that as time went by a number of cultural traits appeared which can or should be linked not least to the kingdom of which Samaria was the capital.[60] So far the state of Samaria or *Samarina*, otherwise known as Bet Omri (*Bit Humriya* in Assyrian sources) or Israel (Mesha's and the Old Testament's nomenclature for this kingdom) may in the course of its history have developed ethnic features (how weak they may have been when seen in the prespective of the Palestinian material culture in general), but these features do not belong to the inceptive period of the state.

To recapitulate: This writer will not produce an argument against social archaeology as such, although he will question the application of so-called holistic models which leave out the human factor and which try to dominate (even master) this factor so such a degree that it becomes predictable. However, in many cases with mute cultures (i.e., cultures without *written* sources) the application of models may be the only way to get beyond the point which is only descriptive and move into the realm of history. That this history is a construed history (even an invented one) is not in discord with modern ideas of history saying that history is always something which is told, i.e., formed in the present for readers living in the present world.

It is, however, a serious mistake not to pay attention to the classic discipline of history for which written sources have always been the most important source material, when such sources (few or many as it may be) are available. Before any other explanation of historical developments

---

[59] The traditional ethnic markers, such as the collared rim jar and the four room house, have all been refuted as ethnic indicators, partly because they should be seen as continuation of the culture of the Bronze Age in the Levant, and partly because their distribution is not limited to the territory of the later Israelite and Judean states. Furthermore, the nomadic origin of the four-room house may be correct; see however, K. W. Schaar, "An Architectural Theory for the Origins of the Four-Room House," *SJOT* 5 (1991) 2.75-98. The argument of the nomadic origins of the occupants of these dwellings by Redford, *Egypt, Canaan, and Israel*, p. 268, that they may have only inherited a house style from the Canaanites, is not legitimate. He cannot argue that the inhabitants were former nomads because they lived in houses! He can only say that there is a possibility that such houses were not always built and inhabited by people belonging to the previously settled part of the population.

[60] For example, an enlarged repertoire of pottery forms, styles of city planning, or the like.

are introduced, the written sources have to be analyzed and explained and eventually disregarded as being of little value. The last thing happened to the biblical narrative about the pre-monarchic history of Israel, simply because it did not fit in with the general historical picture of this era to be glimpsed from ancient Near Eastern written documents and because of the results from archaeological excavations, and it may happen again when it comes to the biblical picturing of the united monarchy. The method to be recommended to social archaeologists is simple. Archaeological excavations have to be executed without a social theory that acts as a Procrustean bed for the archaeologist's interpretation. Archaeology, as such, is a technical discipline aimed at describing facts and is, as such, only descriptive, although it, of course, contains a fair (sometimes more than that) amount of interpretation and even guesswork. In case we have written sources which concern the period being excavated, these sources will be the primary secondary tool for the archaeologist who also wants to be considered a historian. Whenever a social model is introduced to explain the archaeological remains, this model must take into consideration the testimony of the written documents so that it explains as well the archaeological remains as the written documents. Otherwise, the students of social archaeology are simply repeating the mistakes of the former biblical archaeologists, substituting biblical texts with social models in which they have as much faith as formerly in the Bible itself.

In conclusion: The problem of doing sociology with Solomon is not so much connected with the kind of sociology which is applied by the students of this time, it is simply a question of whether there is a problem at all, since it seems highly unlikely that there ever was a Solomon. The archaeological remains which have lately been utilized by social archaeologists may carry historical Solomon to his grave and may refer to a later period in the history of Palestine (i.e., in general to the period of the Omrite dynasty, 9th century BCE). The material may allow the student to reconstruct many aspects of this state, but it has so far failed to give any indications of its ethnic composition.

GLORY LOST: THE REIGN OF SOLOMON IN THE DEUTERONOMISTIC HISTORY

PAULINE A. VIVIANO

INTRODUCTION

The impact of leadership on the history of Israel is a pervasive concern of the Deuteronomistic historian. Stories of great leaders, and not so great leaders, are woven together giving us a history that embodies the theological perspective of the deuteronomic school and provides a lesson for subsequent generations on the necessity of faithfulness to YHWH. Solomon is one such leader whose story revolves around the twin poles of obedience and disobedience. It is a story shaped by the concerns of the Deuteronomistic historian. In his understanding of Israel's history it has become a story of promise denied; a story of glory lost.

1. MULTIPLE EDITIONS

Though Martin Noth had originally argued that the Deuteronomistic History was composed primarily by one author, even Noth maintained that the Deuteronomistic historian used sources and he admitted that later additions were inserted into the history.[1] Though the history may be unified by a deuteronomic ideology, the recognition of sources and additions make unity of authorship difficult to maintain and subsequent scholarship, with rare exceptions,[2] has been trying to determine the sources used by the Deuteronomistic historian or has been arguing for

[1] M. Noth, *Überlieferungsgeschichte Studien I: Die sammelnden und bearbeitenden Geschichtswerke im Alten Testament* (3rd ed.; Tübingen: Max Niemeyer, 1967; originally published in 1943). The English translation appeared in 1981: *The Deuteronomisitc History* (JSOTSup 15; Sheffield: Sheffield Academic, 1981).

[2] H. D. Hoffmann, *Reform und Reformen: Untersuchungen zu einem Grundthema der deuteronomistischen Geschichtsschreibung* (ATANT 66; Zürich: Theologischer, 1980). H. J. Boecker, *Die Beurteilung der Anfänge des Königtums in den deuteronomistischen Abschnitten des I. Samuelbuches* (WMANT 31; Neukirchen-Vluyn: Neukirchner, 1969).

two or even more editions of the history.[3] Such attempts provide valuable insight into the Deuteronomistic History and its composition, but conclusions drawn remain highly speculative. Though it seems reasonable to assume multiple authorship, the criteria used to distinguish various editions are simply inadequate and all attempts to delineate the various editions involve inevitably a certain amount of circularity in their argumentation. Contradictions, repetitions, and different perspectives may indicate the hand of a later editor, but other explanations are possible. Given that we can know so little with certainty about the process of composition in ancient Israel, and given that the Deuteronomistic History works as a unity in spite of some tensions, I will not take multiple editions into account. Rather, I will approach the role of Solomon in the Deuteronomistic History taken as a whole, whether that role is defined by the concerns of the sources used by the Deuteronomistic historian or by a first, second, or even third Deuteronomistic redactor.

2. Theology of the Deuteronomistic Historian

The role that Solomon, or any of the characters found in the Deuteronomisitc History, plays is determined by the theological interpretation of history that comes from the Deuteronomistic historian. This theological interpretation is imbued with deuteronomic ideology in which Israel, YHWH's special people, has an obligation to keep the laws of the covenant. If the laws are obeyed, peace and prosperity follow; if disobeyed, war and disaster follow. This is the deuteronomistic version of the theory of retribution and it is applied throughout the history to the nation as a whole and to prominent individuals. But all the laws of

[3] The concern for sources can be found in nearly every historical-critical commentary of this century on the Books of Deuteronomy, Joshua, Judges, 1-2 Samuel, and 1-2 Kings. Studies on multiple editions include R. Nelson, *The Double Redaction of the Deuteronomistic History* (JSOTSup 18; Sheffield: Sheffield Academic, 1981), and A. D. H. Mayes, *The Story of Israel between Settlement and Exile* (London: SCM, 1983). Several scholars find multiple redactions even though they do not accept Noth's position: A. Jepsen, *Die Quellen des Königsbuches* (Halle: Max Niemeyer, 1956); R. Smend, "Das Gesetz und die Völker: Ein Beitrag zur deuteronomistischen Redaktionsgeschichte," *Probleme biblischer Theologie* (ed. H. W. Wolff; Munich: Chr. Kaiser, 1971) 494-509; and W. Dietrich, *Prophetie und Geschichte* (FRLANT 108; Göttingen: Vandenhoeck & Ruprecht, 1972). For a recent discussion regarding the theories of multiple redactions in the Deuteronomistic History see G. N. Knoppers, *Two Nations under God: The Deuteronomistic History of Solomon and the Dual Monarchies, Vol. 1: The Reign of Solomon and the Rise of Jeroboam* (HSM 52; Atlanta: Scholars, 1993).

covenant do not receive the same attention from the Deuteronomistic historian. It is the first commandment, loyalty to YHWH, the covenant overlord, that has pride of place. For the Deuteronomistic historian that loyalty is expressed in terms of exclusive worship of YHWH. The exhortation to avoid the worship of other gods and the dire consequences of such worship pervade the Book of Deuteronomy (4:15-20, 25-40; 6:10-15; 8:19; 10:12-22; 11:13-17, 26-28; 12:1-14, 29-32; 13:1-18; 16:21-22; 17:2-7, 17; 18:9-14; 27:15; 29:17-19; 29:25ff; 30:17; 31:16ff). In the Book of Joshua the admonition against the worship of other gods is found (23:7-9) and the basis for covenant renewal is the willingness to put aside other gods and worship YHWH alone (24:14-21). The cycle of apostasy-punishment-cry for help-deliverance set out in Judg 2:11-23 dominates the Book of Judges.[4] Though the issue of exclusive worship of YHWH recedes into the background in the Books of Samuel, it is still to be found in recognized Deuteronomistic passages (1 Sam 8:8; 12:9-19). The worship of YHWH and YHWH alone is a central concern of the Books of Kings. Every king is evaluated in terms of the deuteronomistic standard as to what constitutes authentic worship of YHWH. Other sins are mentioned in the history, but none receives the emphasis given to the failure to worship YHWH alone.

It needs to be emphasized that the theory of retribution is ingrained in the core of the theology of the Deuteronomistic historian. It shapes the way he writes the history; it is behind his selection of what to relate and how to relate it.[5] Obedience and success, disobedience and failure are so integrally connected that the converse is also true for the Deuteronomistic historian. That is, failure must always be seen as the result of sin; success as obedience to YHWH's laws. Any time there is failure, it is accounted for in terms of sin; any time there is success, there must have been obedience, or if there was sin, the sinner repented and was forgiven.

---

[4] Each of the stories of the judges is set in this cycle (Othniel, 3:7-11; Ehud, 3:12-30; Deborah, 4:1-23; Gideon, 6:1-7:35; Jephthah, 10:6-12:7; Samson, 13:1-16:31) though the complete pattern of apostasy-punishment-cry for help-deliverance is not found with each story of the judges.

[5] It is increasingly recognized that this is true not only of ancient Near Eastern historiography, but also of biblical historiography; see Knoppers, *Two Nations under God*, p. 33.

3. Application of Deuteronomistic Theology to the History of Israel

It is necessary to situate the Deuteronomistic historian's perspective on Solomon within the larger context of the Deuteronomistic History for the treatment of Solomon is consistent with that of other major figures in the history. The overview that follows is not exhaustive, but focuses only on the application of the theory of retribution to prominent characters or events in the Deuteronomistic History. The presentation of Moses, as the one who led Israel out of Egypt and as the lawgiver, is consistent with the picture of Moses given in the books of Exodus, Leviticus and Numbers. Where the Deuteronomistic historian significantly differs is in the reason given for Moses' failure to enter the land. In Num 20:12 YHWH tells Moses that he will not lead Israel into the land because he doubted YHWH when YHWH commanded him to strike the rock at Meribah to bring forth water. In Numbers Moses does not enter the land because of his own sin of doubt, but in Deuteronomy Moses' fate is determined by the failure of the people, "YHWH was angry with me on your account" (Deut 1:37; 3:26; 4:21ff).[6] Moses, the law giver, the prophet *par excellence*, does not gain entrance into the land, but the fault is not his. He bears the punishment for the sin of the people; his nobility is enhanced for he suffers on behalf of the people. The Deuteronomistic historian is reluctant to attribute any fault to Moses. Moses is for him a paradigm of leadership. He does as YHWH commanded and led Israel out of Egypt and to the promised land. He speaks "just as YHWH had commanded him to speak" (Deut 1:3). Whatever failure is experienced by Moses or the people, the fault rests with the people alone.

Success or failure is more difficult to assess in the Book of Joshua for the book affirms the success of the Conquest (11:23; 21:43-45) and yet acknowledges that the land wasn't entirely conquered (13:1-6) and the inhabitants of the land were not driven off (11:19; 13:13; 15:63; 16:10; 17:12).[7] Studies of the figure of Joshua have been uniformly positive in their assessment of his role,[8] but Joshua does not follow the orders given

[6] That Moses did not enter the land because he doubted YHWH at Meribah is found in Deut 32:51, but this passage is attributed to P, as is Num 20:12; see G von Rad, *Deuteronomy* (OTL; Philadelphia: Westminster, 1966) 45.

[7] For the ambiguity this creates, see L. D. Hawk, *Every Promise Fulfilled: Contesting Plots in Joshua* (Louisville: Westminster/John Knox, 1991).

[8] Joshua as successor of Moses: N. Lohfink, "Die deuteronomistische Darstellung des Übergangs der Führung Israel von Moses auf Josue," *Scholastik* 37 (1962) 32-44; J. R.

by YHWH and the Deuteronomistic historian is strangely silent about this. Joshua is commanded to cross the Jordan and begin the conquest (1:2-9), but instead he sends spies to Jericho initiating a secret mission contrary to the orders given by YHWH in chapter 1. Only in chapter 3 does he do as YHWH commanded. As a result of sending the spies to Jericho, Rahab and her family are spared when the Israelites take over the land. This is a direct violation of the command given in Deut 7:1-2 and 20:16-17, and leads, as noted by Eslinger, "to an intolerable pre-conflict interaction and illegal relationship between Israel and the enemy."[9] Nevertheless, there is no condemnation of Joshua for his failure to follow the orders issued to him by YHWH. In the story of the defeat at Ai and the story of the covenant with the Gibeonites it is Joshua's omissions that stand out. Though the defeat at Ai is blamed on the sin of Achan,[10] Joshua receives no directive from YHWH authorizing the battle as he did before taking Jericho (6:2-5) and engaging in battle against the five kings (10:8). Rather, he again sends out spies and adopts their battle strategy without consulting YHWH.[11] Though it is the leaders who did not consult YHWH regarding the covenant with the Gibeonites (9:14), Joshua is the one who actually makes the covenant with them (9:15) and so should stand condemned. Again the command of Deuteronomy (7:1-2; 20:16-17) has been compromised by Joshua's and the leaders' failure to consult YHWH, but again the Deuteronomistic historian is silent. We are left with a book in which the land is conquered, but it isn't; and Joshua obeys the commands of YHWH, but he doesn't. The theory of retribution is actually applied in the Book of Joshua only to Achan's sin. That sin leads to defeat, but other failings are ignored. For the Deuteronomistic historian the conquest is YHWH's action and the failings of the people and Joshua can delay it, but they cannot annul it entirely.

A strict application of the theory of retribution is nowhere clearer than in the Book of Judges. The repeated apostasy of the people leads to a cycle of oppression by their enemies as punishment. Their return to

---

Porter, "The Succession of Joshua," *Proclamation and Presence* (eds. J. I. Durham and J. R. Porter; Richmond, Vir.: John Knox, 1970) 102-132; Joshua as prototype of Josiah: R. Nelson, "Josiah in the Book of Joshua," *JBL* 100 (1981) 531-40.

[9] L. Eslinger, *Into the Hands of the Living God* (Bible and Literature 24; JSOTSup 84; Sheffield: Almond, 1989) 37.

[10] Though Achan is singled out, the opening verse (Josh 7:1) makes his sin an example of the unfaithfulness of the people.

[11] T. C. Butler, *Joshua* (WBC 7; Waco, Tex.: Word Books, 1983) 79. Butler notes that this suggested battle strategy deviates from the typical spy narrative form and so prepares the way for defeat.

YHWH in their distress leads to their deliverance by a judge, but when the judge dies, apostasy returns and the cycle begins again. Only the behavior of the people is evaluated by the Deuteronomistic historian; questionable behavior on the part of the judges is ignored. Gideon's idol which became a snare to the people, Jephthah's vow and the subsequent sacrificing of his daughter, and Samson's weakness for Philistine women, are passed over without comment. These judges were chosen by YHWH and they successfully delivered Israel from its enemies. Success indicates obedience, so whatever "flaws" the judges may have had, they are ignored. Nevertheless, all is not right with the leadership of the judges. The lack of continuity in leadership results in repeated lapses into apostasy. The last section of Judges, though it may be an addition to the Deuteronomistic History,[12] concludes with the observation, "In those days there was no king in Israel; all the people did what was right in their own eyes" (Judg 21:25). The judges may have delivered the people time and again, but the style of leadership represented by these charismatic figures is not able to deal with the problem of the apostasy of the people and from here the focus of the Deuteronomistic History shifts to the establishment of the monarchy.

Samuel is the last and the greatest of the judges. The importance of Samuel is underscored in the narrative of his birth. His mother was a barren woman and thus God intervened in a special way in his birth; he is dedicated to YHWH as a Nazirite. As a child he is dedicated to the service of YHWH at Shiloh and is raised by the priest Eli. He is called by YHWH and will function as prophet announcing a word of judgment against Eli and his house for the corruption of Eli's sons. He will be successful against the Philistines, though the statement that the Philistines never again entered Israelite territory is countered by the recognition that the Philistines were a threat under Saul (1 Sam 13-14) and David (2 Sam 5:17-25; 8:1). There is never any question of the fidelity of Samuel. He follows YHWH's directives in anointing Saul and David, even though he is against kingship. It is the people who betray a lack of fidelity in asking for a king (1 Sam 10:19) and in worshiping other gods (1 Sam 8:8). Though Samuel, like Eli, has corrupt sons, he is never admonished for his own failure to restrain his sons. Samuel, like Moses, is presented solely in the positive by the Deuteronomisitic historian.

The rise to kingship and the reigns of Saul and David are treated at length in the Deuteronomistic History, but I will focus only on the

---

[12] A. D. H. Mayes, *Judges* (OTG; Sheffield: Sheffield Academic, 1985) 14-15.

Deuteronomistic historian's concern with obedience and success, disobedience and failure in their stories. Up to this point in the history the Deuteronomistic historian was concerned with what the people were doing as well as their leaders, but in these stories the wrongdoing of the people is never directly mentioned.[13] The focus is solely on the kings, Saul and David. The Deuteronomistic historian has grouped all the positive stories surrounding Saul and David at the beginning of the cycles of stories about them. Only after they have sinned will the Deuteronomistic historian introduce the negative aspects of their reigns. This will be the same for both David and Saul, but there the similarity ends. Saul loses his kingdom and dynasty because of his sin; David retains his kingdom and dynasty in spite of his sin. There are two stories of Saul's sin that lead to rejection of him as king (1 Sam 13; 15). His failure to wait until Samuel arrived is spoken of as tantamount to a rejection of YHWH's commands (1 Sam 13:13). That he spared the life of the king of the Amalekites and the best of the sheep and cattle is, according to Samuel, again, a failure to carry out a command of YHWH (1 Sam 15:19). After attempting to shift the blame to the people, Saul admits his transgression and asks for forgiveness, but his request for pardon is denied (1 Sam 15:24-26). For the Deuteronomistic historian Saul is a failure, therefore he must have sinned. There is nothing in the Saul material to suggest that Saul worshiped other gods, so his sin must be found elsewhere. The sin is found in his lack of obedience to YHWH's commands as directed by YHWH's prophet, Samuel. Though Saul remains on the throne, he is a rejected king and his dynasty is rejected; the remainder of his reign is the story of a defeated person.

David's sins, adultery and murder, do not lead to his rejection as king nor to the rejection of his dynasty. We cannot help but wonder at this double standard. Saul's failure to wait for Samuel and to carry out *ḥerem* to its fullest extent, seem insignificant compared to the sins of lust and murder by David, but nevertheless David is forgiven. David's sin is not without its punishment for the child conceived in adultery dies and the rest of his reign is marred by rebellions, one of which is led by his own son. Nevertheless, from the perspective of the Deuteronomisitic historian David is a king whose heart is wholly turned toward YHWH (1 Kgs 11:4; 15:3). This evaluation of David by the Deuteronomistic historian

[13] There is an attempt on the part of Saul to blame the people (1 Sam 15:15, 21), but that blame is swept aside by Samuel. Saul, and Saul alone, is held accountable for preserving the best of the animals from *ḥerem*.

shows how fully the converse of the theory of retribution determines the way the history is written and its kings are evaluated. David does not lose the throne and his dynasty is established, so David must have been faithful to YHWH. Clearly he was not faithful to every one of YHWH's laws, but he is obedient to the only law that is really determinative for the Deuteronomistic historian: the worship of YHWH and YHWH alone. For all of David's indiscretions, the Deuteronomistic historian never accuses him of abandoning YHWH for other gods.

4. The Deuteronomistic Historian's Presentation of Solomon's Reign

Apart from brief acknowledgment of the birth of Solomon and of YHWH's love for him (2 Sam 13:24-25) our first introduction to Solomon is in the story of his accession to the throne (1 Kgs 1-2).[14] The manner in which Solomon secures his throne may strike us as ruthless, but the Deuteronomistic historian does not view his actions in a negative light. There is no hint that he is critical of Solomon's behavior. Indeed, Adonijah, the elder brother of Solomon and presumably legitimate successor, acknowledges that the kingdom is Solomon's "from YHWH" (1 Kgs 2:15). Solomon's successful takeover must mean that YHWH approves of his accession to the throne. Neither the notice that Solomon has married an Egyptian princess (1 Kgs 3:1) nor that he worshiped at high places (1 Kgs 3:2-3) reflect negatively upon Solomon at this point in the narrative. The marriage is simply reported and is probably meant to indicate the prominence to which Solomon had risen that he could marry a daughter of an Egyptian pharaoh. That Solomon worships at high places is excused since the Temple had not yet been built (1 Kgs 3:2).[15] 1 Kgs 3-4 testifies to Solomon's wisdom, his administrative abilities, and the prosperity of his reign. Solomon's building projects occupy 1 Kgs 5-8 with the major focus upon the building, furnishing, and dedication of the Temple.[16] There is some debate as to where the down-

[14] There is some debate as to whether 1 Kgs 1-2 is the conclusion of the David story or the beginning of the Solomon story; see Knoppers, *Two Nations under God*, pp. 60-63, for a detailed argument of this issue.

[15] This verse applies to the people, and may be a later insertion, but its proximity to the statement that Solomon worshiped on high places provides an excuse for his behavior as well.

[16] 1 Kgs 8 is recognized as one of the key passages where the editorial hand and theo-

side of Solomon's reign begins.[17] 1 Kgs 9 contains a second appearance of YHWH to Solomon and the content of Solomon's speech anticipates Solomon's (and the people's) apostasy and punishment. Hiram is dissatisfied with Solomon's payment (1 Kgs 9:10-14) and mention is made of Solomon's program of forced labor (1 Kgs 9:15-22), but it is not clear that either of these reports are intended to reflect negatively upon Solomon. The rest of chapter 9 and chapter 10 report on Solomon's administrative abilities, his cultic activities, his fleet, the spread of his fame and the wealth of his reign. By and large 1 Kgs 1-10 presents Solomon and his reign in a favorable light. The impression given is one of unparalleled peace and prosperity under the reign of a wise king. Nothing in the earlier history and nothing that follows in the history of Israel can compare to this age,[18] but all is lost in 1 Kgs 11. Solomon's idolatry leads, not simply to trouble with Edom and Aram, but more importantly for the Deuteronomistic historian, to the split of the kingdom. The unity of the tribes achieved under David and continued during the reign of Solomon is shattered. The Davidic dynasty will continue to rule "for the sake of David," but it will rule over a diminished kingdom, because of Solomon's idolatry.

Thus we see in broad outline the content of 1 Kgs 1-11. The Deuteronomistic historian arranges his narrative of Solomon's reign in the same manner in which he had arranged the Saul and David material: first the positive, then the negative. The artificial nature of this sequence is apparent in the Solomonic material. Hadad and Rezon are raised up as adversaries after the notice of Solomon's idolatry, but it is clear from the history itself that the trouble Solomon had with Hadad and Rezon lasted throughout his reign (1 Kgs 11:25). There can be no doubt that the

---

logical perspective of the Deuteronomistic historian are evident, but I have not treated it apart from 1 Kgs 5-8 as it focuses more on the place of the Temple in the theology of the Deuteronomistic historian than on Solomon.

[17] This debate is reflected in many recent studies on the structure of the Solomonic narrative: K. I. Parker, "Repetition as a Structuring Device in 1 Kings 1-11," *JSOT* 42 (1988) 19-27; M. Brettler, "The Structure of 1 Kings 1-11," *JSOT* 49 (1991) 87-97; A. Frisch, "Structure and Its Significance: The Narrative of Solomon's Reign (1 Kings 1:1-12:24)," *JSOT* 51 (1991) 3-14, and subsequent rejoinders by Parker, pp. 15-21, and Frisch, pp. 22-24. For a fuller treatment see K. I. Parker, *Wisdom and Law in the Reign of Solomon* (Lampeter, Dyfe, Wales: Edwin Mellen, 1992). For an earlier treatment see B. Porten, "The Structure and Theme of the Solomon Narrative (1 Kings 3-11)," *HUCA* 38 (1967) 93-128.

[18] Knoppers, *Two Kingdoms under God*, pp. 77-134, presents an extensive argument that the age of Solomon is presented by the Deuteronomistic historian as Israel's ideal age.

Deuteronomistic historian's retributive theology has dictated the ordering of his narrative. Early in the narrative the Deuteronomistic historian ignores opportunities to condemn Solomon. That Solomon and the people worship at high places, usually a point of contention for the Deuteronomistic historian, is excused as the "Temple was not yet built." Where the Deuteronomistic historian has the opportunity to fault Solomon for his foreign marriages (1 Kgs 3:1) and buying horses from Egypt (1 Kgs 10:28-29), both of which are forbidden in the deuteronomic law (Deut 17:16-17),[19] he does not do so. Nothing detracts from the positive portrait of Solomon, a king who loves YHWH and walks in the ways of David (1 Kgs 3:3). The accumulation of detail (about his marriage to Pharaoh's daughter, his wisdom, his wealth, his fame, his building projects of which the Temple is particularly noted and described), is evoked to suggest an age unparalleled in its glory.

In the midst of the positive portrait of Solomon, chapter 9 introduces a jarring note: all may be lost. If Solomon is obedient to YHWH's commands then his throne will be established over Israel forever (1 Kgs 9:4-5). Apostasy will result in exile and the Temple will be destroyed (1 Kgs 9:6-9).[20] The retributive theology of the Deuteronomistic historian is clearly set forth: continued peace and prosperity rest upon the faithfulness of Israel's king and its people.[21] Both will fail. Solomon is the first of the kings to be accused of idolatry; neither Saul nor David, for all their wrongdoing, are ever so accused. Solomon's sin brings us back to the days of the judges, but in 1 Kgs 11:1-13 it is not the people who are indicted for their apostasy; it is the king himself. Solomon's kingship is ultimately, for the Deuteronomistic historian, a failure. There is an opportunity for success under Jeroboam, but his kingship will also fail for lack of fidelity in worship. Only as a king stands firm in his opposition to idolatry is there hope for the nation. The severity of Solomon's sin results in a severe punishment: the nation will be torn from Solomon; it is only because of David that the throne is not entirely lost.[22] The

[19] It is difficult to say whether Deut 17:16-17 preceded 1 Kgs 10:28 or was written in light of it.

[20] In verse 6 there is a shift from singular to plural in the pronoun "you" and presumably the plural "you" is the people. This shift may suggest that 1 Kgs 9:6-9 is an addition, but as the text now reads, the king and the people are linked in the same theological frame: turning away from YHWH results in loss.

[21] In the Deuteronomistic History people and king are linked; see G. von Rad, *Old Testament Theology* (New York: Harper & Row, 1962) 1.339.

[22] "For the sake of David" runs the refrain through 1 Kgs 11 (verses 12, 13, 32, 34, 36) and continues in 1 Kgs 15:4; 2 Kgs 8:19; 19:34; 20:6.

Deuternonomistic historian needs to account not simply for the loss of the northern tribes, but for the continued reign of the Davidic kings in the south. He is able to do so by attributing the loss to the sin of Solomon, and the gain to David's faithfulness.

A comparison of the Deuteronomistic historian's presentation of Solomon with that of the Chronicler provides a point of contrast. The difference in the Chronicler's depiction of Solomon is underscored by what he deletes from the Deuteronomistic History. The Chronicler omits any reference to fault or sin on the part of Solomon.[23] In 1 Chr 28:1-29:25 Solomon's accession to the throne is presented as divinely ordained (1 Chr 28:5). There is no palace coup to be crushed as in 1 Kgs 1-2, nor are there any enemies of David for Solomon to take vengeance on in the name of his father. The passing on of rule proceeds without opposition (1 Chr 29:23-24). The Chronicler, by omitting 1 Kgs 3:2-3, avoids the need to excuse what was obviously a problem for the Deuteronomistic historian: worship at high places. The account of Solomon's sin and its consequences (1 Kgs 11:1-40) is completely absent from the Chronicler's history. In the Chronicler's account the split of the kingdom results from Jeroboam's return from exile coupled with Rehoboam's refusal to lighten the "yoke" on the northern tribes (2 Chr 10). The notable omission of the Deuteronomistic historian's negative evaluation of Solomon in Chronicles creates a very different picture of Solomon. He is a king chosen by God and supported by the people. His reign is remembered for its peace and prosperity. His role as Temple builder is highlighted. Even his foreign marriages are viewed positively. The Chronicler presents Solomon "as one who from first to last, was completely faithful to YHWH."[24]

The contrast with the depiction of Solomon found in the Deuteronomistic History is striking. The tendentious nature of each historian is thrown into clear relief. The Chronicler's concern with the Temple dictates his presentation of Solomon as one worthy to build the Temple. Even Solomon's wisdom has its referent in Temple building.[25] The Deuteronomistic historian's presentation of Solomon reveals his concern to use history as a lesson about the evils of idolatry. There was the possibility that kingship could prevent Israel's incessant return to apostasy. Fidelity of the king would result in fidelity of the people. Faithful lead-

---

[23] This is consistent with the manner in which the Chronicler also treats David.

[24] R. L. Braun, "Solomonic Apologetic in Chronicles," *JBL* 92 (1973) 507.

[25] R. B. Dillard, *I Chronicles* (WBC 15; Waco, Tex.: Word Books, 1987) 2.

ers and divinely ordained dynastic succession would bring peace and prosperity. That possibility is realized in the reign of Solomon, only to be lost by his infidelity.

5. Conclusion

The tragedy of "what might have been" is a fitting description of the Deuteronomistic historian's perspective on the age of Solomon. The hopes and expectations surrounding kingship seem realized in the peace and prosperity of his reign, in his wisdom, and in his building of the Temple, only to be eclipsed by his unfaithfulness to YHWH. The king who loved YHWH and foreign women is led by his love for one to betray his love for the other. The disastrous consequences of that unfaithfulness for Israel fill the rest of the Deuteronomistic History. Kingship could have succeeded, but only if the king's heart was "wholly after YHWH" as was David's (1 Kgs 11:4; 15:3). Whatever promise is held out for Solomon in the first part of the Book of Kings, it is lost by his idolatry. Beyond the Books of Kings, Solomon will be remembered for his wisdom (Prov 1:1; 10:1; 25:1) or his wealth and splendor (Cant 3:7, 9, 11; 8:11, 12), but for the Deuteronomistic historian he is remembered as the one who built the Temple (2 Kgs 21:7; 24:13; 25:15) *and* as the one who built high places to the gods of his foreign wives (2 Kgs 23:13) and so strayed in fidelity to the God who loved him.

JOSEPHUS' VIEW OF SOLOMON*

LOUIS H. FELDMAN

1. INTRODUCTION: ISSUES

In his *magnum opus*, the *Jewish Antiquities*, Josephus, in accordance with the Peripatetic tradition (his chief source for the last half of the *Antiquities* was, it appears, Nicholas of Damascus, a well-known Peripatetic),[1] stresses the role of great men in history. The tendency to build up biblical heroes, notably Moses, is to be found in such Hellenistic predecessors as Eupolemus, Pseudo-Eupolemus, Artapanus, Ezekiel the tragedian, and Philo the philosopher.

Though Josephus assures the reader that he will set forth the precise details of the Scriptures, neither adding nor omitting anything,[2] he actually modifies the biblical account in numerous places. This is largely because his primary audience consists of non-Jews, seen from the fact that in the preface he cites as a precedent for his work the translation of the Torah into Greek for King Ptolemy Philadelphus (*Ant.* 1.10). This is confirmed by the fact that he asks whether any of the Greeks have been curious to learn "our" history (*Ant.* 1.9) and that he specifically declares that his history was undertaken in the belief that the whole Greek world would find it worthy of attention (*Ant.* 1.5). Finally, at the end of his work (*Ant.* 20.262), he boasts that no one else would have been equal to the task of issuing so accurate a treatise for the Greeks, which indicates that he directed it to the non-Jewish world, since the term "Greeks" for Josephus is used in contrast to Jews.

Josephus' handling of certain incidents, such as that of Israel's sin with the Midianite women (Num 25:1-9, *Ant.* 4.131-155),[3] does show

---

* A longer presentation of this chapter may be found in L. H. Feldman, "Josephus' Portrait of Solomon," *HUCA* 66 (1995) 103-67.

[1] See my "Josephus' Portrait of Saul," *HUCA* 53 (1982) 46-48.

[2] *Ant.* 1.17. See my discussion of the meaning of this promise in my "Use, Authority and Exegesis of Mikra in the Writings of Josephus," *Mikra: Text, Translation, Reading and Interpretation of the Hebrew Bible in Ancient Judaism and Early Christianity* (ed. Martin J. Mulder and Harry Sysling; CRINT 2.1; Assen: Van Gorcum, 1988) 466-70.

[3] See W.C. van Unnik, "Josephus' Account of the Story of Israel's Sin with Alien

that Josephus is concerned to reach a Jewish audience as well; but, taken as a whole, the first half of the *Antiquites*, in its modified paraphrase of the Bible, is most concerned with the agenda of Josephus' later essay *Against Apion*, namely defending the Jews against the charges of their enemies. In this respect Josephus' portrayal of King Solomon becomes a prime showcase for the defense.[4]

2. The Importance of Solomon for Josephus

The key personality in Josephus' answer to the charge, made by Apion (*Against Apion* 2.135), that the Jews had not produced any eminent sages, was Solomon. In an extra-biblical addition (*Ant.* 8.190) Josephus, summarizing the greatness of Solomon before discussing his deviations from Jewish tradition, asserts that he had been the most illustrious (ἐνδοξότατος) of all kings, the most beloved by G-d (θεοφιλέστατος), and the most outstanding in understanding (φρονήσει) and wealth of those who had ruled the Hebrews before him.

One indication of the importance of Solomon for Josephus may be seen in that he cites more external evidence to support his account of Solomon than he does for any other biblical personality. He devotes no fewer than 8 paragraphs of his narrative (*Ant.* 8.55-56, 144-149) to citing evidence in the Tyrian archives of the correspondence between King Hiram of Tyre and Solomon, informing the inquisitive reader that copies of these letters are available even in Josephus' own day (*Ant.* 8.55). He apologetically explains to the reader (*Ant.* 8.56) that the reason why he

---

Women in the Country of Midian (Num. 25:1ff.)" *Travels in the World of the Old Testament: Studies Presented to Professor M. A. Beek* (Assen: Van Gorcum, 1974) 241-61.

[4] The first attempt to survey Josephus' treatment of Solomon compares Josephus' account with that of the Bible, but the survey is hardly systematic and merely summarizes, without analysis, the high points of Josephus' account where it differs from that of the Bible: W. Sarowy, *Quellenkritische Untersuchungen zur Geschichte König Salomos* (Königsberg: Leopold, 1900) 44-48. My own "Josephus as an Apologist to the Greco-Roman World: His Portrait of Solomon," *Aspects of Religious Propaganda in Judaism and Early Christianity* (ed. E. Schüssler Fiorenza; Notre Dame: University of Notre Dame, 1976) 69-98, is a mere sketch and does not attempt to be exhaustive. H. E. Faber van der Meulen, "Das Salomo-Bild in Hellenistisch-Jüdischen Schriften" (Ph.D. diss., Kampen, 1978), likewise makes no attempt to be exhaustive and is concerned (69-78) primarily with challenging my equation of Solomon with Oedipus. It is surprising that J. Lassner, *Demonizing the Queen of Sheba: Boundaries of Gender and Culture in Postbiblical Judaism and Medieval Islam* (Chicago: University of Chicago Press, 1993) makes no mention at all of Josephus' treatment of the Queen of Sheba narrative.

has dealt with Solomon's relations with the Tyrians in such great detail is that he wants his readers to know that his account is true. He also quotes from two non-Jewish writers, Menander and Dius (*Ant.* 8.144-149), to confirm these statements. Most remarkably, he engages in a long and seemingly utterly irrelevant digression (*Ant.* 8.155-159) to explain why all the Egyptian kings until the pharaoh who was Solomon's father-in-law are called pharaohs; all this establishes the point that the books of the Jews agree with those of the Egyptians in many details.

In his classic apologetic work, *Against Apion*, he has more references to Solomon than to any other biblical figure except Moses. In his effort to prove the antiquity and prominence of the Jews, he devotes no fewer than 22 paragraphs to reproducing the evidence from Phoenician chronicles and from Dius and Menander of Ephesus to confirm the historicity of the friendship between Hiram and Solomon and of the wisdom of Solomon (*Against Apion* 1.106-127). The fact that Josephus reproduces verbatim in the essay *Against Apion* (1.113-115, 117-120) the words of Dius and Menander that are found in the *Antiquities* (8.147-149, 144-146), whereas in no other case does Josephus repeat verbatim material from the *Antiquities,* shows how important he regarded this evidence.

One test of the importance that Josephus attaches to a given pericope is the sheer amount of space he devotes to it as compared with the coverage in the Bible itself.[5] There is a ratio of 3.41 for Josephus as compared with the Hebrew text for the account of Korah, 2.70 for Saul, 2.45 for Eglon and Ehud, 2.21 for Balaam, 2.16 for Jeroboam. 2.01 for Jehu, 2.00 for Joseph (5.45 for the episode of Joseph and Potiphar's wife and 3.28 for the narrative dealing with Joseph's dreams and subsequent enslavement), 1.98 for Ahab, 1.95 for David, 1.93 for Jehoram of Israel, 1.87 for Samuel, 1.83 for Absalom, 1.54 for Samson, 1.52 for Elijah, 1.32 for Daniel, 1.20 for Ezra (.72 compared with the LXX), 1.15 for Jonah. For Solomon (1 Kgs 1:11-11:43 [672 lines], 1 Chr 22:2-23:1, 28:1-29:30 [122 lines]; Josephus, *Ant.* 7.335-342, 348-362, 370-388, 392, 8.2-211 [1721 lines]) the ratio of Josephus' account to 1 Kgs is 2.56; the ratio of Josephus to 1 Kgs combined with 1 Chr is 2:17.[6] Hence, from this point

[5] For the Hebrew I have used the standard edition of the biblical text with the commentary of M. L. Malbim (New York: Friedman, s.a.); for the LXX I have used A. Rahlfs, *Septuaginta* (vol. 1; Stuttgart: Priviligierte Württembergische Bibelanstalt, 1935). For Josephus I have used the LCL text of H. St. J. Thackeray, *Josephus* (vol. 4; London: Heinemann, 1930); Thackeray and R. Marcus, *Josephus* (vol. 5; London: Heinemann, 1934); and Marcus, *Josephus* (vol. 6; London: Heinemann, 1937).

[6] For the Solomon pericope there is evidence that Josephus used both a Hebrew text

of view, the Solomon pericope is clearly one of greatest importance for Josephus. Moreover, because of Josephus' position straddling the Jewish and the non-Jewish worlds, his portrait is of particular significance.

That Josephus (*Ant.* 8.211) assigns to Solomon a reign twice as long as that given to him in both accounts in the Bible (1 Kgs 11:42 and 2 Chr 9:30) and in the LXX adds to the stature of the king, for he is depicted as reigning 80 years, a period exceeded by no Greek, Roman or Oriental sovereign.[7] Rappaport notes that 1 Kgs 11:4 speaks of Solomon's old age and suggests that this is the basis for Josephus' figure;[8] but it is Josephus, and no other extant source, that takes the initiative in doubling the number of years of his reign.

3. SOLOMON'S VIRTUES

If we examine such key figures in Josephus' narrative as Abraham, Isaac, Jacob, Joseph, Moses, Samson, Saul, and David, we see that stress is placed on the external qualities of good birth, upbringing, handsomeness, and the four cardinal virtues of character (wisdom, courage, temperance, justice) and the spiritual attribute of piety.[9] The Jewish hero

(e.g., *Ant.* 8.21 [Josephus follows the Hebrew order; cf 1 Kgs 3:1 ff.], 8.54 [cypresses rather than pines], 8.59 [3,300 rather than 3,600 overseers], 8.64 [the length of the Temple was 30 cubits vs. 25 in the LXX], 8.123 [Solomon celebrated Tabernacles for 14 days vs. 7 in the Vaticanus manuscript of the LXX]) and a Greek text (e.g., *Ant.* 8.13 [Josephus reads Solomon for Absalom], 8.17 [the oath is mentioned at this point], 8.57 [20,000 baths of oil vs. twenty measures of oil in the Hebrew], 8.72 [Josephus closely follows the wording of 2 Chr 3:14], 8.77 [Hebrew omits that the pillars were 4 fingers in thicknesš, 8.81 [the bases of the lavers were 5 cubits in length vs. 4 in Hebrew, 6 cubits in height vs. 3 in Hebrew], 8.140 [head of a calf vs. Hebrew "a rounded top"], 8.202 [LXX on 1 Kgs 11:22 adds "So Ader returned to his country"]), and that he occasionally disagrees with both (e.g., *Ant.* 8.61 [Solomon began to build the Temple 592 (Hebrew and Lucianic 480) years after the Israelites' exodus from Egypt]) 8.64 [the height of the Temple was 60 cubits vs. 30 in the Hebrew and 25 in the LXX]). A. Rahlfs, *Septuaginta Studien* (Göttingen: Vandenhoeck & Ruprecht, 1911) 3.92, notes that for the story of Solomon Josephus follows the MT even though it deviates strongly from the LXX. He is followed by Faber van der Meulen, *Salomo-Bild*, p. 25, who asserts that Josephus in this pericope always follows the MT. Both seem to be mistaken.

[7] Agathonius of Gades, according to Cicero, *De Senectute* 19, reigned for 80 years and lived for 120.

[8] S. Rappaport, *Agada und Exegese bei Flavius Josephus* (Vienna: Alexander Kohut Memorial Foundation, 1930) 58, no. 239.

[9] See my "Hellenizations in Josephus' *Jewish Antiquities*: The Portrait of Abraham," *Josephus, Judaism, and Christianity* (ed. L. H. Feldman and G. Hata; Detroit: Wayne State University Press, 1987) 133-153; "Josephus' Portrait of Isaac," *Rivista di*

must be a Platonic-like philosopher-king and a Pericles-like statesman, all in one. The recitation of his virtues is a veritable aretalogy, such as was popular in Hellenistic times.[10]

David, in Josephus' account, exhorts Solomon to cultivate virtues (*Ant.* 7.338); he is urged to be pious, just, and brave (εὐσεβὴς ὢν καὶ ἀνδρεῖος). They are the same virtues of piety (εὐσεβείᾳ), justice (δικαιοσύνῃ), and fortitude (ἀνδρείᾳ), which, together with obedience (πειθοῖ), are set forth by G-d Himself (*Ant.* 6.160) to Samuel as those which comprise beauty of soul and which He seeks in a king.[11] Solomon's virtues are especially prominent, inasmuch as, whereas in 1 Kgs 5:21, Hiram, king of Tyre, blesses G-d for having given David a wise son, in Josephus' version (*Ant.* 8:53) Hiram praises G-d for having given to Solomon not only wisdom but every virtue. Such praise is especially effective, inasmuch as it comes from a non-Jew.

a. *Upbringing*

One of the typical motifs of the Hellenistic, Roman, Christian, and rabbinic biography of a hero was his exceptional physical development, beauty, self-control, and precocious intellectual development as a child.[12] Solomon's precociousness is highlighted by Josephus (*Ant.* 8.2), through his stress on the fact (not mentioned in 1 Kgs 2:12) that when Solomon took over the rule he was only 14 (*Ant.* 8.211), still a mere youth in age (νέον τὴν ἡλικίαν).[13]

Storia e Leteratura Religiosa 29 (1993) 3-33; "Josephus' Portrait of Jacob," *JQR* 79 (1988-89) 101-51; "Josephus' Portrait of Joseph," *RB* 99 (1992) 379-417, 504-28; "Josephus' Portrait of Moses," *JQR* 82 (1991-1992) 285-328; 83 (1992-93) 7-50, 301-30; "Josephus' Version of Samson," *JSJ* 19 (1988) 171-214; "Josephus' Portrait of Saul," pp. 45-99; and "Josephus' Portrait of David," *HUCA* 60 (1989) 129-74.

[10] See my "Use, Authority and Exegesis of Mikra," pp. 485-94.

[11] Similarly, the qualities of character possessed by Hezekiah which are singled out for special praise by Josephus are his kindly (χρηστή), just (δικαία), and pious (εὐσεβής) nature (*Ant.* 9.260).

[12] See C. Perrot, "Les Recits d'enfance dans la Haggada antérieure au IIe siècle," *RSR* 55 (1967) 481-518, who has collected the haggadic materials relating to the childhood of Noah, Abraham, Isaac, Moses, Samson, Samuel, and Elijah. Furthermore, one may note the examples taken from Plutarch, Quintus Curtius, Philostratus, Pseudo-Callisthenes, 1 Enoch, Philo, and Jubilees, cited by C. H. Talbert, "Prophecies of Future Greatness: The Contribution of Greco-Roman Biographies to an Understanding of Luke 1:5-4:15," *The Divine Helmsman: Studies on G-d's Control of Human Events Presented to Lou H. Silberman* (ed. James L. Crenshaw and Samuel Sandmel; New York: KTAV, 1980) 135.

[13] According to the *Seder Olam* 14, Solomon was only 12 when he succeeded to the

1 Kgs 3:3 declares merely that Solomon loved the L-rd, walking in the statutes of his father, whereas Josephus (*Ant.* 8.21) makes a point of stressing that he was not hindered by his youth from dealing justice, observing the laws, and performing all tasks with as great scrupulousness (ἀκριβείας) as do those of advanced age and mature wisdom. Josephus (*Ant.* 8.23) makes a point of stressing that when G-d offered to give Solomon whatever he might wish, Solomon did not respond by asking for wealth, as one so young might have been expected to do, but rather asked, as only a truly mature person would do, for an understanding mind. The youth of Solomon is likewise stressed in Josephus' account of Solomon's judgment in the case of the two women. There, in an addition to Scripture (*Ant.* 8.32), after he ordered the two children cut in half, all the people secretly made fun of Solomon as a mere lad (μειράκιον).

b. *Wisdom*

The Greeks placed great stress upon wisdom as the *sine qua non* of a leader. This is the distinctive quality of the philosopher-king in Plato's *Republic*. Moreover, one of the characteristics of the μεγαλόψυχος, Aristotle's "great-souled man," is that he is wise; no virtuous man, he says, is foolish (ἠλίθιος, "silly") or unintelligent (ἀνόητος, "senseless").[14]

The chief example to disprove the contention that the Jews had produced no wise men was Solomon. Apparently, if we may judge from the statement of Emperor Julian, who is, on the whole, not unsympathetic to the Jews (though, of course, we must remember that he lived almost a millennium and a half after Solomon), Solomon had his detractors. Julian asks whether Solomon is comparable with the gnomic poets Phocylides and Theognis or the renowned orator Isocrates, proceeding to declare as self-evident that the exhortations of Isocrates are superior in wisdom to Solomon's proverbs.[15] He then reduces Solomon's wisdom to absurdity by noting that he had been led astray by the arguments of a woman.

Solomon's choice of wisdom is highlighted in Josephus to an even

throne. Other sources, cited by L. Ginzberg, *The Legends of the Jews*, (Philadelphia: Jewish Publication Society, 1928) 6.277, nt. 1, indicate he was 13.

[14] Aristotle, *Ethics* 4.3.1123C34-1125A17.

[15] Julian, *Contra Galilaeos* 224C-D

greater degree than it is in the Bible. David's prayer to G-d in 1 Chr 29:19 is that Solomon may be given a perfect *heart* (לבב); but in Josephus (*Ant.* 7.381) his prayer is that he may be given a sound (ὑγιῆ) and just *mind* (διάοιαν). In contrast to Solomon's request in 1 Kgs 3:9 for an understanding heart (לב), Josephus' Solomon (*Ant.* 8.23) requests a sound mind (νοῦν ὑγιῆ) and good practical wisdom (φρόνησιν ἀγαθήν). Later, it is this G-d-given wisdom (κατ' ἐπιφροσύνην τοῦ θεοῦ) that Josephus stresses (*Ant.* 15.398) that led Solomon to surround the Temple mount with great works at the top.

The key incident illustrating Solomon's wisdom is the case (1 Kgs 3:16-28) of two harlots who gave birth to children, one of whom died, both claiming the living child as her own. First, Josephus (*Ant.* 8.26), in an extra-biblical remark, calls attention to the difficulty of the case, adding that it was troublesome to find a solution. To emphasize this difficulty Josephus uses no fewer that three different words (δυσχερής, ἐπίπονον, δύσκολον). Second, in a direct address to his readers in the first person (which he rarely uses), he explains that he has thought it necessary to explain the matter about which the suit concerned that they might have an idea of how difficult (δύσκολον, "troublesome," "harassing") the case was. Finally, true historian that he is (like Thucydides [1.22], who looks upon history as a guide to future decision-making), he mentions a further purpose in recounting this incident at length: when people in the future encounter such an incident they may learn from Solomon's wisdom (ἀγχινοίας, "sagacity," "ready wit," "shrewdness").

To emphasize Solomon's impartial and wise handling of the case, while 1 Kgs 3:22 makes no indication as to how Solomon interrogated the women, in Josephus (*Ant.* 8.30), after the first woman speaks, Solomon takes the initiative asking the other woman to present her rebuttal. 1 Kgs 3:23-27 simply describes the procedure by which Solomon asked for a sword and ordered the living child be cut in two. As the case is described in 1 Kgs 3:27, we hear only the king's decision, with no indication as to how he had arrived at it. Josephus (*Ant.* 8:33) explains that the king recognized the words spoken by each of the mothers as her true sentiments and consequently adjudged the child to the mother who had cried out to prevent the division of the child. There is no indication in the biblical narrative as to what punishment, if any, Solomon inflicted upon the guilty mother, while Josephus (*Ant.* 8.33) records that he condemned her for her wickedness both in having killed her own son and in being eager to see her friend's child destroyed.

There is a significant difference between the biblical version and

Josephus' narrative in the reaction of the people to this judgment. In 1 Kgs 3:28 the response is to fear Solomon because they see that the wisdom of G-d is in him to do justice. In Josephus (*Ant.* 8.34) the reaction is not fear but conviction, since they consider his judgment a great sign (δεῖγμα) and proof (τεκμήριον) of the king's prudence (φρονήσεως) and wisdom (σοφίας). Consequently, they respond by listening to him as to one possessed of a godlike (θείαν) understanding (διάνοιαν).

A key addition in Josephus' version of this incident is his statement (*Ant.* 8.30) that when no one could see what judgment to give but all were mentally blinded as by a riddle, Solomon alone devised a plan. There are, it appears, four key elements in this statement which do not appear in 1 Kgs 3:23-27 (whether in the Hebrew, the LXX or the Lucianic version): one, Josephus indicates that others had attempted and failed to determine who the real mother was; two, these others are spoken of as mentally blinded (τῇ διανοίᾳ τετυφλωμένων); three, to solve the question required the use of intelligence (διάνοια); four, the case is compared to a riddle (αἰνίγματι). Particularly striking is that all four elements are found in Sophocles' *Oedipus the King*. There we find that others had apparently attempted and failed to solve the Sphinx's question; Oedipus solves the riddle of the Sphinx by the use of his intelligence (γνώμη), and the intellectual rivalry between Oedipus and Teiresias culminates in Oedipus' taunting Teiresias with failure of his intelligence (νοῦς); reference is made to Teiresias' blindness in Oedipus' accusation: "You are blind in ears and mind and eyes;" and the Sphinx's question is termed a riddle.[16] Oedipus sarcastically asks the blind prophet Teiresias why he did not solve the riddle (αἴνιγμα) of the Sphinx and thus save the city of Thebes.[17] Most significantly, it is Oedipus alone who solves the Sphinx's riddles (αἰνίγματα), and who, ironically, is to go through a reversal (περιπέτεια) from sight to blindness when he discovers his true identity.[18]

The riddle of the Sphinx is the supreme test of Oedipus' intelligence, as the case of the two harlots is of Solomon's. In both cases it is their self-confident wisdom that is their undoing. For Oedipus, when, as the parts of the puzzle fall into place revealing his real identity, and he begins to lose control of himself, Jocasta comments that Oedipus does not, "like a man in control of his mind (ἔννους) judge the present on the

[16] Sophocles, *Oedipus the King* 391-394, 371, 371, 393, respectively.
[17] Ibid., 391-392.
[18] Ibid., 1524-1525.

basis of the past."[19] As Knox, following a suggestion of Jebb, has remarked, the first part of the very name of Oedipus is close in sound and thus reminiscent of οἶδα, "to know," a word constantly on Oedipus' lips; indeed, as Knox continues, it is his knowledge that makes Oedipus the decisive and confident ruler (τύραννος).[20]

It is instructive to compare Josephus' treatment of this incident with that of the rabbis. The rabbis add a supernatural dimension to the story by presenting the tradition that the two women who claimed the children were not really human at all but rather were spirits who were sent by G-d to exhibit Solomon's wisdom.[21] They add another supernatural dimension by asserting that when Solomon presented his decision a voice from heaven confirmed that this was indeed the mother of the child. In Josephus, on the other hand, the focus of attention is on Solomon and on his human wisdom; the women are more human than ever, and the drama is consequently heightened.

It is not merely in quantity of wisdom that, according to Josephus, Solomon was pre-eminent. Most important, whereas, according to 1 Kgs 5:13, Solomon's wisdom consisted of his speaking in proverbs and parables about beasts, birds, fish, and trees, Josephus, realizing that educated Greeks and Romans looked upon philosophy as the highest form of wisdom,[22] proudly boasts (*Ant.* 8.44) that there was no form of nature with which he was not acquainted or which he passed over without examining. Note that the word which Josephus uses for "without examining" (ἀνεξέταστον) is precisely the word which Socrates uses in his famous phrase at his trial in which he summarizes his mission as a philosopher, ὁ ἀνεξέταστος βίος οὐ βιωτὸς ἀνθρώπῳ, "the unexamined life is not worth living for a man."[23] Josephus then goes on, in an extra-biblical remark, to state that Solomon studied nature philosophically (ἐφιλοσόφησε), that is, presumably, critically, which had been stressed by Josephus' predecessor who had composed the Book of Wisdom, putting into the mouth of his alleged author, Solomon, the statement that G-d had given him "unerring knowledge of existing things, to know the ordering of the world and the working of the elements" (Wisdom 7:17; στοίχείων, presumably the four elements basic to Greek philosophy).

---

[19] Ibid., 915-916.

[20] B. M. W. Knox, *Oedipus at Thebes* (New Haven: Yale University Press, 1957) 183-184.

[21] *Mak.* 23b.

[22] Cf. Cicero, *Tusculan Disputations* 5.3.8-9.

[23] Plato, *Apology* 38a.

Belief in magic (or at least white magic, as Duling, drawing on MacMullen, notes), though always widespread among common folk, had grown considerably among the educated class since the first century.[24] Exorcising demons was a sign of the special power of a wise man, if we may judge from the example of the famous philosopher Apollonius of Tyana, who successfully exorcised a demon from a boy.[25] Lucian, who flourished not long after Josephus, mentions a Syrian from Palestine, who was known to everyone, and who, for a large fee, was alleged to have restored to health through exorcism of foreign spirits, people who were possessed.[26]

Because of parallels of this kind, Josephus apparently felt secure in including such a story. A whole picture, without basis in the biblical text, is developed of Solomon as possessor of G-d-given skill in the art of exorcising demons (*Ant.* 8.45-49).[27] "G-d," he says (*Ant.* 8.45), in an addition to 1 Kgs 5:10, "granted him knowledge of the art used against demons for the benefit and healing of men." He is said to have composed incantations by which illnesses are relieved and to have left behind forms of exorcisms which successfully enable those possessed by demons to drive them out.[28]

Then, in a digression, Josephus (*Ant.* 8.46-49) relates that he himself had seen how a certain contemporary Jew named Eleazar, in the presence of Vespasian, had freed men possessed by demons by putting to their nose a ring which had under its seal one of the roots prescribed by

[24] D. C. Duling, "The Eleazar Miracle and Solomon's Magical Wisdom in Flavius Josephus's *Antiquitates Judaicae* 8.42-49," *HTR* 78 (1985) 1-25, esp. pp. 23-25. R. MacMullen, *Enemies of the Roman Order: Treason, Unrest, and Alienation in the Empire* (Cambridge, Mass.: Harvard University Press, 1966) 95-127.

[25] Philostratus, *Life of Apollonius of Tyana* 4.20.

[26] Lucian, *Philopseudeis* 16. It seems likely that the allusion here is to a Jew, since we find the same phrase, *Palaestino...Syro*, in Ovid, *Ars Amatoria* 1.416, where the reference is definitely to a Jew, since the passage refers to the Sabbath which he observes. See M. Stern, *Greek and Latin Authors on Jews and Judaism* (Jerusalem: Israel Academy of Sciences and Humanities, 1980) 2.221, nt. 4.

[27] For an analysis of this passage see Duling, "Eleazar Miracle," pp. 1-25. For rabbinic parallels see Rappaport, *Agada und Exegese*, p. 131, nt. 241.

[28] Such a book is the *Testament of Solomon*. See version and commentary by D. C. Duling, "Testament of Solomon (First to Third Century): A New Translation and Introduction," *OTP* 1.935-87; and *idem*, "The Testament of Solomon: Retrospect and Prospect," *JSP* 2 (1988) 87-112. F. C. Conybeare, "The Testament of Solomon," *JQR* 11 (1898-99) 11-12, conjectures that the *Testament of the Twelve Patriarchs*, in its original form, may have been the very collection of incantations which, according to Josephus, was composed and bequeathed by Solomon. Ginzberg, *Legends*, 6.291, nt. 48, remarks that the recognized authorities of rabbinical Judaism condemned the use of the conjuring books ascribed to Solomon.

Solomon, drawing the demon out through their nostrils, finally adjouring the demon never to come back into them, speaking Solomon's name and reciting the incantations which Solomon had composed.[29] To prove that it was through him that the demon was expelled Eleazar ordered the demon to overturn a cup full of water that he had placed nearby. When the cup was overturned, he comments, Solomon's understanding (σύνεσις) and wisdom (σοφία) were clearly revealed. Well aware that all this is a digression without Scriptural basis, he remarks (*Ant.* 8.49) that he has recounted this incident so that all men may see from this revelation of Solomon's understanding and wisdom (σύνεσις καὶ σοφία) the greatness of his nature and the extent to which G-d favored him, so that no one under the sun may be ignorant of the king's surpassing virtue of every kind.

A similar story of exorcism, is ascribed to Apollonius of Tyana (including a scene parallel to that of the overturned cup; Philostratus, *Life of Apollonius of Tyana* 4.20), in which Apollonius orders the demon to show by a visible sign that he had indeed quit the possessed man, whereupon the demon threw down a statue. As in other portions of the Solomon pericope, Josephus avoids details that would seem incredible to the sophisticated reader. Hence, we do not find such data (recorded in the rabbinic tradition) as that Solomon had spirits and demons as his personal attendants whom he could send wherever he wished at short notice, that he grew tropical plants in Palestine with the help of ministering spirits who secured water for him from India, that animals also were subservient to him, that eagles transported him wherever he wished, that spirits aided him in the construction of the Temple, that he delivered the land of Arabia from an evil spirit,[30] that he possessed charms against demons and illnesses,[31] and that he had a piece of tapestry no smaller than sixty miles square on which he flew through the air so swiftly that he could eat breakfast in Damascus and supper in Media.[32]

Evidence of Solomon's wisdom is to be seen in that, according to

---

[29] This magic ring is also referred to in the *Testament of Solomon* 5.

[30] See Ginzberg, *Legends*, 4.149-53 and 6.291-93, nts. 48-56.

[31] See Rappaport, *Agada und Exegese*, p. 56, no. 273, and p. 131, nt. 241. The fourth-century *Medicina Plinii* 3.15.7 likewise notes the efficacy of the name of Solomon on amulets as a cure for tertian fever. On the use of the name of Solomon in magical papyri and amulets see C. Bonner, *Studies in Magical Amulets* (Ann Arbor: University of Michigan Press, 1950) 208 ff.; and D. C. Duling, " Solomon, Exorcism, and the Son of David," *HTR* 68 (1975) 235 ff.

[32] See Ginzberg, *Legends*, 4.162.

Josephus (*Against Apion* 1.111), the main bond of friendship between Hiram and Solomon was their passion (ἐπιθυμία) for learning (σοφίας, "wisdom"). Great importance should be attached to Josephus' addition (*Ant.* 8.143) that Hiram, king of Tyre, sent Solomon tricky problems (σοφίσματα, "subtle questions," "sly tricks") and enigmatic sayings (λόγος αἰνιγματώδεις, "riddles"), requesting that he clear them up and relieve his difficulties (ἀπορίας). Here, as in Josephus' version of Solomon's adjudication of the case of the two mothers, he is presented as a kind of Oedipus solving riddles. Josephus proceeds to praise Solomon's wisdom in the highest terms. Inasmuch as Solomon was clever (δεινόν) and keen-witted (συνετόν), none of the riddles proved too difficult for him, and he successfully solved them all by force of reason (λογισμῷ), as did Oedipus, whose bitterest word of condemnation, which he hurls at Teiresias and at Creon, is μῶρος ("stupid") and whose reputation for wisdom is based primarily on his ability to solve the riddle of the Sphinx (a solution which he arrived at through sheer intelligence rather than, as he remarks, by the birds that a seer such as Teiresias might have used).[33]

The most romantic medium through which Solomon demonstrates his wisdom is through the visit of the Queen of Sheba. Ullendorf speaks of Josephus' version of this episode as a slightly expanded and somewhat "smartened up" version of the biblical narrative, doubtlessly reflecting the state of contemporary interpretation, yet essentially faithful to the biblical narrative and completely innocent of the accretions that we find in the Talmudic tradition.[34] In the latter the Queen of Sheba is aggrandized to the point where she is said to have a realm so rich that dust is more valuable than gold, and its trees, dating from the beginning of time, suck up water that flows from the Garden of Eden.[35] Josephus likewise avoids emphasizing the magical element, such as the tale in the Midrash's account of the hoopoe who reported to King Solomon (who understood the languages of birds and beasts) that there existed a land ruled by the Queen of Sheba which was not yet subject to him.[36]

Nevertheless, a number of touches in this pericope lend greater glory to the figure of Solomon. In particular, Josephus' statement that the Queen of Sheba, who, he adds, was thoroughly trained (διαπεπονημέ-

---

[33] Sophocles, *Oedipus the King* 433, 540, 396-398 (respectively). See the discussion by Knox, *Oedipus at Thebes*, p. 18.

[34] E. Ullendorff, "The Queen of Sheba," *BJRL* 45 (1962-1963) 491-92.

[35] See Ginzberg, *Legends*, 4.143.

[36] Ibid., 4.142-44 and 6.289, nt. 39.

νην) in wisdom (σοφίᾳ) and, remarkable in other ways, ruled over Egypt and Ethiopia vastly increases the wisdom of Solomon, inasmuch as Egypt had a reputation of being an extremely ancient land and one that possessed men of the greatest wisdom.[37] As for Ethiopia, its inhabitants were renowned for their wisdom, piety, and bravery and are termed blameless by Homer.[38] Solomon's wisdom is also increased by virtue of Josephus' extra-biblical remark (*Ant.* 8.165-166) that the Queen of Sheba's strong desire to see him arose from reports she heard every day about his country. Believing that hearsay is likely to lead to false belief, she decided to visit Solomon to see for herself.

As to the Queen's method for determining Solomon's wisdom, 1 Kgs 10:1 says that she came to test him with riddles (בחידות). Riddles, as understood in the Bible, cannot be solved without previous knowledge, presumably through divine inspiration, as for example in the case of Samson's riddle in Judg 14:12-17, which could not have been solved except through previous knowledge of the exploit of slaying the lion. Hence, the implication of the Bible's statement is that the Queen wished to find out whether the source of Solomon's wisdom was divine inspiration. On the other hand, in Josephus' formulation (*Ant.* 8.166), the Queen comes not with riddles of this sort but with difficult questions and asks Solomon to solve their difficult (απορον, "impossible") meaning. Thus, very significantly, everything consequently depends upon Solomon's human wisdom rather than divine inspiration.

Josephus (*Ant.* 8.167) further dramatizes Solomon's wisdom in the way by which he solved the Queen's problems. 1 Kgs 10:3 simply says that he answered all her questions, whereas Josephus asserts that Solomon "was studious (φιλότιμος, "eager," "anxious," "zealous," "lavish," "prodigal," "generous") to please her in all ways, in particular by mentally (συνέσει) grasping (καταλαμβανόμενος) with ease the ingenious problems (σοφίσματα) she set him and solving (ἐπελύετο) them more quickly than anyone could have expected." Emphasis here is on Solomon's speed in answering questions, not merely from Josephus' statement that he solved them more quickly than anyone expected but also from Josephus' use of the word σύνεσις to describe Solomon's mental process, since this word refers to the faculty of quick comprehension and mother-wit.[39]

---

[37] See Herodotus, Book 2, *passim.*

[38] Homer, *Iliad* 1.423. See my "Pro-Jewish Intimations in Tacitus' Account of Jewish Origins," *REJ* 150 (1991) 348-49.

[39] See LSJ, s.v. σύνεσις II.

The use of the word σοφίσματα would remind the reader of the use of this word in connection with the tricky problems Hiram, king of Tyre, sent to Solomon, which Solomon solved by force of reason (*Ant.* 8.143). In this respect Solomon would remind the reader of Prometheus, who is said to have discovered numbering, pre-eminent among ingenious devices (σοφισμάτων).[40] The use of the word σόφισμα might also well recall the use of this word in reference to the wily Odysseus' plan whereby he hopes to obtain Philoctetes' bow, which, according to an oracle, is the only weapon with which Troy can be captured.[41]

The scene would likewise remind the reader, as Josephus did in his version of Solomon's decision in the case of the two women claiming the same baby, of Sophocles' Oedipus, whose characteristic action, as Knox points out, is the *fait accompli* and whose characteristic description is ταχύς ("swift").[42] One of the lessons stressed by Sophocles in his *Oedipus the King*, as seen in remarks by the chorus, "Swift (ταχεῖς) thinkers are not safe,"[43] is the danger of making decisions too quickly. Oedipus defensively replies, twice using the word "swift" in the following two lines: "When a swift plotter moves secretly against me, I must be quick with my counterplot." Indeed, the words "speedy" (ταχύς) and "speed" (τάχος) recur as a leitmotif throughout the play, three times by Oedipus, once by the Second Messenger, once by Creon, once by the Chorus, once by Jocasta, and once by the Herdsman.[44] That speed remains the characteristic trait of Oedipus may be seen from the fact that, after his identity has become known, Oedipus uses the phrase "as quickly as possible" on three occasions: "Take me away from this place as quickly as possible;" "Hide me away as quickly as possible;" and "Throw me out of this land as quickly as possible."[45] Indeed, one of the themes of the play is the danger of speed; for those who, like Oedipus, are quick to think things out are not infallible.[46]

c. *Temperance and Modesty*

The cardinal virtue of temperance, with its connected motif of clemency, was a quality of supreme importance to the Greeks, seen in that the pre-

---

[40] Aeschylus, *Prometheus Bound* 459.
[41] Sophocles, *Philoctetes* 14.
[42] Knox, *Oedipus at Thebes*, pp. 15-17, 188.
[43] Sophocles, *Oedipus the King* 617.
[44] Ibid., 142, 430, 1234, 1429 and 765, 945, 1131, 1154 respectively.
[45] Ibid., 1340: ὅτι τάχιστα; 1410: ὅπως τάχιστα; 1436: ὅσον τάχισθ', respectively.
[46] Ibid., 617.

scription to avoid such excess, μηδὲν ἄγαν, was one of the two mottoes inscribed at the most important and unifying religious institution of the Greeks, the Delphic Oracle. Josephus, as can be seen in his account of Saul (*Ant.* 6.63), identifies moderation with modesty. Josephus (*Ant.* 3.74) highlights Moses' modesty in his willingness to take advice from his father-in-law and in his readiness to acknowledge this assistance. Similarly, Moses is said to have modestly recorded the prophecies of Balaam, even though he could just as easily have appropriated them (*Ant.* 4.157), as there were no witnesses to convict him. Josephus was well aware that the pagans frowned upon modesty; Aristotle in particular was critical of the unduly humble man.[47] The virtue of modesty always presents a problem in that excessive modesty, especially in a ruler, is no virtue at all. Josephus' Solomon resolves this problem by following the middle path. Whereas in 1 Kgs 3:7, when G-d appears to Solomon in a dream and offers to give him whatever he wishes, Solomon responds by stating that he is but a little child who does not know how to go out or come in, Josephus, regarding this as excessive modesty, omits this passage altogether.

Because he had already established so solidly Solomon's reputation for wisdom, Josephus (*Ant.* 8.146) felt secure in citing extra-biblical evidence from Menander that Solomon was modest enough to admit that he had been outwitted by the Tyrian lad, Abdemon, who always successfully solved the problems submitted to him by Solomon. He then further cites (*Ant.* 8.149; *Against Apion* 1.114-115) Dius, who composed a history of Phoenicia that asserted that Solomon and Hiram exchanged riddles with the understanding that the one who would be unable to solve them would pay a fine. At first, Hiram paid heavy fines, being unable to solve Solomon's riddles, but afterwards they were solved by Abdemon, who, in turn, propounded others which Solomon was unable to solve, and so in the end Solomon paid back to Hiram more than Hiram had originally paid to him. Thus Josephus graphically demonstrates how honest, honorable and magnanimous Solomon was toward his non-Jewish friends.

d. *Justice*

Justice is the centerpiece of Plato's *Republic*, one of the most influential works throughout the Hellenistic and Roman periods. That Josephus (*Ant.* 6.305, 13.294) identifies justice with law must have made a pow-

[47] Aristotle, *Nicomachean Ethics* 4.1125B7-27.

erful appeal to the Romans in his audience, who placed such a premium upon the rule of law, being proud of their achievements in this field. Not suprisingly, Josephus emphasizes the justice of many of his biblical heroes.[48] In his initial instructions to Solomon, David (*Ant.* 7.338) urges him to try to be worthy of G-d's providence by being pious, just (δίκαιος), brave, and, significantly, in view of the Romans' great respect for law, to keep the commandments and the laws which He gave the Israelites through Moses, not permitting others to transgress them. When David orders that Solomon be anointed king, he instructs him (*Ant.* 7.356) to rule with piety and justice (δικαίως). He reiterates these instructions, in the presence of the national leaders, assuring him prosperity if he will show himself pious, just (δίκαιον), and an observer of the country's laws. In a further prayer by David, whereas 1 Chr 19:29 focuses on the request that Solomon be pious and keep all the commandments of the Pentateuch, Josephus' David (*Ant.* 7.381) emphasizes justice, praying that Solomon might have a sound (ὑγιῆ) and just (δίκαιον) mind, strengthened by all virtuous (ἀρετῆς) qualities. David's dying charge to Solomon is similar. Whereas in 1 Kgs 2:2-3, David urges Solomon to live piously, walking in G-d's ways and keeping His commandments, Josephus' David (*Ant.* 7.384) exhorts Solomon not merely to be pious toward G-d but also to be just (δικαίῳ) toward his subjects, not yielding to favor or flattery.

Whereas 1 Kgs 3:3 states only that Solomon walked in the statutes of David, Josephus (*Ant.* 8.21) stresses that Solomon was not hindered by his youth from dealing justice, observing the laws, or remembering the injuctions of his dying father; rather, he performed all his tasks with as much scrupulousness as do those of advanced age and mature wisdom.

The reader of the Bible might well ask whether Solomon was justified in his seemingly harsh action in punishing Shimei. However, he is more clearly justified in Josephus' version, for whereas 1 Kgs 2:8 says merely that Shimei cursed David, Josephus (*Ant.* 7.388) reports that he did so repeatedly. While in 1 Kgs 2:43 Solomon asks simply why Shimei had not kept "the oath of the L-rd and the commandment that I have charged

[48] See my "Josephus' Portrait of Jacob," pp. 112-13; "Josephus' Portrait of Joseph," pp. 405-13; "Josephus' Portrait of Moses," pp. 32-43; "Josephus' Portrait of Joshua," *HTR* 82 (1989) 362-64; "Josephus' Version of Samson," pp. 190-92; "Josephus' Portrait of Samuel," *AbrN* 30 (1992) 125-29; "Josephus' Portrait of Saul," pp. 82-83; "Josephus' Portrait of David," pp. 150-56; "Josephus' Portrait of Daniel," *Henoch* 14 (1992) 52; "Josephus' Portrait of Hezekiah," *JBL* 111 (1992) 604; and "Use, Authority and Exegesis of Mikra," pp. 492-93.

thee with," Josephus (*Ant.* 8.19) builds up Solomon's defense by stressing that Shimei "had made light of his commands and — what was worse — had shown no regard for the oaths sworn to G-d." Josephus' handling of this case actually enhances the reputation of Solomon for justice. 1 Kgs 2:44 indicates merely that Shimei was being punished for the wickedness that he had done to David. A reader might well ask why, if David had seen fit not to punish Shimei at the time, Solomon should have been so vindictive as to punish him so long afterwards. 1 Kgs 2:44 is silent on this matter, but Josephus was already aware of this objection, for he has Solomon (*Ant.* 8.20) actually teach Shimei (and Josephus' readers) a lesson in the philosophy of punishment; evildoers gain nothing by not being punished at the time of their crimes. During the time in which they think themselves secure because they have suffered nothing, their punishment increases and becomes more serious than that which they would have paid at the time of their wrongdoing.

e. *Piety*

Piety, the fifth of the cardinal virtues in Plato and the Stoics, was especially important for the Romans; the key quality of Aeneas in Virgil's great national poem is *pietas*.[49] It is no surprise that in his portraits of biblical heroes Josephus should emphasize their piety.[50]

An indication of the importance of piety for Solomon may be seen from the fact that the noun "piety" (εὐσέβεια) occurs 6 times and the adjective "pious" (εὐσεβής) occurs 5 times in the Solomon pericope, whereas εὐσέβεια occurs 36 times and εὐσεβής 11 times in the first 11 books of the *Antiquities* (Josephus' paraphrase of the Bible). This means that 23% of the occurrences of these words will be found in connection with Solomon, whereas the Solomon pericope constitutes only approximately 7% (252 paragraphs out of 3777) of Josephus' text relating the biblical period.

A major indication of Solomon's piety is seen in that he applied more energy to the building of the Temple than to the building of his palace.

[49] Plato, *Protagoras* 330B, 349B; *Stoicorum Veterum Fragmenta* 3.64.40.

[50] See my, "Josephus' Portrait of Jacob," p. 113; "Josephus' Portrait of Joseph," pp. 413-16; "Josephus' Portrait of Moses," pp. 43-48; "Josephus' Portrait of Joshua," pp. 364-66; "Josephus' Portrait of Samuel," pp. 129-30; "Josephus' Portrait of Saul," pp. 83-93; "Josephus' Portrait of David," pp. 156-64; "Josephus' Portrait of Hezekiah," pp. 604-07; "Josephus' Portrait of Daniel," pp. 52-54; and "Use, Authority and Exegesis of Mikra in the Writings of Josephus," pp. 493-94.

By deferring the account of the building of the palace until after the completion of his description of the dedication of the Temple, Josephus stresses the importance of the Temple and diminishes that of the palace.[51] In 1 Kgs 9:10 it is simply stated that it took 20 years to build the two houses, 7 years for the Temple (1 Kgs 6:38) and 13 years for the palace (1 Kgs 7:1). Josephus (*Ant.* 8.30), apparently aware of the objection that Solomon devoted almost twice as much time to building his palace for his own glory as to building the Temple for the greater glory of G-d, emphasizes Solomon's piety by adding the significant comment that the palace was not built with the same industry (ἐσπουδάζετο) with which the Temple was built. Josephus (*Ant.* 8.131) adds an extra-biblical remark that the palace was much inferior in dignity (ἀξίας) to the Temple since the building materials had been prepared not so long in advance, with less expense, and was intended as a dwelling place for a king and not for G-d.[52]

4. Contemporary Political Overtones

The underlying theme of Josephus' *Jewish War* is the emphasis on the civil strife (στάσις οἰκεία) engendered by the Jewish "tyrants," responsible for the ill-fated revolt (*War* 1.10). He contrasts the brutal treatment that these tyrants dispensed to their fellow-countrymen with the clemency that the Romans showed toward the Jews, though they were an alien race. This theme would have reminded readers of civil strife at Corcyra so graphically described by Thucydides.[53]

The same theme of the dreadful consequences of civil strife pervades Josephus' paraphrase of the Bible in the *Antiquities*.[54] Josephus constantly, in extra-biblical additions, emphasizes the importance of Solomon's achievement in bringing about peace and avoidance of civil disturbances. Thus he declares (*Ant.* 8.38) that during his reign the people

[51] The LXX and Lucianic texts defer the description of the palace until 1 Kgs 7:38, but Josephus postpones it even further, until after the account paralleling 1 Kgs 8.

[52] Similarly, the rabbinic tradition notes that Solomon was less zealous in building his palace than in constructing the Temple. See *Midrash Song of Songs Rabbah* 1.5, *Sanh.* 104b, *Midrash Numbers Rabbah* 14.1, *Pesiqta Rabbati* 6, *Midrash Proverbs* 22.29, cited by Rappaport, *Agada und Exegese*, p. 132, nt. 242.

[53] *The Peloponnesian War* 3.82-84.

[54] See the discussion of Josephus' treatment of Joab as a lesson in the disastrous consequences of civil strife in my "Josephus' Portrait of Joab," *EstBib* 51 (1993) 335-37.

enjoyed peace and were undisturbed by wars and disturbances (ταραχαῖς, "troubles," "tumults," "uproars," "disorders").

Another theme frequently pursued by Josephus is the importance of liberty. The Israelites, Samuel insists (*Ant.* 6.20), ought not to be content merely to yearn for liberty (ἐλευθερίας), but ought to do the deeds necessary to attain it. Roman readers would recall that in the conspiracy to assassinate the mad Gaius Caligula the password (*Ant.* 19.14) adopted by the conspirators was "Liberty" (ἐλευθερία). It is, therefore, extremely significant that Josephus (*Ant.* 8.38), in an addition to the biblical text, stresses that under Solomon the Jews enjoyed to the fullest the most desirable freedom (ἐλευθερίας) and that none of them was a slave (ἐδούλευεν, *Ant.* 8.161); nor was it reasonable, inasmuch as they had so many nations subject to themselves from whom they could raise a force of serfs.[55]

A persistent charge against the Jews in antiquity was that they were guilty of misanthropy. Even Hecataeus of Abdera,[56] otherwise well disposed toward the Jews, describes Jewish life style as "a misanthropic way of life and one hostile to strangers" (ἀπάνθρωπόν τινα καί μισόξενον βίον).[57]

A number of additions in Josephus' portrayal of Solomon are intented to answer this charge of misanthropy and to demonstrate the excellent relations between Jews and non-Jews. Whereas 1 Kgs 5:15 reads only that Hiram, king of Tyre, sent his servants to Solomon when he heard that he had been anointed king, Josephus (*Ant.* 8.50) adds that Hiram was overjoyed and sent him greetings and congratulations on his good fortune. Solomon, in turn, expresses his gratitude to Hiram for his aid in presenting him with cedar wood for the Temple. Whereas 1 Kgs 5:25 states simply that Solomon gave Hiram 20,000 measures of wheat for food for his household and 20 measures of beaten oil, Josephus' Solomon (*Ant.* 8.57) goes much further in expressing his gratitude, adding 20,000 measures of wine to the gifts specified in the Bible, but also com-

---

[55] C. Begg, *Josephus' Account of the Early Divided Monarchy (AJ 8,212-420): Rewriting the Bible* (Leuven: University Press, 1993) 14, nt. 43, finds a contradiction in a later passage (*Ant.* 8.213), in which the leaders of the people and Jeroboam urge Rehoboam to lighten their bondage (δουλείας) somewhat. But this latter scene, we may remark, takes place after the death of Solomon; and the alleged bondage may reflect the condition of the Israelites in the last years of Solomon's reign. Or, alternatively, we may suggest that the delegation is exaggerating the plight of the people and taking advantage of the relative weakness of the new ruler.

[56] *Ap.* Diodorus Siculus 40.3.4.

[57] On this use of τινα see LSJ. s.v. τις, τι, A, II, 7.

mends (ἐπῄνεσε) Hiram's zeal (προθυμίαν) and goodwill (εὔνοιαν). Finally, 1 Kgs 5:26 states that Hiram and Solomon made a league together, while Josephus (*Ant.* 8.58) elaborates that the friendship of the kings increased through these things so that they swore it should continue forever.

That the friendship between Solomon and Hiram was important in refuting the charge of misanthropy may be seen in that Josephus devotes a goodly portion of his apologetic treatise *Against Apion* (1.100-127) to reproducing evidence from Phoenician archives and from works of Dius and Menander of Ephesus illustrating the excellent relations between the two kings, confirming the antiquity of the Temple (*Against Apion* 1.106-108).[58] There is good reason, says Josephus (*Against Apion* 1.109-110), why the erection of the Temple should be mentioned in the Tyrians' records, since Hiram, king of Tyre, was a friend of Solomon and, indeed, had inherited this friendship from his (Hiram's) father. According to Josephus, it is the non-Jew, Hiram, who inherited the friendship from his father, whereas in 2 Sam 5:11 and 1 Kgs 5:1 it is Solomon who inherits from his father a friendship with Hiram. Josephus (*Against Apion* 1.110), for apologetic reasons, exults in this friendship. Thus, whereas in 2 Sam 5:11 Hiram simply sent cedar trees to David, Josephus (*Against Apion* 1.110) says that Hiram cut down the finest timber from Mount Libanus. That this friendship carried with it a great deal of prestige may be deduced from the fact that the Phoenicians were an ancient people and that Hiram lived more than 150 years before the founding of Carthage (*Against Apion* 2.17-18).[59]

That, according to Josephus (*Against Apion* 1.111), many of the riddles and problems which Hiram and Solomon sent each other were still preserved in Tyre in Josephus' own day is important in building Solomon's reputation for wisdom but also for stressing the friendship and high respect which a Jewish leader had for a non-Jew. While it is true that Josephus does say that Solomon showed greater proficiency and was the cleverer (σοφώτερος) of the two, it is still quite a compliment for Hiram that he could be compared with Solomon and that Solomon found it interesting and challenging to exchange problems and riddles.

---

[58] The correspondence between Solomon and Hiram and their friendship are presented at length by Eupolemus (*ap.* Eusebius, *Praeparatio Evangelica* 34.1-20).

[59] On the great value attached to antiquity in ancient times see my *Jew and Gentile in the Ancient World: Attitudes and Interactions from Alexander to Justinian* (Princeton: Princeton University Press, 1993) 177-200.

The supreme example of Josephus' concern with answering the charge that the Jews were guilty of hating non-Jews is to be found in Josephus' version of Solomon's prayer at the dedication of the Temple. According to 1 Kgs 8:41-43, Solomon prayed that when non-Jews come to the Temple G-d should grant all of their requests so that all the peoples of the earth may know His name and fear Him. Josephus (*Ant.* 8.116-117) says nothing about the peoples fearing Him, perhaps because he thought that this might give the impression that the Jews were seeking proselytes or G-d-fearers, a very sensitive issue for the Romans at this time because they were afraid that the increasing success of Jews in winning such adherents would mean the end of the old Roman way of life.[60] Instead, Josephus adds a new dimension to the discussion by explaining that Solomon's aim in beseeching G-d thus was to demonstrate that Jews "are not inhuman (ἀπάνθρωποι) by nature nor unfriendly (ἀλλοτρίως) to those who are not of their own country, but wish that all men should receive aid from Thee and enjoy Thy blessings." Note that in connection with the rebuilding of the Temple under Zerubbabel, Josephus stresses, in an extra-biblical detail, that the Temple is open to all men, including even the schismatic Samaritans, for worship of G-d (*Ant.* 11.87).

5. Intermarriage and Other Deviations from Jewish Law

Just as Livy, in the preface to his history, laments the decline of morals in the Roman Empire, so Josephus, as a reponsible historian, cites lessons to be learned from his history. One major lesson, perhaps with a view toward what was happening to some of Josephus' contemporaries, is that Jews must avoid assimilation with Gentiles. This may be seen, as Van Unnik has stressed, in Josephus' account (*Ant.* 4.131-155) of the Israelites' sin with the Midianite women (Num 25:1-9), which was expanded from 9 verses to 25 paragraphs.[61] It may likewise be perceived in Josephus' moral of the Samson story that one must not debase (παρεχάρασσεν, used of coins) one's rule of life (δίαιταν) by imitating foreign ways (*Ant.* 5.306). The same theme of moralizing about the effects of assimilation may be seen in Josephus' discussion of Anilaeus and Asinaeus, two Jewish brothers who established an independent state in

[60] Ibid., pp. 288-382.
[61] Van Unnik, "Josephus' Account of the Story of Israel's Sin," pp. 241-61.

Mesopotamia in the first century only to lose it when, at the very peak of their success, Anilaeus had an affair with a Parthian general's wife (*Ant.* 18.340). The closely connected theme, that one must not, as did Samson, submit to one's passionate instincts, is frequent in Josephus.[62] Josephus, however, was confronted with a dilemma, inasmuch as although the Bible itself decisively forbids intermarriage (Deut 7:3), yet he was aware that too strenuous an objection against intermarriage would play into the hands of those opponents of the Jews who charged them with misanthropy.[63] On the one hand, he was especially eager to answer the charge that the Jews hated foreigners. On the other hand, he had to contend with the Bible's strict prohibition of intermarriage. Josephus might have adopted the solution, as he does on numerous other occasions, of simply omitting the references to Solomon's numerous non-Jewish wives. But the *Antiquities*, though directed primarily for apologetic purposes to a non-Jewish audience, is also intended to reach a Jewish audience.[64] Hence, he apparently felt that he could not omit reference to Solomon's indiscretions in marrying foreign women, especially since he apparently felt that a lesson had to be taught to the Jews of his own day.

What Josephus does do, however, is to build up the stature of Solomon more than ever while postponing mention of his marital alliances as long as possible. Thus, whereas 1 Kgs 7:8 mentions the house which Solomon built for Pharaoh's daughter whom he had married, Josephus (*Ant.* 8.134), when first describing the palace which Solomon built for himself, merely states that he adjoined a hall for the queen without identifying the queen as Pharaoh's daughter.

While it is true that Josephus was very eager to show that Jews are not hostile toward non-Jews, nevertheless, one of the dangers of Solomon's close contact and co-operation with non-Jewish kings was that he, in his concern to show how open-minded he was, would compromise some of the tenets of the Jewish religion, particularly in matters of idolatry. In general, however, Josephus' plan in his portrayal of Solomon is to aggrandize him almost to the very end in order both to show what a great and wise king he was and to demonstrate how even such a great man could be misled by intermarriage and the idolatry that was concomitant with it.

---

[62] See my "Josephus' Version of Samson," pp. 211-12, n. 94.

[63] We may here note, of course, that "marrying out" was frowned upon by many ancient nations. In particular, the Greeks disapproved even of marrying citizens of other Greek cities.

[64] See my "Use, Authority and Exegesis of Mikra," pp. 470-71.

When, finally, Josephus comments on Solomon's deviations from biblical law, particularly on intermarriage and idolatry, unlike 1 Kgs 11:1, which, without any introduction or editorial comment, puts into immediate juxtaposition Solomon's tremendous economic achievements and his marriages with numerous foreign women, Josephus (*Ant.* 8.190) begins with an elaborate preface noting the contrast between the time when Solomon was the most illustrious of all kings and most beloved of G-d, surpassing in understanding and wealth all those who had ruled over the Hebrews before him, and the time when he abandoned his fathers' customs (ἐθισμῶν) because he became madly enamored (ἐκμανείς) of women and indulged in excesses (ἀκρασίαν)[65] of passion (the very opposite of the virtue of moderation and wisdom)[66] and, in particular, because he transgressed the laws of Moses who forbade marriage with persons of other nations and the consequent worship of foreign gods in order to gratify his wives and his passion for them.

Thus, Solomon, wisest of all men, was, ironically, carried away by thoughtless (ἀλόγιστον) pleasure.[67] Whereas 1 Kgs 11:3 simply states that his wives turned away his heart, Josephus (*Ant.* 8.193) develops the theme, in the first place remarking that they did so very soon, and in the

---

[65] Cf. Isocrates, *Antidosis* 221: "Perhaps, however, some might venture to reply that many men, because of their incontinence (ἀκρασίας), are not amenable to reason (λογισμοῖς), but neglect their true interests (συμφέροντος) and rush on in the pursuit of pleasure (ἡδονάς).

[66] Cf. Xenophon, *Memorabilia* 4.5.6: "As for wisdom (σοφίαν), the greatest blessing, does not incontinence (ἀκρασία) exclude it and drive men to the opposite? Or do you think that incontinence prevents them from attending to useful things and understanding them by drawing them away to things pleasant, and often so distorts their perception of good and evil that they choose the worst instead of the better?" Again, in the following section, Xenophon (*Memorabilia* 4.5.7) contrasts moderation (σωφροσύνη) and incontinence (ἀκρασία) as exact opposites.

[67] In rabbinic tradition there are differences of opinion as to Solomon's marriages. He is criticized for marrying more than the 18 wives permitted to a monarch (Deut 17:16-17, *Sanh.* 21a). In doing so he thought, wrongly as it turned out, that with his wisdom he would not be affected by his transgression. See Ginzberg, *Legends*, 6.281-82, nt. 16, and 294-295, nt. 59. In particular, the rabbis expand on the dire results of Solomon's marriage with the daughter of Pharaoh. They remark, for example (*Sanh.* 21b, *Shabb.* 56b), that when he married her the archangel Gabriel descended from heaven and stuck a reed in the sea around which accumulated a sand-bank, on which the city of Rome (capital city of the Empire which was to destroy the Temple) was eventually built. Another tradition (*Shabb.* 56b) states that when Solomon married Pharaoh's daughter she brought him a thousand musical instruments, and he did not forbid her to play in honor of her various idols. Again, according to a rabbinic tradition (*Leviticus Rabbah* 12.5), when she spread over his bed a tapestry studded with diamonds and pearls he slept until the fourth hour of the morning, thus preventing the morning sacrifice from being offered, inasmuch as the keys to the Temple lay under his pillow.

second place adding, in language very reminiscent of that which the Midianite women used in seducing the Israelite men (*Ant.* 4.137), that they prevailed upon Solomon to give up his ancestral ways and, as a sign of his favor and affection for them, to live in accordance with their ancestral customs. According to 1 Kgs 11:4, it was when Solomon was old that his wives turned away his heart after other gods; Josephus (*Ant.* 8.194) explains that his reason (λογισμοῦ) became too feeble to oppose to them the memory of his country's practices, and so he adopted their ways. One might think that such an anecdote would reinforce the view that Jews are anti-foreigners, but inasmuch as Josephus places his emphasis on the fact that these foreign wives induced Solomon to deviate from his ancestral customs, Josephus' Roman readers might well have sympathized with his criticism of Solomon in view of Ennius' famous phrase stressing the importance of the old Roman customs as the foundation of the strength of the Romans: *Moribus antiquis res stat Romana viresque*.

It was precisely because of lack of self-control (ἀκρασίας) in revolting against Moses in the wilderness after leaving Egypt that the Israelites were condemned to wander for forty years (*Ant.* 3.314). It was Antiochus Epiphanes' ungovernable (ἀκρασίας) passions that led him to persecute the Jews (*War* 1.34). And it is lack of self-control (ἀκρασίαν) which characterizes the Greek divinities (*Against Apion* 2.244). Above all, Josephus, thinking of the contemporary situation, refers to the intemperatness (ἀκρασίας) of the revolutionaries against Rome whom he despised so greatly (*War* 2.324).

Even so, Josephus realized how destructive to Solomon's reputation was the statement in 1 Kgs 11:7 that Solomon, under the influence of his alien wives, built a high place for Chemosh, the god of Moab, and for Molech, the God of Ammon. Josephus (*Ant.* 8.195) judiciously omits this statement. Instead he recalls that before this time Solomon had sinned by making images of bronze bulls beneath the sea which he had set up as an offering and those of lions around his own throne, acts which are not mentioned as offences either in the Bible or in rabbinic tradition.[68] In order to indicate the gravity of his sins, Josephus adds the

[68] Cf. Ginzberg, *Legends*, 6.280, nt. 12, who remarks that the rabbis, far from blaming Solomon for erecting these images, gave these images an important place in the rabbinic tradition. Cf., however, *War* 1.650, where Josephus states that as Herod lay dying, two highly respected Jewish scholars hinted that this was the proper time to pull down the golden eagle which Herod had erected over the great gate of the Temple in defiance, as they claimed, of the ancestral law prohibiting representations of any living creature.

extra-biblical remark that Solomon died ingloriously (ἀκλεῶς, *Ant.* 8.196). Still, Josephus endeavors to express a more sympathetic attitude toward Solomon even after he had sinned in building altars to alien gods. Whereas after G-d had revealed to Solomon the punishment that would be inflicted upon him for his sins, namely that his kingdom, except for one tribe, would be torn from his son, 1 Kgs 11:14 tells nothing about Solomon's reaction and proceeds immediately to describe the uprising of Hadad the Edomite against Solomon, Josephus describes Solomon's feeling of grief (ἤλγησε) and sore trouble (σφοδρῶς συνεχύθη) at the thought that almost all the good things for which he was envied were changing for the worse.

6. Summary

King Solomon is a major figure in Josephus' attempt, in his rewriting of the Bible in his *Jewish Antiquities*, to answer the anti-Jewish charge that the Jews had failed to produce men of eminence. Whether because he himself was descended from the Hasmoneans or because, as a lackey of the Romans, he opposed the concept of the restoration of a monarchy through a messianic descendant of David, who would overthrow the Roman rule, he focusses more on Solomon than on David. One indication of the importance of Solomon for Josephus may be seen from the fact that he cites more external evidence to support his account of Solomon than he does for any other biblical personality. In terms of the sheer amount of space devoted to him, there are only two other major biblical personalities to whom Josephus gives more attention, namely Korah and Saul.

Josephus, as in the portrayal of other biblical personalities, stresses Solomon's precociousness and wealth and qualities of leadership, notably his concern for his people. Solomon emerges as possessing the four cardinal virtues (wisdom, courage, temperance, justice) as well as the spiritual virtue of piety. Above all, Josephus stresses Solomon's wisdom. Unlike his portrayal in Rabbinic literature, where he emerges as the prototype of the Talmudic sage and where many miraculous and supernatural elements are introduced, Josephus stresses his wisdom as a rational king and judge. There are several indications that when he drew his portrait of Solomon adjudicating the case of the two mothers he had in mind the portrayal of Oedipus, the solver of the riddle of the Sphinx, by Sophocles. Solomon is likewise presented as a kind of Oedipus in the cleverness and speed that he shows in solving the riddles and problems, whose difficulty is stressed, that are presented to him by Hiram the King of Tyre and by the Queen of Sheba. Josephus, like Sophocles, emphasizes that it is the force of human reason, rather than divine inspiration, which brings about a solution to these problems.

Solomon is presented by Josephus as one who had studied the forms of nature philosophically. Because of the popularity of magic in his day, Josephus develops a picture of Solomon as possessing skill in the art of exorcising demons.

Solomon shows exemplary moderation, but coupled with firmness, in his treatment of his brother Adonijah, who had attempted to seize the royal power during David's lifetime. Connected with this moderation is the quality of modesty, which Solomon exemplifies in his admission that he had actually been outwitted by a Tyrian lad named Abdemon, who always succeeded in solving the problems submitted to him by Solomon and who, in turn, submitted others that Solomon was unable to solve.

Solomon's handling of the case of Shimei enhances his reputation for justice. Solomon likewise exhibits the qualities of magnanimity, gratefulness, and generosity, which are closely connected with this virtue.

An indication of the emphasis which Josephus places on Solomon's piety may be seen in the fact that 23% of the occurrences of the words for "piety" and "pious" are found in the pericope dealing with Solomon, which comprises only 7% of Josephus' rewritten Bible. Josephus frequently couples Solomon's justice and piety, just as Sophocles does so often in connection with Oedipus. Solomon, in Josephus' portrait, shows exemplary piety toward his father and his mother, a quality which would have been especially appreciated by Josephus' Roman audience, for whom one of Aeneas' major virtues was his *pietas* toward his parents. Moreover, Josephus adds greatly to the number of details in his description of the beauty and wealth of the Temple, which Solomon built and which was his greatest act of piety. In particular, he stresses that Solomon applied much more energy to the building of the Temple than to that of his own palace.

Josephus is careful not to engage in extravagant statements with regard to G-d's deeds. He presents a rationalized version of the miracle which occured at the time of the dedication of the Temple. Moreover, whereas G-d in the Bible appears directly to Solomon, in Josephus we are told that a dream appeared to Solomon which revealed to him that G-d had heard his prayer.

That the friendship between Solomon and Hiram was important in refuting the charge that Jews hate non-Jews may be seen from the fact that Josephus devotes a goodly portion of his apologetic treatise *Against Apion* (1.100-127) to reproducing evidence from the Phoenician archives and from the works of Dius and Menander of Ephesus to illustrate the excellent relations between Solomon and Hiram. Above all, Josephus, in depicting Solomon as praying that G-d should grant all the requests on non-Jews when they come to the Temple, shows that Jews are not guilty of hating non-Jews.

Josephus, realizing that opposition to intermarriage might be regarded as evidence that Jews in principle hate non-Jews, is careful to base his opposition to Solomon's intermarriages on the ground of his objecting to Solomon's yielding to passion (a point of view which Stoics in his audience would surely have appreciated) and on the ground that intermarriage violated the law of his country.

SOLOMON AND THE WIZARD OF OZ: POWER AND INVISIBILITY IN A VERBAL PALACE

STUART LASINE

It is the glory of God to conceal things;
and the glory of kings is to penetrate (חקר) things.
...
And the heart of kings is impenetrable (אין חקר).
(Prov 25:2,3b)

He who does not know how to dissimulate,
does not know how to rule.[1]

Power is impenetrable.[2]

1. INVISIBILITY AND POWER: DEIOKES, THE WIZARD OF OZ, AND KING SOLOMON

Once there was a Median judge named Deiokes who was in love with royal power.[3] When a gathering of Medes responds to an outbreak of lawlessness and injustice by declaring "Come, let us set up a king for ourselves"[4] and choosing Deiokes, Deiokes immediately has the people build seven concentric ring walls around his royal palace, with the people dwelling outside (I.98-99). He then establishes a new rule, "that no one should come into the presence of the king, but all should be dealt with by...messengers," so that "the king should be seen by no man."[5] Deiokes' motive is to prevent any nobles of his own age and similar background from seeing him and plotting against him because they discovered they were his equal (I.99). By remaining invisible, he hopes that they would assume that he had become different (i.e., superior) to them.

[1] Motto of James I, alluding to Tiberius; see J. Goldberg, *James I and the Politics of Literature* (Baltimore, Md: Johns Hopkins University, 1983) 68.

[2] E. Canetti, *Crowds and Power* (trans. C. Stewart; New York: Continuum, 1981) 292.

[3] Herodotus, I.96.

[4] I.97; A. D. Godley, *Herodotus, Vol I* (LCL; Cambridge, Mass: Harvard University, 1981) 129. Note the uncanny resemblance to the situation in 1 Sam 8, especially v. 5.

[5] Herodotus I.99; Godley, *Herodotus*, p. 131.

Once there was a wizard in Oz who was viewed by his people as both wise and powerful.[6] However, the people's knowledge of Oz's power and knowledge is hardly direct, for no one outside the palace has seen him. Like Solomon's "descendent" Haile Selassie I, the Wizard sits behind a screen when inside the palace, so that "even those who wait upon him do not see him face to face."[7] The Wizard's motive is identical to Deiokes'. After his balloon accidentally lands in this country, his descent from the clouds leads the people to take him for a great Wizard. To maintain this illusion, he has the people build Emerald City and his Palace, so that he can "shut [himself] up and...not see any of [the people]."[8] Invisibility is power: "...I will not see even my subjects, *and so* they believe I am something terrible."[9] The people fill in the gaps created by his invisibility with the assumption that he possesses great power and wisdom.[10]

Traditionally, royal ideology forbids citizens from penetrating the *arcana imperii*, the secrets of political power.[11] With invisible leaders like Deiokes and Oz, the *arcana imperii* become identified with the person of the leader himself. Deiokes and Oz have learned the power inherent in invisibility, or, at least, in managed inscrutability.[12] Even when

---

[6] L. F. Baum, *The Wizard of Oz* (Apple Classics; New York: Scholastic, 1958) 9, 61, 64.

[7] *Ibid.*, pp. 60-61; cf. pp. 11, 67, 69. According to the revised Ethiopian constitution of 1955, the ancestry of emperor Haile Selassie I traces directly back to Menelik I, son of Solomon and the queen of Sheba. The person of the emperor has a quasi-sacred separateness. He is shielded by a screen from the gaze of the populace and does not eat in public. At times, his face is even veiled and he speaks through an intermediary called "mouth of the king;" E. Ullendorff, "The Queen of Sheba in Ethiopian Tradition," *Solomon and Sheba* (ed. J. B. Pritchard; London: Phaidon, 1974) 105-106.

[8] Baum, *Wizard*, p. 113.

[9] *Ibid.*, p. 110; emphasis added.

[10] The power of invisibility sought by Deiokes and Oz resembles the force exerted by Big Brother in Orwell's fantasy-world of *1984*. Here too the people trace "all knowledge, all wisdom, ...all virtue" back to their leader, even though "nobody has ever seen Big Brother." While pictures of Big Brother saturate the landscape, with captions reading "Big Brother is watching you," this ostensibly panoptic leader does not even exist as a person; G. Orwell, *1984* (New York: Plume, 1983) 5, 214. Instead, the idea and image of this invisible ruler act as a "focusing point for love, fear, and reverence" (p. 171).

[11] See C. Ginzburg, *Clues, Myths, and Historical Method* (trans. J. and A. C. Tedeschi; Baltimore, Md.: Johns Hopkins University, 1989) 63; and Goldberg, *James I*, p. 68.

[12] To remain powerful, invisible leaders must at the same time make their followers visible to themselves. Thus, Oz claims to be like a panoptic, omnipresent king or deity (*Wizard*, p. 108) and Deiokes has spies and eavesdroppers everywhere (Herodotus I.100). Sometimes such spies and informers are known as the "King's Eye" or "King's Ear;" see S. Lasine, "Monarchical Dreams and Nightmares: Surveillance, Gossip, and Information Management in 1 Samuel 18-23, 1 Kings, and other Ancient Near Eastern and Greek Texts," presented at the meeting of the Catholic Biblical Association, Albany, New York,

such leaders *are* visible, they remain inscrutable. Everyone who views them may see a different being. For example, Dorothy and her friends are told by the farmer that Oz is a great Wizard who "can take on any form he wishes," appearing differently to everyone.[13] When they are granted separate individual audiences with Oz, they do not converse with him through the screen. Instead, each sees a different, visually entrancing, manifestation, none of which is the true Oz. This elusive Wizard is not only analogous to the European stereotype of shape-shifting witches and wizards, but to such famous and powerful leaders as Alcibiades and Napoleon. According to Plutarch, Alcibiades possessed one special gift which, more than any other, attracted followers to him. He could "submit himself to more transformations than a chameleon."[14] Thus, in Sparta he was austere, in Ionia a hedonist, in Thrace a heavy drinker, and so on. In other words, he "assumed whatever manner or exterior was appropriate to the situation" (23.5-6).[15]

Just as the Wizard of Oz and Alcibiades appear in a variety of different forms, scholars describe Solomon and his reign in so many varying ways that one could almost conclude that the king himself was a shape-shifter. Solomon may appear to be wise or "decadent,"[16] a philosopher king"[17] or a "typical oriental despot,"[18] sultan,[19] or Pharaoh.[20] To some,

August 1995, pp. 5-15. In one post-biblical story tradition, Solomon has a variety of animal assistants, one of which is the hoopie bird. The hoopoe reports to Solomon the existence of a wealthy queen in Sheba who does not acknowledge him or God (see, e.g., *Qur'an* 27:15-44). In these (mostly Islamic) legends, Solomon not only has a royal bird's-eye view of the world, but an actual bird to act as the King's Eye!

13 Baum, *Wizard*, pp. 60-61.

14 *Alcibiades* 23.4; I. Scott-Kilvert, *The Rise and Fall of Athens: Nine Greek Lives by Plutarch* (Baltimore: Penguin, 1960) 267.

15 Similarly, Napoleon allegedly told the Council of State that "it was by becoming a Catholic that I terminated the Vendéen war, by becoming a Mussulman that I obtained a footing in Egypt, by becoming an Ultramontane that I won over the Italian priests, and had I to govern a nation of Jews I would rebuild Solomon's temple;" quoted in G. Le Bon, *The Crowd* (Harmondsworth: Penguin, 1977) 69.

16 M. Noth, *The History of Israel* (2nd ed.; trans. S. Godman, rev. P. R. Ackroyd; New York: Harper & Row, 1960) 216.

17 K. I. Parker, "Solomon as Philosopher King? The Nexus of Law and Wisdom in 1 Kings 1-11," *JSOT* 53 (1992) 76, 89.

18 R. E. Clements, "The Deuteronomistic Interpretation of the Founding of the Monarchy in I Sam. VIII," *VT* 24 (1974) 403; cf. J. L. Crenshaw, *Old Testament Wisdom: An Introduction* (Atlanta: John Knox, 1981) 53.

19 R. Kittel, quoted in H. Donner, "The Interdependence of Internal Affairs and Foreign Policy during the Davidic-Solomonic Period (with Special Regard to the Phoenician Coast)," *Studies in the Period of David and Solomon and Other Essays* (ed. T. Ishida; Winona Lake, Ind.: Eisenbrauns, 1982) 205.

20 E. W. Heaton, *Solomon's New Men: The Emergence of Ancient Israel as a National State* (New York: Pica, 1974) 28.

the account of his accession in 1 Kgs 1-2 appears to be pro-Solomonic, while others see this tale of court intrigue as a "searing indictment"[21] of the monarchy. The fact that Yahweh grants Solomon the riches and honor he did not request may be perceived as an example of "the blessings of free, unsolicited grace"[22] or as a divine "trap" to "unbalance Solomon with temptation that the latter had avoided."[23] Solomon's use of thirty thousand Israelites in the *corvée* may be viewed as an example of the tyrannical rule forecast by Samuel, or as an example of "the justice of Solomon's rule."[24] Some see negative reports about Solomon in chapter 9[25] or as early as chapters 3-5,[26] while to others the narrator appears to be offering an "unambiguous" portrait of Solomon's reign as a "golden age" or "utopia" as late as chapter 10.[27]

Solomon's motives for building his palace do not seem to parallel those of Deiokes and the Wizard. Nor does Solomon express a need to hide from his people. Yet an analogy does exist, once one realizes that Solomon is being kept hidden from readers of 1 Kings, not from the people in the story. In what follows I will argue that readers of Kings and Chronicles are locked out of Solomon's psyche in the same way that citizens are locked out of a palace where a king or tyrant remains invisible, and perhaps for similar reasons. *The text functions as a verbal palace*, with the king mysteriously and provocatively concealed inside. Readers are therefore prevented from knowing Solomon, the ultimate knower.

---

[21] L. J. Hoppe, "Israel, History of (Monarchic Period)," *ABD* 3.561.

[22] S. J. DeVries, *I Kings* (WBC; Waco, Tex.: Word Books, 1985) 53.

[23] L. Eslinger, *Into the Hands of the Living God* (Bible and Literature Series 24; Sheffield: Almond, 1989) 137.

[24] Parker, "Solomon," pp. 80-81.

[25] M. Noth, *The Deuteronomistic History* (2nd ed.; JSOTSup 15; trans. J. Doull, rev. J. Barton and M. D. Rutter; Sheffield: Sheffield Academic, 1991) 97; M. Brettler, "The Structure of 1 Kings 1-11," *JSOT* 49 (1991) 95-97.

[26] Eslinger, *Hands*, pp. 129-43; J. T. Walsh, *I Kings* (Berit Olam; Collegeville, Min.: Liturgical, 1996) 69-101.

[27] G. N. Knoppers, *Two Nations Under God: The Deuteronomistic History of Solomon and the Dual Monarchies* (HSM 52; Atlanta: Scholars, 1993) 1.77, 111, 126, 134; cf. D. Jobling, "'Forced Labor': Solomon's Golden Age and the Question of Literary Representation," *Semeia* 54 (1991) 60, 67.

Portrayals of Solomon in post-biblical traditional religious literature and folklore do not vary as much as these scholarly readings of 1 Kgs 3-11. Differences in the later Solomon's character do exist. However, in much of this (mostly, but not exclusively, Islamic) literature, there is a remarkably uniform tendency to interpret the king's power and wisdom in terms of the esoteric arts of the sorcerer. In other words, Solomon himself becomes a wizard! These later "readers" are projecting *their* images of knowledge and power against the walls of Solomon's verbal palace.

While "our inquiring minds want to know" about the personal life of leaders,[28] the text, and therefore Solomon, remain impenetrable. We are interested in his personality, but are forced to give him one, just as God gave him wisdom, wealth and honor. Speculations about Solomon's personality and knowledge reflect readers' assumptions of what a magnificant and wise king must be like, whether they take their cues from Deut 17 and 1 Sam 8, from traditional descriptions of invisible, all-knowing leaders from the ancient Near East, from the France of Louis XIV,[29] or from modern fantasies about the Wizard of Oz and Kafka's protean official, Klamm.[30]

2. Solomon's Invisibility in 1 Kings 3-11: the Screening Effect of Indeterminacy

> This is what the sovereign displays in public, his own unobservability, observed in his spectacles.[31]

In the Solomon narratives it is the narrator who is the wizard. The way the narrator describes Solomon and his reign is what allows the king to appear so differently to different readers. In *The Wizard of Oz* the dog Toto upsets the screen, exposing the mechanism which produced the Wizard's protean appearance. If Solomon is "screened" by the narrator, we must investigate the nature of this screen and see whether it too can be upset and made to reveal the source and function of Solomon's protean appearance.

One way to gauge the extent to which the character of Solomon is hidden from readers of 1 Kings is by contrasting this account of his life with those of his two royal predecessors. For example, Solomon is the first king of Israel whose physical appearance does not play a role in his early career. In fact, his appearance is not even described, let alone praised as extraordinarily attractive, as is the case for Saul and David. In spite of his thousand wives and concubines, readers do not witness any illuminating exchanges between the king and his famous loves, as one is al-

[28] See S. Lasine, "Invading David's Privacy: Leadership and the Private-Public Distinction in the Court History," presented at the annual meeting of the Catholic Biblical Association, San Diego, Calif., August, 1994, *passim*.

[29] For ancient Near Eastern leaders and Louis XIV, see Lasine, "Monarchical Dreams," pp. 5-24.

[30] On Klamm, see section 4, below.

[31] Goldberg, *James I*, p. 150.

lowed to follow David's interactions with Michal, Abigail, and Bathsheba. None of Solomon's wives is said to love him as David was loved by Michal. None pursues and flatters Solomon as did David's wife-to-be Abigail.

In fact, of Solomon's one thousand wives and concubines only Pharaoh's daughter receives any attention at all in 1 Kgs 3-11, and remarkably little is said about her or about Solomon's alleged love for her. This is most evident when one compares the narrative with other accounts of diplomatic marriages. When the Egyptian king Ramesses II first saw the Hittite princess who was to be his diplomatic bride, he perceived her godlike beauty and "he loved her more than anything."[32] Similarly, when Amenhotep III requested the Mitannian king Tusratta's daughter as a bride, Tusratta enthusiastically agreed to send her, telling the Pharaoh that "he will find that she is exactly what his heart desired."[33] In contrast, the arrival of Pharaoh's daughter is not even reported in 1 Kings, let alone Solomon's reaction to her. In view of the fact that a marriage between a daughter of an Egyptian king and a foreign monarch is almost unprecedented,[34] this silence is particularly striking. While 1 Kings does describe the arrival of one royal woman from another land, that report concerns the only woman in 1 Kgs 3-11 whom Solomon is *not* said to love: the queen of Sheba.

While Solomon's many marriages might lead one to imagine that the halls of his palace would echo continuously with the pitter-patter of little feet, we hear nothing about any sons of Solomon in all of 1 Kgs 3-11, let alone overhear conversations between father and sons such as occurred between Saul and Jonathan, and between David and his sons Amnon and Absalom. Those conversations give readers valuable information regarding the character of the kings, even if all readers do not draw the same conclusions from the reports. In the same way, we are unable to learn about Solomon by listening to his confrontations with strong, named prophets like Samuel and Nathan. There are no such prophets in 1 Kgs 3-11.

Nor are readers granted access to Solomon's private thoughts or feelings in 1 Kgs 4-11, in spite of the fact that these eight chapters focus on Solomon's administration of his empire, his building projects, his inter-

---

[32] J. A. Wilson, "Egyptian Historical Texts," *ANET*, p. 258.

[33] A. R. Schulman, "Diplomatic Marriage in the Egyptian New Kingdom," *JNES* 38 (1979) 184 n. 35.

[34] *Ibid.*, pp. 179-80.

national relations, and ultimately, his harem. While readers hear Solomon speak at length when he is on public display at the dedication of the temple (1 Kgs 8:12-61), they never hear the words spoken by Solomon to any *individual* in face-to-face conversation. Nor does he address any "long-distance" quoted speeches (i.e., messages or letters) to an individual Israelite or to his foreign wives. In fact, the only individual to whom Solomon's quoted words are addressed in these chapters is Hiram of Tyre, to whom Solomon "sends word" from Jerusalem (5:16, Hebrew). Even in the report of Solomon's verbal and economic exchange with the queen of Sheba, it is only *her* words which are quoted directly, and then at some length (10:6-9). Only once does the narrator even report that Solomon responded to her with speech (10:3). No mention is made of Solomon responding to either Hiram's complaint after 9:15 or to the queen's praise after 10:9. Solomon does not even reply to *Yahweh's* warnings at 9:9 or to his condemnation speech at 11:13. This absence of royal direct speech in dialogue is almost unique in 1-2 Kings. All the other kings whose reigns are described at length *are* quoted in such situations, with the exception of the one-dimensional villain Manasseh.[35] The blank spots in the narrator's portrait of Solomon invite the audience to engage in ventriloquism and mind-reading. Those who accept this invitation can then project their biblical Solomon onto the blank screen of history, for Solomon is not mentioned in any contemporary extra-biblical document or artifact.[36]

Another way the narrator keeps Solomon's personal character hidden from readers is by describing the king's activities in terms which are so typical of ancient Near Eastern royal ideology that the description is almost an extended cliché. Readers who note the strong affinities between 1 Kgs 3-10 and ancient Near Eastern royal inscriptions, incubation reports, and building inscriptions may conclude that they should read the biblical text in terms of the genre conventions which govern such texts, as well as royal psalms like Pss 2, 21, and 72. In many of

[35] They include Jeroboam, Rehoboam, Ahab, Jehoshaphat, Jehoram of Israel, Hezekiah and Josiah. On the function of direct quotation in the Jeroboam narrative, see S. Lasine, "Reading Jeroboam's Intentions: Intertextuality, Rhetoric and History in 1 Kings 12," *Reading Between Texts: Intertextuality and the Hebrew Bible* (ed. D. N. Fewell; Louisville: Westminster/John Knox, 1992) 139-45. On the significance of Manasseh's "silence," see *idem*, "Manasseh as Villain and Scapegoat," *The New Literary Criticism and the Hebrew Bible* (ed. J. C. Exum and D. J. A. Clines: JSOTSup 143; Sheffield: Sheffield Academic, 1993) 164-67, 173-75.

[36] G. Garbini, *History and Ideology in Ancient Israel* (New York: Crossroad, 1988) 17, 30-32; T. Ishida, "Solomon," *ABD* 6.105.

these texts the god invites the king to ask for his heart's desire and ultimately grants the king wealth, progeny, wisdom, bliss, or longevity. Wealth and power lead to peace and justice in these texts. By 1 Kgs 11, when readers learn of his many foreign wives and his idolatry, Solomon also comes to resemble biblical, and especially ancient Greek, descriptions of the insatiable and sinful tyrant.[37]

While Solomon's personal character remains hidden from readers, at least we can still point to the king's reputation for knowledge and wisdom as his distinguishing trait. Or can we? Gilgamesh and Odysseus, the most famous knowers in ancient Near Eastern and Greek epic, penetrate to the far reaches of the earth, crossing boundaries behind which the secrets of life and death, and past and future, had remained invisible. They see the cities of many men and know their thought, discover the hidden or bring back knowledge from before the flood. They learn through experience, hard experience. Even the swollen-footed Oedipus, who "learned the hard way" more than anyone else, had traveled many wandering roads of thought (*Oed. Tyr.* 67). Can we say the same of Solomon? Only the "Solomon" of Qoheleth, he who "has been king over Israel in Jerusalem" (Eccl 1:12). Qohelet applies his heart and wisdom to investigate and search out everything done under heaven (1:13). This includes investigating the effects of wealth, pleasure, luxury and women (2:1-10), all things which the Solomon of Kings has at his disposal but with which we do not see him interacting in a way which might grant him "learning by experience." The Solomon of Kings *has* knowledge; he doesn't achieve it. He is *given* wisdom; he is not given an education. Solomon *receives* knowledge; he doesn't earn it. He is given the knowledge that Eve and Adam take. He undergoes no youthful learning by experience, no *Bildung*. He is acquisitive, not inquisitive. With the possible exception of the judgment story, he is not driven to discover what had lain invisible; instead, *he* remains invisible.

The absence of information regarding young Solomon's experiences and education is just as unusual as the other gaps in his biography. To cite just a few contrasting examples, we hear no tales of Solomon's formative years analogous to the wise Joseph's experiences with his brothers or the Egyptians. Nothing like Moses' early career as killer, fugitive, or shepherd. Nothing similar to David's "education" as shepherd and

[37] For a detailed discussion of these positive and negative stereotypical traits, see S. Lasine, "The King of Desire: Indeterminacy, Audience, and the Solomon Narrative," *Semeia* 71 (1996) 89-99.

animal-fighter. And nothing analogous to the early years of his future enemy Jeroboam, the self-made, industrious, leader. For all we know, Solomon might have been sent away to a boarding school for children of the very-rich in Switzerland. His absence from all of 2 Samuel after the report of his birth is total and mysterious. In a sense, Qoheleth's "adult education" retroactively grants Solomon the learning by experience he does not receive as the "young lad"-king of 1 Kgs 3:7.[38]

Here one might object that we can learn much of Solomon's character from the fact that he asks God only for judicial wisdom in his dream at Gibeon. Considering that one of the king's main responsibilities is to establish and maintain justice, Solomon is asking for "work-related" knowledge. He does not even ask for the kind of panoptic knowledge of his people's actions and words which ancient monarchs sought so strenuously to acquire. As far as intelligence concerning foreign monarchs is concerned, the leaders about whom Solomon might want to be informed come to him of their own accord! Nor has he any need to journey to remote exotic locales like Gilgamesh, because everything exotic and remote is brought to him as a gift, without any effort on his part. Even in the story of the two harlots, where Solomon does expose the normally inaccessible workings of the human heart, he does not do so by "exploring" or investigating the women (he significantly chooses not to do so) but by employing a ruse which leads to their true natures being "brought to him" from deep inside, as though their unguarded words in vv. 26-27 were gifts brought from remote Sheba. However, the emphasis on the king's judicial sagacity in chapter 3 is a bit of misdirection, a red herring, because the king's wisdom is not judicial in nature anywhere else in 1 Kgs 1-11.[39]

In fact, the nature of Solomon's "wisdom" becomes increasingly inde-

---

[38] Readers of Samuel-Kings are not even granted enough information about the future king to determine whether his case supports the Athenian in Plato's *Laws*. Plato has the Athenian contrast the bad Persian kings Cambyses and Xerxes to their fathers Cyrus and Darius. The difference is that the fathers were not brought up in an environment of incredible wealth and luxury. No child of excessively rich monarchs who is raised amid royal pampering will ever excel in *arete*; usually they will live an evil life (696a). While the career of Rehoboam might seem to fit this scenario (and perhaps that of Adonijah as well), we simply cannot be sure about Solomon.

[39] For a detailed discussion of the judgment story as a folktale "sound bite" carrying a comforting message about royal wisdom and insight, see S. Lasine, "Solomon, Daniel, and the Detective Story: The Social Functions of a Literary Genre," *HAR* 11 (1987) 247-66; "The Riddle of Solomon's Judgment and the Riddle of Human Nature in the Hebrew Bible," *JSOT* 45 (1989) 61-86; and "The Ups and Downs of Monarchical Justice: Solomon and Jehoram in an Intertextual World," *JSOT* 59 (1993) 42-47.

terminate as the narrative proceeds. By chapter 10 it has become empty of content; it is no longer judicial, proverbial, or economic. It is simply that indeterminate element of Solomon's "character" which makes him desirable, attracting gift-bearing admirers like a magnet. Back in chapter 5 the giving of tribute by the kingdoms was not said to be spurred by Solomon's wisdom (1 Kgs 5:1, Hebrew) and the visits by foreign dignitaries who came to hear his wisdom are not said to include the giving of tribute or gifts (5:14, Hebrew). In chapter 10, on the other hand, when "all the earth" comes to hear the wisdom of the king who exceeds all others in riches and in wisdom, every visitor brings his lavish gift.[40]

Solomon possesses wisdom in the same sense as he possesses gold, silver and wives: in huge quantities. His wisdom is quantified and marketed in the form of proverbs and lectures on botany and zoology (1 Kgs 5:12-13). He "speaks" these pieces of wisdom, but readers do not hear them, just as readers do not hear what he says to his many (politically valuable) foreign wives. Again, the contents are empty. The desirable wisdom and wealth described in 1 Kgs 4-10 could be found in a travel brochure for a golden age paradise. In a sense, the wealth becomes an icon for the wisdom. As such, it is no less vacuous than the images used in marketing consumer products like perfume, beer and ketchup; the products bear no real relationship to the icons used to advertise them.[41] Solomon himself remains empty of personality, although he is the object of the entire world's desire.[42]

3. Solomon's Invisibility and Power in 1 Chronicles 22-2Chronicles 9

> When I was a child, there was a school.... I am a smart scribe whom nothing escapes.[43]

[40] The report of the visit by the queen of Sheba reinforces the idea that Solomon's wisdom simply represents his wealth-enhancing desirability. The queen serves as a focalizer, through whose eyes the narrator invites readers to view and evaluate Solomon's wealth-wisdom.

[41] According to E. Sternberg, in a "postmodern iconic" economy consumer desires are triggered by images which carry no information. Images (simulacra) do the selling. The desirable images convey no information; they have no real content; "The Economy of Icons," *The Truth About the Truth: De-Confusing and Re-Confusing the Postmodern World* (ed. W. T. Anderson; New York: Jeremy P. Tarcher/Putnam, 1995) 84-85.

[42] On the vacuity of desire in 1 Kgs 3-11, see Lasine, "King of Desire," pp. 99-104.

[43] The Sumerian king Shulgi, quoted by M. Civil, "Education (Mesopotamia)," *ABD* 2.304-305.

Scholarly perceptions of the Chronicler's elusive Solomon do not differ as widely, or as profoundly, as is the case with 1 Kings. On the other hand, the unique status of Chronicles generates a cause for indeterminacy absent from Kings. This is because all readers must choose whether to read Chronicles in the light of Samuel-Kings[44] or as what has recently been called "independent" literature.[45] Was the Chronicler *expecting* his audience to have some version of Kings in mind when reading his Solomon story? If so, did he expect those readers to harmonize the two accounts as they proceeded,[46] or to replace the Kings version with his own? Most commentators tend to discuss passages in Chronicles in terms of the extent to which they agree with or deviate from Kings, although others do attempt to describe the contents of Chronicles as though Samuel-Kings did not exist.[47] In this section I will do a little of both.

The Chronicler provides even less insight into Solomon's character and inner life than was the case in Kings. There is no direct quotation of Solomon's words anywhere in 1 Chr 22-29, in spite of the fact that three of these chapters (22, 28, and 29) focus on Yahweh's choice of Solomon to build the temple as David's successor and the affirmation of this choice by David and the people. This silence is even more striking when one notes that David repeatedly exhorts Solomon to "arise and act," "arise and build" or "be strong and act" (22:16, 19; 28:10, 20). Instead, the mentor and "fundraiser"[48] David does *all* the talking to young Solomon in private, and *all* the talking about Solomon in increasingly public forums.

As was the case in Kings, young Solomon is not said to receive an education, even though he no longer seems to possess the political "wisdom" (1 Kgs 2:6; cf. 2:9) which allowed the Solomon of Kings to estab-

---

[44] E.g., T. Willi, *Die Chronik als Auslegung: Untersuchungen zur literarichen Gestaltung der historischen Überlieferung Israels* (Göttingen: Vandenhoeck & Ruprecht, 1972) 66; P. R. Ackroyd, *The Chronicler in His Age* (JSOTSup 101; Sheffield: Sheffield Academic, 1991) 339, 341; B. S. Childs, *Introduction to the Old Testament as Scripture* (Philadelphia: Fortress, 1979) 646-47.

[45] T. Sugimoto, "Chronicles as Independent Literature," *JSOT* 55 (1992) 63, 74; cf. M. Fishbane, *Biblical Interpretation in Ancient Israel* (Oxford: Clarendon, 1985) 382.

[46] E. L. Greenstein, "On the Genesis of Biblical Prose Narrative," *Prooftexts* 8 (1988) 352-53.

[47] E.g., J. W. Wright, "The Innocence of David in 1 Chronicles 21," *JSOT* 60 (1993) 87-88.

[48] H. Tarr, "Chronicles," *Congregation: Contemporary Jewish Writers Read the Jewish Bible* (ed. D. Rosenberg: San Diego, Calif.: Harcourt Brace Jovanovich, 1987) 500.

lish his kingdom and remain in power without much guidance from his father. In Chronicles David justifies his exhaustive preparations for the building of the temple by stressing his son's lack of education, twice describing Solomon as young and inexperienced (or "tender;" נער ורך; 1 Chr 22:5; 29:1; cf. 2 Chr 13:7). Rather than eliminate his son's lack of experience by arranging for him to get the kind of formal schooling obtained by ancient kings like the Sumerian Ur-Nammu's son Shulgi,[49] David commands the princes of Israel to help his son (22:17),[50] and hands Solomon the "blueprints" for the temple (28:11).

Nor does David attempt to increase his son's understanding by composing instructions for his son/successor, in the manner of so many other ancient Near Eastern kings. Instead, he merely tells Solomon that he hopes Yahweh will give him "discretion and understanding" (שׂכל ובינה) so that he might know God, keep his laws and prosper (22:12; 28:9; cf. 29:19). While David does not target judicial understanding, readers of Chronicles may come away with the impression that it is David who inspired Solomon's later request for judicial wisdom and knowledge. When God finally asks Solomon what he wants after David's death, the new king requests wisdom and knowledge to go out and come in before the people and to judge them (2 Chr 1:10). While God tells Solomon that he has granted him his request (1:12), readers are not given the opportunity to witness Solomon acting with judicial wisdom.[51] For these reasons, readers would be hard pressed to specify the precise nature of Solomon's special wisdom, let alone determine the senses in which it might be unique or incomparable.[52]

Scholarly disagreement about the characterization of Solomon in 1 Chr 22, 28-29 usually centers on the issue of whether David is being elevated at the expense of Solomon or vice versa. Some note that David is the one who actively prepares everything for the temple, including funds,

---

[49] This difference goes unnoticed in S. N. Kramer, "Solomon and Šulgi: A Comparative Portrait," *Ah Assyria... Studies in Assyrian History and Ancient Near Eastern Historiography Presented to Hayim Tadmor* (ed. M. Cogan and I. Eph'al; Scripta Hierosolymitana 33; Jerusalem: Magnes, 1991) 193-95.

[50] Apparently they are not to help him personally, for Solomon is not mentioned in David's quoted exhortation to the princes (1 Chr 22:18-19).

[51] The Chronicler does expand one reference to Solomon's wisdom, however, when he has Huram bless Yahweh for giving David a son who possesses wisdom, knowledge, discretion and understanding (חכם יודע שׂכל ובינה; 2 Chr 2:11). Yet Huram goes on to use the same language when praising Huram the craftsman as one who also possesses wisdom, knowledge, and understanding (חכם יודע בינה ; 2:12).

[52] While God says that he is giving Solomon incomparable wisdom in 1 Kgs 3:12, this is not said in the parallel passage in 2 Chr 1:12.

while Solomon apparently just listens to his father expatiate on his extensive preparations and his great generosity. All that is left for Solomon to "arise and do" is to keep fundraising and follow his father's game plan.[53] Others argue that it is Solomon who is glorified at David's expense.[54] They point out that Solomon is now Yahweh's chosen temple builder, while David is disqualified due to the fact that he shed so much blood (22:8; 28:3). In other words, the "man of wars" (28:3) is eclipsed by the "man of rest" and peace (22:9), even if David's wars prepared for that peace. And while David is the active party in chapters 28-29, his activity is focused on grooming the people to view Solomon (if not himself) in an adoring fashion. David's other sons join in as well. Like Esarhaddon's brothers, who all witness Sennacherib's designation of their younger brother as his successor and take a solemn oath to support him,[55] all of young Solomon's brothers give a hand in support (29:24). Finally, in 29:25 the narrator declares that Yahweh magnified Solomon greatly, giving him royal majesty the likes of which had not been bestowed on any king before him [in Israel, MT] (cf. 2 Chr 1:12).

The theme of magnification recalls Yahweh's public relations work on the image of Moses' successor Joshua, as do the repeated admonitions to Solomon and Joshua that they be strong and courageous and not be afraid. However, likening David and the magnified Solomon to Moses and the magnified Joshua strengthens the case of those who view 1 Chronicles as elevating David more than Solomon. Joshua is no Moses, even though Yahweh grooms him to appear Moses-like to his people. As the rabbis put it, Moses is the sun and Joshua the moon (e.g., *B. Bat.* 75a); and light reflected by Joshua has its source in Moses' charisma.

In 2 Chronicles Solomon is no longer silent, although his words are not directly quoted until he responds to Yahweh's gift offer. After that he is quoted on only three occasions: in writing to Huram, in his temple speeches, and in offering a cultic rationale for moving his otherwise unknown Egyptian wife (2 Chr 8:11). On the other hand, Solomon's

[53] E.g., E. L. Curtis and A. A. Madsen, *A Critical and Exegetical Commentary on the Books of Chronicles* (ICC; Edinburgh: T. & T. Clark, 1910) 259.

[54] E.g., R. Braun, "Solomonic Apologetic in Chronicles," *JBL* 92 (1973) 512; J. G. McConville, *I & II Chronicles* (WBC; Waco, Tex.: Word Books, 1987) 3. On Braun's view, see S. J. De Vries, *1 and 2 Chronicles* (FOTL 11; Grand Rapids: Eerdmans, 1989) 228.

[55] R. Borger, *Die Inschriften Asarhaddons Königs von Assyrien* (*AfO* 9; Graz: Ernst Weidner, 1956) 40 (I, lines 8-11).

abbreviated response to Yahweh's offer and his letter to Huram are both more assertive and business-like than their counterparts in 1 Kings. Solomon no longer claims help from Yahweh because he is a little child. Perhaps this is because David has already provided help when he still viewed his son as an inexperienced child, a child who was seen but not heard. Similarly, the Solomon who takes the initiative to contact Huram and set the terms of their building-materials contract does not feel any need to assure Huram that his borders are secure and that he has no enemies. Nor does he explain to Huram why David was unable to build the temple. On the contrary, Solomon is the more powerful party both here and later, when it is Huram who extends the borders of Israel by giving twenty cities to Solomon, not the other way around (2 Chr 8:2; cf. 1 Kgs 9:11).

The Solomon of 1-2 Chronicles is all business; that is, temple business. He has no private life *or* private desires. Gone are the thousand loves of his life. Here he has only two wives and we only learn of them incidentally. We learn of Pharaoh's daughter only because of Solomon's concern not to defile the area in which the ark resides and we learn of the second wife thanks only to his son Rehoboam's later regnal résumé, which includes both his mother's name (Naamah) and her ethnic identity as an Ammonite (2 Chr 12:13).

The fact that this obedient Solomon has only two wives and one named child is significant. In Chronicles a large number of wives and children is a reliable indicator of success and divine approval. Thus, Solomon's father David had many wives and concubines and nineteen sons (1 Chr 3:1-9; 14:3-7). Solomon's son Rehoboam is even more prolific; he has eighteen wives and sixty concubines, including his wife Maacah, whom he loved most of all. These women give birth to twenty-eight sons and sixty daughters (2 Chr 11:18-21). In this key sense, Solomon's own peaceful, obedient kingdom is sterile and unproductive, even more than was the case in Kings.

The Chronicler's Solomon is not only magnified but blameless. Considering that we are told so little about Solomon's personality and personal life, it is hardly surprising that no personal sin is attributed to him. The good news for this blameless and sterile Solomon is that he has no external enemies at the end of his career, precisely because he has no multitude of wives to incite him to idolatry. Nevertheless, rebellion breaks out in the northern half of Solomon's peaceful kingdom immediately after his death, when his "young and tender-hearted" (i.e., faint-hearted or irresolute) son takes the throne (נער ורך-לבב; 2 Chr 13:7; cf.

12:13). When it comes to the cause for the rebellion, the narrator is neither ambiguous nor vague: the blame is laid squarely on the shoulders of a Jeroboam who has been stripped of his divine mandate and on the people who here have no good reason to complain of excessive taxation. Because of the narrator's silences (he never says that Solomon used his own people for the corvée, never says that he formed administrative tax districts to support his extravagant court and his building projects, and never says that he had to sell off part of the holy land), and, it is the sheer perversity of Jeroboam and the Israelites which are, by default, totally responsible for the disastrous schism following the death of this idealized "man of rest."

4. Conclusions

> Some individuals have seen him, everybody has heard of him, and out of glimpses and rumors and through various distorting factors an image of Klamm has been constructed which is certainly true in fundamentals. But only in fundamentals. Otherwise it fluctuates, and yet perhaps it does not fluctuate so much as Klamm's real appearance.[56]

Once there was a castle official named Klamm. In the village below the castle the people say that Klamm is enormously powerful. A man named K. seeks an audience with Klamm as urgently as Dorothy sought an audience with the Wizard. Yet Klamm is as elusive and protean as any panoptic king. While no one can hide from him, he is rarely seen and never speaks to anyone in the village. The two letters which K. receives, apparently from Klamm, are so ambiguous that K. and others engage in intense literary analysis trying to tease out their meaning and intention. When Klamm is seen, it is only for a moment. Even in those moments they are never capable of "really seeing"[57] him. According to a character named Olga, "a man like Klamm, who is so much sought after and so rarely accessible, easily takes on different shapes in people's imagination."[58] Indeed, he is reported to have one appearance when he comes into the village and another on leaving it, one when he is alone and another with people, and so on.

[56] F. Kafka, *Das Schloss* (Berlin: Fischer; New York: Schocken, 1967) 257.
[57] *Ibid.*, p. 74.
[58] *Ibid.*, p. 265.

Given Klamm's inscrutable and protean nature, how can one construct an image of him which is even "true in fundamentals"? According to Olga, the differences in Klamm's appearance "aren't the result of magic;" in other words, Klamm is no more a wizard than is Oz. She believes that they are the result of the momentary mood of the observer (the viewer's "countless gradations" of hope, despair, or excitement) and the fact that Klamm is usually seen only for a moment.[59] This, she concludes, would be sufficient explanation for anyone not personally interested in the matter. For her and K., however, it is a life and death matter.

In a sense, readers of the Solomon narratives share the predicament of K. and Olga, whether they are seemingly disinterested scholars, or observers for whom the question of Solomon's personality is as urgent and vital as Klamm's personality is for K. and Olga. Solomon appears one way in Kings and another in Chronicles, not to mention the variety of different ways he appears to different commentators. Are these varying images of Solomon also a function of the observer's "momentary mood" (or ideology, or hermeneutical habits)? Scholars would not like to say so. Yet if the texts describe the king in such a way that the "real" Solomon (both the literary Solomon and the historical personage) remains invisible, it is unlikely that any academic attempt to bracket out subjective factors will produce an "objective" portrait of the king. The lack of extra-biblical information on Solomon, and the lack of certainty concerning the date and social context of the narratives,[60] only decrease the likelihood of constructing an unambiguous image of the king which is "true in fundamentals."

While the elusiveness of the biblical Solomon might be distressing to readers who want to penetrate the king's public facade, the narratives themselves seem designed to keep Solomon hidden, thereby *encouraging* a variety of subjective responses to the texts. This is hardly suprising, considering the function served by invisibility and protean appearance for leaders like Deiokes, the Wizard, and many others. Whether they are called "court apologetic" or propaganda, the narratives create an indeterminate image of the king which bypasses the dilemma faced by court historians who must otherwise affirm or deny unflattering facts about their monarchs. The solution represented by these narratives is not unlike the strategy called "telling it with discretion" by Ethan,

[59] *Ibid.*, pp. 257-58.

[60] On these problems see Lasine, "King of Desire," pp. 97-99, 103-104.

Solomon's court historian, in Stefan Heym's novel *The King David Report*. Rather than telling all the "undesirable matter" about Solomon's father or denying it (when the audience might learn about it anyway through unofficial channels), Ethan chooses to tell it with discretion. Discretion is "truth controlled by wisdom."[61] In this case, to be discreet and wise means to show a king who is neither invisible nor totally visible. Instead, the king is presented as being discreetly inscrutable, capable of being viewed in many different ways. This means that scholars cannot even determine whether the reconstructions they produce from these textual "glimpses" and age-old "rumors" are even "fundamentally" true. What *can* be determined, however, is that the narratives constitute one of the most unique and complex examples of political rhetoric in ancient literature. And best of all, this rhetoric (Solomon's verbal palace) *is* visible, and therefore available for analysis, if only from the outside.

---

[61] S. Heym, *The King David Report* (London: Hodder and Stoughton, 1972) 84.

SOLOMON'S FALL AND DEUTERONOMY

GARY N. KNOPPERS

In his classic treatment of the Deuteronomistic History, Martin Noth argued that the books of Deuteronomy, Joshua, Judges, Samuel, and Kings constitute a continuous history characterized by a basic consistency in language, style, and content.[1] Noth recognized, however, that Deuteronomy was a special case in that the composition of the deuteronomic law code, defined as Deut 4:44-30:20, predated the composition of the Deuteronomistic History.[2] In Noth's view, the Deuteronomist incorporated the deuteronomic law into the beginning of his history, framing it with speeches by Moses, which introduced the history as a whole.[3] The inclusion of *Urdeuteronomium* was not an afterthought. The Deuteronomist assigned to it "a crucial role, regarding it as a norm for the relationship between God and people and as a yardstick by which to judge human conduct."[4] Noth did not devote a great deal of attention to developing or demonstrating this important point. In fact, as Römer has recently pointed out, Noth did not discuss *Urdeuteronomium* much at all.[5] In some places Noth recognized tensions between the coverage of the Deuteronomist and the standards espoused by Deuteronomy.[6] Nevertheless, most of modern scholarship on Deuteronomy and the Deuteronomistic History has accepted Noth's basic judgment about the relationship between them.

The issues raised by such claims about Deuteronomy and the Deuteronomistic History are, however, many and complex. Some commentators have disagreed with Noth about the date, purpose, and composition

---

[1] *The Deuteronomic History,* (JSOTSup 15; 2nd ed.; Shefield: JSOT Press, 1991) 17-26.

[2] *Ibid.,* p. 31. Noth conceded that there were many later random additions to this original code.

[3] *bid.,* pp. 27-33.

[4] *Ibid.,* p. 124.

[5] T. Römer, "The Book of Deuteronomy" *The History of Israel's Traditions: The Heritage of Martin Noth* (ed. S. L. McKenzie and M. P. Graham; JSOTSup 182; Sheffield: JSOT Press, 1994) 178-83.

[6] For instance, in the deuteronomistic coverage of Josiah, *Deuteronomistic History,* pp. 125-26.

of the Deuteronomistic History.[7] Others have taken issue with him about what is deuteronomic and what is deuteronomistic in Deuteronomy.[8] Despite these important areas of dispute, most have retained Noth's basic notion that the deuteronomistic editor(s) incorporated *Urdeuteronomium* (however one defines this work) into his larger history of Israel. Indeed, some scholars have employed this legal code as a hermeneutical cipher by which to determine the Deuteronomist's posture toward the conduct of characters in the history he narrates.[9]

Noth's influential claim about the Deuteronomist's use of Deuteronomy deserves closer critical scrutiny than it has received. This essay will examine one particular narrative in the Solomon story with a view to evaluating Noth's hypothesis. Solomon's decline and its links to his successors (Rehoboam in Judah and Jeroboam in Israel) present two possible advantages as a test case. First, scholars generally agree that sections of 1 Kgs 11 have been significantly edited by the Deuteronomist(s).[10] Within the first few verses, for example, standard deuteronomistic clichés occur: "to cling to the nations" (דבק בגויים; 1 Kgs 11:2), "to turn a heart after other gods" (הטה לבב אחרי אלהים אחרים; 1 Kgs 11:2,4), and "a perfect heart" (לב שׁלם; 1 Kgs 11:4).[11] Hence, in assessing Solomon's perfidy one is not comparing the standards of *Urdeuteronomium* with what is most likely an unedited source in the Deuteronomist's employ. If there are close connections between Deuteronomy and the Deuteronomistic History, they should be plainly evident in a chapter that bears all the marks of substantial deuteronomistic editing. Second, the narration of the second period in Solomon's reign is one of a relatively few cases in the Deuteronomistic History in which a passage from Deuteronomy seems to be actually quoted. However one defines *Urdeu-*

[7] H. D. Preuss, "Zum deuteronomistischen Geschichtswerk," *TRu* 58 (1993) 229-64, provides an overview.

[8] See the surveys of H. D. Preuss, *Deuteronomium* (ErFor 164; Darmstadt: Wissenschaftliche Buchgesellschaft, 1982) and Römer, "Deuteronomy," pp. 184-99.

[9] Most recently, M. A. Sweeney, "The Critique of Solomon in the Josianic Edition of the Deuteronomistic History," *JBL* 114 (1995) 607-22.

[10] See my *Two Nations Under God: The Deuteronomistic History of Solomon and the Dual Monarchies,* vol. 1: *The Reign of Solomon and the Rise of Jeroboam* (HSM 52; Atlanta: Scholars, 1993) 135-223. In this book I argue that 1 Kgs 11 belongs to a series of deuteronomistic reflections, speeches, and prayers, which the Deuteronomist employs to unify and structure his history of Israel. By the "Deuteronomist" I mean the Josianic Deuteronomist (Dtr^1).

[11] On the deuteronomistic nature and use of these expressions, see M. Weinfeld, *Deuteronomy and the Deuteronomic School* (Oxford: Clarendon, 1972) 341 (#11), 321 (#7a), 335 (#10). The opposite of דבק בגויים is דבק ביהוה, *ibid.*, p. 333 (#5).

teronomium, one knows that the author had in this instance at least a portion of Deuteronomy available to him. Careful study of such a citation may provide important clues to the Deuteronomist's use of and stance toward *Urdeuteronomium*.

To what extent are the standards of Deuteronomy reflected in the deuteronomistic construction and evaluation of Solomon's fall?[12] Any comparison must do justice to both similarities and differences. I will begin by exploring various points of contact between Deuteronomy and the deuteronomistic presentation of Solomon's demise. After documenting what I think are the strongest links that can be made between the two, I will establish some important differences. Both the similarities and the differences point to the Deuteronomist having a much more sophisticated exegetical and heremeneutical stance toward *Urdeuteronomium* than Noth supposed.

1. Solomon, Foreign Women, and Other Gods

In 1 Kgs 11:1-4 the Deuteronomist marks a transition from Solomon's fame to his infamy. To document Solomon's regression, the Deuteronomist draws a series of contrasts with the first period he posits in Solomon's reign. In the first part of his tenure Solomon followed the practices of David his father (1 Kgs 3:3), but in the second part of his tenure Solomon "did not follow YHWH completely as did David his father" (1 Kgs 11:6). Prior to building the temple, Solomon sacrificed and burned incense at the high places (רק בבמות הוא מזבח ומקטיר; 1 Kgs 3:3). When the temple was completed, Solomon regularly sacrificed to YHWH there (1 Kgs 8:5,62-64; 9:25; 10:5). Yet in the second portion of his reign Solomon burns incense and sacrifices (מקטיר ומזבח) to foreign gods at the high places he built for his foreign wives (1 Kgs 11:8).[13]

At first glance, this deuteronomistic narration of Solomon's regres-

---

[12] My concern in this essay is not primarily whether the deuteronomistic treatment of Solomon is consonant with the deuteronomic law of the king (Deut 17:14-20). The relationship between the law of the king and the Deuteronomist and the Deuteronomic treatment of kings is a related issue that I have addressed elsewhere, "The Deuteronomist and the Deuteronomic Law of the King: A Reexamination of a Relationship," *ZAW* 108 (1996) 329-46.

[13] I read with the LXX^{L} the masculine singular מקטיר ומזבח. The MT and the LXX^{B} read the feminine plural מקטירות ומזבחות. The MT and LXX^{B} attempt to soften Solomon's culpability. See also the differences between the MT (plural) and the LXX (singular) in 1 Kgs 11:33.

sion seems to confirm Noth's assessment about the Deuteronomist's use of Deuteronomy. Commentators have long noted that the writer's mention of Solomon's love for foreign women "from the nations" (Moabites, Ammonites, Edomites, Sidonians, Hittites, and the daughter of Pharaoh; 1 Kgs 11:1-2)[14] recalls the deuteronomic prohibition of intermarriage with the indigenous inhabitants of Canaan, "you shall not intermarry with them; you shall not give your daughter to his son, nor shall you take his daughter for your son" (ולא תתחתן בם בתך לא תתן לבנו ובתו לא תקח לבנך; Deut 7:3).[15] Indeed, the reasons given for why such mixed marriages are prohibited in Kings seem to resonate with those offered in Deuteronomy.[16] In 1 Kgs 11:2 the writer uses the citation formula, "YHWH said" (אמר יהוה), to introduce the use of an authoritative *traditum* against Solomon: "You shall not have sexual relations with them nor shall they have sexual relations with you; truly, they will turn your heart after their gods" (לא תבאו בהם והם לא יבאו בכם אכן יטו את לבבכם אחרי אלהיהם).[17] The censure seems straightforward. The Deuteronomist cites Deut 7:4 to explain the consequences of Solomon's actions: "because he will turn (כי־יסיר) your son away from me and they will serve[18] other gods" (אלהים אחרים). Solomon violates the deuteronomic prohibition of exogamy with the seven autochthonous nations of Canaan (Deut 7:1) and his actions exemplify the expected consequences. Solomon's wives "turn (הטו) his heart after other gods" (אלהים אחרים; 1 Kgs 11:4).

If the mechanism by which Solomon regresses confirms the deutero-

---

[14] The inclusion of "and the daughter of Pharaoh" in 1 Kgs 11:2 is syntactically awkward and many scholars delete it as a gloss; most recently, E. Würthwein, *Die Bücher der Könige: 1 Könige 1-16* (ATD 11/1; Göttingen: Vandenhoeck & Ruprecht, 1977) 131. The phrase likely represents a correction by a later scribe to include Pharaoh's daughter among Solomon's foreign wives (1 Kgs 3:1; 9:24). In subsequent discussions of Solomon's perfidy the daughter of Pharaoh plays no role (1 Kgs 11:5 [MT],7-8,33).

[15] E.g., A. Klostermann, *Die Bücher Samuelis under der Könige* (Kurzegefasster Kommentar zu heiligen Schriften 3; Nördlingen: Beck, 1887) 337; G. H. Jones, *1 and 2 Kings* (NCB; Grand Rapids: Eerdmans, 1984) 233-34.

[16] The law of the king in Deut 17:17 prohibits the multiplication of wives (ולא ירבה-לו נשים ולא יסור לבבו). The Deuteronomist, however, lambastes Solomon for worshiping the gods of his foreign wives and not for multiplying the number of his wives; S. J. D. Cohen, "Solomon and the Daughter of Pharaoh: Intermarriage, Conversion, and the Impurity of Women," *JANES* 16-17 (1984-1985) 23-37.

[17] Deut 7:1-6 draws upon and reformulates two different older lemmata (Exod 23:20-33; 34:11-16), G. Braulik, *Deuteronomium 1-16,17* (Die Neue Echter Bibel 15; Würzburg: Echter, 1986) 62-65; M. Weinfeld, *Deuteronomy 1-11* (AB 5; Garden City, NY: Doubleday, 1991) 377-84.

[18] Reading with the MT (*lectio difficilior*). The singular appears in both the LXX and the Samaritan Pentateuch.

nomic inderdictions against marital unions with the indigenous inhabitants of Canaan, the very definition of Solomon's crimes also bears a deuteronomic stamp.[19] Solomon does not "follow YHWH with loyalty" (לא מלא אחרי יהוה).[20] Nor does he keep YHWH's "covenant and statutes" (1 Kgs 11:11).[21] Similarly, YHWH informs Jeroboam, through an oracle delivered by the prophet Ahijah, that Solomon did not "walk in my ways, doing what was right in my eyes" (1 Kgs 11:33).[22] In this perspective, Solomon's conduct contrasts markedly with that of David "who kept my statutes and judgments" (אשר שמר מצותי וחקתי).[23] The standards by which Solomon is judged are couched, therefore, in stereotypical deuteronomic and deuteronomistic clichés.

The specific crimes Solomon commits, apart from intermarriage, are the construction of high places for his foreign wives and the worship of other gods. The latter is not a specifically deuteronomistic sin, but the way in which Solomon's transgression is expressed does resemble the phraseology of Deuteronomy. 1 Kgs 11:5 speaks of "Solomon's following after" (וילך שלמה אחרי) Astarte, the god of the Sidonians, and Milcom, the god of the Ammonites.[24] Similarly, the divine indictment of Solomon in 1 Kgs 11:10 mentions his "following after other gods" (ללכת אחרי אלהים אחרים; 1 Kgs 11:10).[25] Ahijah's royal oracle to Jeroboam in 1 Kgs 11:33 avows that Solomon worshiped (וישתחו) Astrate, the deity of the Sidonians, Chemosh, the deity of Moab, and Milcom, the deity of the Ammonites.[26] Finally, Solomon violates the deuteronomic mandate for

[19] See further my "Sex, Religion, and Politics: The Deuteronomist on Intermarriage," *HAR* 14 (1994) 121-41.

[20] 1 Kgs 11:6 (cf. Deut 1:36). For examples from the Deuteronomistic History, see Weinfeld, *Deuteronomic School,* p. 337 (#19).

[21] *Ibid.*, p. 336 (#17b).

[22] Reading the singular with the LXX (see below). On the expression, see Deut 6:18; 12:25,28; 13:19; 21:9; *ibid.*, p. 335 (#15).

[23] 1 Kgs 11:34. *Ibid.*, pp. 336-37 (#s 16, 21b).

[24] The MT reads Ashtoreth. There is a tendency in both the MT and the LXX of 1 Kgs 11 to replace אלהים as a term for foreign deities with dysphemisms: ειδωλῳ, "idol" and שקץ, "abomination" (cp. vv 8 and 33 with vv 5 and 7). See also Num 25:1,3 and 2 Kgs 23:13. I follow a number of commentators who emend these dysphemisms to אלהים.

[25] See Deut 6:14; 8:19; 11:28; 13:3; 28:14; Judg 2:12,19, and the list of related expressions in Weinfeld, *Deuteronomic School,* p. 320.

[26] Cf. Deut 4:19; 8:19; 11:16; 29:25; 30:17. In 1 Kgs 11:33, the LXX, the Syriac, and certain manuscripts of the Vg. all read the masculine singular with the 1 masculine singular suffix. The plural of the MT is grammatically inconsistent (compare the beginning of v 33 with כדוד אביו at the end of v 33). The reading of the versions also agrees with the antecedent (שלמה of v 31) and with מידו of v 34. The MT probably represents an attempt to soften Solomon's culpability by making the Israelites themselves responsible for his

centralization (Deut 12:2-14,29-31). 1 Kgs 11:7 describes how Solomon built a high place for Chemosh, the god of Moab, and for Milcom,[27] the god of Ammon.[28] 1 Kgs 11:8 elaborates, declaring that Solomon did this for all of his wives. By sacrificing and burning incense at all these sanctuaries, the builder of Israel's long awaited central sanctuary himself defies its exclusive status.

Beyond phraseology and specific infractions one may notice broader conceptual parallels between Deuteronomy and the Deuteronomistic History. Deuteronomy evinces what Noth calls a "legal" notion of the factors that determine the course of history.[29] Transgressing divinely set limits elicits divine wrath and punishment (Deut 7:4). Disobedience, in particular the worship of other gods, has disastrous consequences. Although a legal conception of history is not exclusive to the deuteronomic and deuteronomistic writers,[30] there is something to Noth's assertion. One is struck by the judicial way in which the Deuteronomist orders his presentation: a catalogue of crimes (1 Kgs 11:1-8), accusations (1 Kgs 11:11,33), divine judgment (1 Kgs 11:12-13,31-32,34-36), and the implementation of penalties (1 Kgs 11:14-25; 12:1-20). Solomon's misconduct infuriates YHWH, the deity who "appeared to him twice" (1 Kgs 11:9; cf. 1 Kgs 3:4-14; 9:1-9), who decides to punish him.[31]

Critical to the deuteronomic understanding of law is its application to various sectors of society. The only mediation between God and his privileged people (Deut 7:5-6) is supplied by (deuteronomic) laws that struc-

misdeeds. For further details on the textual criticism of this verse, see my *Two Nations Under God, 1,* pp. 186-88.

[27] Reading with the LXX^L (cf. 2 Kgs 23:13). The MT reads מֹלֶךְ. As B. Stade, and F. Schwally (*The Book of Kings: Critical Edition of the Hebrew Text* [Sacred Books of the Old Testament 9; Leipzig: Hinrichs, 1904] 125) point out, the reading of the LXX και τῳ βασιλει αυτων interprets an original מלכם. See also v 5 (מלכם), the various witnesses to the MT's מַלְכָּם in 2 Sam 12:30, Jer 49:1,3, and Zeph 1:5.

[28] Reading with the MT (*lectio brevior*). The LXX adds και τῃ Ασταρτῃ Βδελυγματι Σιδωνιων (ולעשתרת אלהי צדנים), which assimilates to לעשתרת שקץ צדנים in 2 Kgs 23:13.

[29] Noth, *Deuteronomistic History,* pp. 120,124.

[30] One also finds such a view of history in the Priestly work and the Chronicler's History.

[31] In the Deuteronomistic History the anger formula, "YHWH became incensed" (התאנף יהוה ב־) and its alloform (חרה אף יהוה ב־), are one means by which the author structures major transitions within history; D. J. McCarthy, "The Wrath of Yahweh and the Structural Unity of the Deuteronomistic History," *Essays in Old Testament Ethics* (ed. J. L. Crenshaw and J. T. Willis; New York: KTAV, 1974) 97-110. Israelite disobedience is linked to the incitement of divine wrath and an ensuing penalty. But, in this case, the penalty is delayed (see section 2 below).

ture the divine-human relationship.[32] This legal code is not promulgated by a human king, nor are human kings exempt from its stipulations (Deut 17:14-20).[33] Israelite institutions, groups, and individuals all fall under the scope of YHWH's statutes and commandments.[34] In this context, one may observe that the *topos* of mixed marriages explains a reversal in the course of Solomonic rule, but it does not excuse it. Solomon's foreign wives catalyze his decline, but YHWH becomes enraged with Solomon, and not his wives, "because he turned (נטה) his heart from YHWH, the God of Israel" (1 Kgs 11:9). Similarly, the judgment oracle of 1 Kgs 11:11-13 accuses Solomon, and not his wives, of malfeasance. The refusal to excuse Solomon underscores the force of the prohibitions he violates. In his dotage (1 Kgs 11:4) Solomon flounders because he flouts established divine commands. Under the rule of law even one of Israel's most distinquished monarchs can be judged and found wanting.

In short, it is difficult to deny that some sort of relationship exists between *Urdeuteronomium* and the deuteronomistic narration of Solomon's fall. Not only is the language and style similar, but the deuteronomistic indictment of Solomon seems to quote Deuteronomy directly. Finally, some cardinal tenets of Deuteronomy reappear, albeit negatively, in 1 Kgs 11. The mandate for centralization is dishonored by the construction of high places and the call for exclusive worship of YHWH is abrogated by Solomon's worship of other gods. The deuteronomic rule of law is vindicated in the judgments assessed against Solomon. Given the evidence, one might be tempted to agree with Noth that *Urdeuteronomium*, of fundamental importance to the Deuteronomist, was used by him to evaluate Solomon. But are such sweeping conclusions justified? Upon close scrutiny of the Deuteronomist's narrative, a series of major difficulties emerge.

---

[32] E.g., Braulik, *Deuteronomium*, pp. 15-17; Römer, "Deuteronomy," pp. 201-202.

[33] This is not to say that Deuteronomy exhibits an entirely consistent presentation of what YHWH's statutes and commandments are. N. Lohfink argues, for example, that in certain texts (Deut 7:4 included) the decalogue is in view, "Die These von deuteronomischen Dekalogabfang—ein fragwürdiges Ergebnis atomistischer Sprachstatistik," *Studien zum Pentateuch* (ed. G. Braulik; Wien: Herder, 1977) 99-109. This essay is reprinted in his *Studien zum Deuteronomium und zur deuteronomistischer Literatur, 1* (SBAB 8; Stuttgart: Katholisches Bibelwerk, 1990) 363-78.

[34] This is especially clear in Deut 16:18-18:22. See N. Lohfink, "Die Sicherung der Wirksamkeit des Gotteswortes durch das Prinzip der Schriftlichkeit der Tora und das Prinzip der Gewaltenteilung nach den Ämtergesetzen des Buches Deuteronomium (Dt 16:18-18:22)," *Testimonium Veritati* (ed. H. Wolter; Frankfurter Theologische Studien 7; Frankfurt: Knecht, 1971) 143-55; U. Rüterswörden, *Von der politischen Gemeinschaft zur Gemeinde: Studien zu Dt 16,18-18,22* (BBB 65; Frankfurt am Main: Athenäum, 1987).

2. FOREIGN WIVES, DAVID, AND TRANSGENERATIONAL PUNISHMENT

In discussing the discrepancies between the standards of Deuteronomy and the deuteronomistic story of Solomon's fall, I will begin with the description of Solomon's sins and then turn to the nature of the penalties imposed upon Solomon. We have seen that some commentators construe, "You shall not have sexual relations with them nor shall they have sexual relations with you" (לא תבאו בהם והם לא יבאו בכם; 1 Kgs 11:2) as a quote of Deut 7:3, "you shall not intermarry with them; you shall not give your daughter to his son, nor shall you take his daughter for your son" (ובתו לא תקח לבנך ולא תתחתן בם בתך לא תתן). But the two lemmata are not strictly parallel.[35] Not only does the phraseology differ, but the subject matter does as well. 1 Kgs 11:2 deals with sex, while Deut 7:3 refers to mixed marriages.[36] Indeed, comparative analysis reveals that the precise text the author of 1 Kgs 11:2 introduced by the citation formula, "YHWH said," appears neither in the Pentateuch nor elsewhere in the Former Prophets. The closest parallel to the citation in 1 Kgs 11:1-2 can be found in the deuteronomistically edited farewell speech of Joshua (Josh 23:2-16).[37] The Deuteronomist ironically engages not the divine voice of Deuteronomy 7, but the admonition of Josh 23:11-12, "watch your lives carefully to love YHWH (לאהבה את-יהוה) your God, because if you turn away and cling to the remainder of these nations with you,[38] and you intermarry with them and have intercourse with them and they with you (והתחתנתם בהם ובאתם בהם והם בכם), surely know that YHWH your God will not continue to dispossess these nations from before you." The Deuteronomist is selective, citing only that portion of Joshua's warning that deals with sexual intercourse.

To this problem another can be immediately added. The authors of Deut 7:1-4 prohibit exogamy, but solely with the seven autochthonous Canaanite nations. Only one of the nations appearing in the MT of 1 Kgs 11:1-2 (the Hittites) actually appears in those Pentateuchal passages (Exod 34:11-16 and Deut 7:1-4) that prohibit Israelites from intermarry-

[35] The idiom -בא אל\ב with the object of person(s) consistently refers to sexual relations (e.g., Gen 6:4; 16:2,4; Deut 22:13; Josh 23:12; Judg 16:1; Ezek 23:44).

[36] Hence, M. Fishbane refers to 1 Kgs 11:2 as a "pseudo-citation" of Deut 7:3, *Biblical Interpretation in Ancient Israel* (Oxford: Clarendon, 1985) 125.

[37] On Josh 23:2-16 as a deuteronomistic composition, see Noth *Deuteronomistic History*, pp. 45-60; J. A. Soggin, *Joshua* (OTL; Philadelphia: Westminster, 1972) 217-19; R. Boling and G. E. Wright, *Joshua* (AB 6; New York: Doubleday, 1982) 522-26.

[38] Reading with the LXX^B (*lectio brevior*). The MT adds הנשארים האלה.

ing with any one of the native Canaanite nations.[39] If the author of 1 Kgs 11:1 were directly quoting Deut 7:1, one might expect him to include more peoples from Deuteronomy's standard register of nations. Both the non-appearance of six of seven nations and the appearance of the Moabites, Ammonites, Edomites, and Sidonians in 1 Kgs 11:1-2 are surprising.

This is not to say that there is no connection with Deut 7 whatsoever. The consequences of Solomon's relations to foreign women recall the consequences outlined in Deut 7:4. Josh 23:13 speaks of the remaining nations as a snare and a trap, but Deut 7:4 forbids intermarriage, "because he will turn (כי־יסיר) your son away from me and they will serve other gods" (אלהים אחרים). Hence, the writer selectively develops two different sources.[40] But if the Deuteronomist had access to Deut 7:1-6, why does he cite the *traditio* of Josh 23:11-13, and not the *traditum* of Deut 7:1-6, to condemn Solomon? Joshua's farewell speech offers three advantages. First, by citing only the general command against sexual relations with members of "the nations," 1 Kgs 11:2 exploits an ambiguity inherent in Josh 23:11, facilitating an adjustment in the original repertoire of autochthonous nations to include others not previously listed. Joshua's speech is ambiguous. He warns Israel about "the remainder of these nations" (ביתר הגוים האלה) left to be dispossessed, but never identifies them (Josh 23:4,7,12,13). 1 Kgs 11:2, like Josh 23:11, does not delimit the peoples with whom the Israelites are not to intermarry. This explains why the writer includes only one (MT) or two (LXX) nations from Deuteronomy's standard repertoire of authochthonous peoples. The author provides a sample of the nations with whom Solomon had become related, naming those peoples of particular interest to him. The Moabites, the Ammonites, the Edomites, the Sidonians, and the Hittites (1 Kgs 11:1) are a sub-group of those nations (מן־הגוים) with whom YHWH forbids conjugation (1 Kgs 11:2).

Second, the Deuteronomist opines that Solomon had both hundreds of wives and hundreds of concubines (1 Kgs 11:3). The selective citation (לא־תבאו בהם לא־יבאו בכם) of Joshua's parenesis covers both types of paramours. Third, the Deuteronomist employs Joshua's admonitions to draw a parallel with another major shift in Israelite history. The bifurcation in

---

[39] The LXX of 1 Kgs 11:1 mentions another aboriginal people, the Amorites. The Amorites also appear in Deut 7:1 and Exod 34:11.

[40] The pericope of Deut 23:4-9, which refers to admittance into the assembly, is not in view, Knoppers, "Sex, Religion, and Politics," pp. 123-28.

the presentation of Solomon's reign is informed by the fundamental decision the Deuteronomist champions in Joshua's speech: love either YHWH or the nations. Solomon attempts both, but not simultaneously. Solomon's love for foreign women catalyzes a reversal of his erstwhile love for YHWH. The appeal to cling to YHWH is found many times in Deuteronomy and the Deuteronomistic History, but the alternation between clinging to YHWH and clinging to the nations is characteristic of only two parts of this extensive work: Joshua's farewell speech and Solomon's reign.[41] Joshua summons Israel to cling to YHWH (ביהוה אלהיכם תדבקו) and love (לאהבה) him and not to cling (ודבקתם) to the nations (Josh 23:8,12). Having earlier loved YHWH (ויאהב שלמה את-יהוה; 1 Kgs 3:3), Solomon clings (דבק) to his foreign wives and concubines in love (לאהבה; 1 Kgs 11:2). In this manner, the Deuteronomist draws upon Deut 7 to create a *topos*, expounding on the ramifications of intermarriage.[42] This *topos* explains two critical junctures in Israelite history: Israel's metamorphosis from a victorious people in Joshua to a disorganized one in Judges and the transition from a peaceful united kingdom under Solomon to a troubled divided kingdom under Rehoboam and Jeroboam. In each case, foreign wives are a conduit by which heteropraxis reappears in Israelite life.

Close examination of the indictment of Solomon has revealed considerable freedom in the Deuteronomist's handling of Deuteronomy. The Deuteronomist draws upon both *traditum* and *traditio* to orchestrate a major turning point in Israelite history. The authoritative standard employed to judge the actions of major characters comprises both deuteronomic law and deuteronomistic parenesis. Nevertheless, by bringing together two disparate sources, the Deuteronomist has created something new. The exegetical blend of Deut 7:4 and Josh 23:11-13 modifies both *traditum* and *traditio*, creating a *tertium quid*. Yet, as Fishbane observes, the use of a citation formula (אמר־יהוה) has its benefits.[43] The citation formula bestows legitimacy to a *traditio*, making the innovation contextual with the *traditum* itself.

If the Deuteronomist's criticism of Solomon is only partially informed by Deuteronomy, this is true also for the standards by which Solomon and his successors are judged. Solomon, Jeroboam, and Rehoboam are all subject to the rule of law. Yet one must ask what loyalty to YHWH's

---

[41] Deut 4:4; 10:20; 11:22; 13:5; 30:20; Josh 22:5; 2 Kgs 18:6.

[42] Knoppers, "Sex, Religion, and Politics," pp. 129-33.

[43] *Biblical Interpretation*, pp. 267-68.

"statutes" and "commands" involves.[44] Solomon's infidelity is construed as abrogating the temple's exclusive claim to royal allegiance: constructing the high places, worshiping at the high places, and worshiping other gods (1 Kgs 11:1-11,33). Jeroboam is charged with establishing a counter-cultus to the temple cultus in Jerusalem (1 Kgs 12:25-33), supporting northern high places (1 Kgs 13:33-34), and, more specifically, with making other gods and molten images (1 Kgs 14:9). Judah under Rehoboam is charged with construction of high places, asherim, standing stones, and toleration of male officiants (קדשים).[45] To be sure, the Deuteronomist does not always define what the "statutes and commands" are; but, as commentators have generally recognized, their primary reference is cultic.[46] By comparison, the deuteronomic law code contains a wide range of legislation affecting social, economic, cultic, and political circumstances.

Two issues, one specific and the other more general, arise from the deuteronomistic construal of law as cultic law. First, the Deuteronomist indicts Solomon and a succession of Judahite kings for constructing high places, tolerating high places, and worshiping at them, but high places (with a cultic designation) are never mentioned in Deuteronomy. As Hölscher and Mullen observe, Deuteronomy only mentions high places in the Song of Moses (32:13) and the Blessing of Moses (33:29).[47] But the "high places" in these older poems refer to places of battle, not to places of worship.[48] Given the consistent concern with high places in the Deuteronomistic History, especially in the history of the Judahite monarchy, the discrepancy between Deuteronomy and the Deuteronomistic

---

[44] The terms of Jeroboam's mandate are virtually identical to the terms used to describe Solomon's charge and infidelity. Like Solomon, Jeroboam is instructed "to heed all what I [YHWH] commanded you" (1 Kgs 11:10,38), to "walk in my ways" (1 Kgs 2:3; 11:13,38), "to do what is right in my sight" (1 Kgs 11:33,38), and "to observe all my statutes and commandments" (1 Kgs 2:3; 11:11,38). See further my *Two Nations Under God, 1*, pp. 199-206.

[45] 1 Kgs 14:22-24. The MT of 1 Kgs 14:22 has Judah as the subject, but 3 Rgns 12:24a has Rehoboam. The record of infidelities serves as a minor counterpoint to the infidelity of Jeroboam in the northern kingdom, H. D. Hoffmann, *Reform und Reformen: Untersuchungen zu einem Grundthema der deuteronomistischen Geschichtsschreibung* (ATANT 66; Zürich: Theologischer Verlag, 1980) 77.

[46] The point is conceded by Noth, *The Deuteronomistic History*, pp. 124-25.

[47] G. Hölscher, "Komposition und Ursprung des Deuteronomiums," *ZAW* 40 (1922) 182; E. T. Mullen, "The Sins of Jeroboam: A Redactional Assessment," *CBQ* 49 (1987) 218-19.

[48] S. R. Driver, *A Critical and Exegetical Commentary on Deuteronomy* (ICC; Edinburgh: T. & T. Clark, 1895) 358-59.

History is striking.[49] Even though the Deuteronomist applies the law of centralization to cover במות, the very fact that Deuteronomy does not mention them suggests some distance between this work and the Deuteronomistic History.

Second, in holding Solomon, Rehoboam, Jeroboam, and other kings responsible for centralization, the Deuteronomist imputes an enormous amount of power to the monarchy. The Deuteronomist expects kings to secure both *Kultuseinheit* and *Kultusreinheit.* The very measure of assessing royal conduct, whether a king provides exclusive support for the Jerusalem temple cultus and destroys all other cult places, Yahwistic or otherwise, is predicated upon pervasive royal supervision and control of religious affairs. Even those kings whom the Deuteronomist deems to have "done what is right in the sight of YHWH," but who have allowed the high places to survive have not done well enough.[50] By holding monarchs accountable to such stringent criteria, the Deuteronomist makes kings responsible for preserving the relationship between God and people. Such a strong monarchical stance contrasts with the two related features of Deuteronomy: the primacy placed on the relationship between God and people and the program for a (re)distribution of powers among a variety of office-holders (Deut 16:18-18:22).[51] Within Deuteronomy's carefully balanced polity, a kingship of very limited powers is permitted (Deut 17:14-20), but the institution of kingship is only a possible and not a necessary factor in Israel's constitution.[52]

In his narrow definition of law, as in his selective use of Deuteronomy 7 to indict Solomon, the Deuteronomist has proved himself to be the

---

[49] The discrepancy becomes even more startling the more deuteronomistic editions one posits within Deuteronomy. If one believes that the deuteronomistic law code was subject to a series of major and minor deuteronomistic reworkings, one has to reckon with the fact that none of these editors saw fit to confront what the deuteronomistic editor(s) of Kings viewed as one of Judah's most persistent problems.

[50] 1 Kgs 15:14; 22:44; 2 Kgs 12:4; 14:4; 15:4,35.

[51] A. D. H. Mayes, *Deuteronomy* (NCB; Grand Rapids: Eerdmans, 1979) 55-57; Braulik, *Deuteronomium*, pp. 16-17.

[52] The composition of Deut 16:18-18:22 is debated, R. Albertz, *A History of Religion in the Old Testament Period, I: From the Beginnings to the End of the Exile* (OTL; Louisville: Westminster/John Knox, 1994) 195-226. Mayes views most of this material as deuteronomic, *Deuteronomy*, pp. 261-84. In the opinion of Albertz and U. Rüterswörden (*Gemeinschaft*, pp. 89-93,106-11), Deut 16:18-18:22 contains both preexilic and exilic elements. Lohfink thinks that Deut 16:18-18:22 was a late exilic addition to the deuteronomic corpus, "Sicherung," pp. 143-55. Even if Lohfink were right, the tension between *Urdeuteronomium* and Kings would not disappear entirely, because of the emphasis on the primacy of the divine-human relationship elsewhere in Deuteronomy.

master of *Urdeuteronomium*, rather than its servant. The Deuteronomist innovates by appealing to the very authority he subverts.[53] By narrowing the range of the "statutes" and "commandments" to cultic issues, he ties national fortunes to cultic (dis)obedience. By holding monarchs responsible for centralization the Deuteronomist makes Deuteronomy speak with a new royal voice.

Having examined varying notions of law and the monarchical role in enforcing law, this essay now turns to the penalties for violating law. The author of Deut 7:4 threatens that "the anger of YHWH will flare up against you and he shall destroy you quickly," if Israelites intermarry and worship other gods. The close link between a crime and the punishment of the perpetrator of that crime is made even more explicit a few verses later in Deut 7, in a text that both cites and revises Exod 20:5 (= Deut 5:9).

> Know that YHWH your God is God, the trustworthy God who keeps his gracious covenant with those who love him and observe his commandments to the thousandth generation, but who repays those who hate him to his face, causing him to perish. He does not delay with those who hate him; he repays them to his face. (Deut 7:9-10)

This pronouncement on the nature of divine grace and retribution constitutes a "radical deviation" from the original formula justifying divine punishment to the third or fourth generation.[54] The writer cites the *traditum* through the technique of inverted quotation, but only to revise its original force.[55] Transgenerational divine loyalty still obtains for those who love YHWH, but YHWH penalizes evildoers immediately. As Levinson remarks, "The progeny, here strikingly unmentioned, are not explicitly visited with divine punishment."[56] Instead, the lemma proclaims swift justice for the sinner. In the realm of human justice, the stress on single generation justice is also found in Deuteronomy.[57]

---

[53] In so doing, the Deuteronomist is not breaking new ground. The deuteronomic writers employ similar exegetical strategies in their reuse of older law, B. M. Levinson, "The Human Voice in Divine Revelation: The Problem of Authority in Biblical Law," *Innovation in Religious Traditions* (ed. M. A. Williams, C. Cox, and M. S. Jaffee; Religion and Society 31; Berlin: De Gruyter, 1992) 46-61.

[54] Weinfeld, *Deuteronomy*, p. 371, calls attention to Exod 34:6-7, Num 14:18, and the reformation of divinely administered punishments in Deut 6:14-15.

[55] Levinson, "Human Voice," pp. 54-56.

[56] *Ibid.*, p. 54.

[57] Deut 24:16, quoted in 2 Kgs 14:6. A similar pronouncement against transgenerational consequences of Israelite sins occurs in Jer 31:28, while the concept of single generation repentance and retribution is systematically worked out in Ezek 18.

The divinely inflicted punishments upon Solomon are, however, primarily transgenerational, focussed upon his son Rehoboam and with lasting consequences for generations thereafter. The judgment oracle of 1 Kgs 11:11-13 announces that YHWH will take the kingdom, minus one tribe, and give it to one of Solomon's servants. This message is soon conveyed by the prophet Ahijah to the servant himself, Jeroboam, whose future kingship is authorized and defined (1 Kgs 11:31-38). The parameters of division are established before Rehoboam even ascends to the throne. To be sure, Solomon does not emerge unscathed. The revolts of foreign monarchs formerly under the hegemony of David and Solomon end the *Pax Solomona* (1 Kgs 11:14-25). But the primary assessment is tempered and delayed by recourse to ancestral and civic merit: "for the sake of David my servant and for the sake of Jerusalem, which I have chosen" (1 Kgs 11:13). In deuteronomistic perspective it is ironically a mark of divine leniency to impose the punishment due to the father upon the son. The delay works to the advantage of Solomon, who dies while his kingdom is still intact (1 Kgs 11:41-43), but to the disadvantage of Rehoboam, who takes office only to see his realm quickly torn asunder (1 Kgs 12:1-20). When Rehoboam stubbornly refuses to heed the advice of his elders, the Deuteronomist comments:

> But the king would not listen, because it was a turn of events from YHWH in order to establish the word that he had spoken through Ahijah, the Shilonite to Jeroboam, the son of Nebat.[58]

The deuteronomistic emphasis upon the transgenerational consequences of sin is not unique. It also applies to Jeroboam, who transgresses the imperative for centralization by establishing his own state cultus at Bethel and Dan (1 Kgs 12:25-33).[59] In the judgment oracles of Ahijah (1 Kgs 14:7-11, 12-16), both of which are heavily edited by the Deuteronomist, the prophet proclaims the demise of Jeroboam's house (vv 7-11),

[58] 1 Kgs 12:15. I am reading with LXX and the Syriac. The MT explicates by adding יהוה before ביד אחיה השילני. The first part of this verse differs somewhat from its approximate parallel in 3 Rgns 12:24r. 3 Rgns 12:24a-z also lacks any notice of a fulfillment of Abijah's prophecy.

[59] The judgment oracles against later northern dynasties are also relevant (1 Kgs 16:1-4; 21:21-24; 2 Kgs 9:6-10). Like 1 Kgs 14:7-11, these oracles legitimate the transfer of the realm from one northern king or house to another and comment upon the fate of the deposed. See W. Dietrich, *Prophetie und Geschichte* (FRLANT 108; Göttingen: Vandenhoeck & Ruprecht, 1972) 9-13; H. Weippert, "Die 'deuteronomistischen' Beurteilungen der Könige von Israel und Juda und das Problem der Redaktion der Königsbucher," *Bib* 53 (1972) 301-39; S. L. McKenzie, *The Trouble with Kings: The Composition of the Book of Kings in the Deuteronomistic History* (VTSup 42; Leiden: E. J. Brill, 1991) 61-80.

announces a death sentence on Jeroboam's son (vv 12-13), predicts an imminent *coup d'état* (v 14), and pronounces a judgment of exile against the entire northern kingdom (vv 15-16). The surprising death of Jeroboam's sick son prefigures the demise of Jeroboam's house and Israel itself (1 Kgs 14:12,18).[60] In spite of the severity of these disparate penalties, one cannot help but be struck by their communal nature, pertaining to Jeroboam's family, dynasty, and kingdom. Jeroboam does not himself die an unnatural death. In his concluding formulae to Jeroboam's reign, the Deuteronomist acknowledges that Jeroboam actually ruled Israel for twenty-two years (1 Kgs 14:19-20). His reign shows no ill efects of the cultus he established. Jeroboam's house is only overturned during the reign of his son, Nadab (1 Kgs 15:29). Even more so than with Solomon's sins, the consequences of Jeroboam's sins are transgenerational.

To appreciate the force of the deuteronomistic presentation, it will be useful to compare, however briefly, its treatment of Solomon, Rehoboam, and Jeroboam with the Chronicler's presentation. The Chronicler eliminates all explicit references to Solomon's sins from his history and presents the division as primarily a dispute between Rehoboam and Jeroboam.[61] In the Chronicler's judgment, Jeroboam and the "scoundrels" accompanying him took advantage of a naïve and inexperienced Rehoboam to wrest most of the kingdom away from him.[62] In spite of his blunder, Rehoboam recovered by heeding Shemaiah's warning (2 Chr 11:1-4 // 1 Kgs 12:21-24) and rebuilding what was left of his realm (2 Chr 11:5-11). By reversing his earlier course, Rehoboam was able to consolidate his rule over Judah and Benjamin (2 Chr 11:12,17). In Chronicles even Jeroboam meets his due. After the forces of Rehoboam's son Abijah humiliate Jeroboam's forces in holy war (2 Chr 13:2-3,13-19), Jeroboam never recovers.[63] "YHWH struck down Jeroboam and he died" (2 Chr 13:20).

When one recognizes the degree to which the Chronicler has reworked the Kings material in his own narrative, one comprehends a distinctive feature of his history: reciprocity in divine-human relations. A multi-

[60] G. N. Knoppers, *Two Nations Under God: The Deuteronomistic History of Solomon and the Dual Monarchies, vol. 2: The Reign of Jeroboam, the Fall of Israel, and the Reign of Josiah* (HSM 53; Atlanta: Scholars, 1994) 73-120.

[61] Knoppers, "Rehoboam in Chronicles: Villain or Victim?" *JBL* 109 (1990) 423-40.

[62] 2 Chr 13:5-7; cf. 2 Chr 10:1-19 // 1 Kgs 12:1-20.

[63] H. G. M. Williamson, *1 and 2 Chronicles* (NCB; Grand Rapids: Eerdmans, 1982) 250-55; S. Japhet, *I & II Chronicles* (OTL; Louisville: Westminster/John Knox, 1993) 685-700; G. N. Knoppers, "'Battling against Yahweh': Israel's War against Judah in 2 Chr 13:2-20," *RB* 100 (1993) 511-32.

generation punishment has given way to a sequence of punishments and rewards tailored toward the actions of pivotal individuals within the span of a single generation. In contrast with the Deuteronomist for whom the judgment of Solomon and Jeroboam is deferred, the Chronicler is at pains to demonstrate that perfidy soon results in the punishment of the guilty party, while allegiance results in peace, prosperity, and success.[64] The implications of the comparison should be clear. In narrating the consequences of human rebellion against the deity, the Chronicler's History is more deuteronomic than the Deuteronomistic History.

The comparison between Kings and Chronicles is subject to two possible objections. First, one could assert that the Deuteronomist lacked Deut 7:4 or Deut 7:9-10 in his *Vorlage*. This is entirely possible. Scholars differ greatly in their stratification and dating of Deut 7.[65] Nevertheless, some caution is in order. The author of 1 Kgs 11 clearly had some portions of Deut 7 before him. Given this evidence, the burden of proof is on those who would argue that the Deuteronomist lacked access to other sections of the chapter. One has also to recognize the extent to which the Deuteronomist can be selective in his use of *Urdeuteronomium* and of his ability to adapt it to his own ends. As we have seen, the Deuteronomist exercises considerable freedom in his use of Deuteronomy.

A second objection involves the nature of the history the Deuteronomist recounts. Is it not possible that the Deuteronomist is simply reporting what he believed to be actual reality?[66] Perhaps the Deuteronomist held to the strictures of Deuteronomy about individual retribution, but was too good a historian to deny that Solomon and Jeroboam themselves suffered no ill effects from the policies they implemented. Yet such a stance overlooks the Deuteronomist's own historiographical

---

[64] J. Wellhausen, *Prolegomena to the History of Ancient Israel* (Edinburgh: Adams and Charles Black, 1885) 203-11; S. Japhet, *The Ideology of the Book of Chronicles and Its Place in Biblical Thought* (BEATAJ 9; Frankfurt am Main: Lang, 1989) 150-98; R. B. Dillard, "Reward and Punishment in Chronicles: The Theology of Immediate Retribution," *WTJ* 46 (1984) 164-72.

[65] Recently, Mayes, *Deuteronomy*, pp. 181-86; F. García López, "Un peuple consacré: Analyse critique de Deutéronome vii," *VT* 32 (1982) 438-63; Weinfeld, *Deuteronomy*, pp. 377-84; R. H. O'Connell, "Deuteronomy vii 1-26: Assymetrical Concentricity and the Rhetoric of Conquest," *VT* 42 (1992) 248-65; E. Nielsen, *Deuteronomium* (HAT 1/6; Tübingen: Mohr, 1995) 94-99.

[66] Noth, for example, declares that the Deuteronomist's recourse to Davidic merit to explain the delay of punishment corresponded with what happened historically, namely that the division was largely Solomon's fault but occurred in the early reign of Rehoboam; *Deuteronomistic History*, pp. 97-98.

assumptions and the manner in which he has structured his history with long-term historiographical objectives in view. Given Rehoboam's less than dazzling performance at the assembly at Shechem, it by no means follows that the Deuteronomist should have thought that Solomon was primarily responsible for disunion.[67] Similarly, given the Deuteronomist's antipathy toward Jeroboam's cultic initiatives in the early northern kingdom, it would hardly be irrational for the author to assign some blame for the division itself on Jeroboam and the northern representatives.[68] One can even argue that the Deuteronomist strains to hold Solomon responsible for Israel's defection. The reason the Deuteronomist gives for the delay of punishment on Solomon is artificial. The Davidic promises temper the exercise of divine wrath against the sons of David, should they sin (2 Sam 7:14-15). His throne shall endure despite such setbacks (2 Sam 7:16). But Nathan's dynastic oracle nowhere mentions the prospect of a postponement of divine retribution against errant Davidic descendants.

The transgenerational punishments against Solomon and Jeroboam are not ill-considered. They are integral to the deuteronomistic record of the monarchy. The writer establishes an elaborate coherence between the sins of Solomon in the 10th century and the reform of Josiah in the 7th century (2 Kgs 23:13-14).[69] By blaming Solomon and associating Solomon's construction of high places with Israel's secession, the Deuteronomist subordinates the division to Solomon's perfidy. Solomon's sins are more foundational than disunion itself. In this manner, the Deuteronomist is able to portray Josiah's reforms as striking at the heart of what ails Judah. The Deuteronomist's coverage of Jeroboam also manifests long-range concerns. By tying the death of Abijah, the fall of Jeroboam's house, and the demise of Israel to the perpetuation of Jeroboam's cultus, the Deuteronomist contrasts David's positive precedent in Judah with Jeroboam's negative precedent in Israel.[70] Whereas the Davidic promises being continuity of leadership and divine restraint

[67] Along with almost all commentators, I am assuming that the Deuteronomist had access to a source for his narration of the events described in 1 Kgs 12:1-20.

[68] Indeed, the "supplement" to the LXX (3 Rgns 12:24b-f) accords to Jeroboam some building and martial activities not attested in the MT. See J. C. Trebolle Barrera, *Salomón y Jeroboán: Historia de la recensión y redacción de 1 Reyes 2-12, 14* (Insitución San Jeronimo 10; Valencia: Investigación Biblica, 1980); Knoppers, *Two Nations Under God, 1*, pp. 174-79.

[69] Knoppers, *Two Nations Under God, 2*, pp. 175-96.

[70] *Ibid.*, pp. 73-120.

in dealing with Judah's sins, the divine judgments against Jeroboam bring discontinuity of leadership and the actualization of divine wrath against Israel. Motifs of transgenerational merit and demerit are not ancillary to the Deuteronomist's presentation, but essential to his history of the united and divided monarchies.

Conclusions

The Deuteronomist is indebted to *Urdeuteronomium* in language, style, exegetical technique, historiography, and theology. The Deuteronomist enlists *Urdeuteronomium* to criticize the actions of major figures, such as Solomon, Rehoboam, and Jeroboam. Indeed, in condemning Solomon's mixed marriages, the Deuteronomist's exegetical blend of Deut 7:4 and Josh 23:11-13 revises the force of Deuteronomy's provisions to widen their application. The appeal to *Urdeuteronomium* has its advantages. Alluding to the precedent of YHWH's "statutes," "decrees," and "commandments" lends a certain authority to the Deuteronomist's own judgments. Yet the Deuteronomist's use of Deuteronomy is sophisticated hermeneutically. His use of stock deuteronomic phraseology obscures the extent to which he departs from his deuteronomic predecessors. In this regard, the many references within the Deuteronomistic History to YHWH's "statutes," "decrees," and "commandments" have misled scholars into thinking that a tighter relationship exists between *Urdeuteronomium* and the Deuteronomistic History than is either necessary or warranted by the evidence. The Deuteronomist is an independent author, who often goes his own way. Even in those cases in which one can demonstrate the Deuteronomist's textual dependence upon Deuteronomy, the Deuteronomist shows remarkable hermeneutical freedom. The Deuteronomist is perfectly capable of subverting the very code he incorporates and cites within his history.

A related and even more basic issue is whether the Deuteronomist held to a static view of revelation. Did *Urdeuteronomium* function by itself "as a norm for the relationship between God and people," or did the Deuteronomist hold to a more dynamic view of revelation? The citation of Josh 23:12 in 1 Kgs 11:1-2 as an authoritative divine pronouncement raises the question of what a *traditum* is for the Deuteronomist. The Deuteronomist's citation, reuse, and qualification of the Davidic promises raises a similar question. Nathan's dynastic oracle is depicted as a divine revelation to David (2 Sam 7:5-16) and David's prayer assumes as much (2 Sam 7:18-29). The Deuteronomist subsequently refers to and redefines these promises in his narration of Judahite history.[71] Given that the author employs the Davidic promises as a normative means by which to explain the course of Judahite history, it is understandable that scholars have debated the relationship between the Davidic covenant and the Sinaitic covenant.[72] But the Deuteronomist's reworking of the Davidic promises and his assigning to them "a crucial role" in discussing Judahite history also raises the question of what legal exegesis is for the Deuteronomist.

This study also has implications for scholarly investigations of the deuteronomistic editing of Deuteronomy. The last few decades have witnessed numerous attempts to locate evidence of deuteronomistic editing within the deuteronomic law code itself (Deut 12-26) and not simply in the speeches that frame the code, as Noth originally alleged.[73] Such efforts may be completely justified, yet one may ask what "Deuteronomists" are represented in such reworkings? For Noth the deuteronomistic editing of Deuteronomy, excepting miscellaneous additions, could only point to the author of the Deuteronomistic History. If, for example, much of the law of the king (Deut 17:14-20) or the constitution for office holders of which the law of the king is a part (Deut 16:18-18:22), stemmed from deuteronomistic hands, how likely is it that the Deuteronomists who edited Kings wrote such texts? It may be more helpful to ask whether some deuteronomistic editing of Deuteronomy is distinct from the editing of the Deuteronomistic History. The Book of Jeremiah may provide a useful analogy. Most scholars recognized that the deuteronomistic editing of Jeremiah manifests its own particular ideological concerns, even though it shares some linguistic and stylistic traits with Deuteronomy and the Deuteronomistic History.[74] If the deuteronomistic redaction(s) of Jeremiah stem from different editors than those of the Deuteronomistic History, could this not also be true, at least in part, of the deuteronomistic editing of Deuteronomy?

---

[71] Knoppers, *Two Nations Under God, 1,* pp. 151-59.

[72] J. D. Levenson, "The Davidic Covenant and Its Modern Interpreters," *CBQ* 41 (1979) 205-19.

[73] Preuss, "Geschichtswerk," pp. 230-45; Römer, "Deuteronomy," pp. 192-94.

[74] W. Thiel, *Die deuteronomistische Redaktion von Jeremia 1-25* (WMANT 41; Neukirchen-Vluyn: Neukirchener, 1973); *idem, Die deuteronomistische Redaktion von Jeremiah 26-45* (WMANT 52; Neukirchen-Vluyn: Neukirchener, 1981); R. Albertz, *A History of Religion in the Old Testament Period, Volume II: From the Exile to the Maccabees* (OTL; Louisville: Westminster/John Knox, 1994) 384-87.

THE IDEALIZATION OF SOLOMON AS THE GLORIFICATION OF GOD IN THE CHRONICLER'S ROYAL SPEECHES AND ROYAL PRAYERS

MARK A. THRONTVEIT

Scholars have long recognized that the books of Kings and Chronicles differ in their depictions of the reign of Solomon.[1] Typical analyses of the deuterononomistic presentation emphasize the division of Solomon's reign into two distinct periods.[2] The first period (1 Kgs 1-10) is usually seen as a positive portrayal of Solomon that emphasizes his obedience and the blessing that such obedience rewards. The second period (1 Kgs 11) relates Solomon's tragic apostasy, seeing it as the reason for the divine judgment that came in the form of the schism that divided Israel into Northern and Southern Kingdoms. As such, the deuteronomistic portrayal of Solomon functions as yet another factor in the complex exilic explanation of the destruction of Jerusalem. While the positive aspects of the early part of Solomon's reign would encourage those exilic readers with the reminder that the Davidic dynasty had begun in fulfillment of God's promise to David through Nathan, the final chapter in Solomon's story serves to introduce the theme that will occupy the author for the rest of Kings, namely, the failure of the kings to live in accordance

[1] See, for example, the classic expressions of P. R. Ackroyd, "History and Theology in the Writings of the Chronicler," *CTM* 38 (1967) 501-15; R. L. Braun, "The Message of Chronicles: Rally 'Round the Temple," *CTM* 42 (1971) 502-14; *idem*, "Solomonic Apologetic in Chronicles," *JBL* 92 (1973) 503-16; *idem*, "Solomon, the Chosen Temple Builder: The Significance of 1 Chronicles 22, 28, and 29 for the Theology of Chronicles," *JBL* 95 (1976) 581-90; A. M. Brunet, "La theologie du Chroniste: Theocratie et messianisme," *Sacra Pagina* 1 (1959) 384-97. R. B. Dillard, *2 Chronicles* (WBC 15; Waco, Tex.: Word Books, 1987) 1-7; D. N. Freedman, "The Chronicler's Purpose," *CBQ* 23 (1961) 436-42; S. Japhet, *The Ideology of the Book of Chronicles and Its Place in Biblical Thought* (BEATAJ 9; Frankfort: Peter Lang, 1989) 478-89; H. G. M. Williamson, "The Accession of Solomon in the Books of Chronicles," *VT* 26 (1976) 351-61; *idem*, "Eschatology in Chronicles," *TynBul* 28 (1971) 115-54; *idem*, *1 and 2 Chronicles* (NCB; Grand Rapids: Eerdmans, 1982) 192-237.

[2] R. B. Dillard's summary is especially clear and concise, "The Chronicler's Solomon," *WTJ* 43 (1980) 290-91. A more detailed presentation of the Chronicler's use of Kings in the Solomonic material can be found in S. L. McKenzie, *The Chronicler's Use of the Deuteronomistic History* (HSM 33; Atlanta: Scholars, 1985) 83-99.

with the covenant, a failure that ultimately results in the catastrophes of 721 and 587, the destruction of Israel and Judah.

Typical analyses of the Chronicler's presentation of Solomon's reign draw attention to the omissions that are immediately evident to anyone familiar with the account in Kings. These tend to cluster at the beginning and the end of the story, most notably the intrigue and violence associated with Solomon's accession (1 Kgs 1-2), his judicial ruling in the case of the harlots (1 Kgs 3:16-28), and the events that characterize his final years as king: marriages to foreign women, cultic apostasy, and conflicts with neighboring kings (1 Kgs 11). This is not to deny that the Chronicler has meticulously "retouched" the portrait he received from his deuteronomistic sources at other junctures in the narrative. The omissions of Solomon's conscription of Israelite labor for the building of the temple (1 Kgs 5:13-18), and the notice that the construction of his own house took nearly twice as long as the building of the temple (1 Kgs 6:38; 7:1), as well as the reversal of the report concerning Solomon's gift of twenty cities to Hiram (1 Kgs 9:10-14) so that Hiram gives twenty cities to Solomon (2 Chr 8:1-2) are clear testimony to tendentious, editorial activity in the central sections of the story. As such, the case is often made that the chronistic presentation "omits or recasts any item that might be taken to suggest less than ideal circumstances."[3] Japhet's conclusion in this matter, that the Chronicler has simply replaced 1 Kgs 1-2 with his own account of Solomon's accession (1 Chr 29) and omitted 1 Kgs 11, so that "what remains of Solomon's history is well suited to the Chronicler's own views," while somewhat overstated in light of these other omissions and reworkings of the text, is therefore essentially accurate.[4]

These observations have led to something of a consensus regarding the Chronicler's depiction of Solomon. McConville's is perhaps the most eloquent statement of this consensus position, "The Chronicler's aim in his portrayal of Solomon is to show how God governed the events of history to impart to the kingdom of Israel, at least once, a splendour that was fit to symbolize his own."[5] Williamson is more concerned to relate the promises made to David, "... the Chronicler wished to present

---

[3] J. M. Miller and J. H. Hayes, *A History of Ancient Israel and Judah* (Philadelphia: Westminster, 1986) 197.

[4] S. Japhet, *I & II Chronicles* (OTL; Louisville: Westminster/John Knox, 1993) 632-33.

[5] J. G. McConville, *I & II Chronicles* (DSB; Philadelphia: Westminster, 1984) 110.

Solomon as one man who fulfilled the conditions of obedience to the will of God that were necessary for the permanent establishment of the dynasty."[6]

Recent investigations of the Chronicler's presentation have come to similar, positive opinions. Duke's investigation of the rhetorical motivation behind the Chronicler's presentation concludes, "As with the portrayal of David, that of Solomon is positive and idealistic."[7] While Riley's examination of Solomon from a cultic point of view suggests that the non-monarchical situation of post-exilic Israel demanded a re-evaluation of former kings that emphasized the theological significance of the monarchy at the expense of the political, he still claims that, "In many ways the Chronistic Solomon, cleansed of the sins and failures of the Deuteronomistic History (1 Kgs 11:1-8), provides a picture of the true Davidide."[8]

Recently, this broad consensus that the Chronicler has idealized the figure of Solomon, and therefore his vision of Solomon's reign, has been challenged as "a subjective interpretation" that "does not stand up to close scrutiny," by Kelly, who cites the retention of *Vorlage* material critical of Solomon (2 Chr 10:4, 10-11, 14) as indicative of a more balanced approach by the Chronicler.[9] Less convincing, for its lack of evidence, is his plea for reading the references to "the records of Nathan the prophet" and "the prophecy of Ahijah the Shilonite" (2 Chr 9:29) as denoting accounts in 1 Kgs 1 of the accession and consequences of Solomon's apostasy (1 Kgs 11:29-39).[10]

My purpose in this essay is to look at this idealization of Solomon through the lens of the literary discourses in Chronicles with a view to

---

[6] Williamson, *1 and 2 Chronicles*, p. 236.

[7] R. K. Duke, *The Persuasive Appeal of the Chronicler: A Rhetorical Analysis* (JSOTSup 88; Sheffield: JSOT, 1990) 66.

[8] W. Riley, *King and Cultus in Chronicles: Worship and the Reinterpretation of History* (JSOTSup 160; Sheffield: JSOT, 1993) 96. Mosis's suggestion that Solomon's reign is presented as a "type" of end-time expectation in Chronicles has not won general acceptance; R. Mosis, *Untersuchungen zur Theologie des chronistischen Geschichtswerkes* (FTS 92; Freiburg: Herder, 1973) 164-69, 211-14. For a recent critique of Mosis see B. E. Kelly, *Retribution and Eschatology in Chronicles* (JSOTSup 211; Sheffield: JSOT, 1996) 151-53.

[9] See B. E. Kelly, "Messianic Elements in the Chronicler's Work," *The Lord's Anointed: Interpretation of Old Testament Messianic Texts* (eds. P. E. Satterthwaite, R. S. Hess and G. J. Wenham; Grand Rapids: Baker, 1996) 257-58.

[10] To be fair, Kelly is following Williamson here (*1 and 2 Chronicles*, pp. 236-37) and registers Japhet's challenge of this interpretation (*I & II Chronicles*, p. 646); Kelley, "Messianic Elements," p. 258.

shedding light on the Chronicler's vision of Solomon and his age. Three moments in the narrative, all directly related to the Chronicler's crucial reinterpretation of the promises contained in Nathan's oracle (2 Sam 7 // 1 Chr 17), are especially fruitful in this regard: the dynastic oracle itself; David's recalling of the promises made in the oracle at various junctures in his final addresses; and Solomon's allusions to the oracle at the time of the dedication of the newly built temple.

The importance of the speeches and prayers for discerning the theological intention of the Chronicler needs no justification. Towards the end of the 19th century, Driver concluded his analysis of the speeches by stating, "It would have been interesting to point out how the speeches peculiar to the Chronicler reflect, in almost every case, the interests and point of view of the Chronicler himself; but space has obliged me to confine myself to the linguistic argument."[11] Noth's investigation clearly established the view that the Chronicler was responsible for the speeches themselves and Plöger demonstrated their chronistic placement at strategic points in the narrative.[12] These pioneering works in the area of the Chronicler's speeches have been enhanced by the more recent work of Braun, Newsome, Saebø, Mathias, Throntveit, Duke, Mason, and Schniedewind, all in basic agreement as to the use, function, and historicity of these addresses.[13]

1. The Dynastic Oracle: 1 Chronicles 17 // 2 Samuel 7

Schniedewind provides us with a convenient starting point for the discussion of this royal speech placed upon the lips of David by the authors of both Samuel and Chronicles:

---

[11] S. R. Driver, "The Speeches in Chronicles," *The Expositor* 1, 5th series (1895) 255.

[12] M. Noth, *Überlieferungsgeschichtliche Studien* (Wiesbaden-Biebrich: Becker, 1943); O. Plöger, "Reden und Gebete im deuteronomistischen und chronistischen Geschichtswerk," *Aus der Spätzeit des Alten Testaments* (Göttingen: Vandenhoeck & Ruprecht, 1971) 50-66.

[13] R. Braun, "The Significance of I Chronicles 22, 28, and 29 for the Structure and Theology of the Work of the Chronicler" (dissertation, Concordia Seminary, 1971); J. D. Newsome, "The Chronicler's View of Prophecy" (dissertation, Vanderbilt, 1973); M. Saebø, "Taler og bønner hos Kronisten og I Esra/Nehemja-boken: Noen bemerkninger til et aktuelt tema," *Norsk Teologisk Tidsskrift* 83 (1982) 119-32; D. Mathias, "'Levitische Predigt' und Deuteronismus," *ZAW* 96 (1984) 23-49; M. A. Throntveit, *When Kings Speak: Royal Speech and Royal Prayer in Chronicles* (SBLDS 93; Atlanta: Scholars, 1987); R. K. Duke, *Persuasive Appeal*; W. M. Schniedewind, *The Word of God in Transition: From Prophet to Exegete in the Second Temple Period* (JSOTSup 197; Sheffield: JSOT, 1995); R. Mason, *Preaching the Tradition: Homily and Hermeneutics after the Exile* (Cambridge: Cambridge University, 1990).

> The Chronicler rewrites and recontextualizes the dynastic oracle so that it justifies the building of the temple and introduces his comprehensive description of the temple and its institutions ... The Chronicler then reappropriates the dynastic oracle within the process of temple building by recalling the dynastic oracle in speeches and narratives.[14]

While the Chronicler has been remarkably conservative in his appropriation of the speech one omission and three alterations provide us with some insight into his vision of Solomon.[15]

2 Samuel 7:1 ≠ 1 Chronicles 17:1

First, the statement that "YHWH had given him [David] rest from all his enemies," (2 Sam 7:1) is omitted in 1 Chr 17:1 and a similar notice from 2 Sam 7:11 in 1 Chr 17:10 is reworded. It is certainly possible that this omission is due to the Chronicler's desire to avoid a chronological conflict with the later references to David's wars in verse 10 and chapters 18-20. Braun, however, building upon the earlier studies of von Rad and Carlson, has pointed to the significance of this concept of "rest" in Deuteronomy and the deuteronomistic history.[16] He concludes that while the usages of the term cluster around three important events, the conquest of the land by Joshua, the dynastic promise to David, and the building of the temple by Solomon, "the singular importance of *menuha* for our study is most apparent from Deut 12, where the unification of the cult is specifically related to Israel's rest in the promised land."[17] For the Chronicler, this concept of a God-given rest in the promised land was the necessary prerequisite for the building of the temple, since it marked the fulfillment of the promises to Israel. As such, it is regularly applied to

[14] Schniedewind, *Word of God*, pp. 143-44. His judicious discussion of the relative merit of the LXX, especially over against the somewhat optimisitc use of the Greek tradition by McKenzie, is as refreshing as it is provocative.

[15] Comparisons of these parallel passages are legion with debate raging over priority, *Vorlage*, and the lack or presence of *Tendenz*. See H. van den Busche, "Le texte de la prophetie de Nathan sur la dynastie davidique (II Samuel VII-I Chronicles XVII)," *ETL* 24 (1948) 354-94; McKenzie, *Chronicler's Use*, pp. 63-64; and Williamson, *1 and 2 Chronicles*, pp. 132-33. This study agrees with Lemke that the chronistic divergences from Samuel derive from the Chronicler's agenda rather than disturbances in the underlying texts; W. E. Lemke, "Synoptic Studies in the Chronicler's History" (dissertation, Harvard Divinity School, 1963) 40-46.

[16] Braun, "Chosen Temple Builder," pp. 582-86. G. von Rad, "There Remains a Rest for the People of God: An Investigation of a Biblical Conception," *The Problem of the Hexateuch and Other Essays* (ed. E. W. T. Dicken: Edinburgh: Oliver & Boyd, 1966) 94-102; R. A. Carlson, *David, the Chosen King* (Stockholm: Almqvist & Wiksell, 1964) 97-106.

[17] Braun, "Chosen Temple Builder," p. 583.

Solomon, the chosen temple builder (especially in the royal speeches at 1 Chr 22:8-9, 18; 28:2; 2 Chr 14:6), and deleted from descriptions of David in the *Vorlage*.[18] In addition it provides a crucial interpretive key for the other modifications made in this passage.

2 Samuel 7:5 ≠ 1 Chronicles 17:4

A second alteration of the dynastic oracle in Kings occurs in verse 4. The Chronicler recasts YHWH's rhetorical question, "*Shall you* build me *a* house for me to live in?" (2 Sam 7:5) into the indicative, "*You shall not* build me *the* house to live in," (1 Chr 17:4). While scribal error in either direction between האתה (Samuel) and לא אתה (Chronicles) is possible, the alteration sets the agenda for the rest of the oracle and, at the very least, suggests that a strong contrast is being drawn between David and Solomon with regard to the actual construction of the temple. In this regard the Chronicler's addition of the definite article to the word "house" would seem to argue for a more precise determination of the temple in Jerusalem.[19]

Furthermore, no censure of David is intended. As Japhet has demonstrated, only at a later stage in the tradition does the rejection of David's "offer" to build a house for God in verse 1 become a matter of precedence, while for the Chronicler, "the emphasis is different. From the outset the determining factor is that of timing: not you but your successor will build a house. The days of peace and 'rest' have not yet come; when they do my house shall be built."[20] As we have seen, the Chronicler's theology of rest and the alterations he makes in his sources that stem from this perspective, indicate that the Chronicler believes those days of peace and rest came in the time of Solomon.

2 Samuel 7:11 ≠ 1 Chronicles 17:10

Yet another alteration is evident in 1 Chr 17:10. The Chronicler's source read, "*YHWH* declares to you that YHWH shall *make* a house for you" (2 Sam 7:11). Chronicles reads, "*I* declare to you YHWH shall *build* a house for you" (1 Chr 17:10b). The change to first person is probably insignificant, in that it merely smoothes out the connection between the first person verbs in verses 7-10 and 11-14.[21] More, however, can be said

[18] For a fuller summary of the theme of rest in Chronicles along similar lines see Kelly, *Retribution*, pp. 196-99.

[19] Williamson, *1 and 2 Chronicles*, p. 134.

[20] Japhet, *I & II Chronicles*, pp. 329-30.

[21] Mosis, *Untersuchungen*, p. 82.

about the change from "make" (עשׂה) to "build" (בנה). The Samuel text is clearly about the establishment of a family since this verb only appears with "house" with the idiomatic sense, as, for example, when God promises to "give" (עשׂה) the midwives Shiphrah and Puah "families" (בתים) as a reward for their faithful service (Ex 1:21). By altering his source to "build a house" the Chronicler allows the meaning of the "building of a house" to include both the establishment of a dynasty and the construction of the temple. In addition, the alteration solidifies the literary echoes between "You shall not build me a house" (v 4) and "He shall build me a house" (v 12), both places where the Chronicler has been especially active in his appropriation of the *Vorlage*.

2 Samuel 7:16 ≠ 1 Chronicles 17:4

The passages disagree in a number of instances. Samuel reads, "But *your* house and *your* kingdom shall be made sure forever before [me]; *your* throne shall be made firm forever" (2 Sam 7:16). The contrast in the verse is to Saul and his kingdom, mentioned in the previous verse. The second person pronominal suffixes refer unambiguously to David. The Chronicler radically alters the first two to first person ("my" i.e. "God's") and the third to the third person ("his") so that the promise applies to Solomon, "I shall establish him in *my* house and in *my* kingdom forever and *his* throne shall be made firm forever" (1 Chr 17:14). The changes are indicative of the Chronicler's differing perspective on the institution of kingship and the role of David and Solomon. In stark contrast to the deuteronomistic view, where David is the paradigmatic ruler to whom subsequent rulers in Judah are compared, the Chronicler sees the united monarchy of David and Solomon as the climactic event in the history of Israel.[22]

Interestingly enough, these alterations combine to reveal the concentric structuring of the Chronicler's texts.[23] Based upon the repetition of the trope "to build a house," the chronistic structuring is tighter and more unified than that of the *Vorlage*:

A Narrative frame introducing Nathan's oracle (3-4a)
  B "*You* shall not build me the house to dwell in" (4b-6)
    X Promise of dynasty: "*The Lord* will build you a house" (7-10)

[22] Japhet, *I & II Chronicles*, p. 335.

[23] S. De Vries, *1 and 2 Chronicles* (FOTL; Grand Rapids: Eerdmans, 1989) 153, has noted the probable inclusio provided by ישׁב in verses 1 and 16.

B' "*He* shall build a house for me" (11-14)
A' Narrative frame concluding Nathan's oracle (15)

The narrative frame (A, A') simply serves as an introduction and conclusion for the oracle itself. The inner frame (B, B'), however, contrasts the denial of David's construction of the temple (v 4b) with the indication, at this stage of the narrative somewhat cryptic, that Solomon will indeed be the chosen temple builder (v 12a). Thus, these segments of the passage, when taken together, focus upon the physical building of the temple itself, without obstructing the promise of a secure dynasty in B'. The central segment, indicated by the rhetorical ועתה ("And now") as well as a second introduction by means of a messenger formula, provides the transition between the dual emphasis on temple and dynasty that has been at the heart of the Chronicler's paranomasia in this section. A historical retrospect of divine favor towards David in the past (vv. 7-8a) is matched by the promise of God's future care and provision for people (vv. 8b-10a) that climaxes in the dynastic promise to David that "YHWH will build you a house" (v 10b).

2. David's Speeches of Encouragement: 1 Chronicles 22, 28 and 29

The Chronicler has provided much of his unique theological interpretation in the form of fourteen royal speeches that do not have a parallel in the synoptic material contained in Samuel-Kings.[24] Saebø has suggested that a primary function of the speeches is to invest the speakers with authority and since only the Chronicler's favorites (David, Abijah, Asa, Jehoshaphat, Hezekiah and Josiah) deliver royal addresses and then only in that part of their reign that is presented in a favorable light (if the particular reign receives a mixed judgment); one would have to agree.[25] Almost half of these royal speeches have been placed on the lips of David (1 Chr 13:2-3; 15:2,12-13; 22:6-16; 22:17-19; 28:2-10; 28:20-21; [29:1-5]) and the last five have a direct bearing on the concerns of this investigation.

[24] See Throntveit, *When Kings Speak*, pp. 11-50. Mason, *Preaching the Tradition*, pp. 133-35, finds fifteen such addresses. Mosis, *Untersuchungen*, pp. 105-107, however, considers all of 1 Chr 29:1-19 to be redactional. I would agree that at least David's royal speech (1 Chr 29:1-5) and thus the people's response (vv 6-9) are later expansions, see Throntveit, *When Kings Speak*, pp. 92-93; however, these verses do play a significant structural role in the final form of the text as seen below.

[25] Saebø, "Taler og bønner," p. 125.

The initial form-critical classifications of Braun and Throntveit (edict, rationale, and oration) now appear to be much too rigid.[26] Nine of the addresses can be grouped under the more general classification: Encouragement for a Task, which would include "a call to a specific enterprise, a reason for undertaking it and/or grounds of encouragement which make the task a hopeful one."[27] David's last speeches in 1 Chronicles dominate here and set the pattern for future instances among his heirs. The task that is encouraged is the preparation of Solomon for the building of the temple. Braun has led the way in the contemporary understanding that argues ultimately for our seeing the reigns of David and Solomon as essentially one moment focused upon the temple, with David preparing for its construction and Solomon completing the task.[28] This means that these three chapters at the close of 1 Chronicles are in effect a transitional unit bridging the artificial gap between David and Solomon occasioned by the later division of the books of Chronicles.[29]

1 Chronicles 22:6-10

> 6 Then he called for his son Solomon and charged him to build a house for the Lord, the God of Israel. 7 David said to Solomon, "My son, I had planned to build a house to the name of the Lord my God. 8 But the word of the Lord came to me, saying, 'You have shed much blood and have waged great wars; you shall not build a house to my name, because you have shed so much blood in my sight on the earth. 9 See, a son shall be born to you; he shall be a man of peace. I will give him peace from all his enemies on every side; for his name shall be Solomon, and I will give peace and quiet to Israel in his days. 10 He shall build a house for my name. He shall be a son to me, and I will be a father to him, and I will establish his royal throne forever.' " (NRSV).

---

[26] Braun, *Significance*, pp. 225-49; Throntveit, *When Kings Speak*, pp. 20-50. The same may be said for the complex suggestions of De Vries, *1 and 2 Chronicles*.

[27] Mason, *Preaching the Tradition*, p. 18. Mason was anticipated in this regard by O. Plöger, "Reden und Gebete," p. 57, who speaks of David's speeches as "*Ermunterungsreden*."

[28] Braun, "Solomonic Apologetic;" *idem*, "Solomon, the Chosen Temple Builder;" *idem*, *1 Chronicles* (WBC 14; Waco, Tex: Word Books, 1986) xxxiii-xxxv, 219-27, 265-93.

[29] Braun, *1 Chronicles*, xxxv. The thorny problem of chapters 23-27 which many, including Braun, view as secondary, cannot engage us at this time, For conflicting, yet well argued views, see H. G. M. Williamson, "The Origins of the Twenty-Four Priestly Courses: A Study of 1 Chronicles xxiii-xxvii," *Studies in the Historical Books of the Old Testament* (ed. J. A. Emerton; VTSup 30; Leiden: E. J. Brill, 1979) 251-68; and J. W. Wright, "The Legacy of David in Chronicles: The Narrative Function of 1 Chronicles 23-27," *JBL* 110 (1991) 229-42.

David's speech is laced with echoes of the dynastic oracle. Schniedewind conveniently lists three direct borrowings and four expansions to the previous material:[30]

1. David's desire to build a temple (v 7) recalls 1 Chr 17:1-2
2. YHWH's prohibition (v 8) paraphrases 1 Chr 17:4
3. The promise of a son (v 10) follows the wording of 1 Chr 17:12-13
4. YHWH had justified his refusal to David by explaining he had no need of a temple (1 Chr 17:5-6). Verse 8 adds his military activity as further justification for the refusal
5. The designation of Solomon (v 9) corrects the oracle's lack of specificity regarding which of David's sons would follow him 1 Chr 17:9
6. The pun between Solomon's name (שלמה) and "peace" (שלום) (v 9) 1 Chr 17:9
7. The promise of peace/rest in 1 Chr 17:9 has been moved from David's reign (2 Sam 7:1, 11, where it was omitted by the Chronicler in the parallel 1 Chr 17) to that of Solomon (v 9)

Essentially, the passage seeks to provide an explanation for the historical fact that David did not construct the temple. This is accomplished by means of a judicious application of the Chronicler's theology of rest, as adapted from the principles set forth in Deut 12:10-11 (see above). By applying the concept of "rest" (not "peace" as in the NRSV) to Solomon in verse 9, the Chronicler has effectively drawn a contrast between David, whose time was spent in military pursuits that consolidated the kingdom, and Solomon, his "peaceful" son. Rather than disparaging David, however, this approach seeks to emphasize that God, as the primary actor in the narrative, has now determined the time is ripe for the construction of the temple, as indicated by his gift of "rest," the precursor of the project. Neither does the text seek to glorify Solomon. If David cannot build, Solomon cannot plan due to his "youth and inexperience" (v 8).[31]

As in the last section, this passage can be seen to have a concentric structure that emphasizes these very points (David's preparations, Solomon's youth, and the glorification of the temple):

---

[30] Schniedewind, *Word of God*, p. 156.

[31] McConville, *I & II Chronicles*, p. 78.

[32] ויאמר followed by an infinitive signifies a command, especially in the Chronicler's syntax; BDB, 56.

A David commands (אמר)[32] the resident aliens (2a)
B Stonecutters (2b)
C David's preparations (3-4)
D Solomon's youth as reason for David's preparations (5a)
X Glory of the temple (5b)
D' Solomon's charge (6-13)
C' David's preparations (14)
B' Stonecutters and other workers (15-16)
A' David commands (צוה) all the leaders of Israel (17-19)

1 Chronicles 28:2-5

2 Then David rose to his feet and said: "Hear me, my brothers and my people. I had planned to build a house of rest for the ark of the covenant of the Lord, for the footstool of our God; and I made preparations for building. 3 But God said to me, 'You shall not build a house for my name, for you are a warrior and have shed blood.' 4 Yet the Lord God of Israel chose me from all my ancestral house to be king over Israel forever; for he chose Judah as leader, and in the house of Judah my father's house, and among my father's sons he took delight in making me king over all Israel. 5 And of all my sons, for the Lord has given me many, he has chosen my son Solomon to sit upon the throne of the kingdom of the Lord over Israel" (NRSV).

Once again, Schniedewind has conveniently collected the Chronicler's echoes of 1 Chr 17 in this particular royal address and convincingly argues that the Chronicler has developed the themes of the dynastic oracle to a greater degree than its presentation in 1 Chr 22:6-10.[33] This development is accomplished by the repetition and expansion of three of the prior speeches' main points:

1. David's inability to build the temple (vv 2-3, see 22:7-8)
2. Solomon as David's chosen successor (vv 4-5, see 22:9)
3. Solomon as the divinely appointed temple builder (v 6, see 22:10)

The first expansion comes in David's reference to the temple as a "house of rest" (בית מנוחה, v 2). This is a new development in the Chronicler's theology of rest in these passages where, as we have seen, an initial omission of the concept in the Chronicler's version of the dynastic oracle (cf. 1 Chr 17:1 with 2 Sam 7:1-2) in order to remove the period of rest

[33] Schniedewind, *Word of God*, pp. 156-60.

from the time of David, was followed by the designation of Solomon as the "man of rest" (איש מנוחה, 1 Chr 22:9) thereby attributing the time of rest to Solomon's rule. Now it becomes clear that the Chronicler's theology of rest is to reach its culmination in the building of the temple, the house of "rest." Further expansions on this theme include David's designation as a "man of war" (איש מלחמות)[34] who shed blood, thereby heightening the contrast between David and Solomon. This concept of rest was so important for the Chronicler's vision that David's military activity disqualified him from the temple's construction, despite the vital role that this military activity played in creating the necessary conditions for the project.[35]

The second expansion has to do with the divine election of Solomon. Although Braun rightly regards verses 4-6a, 8, and 12b-18 as part of a later expansion,[36] the expansion is not contrary to the Chronicler's intent at this juncture, namely to emphasize the choice of Solomon to "sit on the throne of the kingdom of the LORD" (v 5), to be God's son (v 6), and to build the temple (v 10). This is the only instance of the divine choice of a post-Davidic king in the Old Testament.[37]

In a similar fashion, the Chronicler develops the concept of "the kingdom of God." In the dynastic oracle God refers to the kingdom as "my kingdom" (1 Chr 17:14) with the implication that the kingdom is God's and the throne is Solomon's. The throne and the kingdom, however, are combined in David's first address with the announcement of God's decision "to establish the throne of his [i.e. Solomon's] kingdom over Israel forever" (1 Chr 22:10). Finally, in his present address, David again refers to the dynastic oracle, this time asserting that Solomon was chosen "to sit upon the throne of the kingdom of the Lord over Israel" (1 Chr 28:5). As Schniedewind perceptively concludes, "Again, the throne and the kingdom are placed together; however, now it is the 'throne of YHWH's kingdom.' The idea that the earthly kingdom of the Davidic ruler

---

[34] NRSV's translation ("warrior") at this point gives up too much of the symbolism inherent in the more literal translation. The argument that it eliminates an unnecessary occurrence of "man" overlooks the fact that Solomon's designation ("man of peace," 1 Chr 22:9, though we should read "man of rest") was not treated in this fashion.

[35] M. Selman, *1 Chronicles: An Introduction & Commentary* (TOTC 10a; Downers Grove, Ill.: Inter-Varsity, 1994) 250.

[36] The later expansion interrupts the divine address in vv 3 and 6, is concerned with Solomon as king and not as temple builder, and contains the unprecedented notion of Judah's election; Braun, *Significance*, p. 41.

[37] Braun, "Chosen Temple Builder," p. 589.

belongs to God is implicit in the Chronicler's version of the dynastic oracle."[38]

With the ponderous passage contained in 1 Chr 28:11-19 concerning the pattern of the temple,[39] the Chronicler emphasizes the transitional nature of the relationship between David and his son. David, in receiving the pattern from God and passing it on to Solomon has done all that he can to assure a smooth transference of power. Here, as well, it should be noticed that God, the designer of the pattern and the pattern of the temple itself are at least as prominent as David and his son.

Once again, the obvious concentric structuring of chapters 28-29 highlights the importance of the speeches for this transitional unit in the Chronicler's presentation:

A Princes; gifts (28:1)
  B People addressed (28:2-8)
    C Solomon charged (28:9-10)
      X Pattern of temple delivered (28:11-19)
    C' Solomon charged (28:20-21)
  B' People addressed (29:1-5)
A' Princes; gifts (29:6-8)

3. Solomon's Prayer: 2 Chronicles 6:40-42 = Psalm 132:8-10, 1 ≠ 1 Kings 8:52-53

These thematic expansions introduced by the Chronicler reach their conclusion in the Solomonic material dealing with the construction and dedication of the temple. Solomon's prayer at the dedication of the temple (2 Chr 6:12-42) is the third of three Solomonic addresses (vv 12; 3-11) that have been taken over from 1 Kgs 8:12-50. The two versions of the prayers are very similar and remarkably free of alterations, apart from the minor orthographic and linguistic modifications that regularly appear in Chronicles, until the appeals with which each version of the prayer ends. In Kings the appeal reads:

> 52 "Let your eyes be open to the plea of your servant, and to the plea of your people Israel, listening to them whenever they call to you. 53 For you have

[38] Schniedewind, *Word of God*, pp. 157-58. Selman, *1 Chronicles*, p. 251, makes similar points in his treatment of the same material.

[39] Reading του ιερου "the temple" with the Greek tradition instead of the MT אולם "porch."

> separated them from among all the peoples of the earth, to be your heritage, just as you promised through Moses, your servant, when you brought our ancestors out of Egypt, O Lord God." (1 Kgs 8:52-53, NRSV)

Here Solomon uses God's earlier deliverance of the people at the Exodus as the warrant for his request that God be attentive to his prayers and the prayers of Israel. This is in full accord with the themes of the dedication prayer in general and, as such, adds nothing new. The version in Chronicles, however, has been dramatically expanded:

> 40 "Now, O my God, let your eyes be open and your ears attentive to prayer from this place. 41 Now rise up, O Lord God, and go to your resting place, you and the ark of your might. Let your priests, O Lord God, be clothed with salvation, and let your faithful rejoice in your goodness. 42 O Lord God, do not reject your anointed one. Remember your steadfast love for your servant David." (2 Chronicles 6:40-42, NRSV)

Here, in addition to the request that God be attentive "to prayer *from this place*" (v 40) a subtle change favoring the temple and all that it stands for over against the people, the warrant for such a request (vv 41-42) is entirely different. Based upon Ps 132:8-10, 1, this change shifts the focus away from Solomon, who has been literally the center of attention in terms of the concentric structuring of the first nine chapters of 2 Chronicles, and back to David. Both his faithfulness with regard to the ark (2 Sam 6) and God's promise of an eternal dynasty (2 Sam 7; 1 Chr 17) are recalled in the fulfillment of those promises in the building of the temple. That this shift back to David is not intended to nullify Solomon is shown by the modification of "your anointed one" (Ps 132:10 [and 2 Chr 6:42 NRSV]) to "your anointed ones" (2 Chr 6:42). Although "your anointed ones" could refer to the priests mentioned immediately before, as Dillard has aptly remarked, "... it would appear better to refer to David and Solomon: the singular of Ps 132:10 which clearly referred to a king has been made plural in Chronicles to embrace both kings."[40] This in turn augments the well known chronistic understanding of the reigns of David and Solomon as a united monarchy centered in the construction of the temple.

The omission of "today" (היום) in verse 19, where the *Vorlage* reads, "Regard your servant's prayer and his plea, O Lord my God, heeding the cry and the prayer that your servant prays to you *today*" (1 Kgs 8:28), is best explained as an attempt to release the prayer from its chronological

[40] Dillard, *2 Chronicles*, p. 51.

moorings. In this way the prayer functions as a "timeless paradigm" applicable to any period in history, especially the post-exilic period in which the Chronicler is writing, and not simply that of Solomon. God's people in all times and in all places can be assured of having their prayers heard when they are offered at or toward this temple.[41]

4. Conclusions

It is difficult to say whether the evidence gleaned from an examination of the Chronicler's royal speeches argues for the idealization of Solomon or not. In every instance the emphasis fostered by the text can be attributed to the glorification of God, God's election, or God's kingdom with as great or greater a degree of probability than as an idealization of Solomon. In the conclusion of her discussion of Solomon, Sara Japhet speaks of two, apparently contradictory tendencies at work in the Chronicler's vision of Solomon. The emphasis placed upon his role as temple builder has resulted in the omission of many other matters, but much of his work as temple builder is attributed to David. This reworking of the text provides a measure of balance in the relative contributions of both kings so that their two reigns in essence become one period where the son's achievements draw upon and complement the work of his father. But this striving for parity can hardly be called idealization:

> Even when it comes to his greatest achievement, Solomon is merely following his father's instructions, using the manpower, tools, and materials provided by David. As individual characters, neither David nor Solomon is idealized in the book of Chronicles, but when the two figures are united by one central idea, their period becomes the golden era of Israelite history.[42]

The "one central idea" that unites David and Solomon is the construction of the temple. And it is precisely in the temple that these themes coalesce:

1. Williamson is surely correct in his assessment that, "The Chronicler also stresses over against Sam./Ki. that it is especially in the building of the temple that the promises to David mediated through Nathan will have their initial fulfillment. This is the main purport of the

[41] See Throntveit, *When Kings Speak*, pp. 58-61; Williamson, *Israel in the Books of Chronicles* (Cambridge: Cambridge University, 1977) 64-66.

[42] Japhet, *Ideology*, p. 489; for her discussion see pp. 478-89.

speeches of David in I Chr. 22:7-19, 28:2-10, 29:1-5 and his prayer in 29:10-19, all of which are peculiar to Chr."[43]

2. Recent scholarly treatments of the Solomon narrative agree that the material in 2 Chr 1-9 has been structured in a concentric, chiastic, or otherwise palistrophic literary architecture and, while there is some disagreement as to the precise arrangement of the individual elements, there is unanimity on the fact that the narrative centers on the construction and dedication of the temple.[44]
3. Significant chronistic alteration of the deuteronomistic Vorlage in the Solomon story is not only concerned with removing those remembrances deemed to blemish his character. Several accounts that would have enhanced a glorification of the king have been removed because they do not serve the Chronicler's ultimate purpose in this material which is to glorify the temple. Even as staunch a supporter of the idealization of Solomon as Dillard can conclude, "... narratives not showing any involvement with the cult are omitted. Even the enduement with wisdom is not wisdom in the abstract (1 Kgs 3:16-4:34) but is specifically wisdom to build the temple."[45]

Thus, it seems the Chronicler's view of Solomon and his age, at least as far as that is recoverable from an examination of his royal speeches and prayers, is hazy at best. The accounts available to the Chronicler in Kings have been utilized to produce a picture of Solomon that portrays him as the builder of God's temple, at a time determined by God, in a place determined by God, to fulfill God's promise, and according to a pattern delivered by God through David. This emphasis on God and God's temple forms the true thrust of the Chronicler's message to post-exilic Israel. As Selman reminds us, "This divine right of kings, as it is

---

[43] Williamson, *Israel*, p. 65.

[44] See Dillard, *2 Chronicles*, pp. 5-7; De Vries, *1 and 2 Chronicles*, p. 233; Duke, *Persuasive Appeal*, p. 65; Selman, *2 Chronicles*, pp. 285-86; Kelly, *Retribution*, pp. 87-88. Dillard's arrangement is by far the most intricate and widely quoted. Duke's modifications with regard to the crucial central material are convincing and have the advantage of maintaining the intricacy of Dillard's arrangement as over against the very basic structure envisioned by De Vries. Selman, who is critical of Dillard's failure to account adequately for 2 Chr 3-5, has proposed a radically simplified arrangement that is preferred and adopted by Kelly. On the matter of chiasmus in Chronicles see I. Kalimi, *Zur Geschichtsschreibung des Chronisten* (BZAW 236; Berlin: Walter de Gruyter) 191-234. For a similar concentric arrangement of the Solomon story in Kings see J. T. Walsh, *1 Kings* (Berit Olam; Collegeville, Minn.: Liturgical, 1996) 151.

[45] Dillard, *2 Chronicles*, p. 2.

developed here, is far from giving unqualified approval to the king's every move. Rather it confirms that despite Solomon's weaknesses, God was still working out his own purposes through him."[46]

---

[46] Selman, *1 Chronicles*, p. 251.

A WEALTH OF WOMEN: LOOKING BEHIND, WITHIN, AND BEYOND SOLOMON'S STORY

LINDA S. SCHEARING

No other biblical story can match Solomon's for its sheer wealth of women. 700 royal wives, 300 concubines, 3 royal mothers, 2 daughters, 2 prostitutes, 2 foreign queens, 2 widowed mothers, and an enemy's high-born wife; all these populate Solomon's story in 1 Kgs 1-11.

In the last decades of the 20th century new interest in, and approaches to, these women's stories blossomed. The feminist revival of this period, with its emphasis on recovering women's presence in history, drew attention to women's biblical presence as well as their roles in ancient Israelite society. Moreover, modern women, enrolling in biblical studies doctoral programs in record numbers, began publishing their own research, often focusing on biblical stories about women. Indeed, by the 1990s, Elizabeth Cady Stanton's dream of a cadre of female biblical commentators edged closer and closer to reality. Aside from this influx of female scholars, however, Hebrew Scripture studies changed in other ways as well. Challenges to traditional constructions of Israelite history and religion, for example, attacked the very way scholars perceived ancient Israel. At the same time scholars were reimaging Israel, they were rethinking textual methods. The methodological shift from the "world behind the text" (historical reconstruction; preliterary and source analysis) to the "world within the text" (literary analysis)[1] produced new approaches to biblical stories. By the end of the 2nd millennium all these factors united to provide new interest in, and new readings of, the wealth of women associated with Solomon.

As we stand on the brink of the 3rd millennium, a third world is opening for many biblical scholars, the "world *beyond* the text" (the history of biblical texts' interpretation). Implicit in this growing interest is the

[1] P. House traces this shift in his article, "The Rise and Current Status of Literary Criticism of the Old Testament," *Beyond Form Criticism: Essays in Old Testament Literary Criticism* (ed. P. House; Winona Lake, Ind.: Eisenbrauns, 1992) 3-22.

recognition and affirmation of an old truth: the lives of scriptural stories are ongoing, fashioned and understood in dialogue with their historical readers. Moreover, thanks to 20th century ecumenism, we are increasingly aware of this reading audience's diversity. Just as 19th century scholars mined the text's preliterary life, perhaps 21st century ones will excavate the multicultural strata of its postcanonical life.

This study is divided into four sections. First, we will identify the women connected with Solomon in 1 Kgs 1-11. Second, we will briefly discuss how recent changes in our understanding of Israelite history and religion call for a reevaluation of these women's significance. Third, we will examine how literary approaches emphasize previously ignored dimensions of their stories. Lastly, we will examine scriptural and post-scriptural treatments from Jewish, Christian, and Muslim traditions and explore how readers culled, clarified, and expanded stories of Solomon and women.

1. The Women of Solomon's Story

A. *Bathsheba*

Although Bathsheba (daughter of Eliam, wife of Uriah the Hittite and of David) is introduced in 2 Sam 11, our interest in her begins with Solomon's birth. Solomon's birth announcement (2 Sam 12:24-25) follows the death report of Bathsheba's first child (12:15b-23) and distinguishes him from the child conceived through David's rape (?) of Bathsheba (11:2-5). While Bathsheba encounters David sexually in 12:24 and 11:4-5, there is an important difference in the events' presentation. David goes to his own wife in 12:24, while in 11:4 he has Uriah's brought to him. Thus, Solomon is imaged as the legitimate offspring of Bathsheba and David, a son "beloved of the Lord" (12:25). In both incidents, Bathsheba is silent, a passive figure standing in stark contrast to her activity in Solomon's later accession.

B. *Haggith versus Bathsheba*

Solomon's accession takes place in 1 Kgs 1-2. While it involves a power struggle between Adonijah and Solomon (and their respective court factions), it also alludes to a struggle between their mothers, Haggith and Bathsheba. After David failed to get "warm" with Abishag (1 Kgs 1:1-

4), his son Adonijah declared himself king (1:5) and sacrificed at the stone Zoheleth with his supporters (1:9-10). The narrator introduces this incident with the note that "Adonijah *son of Haggith* exalted himself" (1:5). Immediately following Adonijah's declaration, Nathan conferred with Bathsheba. According to the narrator: "Nathan said to *Bathsheba, Solomon's mother*, 'Have you not heard that *Adonijah son of Haggith* has become king ...?'" (1:11). Thus, at the level of literary epithets, the explicit rivalry between half-brothers in David's court is now implicit between the wives of David's harem. This "battle of epithets" between Haggith and Bathsheba occurs twice, both times outside David's narrative presence. While the first is preparatory to Nathan and Bathsheba's audience with (manipulation of?) David (1:15-31), the second immediately follows David's death notice (2:10-12). In 1 Kgs 2:13 we are told that "*Adonijah son of Haggith* came to *Bathsheba, Solomon's mother*." Since this note introduces Adonijah's request for Abishag as wife (2:14-18), it is interesting that both epithet "battles" occur within a context of threat to Solomon's kingship. That is, it is only when Adonijah declares himself king or when he asks for Abishag as wife that the narrator raises the competition between brothers to the level of their mothers as well.

C. *Solomon's Wives and Concubines*

1) Abishag. 1 Kings 1 introduces Abishag, a very beautiful Shunammite woman who is brought in to comfort (test?) a very old and impotent David (1:1-4). David's impotence prompts the succession battle between Adonijah and Solomon in 1 Kgs 1:5-53, a battle that ultimately results in Solomon's kingship. The last reference to Abishag occurs in Adonijah's request in 1 Kgs 2:13-18. Adonijah solicits Bathsheba's help in approaching Solomon for Abishag. But when Bathsheba relays Adonijah's request, Solomon interprets it as a bid for the throne and executes him (2:19-24). Abishag's actual status is unclear in the text. Is she part of David's or Solomon's harem? Or is she simply a marriageable woman in Solomon's court? One thing can be said for certain; although she never speaks in 1 Kgs 1-2, she is the agent through whom Adonijah's hopes for the throne are born and, ironically, the one through whom his death is sealed.

2) Daughter of Pharaoh. References to Solomon's wife, the daughter

of Pharaoh, occur five times in 1 Kings (3:1; 7:8; 9:16,[2] 24;[3] and 11:1). In all five she is nameless, identified only by her father's rank. We first learn of her marriage to Solomon in 1 Kgs 3:1 where we are told she resides in the "city of David" awaiting the construction of her own domicile. Although her house is finally completed in 1 Kgs 7:8 (after the building of Solomon's palace, Yahweh's Temple, and Jerusalem's wall), she does not move into it until 1 Kgs 9:24. Although it is similar in some ways to Solomon's house, her dwelling stands outside the city of David. The last mention of Pharaoh's daughter is in 11:1 where she is first on the list of Solomon's foreign wives blamed for his downfall. Her presence at the conclusion of Solomon's story echoes that at its beginning (3:1) with one important difference. Of all five references, only 11:1 explicitly presents her in a pejorative light.

3) His Foreign Wives. Solomon's love of "foreign women" (1 Kgs 11:1) marks the beginning of his downfall. Aside from the Egyptian daughter of Pharaoh, he loved "Moabite, Ammonite, Edomite, Sidonian, and Hittite" women as well. While his harem is legendary (700 princesses and 300 concubines; 11:3), it is condemned, not for its excessive size,[4] but for its multicultural content (11:2). Of this multitude of foreign wives, only one name survives: Naamah, the Ammonite (see following section).

Solomon is severely criticized for following his foreign wives' gods (11:4-12). His apostasy includes worship of "Astarte, goddess of the Sidonians" (11:5), "Milcom, the abomination of the Ammonites" (11:5), "Molech, the abomination of the Ammonites" (11:7), and "Chemosh, the abomination of Moab" (11:7). Of the four deities named, only the males (Milcom, Molech and Chemosh) are given pejorative epithets ("abomination of ...") while the female (Astarte) is referred to more neutrally ("goddess of ...").[5] The summary statement in v. 8 implies his wives' (and perhaps Solomon's?) worship of other deities as well. Reference to Solomon's harem occurs only once in 1 Kgs 1-11 outside of chapter 11. As part of the Queen of Sheba's overall praise of Solomon's court, she

---

[2] 1 Kgs 9:16 mentions that her father captured, burned, and decimated the city of Gezer before giving it to Solomon as part of her dowry. The LXX groups 3:1b and 9:16 together and places them in 4:31-32 creating a summary of queen-related references. See D. W. Gooding, "The Septuagint's Version of Solomon's Misconduct," *VT* 15 (1965) 327.

[3] LXX 9:9b.

[4] Later commentators would conclude it was in open defiance of the Deut 17:17 injunction against large royal harems.

[5] G^{BL} reads "Astarte the abomination of the Sidonians."

proclaims his wives fortunate,[6] but she does not explain why.

4) Naamah. Naamah is the only named wife of Solomon. Her name occurs in the introductory and concluding regnal formulas of her son, Rehoboam (1 Kgs 14:21-24 and 29-31 respectively). While the name of the king's mother is a standard feature of Judean introductory regnal formulas, it is not part of the standard concluding formula. Thus, "His mother's name was Naamah the Ammonite" in vv. 21 and 31 functions as an unusual inclusio to this last segment of Rehoboam's account (14:21-31). The identification of Naamah as an Ammonite echoes the reference to Solomon's love of foreign women (Ammonites being second on the list found in 1 Kgs 11:1).

D. *Solomon's Daughters*

Of all the offspring we might expect from Solomon's many unions, we are told of, and given the names of, only three: a son (Rehoboam) and two daughters (Taphath and Basemath).[7] While the story of Solomon's son spans several chapters (1 Kgs 11:43-14:31) and includes his mother's identity (Naamah), mention of Solomon's daughters occurs only in the list of his administrative officers (4:1-19)[8] and omits their mothers' names.

1) Taphath. The only reference to Solomon's daughter Taphath occurs in a remark about her husband, Ben-abinadab (1 Kgs 4:11). Ben-abinadab is fourth on the list of twelve officials who "provided food for the king and his household" (4:7). His administrative area, Naphath-dor, supported the palace for one month each year. As an aside, we learn that Ben-abinadab "had Taphath, Solomon's daughter, as his wife" (4:11).

2) Basemath. Reference to the second of Solomon's daughters, Basemath, occurs in the administration list as an aside to her husband, Ahi-

[6] 1 Kgs 10:8 reads: "Happy are your wives!" The Greek and Syriac traditions, however, contain the variant: "Happy are your men!"

[7] An interesting literary approach to Solomon's children is taken by D. Jobling. He suggests the text leaves open the possibility that all three children were conceived before Solomon's accession. According to Jobling, the literary absence of other children heightens Solomon's "golden age," an age when there was no war and, for Jobling's Solomon at least, no sex as well. According to Jobling, this age came to an end in 1 Kgs 11 when Solomon becomes sexually active (v. 1) and goes to war (vv. 14ff); D. Jobling, "Forced Labor: Solomon's Golden Age and the Question of Literary Representation," *Semeia* 54 (1991) 57-76, especially 63.

[8] Their presence in the list is usually seen as significant for its dating. Rather than concluding it comes from early in Solomon's reign (due to its textual location), it is often assigned to a later date to allow Taphath and Basemath time to reach marriageable ages; see P. Ash, "Solomon's? District? List," *JSOT* 67 (1995) 67-86.

maaz. Ahimaaz, eighth on the list of officials, oversaw Naphtali and took "Basemath, Solomon's daughter, as his wife" (1 Kgs 4:15). No subsequent mention is made of Basemath, Taphath, or their husbands in the rest of Solomon's story.

E. *Other Women and Solomon*

In addition to the women intimately related to Solomon (his mother, wives, concubines, and daughters) there are two other categories of women in his story: 1) those associated with Solomon's wisdom (the two prostitutes and the Queen of Sheba), and 2) those named in connection with Solomon's friends and enemies (Hiram's mother, Hadad's wife, Queen Tahpenes, and Zeruah). Whereas those in the first category come into direct contact with Solomon, the women of the second form the backdrop to his story.

1) Two Prostitutes. The account of Solomon and the two prostitutes (3:16-28) occurs immediately following the Gibeon incident (3:3-15) where Solomon acquired wisdom (3:12) in a dream sent by Yahweh. According to v. 16, sometime "later" two prostitutes came to Solomon with a dilemma. Both lived in the same house, by themselves, and had recently given birth to a son. Following one of the boys' deaths, both women claimed the living child as theirs (3:17-22). After listening to both sides, Solomon called for a sword to divide the living son in half (3:23-25). When one woman protested, Solomon declared her to be the mother and awarded her custody of the child (3:26-27). According to v. 28 "all Israel" stood in awe of Solomon "because they perceived that the wisdom of God was in him, to execute justice."

2) Queen of Sheba. The account of Solomon and the Queen of Sheba occurs in 1 Kgs 10:1-13 following reports of Solomon's building and commercial activities (9:15-28) and is set within the context of Solomon's great wealth and achievements (10:11-12, 14-29). In response to accounts of Solomon's fame, the Queen (accompanied by a large and costly retinue, 10:2) came to Jerusalem to "test him with hard questions" (10:1). Not only did Solomon answer her questions satisfactorily (10:3), but he so impressed her with the quality of his household that there "was no more spirit in her" (10:4-5). After praising Solomon at great length (10:6-9) the queen gives Solomon numerous and costly gifts (10:10). In turn, Solomon gives the Queen of Sheba "every desire that she expressed" (the content of this gift is not specified) and she "returned to her own land, with her servants" (10:13).

3) Hiram's Widowed Mother. According to 1 Kgs 7:13-14, Solomon assigned a bronzeworker named Hiram to work on the Temple's pillars (7:15-22). In an unusual genealogical note, we are told that Hiram is a widow's son whose father was an artisan from the tribe of Naphtali (7:14). Such a note informed (and assured) readers that Hiram, the temple worker, was part Israelite.

4) Hadad's Wife and Pharaoh's Queen. In 1 Kgs 11:14-22 we are told that the Edomite prince Hadad survived a purge of Edomite males during David's reign. Fleeing to Egypt, he married Pharaoh's sister-in-law (Queen Tahpenes'[9] sister) and fathered a son, Genubath (11:17-19). Queen Tahpenes weaned Genubath and raised him in the royal household (11:20). Although both Pharaoh's Queen and Hadad's son are named, Hadad's wife and the Queen's husband remain nameless. Ironically, by providing information about Genubath's birth and youth, the text gives Solomon's enemy's son something it denies Solomon's own son.

5) Zeruah, Jeroboam's Widowed Mother. Solomon employed Jeroboam, son of Nebat (an Ephraimite of Zeredah), as head of the forced labor responsible for Solomon's building projects. The account of Jeroboam's rebellion against Solomon (11:26-40) is the third of three reports of adversaries raised by God in 1 Kgs 11 to punish Solomon for his apostasy (Hadad, 11:14-22; Rezin, 11:23-25; and Jeroboam 11:26-40). The reference to Jeroboam's widowed mother occurs in the opening verse of Jeroboam's section (v. 26). While we are informed of Jeroboam's father's tribe and place of origin, no such information is given for his mother. In LXX 12:24e, Jeroboam (like Hadad in 1 Kgs 11:19) marries Pharaoh's wife's sister).

2. Looking Behind the Text

Once upon a time, reconstructing the reign of Solomon was relatively simple. One read 1 Kgs 1-2 (Solomon's accession) with 3-11 (Solomon's reign) and then drew from these texts a picture of life in 10th century Israel. At the end of the 2nd millennium, however, reconstructing Solomon's historical reign (and the women in it) is far removed from this naive vision. In the last thirty years, challenges both outside and within

[9] J. Gray suggests that "Tahpenes" is not a name but a corruption of "*t.hmt.nsw* 'the wife of the king')" *1 & 2 Kings* (OTL; 2nd ed.; Philadelphia: Westminster, 1970) 285.

biblical studies have questioned: 1) the possibility of gleaning history, in general, from artistically crafted texts, as well as 2) recovering women's history, in particular, from texts shaped and transmitted by patriarchal hands. Moreover, recent attacks on traditional reconstructions of 10th century Israel raise serious questions concerning the historical accuracy (and thus significance) of references to women in 1 Kgs 1-11. While we do not wish to repeat arguments previously made in this volume concerning the world behind 1 Kgs 1-11, there are several points at which such discussions intersect with our interests concerning women.

A. *Bathsheba and the Position of Queen Mother*

While the biblical text never refers to Bathsheba as *gebira*, Solomon's treatment of her in 1 Kgs 2:19 (rising, bowing, seating her on a throne beside his) is seen as proof, at the very least, of Bathsheba's exalted status in Solomon's 10th century court; or, at the very most, as evidence of an official position occupied by the king's mother.[10] The recent work of Zafrira Ben-Barak[11] and Susan Ackerman[12] illustrates the poles of the current debate.

Ben-Barak champions the idea that Solomon's deference was due to Bathsheba's personal power. She finds the biblical evidence for an institutional office of Queen Mother "sporadic and insubstantial."[13] Rather than extrapolate from the few biblical examples for which we have any detail (Bathsheba, Maacah, Hamutal, and Nehusta) to a general state office, Ben-Barak suggests that each woman's case be considered separately. After doing this she concludes that "each of these queens was the mother of a younger son who was without right to the succession" and that "each succeeded in recruiting a powerful following of ambitious adherents who helped make it possible to place a younger son at the head of the kingdom."[14] For Ben-Barak, these women were exceptions to the rule rather than examples of it. They were rare women who, by sheer

[10] Those who argue for an office of "Queen Mother" find additional evidence in: 1) the king's mother's inclusion in Judean introductory regnal formulas; 2) actions of kings' mothers (Maacah, Athaliah, etc.); and, 3) the presence and activities of kings' mothers in other ANE courts. Other areas of debate involve the origin of her position, her primary duties, and her religious function.

[11] Z. Ben-Barak, "The Status and Right of the *Gebira*," *JBL* 110 (1991) 23-34.

[12] S. Ackerman, "The Queen Mother and the Cult in Ancient Israel," *JBL* 112 (1993) 385-401.

[13] Ben-Barak, "Status and Right," p. 117.

[14] *Ibid.*, pp. 181-82.

"force of their personality and command of power and influence" were able to grasp and wield power *normally outside* the reach of kings' mothers.[15] Thus, while Bathsheba wielded political power, it was personally, rather than institutionally or religiously, derived.

Susan Ackerman disagrees with Ben-Barak. Ackerman argues that Bathsheba's duties were both political (king's advisor) and cultic (Asherah's representative in the Judean royal court). Unlike Ben-Barak, who minimizes the Queen Mother's religious function, Ackerman views it as the primary source of her power. Positing widespread Asherah worship in Israel and Judah, Ackerman suggests the Queen Mother was "the human representative, even surrogate, of Asherah." Such "divine legitimation," according to Ackerman, undergirded the Queen Mother's position as "second most powerful figure in the royal court, superseded only by her son, the king."[16]

Since the differences between Ben-Barak (a minimalist) and Ackerman (a maximalist) show no signs of quick resolution, the debate concerning Queen Mothers and their function will no doubt continue into the next millennium with no clear consensus in sight. Ackerman herself suggests that the changing climate in the study of Israelite religion makes this ongoing discussion especially timely.[17]

B. *Foreign Wives, Diplomatic Marriages and Solomon's Wealth*

Are Solomon's foreign wives proof of an extensive web of political alliances holding his vast empire together, alliances that, in part, were responsible for Solomon's wealth and the "pax Solomona" of 1 Kgs 3-10? Supporting such a reading is Solomon's marriage to Pharaoh's daughter, his alleged marriages to 700 foreign princesses, and the multicultural nature of his harem.[18] (The latter is considered historical by some in spite of 1 Kgs 11:3's obvious hyperbole and literary function.[19])

---

[15] *Ibid.*, p. 185.

[16] Ackerman, "Queen Mother," pp. 400-401.

[17] *Ibid.*, pp. 387-88.

[18] A good example of this argument is found in A. Malamat, "Aspects of the Foreign Policies of David and Solomon," *JNES* 22 (1963) 1-17.

[19] Gray, *1 & 2 Kings*, pp. 274-75, for example, asserts that although "historical fact has been magnified and stylized" in 1 Kgs 11:3, there is still a "historical basis" to Solomon's diverse harem; while J. B. Burns, "Solomon's Egyptian Horses and Exotic Wives," *Foundations & Facets Forum* 7 (1991) 33, admits that the "exaggerated numbers of wives and concubines would not have appeared in any formal chronicle" yet goes on to argue that "nonetheless, it is conceivable that Solomon wed foreign princesses to weave a strong web of alliances."

Understanding the significance of Solomon's marriages in this light, however, is predicated on the assumption that there *was* a vast Solomonic empire; an assumption currently under siege. On the one side of the debate are those who feel, despite the text's use of hyperbole, that Solomon's empire was extensive and economically prosperous.[20] On the other side are those who doubt seriously whether the text's presentation of Solomon can be wholly trusted.[21] If Solomon's splendor continues to crumble under scholarly onslaught, then the existence and diplomatic significance of Solomon's marriages may also disappear amid the shambles of his once great empire.

C. *Solomon and His Wives' Gods*

Does the condemnation of Solomon's marriages and his apostasy indicate that 10th century Israel was monotheistic? While critical scholars have long dismissed 1 Kgs 11:1's idea of historical causation (the kingdom fell because God punished Solomon), some nevertheless continue to accept Solomon's apostasy as if 10th century Israelite religion was monotheistic. Scholars in the 1990s no longer share their predecessors' optimism that 10th century Israel was either monotheistic[22] or that the "Yahweh alone" party dominated religious politics.[23] At the very least, this means that the text's pejorative presentation of Solomon's mar-

[20] See, for example, A. R. Millard, "Does the Bible Exaggerate King Solomon's Golden Wealth?" *BAR* 15 (1989) 15, 20-29, 31, 34, and his response to M. Miller in *PEQ* 123 (1991) 117-18; and C. Meyers, "The Israelite Empire: In Defense of King Solomon," *Michigan Quarterly Review* 22 (1983) 412-28.

[21] See, for example, M. Miller's response to Millard in "Solomon: International Potentate or Local King?" *PEQ* 123 (1991) 28-31. Others who challenge particular aspects of Solomon's reign are D. J. Schley, "1 Kings 10:26-29: A Reconstruction," *JBL* 106 (1987) 595-601; and J. K. Kuan, "Third Kingdoms 5.1 and Israelite-Tyrian Relations During the Reign of Solomon," *JSOT* 46 (1990) 31-46. B. Halpern calls for a more "reasoned deconstruction" of this period in "Erasing History: The Minimalist Assault on Ancient Israel," *BibRev* 11 (1995) 26-35, 47.

[22] For example, L. K. Handy, "The Appearance of Pantheon in Judah," *The Triumph of Elohim: From Yahwisms to Judaisms* (ed. D. V. Edelman; Grand Rapids: Eerdmans, 1996) 27, observes that it "is fairly well established by now that the narrative of the book of Kings cannot be taken as an accurate reflection of the religious world of the nations of Judah and Israel ... this picture should be seen as the product of an exilic or postexilic theology rather than a reflection of a real religious past."

[23] See, for example, M. J. Mulder, "Solomon's Temple and YHWH's Exclusivity," *New Avenues in the Study of the Old Testament: A Collection of Old Testament Studies Published on the Occassion of the Fiftieth Anniversary of the Oudtestamentisch Werkgezelschap and the Retirement of Prof. M. J. Mulder* (ed. A. A. Van der Woude; Leiden: E. J. Brill, 1989) 49-62.

riages, as well as his foreign wives' religious practices, needs reevaluation. If neither reflects 10th century realities, then 1 Kgs 11:1-13's historical significance has little to say about Solomon's wives and 10th century religious orthodoxy.

D. *Solomon, Women and the Deuteronomistic Historians*

If some stories of women in 1 Kgs 1-11 say little about Solomon's Israel, can they be used to understand Josiah's? The work of Gary Knoppers[24] and Marvin Sweeney[25] furnish us with good examples of how the historical significance of Solomon's foreign wives can be relocated from the 10th to the 7th century.

Gary Knoppers' two volume work, *Two Nations Under God: The Deuteronomistic History of Solomon and the Dual Monarchies* (1993), examines Solomon's role in the DH. According to Knoppers, "most, if not all" of 1 Kgs 11:1-10 is from the hand of Dtr. The prohibition of intermarriage, the championing of montheism, and the centralization of worship (all priorities for Dtr), are the foundation of Solomon's condemnation in 1 Kgs 11. Knoppers concludes from this that the "golden age of David and Solomon attributes seventh century problems to the era of the dual monarchies." For Knoppers, Josiah's 7th century reforms are imaged as "an attempt to reclaim the heritage of the united monarchy."[26]

Unlike Knoppers who argues that 1 Kgs 3-10 idealizes Solomon, Marvin Sweeney argues that Solomon is a literary foil to Josiah. According to Sweeney, "Solomon causes the fundamental problems within the kingdoms of Israel and Judah that Josiah attempts to set aright."[27] It is Josiah (not Solomon) that is Dtr's ideal king and, therefore, all references to Solomon's foreign wives and Pharaoh's daughter emphasize Solomon's failure in comparison with Josiah's success.

For both Knoppers and Sweeney, Solomon's foreign wives and their religious practices are literary constructs addressing social realities well beyond the 10th century. While they contribute little to reconstructions of Solomon's Israel, they say a lot about the priorities of Josiah's.

---

[24] G. Knoppers, *Two Nations Under God: The Deuteronomistic History of Solomon and the Dual Monarchies* (HSM 52; Atlanta: Scholars, 1993) vol. 1.

[25] M. Sweeney, "The Critique of Solomon in the Josianic Edition of the Deuteronomistic History," *JBL* 114 (1995) 609.

[26] Knoppers, *Two Nations Under God*, p. 134.

[27] Sweeney, "Critique," p. 609.

3. Looking Within the Text

By the late 1980s, scholars like David Gunn proclaimed the ascendancy of literary approaches to the Bible over historical ones:

> Plainly things have changed. The study of narrative in the Hebrew Bible has altered dramatically in the past ten years, as least as far as professional biblical studies is concerned. That is now a truism ...
> So striking is the change, it has led me on more than one occasion to suggest that 'literary criticism' was becoming, has become perhaps, the new orthodoxy in biblical studies ...[28]

While not all agreed with Gunn's assessment (even Gunn admitted that he enjoyed "overstating the position"[29]), it was clear that the winds of biblical studies were shifting. Scholars' preoccupation with historical reconstruction and with preliterary and source questions was being replaced with an interest in the text's final form. This methodological shift inevitably left its mark on readings of 1 Kgs 1-11's female characters. Studies analyzing characterization, for example, emphasized textual elements in these women's stories previously ignored in historical approaches.

A. *Women's Characterization: Typecasting*

Scholars such as Athalya Brenner grouped female biblical characters into types, identified each type's basic elements, and then decided whether specific texts reinforced, countered or added a significant variant to the core type.[30] Brenner's interest lay in two questions: 1) "Can we define, on the basis of biblical literature, women's position in the socio-political sphere beyond their traditional domestic function?" and 2) "Can we trace the development of stereotypes and paradigms which are used, again and again, for the description of women, to the extent that many individual portrayals contain strong elements of literary conventions or cliches?"[31] Although Brenner examined four female literary types (the hero's mother, the temptress, foreign women, and the ancestress), it is

---

[28] D. M. Gunn, "New Directions in the Study of Biblical Hebrew Narrative," *JSOT* 39 (1987) 65.

[29] *Ibid.*, p. 65.

[30] A. Brenner, *The Israelite Woman: Social Role and Literary Type in Biblical Narrative* (Biblical Seminar 2; Sheffield: JSOT, 1985).

[31] *Ibid.*, p. 9.

her treatment of "foreign women" that concerns our study of Solomon. Brenner observed that, as is the case with other literary types, foreign women in the Bible are imaged both positively (Tamar, Ruth, Rahab, and Jael) and negatively (Potipher's wife, Samson's women, the Foreign Woman in Proverbs). According to Brenner, the negative foreign woman is: 1) inherently religious; 2) remains loyal to her pre-marital gods and people (this distinguishes her from the positive type); and 3) often associated with "seduction, prostitution, and sexual disloyalty."[32] Not surprisingly, Brenner identified the foreign women in 1 Kgs 11:1-3 as the "negative foreign woman" type. While this type's socio-cultural significance, Brenner argued, dealt with fertitlity worship, she did not address how this observation pertained to 1 Kgs 11:1-3.[33]

Another example of type analysis during this period is Phyllis Bird's work on biblical prostitutes. Whereas Brenner examined several literary types and social roles, Bird focused on one: the Harlot as Heroine.[34] Bird submitted the stories of Judah and Tamar (Gen 38:1-26), Rahab (Josh 2:1-24), and the two prostitutes (1 Kgs 3:16-27) to two questions: 1) "What is the image of the harlot assumed in the text?" and 2) "How does that image of understanding affect the construction or narration of the story?"[35] After analyzing the Judah/Tamar and Rahab stories, Bird concluded with the account of Solomon and the two prostitutes in 1 Kgs 3:16-27. According to Bird, Solomon's judicial task is complicated precisely because the plaintiffs are both mothers *and* harlots. Since the ruling stereotype of a harlot is "a woman of smooth and self-serving speech" from whom one does not "expect truth," the audience also expects these harlots to be self-motivated liars. But, Bird argues, the audience also expects mothers to be women who are connected "by the deepest emotional bonds" to the fruit of their womb. Since the account concludes with a lying harlot and a selfless mother, the resolution of Solomon's judicial dilemma reinforces (rather than challenges) both of these stereotypes. Indeed, as Bird observes, "The case is built on the one [the harlot type] and resolved on the other [the mother type]." Yet even

---

[32] *Ibid.*, pp. 115-22.

[33] While Brenner argued that a woman's foreignness is often secondary to a more primary element of her characterization (i.e. the Temptress), she did not make the case for 1 Kgs 11:1-3, perhaps because there is no explicit sexual reference in these verses; Brenner, *Ibid.*, p. 122.

[34] P. Bird, "The Harlot as Heroine: Narrative Art and Social Presupposition in Three Old Testament Texts," *Semeia* 46 (1989) 119-39.

[35] *Ibid.*, p. 119.

the mother, when all is said and done, "remains a harlot" relegated to the "shadows of Israelite society."[36]

B. *Women's Characterization: Anonymity*

Of the numerous women in Solomon's story only eight have names: Abishag, Basemath, Bathsheba, Haggith, Naamah, Taphath, Tahpenes, and Zeruah. The remaining characters (700 royal wives, 300 concubines, 2 prostitutes, a bronzeworker's widowed mother, a foreign queen, a daughter of Pharaoh and Hadad's wife) are anonymous. In the last decade, however, these faceless female characters have gained scholars' attention in spite of their anonymity. In her work on women in 1-2 Kings, for example, Adele Reinhartz explores anonymity as a literary technique.[37] According to Reinhartz, anonymity detracts from female characterization in two ways: 1) it encourages readers to typify anonymous female characters (i.e. harlots, queens, or mothers) rather than viewing them as individuals,[38] and 2) it draws readers to the text's named (male) characters instead of its unnamed (female) ones.[39] Reinhartz identifies three categories of anonymous females in 1-2 Kings:

[36] *Ibid.*, pp. 132-33. Esther Fuchs also thought the harlots of 1 Kgs 3:16-28 represented negative types, but for different reasons. Fuchs saw the story as a parody of the "mother-figure as unmarried woman" type. Though the victim's characterization is less harsh than the perpetrator's, neither woman is heroic or even admirable because neither has a husband. According to Fuchs, the story's message is clear: when women give "birth outside of wedlock, there is bound to be trouble." E. Fuchs, "The Literary Characterization of Mothers and Sexual Politics in the Hebrew Bible," *Feminist Perspectives on Biblical Scholarship* (ed. A. Y. Collins; SBL Centennial Publications; Chico, Calif.: Scholars, 1985) 131.

W. A. M. Beuken's approach to the two harlots is more positive. Beuken argued that while the story begins by identifying both women as the same type (whore), it ends by presenting them as "diametrically different women." By choosing to protect the life of her child, one of the women "becomes a mother" and, in following "the dictates of her motherly feelings," this woman "becomes wise as a result of it." Thus the story concludes with two women who personify two different types (whore and mother) that, in turn, typify folly and wisdom. W. A. M. Beuken, "No Wise King Without a Wise Woman (1 Kings III 16-28)," *New Avenues in the Study of the Old Testament: A Collection of Old Testament Studies Published on the Occassion of the Fiftieth Anniversary of the Oudtestamentisch Werkgezelschap and the Retirement of Prof. M. J. Mulder* (ed. A. S. Van der Woude; Leiden: E. J. Brill, 1989) 1-10.

[37] A. Reinhartz, "Anonymous Women and the Collapse of the Monarchy: A Study in Narrative Technique," *Feminist Companion to Samuel and Kings* (ed. A. Brenner; FCB 5; Sheffield: Sheffield Academic, 1994) 43-67.

[38] *Ibid.*, p. 63.

[39] *Ibid.*, p. 64; Reinhartz calls these unnamed female characters the "narrative antonyms of the major players — named male kings and prophets."

kings and consorts, mothers and kings, and mothers and prophets. Of these, only the first two categories concern our study.

Reinhartz argues that the narrator of 1-2 Kings compares and contrasts characters in order to pass "negative judgment on those he considers responsible for the collapse of the monarchy."[40] Concerning kings and consorts, for example, Solomon's unnamed "narratively barren" wives and concubines stand in stark contrast to the named, fruitful wives of David. This contrast, according to Reinhartz, underscores the "downhill process" in Israel (from the righteousness of David to the folly of Solomon) that eventually results in Israel's destruction. Concerning mothers and kings, a similar contrast is found between the harlot mothers of 1 Kgs 3:16-28 and the cannibal mothers of 2 Kgs 6:26-30. While the first illustrates Solomon's wisdom, the second emphasizes Joram's helplessness and the "despair and destruction" that marked the later years of the monarchy (see Deut 28:25-57 and maternal cannibalism). Thus 2 Kgs 6:26-30, with its two sets of unnamed women, really compares Solomon with Joram and serves as a microcosm of the "divine judgment against the people of Israel."[41]

Discussions concerning characterization (of which the above is a mere sample) and other such literary emphases furnished fresh readings of 1 Kgs 1-11 at precisely the time its historical dimensions were being challenged. Along with these new interpretive options, however, came a growing interest in another area rich with fresh readings: the world beyond 1 Kgs 1-11.

4. Looking Beyond 1 Kings 1-11

Though certainly not a "new" approach, interest in the history of biblical texts' interpretation is increasing and gaining respectability as an area of study for biblical scholars.[42] The legitimacy and worth of such

[40] *Ibid.*, p. 44.

[41] *Ibid.*, pp. 48-55.

[42] Over twenty years ago J. Pritchard edited *Solomon & Sheba* (London: Phaidon, 1974), a collection of essays tracing the story of Solomon and the Queen of Sheba through Jewish, Christian, and Muslim traditions. Within the last decade, studies such as *Die Königin von Saba: Kunst, Legende und Archäologie zwischen Morgenland und Abendland* (ed. W. Daum; Stuttgart: Belser, 1988); M. Delcor, "La Reine de Saba et Salomon: Quelques aspects de l'origine de la légende et de sa formation principalement dans le mond juif et éthiopien, à partir des texts bibliques," *Tradicio i traduccio de la paraula* (ed. F. Raurell and others; Montserrat: Publications de l'Abadia de Montserrt,

studies has not always been appreciated by past biblical scholars. Simon DeVries, for example, after briefly identifying Jewish and Muslim interpretations of the Queen of Sheba in his commentary on 1 Kings, remarked that, "All this is irrelevant to the biblical account."[43] DeVries' comment reflects a privileging of stories' pre-literary and canonical dimensions over their postcanonical ones. At the turn of the millennium, however, there is a growing realization that readers stand within a continuum of interpretation, and that all points on that continuum are a part of a story's "life" and "truth." The following represents a limited selection of biblical and pre-10th century postbiblical treatments as well as Qur'anic and medieval post-qur'anic treatments. As we skim the surface of this fascinating interpretive pool we will see how subsequent commentators culled, clarified and expanded the relationship between Solomon and the women associated with him.

A. *First Testament: 1-2 Chronicles (ca. 4th century BCE)*[44]

When compared to Kings, Solomon's account in Chronicles is notable for its lack of female characters. Absent are Solomon's 700 wives and 300 concubines, his 2 daughters, the 2 prostitutes, Abishag, Hadad's wife (Queen Tahpenes' sister), and Jeroboam's widowed mother. In fact, of the wealth of women found in the Kings' account, only five remain: Bathshua (= Bathsheba), Pharaoh's daughter, the bronzeworker's mother, the Queen of Sheba, and Naamah. Yet even these figures are different from their Kings' counterparts. For example, in comparison to the five references to Pharaoh's daughter in Kings, Chronicles has only one. It informs us that Solomon moved[45] his wife outside the city of David because "the places to which the ark of the Lord has come are holy" (2 Chr 8:11). Thus Chronicles explains what Kings leaves unsaid: that

1993); and J. Lassner, *Demonizing the Queen of Sheba: Boundaries of Gender and Culture in Postbiblical Judaism and Medieval Islam* (Chicago Studies in the History of Judaism; Chicago: University of Chicago, 1993), explored the "life" of 1 Kgs 10:1-13 far beyond its textual boundaries. Another example of this interest in the postcanonical life of biblical texts is the series published by Westminster/John Knox (Gender and Biblical Traditions) that focuses exclusively on early post-canonical interpretations of biblical women's stories.

[43] S. J. DeVries, *1 Kings* (WBC; Waco, Tex.: Word, 1995) 139.

[44] Those points where Chronicles is thought to preserve a tradition older than Kings are identified in the footnotes.

[45] In 1 Kgs 9:24 she goes of her own accord, while in 2 Chr 8:11 Solomon initiates her move.

Solomon's high born Egyptian wife was a threat to the Holy City's purity.[46] There are other differences between the Kings and Chronicles accounts as well: 1) in Kings, references to Bathsheba occur in Solomon's birth and succession, but in Chronicles her presence is limited to a genealogical note (1 Chr 3:5) that identifies her as "Bathshua"[47] the daughter of Ammiel (instead of Eliam) and the mother of three sons besides Solomon (Shimea, Shobab, and Nathan); 2) the bronzeworker's[48] mother, who in 1 Kings is "a widow from Naphtali," becomes in the Chronicler's account "one of the Danite women" (2 Chr 2:13-14);[49] 3) in Kings, the number and nationality of Solomon's wives are emphasized, while no mention of these are made in Chronicles aside from the Queen of Sheba's brief remark in 2 Chr 9:7 (= 1 Kgs 10:8),[50] and 4) in Kings, Naamah's name occurs in Rehoboam's introductory and concluding regnal formulas, while in Chronicles it appears only in his introduction (2 Chr 12:13–1 Kgs 14:21).[51]

---

[46] S. Japhet, *I & II Chronicles* (OTL; Louisville: Westminster/John Knox, 1993) 626, suggests that "it is not human residence in a holy precinct *per se*, nor the fact that the queen is a foreigner which prohibits her dwelling within a certain proximity to the ark, but an implication of impurity, specific to her *as a woman*." Japhet finds a similar injunction in the *Damascus Covenant* 12.1-2, which prohibits intercourse with a woman within the city of the sanctuary. A similar injuction is found in the *Temple Scroll* 45.11. Another suggestion is that Solomon is trying to preserve the ark from menstrual pollution; J. M. Myers, *II Chronicles* (AB 13; Garden City, NY: Doubleday, 1965) 49-50. H. G. M. Williamson, *1 and 2 Chronicles* (NCB; Grand Rapids: Eerdmans, 1982) 230.

[47] The LXX and the Vulgate of this verse have "Bathsheba."

[48] In 1 Kgs 7:13-14 he is called Hiram while in 2 Chr 2:13-14 he is identified as Hurambi.

[49] Whether or not this change is due to an alternate tradition or the writers' *tendenz* is difficult to determine. Japhet, *I & II Chronicles*, p. 545, suggests that, while both locations (Naphtali and Dan) are in the north and thus "historically viable" (the father remains Phoenician in both accounts), it is possible that the change was influenced by 'Oholiab the son of Ahisamach of the tribe of Dan (Exod 35:34) who helped Bezalel build the tabernacle.

[50] MT reads "your men" instead of "your wives" (see also the MT of 1 Kgs 10:8). Japhet suggests that the MT preserves the better reading and identifies "your wives" as a "later homiletical expansion;" *ibid.*, p. 636. The NRSV reads "your wives" in 1 Kgs 10:8, but "your people" in 2 Chr 9:7.

While the Chronicler does not dwell on Solomon's harem, he shows no such reticence with Solomon's son, Rehoboam. According to 2 Chr 11:18-23, Rehoboam had 18 wives and 60 concubines, and fathered 28 sons and 60 daughters. While Rehoboam's "fall" is not explicitly linked to these marriages (note that no foreign ancestry is ascribed to his wives), immediately following we are told that Rehoboam "abandoned the law of the LORD" (2 Chr 12:1). Unlike the Solomon of 1 Kgs 11, however, the Rehoboam of 2 Chr 12 repents (12:6-8).

[51] Since the second reference to Naamah in 1 Kgs 14:3 is also missing from the Peshitta of Kings and from some LXX manuscripts, Japhet suggests that the reading in Chronicles is to be preferred; *ibid.*, p. 683.

Indeed, of all the women in 1 Kgs 1-11, only the Queen of Sheba's account in 2 Chr 9:1-12 remains relatively untouched.[52] Yet, since the Chronicler omits several examples of Solomon's wisdom found in 1 Kings (3:16-28 and 4:29-34), the visit takes on a new significance, and, as Japhet observes, becomes "a major demonstration of Solomon's political and economic sagacity."[53] In addition, since the Chronicler omits 1 Kgs 11 (as well as the acrimonious aspects of Solomon's accession in 1 Kgs 1-2; see 1 Chr 29), the visit becomes the climax of Solomon's peaceful and prosperous reign, with only the notes on his wealth and fame (2 Chr 9:13-28) and the concluding regnal formula (9:29-31) following.

While Solomon's account in Chronicles has less female characters than its parallel in Kings, their overall presentation is more positive. Whereas in Kings their nationalities and faith are problematic, in Chronicles only Pharaoh's daughter is dangerous (and then only to the city's purity not to Solomon himself).

Although scholars continue to debate the relationship between 1-2 Chronicles and Ezra/Nehemiah,[54] it is interesting to note that Nehemiah 13:23-27 does what 2 Chronicles avoids; it condemns Solomon's foreign marriages. According to Nehemiah, Solomon is an object lesson to men in Nehemiah's time who are marrying women of Ashdod, Ammon, and Moab. If the mighty Solomon could not marry outside his faith and remain true to his god, how can Nehemiah's male audience imagine they will be different?

B. *First Testament: The Song of Solomon (Date uncertain)*

According to tradition, Solomon wrote the biblical books of Proverbs, Ecclesiastes, and the Song of Solomon.[55] While modern critical scholars

---

[52] What minor differences exist between accounts may (or may not) be significant. Williamson, for example, observes that the Chronicler has the Queen talking "with" Solomon rather than "to" him and wonders if this is an attempt to put Solomon on a more equal footing with the Queen than that found in 1 Kgs 11; *1 and 2 Chronicles*, p. 234.

[53] Japhet, *I & II Chronicles*, p. 634.

[54] See, for example, K. Richard, "Reshaping Chronicles and Ezra-Nehemiah Interpretation," *Old Testament Interpretation, Past, Present, and Future: Essays in Honor of Gene M. Tucker* (ed. J. L. Mays and others; Nashville: Abingdon, 1993) 211-24.

[55] R. Jonathan, for example, suggested that Solomon wrote the Song of Songs in his youth, Proverbs in his middle age, and Ecclesiastes in his cynical last years. Not all of his rabbinical colleagues, however, agreed with his developmental schema (see *Songs R.* 1.1.10).

no longer assume Solomonic authorship for any of these, it is important to remember that for centuries these books provided a filter for understanding Solomon's story (and the women in it). A good example of this intertextual reading can be seen between 1 Kgs 1-11 and the Song of Solomon.

While it is true that allegorical readings of the Song predominated in Jewish and Christian tradition until relatively recently,[56] there has nevertheless been a persistent minority throughout the centuries that read the Song literally and found within it historical references to Solomon's love life. For example, Theodoret, Bishop of Cyprus in Syria (*ca.* 393-466 CE), a keen proponent of the Song's allegorical interpretation, complained in the preface to his commentary on the Song that some said "that Solomon the Wise wrote it [the Song] concerning himself and Pharaoh's daughter." Such an association, in Theodoret's estimation, was "slander."[57] Years earlier, Origen (*ca.* 185-253 CE) conceded the Song's connection with Pharaoh's daughter, but insisted that such a literal reading was inferior to the Song's allegorical dimensions.[58] Another candidate for the object of Solomon's alleged attentions in the Song was Abishag. Since Song 6:13 [Hebrew 7:1] refers to a beautiful Shulammite (thought by some as a variant of "Shunammite") and 1 Kgs 1:3-4 describes Abishag as both beautiful and a Shunammite, readers concluded that the Song described Solomon's love for Abishag. This allowed readers to explain Solomon's reaction to Adonijah's request in 1 Kgs 2:22-25 as impassioned jealousy.[59] Yet another candidate for Solomon's affections was the Queen of Sheba. The woman's words in Song 1:5 ("I am black, but comely") paved the road for her identification by medieval commentators, for example, as the Queen of 1 Kgs 10.[60] Passages such as Song 6:8 also drew scholars' attention to the women of 1 Kgs 1-11. In Song 6:8, the male speaker refers to his harem of 60 queens, 80 concubines, and maidens without number. In spite of its numerical discrepancy with 1 Kgs 11:3 (700 princesses and 300 concu-

---

[56] M. H. Pope, *Song of Songs* (AB 7C; Garden City, NY: Doubleday, 1977) 89.

[57] Theodore, Bishop of Mopsuestia (*ca.* 350-428 CE) suggested that Solomon wrote the book in defiance of the criticism evoked by his marriage to Pharaoh's daughter; Pope, *Song*, pp. 119-20.

[58] *Ibid.*, p. 89.

[59] *Ibid.*, p. 598.

[60] M. Warner, "In and Out of the Fold: Wisdom, Danger, and Glamour in the Tale of the Queen of Sheba," *Out of the Garden: Women Writers on the Bible* (eds. C. Buchmann and C. Spiegel; New York: Fawcett Columbine, 1994) 154.

bines), readers developed ingenious ways of harmonizing the two verses.[61]

While the above examples are only a few of the many that could be mentioned, they serve as a reminder that First Testament books other than Chronicles shaped subsequent interpretations of Solomon's relationship with the women of 1 Kgs 1-11.

C. *Second Testament: A Solomon With One Woman (1st century CE)*

There is only one reference to the women of Solomon's story in the Second Testament. Indeed, Solomon's presence in the Second Testament itself is minimal, with comments on his ancestry (Matt 1:6-7), glory (Matt 6:29 = Luke 12:27), wisdom (Matt 12:42 = Lk 11:31), and building projects (Acts 7:47)[62] constituting the bulk of his treatment. Subsequent readers of the Second Testament, however, found references to the Queen of Sheba in Acts 8:27 (with its reference to Candace, Queen of the Ethiopians[63]) and in Matt 12:42 = Luke 11:31 (with its mention of the "Queen of the South" who "came from the ends of the earth to listen to the wisdom of Solomon"[64]). A good example of the blending of these two readings is found in the *Kebra Nagast* ("Glory of Kings," Ethiopic national saga, *ca.* 6th-14th centuries CE).[65]

D. *Josephus, Antiquities (1st century CE)*

While several sources during the postbiblical period contain references to Solomon and women,[66] one of the most sustained treatments is found

---

[61] F. Delitzsch (1891) argued that Song 6:8 referred to Solomon's youth while 1 Kgs 11:3 referred to the excesses of his old age. Others saw behind the vagueness of Song 6:8c an attempt by Solomon to hide the excessive number of women in his harem; Pope, *Song*, pp. 567-68.

[62] John 10:23, Acts 3:11, and 5:12 mention the portico of Solomon, a part of the Jerusalem Temple complex. While not built by Solomon, it was linked by tradition to him; see Josephus, *Ant.* 20.9.7.

[63] See the discussion in E. Ullendorff, "Candace (Acts VIII.27) and the Queen of Sheba," *NTS* 2 (1955) 53-56.

[64] P. F. Watson, "The Queen of Sheba in Christian Tradition," *Solomon & Sheba* (ed. J. B. Pritchard; London: Phaidon, 1974) 115-45; as well as Pritchard's "Conclusion" to the same volume, pp. 146-51.

[65] Ullendorff, "Candace," p. 54. According to the saga, the queen bore Solomon a child who became the founder of Ethiopia's royal house.

[66] For example, according to *The Lives of the Prophets* (*ca.* 1st century CE) the prophet Ahijah foretold that Solomon would "give offense to the Lord" (18.2) and that

in Josephus' *Ant.* 7.14.2-8.7.8. Although Josephus' account of Solomon's reign contains many of the same female characters found in 1 Kgs 1-11, significant changes occur in their stories and characterization. Abishag (= Abisake) in 7.14.3 and 8.1.2-3 is a good case in point. Josephus emphasizes that Abishag neither had sex with David nor was she ever supposed to. Indeed, David's body was so "cold and numb" that the "heaping on of many garments" did little to alleviate his chill. Abishag's task, no more or less, was to "help him against the cold," to keep him, quite literally, "warm." To emphasize the nonsexual nature of this warmth, Josephus explicitly mentions that she "merely slept in the same bed ... for at his age [David] was too feeble to have sexual pleasure of intercourse with her."[67] Later, Adonijah asks for Abishag "who had lain with his father" but who "by reason of his age had not had intercourse with her." When Bathsheba intercedes for Adonijah, Solomon gets angry with her and sends her away (8.1.3).

An intriguing contrast is found between Josephus' account of the Queen's visit to Solomon (in Josephus she is Nikaule, the Queen of Egypt and Ethiopia) and that of Solomon's many wives. Josephus' meeting of Solomon and the Queen of Egypt and Ethiopia (8.6.5) is one of like-minded intellectuals: 1) the Queen is "thoroughly trained in wisdom;" 2) her motivation for coming to Solomon is based on logic and reason (she wishes to be "convinced by experience" and not dependant merely on hearsay; 3) her intent is to test Solomon's wisdom by "propounding questions and asking him to solve their difficult meaning;" and 4) in response, Solomon "was studious to please her" and mentally grasped "with ease the ingenious problems" she presented. This rea-

Solomon's "wives would change him and his posterity" (18.4). No mention is made, however, of the wives' nationality nor the nature of the threat they presented. Another example is found in *The Apocalypse of Adam* (*ca.* 1st-4th centuries CE). A list in *ApAdm* 7.1-48 gives thirteen false explanations concerning the birth of a savior figure ("the Illuminator"). The fourth explanation (7.13-16) describes how Solomon sent his demons to bring him a certain virgin. They failed to find her and instead substituted another whom Solomon had intercourse with and who bore his son. According to the explanation, she raised the boy at the desert's fringe and he later became the "Illuminator."

[67] Another example of how Josephus' account differs from that in 1 Kgs 1-11 is his treatment of Solomon and the two harlots (*Ant.* 8.2.2). According to Josephus: 1) the women lived in the same room and gave birth at the same hour; 2) the mother discovered the child's death when she went to nurse him; 3) Solomon delivered judgment after all in attendance had failed to solve the "riddle;" 4) Solomon ordered both sons be divided so that each mother got two halves; 5) those in attendance thought Solomon's judgment foolish, the words of a mere boy; 6) the real mother is determined and the guilty woman condemned; and 7) people thought Solomon's wisdom was "godlike."

soned intellectual exchange between Solomon and the Queen stands in stark contrast to the passion of Solomon's interaction with his foreign wives (8.7.5). According to Josephus, Solomon became "madly enamored of women and indulged in excesses of passion" and "carried away with thoughtless pleasure" disregarded God's warnings. Moreover, as he got older, "his reason became ... too feeble to oppose" his wives' wishes. Thus Josephus' account of the Queen's visit, when read alongside that of his foreign wives, traces Solomon's movement from reason into passion; a movement that ultimately contributed to his downfall. Yet, unlike other 1st century writers, Josephus presents women in terms other than passion, pleasure, and danger. While it is true such imaging exists with Solomon's foreign wives, Josephus' portrayal of the foreign Queen reflects a woman guided by logic and reason as well.

E. *The Testament of Solomon (ca. 1st-3rd centuries CE)*

Written or edited by a Greek speaking Christian,[68] *The Testament of Solomon* is a tale focusing on Solomon's magical wisdom. It begins with a demonic attack on his master workman's son, a boy "much loved" by Solomon (*TSol* 1.1). Two incidents involving Solomon and women are specially interesting for our purposes: 1) Solomon and Sheeba (Queen of the South), and 2) Solomon's unnamed Shulammite wife.[69]

---

[68] D. C. Duling, "*The Testament of Solomon*: A New Translation and Introduction," *OTP* 1.943.

[69] Females also occur as both victims and victimizers in Solomon's interrogation of the demons. After Solomon learns from the boy the true nature of his illness (a demon is sucking his life essence from the boy's thumb each evening; 1.3-4), the archangel Michael gives Solomon a magical ring that gives Solomon control over all demonkind (1.5-7). One by one, Solomon calls in demons, questions them about their functions and weaknesses and binds them into Temple service. Three of the demons he summons are female: Onoskelis (4.1-12), Obyzouth (13.1-7), and Enepsigos (15.1-12). Onoskelis is "very beautiful" and, among other things, strangles men and perverts their natures. Obyzouth has "disheveled hair" and is a denizen of the night who strangles newborns, while the two-headed Enepsigos is an expert in deception (a shapeshifter) appearing as a goddess one moment and then changing her appearance in the next.

As demons, females victimize humankind, but as humans, females fall victim to male and female demons alike. Male demons, for example, wreck sexual and social havoc. They: 1) kill Aquarian men who lust after Virgo women (2.2); 2) desire young men (or women?) (2.3); 3) sow discord with newlyweds (5.7); 4) make cold hearted virgins (5.7); 5) cause women's madness (5.8); 6) cause holy men and select priests to lust (6.4); 7) inflect jealousy (6.4); 8) cause housholds to be nonfunctional (7.5; 18.15,22); and 9) rape beautiful women anally (14.3-4). Unlike the male demons to whom Solomon assigns construction tasks, Solomon orders that Obyzouth (the female demon who kills newborns) be hung by her hair in front of the Temple (13.7). No such violent punishment is given male demons.

The story of Sheeba, Queen of the South, is built upon the biblical story of the Queen of Sheba (1 Kgs 10:1-13).[70] Like the biblical queen, the Sheeba of *TSol* 19.1-3 comes to Solomon bearing gifts. Unlike her biblical counterpart, this Sheeba is a witch who bows to Solomon only after a display of arrogance (19.3). This incident precedes (and stands in tension with) the account of her awe and support of the Temple (she contributes 10,000 copper shekels towards its construction) as well as her visit to the Temple's inner and outer courts (21.1-4).

Another interesting allusion to 1 Kgs 11:1ff is *TSol* 6.1 where Solomon admits to taking "countless wives from every land and kingdom." Yet, like the account of the Queen of Sheba, this too is supplemented by haggadic expansion, this time in the form of a lengthy narrative concerning an unnamed Shummanite woman (vv. 1-8). Although Solomon was "madly in love" with the girl (v. 2), her parents threatened her with violence if she went to bed with him before he sacrificed to their gods, Raphan and Moloch (v. 4). Since Solomon was "out of [his] senses" with lust, he sacrificed five locusts to the idols, and took the girl to his palace (v. 5). Once in his palace, the girl convinced Solomon to build temples to the idols (v. 6). As a result, the spirit of God departed from Solomon (v. 6), God's glory departed (v. 7), Solomon's spirit darkened (v. 7), his words became like "idle talk" (v. 6), and he became a "laughingstock" to both idols and demons (v. 7).

F. *The Rabbinic Solomon and Women*

Tracing the women of Solomon's story through rabbinical materials is a far reaching, but exciting adventure. The paragraphs that follow summarize interpretive developments in these materials concerning: 1) the two prostitutes, 2) the Queen of Sheba, 3) Solomon's foreign wives, and 4) Solomon's marriage to Pharaoh's daughter.

1) The Two Prostitutes. In the case of the two prostitutes, rabbinic writers both praised and criticized Solomon's judicial wisdom. On the positive side, Solomon's acumen was reportedly so sharp that he was able to judge the women without "witness" or "warning" (*Song R.* 1.1.10; *Eccl R.* 10.16.1), his decision being either spoken by, or verified through, the Holy Spirit (*Gen R.* 85.12; *Eccl R.* 10.17.1). On the negative side, some rabbis saw behind Solomon's arbitrary ruling a note of aro-

[70] Note that in *TSol* Sheeba becomes the Queen's name while in 1 Kgs 10 the queen is nameless.

gance, even cruelty. The idea of cutting a child in half did not sit well with one rabbi who remarked that Solomon ought to have been strangled for putting the true mother through such an ordeal (*Eccl R.* 10.16.1). Other rabbis suggested that the two "women" were not human at all, but spirits. Since rabbinic tradition expanded Solomon's kingdom into the spirit world, interpreters were able to define "prostitutes" supernaturally; that is, as beings who seduced men's spirits rather than their bodies (*Song R.* 1.1.10; *Eccl R.* 10.16.1).[71]

2) The Queen of Sheba. Unlike the other female characters in Solomon's history, there is little expansion of the Queen of Sheba in talmudic materials. In fact, b. *B.Bat.* 15b suggests that *malkath* (queen) should be translated "kingdom," leaving readers with a "kingdom of Sheba" and no queen at all!

No such reticence is found in writings outside the Talmud. The *Midrash Mishle* and *Midrash ha-Hefez*, for example, give specific examples of the riddles and tests with which the queen "tested" Solomon. While the former contains four riddles, the latter expands on these four by adding fifteen more.[72] In addition, the *Targum Sheni* (the second Aramaic translation of Esther) both expands[73] and supplements[74] the biblical account of the queen's visit. In all three, the development of the riddles highlights Solomon's prowess and, other than drawing the reader's attention to Solomon rather than the queen, are not particularly pejorative to her characterization. The same cannot be said for some of the supplementary materials found in *Tarqum Sheni*. In these materials, the

---

[71] According to the footnote on this verse in the Socino translation, the logic behind this development is that the rabbis assumed that real prostitutes were devoid of maternal feelings and would not have brought the case to Solomon in the first place; M. Simon, tr., *Midrash Rabbah: Song of Songs* (London: Socino, 1983) 14, n. 2.

[72] Several of these portray Solomon's knowledge of female anatomy. For example, a riddle in the *Midrash Mishle* states: [Queen] "What are they? Seven depart and nine enter, two give drink but only one partakes." [Solomon] "No doubt, seven are the days of the menstrual cycle, nine are the months of pregnancy, two [refers] to the breasts that succor and one to the child born [who drinks from them]." Moreover, in the *Midrash ha-Hefez*, when the queen queries: "What is the enclosure with ten gates—When one opens, nine are shut. When nine open, one is shut?" Solomon answers: "That enclosure is the womb of a woman." Lassner, *Demonizing the Queen of Sheba*, pp. 161-65

[73] Expansions of the biblical account primarily concern the wealth she gave Solomon (6,000 boys and girls matched in age, stature and purple clothes) and the three riddles she poses to Solomon.

[74] Supplementary material includes: 1) Solomon's initiation of the encounter; 2) the queen's mistaking Benayahu, a handsome courier, for Solomon; and 3) an encounter between Solomon and the queen in a bathhouse.

queen is robbed of her autonomy (her visit is in response to Solomon's threat) and insulted as well:

> Now when King Solomon heard that she was coming to him, King Solomon arose and went to sit down in a bathhouse. When the Queen saw that the king was sitting in a bathhouse, she thought to herself the king must be sitting in water. So she raised her dress in order to wade across. Whereupon he noticed the hair on her leg, to which King Solomon responded by saying: "Your beauty is the beauty of women, but your hair is the hair of men. Now hair is beautiful for a man but shameful for a woman." (*Targum Sheni*, ch. 1)

Jacob Lassner, who analyzes both the Jewish and Muslim development of this story, argues that the above transformation of the biblical tale served to humiliate the queen and thus restore Solomon's superiority; a superiority that was open to question in the biblical version.[75]

3) The Foreign Wives. Rabbinic commentators were quick to criticize the number of Solomon's alleged wives, repeatedly referring to his triad of sins: too much wealth, too many horses, and too many wives (*Song R.* 1.1.10; *Eccl R.* 2.2.3; *Lev R.* 19.2; b. *San.* 21a; *Num R.* 10.4). As Solomon reportedly mounted the steps to his throne, a herald would call out the injunctions of Deut 17 as a poignant reminder to Solomon (*Num R.* 12.17). Another point of rabbinic criticism was his wives' nationalities (*Song R.* 1.1.10). According to rabbinic opinion, Solomon's marriages reflected a naive arrogance that assumed while others might be seduced, Solomon himself was too strong and wise to be caught (*Exod R.* 6.1; b. *San.* 21b; *Eccl R.* 1.2-2; *Num R.* 10.4). Such was the magnitude of his sin that some suggested it was better to clean sewers than to have been guilty of Solomon's actions (*Exod R.* 6.1). While the number and nationalities of Solomon's wives were problematic to rabbinic readers, there were other aspects of these liasons they found disturbing as well. Some thought them lustful ("harlot-love," *Songs R.* 1.1.10), unclean (consummated during menstruation; *Songs R.* 1.1.10), or economically disastrous.[76] Attempts to soften these harsh criticisms of Solomon: 1) exonerated Solomon of apostasy (his wives failed to seduce him, he failed to restrain them; b. *Šabb.* 56b); 2) presented a pious reason for his marriages to foreign women (he wanted to convert them; *Songs R.* 1.1.10);

[75] Lassner, *Demonizing the Queen of Sheba*, pp. 1-7.

[76] We are told that each woman vied for Solomon's attention by daily cooking him meals (*Eccl R.* 9.11.1), making the expense to the palace enormous (*Num R.* 21.19), and ultimately contributing to the economic unrest that split the kingdoms after Solomon's death.

or 3) insisted that, while Solomon loved foreign women, he did not actually marry them (y. *Sanh.* 2.6.20c).

4) Daughter of Pharaoh.[77] Unlike the biblical tradition, rabbinic writers provided names for both Pharaoh and his daughter. "Pharaoh" became Pharaoh Necho (*Songs R.* 1.6.4; *Eccl R.* 9.2.1) or Shishak (*Esth R.* 1.12), while his daughter was either "Bathiah" (*Num R.* 10.4) or "Bithiah" (*Lev R.* 12.5). Solomon's marriage to Pharaoh's daughter fascinated rabbinic writers who suggested Solomon waited to marry her until after the Temple was built (*Lev R.* 12.5; *Num R.* 10.4). At the wedding feast, Pharaoh's daughter: 1) danced 80 dances (*Lev R.* 12.5), 2) brought in 1,000 musical instruments, each dedicated to a different god (b. *Šabb.* 56b; *Num R.* 10.4), and 3) persuaded Solomon to drink heavily after being abstinent for seven years (*Lev R.* 12.5); thus causing him to sleep late and neglect his religious duties.

Neither heaven nor earth was pleased with Solomon's marriage to Pharaoh's daughter.[78] God decided that evening to destroy Jerusalem (*Lev R.* 12.5; b. *Nid.* 70b; *Num R.* 10.4); and an angel, either Michael (*Songs R.* 1.6.4) or Gabriel (b. *Šabb.* 56b; b. *Sanh.* 21b), founded Rome for that purpose. On earth, Solomon's subjects could not sacrifice while Solomon slept off his inebriation (the Temple's keys were under his pillow; *Lev R.* 12.5). Bathsheba and Jeroboam rebuked Solomon for his drunkenness (*Lev R.* 12.5; *Num R.* 10.4). Thus, Pharaoh's daughter caused him to sin the most (*Sifre Deut* 52). After Solomon's death, his father-in-law seized Solomon's ornate throne, but, being unfamiliar with the throne's mechanisms, was himself killed (*Eccl R.* 9.2.1).

G. Islam and Solomon (= Sulayman)

In Muslim tradition, Solomon is king, warrior, prophet, and wise servant of Allah. Traditions concerning his relationship with women are found in the Qur'an and in post-qur'anic commentaries.

1) The Qur'an. Of all the women associated with Solomon in the Hebrew Bible, only the Queen of Sheba appears in the Qur'an. Surah 27.15-44 ("The Ant") reports the story of how a bird (the hoopoe) tells

[77] For an interesting history of interpretation of Pharaoh's daughter see S. J. D. Cohen, "Solomon and the Daughter of Pharaoh: Intermarriage, Conversion, and the Impurity of Women," *JNES* 16-17 (1984-1985) 23-37. For a discussion of the sympathy between the LXX reading and rabbinic tradition see Gooding, "Septuagint's Version," pp. 328-31.

[78] For a rabbinic discussion concerning the legality and validity of his marriage to her see Cohen, "Solomon and the Daughter of Pharaoh," pp. 30-32.

Solomon of a southern country ruled by a sun-worshiping woman. Solomon sends her a letter demanding both her attendance at his court and her conversion to Islam. In response, she sends Solomon gifts, which he subsequently spurns (he has better than anything she can possibly give him!). An'ifrit (one of the jinn) brings Solomon her throne and disguises it to test her. Not only does she recognize the throne, but she submits to both Solomon and Allah, and becomes a Muslim.

Unlike the queen in the Jewish *Targum Sheeni*, the Qur'anic Sheba: 1) is an unbeliever who converts to Islam; 2) is the examinee rather than the examiner (she is tested by Solomon rather than being the one who tests him); and 3) uncovers her ankles (Surah 27.44), but is not subsequently insulted and humiliated by Solomon. Thus, in the Qur'anic account, the Queen's religious preference takes priority over other aspects of the story.

2) Post-Qur'anic Treatments. Although the Queen of Sheba (named Bilkas by commentators) evoked the most comment in the post-qur'anic period, qur'anic commentators drew attention to other women in Solomon's life as well. Since Jacob Lassner has done a superb job of analyzing Bilkas in his book *Demonizing the Queen of Sheba: Boundaries of Gender and Culture in Postbiblical Judaism and Medieval Islam*, the following paragraphs will discuss lesser known post-qur'anic traditions concerning Solomon and women.

a) Solomon's Harem, Potency and Pride. While many commentators refer to Solomon's harem and echo the numbers found in 1 Kgs 11:3 (700 princesses, 300 concubines), others reverse the ratio (300 wives, 700 concubines) or suggest a different one (600 wives/400 concubines; 400 wives/600 concubines).[79] Solomon's sexual performances with such a large number of women became legendary, servicing, in a single night, either 70, 90, 100, or all 1,000![80] But since Solomon boasted of his prowess (from each wife he would produce a warrior son) and did not say "if Allah wills," he had only one deformed son (having only one

---

[79] I. b. U. Ibn Kathir, *Al-Bidāyah wa al-nihāyah* (Cairo, 135-1359/1932-1940) 2.29-30; *idem*, *Qiṣaṣ al-anbiyā'* (Beirut: [Dār al-Qalam], 1405/1985) 511-12. As cited in Lassner, *Demonizing the Queen of Sheba*, p. 239.

[80] Ibn Kathir, *Qiṣaṣ al-anbiyā'* , p. 446, (70 women > Boechari, 90 > Shu'ayb, 100 > Abu Ya'lā and Aḥmad b. Ḥanbal); M. b. U. al-Zamakhsharī, *Al Kashshāf fi ḥaqā'iq al-tanzīl wa 'uyūn al-aqā-wīl fī wujūh al-ta'wīl* (W. N. Lees and others; Calcutta, 1956) 1036. As cited in Lassner, *Demonizing the Queen of Sheba*, p. 239, n. 80; see p. 241, n. 32, for more post-qur'anic references.

hand, eye, ear, and foot). Only after Solomon humbled himself before Allah was the boy made whole.[81]

b) Solomon, Two Women, and a Baby. According to commentators, a wolf carried off one of two babies, the result being that both mothers claimed the remaining baby as theirs. The case was brought before David who found in favor of the older mother. Solomon, however, intervened by suggesting that the baby be cut in two. The younger mother protested, and thus Solomon declared her the true mother and awarded her the child.[82]

c) Solomon the Apostate Who Repents. Surah 38.33-35, with its reference to Solomon's punishment, became the point of departure for post-qur'anic commentators who preserved a two-part story of Solomon's apostasy and forgiveness. Accordingly, Solomon married a king's daughter whose father Solomon defeated and killed in battle. The girl, young and beautiful, was converted to Islam, though not without hesitation on her part. Though Solomon loved her more than any of his other wives, she continually grieved for her father. In order to appease her, Solomon let her fashion an effigy of her dead parent, which she clothed and subsequently worshiped for the next forty days whenever Solomon was not around. Through the intervention of a holy man, Solomon learned of her actions and dealt with her and her daughters accordingly. Sometime afterward, Solomon was bathing and gave his ring of power to Amina, a trusted wife, for safe keeping. A demon masquerading as Solomon deceived Amina into giving him the ring of power and then ruled for forty days in Solomon's stead, while Solomon wandered in exile. Such was Solomon's punishment for allowing his wife's apostasy.[83]

5. Conclusion

Scholars have come a long way in the last century in their treatment of 1 Kgs 1-11's female characters. From a preoccupation with these

[81] I. I. Al-Boechari, *Recueil des Traditions Mahometanes* (ed. Krehl; Leiden, 1864) ii.364; Ibn Kathīr, *Al-Bidayah*, ii.187.

[82] Boechari, *Recueil*, ii.364.

[83] See, for example, *al-Kisā'ī*, in Lassner, *Demonizing the Queen of Sheba*, pp. 212-14. Another version is found in Ibn Isḥāq's *Sîrah* (written sometime before 767 CE) in G. D. Newby, *The Making of the Last Prophet* (Columbia: University of South Carolina, 1989) 167-69.

women's historical significance, scholars have grown appreciative both of the literary artistry their stories display, as well as the artful creativity with which postcanonical readers understood these stories. As this millennium draws to a close and the next century of scholarship begins, 1 Kgs 1-11's wealth of women will no doubt be matched by a wealth of interpretations as scholars continue to explore the worlds behind, within, and beyond these rich chapters.

THE HELLENIZATION OF SOLOMON IN RABBINIC TEXTS

SANDRA R. SHIMOFF

1. THE NATURE OF AGGADA

Rabbinic literature can be divided into two broad categories: halakha and aggada. Halakhic material relates to issues in Jewish law, ritual, jurisprudence and practice. Aggadic material includes a broad range of topics, including history, homiletics, legend, lore, medicine, moral lessons, and mysticism, as well as social and political commentary.

Halakhic discussions were necessarily closely tied to the real world; it was halakha that set the legal boundaries defining the immediate daily life of the Jews. Rabbinic discussions of halakhic issues were constrained by the rabbinic view that halakha ultimately determined how Jews were to observe the 613 commandments of the Torah.

But aggadic discussions had no such limitations and the rabbis were free to include imaginative flights of fancy, novel interpretations, and creative reconstructions. Halakha was the heart of rabbinic Judaism, but aggada was its soul. Halakha may have defined how a Jew was to act, but it was aggada that captured the imagination of the people, that expressed the nature and spirit of Judaism. And it is in the corpus of aggadic literature that we can most readily see the rabbinic perspective on Solomon. The rabbis of the hellenistic era recreated Solomon in their own image so that the aggadic narratives tell us, in a sense, more about the rabbinic response to Hellenism than they tell us about the biblical Solomon.

In the course of this chapter, we will examine some of the most prominent Solomonic aggadic themes, describing his wisdom (and its limits), his role as judge, his wealth, his throne, his personal life, and his building of the Temple. These aggadic themes exemplify the rabbinic image of Solomon and how he was presented to the people. However, these themes also reflect the rabbinic response to the challenge of Hellenism. Many of the aggadic narratives were not just "legends of

Solomon," but were instead homiletic lessons and political commentary.[1]

2. SOLOMON'S EDUCATION

Rabbinic tradition places great emphasis on the importance of education and on respect for one's teachers. Given that background, it is not surprising to see that some aggadic narratives describe Solomon's exemplary behavior towards his teachers. In some instances these aggadic narratives appear to carry a subtle political message.

Rab Hiyya b. Ammi (a third generation Babylonian amora), citing Ulla, indicated that Shimei b. Gera was an important educational influence on Solomon; Solomon did not marry Pharaoh's daughter during Shimei b. Gera's lifetime, presumably out of respect for his teacher (*b. Ber.* 8a). This may well represent a subtle criticism of the Patriarch Judah II (Nesi'a), who flourished in the middle of the 3rd century CE. The Patriarch in Palestine and the Exilarch in Babylonia were the political and social leaders of their communities; in addition to their hereditary status, they claimed Davidic descent. The political power of the Patriarchate and Exilarchate made direct criticism by other sages and rabbis unwise. Rather than directly criticizing these powerful figures, unflattering comments were often veiled as criticisms of David or Solomon. This narrative may be a veiled reference to the fact that Rabban Gamaliel III, the father of Rabbi Judah II (Nesi'a) never accepted anything from Rome, while Rabbi Judah II himself did, and collected taxes for the Romans as well as requiring contributions by the sages themselves.[2]

Rab Hiyya's message may be subtle to the modern reader, but was probably quite clear to his audience; just as Solomon's improper acts stemmed from a failure to follow from his teacher's example, so did Rabbi Judah II err in straying from his teacher's ways. Thus R. Simeon b. Lakish said to Rabbi Judah II, "Take nothing from anyone and then you will not have to give anything" (*Gen. R.* 78:12).

Rab Hiyya's lesson was aimed not only at Rabbi Judah II, but at all

[1] S. R. Shimoff, "Hellenization among the Rabbis: Some Evidence from Early Aggadot Concerning David and Solomon," *JSJ* 18 (1988) 168-87.

[2] M. Avi-Yonah, *Bi'Ymei Roma u-Byzantium* (Jerusalem: Mosad Bialik, 1970).

those Jews who were tempted by hellenization and encouraged by the Patriarch's model. Too much hellenization was not acceptable.

3. Solomon's Wisdom

For the rabbis, the scriptural praise for Solomon's wisdom was inadequate. They commented that his knowledge exceeded that of Adam, Abraham, Joseph, Moses, and the generation of the wilderness (*Pesikta de-Rabbi Kahana* 4:3).

It was only because Solomon taught Torah in public, according to R. Judah (a second generation Palestinian amora), that the Holy Spirit rested upon him (*Songs R.* 1:1:8). It would seem likely that the sages were encouraging public discourse and reminding scholars that great reward is in store for those who give of their time to teach the masses. Thus, in a very real sense, the rabbis were suggesting that Solomon's greatest spiritual achievements came about not for his monarchic role, but when he adopted the rabbinic role of teacher.

Solomon's knowledge was not limited to religious and spiritual matters but extended to all other disciplines, too (*Songs R.* 1:1:7). But when it came to halakhic matters, Solomon consulted rabbinic authority. Perhaps the most dramatic aggadic description of the monarch deferring to rabbinic authority involves the death of David. According to the aggadic narrative David died on the Sabbath, and halakha did not allow Solomon to move the body despite the heat of the sun and menacing dogs. Solomon had to consult the Sanhedrin (an obvious anachronism) in order to obtain its halakhic approval (*Ruth R.* 3:2; *b. Šabb.* 30b).

In another instance of rabbinic authority superseding monarchic status, Solomon was credited with intercalating the year only in concert with seven scholars (*Exod. R.* 15:20). He was not to intercalate the year on his own initiative.

While the rabbis recognized the great power of the monarchy, some perogatives and responsibilities were reserved for scholars; under these conditions the power of the monarchy bowed to the knowledge of the sages. Only rabbis may decide questions of halakha and even the monarch must defer to rabbinic judgment of halakhic matters. Again, the subtle political and social message is clear. Rome (and the Patriarch) may hold temporal power, but halakhic decisions abide in the rabbinic domain.

4. Limitations on Solomon's Knowledge

How could Solomon, the righteous and wise king, have trangressed the three biblical prohibitions specifically and explicitly directed to kings of Israel: not to maintain too many horses, not to have too many wives, and not to accumulate excessive wealth (Deut 17:16-17)? In an apologetic exercise the rabbis deduced that Solomon must have studied these laws and reasoned that he was justified in his transgression and that "his heart would not be turned away" (*Exod. R.* 6:1). Solomon himself is reported to have attributed his downfall to his conviction that he understood the intention of biblical laws (*Exod. R.* 6:1). R. Simeon b. Yohai (a mid-2nd century tanna), who often advocated extreme positions, states that it would have been better for Solomon to have cleaned sewers than to have been misled (*Exod. R.* 6:1) and attributed Solomon's errors to his interest in needless knowledge (*Tanhuma Buber* 2:18).

The message in these aggadic narratives is clear; if scholarly hubris could lead to Solomon's downfall, how much moreso might it threaten those of lesser intellect. Hellenistic intellectualism was not simply a waste of time, it could represent a real and immediate threat! The rabbis were suggesting that even Solomon needed to consult the sages before acting.

R. Joshua b. Levi (a Palestinian amora of the first half of the 3rd century) said that the rabbis sought to exclude Solomon from the world to come because of his sins but a Heavenly Voice cancelled the plan (*Songs R.* 1:1:15). A similar account was attributed to Rab Judah (a Babylonian amora who flourished in the latter part of the 3rd century) in the name of Rab (*b. Sanh.* 104b; *Songs R.* 1:1:15; *Pesikta Rabbati* 6:4).

This account suggests that the sages had authority in most matters of law, but had no authority over the House of David. The rabbis, in this account, do not have the final word. Rab Judah was a disciple of Rab, who traced his lineage to David and felt constrained to clear the Davidic dynasty of any stain. While defending Solomon, he was asserting the supremacy of the Exilarchate over rabbinic objections and protestations.

R. Joshua b. Levi (a first generation Palestinian amora known for his piety) represented his people to the Roman government at Caesarea[3] and thus had good reason to support the Patriarch; rabbinic support and popular appeal were vital for the Patriarch's official position. Although

[3] M. Margalioth, *Encyclopedia le-Hahme ha-Talmud ve-ha-Geonim* (Tel Aviv: Yavneh) 463-64.

some rabbis may have disapproved of Solomon, he was ultimately supported by a Heavenly Voice. Similarly, contemporary rabbinic disapproval of the Patriarch may have been, according to R. Joshua b. Levi, ill-advised.

A more striking apologetic tendency was shown by those sages, however, who maintain that Solomon never committed any transgression whatsoever. These assertions are particularly remarkable since Solomon's sins are explicit in the scriptural account. Yet R. Samuel b. Nahmani (a Palestinian amora whose life bridged the 3rd and 4th centuries) quotes R. Jonathan's statement that anyone who asserts that Solomon sinned is in error (*b. Šabb.* 56b). And R. Nathan (a fourth generation tanna) notes that the statement that Solomon's wives turned him towards other gods means that they attempted unsuccessfully to have him participate (*b. Šabb.* 56b).

R. Samuel b. Nahmani was a noted aggadist who was on very cordial terms with R. Judah II (Nesiʾa); they frequented the warm baths of Tiberias together and the Patriarch chose him to accompany Emperor Diocletian on his visit to the East.[4] His defense of Solomon is readily predicted on the basis of his relations with the Patriarch.[5] His defense of Solomon was, in fact, a defense of the Patriarch.

R. Nathan was the son of the Exilarch and thus of Davidic descent himself and had served as Av Beth Din (chief judge of the rabbinic court) under the Patriarch Rabban Simeon ben Gamaliel at Usha.[6] He would then understandably be concerned with clearing Solomon of wrong-doing and taught that the attempts of Solomon's wives to seduce him into idolatry were unsuccessful, scriptural suggestions notwithstanding (*b. Šabb.* 56b).

5. Solomon as Judge

Rabbinic jurisprudence demands that judgments of criminal acts be made only if the perpetrator had been warned before the crime and only if there were valid witnesses to the act. Yet *b. Rosh Hashannah* 21b depicts Koheleth (Solomon) pronouncing verdicts using only his insights without benefit of witnesses or warnings. How could Solomon have acted contrary to rabbinic law?

---

[4] *Ibid.*, p. 831.
[5] *Ibid.*, p. 832.
[6] *Ibid.*, p. 680.

The explanation is provided by R. Jose in the name of R. Hanina based on the passage "And Solomon sat on the throne of the Lord" (1 Chr 29:23) indicating that Solomon was able to render judgments with neither witnesses nor warnings (*Midrash Pss.* 72:2; *Songs R.* 1:1:10). R. Isaac commented that David prayed that Solomon should be able to judge without witnesses or warnings, just as God judges, and that David's request was granted (*b. Ros. Has.* 21b). Therefore no contradiction exists; Solomon was not arrogantly petitioning for Divine permission to judge without witnesses and warnings.

6. Solomon's Wealth

Given the scriptural descriptions of wealth and economic prosperity during Solomon's reign, rabbinic homiletic exaggeration is not surprising. Some of these aggadic narratives appear to reflect hellenistic influence. The rabbis taught that the coin of Jerusalem had "David and Solomon" inscribed on one side and "Jerusalem" on the other (*b. B. Qam.* 97b). However, there are no coins extant from the days of David and Solomon and it is unlikely indeed that, had there been any, these would have remained to be seen by the rabbis.[7]

Why would the rabbis have "invented" such a coin and why would its description be included in this aggadic narrative? The "rabbinic" coin bore no images and this aggadic narrative probably dates from a period in which representations were less likely to be acceptable to the rabbis. It was probably at a time when nationalistic aspirations and hope for the restoration of independence were still fierce, offering pride in a glorious past and hope for a vibrant future. It is possible that this aggadic narrative is encouraging the use of coins, as if to say that coins are not a foreign innovation but rather a convenience dating from the early days of the nation.[8]

R. Hiyya b. Nehemiah (a Palestinian amora, date uncertain) offers yet another analysis of Solomon's wealth; he asserts that it refers to wealth of Torah (*Eccl. R.* 2:8:2). Solomon is credited with building many

[7] E. R. Goodenough, *Jewish Symbols in the Greco-Roman Period* (New York: Pantheon, 1954) 1.21.

[8] This is not the only coin from antiquity described by the rabbis. See Shimoff, "Hellenization," pp. 180-82 for discussion on why coins posed a dilemma for hellenistic Jewry.

synagogues and houses of study (*Eccl. R.* 2:8:2 explaining Eccl 2:4 "I built houses..."). The vineyards planted (Eccl 2:4) refer to rows of disciples seated in tiers as in a vineyard (*Eccl. R.* 2:8:2). R. Eleazar b. Azariah (a tanna whose life bridged the 1st and 2nd centuries CE) offered this comment in the presence of the sages in the vineyard of Jabneh, where, too, it is said that the disciples sat in tiers as in a vineyard. Therefore, what was instituted at Jabneh was not an innovation, but was the continuation of a respected tradition from the time of Solomon.

The rabbis also comment that Solomon's wealth was reflected in his eating habits. Gorian b. Astion indicates that the large quantity of food mentioned in 1 Kgs 5:2 was for the cook's dough, which was placed above the pot to absorb the steam and vapors (*b. B. Meṣ.* 86b). R. Isaac (a second to third generation Palestinian amora) said that the animals mentioned were intended for the mincemeat puddings (*b. B. Meṣ.* 86b). He further stated that each of Solomon's thousand wives prepared this enormous quantity of food in her own house, hoping that Solomon would choose to dine with her (*b. B. Meṣ.* 86b; *Midrash Pss.* 50:2; *Num. R.* 21:19; *Pesikta de Rab Kahana* 4:3). These obvious exaggerations were purposely inserted to stress the luxury and opulence of Solomon's court.

Historically-based legends were often extended homiletically. The midrash interprets Ruth 2:14 as referring to the economic prosperity of Solomon's reign. The same midrashic statement is then extended into the political realm with the note that similar prosperity was characteristic of the "reign" of Rabbi, who claimed Davidic descent.

R. Hamma b. Hanina (a 3rd century Palestinian amora) maintains that Solomon was supplied with beets during the summer and cucumbers in the winter (*Deut. R.* 1:5) and that Solomon's table always featured fresh vegetables out-of-season. He also states that Solomon's table never lacked roses, which he enjoyed year-round (*Eccl. R.* 2:1:7).

R. Hamma b. Hanina was on friendly terms with Resh Lakish and R. Jonathan, both general supporters of the Patriarch Rabbi Judah II (Nesiʾa). Rabbi Judah Nesiʾa's grandfather also apparently enjoyed fresh vegetables throughout the year. In describing Solomon's table, he is probably referring to the table of the Patriarch (or what was expected at the table of a Patriarch). This might in fact have been a description of opulence worthy of monarchy and thus a source of national pride.

The culinary emphasis clearly indicates that at least some of the rabbis were sufficiently hellenized to adopt the Roman attitude towards din-ing. That Rabbi (R. Judah the Patriarch, grandfather of R. Judah Nesi'a) himself had adopted hellenistic culinary practices coupled with the description of his great wealth underscores that this was a source of national pride.

7. Solomon's Reign

According to R. Isaac, Solomon reigned *imitatio Dei* over the whole earth (*Songs R.* 15:26) and over all kings (*Songs R.* 15:26, based on 2 Chr 9:23-24). It was said of Solomon's throne that only one who ruled over the entire world could sit upon it (*Esth. R.* 1:12). The concept of world domination and imperial might was hellenistic rather than Jewish. There is no mention in biblical texts of Solomon achieving world dominion or even that such dominion was valued; Jewish rule over Israel (Deut 17:14), not the world, was the ideal. Clearly, the rabbis had accepted the hellenistic notion of world domination as appropriate not only for Romans, but for their own historical monarchs as well (*Esth. R.* 1:13).

The description of Solomon's throne (*Esth. R.* 1:12) adds evidence that ancient Jewish proscriptions against images were weakened under the influence of Hellenism. There is substantial evidence that the rabbis passively accepted the use of such images (*Esth. R.* 1:12) despite Josephus' assertion that Solomon sinned in fashioning lions for his throne (*Ant.* 8:7:5). Some Rabbis did not condemn the use of wall-paintings and mosaics (*j. Abod. Zar.* 42d). Even statuary was acceptable as long as it wasn't the image of a human.[9] The leniency of the Patriarchate on this matter may be related to the desire for support from wealthy hellenized families who were willing to finance such art.[10] In the description of Solomon's throne by the rabbis in the narratives above, the rabbis stepped (perhaps subconsciously) from passive acceptance of hellenization to its implicit encouragement.

---

[9] *b. Ros. Has.* 24b. See E. E. Urbach, "The Rabbinic Laws of Idolatry in the Second and Third Centuries in the Light of Archaeological and Historical Facts," *IEJ* 9 (1959) 149-65. See this same article for an account of Babylonian amoraim praying in a synagogue which contained a human figure.

[10] J. M. Baumgarten, "Art in the Synagogue: Some Talmudic Views," *The Synagogue: Studies in Origins, Archaeology and Architecture* (ed. J. Gutmann; New York: KTAV, 1975) 88.

8. Solomon's Wives

The scriptural narrative (1 Kgs 11:1-2) notes Solomon's many wives: "Solomon did cleave unto them in love." The rabbis differ in their evaluation of the monarchic polygamy.[11]

Some adopted a strongly negative perspective. R. Simeon b. Yohai interprets "in love" to mean "harlot-love" (*Songs R.* 1:1:10; *j. Sanh.* 2:6) and thus sinful. R. Eleazar b. R. Jose the Galilean said that these women caused him to sin by having marital relations with him without warning him when they were ritually impure (*Songs R.* 1:1:10).

Others sought to exonerate Solomon of any wrong-doing. R. Joshua b. Levi said that the biblical injunction was only against marriage (*Songs R.* 1:1:10) while 1 Kgs 11:1-2 does not necessarily indicate marriage. And still others find Solomon praiseworthy. R. Jose b. Halafta (a fourth generation tanna) translated "in love" to mean that Solomon converted them to Judaism and thus made them beloved of God (*Songs R.* 1:1:10; *j. Sanh.* 2:6).

Again, the various rabbinic views of this aspect of Solomon's life can be most readily accounted for by examining the political positions of the aggadists with respect to hellenization and relations with governmental authorities (both the Romans and their representatives, the Exilarch and Patriarch). R. Simeon b. Yohai violently hated the Romans (*Mekhilta BeShalakh* 2:1), comparing the Romans to serpents and asserting that the best of them was to be killed. In view of his background it is possible to understand his disapproval of Solomon, who dealt extensively with idolaters, as well as his dissatisfaction with the Patriarch who negotiated extensively with Rome.

The Patriarch Rabban Gamaliel maintained relations with other nations to such an extent that permission was granted to him and his family to study Greek, a privilege not granted to others (*b. Soṭa* 49b). It is in view of this information that one can understand R. Simeon b. Yohai's negative assessment of Solomon; just as Solomon was misled in foreign affairs (Tanhuma Buber 2:18), so was Rabban Gamaliel. R. Simeon b. Yohai accuses Solomon of dealing with needless knowledge, a guarded criticism of Rabban Gamaliel's preoccupation with the study of Greek and arguing with philosophers and early Christians. These intellectual endeavors and dealings with leaders of Rome would have been anathema to the extremist R. Simeon b. Yohai. In line with his

[11] See A. A. Halevi, *Aggadot ha-Amoraim* (Tel Aviv: Dvir, 1978) 421-22.

religious extremism and critical attitude towards the Patriarch, he says that Solomon's love for his many foreign wives was harlot-love, therein being his sin (*Songs R.* 1:1:10).

Similarly, R. Simeon b. Yohai's colleague, R. Jose the Galilean, supported the ideology of his good friend; neither had kind words for Rome or for non-Jews in general. It was R. Jose the Galilean who said that Solomon had intercourse with his foreign wives while they were ritually forbidden to him.

R. Jose bar Halafta, who actually supported Solomon's taking foreign wives (by interpreting "in love" to mean that he made them beloved to God), was on cordial terms with the Patriarch Rabban Simeon b. Gamaliel and also taught Rabbi, who likewise admired R. Jose b. Halafta to such an extent that Rabbi deferred to his judgment (*b. Šabb.* 51a; *b. Yebam.* 105b).[12] R. Jose b. Halafta might well be expected to give unflinching support to the Patriarch even under difficult circumstances such as these. Of all Solomon's wives, none aroused as much rabbinic ire as Pharaoh's daughter. It is reported that when Solomon married Pharaoh Necho's daughter it infuriated God and set him against Jerusalem (*b. Nid.* 70b; *Lev. R.* 12:5). R. Levi (a Palestinian amora who flourished in the third quarter of the 3rd century) said that on their wedding day the angel Michael descended and planted a reed in the sea which gathered mud around it and eventually it became the site of Rome (*j. Abod. Zar.* 1:2; *b. Sanh.* 21b; in *b. Šabb.* 56b, the same comment is attributed to Rab Judah instead of R. Isaac). This may allegorically indicate that the marriage heralded a weakening of Israel's moral fiber which eventually resulted in the conquest of Jerusalem by the Roman Empire.

According to another opinion, Solomon caused Pharaoh's daughter to convert. Although there was a practice not to accept converts during the reigns of David and Solomon (lest the conversion have been motivated by hopes of economic prosperity), an exception was made in the case of Pharaoh's daughter, whose own wealth was enough to ensure that financial benefits were not a factor (*b. Yebam.* 76b). Even as a convert, however, Pharaoh's daughter would have been a first-generation proselyte, while only third-generation proselytes were permitted in marriage to Israelites (*b. Yebam.* 76b). Since this restriction was still in force in the rabbinic era (*b. Yebam.* 78a), even her conversion would not have qualified her to be joined in marriage to Solomon.

---

[12] See also Margalioth, *Encyclopedia*, p. 753.

Rab Papa (a 4th century, fifth generation Babylonian amora) maintained that Solomon's marriage to Pharaoh's daughter was never carried out according to Jewish law, and was thus invalid (*b. Yebam.* 76b). Although 1 Kgs 11:12 uses the term "in love," allowing considerable rabbinic latitude in interpretation, 1 Kgs 3:1 refers specifically to marriage and is not so readily circumvented. Rab Papa explains that Solomon's love was so great that Scripture regards them as if they were married even though the actual ritual never took place (*b. Yebam.* 76b); this, too, seems designed to exculpate Solomon.

9. The Temple

The building of the Temple was regarded by the rabbis as the pinnacle of Solomon's accomplishments. When Solomon completed the Temple, the work of Creation was finally considered complete; hence his name: Shlomo = shalem = complete (*Pesikta Rabbati* 6:6). Solomon accomplished the building in seven years, even though it took thirteen years to build his own house (*Songs R.* 1:1:5). This is regarded as a credit to Solomon, indicating that he did not tarry in building the Temple in contrast with David who first built his own house and only later wished to secure a House of God.

R. Judah relates that during the building of the Temple Solomon did not drink any wine. After its completion, he took Bethiah, Pharaoh's daughter as a wife, drank wine that night and overslept, delaying the dedication of the Temple. R. Haggai (a third-fourth generation Babylonian amora emigré to Palestine) reported in the name of R. Isaac that Jeroboam, in the company of one thousand members of his tribe, entered the royal chambers and reprimanded him (*Lev. R.* 12:5). Jeroboam was sharply rebuked by God for this lapse in manners; public criticism of the king was under no conditions acceptable (*Lev. R.* 12:5).

Aberbach and Smolar suggest that "the defence of the constituted authorities and especially of the Davidic dynasties—as continued by the Patriarchate in Palestine and the Exilarchate in Babylonia—against all critics and detractors, is the primary motive of this 'interpretation' of history which bears no relationship whatever to the historical persons of Solomon and Jeroboam."[13] According to their analysis, Solomon

[13] M. Aberbach and L. Smolar, "Jeroboam and Solomon: Rabbinic Interpretations," *JQR* 59 (1968) 118-152; quote, p. 131.

represents the Patriarch Judah II. If the Patriarch assumes the wrong course, his public has the right to criticize him, but only in private, as public reprimand was likely to undermine the dignity and authority of the Patriarch.

The authors suggest that this was veiled criticism of popular preachers such as R. Jose of Maon (a second generation Palestinian amora) who stirred discontent and unrest among the people. Jeroboam's removal of his phylacteries in the presence of Solomon is considered an act of disrespect. Rab Nahman, according to Aberbach and Smolar, "sharply insisted that even a minor act of disrespect—such as taking off his phylacteries in Solomon's presence—constituted an act of rebellion."[14]

R. Oshaia (a third generation Palestinian amora) said that when Solomon built the Temple he placed in it precious golden trees which produced fruit in the same season as the trees of the field. When the wind blew, it caused the fruit to fall (or they dropped off) (*b. Yoma* 21b; *Songs R.* 3:10:3) and these were a source of income for the priests (*b. Yoma* 39b). According to *Songs R.* 3:10:3, the income from the sale of the fruit was used for the repair of the Temple. These trees dried up when idolaters entered, but will be restored in the future (*Songs R.* 3:10:3; *b. Yoma* 21b).

R. Oshaia (a poverty-stricken Palestinian amora) was generally critical of the Patriarch. R. Oshaia did not approve of the taxes imposed by Rabbi Judah II (Nesi'a), or of the lavish lifestyle he enjoyed. He understood the fact that the priests in Solomon's day were independent of Solomon's unfair taxation and did not benefit from his ill-gotten wealth. Wise members of his audience might have concluded that there was merit in such independence. The comment was at once both subtly critical of Solomon and laudatory of those priests independent of him. By analogy, it is critical of Rabbi Judah II (Nesi'a), who imposed and extended taxes, and lauds Rabbi, who refused to benefit from them. R. Oshaia's message was that scholars like himself (subsisting without much help from the Patriarch) were in the tradition of the priests of the Temple. It is important to note, however, that there are many stories recounting prosperity of the past in contrast to the poverty of the present; the concept of decline following the destruction of the Temple was a recurring rabbinic theme (e.g. *b. Soṭa* 49a).

Another instance of ancestral merit was in Solomon's thwarted attempt to bring the Ark into the Sanctuary; the dimensions of the Holy

---

[14] *Ibid.*, p. 130.

of Holies proved to be too snug a fit. Solomon called upon the merit of David and God saved him from national public embarrassment by allowing the Ark to enter (*b. Sanh.* 107b; *Tanhuma Buber* 2:22; *Midrash Pss* 24:1; *Num. R.* 14:3; *Exod. R.* 8:1). R. Berekiah (a fourth generation Palestinian amora) indicated that, in fact, David came to life and pleaded on Solomon's behalf (*Songs R.* 7:8:8:1). Solomon was also forced to call on David's merit during the dedication of the Temple; he prayed that fire descend upon the altar, but he was not answered until he called in his father's name (*Exod. R.* 44:2).

It is possible that here Rabbi Judah II (Nesi᾽a) is again being compared with Solomon. Just as Solomon required the merit of his ancestor David to save him from national disgrace, so too should the Patriarch Judah II avoid unpatriotic collaboration by following the model of his father Rabban Gamaliel III, who never collaborated with Rome.

10. Conclusion

How was Solomon represented in Jewish texts of the hellenistic era? Jewish traditions did not exist in (or develop in) a vacuum. The hellenized narratives described in this chapter were developed by and presented to people who were familiar with the biblical account as well as with earlier oral traditions.

But in the era of hellenization, Solomon was portrayed in Jewish tradition not simply as an ancient monarch or as the king of Israel in its greatest era. Instead, he was an individual whose successes and failures in religious, moral, and political domains were similar to situations that arose in the hellenistic era. In a very real sense, these aggadic narratives teach us more about the rabbinic response to hellenization than about the details of Solomon's life. Ultimately, that is the essence of both the aggadic enterprise and of modern scholarship.

THE VALUE OF SOLOMON'S AGE FOR THE BIBLICAL READER

DAVID JOBLING

My title was kindly supplied for me by the editor, though he knew that what I would offer under this title would be an only lightly revised version of an earlier essay with a different title.[1] But I am happy with the new title. It implies that "Solomon's Age" is not a preserve of historians, but is the name of a piece of literature constructed for real ancient readers. (These readers, I believe, lived nowhere near to the time of the historical Solomon. The literary text of Solomon's Age in 1 Kings, like the rest of biblical narrative, I assume to have reached a stable form only in very late post-exilic times.) And of course Solomon's Age has had readers ever since, including you, my readers.

The word "value" is also apt for a text which includes, as I will show, so very much economic discourse. What is the value of a literary *work*? For its first readers, for its readers now? How is that value related to my work of writing, your work of reading? In the terms I shall later propose, is the economics of reading the Bible a real or an ideal economics? These are questions directly related to our text, particularly to its economic reading of wisdom.

My text, like the biblical one (see 1 Kgs 3:5), is a product of dreamwork. The shape of this essay came to me, more or less whole, in a dream. This occurred the night after I delivered the first oral version of an essay on Psalm 72. That essay, in its eventually published form, is a precursor and companion piece to the present essay.[2]

In that essay, I applied to Ps 72 a method of Marxist literary reading suggested by Fredric Jameson. Based on the theory of historical "modes of production," the method consists of reading a text in relation to the social formation which generated it, and in particular of correlating its semantic contradictions with social contradictions (whether these be

---

[1] D. Jobling, "'Forced Labor': Solomon's Golden Age and the Question of Literary Representation," *Semeia* 54 (1991) 57-76.

[2] D. Jobling, "Deconstruction and the Political Analysis of Biblical Texts: A Jamesonian Reading of Psalm 72," *Semeia* 59 (1992) 95-127. That the two essays were published in reverse order is an accident of history.

analyzed as inherent in a given mode of production, or as the result of conflict, within a given social formation, between the dominant mode of production and traces of other modes). Taking the psalm as a rather pure expression of the ideology of the "Asiatic" or "tributary" mode of production,[3] I relate tensions in it to contradictions inherent in that mode, but also to the possible continuing ideological power of an earlier "egalitarian" mode.[4] The first part of the psalm (vv. 1-7), I suggest, creates out of three terms (king, people, God) a system for perfect and permanent prosperity (what in the present essay I shall call "ideal" economics). The second part (vv. 8-17) adds another term (foreign nations) and cannot evoke to the same extent an ideal state of affairs (the contradictions stand out more clearly).

This essay is a direct continuation of the same program of work. My text, the 1 Kings account of Solomon's reign, stands, I shall claim, in ideological continuity with Ps 72, manipulating mostly the same terms (king, God, Israel, foreign nations) to the same end, the evocation of an ideal state of affairs. But the work going on here is much more complex and conflictual than in the psalm for at least two reasons. First, a long narrative text (itself only one section of a very much longer one) is less apt for evoking a closed system than a short piece of liturgy. Second, the narrating voice in 1 Kings is much less caught up in the system it evokes than is the praising voice in the psalm. It acknowledges a long span of time and a radical change of circumstances between the time of the telling and the time of which it tells. Unlike the psalm, the narrative refers to an ideal *which has been lost*, evokes it precisely *as lost*.

The account of Solomon's reign belongs to the genre of narrative which tells of a past Golden Age and a subsequent fall. The term "Golden Age" comes from classical mythology.[5] I exploit it here, as I did in an earlier reading of Gen 2-3,[6] not for specific themes which classical and biblical texts have in common (though I shall note a few), but

[3] See also D. Jobling, "Feminism and 'Mode of Production' in Ancient Israel: Search for a Method," *The Bible and the Politics of Exegesis: Essays in Honor of Norman K. Gottwald on His Sixty-Fifth Birthday* (eds. D. Jobling, P. L. Day, and G. T. Sheppard; Cleveland: Pilgrim, 1991) 239-51.

[4] See N. K. Gottwald, *The Tribes of Yahweh: A Sociology of the Religion of Liberated Israel, 1250-1050 B.C.E.* (Maryknoll, NY: Orbis, 1979).

[5] For a full treatment, see A. O. Lovejoy and G. Boas, *Primitivism and Related Ideas in Antiquity* (Baltimore: Johns Hopkins University, 1935). The supplementary essays there extend the scope to other ancient literatures, including biblical.

[6] D. Jobling, *The Sense of Biblical Narrative II: Structural Analyses in the Hebrew Bible* (JSOTSup 39; Sheffield: JSOT, 1986) 17-43.

for structural features. All Golden Age mythology entails, in one way or another, an essential contradiction. If the Golden Age represented the absolute ideal, then it could not have come to an end. For if it came to an end, there must have been something in it that was susceptible of change. But this implies that it was not the absolute ideal. *Reductio ad absurdum.* To say that it came to an end through external causes is merely to shift this contradiction to another place. Thus any depiction of a primal Golden Age will contain, and can be analyzed to expose, elements or germs of that diminished, "real," present world to which it is supposed to stand in utter contrast. The contrast between ideal and real must inevitably prove partial, forced, artificial. But the analysis will be intricate, for the myth will tend to cover its tracks, to obscure the contradiction which generates it.[7]

In Gen 2-3, I traced in a number of semantic fields (culture, society/sexuality, vitality, knowledge) the attempt to depict the ideal of the past as the opposite of present reality. I showed how the attempt always failed because the real was always already present in the supposed ideal. The implicit ideal, I argued, was humanity without sexuality or sexual difference (but *male*, since this is the default value of "human" in the mindset at work), immortal, culturally undeveloped (a primitive agricultural existence), and lacking in knowledge (i.e., awareness that life could be other than this). But this ideal was of necessity never clearly defined in the text. It had to be established by analysis. Above all, it was obscured by the inevitable importation into the ideal state of affairs in the Garden of alien (real) features (above all, humanity as two sexes) which must inevitably lead to the fall.

I concluded my treatment of Gen 2-3 by suggesting that the text "works as a means of sorting out experience and dream, living with both, but opting for experience."[8] Golden Age mythology can be thought of as cultural dream-work, as wish-fulfillment.[9] In one of its most popular classical versions, the virgin Justice, who ruled over the Golden Age but has since withdrawn, "still at night ... appears to men."[10] Solomon's Golden Age begins with an appearance to the king in a dream by night

---

[7] C. Lévi-Strauss, "The Structural Study of Myth," *Structural Anthropology* (New York: Basic Books, 1963) 206-31.

[8] Jobling, *Sense of Biblical Narrative*, p. 40.

[9] S. Freud, *The Interpretation of Dreams* (Pelican Freud Library 4; Harmondsworth: Penguin, 1976) 200-13 and *passim*.

[10] Aratus, *Phaenomena* 96-136, in Lovejoy and Boas, *Primitivism*, pp 34-36; quote line 135.

(1 Kgs 3:5-14). The account of his reign is, I suggest, someone's troubled dream of national glory.

But whose? My purpose here, in addition to continuing the analysis of royal ideology in biblical texts, is to respond to a concern, voiced by some colleagues who read my work on Ps 72, that I am reverting to an outworn historicism. At issue here is the relationaship between history and literary representation. Jameson's slogan is "Always historicize!"[11] and having come to accept much of his interpretive framework, I can no longer bracket the historical question. But his is not the old liberal historicism. Rather, it is a materialist history borne along by ideological conflict, and it has come to terms (in various uneasy ways) with post-modern literary theory. Neither he nor I read a text as "representing" historical data. What the text represents is *the historical necessity of its production* (and, especially in the case of an ancient canonical text, its subsequent *reproduction*). The complex textual work going on in, say, a myth of a Golden Age is historically contingent, not universally predictable (though more or less similar features will occur from case to case). And the *particularity* of the work will correlate with the text's particular ideological location.

One particularity of 1 Kings is that, although it evokes a past ideal, it is not (in contrast to Gen 2-3 and the classical sources) a myth of *origins*. In its larger narrative context, Solomon's reign consummates an already long story. It is vital to realize how fundamental an ideological difference this creates between 1 Kings and Ps 72. 1 Kings is part of a narrative which tells of the origin of Israel's monarchy (1 Samuel). But the psalm, I argue, posits monarchy as eternal and changeless, as having had no historical beginning.[12] These different relationships in which the two texts stand to their common ideal is a *literary* finding, but it requires an *historical* accounting. I have little doubt that the deuteronomic text has imposed an historical framework on a preexisting monarchical ideology, for which Solomon was a unique emblem, and which was in essence and origin ahistorical.

I cannot, therefore, work in isolation from the developing hypotheses about the history of Israel and the history of the text (precarious as these

---

[11] F. Jameson, *The Political Unconscious: Narrative as a Socially Symbolic Act* (Ithaca, NY: Cornell University, 1981) 9.

[12] Jobling, "Deconstruction." Compare the understanding of kingship as a primal divine gift to humans in the Sumerian King List; A. L. Oppenheim, "Babylonian and Assyrian Historical Texts," *ANET*, pp. 265-66.

may be) which are implied in the very term "deuteronomic." I shall begin with literary analysis, using my usual idiosyncratic structuralist method. But in the latter part of the essay, I shall begin to consider the historical-ideological location of this text and resume discussion of the hermeneutical issues in relation to a recent discussion by Kim Parker and others[13] which seems to me to short-circuit historical analysis in a way which prejudices literary hypotheses.

1. The Literary Structure of the Narrative of Solomon's Reign

The 1 Kings account of Solomon's reign runs from 2:12 through chapter 11. My main thesis is that the narrative works to confine to the frame sections (2:12-46 and 11) anything negative about Solomon. 1 Kgs 2:12-46 depicts the beginning of his reign as a bloodbath, while chapter 11 records its end in equally negative terms, as the old king falls from grace. The result of this framing is that the long central section (chapters 3-10) can present the time of Solomon as a monarchical Golden Age. Formally speaking, 2:46b serves as an opening frame for this central section. A closing frame is less clear, but 11:4, "when Solomon was old," creates a temporal separation from what has preceded.

This framing of chapters 3-10 is artificial and tendentious. At the beginning, the artifice is patent in the use of the technique of "resumption," whereby 2:46b repeats 2:12b.[14] This technique enables Solomon's reign to begin again from scratch, as it were, in an appearance of innocence. The artificiality at the end, in the separation of chapter 11 from chapters 3-10, will appear in various features of the analysis. But I shall maintain (against Parker) that the text works to establish exactly this separation.

That chapters 3-10 function as unit is further indicated by an intricate literary structuring based on major themes: Solomon's wisdom, his building work, and his relations (in economic and other ways) to his own people and to foreigners, particularly women. The following structure emerges:

---

[13] K. I. Parker, *Wisdom and Law in the Reign of Solomon* (Lewiston, NY: Edwin Mellen, 1989).

[14] Compare my remarks on a similar case, Josh 24:29-30 = Judg 2:8-9, in Jobling, *Sense of Biblical Narrative*, p. 62.

A Dream-theophany at Gibeon (3:1-15)
B Women and Wisdom (3:16-28)
C Administration and wisdom (chapter 4)
D Contract with Hiram of Tyre (5:1-12)[15]
E Corvée[16] (5:13-18)
F Building of temple and palace (chapters 6-8)
A' Theophany (dream?) (9:1-9)
D' Contract with Hiram (9:10-14)
E' Corvée (9:15-28)
B' Woman and wisdom (10:1-13)
C' Wealth and wisdom (10:14-29)

This scheme oversimplifies in places (notably in C and E'), but the pattern that emerges is convincing. Around a center (F) are arranged two sections, each of which begins with a theophany (A, A'), and which, to a striking degree, cover the same issues. The first theophany is in a dream. The second is not specifically said to be a dream, but the words "as he had appeared to him at Gibeon" (9:2) might imply this.

2. Analysis by Semantic Fields

In this section I shall begin by analyzing in our text the semantic fields of economics and sexuality to show how the Golden Age conceptuality fares in each. I shall then turn to the field of wisdom, which seems to me to provide the clue to what is going on in the first two fields.

A. *Economics*

There is a vast amount of economic discourse in 1 Kgs 3-10. An *ideal* economics of natural abundance predominates.[17] But it stands in tension with a secondary economics built on the "reality principle." In real economics any acquisition by one party diminishes another's store. Ideal economics, on the other hand, allows for one party to win without anyone else losing (Ps 72:1-7 develops a mechanism for ideal economics[18]).

[15] In chapters 4-5, I use the NRSV's versification and chapter division, which is more appropriate to the content than the MT tradition.

[16] Corvée is the standard term for forced labor.

[17] This is in line with the major strand of Golden Age mythology that Lovejoy and Boas, *Primitivism*, 10 and *passim*, refer to as "soft primitivism."

[18] See Jobling, "Deconstruction."

In fact, this dual economics repeats itself in two different spheres: the internal economics of Israel and external (international) trade. Hence we need to identify four clusters of texts.

1) Under ideal internal economics, all of Israel prospers by Solomon's accumulation of wealth. This is most plainly stated in 4:20, 25, but a general prosperity seems to be celebrated also in 10:21, 27.

2) Under ideal external economics the nations of the world are glad to increase the wealth of Solomon and there is no indication that this is a hardship or a diminution of their own wealth. This is particularly the tenor of chapter 10 (cf. vv. 10, 24-25), but 4:21, 24 suggests something similar.

3) Under real internal economics, Solomon sets up a powerful administrative apparatus throughout Israel, geared in particular to the provisioning of the royal court (4:1-19) and imposes forced labor (corvée) on the people (5:13-18, cf. 4:6). In this perspective, Israel does not bask in Solomon's wealth, but is forced to create it.

4) Under real external economics, Solomon enters into trading deals with Hiram, King of Tyre (5:7-12, 7:13-14, 9:10-14). The general impression is that these deals were unfavorable to Solomon. In 5:7-12 we find Israel exporting staples and importing luxury goods, a classic situation of economic weakness. The same weakness is suggested by the necessity, in 7:13-14, of importing skilled labor. 9:10-14 leaves an unclear impression as to who came off best in the last encounter between Solomon and Hiram, but by any account it was a hard-headed business deal.

In relation to these clusters, 9:20-22 seems to play a special role. By its claim (in defiance of 5:13-18) that corvée was imposed only on the former inhabitants of the land, and not on Israelites, it functions as a sort of safety valve for the economic tensions. The peoples "left in the land" when Israel arrived are in a sense neither Israelites nor foreigners. This perhaps means that their labor can be exploited without prejudice to ideological statements about either internal or external economics.

Ideal economics entails a theory of surplus value, according to which wealth can generate, of its own accord, a surplus over and above the value of anyone's labor. Such a theory allows for one class to prosper without their prosperity's being at anyone else's expense.[19] The text gen-

[19] The separation of prosperity from labor is a recurrent theme of Golden Age mythology. See, for example, Hesiod, *Works and Days* 112-13, 117-19: "Like gods they lived ... remote from toil and grief ... For the fruitful earth spontaneously bore them abundant fruit

erates a fiction in which, under the aegis of Solomon, everyone prospers, whether Israelite or foreigner, while at the same time an unlimited surplus accrues to Solomon himself. But the text also subverts this fiction through its real economics, in the sections which suggest that wealth comes only by exchange.

After all this economic discourse in chapters 3-10, it is striking that there is none in chapter 11. Though in a general sense prosperity was no doubt a casualty of Solomon's fall from grace, neither his offence nor its consequences are given any specifically economic dimensions. This seems remarkable in view of the Golden Age conceptuality in which the fall from the ideal is precipitated by the subversive presence of "real" features within the ideal state. In the Kings narrative, real economic features have been incorporated rather comfortably, it seems, into the ideal. It is not the tension between ideal and real *economics* that precipitates the fall. It is something else.

B. *Sexuality*

Just as Gen 2-3, in my analysis, evokes an ideal of asexuality, so 1 Kgs 3-10 excludes, in a remarkable way, any sexual activity on Solomon's part (belying his traditional reputation, based on chapter 11 and also on the Song of Solomon).[20] The reader can hardly fail to be struck by the absence of the theme of royal succession, so central to chapters 1, 2, and 11 (and, of course, to the David narrative). But something more radical is going on, which can be best appreciated by looking at the annalistic notes in 11:42 and 14:21. Solomon reigned 40 years. His son Rehoboam was 41 when he succeeded. *Ergo*, Rehoboam was not conceived during Solomon's reign! 4:11, 15 refer to "daughters" of Solomon. But they are introduced very early in the account as being already of marriageable age, so that they too can easily be assumed to have been born before Solomon's accession. Without directly affirming Solomon's sexual inactivity during the Golden Age, the text works hard to keep it as a possibility.

The opening of chapter 11 reveals the artificiality of this textual work. 11:1-4 indicates a state of affairs (liaison with foreign women) which

---

without stint. And they lived at ease ...;" translation from Lovejoy and Boas, *Primitivism*, p. 27.

[20] In one of Hesiod's scenarios there were no women in the Golden Age, Pandora being the origin of both women and evil; Hesiod, *Works and Days* 42-105, see Lovejoy and Boas, *Primitivism*, pp. 24, 196-99.

must have obtained throughout Solomon's reign. If having foreign wives is a cause of apostasy (11:2), and if Solomon had them all along, the claim that it was only in his old age that they led him astray lacks plausibility. But this artificiality only underlines the importance of the issue. Cutting the Gordian Knot, the text has simply expelled the foreign women from the narrative of chapters 3-10.

This procedure can be illuminated by analogy with a different semantic field, that of war and peace. According to 4:24, Solomon enjoyed universal peace. The reader anticipates that the account of the fall in chapter 11 will tell how peace turned to war. So it does (11:14-25), but it gives the game away by admitting that Rezon was an enemy "all the days of Solomon" (11:25)! Just as with the theme of sexuality, the Golden Age chapters have attempted to expel the theme of warfare beyond their boundaries and into Solomon's old age. But the attempt is equally implausible and even less successful.

There is, though, an apparent exception to the exclusion of sexuality. The Solomon of the Golden Age does have a consort, the daughter of Pharaoh (3:1). Still, there is no indication of sexual relations (in sharp contrast to the references to "love" in 11:1-2), and, of course, nothing of the birth of children. All Pharaoh's daughter does, after she is first introduced, is to move house (7:8, 9:24).[21] But why, if she subverts the work of the text, is she introduced at all, and indeed *at the first possible moment* (3:1)? I suggest that we have here a striking example of how Golden Age thinking has formed our text. The negative/real must be already present in representations of the Golden Age, and Pharaoh's daughter functions in chapters 3-10 to establish that the course of Solomon's eventual fall is already present in the time of his glory. When his fall does come, she is again the very first person mentioned (11:1).

If economic discourse is absent from the account of the fall in chapter 11, sexual discourse is central to it. Sexuality not only marks, but in some ways causes, the fallen state. Though the text tries to insist that *foreign* women were the problem, it is hard to make mere foreignness into a negative after all the positive treatment of foreigners in chapters 3-10. The problem the text defines (the power of female wiles over an aging man) is a problem of sexuality as such. The semantic field of sexuality, unlike that of economics, fits convincingly into the typical Golden Age conceptuality.

---

[21] The version in 2 Chr 8:11 captures and even extends the misogynist tendency; it is not fitting for a woman to dwell in holy space.

C. *Wisdom*

Solomon's wisdom is a pervasive theme in 1 Kgs 3-10, specifically in the following sections: 3:5-14, 16-28; 4:29-34; 5:7, 12; 10:1-10, 23-25. It is put forward, in a very clear way, as the thing that drives the ideal economics. It is the surplus value which, residing in Solomon, enables him to accomplish his economic miracle. Wisdom is implicated to an extraordinary degree in the economic organization of our text, including the economic tensions.

I begin by noting, at the end of chapter 4, the quantification of wisdom. "And God gave Solomon wisdom and understanding beyond measure, and largeness of mind like the sand on the seashore" (4:29). This metaphor was used just a few verses earlier (4:20) for the exploding population of Judah and Israel in Solomon's time. His wisdom, like the population of his domain, is a *quantity*, even if both exceed the scope of any census.[22] But, oddly, there is a "census" of Solomon's wisdom, just a few verses later: "He also uttered three thousand proverbs; and his songs were a thousand and five" (4:32).

This quantification enables wisdom to be related to quantifiable economic values. There are several places where it appears alongside, and at the same level as, other commodities. Most of these references are in chapter 10; "wisdom and goods" (10:7), "in riches and wisdom" (10:23), and above all 10:4-5, where "the wisdom of Solomon" which the Queen of Sheba "saw" is juxtaposed to a whole series of goods: "the house that he had built, the food of his table, the seating of his officials,[23] the attendance of his servants ..., and his burnt offerings which he offered at the house of Yahweh." But the same logic governs 4:20-34, where the enumeration of Solomon's wisdom in verses 29-34 follows naturally upon the enumeration of other blessings of his reign in verses 20-28.

The possibility of *exchanging* wisdom for other goods is a further step in the same direction. Again, it is in chapter 10 that this happens most clearly. How else can verses 24-25 be read than as a fair exchange of luxury goods for wisdom? Likewise, the material goods which the Queen of Sheba gives to Solomon (10:10) seem to be in recompense for all the wisdom she has seen. Similarly, if less tightly, chapter 4 relates

---

[22] It is fascinating to compare 1 Kgs 4:20 with David's disastrous attempt to take a census just a few chapters earlier, in 2 Sam 24!

[23] I take this to be a reference to the scope and hierarchical organization of Solomon's bureaucracy, the most prominent political feature of the tributary state.

the tribute paid by the nations (4:21) to their hearing Solomon's wisdom (4:34). One is tempted to ask how many proverbs (4:32) one could get for a talent of gold.

Does anything in Israel's internal economics correspond to this very clear exchange value of wisdom in external economics? Solomon's wisdom certainly represents a benefit to Israel. But this is usually expressed in a general, not overtly economic, way (3:8-9, 28; 4:20, 25 in relation to 4:29-34; 10:9). 1 Kgs 10:8, however, hints at something more specifically economic. When the Queen of Sheba exclaims, "Happy are your men; happy are these your servants, who continually stand before you and hear your wisdom!" she posits a sort of surplus in the economic relationship between master and servant. Servants so uniquely privileged ought not to demand much in the way of material pay! Perhaps Israelites will even march off more willingly to the labor gangs (5:13-18) when they know (from the immediately preceding verse) that "Yahweh [has given] Solomon wisdom!"

The capstone to this analysis is 3:5-14, the first mention of wisdom in our text. Here, wisdom appears as surplus value in the most direct way. The whole point of the passage is that if one gains wisdom one also gains other goods as a natural surplus. The logic at work here will not, of course, bear much examination, for the exchange of wisdom is not like the exchange of wealth. Solomon can exceed all others in both wisdom and riches only because he grows rich at real expense to them, while they grow wise at no expense to him. In reality, wisdom *exceeds* the system of exchange. The trick accomplished in 3:5-14 is to make it into *a symbol of excess within the system of exchange*. The uniqueness of wisdom, its incommensurability with other values, is maintained. But at the same time it acquires a unique *commodity* value, a special "exchange but over-above exchange" value which renders ideal economics plausible in the presence of real economic conditions.

The logic of 3:5-14 can scarcely be maintained in a context of real economics, as the references to wisdom in 5:7, 12 suggest. These two verses frame a piece of real external economics, Solomon's deal with Hiram. First Hiram (5:7), and then the narrator (5:12), laud Solomon's wisdom in making this deal, despite the fact that it is clearly a disadvantageous one. Surely Hiram's praise is tongue-in-cheek. Whether or not the text intends it, a modern sensibility sees irony here. The high-flown wisdom of the rest of our text is made to look ridiculous.

I entitled an earlier version of this part of my essay "The Commodification of Wisdom in 1 Kings 3-10."[24] Arguably an even better title would be "The Sapientialization of Wealth." At any rate, wisdom is correlated positively with wealth. On the other hand, it is correlated negatively with sexuality. The links here are less pervasive, but I note the following points. First, the account of Solomon's senile sexual folly in chapter 11 makes no reference to wisdom. Second, it is surely significant that Solomon proves his wisdom to or through women (3:16-28; 10:1-13). This form of relationship with women perhaps takes the place of a sexual one; indeed this dynamic seems close to the surface of the Queen of Sheba account. Third, Wisdom as sex-substitute may be present also at the very beginning of the account of Solomon's Golden Age. The wisdom literature sexualizes wisdom by the contrast and competition it often imagines between Dame Wisdom and the sexually seductive Foreign Woman.[25] We can easily read this contrast behind 1 Kgs 3. Though Solomon has a new bride, a foreign woman (3:1), it is Dame Wisdom who has his attention at night (3:5-14)! Fourth, is there not a resonance between the quantification of Solomon's women after the fall (11:3) and the quantification of his wisdom before (4:32)? In the fall, sex has been resubstituted for wisdom.

These contrasting linkages with wisdom mark the strikingly different treatments of economics and sexuality in relation to the Solomonic Golden Age. *All* that Solomon does economically, including the "real" and sometimes apparently stupid (5:7-12), is done "in wisdom" and can be contained within the ideal. On the other hand, sexuality *as such* is antithetical to wisdom, so that it must be radically excluded from the ideal.

---

[24] T. Bottomore, ed., *A Dictionary of Marxist Thought* (Oxford: Blackwell, 1983) s.v. "Commodity."

[25] See especially Prov 1-9, and on this, C. V. Camp, *Wisdom and the Feminine in the Book of Proverbs* (Bible and Literature 11; Sheffield: Almond, 1985); and C. Newsom, "Women and the Discourse of Patriarchal Wisdom: A Study of Proverbs 1-9," *Gender and Difference in Ancient Israel* (ed. P. L. Day; Minneapolis: Fortress, 1989) 142-60. In the section of Aratus' *Phaenomena* already referred to, in lines 105-107, it is said of the virgin who presided over the Golden Age, "They called her justice; and assembling the elders, either in the market place or in the wide streets, she spoke aloud urging judgments more advantageous to the people;" Lovejoy and Boas, *Primitivism*, pp. 34-35. Compare with this the depiction of Wisdom in Prov 1:20-21; 8:1-3.

3. An Alternative View of the Structure of the Solomon Traditions

In a book on which I have drawn considerably for my outline of 1 Kgs 3-10, Kim Parker reaches a different view of the structure of our text and exploration of the difference will help lead to the next stage of my discussion.[26] Parker includes in his scheme the whole of chapters 1-11. Chapters 1-2 and 11:14-43 he takes as a "frame story" and the rest he divides into two parts: chapters 3-8, "favorable to Solomon," and 9:1-11:13, "hostile to Solomon."

The point of difference between us lies in Parker's view of chapters 9-10 as entirely negative in their view of Solomon. The following comments cover his main arguments.[27] First, the theophany in 9:1-9 has a threatening tone, in sharp contrast to 3:5-14. I agree. Second, I tend to agree also that 9:10-14 gives the reader a negative impression of Solomon. Even if we see him here as gaining revenge, by getting the better of Hiram in an economic transaction, the episode certainly takes some of the glitter from the Golden Age. Third, I begin to disagree sharply with Parker over 9:15-23 and the issue of the corvée. He regards the earlier reference (5:13-18) as more positive towards Solomon, for example because it allows for breaks between periods of labor. But a stronger argument can surely be made for reading chapter 9 more positively than chapter 5. Chapter 5 indicates that the corvée was imposed on *Israelites*, which must be worse than imposing it only on foreigners (chapter 9). Fourth, while one can certainly read the reference to Pharaoh's daughter in 9:24 negatively, it is no more negative than those in 3:1 and 7:8. Fifth, Parker claims that in chapter 10 "A concern for the welfare of the people is transformed to a concern with self-glory and wealth."[28] But concern for the people's welfare is present in 10:9.

I agree with Parker that chapters 9-10 require special treatment. But I disagree with his claim that they transform into the negative, point by point, everything positive that was previously said about Solomon. The textual effects are much more complex than this. There is a perceptible downturn in the view of Solomon in 9:1-24. But for me this is canceled by what follows. 9:25-10:29 expresses towards Solomon an adulation certainly no less than that of chapters 3-8. If the Solomon market turns

[26] Parker, *Wisdom and Law*, pp. 39-56.
[27] *Ibid.*, pp. 85-96.
[28] *Ibid.*, p. 92.

briefly bearish, his shares by the end are of greater value than ever. The bottom line for me is that *any* negativity towards him in chapters 3-10 pales into insignificance when compared with the massive negativity of chapter 11.

4. Towards a Historical-Ideological Concept of the Deuteronomic Text

One of Parker's arguments is of particular interest, since it takes us out of the Solomon traditions in particular and into the "deuteronomic" in general. He invokes "the law of the king" (Deut 17:14-20), with its injunctions that the king not accumulate for himself "horses" (with reference presumably to military capability), "women," or "silver and gold."[29] In 1 Kgs 9-10, Solomon certainly accumulates plenty of gold and silver, and even horses (10:25-29). This links these chapters, in Parker's scheme, to the accumulation of women in chapter 11; all under the sign of the negative.

I disagree that chapters 9-10 differ qualitatively in these respects from chapters 3-5.[30] But to read the text my way is to create a contradiction which Parker avoids: How can it be right to accumulate gold, silver, and horses, but wrong to accumulate women? To establish my case, I have to explain why the deuteronomic account of Solomon is so selective in measuring him against the Mosaic charter in Deut 17:14-20. To be consistent, the text *ought* to assess Solomon Parker's way, ought to condemn the riches which (in my view) it celebrates. My response is implicit in the earlier part of this essay, but I need now to develop further a framework for understanding this contradiction between wealth and women, between economics and sexuality.

A. *The Conditionality Versus the Unconditionality of Divine Blessing*

As a preface, we need to consider another even more basic contradiction, between conditional and unconditional understandings of divine blessing. This, of course, is a major topic of all the deuteronomic work.

---

[29] *Ibid.*, p. 96. I used this passage similarly myself in Jobling, *Sense of Biblical Narrative* II, pp. 58-59.

[30] See my arguments in the preceding section; for riches, cf. 1 Kgs 4:21, for horses, 4:26, 28.

In my analysis of Gen 2-3, I suggested that the very first intrusion of the semantics of the "real" into the "ideal" is when Yahweh makes human existence in the garden conditional (Gen 2:17). For conditionality negates in principle the notion of a Golden Age. A conditional ideal is not ideal, for an unconditional one would be even better! Classical myths of the Golden Age scarcely ever use conditional formulations. But the conditional is characteristic of biblical, and above all of deuteronomic, discourse. It often comes into collision, though, with unconditional divine promises, such as those which guarantee the perpetuity of temple and monarchy.[31]

In 1 Kgs 3-10 (unusually in the deuteronomic work) the unconditional reigns, but not without subversion from the conditional. It is important to look closely at these dynamics. The Solomonic Golden Age comes in the wake of the most powerful assertion of the unconditional ever found in the deuteronomic work: the covenant with the house of David (2 Sam 7:11b-16). It is this unconditional which creates the very possibility of a monarchical Golden Age. But, as if 2 Sam 7 has conceded too much to the unconditional, typical deuteronomic conditional formulations intrude into the depiction of the Golden Age, with subversive effect. Nonetheless the unconditional (grounded not only in the monarchy, but also in the traditions surrounding Solomon's temple) remains in control.

For example, we can observe the unconditional beating back the threat of conditionality in 6:11-13. This is clearly a conditional formulation. Blessing for Israel depends on Solomon's obedience to Yahweh. But, by its allusion to 2 Sam 7, this passage ends up saying, in effect, "If you obey, then I will activate the promise which [according to 2 Sam 7:14-15] doesn't depend on your obedience." Unconditionality holds. We see a similar dynamic in Solomon's dedication speech in chapter 8. The speech repeatedly admits the logic of the conditional, when it refers to disasters which may happen "because [the people] have sinned" (8:33, for example). But the unconditional still triumphs, since remedy will be available through the influence of the temple (i.e., within the unconditional system). Even exile from the land (8:46-53) is boldly included among the things the temple can put right.

But the dynamic is different in 9:4-9. This passage begins with the unconditional, expressed in relation to both temple (9:3) and monarchy (9:4; cf. 6:12). But it turns the tables by threatening *the destruction of the*

[31] W. L. Humphreys, *Crisis and Story: Introduction to the Old Testament* (2nd ed.; Mountain View, Calif.: Mayfield, 1990) 33-43, 60-72, 168-75.

temple itself "if you turn aside" (9:6). Here it is the conditional which subverts the logic of the unconditional. I believe it is this triumph of the conditional which allows for the accumulation in chapter 9 of a considerable amount of material relatively negative to Solomon. But it is, as I have argued, a temporary triumph. The threats and problems pass and the king is back on his pedestal in chapter 10.

These passages leave the reader with the impression of an aimless back-and-forth between two powerful textual drives. Despite repeated attempts, deuteronomic conditionality is unable to finally call the shots in a text which is under the charm of the Golden Age. But there is perhaps a deeper logic, for which we must turn to the dream-theophany of chapter 3. "Dreams are unable to express an if," says Freud.[32] But chapter 3 does include a conditional, though it is a most peculiar one. Solomon, having chosen wisdom, is granted it, with riches and honor as surplus, unconditionally. Only at the very end (3:14) does a conditional appear and the only thing that is conditional is a long life to maximize his enjoyment of these unconditional blessings!

The reader may at first feel that this conditional is just a vacuous deuteronomic gesture. Yet it enters into a curious collusion with chapter 11. Solomon *does* live into old age (11:4), which implies (3:14) that he must have "walked in Yahweh's ways" throughout chapters 3-10. But precisely when he has achieved old age, he ceases so to walk! The logic is indeed dream-like, yet oddly compelling. The inaugural dream-theophany allows for Solomon's wisdom, riches, and honor to stand throughout chapters 3-10 under the sign of the unconditional. But conditionality is not abolished, merely deferred or marginalized. It is pushed to the end of the dream-theophany and it is kept at bay throughout chapters 3-10. When we reach chapter 11, though, we find that everything was conditional after all; conditional on something which up to that point had been successfully repressed, namely sexuality!

B. *Economics versus Sexuality*

After this detour, I return to the question from which this section began. To be true to their tradition, the deuteronomists ought to reject Solomon's accumulation of riches, horses, and wives. Their assessment of his reign ought to be *conditional* on his conduct in these matters. But in fact

[32] Freud, *Interpretation of Dreams*, p. 558.

(I summarize my earlier discussion) they take completely different views of economics and sexuality. The "reality principle" in economics appears freely and frequently in chapters 3-10, but real economics is kept subordinate to the ideal economics of the Golden Age. By contrast, no reality principle can be admitted for sexuality. The fiction is splendidly maintained, as far as chapter 10, that Solomon was not sexually active. When real sexuality appears at the beginning of chapter 11, it instantly breaks the spell and the "fall" occurs.

In terms of "the law of the king," the deuteronomists can live with, even celebrate, Solomon's multiplying of horses, silver, and gold, but they cannot stomach his multiplying wives. What Yahweh hates, what spoils his ideal order, is not economic offence, social injustice, and the like, but sexual offence, or even (as in Gen 2-3) sexuality as such. The theme of wisdom, as we have seen, fits perfectly into this divided attitude.

Our text, then, displays a powerful concern with economic matters, but displaces Solomon's fault from the economic into another sphere. This fits in with a sense I have of the deuteronomic work as coming out of an egalitarian ideology, but as having lost touch with it. The deep concern for economic and social justice which marks the legislation in Deuteronomy finds an echo in only a few sections of the Deuteronomic History (Judg 5; 1 Sam 2:1-10; 8:11-18; 1 Kgs 21, and, though more implicitly than explicitly, the Elijah and Elisha cycles). The deuteronomists, though they are (in the view of most historians of Israel) heirs of a tradition at best lukewarm to monarchy, have come to accept monarchy as representing the divine will for Israel. They accept the unconditional covenant with the house of David and when they try to posit an ideal past, a Golden Age, they put the 40 years of the reign of Solomon at least on a par with the 40 years of wandering in the desert.

Another sign of how deeply immersed our text is in the monarchical ideology lies in its assumption that the fate of the people depends on the king. The fall from the Golden Age must be accounted for in terms of *royal* fault. But what, in summary, is this fault? From the ideological location just outlined, it is not possible to locate the fault in normal monarchical practice, in any feature of the way monarchy systemically works (even though a passage like 1 Sam 8:11-18 could form the basis for such a critique). The fall must be "explained" in terms of something which is related to the king, but which is as marginal, accidental, and asystemic as possible.

The economic sphere is not available for this explanatory purpose, since it has been accepted as belonging to the essence of monarchy. But sexuality is readily available to account for the royal fault.[33] In a culture never far from misogyny, it possesses great potential for shifting the blame. Like the fall of the man in Gen 3, Solomon's fall takes on an accidental, or fatalistic, cast: not quite within his own power, not quite his own fault. Indeed, he almost reached the finishing line! After an exemplary sexual career (absurdly dressed out with the Golden Age theme of asexuality), it was only in old age that he allowed himself to be seduced.

Such fantasies falter, of course, as soon we realize that Solomon's sexual activity was, in fact, entirely systemic. As Deut 17:14-20 well knows, a king does not accumulate women because his lust just happens to be less controllable than other men's. Nor do the ones he accumulates just happen to include foreigners. This accumulation is no less systemic than gathering wealth or military capability.[34]

In line with a widespread trend in current biblical scholarship, I now see the deuteronomic work, and the biblical narrative in general, as reaching its canonical form very late, when Israel was part of the Persian or even Greek empire. I see it as the result of a centuries-long process of revision, designed to make it usable in a series of changing historical circumstances. The recreated past needs to satisfy two needs which are in uneasy relation to each other. It must provide both a way of accommodating to a problematic present, and a basis for future-oriented, utopian imagining. The creation of a past Golden Age serves this double purpose and I believe that, in the late post-exilic context I have described, Israelite historiography came powerfully under the charm of the Age of Solomon. The ideal past was monarchical, even imperial, like the experienced present. But the ideal empire was an Israelite, Yahwistic one. If all that stood, back then, between Israel and the indefinite continuance of the Golden Age was an old man's sexual weakness, need a new Golden Age be far away?[35]

---

[33] The treatment of sexuality is, of course, always political; see M. Bal, *Death & Dissymmetry: The Politics of Coherence in the Book of Judges* (Chicago: University of Chicago, 1988); Jobling, "Feminism;" and R. M. Schwartz, "Adultery in the House of David: The Metanarrative of Biblical Scholarship and the Narratives of the Bible," *Semeia* 54 (1991) 35-55.

[34] The deuteronomists, of course, express Solomon's fault in very general terms, as "going after other gods" (1 Kgs 11:4). But when they look for a more specific cause, their choice is instructive. There is no suggestion that trade, or international wisdom conferences, entail "going after other gods." But marrying foreign wives automatically does.

[35] In a soon to be published book on 1 Samuel (in the series *Berit Olam*, ed. David Cotter; Minneapolis: Liturgical), I take these thoughts in a different direction. Under the

5. Concluding Hermeneutical Thoughts

A. *Text and History*

Recently, many of us have determined to take as the object of our research "the text itself," rather than some history to which it might refer. To the extent that this is a reaction against tying meaning to the short-term details of history, I am still very much a part of it. The world of meaning which the text creates is not very bound to such details (too bad for us if it were, since we have little historical access to them). The world of meaning created by, say, an Israelite psalm of 800 BCE will scarcely differ from one of 700 BCE, though a century's worth of happenings intervened.

On the other hand, some literary approaches seem to assume that worlds of meaning don't change at all, that the symbolic values with which literature operates transcend the flux of history. This can lead to a questionable shortcut in interpretation, an assumption that the symbol-making and -breaking going on in the text can fuse, without further ado, with our own symbol-making and -breaking.

It is against this assumption that Jameson takes up arms.[36] His view of history identifies a multiplicity of modes of production and, in his analysis, a given mode of production constrains the entire processes of production, distribution and consumption of symbolic values (in the ideological process), as well as of material products (in the economic process). It constrains the production of consciousness itself, since consciousness is dialectically related to ideology, as its product and producer. The "same" symbolic values will not be really the same in texts produced within different modes of production. By the same token, the values of any given text will not *remain* the same when it is read within different modes of production. Hence it is illegitimate to separate literary analysis from historical hypotheses.

Such a point of view, of course, raises immediately the question of our

---

influence of Jacques Derrida's book, *Spectors of Marx*, I suggest that Israel is at some level aware of an entirely different kind of ideal past, an egalitarian pre-monarchical order like the one which Gottwald posits. But Israel is "aware" of this past as something *lost*, to such an extent that the awareness itself has been culturally repressed. Hence the compensatory need to exalt the time of the kings and belittle the time of the judges. But Israel continues always to be "haunted" (Derrida's key word, taken from the opening sentence of the Communist Manifesto) by this dim alternative past.

[36] Jameson, *Political Unconscious*, p. 283.

own consciousness as interpreters, and the ideological assumptions which produce it. Unless these are being examined, as part of the interpretive process itself, we must inevitably modernize. We will read the symbol-making and -breaking in an ancient text in terms of our own and suppose that we have identified the text's implicit view when we have rather projected our own view onto it.

B. *Reading the Solomon Traditions*

1 Kgs 3-10 is a text which looks back, from the perspective of a (sometime) present state of affairs, at a past state of affairs under King Solomon.[37] As I read this text, I perceive at least three consciousnesses. The first is not very different from that of Ps 72 and I suppose it to have been generated in the context of the pre-exilic Israelite attempt to function as a state under the tributary mode of production (see my analysis of the psalm).[38] The second consciousness, generated out of a radically different, egalitarian, mode of production,[39] presents claims which cannot be met within the constraints of the first. The third consciousness is a divided one, generated out of the attempt, only partially successful, to repress the second consciousness in favor of the first.

But there is another consciousness (or a variety of them) to be accounted for in the interpretive process: our own. The temptation to modernize the text, to relate its production of meaning to ours, is ever present. I have suggested a deuteronomic displacement of the critical issues in 1 Kgs 3-10 from the economic to the sexual realm. In connection with this I cannot help but think of religious groups in our own day which live with vast social crime more easily than with sexual peccadillos. Again, in identifying a "surplus value" in the economics of 1 Kgs 3-10, I deliberately reach out to the theory of surplus value proposed in Marx's critique of capitalism.[40] But any such connections must be made

---

[37] "Past" and "present" refer in the first instance to narrative time; the text's own production of temporality. The Solomon text does not indicate *how much* time has passed between its own present and the past of which it tells, nor specify qualitative differences between "then" and "now." But the Jamesonian mode of historical criticism is not content merely to live with this lack; it seeks to supply the lack.

[38] On Ps 72, Jobling, "Deconstruction." Though I have no interest in its literary reconstruction, I find it hard to doubt that this consciousness expressed itself in some earlier form, known to the deuteronomists, of the tradition of Solomon's reign as a Golden Age.

[39] Jobling, "Feminism."

[40] T. Bottomore, ed., *A Dictionary of Marxist Thought* (Oxford: Blackwell, 1983) s.v. "Surplus value," "Surplus value and profit."

only in the awareness that these apparently similar features exist within different sets of laws, within different consciousnesses. For example, the surplus value in 1 Kings is produced and processed within a consciousness which can hold mythic and realistic together in a way not available to us. Comparative analysis of our own and the text's ideological frameworks will therefore be indispensible.

These considerations provide a framework for reconsidering Parker's analysis. When he reads 1 Kgs 9-10 as negative to Solomon, it is on basically economic grounds (that Solomon pursued his own interests rather than the people's, for example). It seems to me likely that Parker is here modernizing. He is reading the text from a leftish academic perspective and therefore with eyes apt to take a certain view of its economics. From this perspective, which many of us share, we read about the corvée, or about unlimited accumulation of wealth, with distaste. Parker correctly senses a clash of consciousnesses in our text, but does not examine his assumptions about the (dis)similarities between these consciousnesses and his own. So he ascribes to the text the same sensitivities to economic data that people like himself have. Put another way, he reads the text with eyes prepared by Gottwald's unearthing of biblical egalitarianism, missing the question of whether the deuteronomists were any longer capable of reading their past in this way.

C. *"Forced Labor"*

I concluded the first version of this essay with a contrast between two kinds of literary hermeneutic in biblical studies. The first is a hermeneutic of "every man under his vine and under his fig tree" (1 Kgs 4:25; I retain the sexist language deliberately). This is a way of describing recent approaches to the Bible as "pure" literature, approaches which are informed by a high literary aesthetic (often derived from the New Criticism), and which find in the Bible literary values of the highest order. Such readings pluck fruit that the Bible as literary text freely offers, and the fruit is abundant, since until a couple of decades ago few were harvesting it! I suggested that this sort of work is done under the protection of a cultural and academic system which is quite content that we not explore the text's historical conditioning, or our own. Against it I set a literary hermeneutic of "forced labor;" the labor of interpreting the text and ourselves as involved in ideological systems of production, distribution, and consumption. The labor involved in comparative analysis of the modes of literary production, within the Bible and within the hermeneutical process, is not to be shirked, even though it divert us from admiration of the text's high literary qualities.

This ploy, which was already given to me in the dream that generated the essay and which provided the earlier title, "Forced Labor," is neat enough. It enables me to connect the dynamics in the text with the dynamics of its interpretation, as I try to do in all my readings. But it falls into the very trap against which I have been warning, for it assumes that metaphors like "every man under his vine and under his fig tree" and "forced labor" can simply be borrowed from the ancient text and applied to our own situations. What happens to such metaphors if we translate them into categories emerging from real analysis of our own capitalist mode of production? Will they function symbolically in ways compatible with how they functioned in ancient times?

The terms conjure readily the Marxist categories of "alienated" and "unalienated" labor.[41] Alienated labor is work done for mere survival in the capitalist system, work which disregards the workers' subjectivity and turns them into objects. If I try to relate this term to my own history, what comes first to mind is my gut reaction to traditional historical criticism. Early in my career I came to experience it as a set of alien(ating) assumptions under which I had been trained and indentured to work. In that situation serious literary approaches of any kind seemed to offer the possibility of unalienated labor on the Bible.

That experience was an authentic one and it remains a critical moment in my history. But my response to it no longer satisfies me. To think in these terms seems like a false appropriation of the historical privilege of those whose labor is really forced, those who by reason of class, race, gender, nationality, and so on, have little or no choice about their labor. (Of course, these categories define effective power structures also within academic biblical studies. Nonetheless, anyone who has achieved even a lowly position within academia has done so on the backs of others who have still less power). As one with the privilege of spending my life at relatively unalienated labor, I feel "forced" to work in solidarity with those who have less or none of this privilege.

A revolution is going on in biblical studies and the turn towards literature, or "reading," is a major part of it. But unless this revolution stays linked with political transformation, it can only be seen as the work of

[41] T. Bottomore, ed., *A Dictionary of Marxist Thought* (Oxford: Blackwell, 1983) s.v. "Alienation."

an intellectual class which accepts its leisured marginalization. The reader for whom I have tried in this essay to assess the value of Solomon's age is not, therefore, some "general reader" with no particular location, but one who is asking questions about what it means to read the Bible within the culture we all inhabit.

POSTLUDE AND PROSPECTS

LOWELL K. HANDY

1. POSTLUDE: WHERE WE STAND

The "Age of Solomon" exists as a historical construct. No matter what happened during the reign of the king of Judah and Israel known as Solomon, the reconstruction of that period of time in that place determines what the "age" was like. Little data remains from which to produce an accurate representation of the kingdoms of Judah and Israel under this ruler. The most extensive portrayals will continue to be those that take the majority of the biblical accounts and the maximum amount of archaeological data together as a mutually supportive foundation for forming their picture of Solomon and his kingdom. Those who find the biblical narratives totally untrustworthy and insist on finding actual undisputed contemporary references to Solomon in the archaeological record will continue to reject the possibility of knowing what the reign of Solomon was actually like, or even rejecting a historical figure of Solomon altogether. All possibilities between these approaches can and will continue to be pursued.

The whole area of study concerning sources for the historical reconstruction of the United Monarchy expands. The long-held theory that the reigns of David and Solomon as presented in the books of Kings and Chronicles are based on reliable court documents has come under increasing scrutiny recently; however, ever new theories are devised to explain the retention of accurate material in the received texts. The myriad attempts to reconstruct the editions of the Deuteronomistic History reinforce the notion that the histories contained in the MT are based on generations of historical consciousness in the courts of Judah and Israel. However, the very existence of a myriad of theories undermines the certainty that any of these theories has a basis in historical reality. In short, the scholar is left with the earliest extant versions of Kings and Chronicles as the earliest sources for Solomon; since neither is contemporary to the ruler nor represents an attempt at objective history, the information in both texts cannot be taken at face value without corroborating data, which remains non-existent for Solomon.

The continuing search for points of view from which to question the data for possible origins will undoubtedly be maintained. However, it cannot be forgotten that the date of data tells us nothing about its reliability. Contemporary narratives may be polemical, propaganda, cover-ups, lies, or just plain literary fiction, while original compostions of a few (or several) hundred years after an event may contain accurate materials received not only from official documents, but legends, common knowledge (passing on true and false information), family oral histories, or suppositions formed by theoretical reconstruction. Any attempt at this juncture to recover data or documents of an earlier time from the texts of Kings and Chronicles will result in hypotheses which may be accepted or rejected by the members of the academic community morc or less on whim.

The historical investigation of Solomon's reign remains an investigation of biblical narratives and archaeological data; a situation which is not likely to change in the foreseeable future. The biblical texts are not likely to change significantly, but archaeological excavations at any site in the areas of ancient Judah and Israel (not to mention the surrounding regions) always have the possibility of bringing new and useful data to light. It is not reasonable to expect to recover a Solomonic archive, the foundations of the royal palace, or anything related to the building of the Solomonic temple. It is not out of the question to hope for some reference to the ruler Solomon in some epigraphic text either from Judah or the surrounding small states of the time. Unless such material appears, however, all excavations assigned to the time of Solomon will remain debated.

The theoretical social science approaches to the reign are beginning even now to enter into the self-criticism which is endemic throughout the social sciences themselves. The origins of anthropology, sociology, economics, political science, and others, can be readily traced. Many of the most dearly held assumptions of the philosophical sciences have been unravelling before the critical assaults of post-modernists, feminists, post-marxists, and traditions which never took part in the scientific venture at all. Some of these assumptions arose as attempts to demean others with whom the authors were in debate. Notions of cultural, social, gender, and ethnic superiority have shaped much of the foundational materials and these need to be addressed, even as to the question of the validity of the various models. There is little chance that the idea of change will disappear, but the notions of progress and social evolution have both come in for severe criticism in the past couple decades; both ideas are, nonetheless, more apt to survive than to be dismissed. Nevertheless the structured notions of social change, familiar in biblical studies as currently pursued, are apt in the near future to be relegated to amusing footnotes if not forgotten altogether in future Bible interpretation. There is nothing special about our moment in time along the hermeneutical tradition which will hold our methods valid for long. Yet, clearly, the social science fields are not going to disappear from the study of Solomon, but they will be redefined and the discussions currently taking place within the disciplines themselves will need to be recognized in such other disciplines as they are cited (including biblical studies).

Moving from the investigation of history itself, the field of historiography is expanding and any narrative may be studied from an almost infinite series of points of view. Solomon's reign, as presented in the biblical texts, is open to numerous serious historiographical questions. Some of this material is presented here, but there is reason to approach the texts from the point of view of those who opposed Solomon, both in his own time and in the guise of the "historical" Solomon invented for the Kings or Chronicles texts. One may read Solomon positively or negatively from the same texts, but why one should do one or the other needs to be systematically set forth. If political, economic, and social classes can be the object of intense study, so can everyday life, the work of slaves, commoners and lower officials; any portion of society may be used as a lens to the era. The study of both those who are thought to have lived in Solomon's time and those who are thought to have written the texts needs both a context and a sense of the purpose for writing the narratives. And, of course, the context and purposes of those doing the modern studies needs to be investigated as well.

2. Islam

There is a large literature in Islam concerning Solomon which awaits systematic research by scholars in the Jewish and Christian traditions. The correlations of Muslim traditions and those of Judaism and Christianity might well be profitably investigated. Islam, as well, has its own historical tradition for the reconstruction of the reign of this king in Judah and Israel. Also, just the figure of Solomon himself in Islamic tradition would be an extensive study. An extremely popular figure in the Muslim world, Solomon has become more than just a historical character from the Qur'an; he appears in the culture as a model for numerous aspects of proper Islamic life.

The Qu'ran contains stories of Solomon at several places.[1] These Qu'ranic texts present Solomon as a prophet who never disbelieved or disobeyed God; in this he is shown to be like his father David. God had revealed the truth to this king that he might tell it to his subjects, though there were those in his kingdom who disbelieved both God and their ruler. Moreover, Solomon is presented as wiser than most persons. His knowledge extends beyond the normal areas of human knowledge to include the language of birds, magic, and the control of jinn. These are all gifts from God. Unquestionably the most popular story is that of the Queen of Sheba (told in The Ant) in which Iblis (Satan) has held her nation in bondage to idols, but Solomon convinces her to surrender herself to God through diplomacy and magic.[2] Thus, the sacred textual tradition of Islam has a Solomon who is among the true prophets and a great ruler.

In the Islamic tradition Solomon takes on the image of paradigms for proper behavior. These models include Solomon as the exemplar of the Muslim missionary who uses diplomacy and reason to convert those who are not Muslims to the truth of submission to God.[3] He is also presented as only one of four persons who ruled over both the East and West, and one of only two who were believers; in this he is an examplar of the just ruler.[4] Solomon is also presented as the paradigm for proper behavior toward women and as the example for showing the high status of women in Islam.[5] The wisdom and rule of Solomon also permeated the royal architecture at certain times and places; the most significant

---

[1] See especially, The Cow, Women, The Ant, Sad, The Prophets, and Sheba.

[2] See also, W. M. Watt, "The Queen of Sheba in Islamic Tradition," *Solomon and Sheba* (ed. J. B. Pritchard; London: Phaidon, 1974) 85-103.

[3] K. Steenbrink, "Interactive Use of Scriptures within an Interreligious Network," *Exchange: Journal of Missiological and Ecumenical Research* 24 (1995) 120.

[4] See, for example, *The Sea of Precious Virtues* (*Bahr al-Fava'id*)*: A Medieval Islamic Mirror for Princes* (ed. and tr. J. S. Meisami; Salt Lake City: University of Utah, 1991) 217, 321. To praise an Islamic ruler one might simply state that the "magnificence is equal to that of Solomon;" N. R. Farooqi, "Six Ottoman Documents on Mughal-Ottoman Relations during the Reign of Akbar," *Journal of Islamic Studies* 7 (1996) 32-33.

[5] See, for example, A. A. Thānvī, *Perfecting Women: Maulana Ashraf 'Ali Thanawi's* Bihishti Zewar*: A Partial Translation with Commentary* (ed. and tr. B. D. Metcalf; Berkeley: University of California, 1990) 268

being the Alhambra, built on notions of Solomon's building activities.[6] This is a sample derived essentially at random of the place of the figure of Solomon within Islamic tradition; much research awaits.

Finally, Solomon fits into a historiographical vision of the past of true believers in Islam. In much the same way that one can set out the use of Solomon in the historical presentations of Kings, Chronicles, or Josephus, the reconstructions of religious and political history in Islamic tradtions needs to be considered. In the Qur'an he can be shown to display the recurring motif of the Israelites who had been given the true revelation, but fell away and could not/would not listen to the revelation of God presented by a long series of true prophets sent for their benefit, even if the message gets across to others to whom it was not necessarily sent (e.g., the Queen of Sheba narrative). Islamic historians have produced their own histories with their own purposes; Solomon's place in these texts is a useful area for research.

3. Solomon in Religious and Secular Culture

Mieke Bal has demonstrated the worth of investigating the manner in which biblical characters are presented to the religious traditions and the manner in which these characters have been understood. Solomon would appear to be a perfect topic for extensive study. His place in the history of Judah and Israel is clear in the narratives, yet he is not as well known as David or Moses.

A quick survey of an adult Sunday school class, demonstrated that what was generally known of Solomon was fairly little. From the five respondents to eight supplied questionaires there were only four items concerning Solomon of which more than one person was aware, and, of these, three was the highest number of persons for any given item: he was King of Israel (2), he was wise (3), he built the temple (3), and the incident of the judgment of two women and the baby (2). Other items known by one each of the respondents included: fortification construction, palace construction, fame, son of David, wrote songs, ruled over happy people, caused downfall of Israel by listening to his wives, and he

---

[6] F. P. Bargebuhr, *The Alhambra: A Cycle of Studies on the Eleventh Century in Moorish Spain* (Berlin: Walter de Gruyter, 1968) 2, 120-23, 136-40; note that the Muslims relied on Jewish expertise concerning the biblical Solomon for construction models.

had mines (though this last was correctly noted to be something picked up from non-biblical sources). All these items reflect the basically "good" Solomon. Once the texts in 1 Kings and 2 Chronicles were read by the respondents, the impressions of Solomon changed. Three noted that the succession to the throne of David was not smooth and seemed merciless on the part of the new king. Again, three noted that he had a "weakness" for both women and wealth, though one noted that the wealth was a gift from God. All respondents remarked in one way or another on Solomon's wisdom. Several incidents of the reign were mentioned, but suprisingly not one reference to the Queen of Sheba. One noted that Solomon's method of rule seemed as merciless as his method of attaining the throne, though another two noted that he ruled fairly. It was also noted by one that the Kings' version of Solomon and the Chronicler's version did not seem to be about the same person. In general, the traditional received vision of Solomon appeared to be slightly different from and more favorable than the version found in the Bible itself.[7]

Along the same line, it would be worth studying the appearance of Solomon in the materials used to teach members of the religious communities. A totally unscientific survey of children's Bibles as found on the shelf of a local chain book store disclosed the following items presented to teach young children about Solomon:[8]

---

[7] I wish to thank the members of the adult Sunday school class of the First Christian Church, Fort Dodge, Iowa, who filled out these forms for me: Donna Bonnel, Ardy Fortune, Darrel Grossnickle, Sr., H. R. Hager, O. A. Handy.

[8] The volumes consulted were: V. G. Beers, *The Early Reader's Bible* (revised ed.; Sisters, Ore.: Gold 'n' Honey Books, 1995) 178-91; *idem.*, *Preschoolers Bible* (Wheaton, Ill.: Victor Books, 1994) 172-79; M.-H. Delval, *Reader's Digest Bible for Children: Timeless Stories from the Old and New Testaments* (N.p.: Reader's Digest Young Families, 1995) 80-85; R. Hannon, *My First Bible* (New York: Regina, 1993); S. Hastings, *The Children's Illustrated Bible* (London: Dorling Kindersley, 1994); L. Hayword, *My First Bible* (New York: Random House, 1994); K. Henley, *The Beginners Bible: My Favorite Bible Stories* (Brentwood, Tenn.: Performance Unlimited, 1995) 117-121; M. Hollingsworth, *My Little Bible* (Dallas: Word, 1991) 36; D. F. Kennedy, *My Very First Golden Bible* (Racine, Wis.: Western, 1991) 67-73; S. Stoddard, *The Doubleday Illustrated Children's Bible* (New York: Doubleday, 1983) 141-54; K. N. Taylor, *My First Bible: In Pictures* (Wheaton, Ill.: Tyndale House, 1989) unpaginated; J. Winkler, *Saint Joseph Illustrated Children's Bible: Popular Stories from the Old and New Testaments* (New York: Catholic Book, 1991) 59-63.

Story	No. of Bibles
Solomon made wise by God because he asked	9
Solomon built temple (usually referred to as a church)	9
Solomon's judgment of the 2 women and the baby	5
People worshiped in the temple	4
Son of David and Bathsheba	2
Solomon wisest king in the world	2
Visit by Queen of Sheba	2
God gave him wealth	2
Wives made him worship other gods	2
Solomon worshiped golden animals	1
Solomon enslaved people to work for him	1

Two of the books had no reference to Solomon and the citations of people worshiping in the temple are inaccurate, of course. The citations of God giving Solomon wealth, his *wives* making him go astray, and the enslavement of people may well appear in the texts as part of the beliefs of the authors and the intentions of instruction for particular religious groups. One might also wonder about the need to teach small children about the "wise" Solomon threatening to cut a small child in half during a confrontation between two adults, but that's another matter.

Biblical scholars should find similar research into Sunday school materials, popular religious books on Israelite-Judean history and common reference works both informative and interesting. What is considered important and unimportant in the reign of this king, in a wider context, would help explain the use made of Solomon in the teaching of the church and synagogue. Such investigations should extend even into scholarly presentations of Solomon in academic work. In this latter material, the amount of information added to the biblical narratives or subtracted from it would also be revealing, as would an investigation into how the extant scholarship has been used to bolster opinions developed by the religious traditions of the scholars.

Solomon has never been as popular as Moses, David, or Jesus in the popular literature on biblical themes.[9] The one exception to this is the

[9] One might note C. R. LaBossière and J. A. Gladson, "Solomon," *A Dictionary of Biblical Tradition in English Literature* (ed. D. L. Jeffrey; Grand Rapids: Eerdmans, 1992) 721-723, where it is fairly clear that Solomon plays a minor passing role in literary works except as the "author" of proverbs or the "Song of Songs." The Queen of Sheba has been a more popular character for novelization and Solomon appears in "her" stories.

fabulous notion of King Solomon's mines which appear in novels, movies, and comic books.[10] However, Solomon himself seems to have been a bit boring for the Hollywood treatment; the most successful Solomon film, *Solomon and Sheba*, takes such liberities with the biblical narratives that the references are hardly recognizable, as well as spending more time with the Queen of Sheba (Gina Lollobrigida) than with Solomon (Yul Brynner) while Adonijah (George Sanders) is kept alive as a foil to the glowering hero.[11] Otherwise Solomon appears as a subsidiary character in films dedicated to the Queen of Sheba: *The Queen of Sheba* (1921) clearly provided the foundation for the later *Solomon and Sheba* with its focus on the sexy Queen (Betty Blythe) and enamored Solomon (Fritz Leiber) while having Adonijah (G. Raymond Nye) around as a foil; however, *La Regina di Saba* (1952), has Solomon (Gino Cervi) as a minor character to the heroine Queen (Leonora Ruff), who is courted successfully by none other than Rehoboam.[12] The Solomon of these productions has little to do with any historical person, but does illustrate what was envisioned of him in cinema/Hollywood adaptations for a popular market. There are also children's videos of biblical narratives which contain Solomon.

---

[10] This topic got its popular foundation in the adventure novel by H. R. Haggard, *King Solomon's Mines* (World's Classics; Oxford: Oxord University, 1989), first published in 1885; the movies (there have been five productions of the Haggard novel as commercial films in Great Britain and the United States); and the comic books: in 1951 a comic was based on the just released American film made from the novel, but the premise appears elsewhere: see, for example, C. Barks, "The Mines of King Solomon," *Uncle Scrooge* 19 (September 1957), who actually moves the mine to the west coast of the Red Sea and makes it the gift of the Pharaoh of Egypt to his son-in-law Solomon (incorporating an unrelated biblical tradition), and P. Murry and D. Spiegle, "The Mystery at Misty Gorge," *Mickey Mouse* 610 (October 1966), who follow the Haggard novel by having the mine in Sub-Saharan Africa.

[11] T. Richmond (producer), *Solomon and Sheba* (Santa Monica, Calif.: MGM/UA Home Video, 1993); the movie was released in 1959. Needless to say, the film provides romance, battle scenes, intrigue, lots of partially-clad young women, and a special-effects destruction of the temple (which looks like no possible biblical representation of Solomon's temple). On the transformation of the biblical text into a very different movie script, see B. Babington and P. W. Evans, *Biblical Epics: Sacred Narrative in the Hollywood Cinema* (Manchester: Manchester University, 1993) 47-48. On the centrality of the sexuality of the Queen for the picture (and the almost insignificance of Solomon), see G. E. Forshey, *American Religious Biblical Spectaculars* (Media and Society; Westport, Conn.: Praeger, 1992) 55, 75-77.

[12] R. H. Campbell and M. R. Pitts, *The Bible on Film: A Checklist, 1897-1980* (Methuchen, NJ: Scarecrow, 1981) 11-12, 33-34. The volume also mentions two television programs devoted to Solomon: "The Plot Against Solomon," a segment of CBS's "You Are There," November 28, 1954; and "The Judgment of Solomon," a segment of NBC's "Greatest Heroes of the Bible," November 21, 1978. More recently the series "Biography" carried "Solomon & Sheba," A&E, 1996.

If Solomon has been unpopular as a dramatic figure, he has been popular as an object of artistic representation. The chance to display grandeur and opulence in an "oriental" (as envisioned by "occidental") setting has made Solomon very common in the portfolios of biblical artists. Both renowned painters and the famous illustrators have multiple reditions of the wise and wealthy ruler of Israel.[13] One could add to the works of the more famous illustrators the series of cartoons concerning Solomon and his wives which have graced joke magazines and "men's" magazines for over a century; though their concern is decidedly not to display Solomon.

4. Prospects: Where We're Going

The use of the past to frame the future has long been a central purpose of historical writing. In this regard we can divide current biblical historical endeavors into three rather broad purposes: 1) Attempts to recover the past as it happened in the most accurate fashion possible [impossible to complete as there is by definition insufficient data]; 2) Attempts to create a past which displays the lessons of society, behavior, or culture which we wish to instill into those who read (or are taught) that history [possible because we may be highly selective about the past, the future is what emerges as important]; 3) Attempts to demonstrate that the past fits formulas already developed about historical/social/economic progression [possible, and popular, because the outlines are already determined and missing information may be invented without having the data]. The three overlap, but in sum cover the biblical historical endeavor as currently pursued.

Each approach is constantly in the process of changing. Any new data discovered or retrieved from the extant materials modifies the vision of events as they occurred. Moreover, the focus of historical reconstruction allows numerous renditions of the same events as being historically valid. History as prologue to the future changes everytime the notion of

[13] Doré's Bible illustrations, for example, include four Solomon plates; G Doré, *The Doré Bible Illustrations* (New York: Dover Publications, 1974) 90-93. On the use of Solomon to display wealth and oriental splendor, see note on this in A. Schorsch and M. Grief, *The Morning Stars Sang: The Bible in Popular and Folk Art* (New York: Universe Books, 1979) 77, with examples pp. 77-79; other examples are presented in C. Harby (pseud.), *The Bible in Art: Twenty Centuries of Famous Bible Paintings* (New York: Covici Friede, 1936) 99-100.

what the future ought to be changes. The many groups who see their future possibilities in as many different ways can (and will) envision the past to suit their vision and as their vision changes so will their teaching of the past. As formulaic material, historical resconstruction will adapt to the changing paradigms of the models used. There is no danger in the foreseeable future of formulas coalescing into one agreed upon paradigm or even of any of the formulas remaining as the same structure they are at this time; thus, likewise, the historical material will need to be constantly updated as well as compared with yet other and newer such formulas.

What this means for Solomon is that the reconstruction of his reign is still an open investigation. There is plenty of room for new, creative, and insightful scholarship. Surely enough to keep academics and others busy for another millennium.

INDEX OF SUBJECTS

INDEX OF AUTHORS

INDEX OF SCRIPTURE CITATIONS

STUDIES IN THE HISTORY AND CULTURE OF THE ANCIENT NEAR EAST

EDITED BY

B. HALPERN AND M.H.E. WEIPPERT

ISSN 0169-9024

1. G.W. Ahlström. *Royal Administration and National Religion in Ancient Palestine.* 1982. ISBN 90 04 6562 8
2. B. Becking. *The Fall of Samaria.* An Historical and Archaeological Study. 1992. ISBN 90 04 09633 7
3. W.J. Vogelsang. *The Rise and Organisation of the Achaemenid Empire.* The Eastern Iranian Evidence. 1992. ISBN 90 04 09682 5
4. T.L. Thompson. *Early History of the Israelite People.* From the Written and Archaeological Sources. 1992. ISBN 90 04 09483 0
5. M. el-Faïz. *L'agronomie de la Mésopotamie antique.* Analyse du «Livre de l'agriculture nabatéenne» de Qûṯâmä. 1995. ISBN 90 04 10199 3
6. W.W. Hallo. *Origins.* The Ancient Near Eastern Background of Some Modern Western Institutions. 1996. ISBN 90 04 10328 7
7. K. van der Toorn. *Family Religion in Babylonia, Syria and Israel.* Continuity and Change in the Forms of Religious Life. 1996. ISBN 90 0410410 0
8. A. Jeffers. *Magic and Divination in Ancient Palestine and Syria.* 1996. ISBN 90 04 10513 1
9. G. Galil. *The Chronology of the Kings of Israel and Judah.* 1996. ISBN 90 04 10611 1
10. C.S. Ehrlich. *The Philistines in Transition.* A History from ca. 1000-730 B.C.E. 1996. ISBN 90 04 10426 7
11. L.K. Handy (ed.). *The Age of Solomon.* Scholarship at the Turn of the Millennium. 1997. ISBN 90 04 10476 3